First Aid
for Colleges
and Universities

First Aid for Colleges and Universities

Seventh Edition

Brent Q. Hafen

Keith J. Karren
Brigham Young University

Kathryn J. Frandsen
Novell, Inc.

Allyn and Bacon

Boston   London   Toronto   Sydney   Tokyo   Singapore

Publisher: Joseph E. Burns
Vice President: Paul A. Smith
Series Editorial Assistant: Sara Sherlock
Marketing Manager: Rick Muhr
Composition Buyer: Linda Cox
Manufacturing Buyer: Megan Cochran
Cover Administrator: Linda Knowles
Editorial Production Service: Lifland et al., Bookmakers
Text Designer: Wendy LaChance/By Design
Electronic Composition: Omegatype Typography, Inc.

Library of Congress Cataloging-in-Publication Data

Hafen, Brent Q.
    First aid for colleges and universities / Brent Q. Hafen, Keith J.
Karren, Kathryn J. Frandsen. -- 7th ed.
        p.   cm.
    Includes index.
    ISBN 0-205-29123-6
    1. First aid.   2. Emergency medicine.
    I. Karren, Keith J.   II. Frandsen, Kathryn J.   III. Title.
RC86.7.H339   1998
616.02'52--dc21   98-31203
                                                  CIP

Printed in the United States of America

10 9 8 7 6 5 4 3 2   03 02 01 00 99

Photo Credits
Rick Nye: pp. 4, 17, 44, 61, 65–66, 82, 83–85, 109–110, 136, 158,
159 (top left), 164, 166, 198, 200 (left), 207, 215, 225, 236, 250,
263–265, 279, 314 (left), 315, 328, 330, 385, 399 (top), 400,
449–451, 462, 463, 477–488, 495 (bottom); Anthony Neste: p. 208;
Scott Camazine/Photo Researchers: p. 378; Larry Miller/Photo
Researchers: p. 378; Kenneth Murray/Photo Researchers: p. 495;
Terry Wild: pp. 42, 392, 416.

Notice on Care Procedures
It is the intent of the authors and publisher that this
textbook be used as part of a formal First Aid education program taught by a qualified instructor. The
procedures described in the textbook are based on
consultation with First Aid, First Responder, and
medical authorities. The authors and publisher have
taken care to make certain that these procedures reflect currently accepted practice; however, they cannot be considered absolute recommendations.

The material in the textbook contains the most
current information available at the time of publi-
cation. However, federal, state, and local guidelines
concerning first aid practices, including, without
limitation, those governing infection control and
universal precautions, change rapidly. The reader
should note, therefore, that new regulations may
require changes in some procedures.

It is the responsibility of the reader to become
familiar with the policies and procedures set by
national, state, and local agencies as well as the
institution or agency where the reader is being
trained. It is the reader's responsibility to stay informed of any new changes or recommendations
made by any of these agencies. The authors and the
publisher of this textbook and supplements written
to accompany it disclaim any liability, loss, or risk
resulting directly or indirectly from the suggested
procedures and theory, from any undetected errors,
or from the reader's misunderstanding of the text.

Contents........................

v

Preface . . . .

Why Study First Aid?

How people respond to an emergency before medical help arrives often determines how well a victim recovers and, in extreme cases, can spell the difference between life and death. Since you are the person most likely to be first on the scene of an emergency, you need to know how to recognize emergencies and how to respond in a way that best protects the victim. This text and course will prepare you to make appropriate decisions regarding first aid care and to act skillfully on those decisions.

Approach

Meeting the standards of Red Cross National Safety Council and all other first aid training courses, *First Aid for Colleges and Universities,* Seventh Edition, provides the most complete coverage of certification-level instruction. Written particularly with college and university courses in mind, this comprehensive text is the only first aid text on the market that contains enough material to fill a semester-long college course in first aid. It also serves as a valuable resource after completion of a first aid training course.

Obtaining American Red Cross Certification

You can use what you learn in *First Aid for Colleges and Universities,* Seventh Edition, to obtain an American Red Cross First Aid/CPR certificate. Study the text and correctly answer the Progress Checks in each chapter. After mastering the chapter content and completing all the Progress Checks, test yourself at the end of each chapter by taking the Chapter Self-Test. Then contact the local branch of the American Red Cross

(local chapter information is available on the American Red Cross Web site < http://www.crossnet.org >) and request an appointment with the Health and Safety Director to take a Challenge test. Once you successfully complete this skills and written test, the American Red Cross will issue you a certificate.

What's New in This Edition

Along with offering the most complete coverage of certification-level instruction in first aid, the seventh edition has been thoroughly updated and incorporates the following material and learning aids:

- The most recent protocols for first aid care as well as the latest CPR guidelines for first aid providers.

- The latest information on protecting yourself from infectious diseases such as AIDS and hepatitis. A new section on bloodborne pathogens has been added.

What's Unique in This Text

- Chapter 12, Common Sport and Recreational Injuries, discusses the most likely mechanisms of injury in sports and recreational activities, lists the most common signs and symptoms, and outlines valuable first aid techniques that can prevent further injury.

- Chapter 27, Wilderness Emergencies, gives valuable information on how to care for victims who are at risk of further injury when you are far from the safety of the 9-1-1 system, in a potentially hostile environment. This important chapter also describes how to prevent problems in the wilderness setting, covers the basics of survival, and details common wilderness problems. Finally, it describes special considerations in assessing and caring for victims when you have limited equipment and supplies.

- An innovative learning technique, SQ3R Plus (survey, question, read, recite, review, write, and reflect), has been incorporated into every chapter to encourage active participation in learning, studying, and reviewing and to reinforce the key points in each chapter.

- A margin glossary defines key terms where they first appear in the text, assuring understanding of the material as it is presented.

The SQ3R Plus System

The SQ3R Plus system provides structured learning aids throughout each chapter that can boost your effectiveness, enhance your learning, and increase your retention. The following learning aids comprise the SQ3R Plus system.

- Learning objectives, presented at the beginning of each chapter, are used to organize the text and focus on major concepts. These objectives are repeated in the chapter to introduce the material to which they refer.

- Progress Checks at the end of each major section of the chapter immediately reinforce the material just covered and check your comprehension.

- Self-Tests at the end of each chapter provide a review of the material by testing your retention and offer an excellent study tool for exams.

Effective Use of This Text

We've structured the seventh edition so you can use the SQ3R Plus system—*survey, question, read, recite, review*, plus *write* and *reflect*—as you study the material.

The following steps will help you get the most out of this text.

- **Survey.** Before you start reading a chapter, take a few minutes to scan it. Read the case study that begins each chapter to get a sense of how the principles apply to real-life examples. Then flip through the pages, reading the section headings and subheadings. Finally, look at the illustrations and tables. When you're finished, you'll have a good idea of what lies ahead.

- **Question.** Write down some questions you'd like answered by the material you'll study in each chapter. Need help? Look at the detailed learning objectives listed at the beginning of each chapter and the Progress Checks at the end of each section. You might also turn section headings or subheadings into questions. Developing your own list of questions makes the information more relevant and interesting. And because you have a goal, it gets you more involved!

- **Read.** Now read the text and find the answers to the questions you wrote down. Use the Learning Objectives as prompts and pointers—they'll guide you to information and key terms. As you read, pause often to determine how the material is personally relevant.

- **Recite.** Each time you finish reading the material under a heading, stop and *recite*. How? Mentally rehearse what you just read—this time, in your own words. Think of your own examples and metaphors.

- **Review.** To begin, look at your list of questions; answer them from memory. Now look at the list of learning objectives; write a summary for each from memory. Next, look at the list of key terms at the end of each chapter; write a definition for each from memory. Finally, answer the questions in the Progress Checks if you haven't already done so, and take the Self-Test at the end of the chapter. These give you immediate feedback on how well you learned the key concepts. If you're unsure about some of the questions, go back and study those sections in the chapter again.

- **Write and Reflect.** You've already started writing a summary of what you've learned; make sure you really understand and that you've covered all the key points. As a final step, reflect on how you personally can use this material and apply what you've learned. Write down the specifics to make them more meaningful and to increase your involvement in what you've studied.

Acknowledgments ·····················

We would like to thank Terry F. Scott of California University of Pennsylvania and Carolyn Gerdes of Kean College of New Jersey for their input into the seventh edition, and the following reviewers for their valuable suggestions and input into the sixth edition: Kevin Brown, Belleville Area College; Joan Couch, University of Delaware; Peter Koehneke, Canisius College; Robert May, University of Southwest Louisiana; Mathew McIntosh, Hagerstown Junior College; Corey Stanbury, El Camino College; Richard Travis, James Madison University.

We would like to offer our special thanks to Susan Duane, Photo Director, for her creativity, enthusiasm, and support. We would also like to thank Rick Nye, who shot many of the photos; Sharon RaNea Hinckley, for her technical help with the photoshoot; Ellen Martin, who coordinated and arranged models for the photos; and the models—Judy Berryessa, Kevin Crawford, Jeff Francom, Ron Hammond, Steve Hawkes, Gary Jolley, Jane Johnson, Brady Karren, James Karren, Ted and Alice Malquist, Joe McRay, Chuck Tandy, Sharon RaNea Hinckley, Ellen Martin, Mindy Shoemaker, Jennifer Hinckley, Jamie Cook, Doreena Ng, Janeth Caizalitin, Kingsley Ah You, Kyung-Hee Lee, Calvin Rivers, and Alison Nye.

We extend special thanks to Blayne Hirsch, M.D.; James Clayton, M.D.; and Spenco Medical Corporation for allowing us to use their color photographs. Other companies and individuals that generously assisted with photographs include Terry Wild Studio; California Medical Product, Inc.; REEL Research and Development; Philip C. Anderson, M.D.; Paul S. Auerbach, M.D.; Cameron Bangs, M.D.; W. Henry Baughman, H.S.D.; Robert Biehn; John A. Bostwick, Jr., M.D.; Jim Bryant; N. Branson Call, M.D.; Douglass C. Cox, Ph.D.; Drug Intelligence Publications, Inc.; Corine A. Dwyer; Larry Ford; Dyna Med Industries; Michael D. Ellis; Bruce Halstead, M.D.; Niles W. Herrod, D.D.S.; Glen R. Hunt, M.D.; Renner Johnson, M.D.; Arthur K. Kahn, M.D.; Thomas Morton, M.D.; Eugene Robertson, M.D.; Pat Sullivan; Lawrence Wolheim, M.D.; World Life Research Institute; Michael and Jacqueline Gelotte; and Mark and Sharlene Sumsion.

We gratefully acknowledge the following REGENTS/PRENTICE HALL authors for their generous permission to use selected pieces of artwork: Bryan Bledsoe, Robert Porter, and Bruce Shade: *Paramedic Emergency Care* (Brady, 1991), Figures 2-7, 2-8, 2-11, 2-12, 2-13, 2-14, 2-15, 2-18; and Harvey Grant, Robert Murray, and J. David Bergeron: *Emergency Care*, 5th edition (Brady, 1990), Figures 5-37, 8-16, 8-17, 18-5, 24-20, 24-21, 24-22, 30-4.

Additional appreciation is expressed to Lifland et al., Bookmakers for coordinating the text production, to Jay Alexander of I-hua Graphics and Precision Graphics for their outstanding artwork, and to Wendy LaChance of By Design for her design expertise.

First Aid
for Colleges
and Universities

1

Introduction to First Aid and Emergency Care

Learning Objectives

When you have mastered the material in this chapter, you will be able to

1 Identify the need for properly prepared First Aiders

2 Identify the principal aims of first aid

3 Understand the skills of a First Aider

4 Understand the legal aspects of first aid and emergency medical care

5 Explain the factors that constitute negligence on the part of a First Aider

6 Understand how infections are transmitted

7 Identify the infectious diseases that are of concern in an emergency setting

8 Describe ways to prevent the spread of AIDS and other infectious diseases in an emergency setting

SQ3R Plus

- **Survey** to set goals for studying.
- Ask **questions** as you **read.**
- Stop frequently to **recite** and **review.**
- **Write** a summary of key points.
- **Reflect** on the importance of this material and its relevance in your life.

I remember the first serious victim I ever cared for. I had been trained in first aid at my local community college. A friend and I were driving down a country road and observed an older lady standing by her parked car, frantically waving to us. As we pulled closer I saw a man slumped in the front seat. My mind began racing: "Would I remember everything from class? What if the man is unconscious? Worse yet, what if he needs CPR?"

As we rolled to a stop behind the parked car, the woman came to us and said that her husband was experiencing terrible chest pain. He looked pale and ashen and had broken out in a sweat. Recognizing these as signs of a possible heart attack, we hurried to the parked car.

I felt myself rushing, losing my concentration. Fortunately, I remembered my first aid instructor's words: "Sometimes it feels like you're going to lose it. If that happens, stop briefly. Recite the letters A, B, C, D a few times to yourself." He said it would keep me from jumping in too fast and losing the big picture. He also said it would remind me of my priorities in caring for any victim. It worked.

I introduced myself to the victim. He had all the classic signs of a heart attack (myocardial infarction). I tried to reassure him. He was clutching his chest and told me that he felt like there was a huge band pulling tightly around it. I began taking vital signs, and I sent my friend to call 9-1-1 and get paramedics on their way.

When the paramedics arrived, we were ready for them with a complete set of vitals, information on the victim's complaint, and a medical history. I gave all the information to the ambulance crew chief. The patient was now theirs, but my friend and I stuck around to help until he was wheeled into the ambulance.

Although it was my first serious call, it went pretty well. Since then, there have been many opportunities to give first aid. I've learned that being prepared to give first aid is important: Giving early first aid at the scene of an emergency not only helps injured victims, it also saves lives.

AMONG THE MOST CRITICAL AND VISIBLE HEALTH PROBLEMS in America today are catastrophic accidents and illnesses and the resultant disabilities and/or sudden loss of life. More than 70 million Americans receive hospital emergency care each year. One American in three suffers a nonfatal injury.

Too often, those who arrive first at the scene of an accident are not trained sufficiently to give proper, on-the-scene emergency care or in-transit emergency assistance. Often, too much time passes before proper emergency care is given, and victims who might have been saved die as a result of a lack of necessary care (see Figure 1-1).

Learning Objective 1 Identify the need for properly prepared First Aiders.

The first people on the scene, the First Aiders, can initiate various life-saving procedures:

- Airway and respiratory intervention
- Cardiopulmonary resuscitation
- Bleeding control
- Special wound care
- Stabilization of spinal injuries
- Splinting of fractures

As a First Aider, you become an important part of the emergency care team, prepared with the knowledge and the skills to render appropriate life-saving care.

Figure 1-1. Victims of severe trauma have enhanced chances of survival if they can be delivered to the operating room within one hour after their accident (the "Golden Hour").

● Section 1 ●
WHAT IS FIRST AID?

Learning Objective 2 Identify the principal aims of first aid.

First aid is the temporary and immediate care given to a person who is injured or who suddenly becomes ill. It can also involve home care if medical assistance is delayed or not available. First aid includes recognizing life-threatening conditions and taking effective action to keep the injured or ill person alive and in the best possible condition until medical treatment can be obtained.

First aid does *not* replace the physician, nurse, or paramedic. In fact, one of the primary principles of first aid is to obtain medical assistance in all cases of serious injury.

The principal aims of first aid are to

- Recognize life-threatening situations
- Supply artificial ventilation and circulation when needed
- Control bleeding
- Care for other life-threatening conditions
- Minimize further injury and complications
- Prevent infection
- Make the victim as comfortable as possible
- Arrange for medical assistance and transportation

Your first aid training will be of obvious benefit to those you treat—from your friends and family members to co-workers and strangers. It will be of particular value when you use it to help those who will not have access to medical care for an extended period—such as someone camping in the wilderness or working on a remote farm. But it will also be of tremendous benefit to you, as you will be able to provide immediate care for your own sudden injuries and illnesses.

As a First Aider, you need to be able to take charge of a situation, keep calm while working under pressure, and organize others to do the same. By demonstrating competence and using well-chosen words of encouragement, First Aiders should win the confidence of others nearby so that they can do everything possible to reassure the victim.

first aid The temporary and immediate care given to a person who is injured or who suddenly becomes ill

• Section 2 •
GENERAL PROCEDURES

Being involved in a sudden injury or illness situation requires fast thinking and action. Consider the following plan of action:

- Observe the accident scene as you approach it.

- Keep yourself and others at the scene safe; if necessary, assign a bystander to direct traffic away from the accident scene, position safety flares, keep bystanders at a safe distance, turn off any engines that are still running, and so on.

- Gain access to the victim(s) and determine any immediate threats to life.

- Provide basic life support to those whose lives are threatened; always give first aid to the most seriously injured victims first.

- Summon more advanced medical help if needed. You should activate the EMS system if childbirth is imminent; a victim has been drowned, electrocuted, burned, or poisoned; you suspect heart attack or spinal injury; or the victim is bleeding profusely, has difficulty breathing, is choking, has any paralysis, has an altered level of consciousness, or has more than one seizure.

Arranging for Medical Assistance (Activating the EMS System)

During the first minutes after an accident, it is essential that the Emergency Medical Services (EMS) system be activated. In most areas of the United States, you can activate the EMS system by dialing 9-1-1; learn how to access the system in your area (see Figure 1-2). Give the following information to the dispatcher:

- The exact location of the victim—for example, the complete address and, if applicable, the number of the floor or office in the building

- The phone number where you can be reached

Figure 1-2. By dialing the emergency response system, 9-1-1, you activate Emergency Medical Services.

- Any information about the victim that will help the dispatcher send appropriate personnel and equipment

If at all possible, send a responsible bystander to telephone with the above information. If you're alone, activate the EMS system immediately after you determine unresponsiveness in an adult; in the case of an unconscious infant or child, provide 1 minute of rescue support before you activate the EMS system.

If no telephone is available, continue giving emergency care until a bystander is available to activate the EMS system.

• Section 3 •
ASPECTS OF FIRST AID

First Aider Skills

Learning Objective 3 Understand the skills of a First Aider.

When you have finished the first aid course, you should be able to

- Control an accident scene to prevent further injury
- Gain access to victims in the easiest and safest ways possible
- Open a victim's airway
- Perform rescue breathing
- Provide one- and two-rescuer cardiopulmonary resuscitation.
- Control bleeding by direct pressure, elevation, pressure points, and tourniquets
- Detect and care for shock
- Detect and care for soft-tissue and internal injuries
- Perform basic dressing and bandaging techniques
- Detect and care for open and closed fractures
- Detect and care for poisoning, including poisoning by alcohol or drugs
- Detect and care for heart attack, stroke, diabetic coma, insulin shock, and seizures
- Detect and care for facial and head injuries and chest injuries (including fractured ribs, flail chest, and penetrating chest wounds)
- Detect and care for first-, second-, and third-degree burns and smoke inhalation
- Detect and care for heat- and cold-related injuries
- Assist in childbirth and care of the newborn
- Give psychological support to victims of crises and disasters
- Perform emergency and nonemergency moves

Legal Aspects of First Aid

Learning Objective 4 Understand the legal aspects of first aid and emergency medical care.

First Aiders are bound by the same legal statutes as other emergency care providers. Every state has laws that govern these providers; find out what the laws are in your state.

Basically, the First Aider's duty can be legally defined as follows:

- The First Aider should not interfere with the first aid being given by others.
- The First Aider should follow the directions of a police officer and do what a reasonable First Aider would do under the circumstances.
- The First Aider should not force help on a victim who is unwilling to be treated unless the situation is life-threatening.
- Once a First Aider has *voluntarily* started care, he or she should not leave the scene or stop the care until relieved by a qualified and responsible person *who renders care at the same or a higher level of care.* Otherwise, leaving the scene or stopping care is legally considered *abandonment* and places the First Aider at risk of litigation.
- The First Aider should follow accepted and recognized emergency care procedures taught in first aid texts.
- The First Aider should respect the victim's privacy and should disclose confidential information—such as a victim's medical condition, injury, physical condition, or medications—only to those with a medical need to know.
- Any First Aider involved with a victim at a crime scene should document and preserve evidence and should comply with state laws requiring the reporting of specific criminal incidents (such as abuse, rape, and gunshot wounds).

Duty to Act

Duty to act means there is a legal obligation to give aid or perform emergency care. This legal obligation may exist in the following situations:

- When you have a preexisting responsibility—you have an already established relationship that legally binds you to give aid, such as the relationship between driver and passenger or between parent and child.
- When your employment requires it—as in the case of school teachers, park rangers, lifeguards, and police and fire personnel
- When first aid has begun—once you have started, you must continue administering first aid until you have done all you can do.

duty to act The legal obligation to give aid or perform emergency care

As part of the duty to act, a First Aider must follow guidelines for the standard of care. Essentially, a First Aider is legally expected to provide the level and type of care consistent with his or her training. A First Aider has a different standard of care, for example, than a physician or an emergency medical technician.

Good Samaritan Laws

Learning Objective 5 Explain the factors that constitute negligence on the part of a First Aider.

To protect health care personnel from being sued, many states have enacted **Good Samaritan laws.** In essence, these protect you as a First Aider unless you are found guilty of **negligence**—carelessness, inattention, disregard, inadvertence, or oversight that was accidental but avoidable. In order to establish negligence, the court must decide that

- The victim was injured
- Your actions or lack of action caused or contributed to the injury
- You had a duty to act
- You acted in an unusual, unreasonable, or imprudent way

"Reasonable-Man" Test

Your defense against a charge of negligence is the **"reasonable-man" test**—did you act the same way a normal, prudent person with your same background and training would have acted under the same circumstances? Essentially, the burden of proof is on the victim; you can be prosecuted only if the victim can prove that you are guilty of gross negligence, recklessness, willful or wanton conduct, or causing intentional injury.

Right to Refuse Care

A competent adult has the right to refuse emergency care and/or transportation for himself or herself or a minor in need of such care. If the victim or guardian refuses to consent, *you may not give emergency care or forcibly transport the victim.* If you do, you can be legally charged with battery. Generally, law enforcement personnel are the only people who can touch, restrain, or transport someone against his or her will. There are four different kinds of consent:

1. **Actual consent.** The consent must be informed; you need to explain the care you will provide. Oral consent is valid.

2. **Implied consent.** In a true emergency, with significant risk of death, disability, or deterioration, the law assumes the victim would give consent.

3. **Minor's consent.** The right to consent is usually given to the parent or guardian of a minor.

4. **Consent of the mentally ill.** The right to consent is usually given to the parent, guardian, or permanent caregiver of the mentally ill.

If a victim or guardian will not give consent and you believe that a life is at stake, summon the police. If injuries are serious but not life-threatening, explain the possible consequences of refusing treatment and try to persuade the victim to consent; enlist the help of family members or friends if necessary. If the victim still refuses, make sure there are witnesses who can verify that the victim refused care, then activate the EMS system.

Controversies in First Aid Care

The first aid and emergency-care procedures in this text are accepted practices in the United States. However, there are still some areas of controversy in first aid care. When controversies exist, you should follow local protocol as outlined by your instructor.

Progress Check

1. *Duty to act* means you have a _____ to give aid. (*responsibility/legal obligation/choice*)

2. The "reasonable-man" test shows that you acted as a normal, prudent person would have acted under the _____ . (*same circumstances/law*)

3. _____ means you acted with carelessness, inattention, disregard, or oversight. (*Imprudence/Negligence/Recklessness*)

4. Every competent adult has the right to give _____ to treatment. (*approval/permission/consent*)

• Section 4 •
INFECTIOUS DISEASE TRANSMISSION

An **infectious,** or communicable, **disease** is one that can be transmitted from one person to another or

HOW INFECTIOUS DISEASES CAN SPREAD

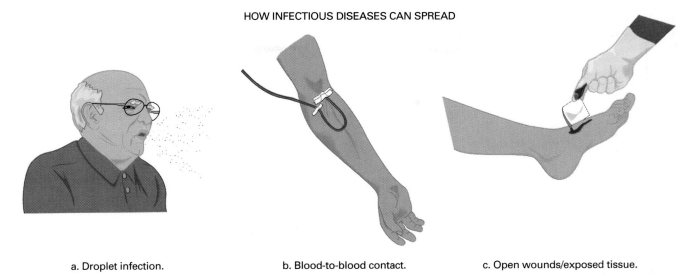

a. Droplet infection.   b. Blood-to-blood contact.   c. Open wounds/exposed tissue.

Figure 1-3. You can pick up and spread infections through physical contact with blood and other body fluids.

from an infected animal or the environment to a person. All kinds of body fluids should be considered infectious, including saliva, blood, vaginal secretions, semen, amniotic fluid (the fluid that surrounds a fetus in the uterus), and fluids that lubricate the brain, spine, lungs, heart, abdominal organs, and joints and tendons.

Transmission of Infectious Disease

Learning Objective 6 Understand how infections are transmitted.

For disease to spread, three things must happen:

1. Infecting organisms, such as bacteria and viruses, must survive outside their host—an infected person, an animal, or an insect. Bacteria and viruses can also survive on inert objects, such as surfaces in the environment or discarded needles.

2. The infecting organism must then move from one place to another. Some organisms, such as the cold viruses, are easily transmitted; others, such as tuberculosis bacteria, are relatively difficult to transmit (see Figure 1-3).

3. The infecting organism must then invade a new person's body and begin to multiply there. Inadequate nutrition, poor hygiene, crowded or unsanitary conditions, and stress can all increase a person's susceptibility to infection.

Identifying Infectious Diseases

A victim with any of the following should be considered infectious:

A rash or skin lesion
An open sore
Diarrhea
Vomiting
Coughing or sneezing
Draining or oozing wounds
Profuse sweating
Abdominal pain
Headache with stiff neck
Yellowish skin or eyes

Good Samaritan laws Laws that protect health care personnel and provide guidelines for care

negligence Acting with carelessness, inattention, disregard, inadvertence, or avoidable oversight

"reasonable-man" test Did the First Aider act the same way a normal, prudent person with similar training would have acted under the same circumstances?

actual consent Informed consent

implied consent Assumption that a victim of life-threatening injury or illness would give consent

minor's consent The right of consent given to a parent or guardian

infectious disease A disease that can be transmitted from one person to another or from an insect or animal to a person

Diseases of Concern in the Emergency Setting

Learning Objective 7 Identify the infectious diseases that are of concern in an emergency setting.

Bloodborne Pathogens

Of greatest concern to First Aiders and others in emergency settings are *bloodborne pathogens,* or diseases that are caused by microorganisms that are carried in the blood. You can be exposed to these any time you come in contact with a victim's blood or any other body fluid that contains blood; you can minimize your risk by using protective equipment, such as latex gloves, to avoid contact with the victim's blood.

Three bloodborne pathogens are of particular concern:

- Hepatitis B. The most common type of hepatitis, Hepatitis B, is a viral infection of the liver; symptoms may resemble those of the flu, but many victims do not have symptoms at all. Even those without symptoms can still pass the infection on to others, however. The infection causes inflammation of the liver and can in some cases lead to permanent liver damage or even cancer of the liver. A vaccine for Hepatitis B is available, and is recommended for all those who may come in contact with the blood of others.

- Hepatitis C. Caused by a different virus than Hepatitis B, Hepatitis C can also lead to permanent liver damage or cancer of the liver. Like Hepatitis B, it may not cause symptoms, but the victim remains contagious even without symptoms. There is currently no effective treatment for or vaccine against Hepatitis C.

- HIV. The HIV virus suppresses the immune system and interferes with the body's ability to defend itself against other diseases. People infected with HIV almost always eventually develop AIDS, which is fatal. HIV is spread by contact with infected blood or blood products, needles, urine, feces, or by sexual contact. People infected with HIV may have no symptoms, but even symptom-free victims can pass the virus to others. There is no vaccine against HIV, and there is no effective way of removing the virus from the body. The best defense against HIV is to avoid infection; always wear protective equipment, such as gloves, when caring for victims. Because the virus lives only a few hours in a dry environment and can be killed by common dis-

infectants, you should always be especially careful to clean any areas or equipment that have been contaminated by body fluids.

Several other diseases are of particular concern to First Aiders and others in an emergency setting.

- Herpes. A highly contagious viral infection of the skin and mucous membranes, herpes is spread through contact with active lesions. Genital herpes is also spread through contact with active lesions.

- Tuberculosis. Tuberculosis is a severe lung infection spread through the air or through direct contact with nasal or oral secretions. You can be infected by someone who is coughing, spitting, or simply speaking.

- Meningitis. Meningitis is an infection of the membranes lining the brain and spinal cord that is spread through infected water, food, air, or direct contact.

Protecting Yourself from Risk of Infection

Learning Objective 8 Describe ways to prevent the spread of AIDS and other infectious diseases in an emergency setting.

The following guidelines will help you avoid being infected by contact with blood, body fluids, secretions, sores, droplets, and bites.

- Make sure your immunizations are up to date. Adults who may render first aid should have the MMR (measles, mumps, rubella), DPT (diphtheria, pertussis, tetanus), varicella (chicken pox), Hepatitis B, and influenza immunizations.

- Wear disposable latex gloves whenever you have direct contact with a victim (see Figure 1-4). Do not use gloves that are discolored, brittle, punctured, or torn.

- If a victim's body fluids spill, wipe them up with paper towels and then flood the area with a solution of household bleach in water. Let the solution soak for at least 10 minutes, then wipe up the solution with clean paper towels.

- Remove contaminated gloves by turning them inside out; grab the inside edge of the second glove with your bare hand, and avoid touching contaminated surfaces of the gloves.

- Wash your hands thoroughly with soap and hot water or an antibacterial agent immediately after

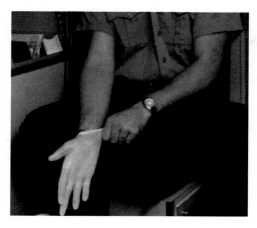

Figure 1-4. An Emergency-Care Provider using surgical gloves for infectious disease protection

Figure 1-5. Pocket masks with one-way valves can be used to reduce the risk of cross-contamination. Many disposable types are also available.

providing care, even if you were wearing gloves; be sure to scrub under your fingernails. Scientific tests show that 9 percent of all latex gloves and 43 percent of all vinyl gloves leak.

- Avoid touching your mouth, nose, or eyes or any personal items (such as a comb, car keys, or food) until you have washed your hands.

- Cover any abrasions or skin conditions you have with protective clothing and/or latex gloves.

- Use a pocket mask if possible when giving mouth-to-mouth resuscitation (see Figure 1-5).

- If there is a risk of significant body fluid contact, wear additional disposable protective gear, such as a face mask, protective goggles, and a gown (see Figure 1-6).

- Report all incidents of exposure to body fluids.

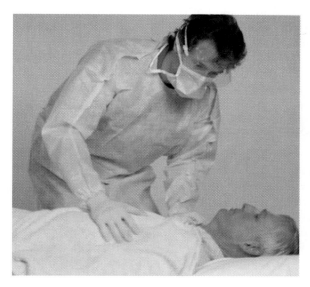

Figure 1-6. Emergency-Care Provider wearing appropriate infection-control gear while treating a victim with an infectious disease

Progress Check

1. To prevent the risk of bloodborne infection, you should always wear _____ when caring for a victim.
   (a face mask/a gown/latex gloves)

2. Use a _____ when giving mouth-to-mouth resuscitation.
   (face mask/pocket mask/face shield)

3. The best protection against disease you have is to _____ after giving treatment.
   (wash your hands/take an antibiotic/ use antiseptic)

• Section 5 •

SAFETY AT THE SCENE

One of the first things you will need to deal with at many scenes is safety—not just for the victim, but for you and for bystanders at the scene. *Staying safe is your first priority;* you won't be able to help someone else if you become a victim yourself.

As soon as you arrive at a scene, assess the situation from a safety standpoint. Do not enter an unsafe situation unless you have been properly trained and have proper protective equipment. In addition to activating the EMS for a victim, you may need to send for specialized personnel who can move wreckage, take care of downed power lines, put out a fire, and so on.

Fire

Immediately call the fire department, regardless of how small the fire is—fire of any size can get out of control, threatening life and property. Unless you have been specifically trained, never approach a burning building or a burning vehicle; stay a safe distance away, upwind from any smoke or fumes, until the fire has been contained.

Unstable Structures

An unstable structure is defined as one in which you may become trapped or injured because of weak floors or ceilings, partially collapsed walls, debris, hazardous gases in the air, or the threat of explosion or fire. And instability is not limited to buildings—it can also involve wells, trenches, silos, vats, pits, and mines, in which you could be buried or trapped. Call the fire department for help; in the meantime, figure out the probable location of any victims so you can offer help as soon as the structure is stabilized.

Motor Vehicle Accidents

One of the greatest threats related to a motor vehicle accident is that posed by oncoming traffic. As soon as you arrive at the scene, park where you will not interfere with an ambulance and where you will be least likely to cause increased traffic problems. Assign a bystander to direct traffic as far away from the accident as possible. If they are available, place safety flares or reflectors well beyond the accident in both directions.

Other safety threats at the site of an accident include spilled gasoline (which can cause fire or explosion), hazardous materials, and unstable wreckage. Methods of stabilizing a vehicle and extricating a victim from wreckage are discussed in Chapter 30.

People who transport or store hazardous materials are required by law to post placards on their vehicles identifying the hazardous materials. Even if you do not see such a placard, you may suspect the presence of a hazardous material because of leaking containers or an unusual odor, liquid, or vapor. If you suspect a hazardous material, alert the fire department or a HAZMAT team, then wait a safe distance upwind and take care not to create sparks.

Electrical Hazards

Look for downed power lines at the scene of *every* motor vehicle accident, and always consider downed power lines to be "live." Immediately notify the local power company and fire department, and wait for trained personnel to shut off the power source before you get close to the wires. *Never try to move downed wires yourself.*

Never touch a vehicle, body of water, or metal object that is in contact with a downed wire. If power lines are touching a vehicle, tell victims—even those who seem seriously injured—to stay inside until help arrives. Keep all bystanders a safe distance from downed wires; live wires can whip and lash about, so as a general rule, stay at a distance at least twice as long as the span of wire.

Water

Never enter the water or venture out onto ice to rescue someone unless you have been specifically trained in water rescue—and, even then, do it only as a last resort. Call for help, then follow these guidelines while you wait for help to arrive:

- If the victim is near enough to reach you, hold out your hand, a pole, a branch, or some other object; once the victim grabs it, pull the victim to shore. Make sure your footing is stable so that you are not pulled into the water.

- If you can not reach the victim, tie a buoyant object to the end of a rope and throw the object to the victim. You can use an ice chest, a milk jug, an inflated toy, a branch, a life jacket, or anything else that floats. Tell the victim to hold on to the floating object, then tow the victim to shore. Again, check your own footing to avoid being pulled into the water.

Hostility and Violence

Stay a safe distance from a hostile victim while you calmly explain who you are and what you want to do to help; if possible, enlist the help of a family member or friend to try to defuse the situation. If a victim remains hostile, retreat and call for help. *Never* approach a hostile crowd; call the police and wait until the situation is under control.

Never approach a victim of violence—even one with life-threatening injuries—until you are sure that the perpetrator has left the scene. Likewise, never approach an armed person who is threatening suicide. Immediately call the police and wait for them to secure the scene; do not touch anything or disturb any evidence while you wait.

Progress Check

1. Your first priority at the scene of an accident is

_____ .

(reaching the victim/staying safe/preventing further injury to the victim)

2. You should call the fire department in case of

_____ .

(any fire/a fire that is out of control/a fire that is creating toxic fumes)

3. One of the greatest threats to safety from a motor vehicle accident is _____ .
(fire/gasoline fumes/oncoming traffic)

4. You can touch a downed power line _____ .
(with a stick/if you are wearing rubber-soled boots/only after the power company has turned off the power)

5. If a victim is hostile, _____ .
(restrain the victim yourself/ have bystanders help you restrain the victim/call the police)

• SUMMARY •

- First aid is the temporary and immediate care given to a person who is injured or who suddenly becomes ill; it does not replace the care of a physician, nurse, or paramedic.

- A primary principle of first aid is to obtain medical assistance in all cases of serious injury.

- First Aiders should be able to recognize life-threatening problems, supply artificial ventilation and circulation, control bleeding, prevent further injury, and minimize complications.

- You should always provide care to the most seriously injured victims first.

- You have a duty to act—the legal obligation to give aid or perform emergency care—if you have a preexisting responsibility, your employment requires it, or you have already started first aid.

- As a First Aider, you are protected under the law as long as you act the same way that a normal, prudent person with your background and training would have acted under the same circumstances.

- Any competent adult has the right to refuse emergency care and/or transportation; you must obtain consent before beginning treatment.

- Infectious diseases—especially Hepatitis B, meningitis, tuberculosis, and AIDS—are of particular concern in the emergency setting.

- You can minimize your risk of infection by wearing latex gloves; wearing other protective gear as appropriate; using a pocket mask during mouth-to-mouth resuscitation; and washing your hands thoroughly after any contact with a victim.

• KEY TERMS •

Make sure you understand the following key terms:

- first aid
- duty to act
- Good Samaritan laws
- negligence
- "reasonable-man" test
- actual consent
- implied consent
- minor's consent
- infectious disease

Student: _____   Date: _____

Course: _____   Section #: _____

PART 1 • True/False

If you believe the statement is true, circle the T. If you believe the statement is false, circle the F.

T   F   **1.** One in five Americans is injured each year.

T   F   **2.** Two important words in a definition of first aid are *immediate* and *temporary*.

T   F   **3.** Activating the EMS system is an important part of first aid.

T   F   **4.** The first thing to do for an injured person is to control bleeding.

T   F   **5.** One of the main concerns of a First Aider is to prevent added injury or death.

T   F   **6.** You should not activate the EMS system until you have rendered all possible emergency care.

T   F   **7.** A person who receives first aid training is required by law to stop and help at an accident scene.

T   F   **8.** You have to receive a person's consent for treatment before you can render first aid care.

T   F   **9.** A First Aider should take specific precautions against infectious disease.

T   F   **10.** If you wear latex gloves while treating a victim, you don't need to wash your hands.

PART 2 • Multiple Choice

For each item, circle the correct answer or the phrase that best completes the statement.

1. First aid is the immediate action taken to
   a. care for the injured until medical help is available
   b. supplement proper medical or surgical treatment
   c. preserve vitality and resistance to disease
   d. rescue and transport the injured

2. When administering first aid, the condition that should be cared for first is
   a. the most painful one
   b. the most life-threatening one
   c. the most obvious one
   d. bleeding

3. The most correct definition of first aid is
   a. immediate care given to someone who is ill or injured
   b. care administered at home
   c. self-help
   d. all of the above

4. Under normal circumstances, the best first contact for help in case of accident is
   a. the hospital emergency room
   b. the first response department
   c. the police or highway patrol
   d. the Emergency Medical Services (EMS) system

5. The "reasonable-man" test is
   a. given to First Aiders to test their skills
   b. given to First Aiders to test personality traits
   c. used to ascertain whether a First Aider provided care that was fair, reasonable, and unbiased
   d. used to ascertain whether a First Aider acted as a normal, prudent person with first aid training would have acted

6. Infectious disease is a disease that
   a. always causes permanent disability or death
   b. can be spread from one person to another
   c. must be reported to state or federal agencies
   d. cannot be prevented

PART 3 • Matching

Match the terms on the right with their proper definition.

A. In a true emergency, the law assumes an unconscious person would give consent.
B. The right to consent is given to the parent or guardian.
C. An informed consent.

Actual consent _____

Implied consent _____

Minor's consent _____

_____ has satisfactorily demonstrated the following practical skills:

Student's Name

Read the following list of first aid and emergency-care skills; indicate with a checkmark those you feel prepared to perform. At the end of this course, go back over the list to determine your preparedness.

First Aid Skills

Do you know how to	Now	End of Course
Control the accident scene so further injury will not occur?	❏	❏
Gain access to victims in the safest and easiest way possible?	❏	❏
Effectively and quickly evaluate an accident scene for cause, then control the scene for safety?	❏	❏
Perform quick, effective primary and secondary victim surveys, including vital signs (breathing, pulse, skin temperature)?	❏	❏
Obtain information about the accident or sudden illness from bystanders and the victim?	❏	❏
Determine any diagnostic signs and relate them to possible injuries or sudden illnesses that require emergency care?	❏	❏
Open an airway, provide rescue breathing, provide one- and two-rescuer CPR, and control bleeding?	❏	❏
Detect and care for shock?	❏	❏
Detect and care for soft-tissue and internal injuries, including using basic dressing and bandaging techniques?	❏	❏
Detect and care for open and closed fractures, sprains, and dislocations, including splinting?	❏	❏
Detect and care for poisoning, including poisoning by alcohol and drugs?	❏	❏

Anatomy and Physiology of Body Systems

Learning Objectives

When you have mastered the material in this chapter, you will be able to

1   Define and use the common anatomical terms of body position

2   Define and use the common topographic terms of direction and location

3   Describe the main structures and functions of the skeletal system

4   Describe the main structures and functions of the muscular system

5   Describe the main structures and functions of the circulatory system

6   Describe the main structures and functions of the respiratory system

7   Describe the main structures and functions of the digestive system

8   Describe the main structures and functions of the urinary system

9   Describe the main structures and functions of the endocrine system

10   Describe the main structures and functions of the nervous system

11   Describe the main structures and functions of the skin

SQ3R Plus

- **Survey** to set goals for studying.
- Ask **questions** as you **read.**
- Stop frequently to **recite** and **review.**
- **Write** a summary of key points.
- **Reflect** on the importance of this material and its relevance in your life.

On August 12, 1998, Jim Stewart was a volunteer in a first aid station during a bike marathon. Shortly after the race began, he received a report of a fall. It occurred close to his station, and he went to check it out. The course was partially on paved road and partially on special bike trails, which were not wide enough for cars. Jim took his bicycle and first aid kit.

When Jim arrived, a few of the riders were gathered around the woman who had fallen, so he sent one of them to activate the EMS system and another to the head of the trail to direct the ambulance to them.

The woman had somehow lost control of her bike, gone off the trail, and hit a tree. She was conscious and alert, but complained of pain in several places. Jim had one of the onlookers keep her head and cervical spine stable without removing the helmet she was wearing, while he continued to evaluate her other injuries.

Jim found the woman in a supine position, though she had fallen on her left side. She complained of pain in her lower ribs and left arm. She also had numerous abrasions and one laceration approximately 2 inches long on the medial aspect of her left lower leg, which was still bleeding. Jim applied a dressing and had a bystander apply pressure to the wound so he could check the woman's vital signs.

Jim was concerned about the pain in the woman's left upper quadrant—which could indicate a potentially serious injury. He continued to monitor her vital signs very closely. He also had time to dress and bandage the laceration on her leg while waiting.

When the EMS crew arrived, they removed the victim's helmet, immobilized her on a backboard, applied an oxygen mask, splinted her arm, and otherwise made her ready for transport. Jim walked beside them on the way to the ambulance, wheeling both of the bikes. He assured the victim that he would notify family members who were waiting for her at the end of the course and give them her bike.

TO RENDER FIRST AID EFFECTIVELY, YOU NEED TO HAVE a knowledge of the basic structures of the human body. A *cell* is the basic unit of all living tissue, and *tissues* are collections of similar cells. A *system* is a group of organs that work together to perform a specific function. *Anatomy* deals with the structure of the body and the relationship of its parts to each other. *Physiology* deals with the function of the living body and its parts—in other words, how the body works.

• Section 1 •
ANATOMICAL TERMINOLOGY

When you seek medical assistance, you need to use correct anatomical terms to describe the victim's position, direction, and location—a practice that eliminates confusion and helps you communicate the extent of injury.

Terms of Position

Learning Objective 1 Define and use the common anatomical terms of body position.

The terms of position include

- **Anatomical position**—the victim is standing erect, arms down to the sides, the palms facing you. "Right" and "left" refer to the victim's right and left.
- **Supine position**—the victim is lying face up (on the back) (see Figure 2-1).
- **Prone position**—the victim is lying face down (on the stomach) (see Figure 2-2).

- **Lateral recumbent position**—the victim is lying on the left or right side (see Figures 2-3 and 2-4).

Terms of Direction and Location

Learning Objective 2 Define and use the common topographical terms of direction and location.

Terms of direction and location (see Figure 2-5) include

- **Superior**—toward the head
- **Inferior**—toward the feet

anatomical position Standing erect with the arms down at the sides, the palms facing forward

supine position Lying on the back

prone position Lying on the stomach (face down)

lateral recumbent position Lying on the right or left side

superior Toward the head

inferior Toward the feet

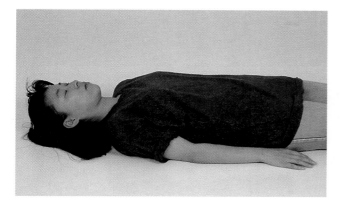

Figure 2-1. Supine position

Figure 2-2. Prone position

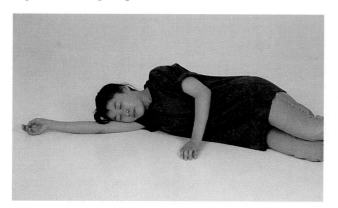

Figure 2-3. Right lateral recumbent position

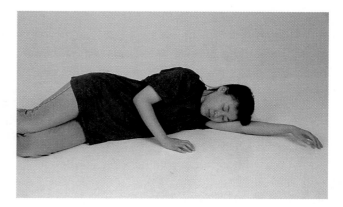

Figure 2-4. Left lateral recumbent position

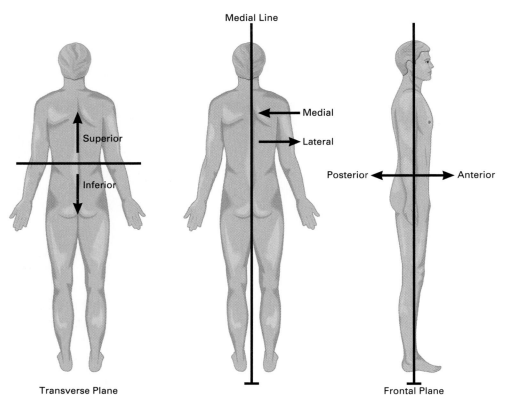

Figure 2-5. Anatomical planes

- **Anterior**—toward the front
- **Posterior**—toward the back
- **Medial**—toward the midline or center of the body
- **Lateral**—to the right or left of the midline
- **Proximal**—near the point you are referring to
- **Distal**—far away from the point you are referring to
- **Superficial**—near the surface
- **Deep**—remote from the surface
- **Internal**—inside
- **External**—outside

Progress Check

1. A victim lying on his or her back is in the _____ position.
   (supine/prone/lateral)

2. A victim lying on her or his stomach is in the _____ position.
   (supine/prone/lateral)

3. _____ means toward the victim's head.
   (superior/anterior/posterior)

4. _____ means toward the victim's feet.
   (superior/inferior/posterior)

5. A wound near the surface is a _____ wound.
   (internal/external/superficial)

• Section 2 •

THE BODY'S FRAMEWORK

The Skeletal System

Learning Objective 3 Describe the main structures and functions of the skeletal system.

The human body (see Figure 2-6) is shaped by a framework of bones held together by ligaments that connect bone to bone; layers of muscles; tendons, which connect muscles to bones or other structures; and various connective tissues. Bones and their adjacent tissues help to move, support, and protect the vital organs.

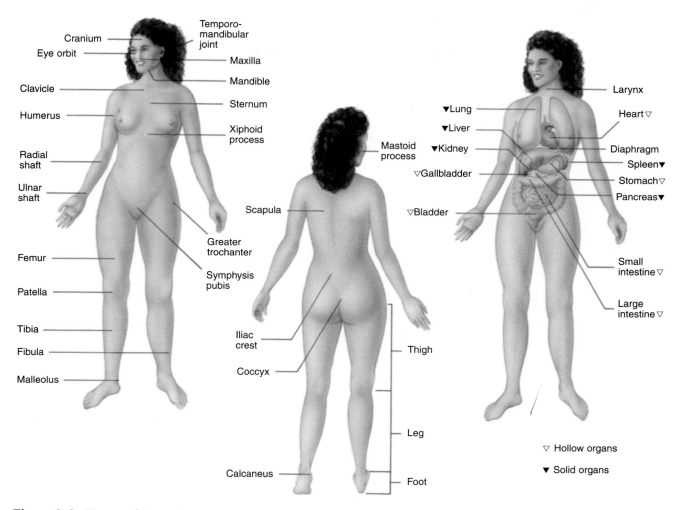

Figure 2-6. Topographic anatomy

The skeleton (see Figure 2-7 on page 20) is

- Strong, to provide support and protection
- Jointed, to permit motion
- Flexible, to withstand stress

Bones are made up of living cells that are surrounded by dense deposits of calcium; all cells in the bone are richly supplied by nerves and blood vessels. The adult skeleton has 206 bones that are classified by size and shape as long, short, flat, or irregular.

Joint Movements

The structure of the joint (see Figure 2-8 on page 21) determines the kind of movement that is possible, because the bone ends **articulate**—or fit into each other—at the joint. Each joint is enclosed in a tough,

anterior Toward the front

posterior Toward the back

medial Toward the midline (center) of the body

lateral To the right or left of the midline (center) of the body

proximal Near the point you are referring to

distal Farther from the point of reference

superficial Near the surface

deep Remote from the surface

internal Inside

external Outside

articulate To fit into each other

THE SKELETON

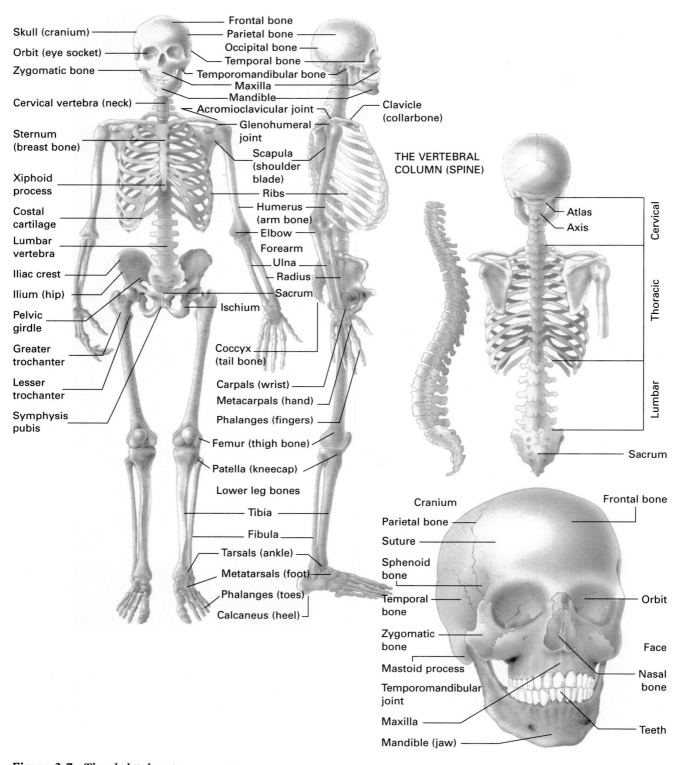

Figure 2-7. *The skeletal system*

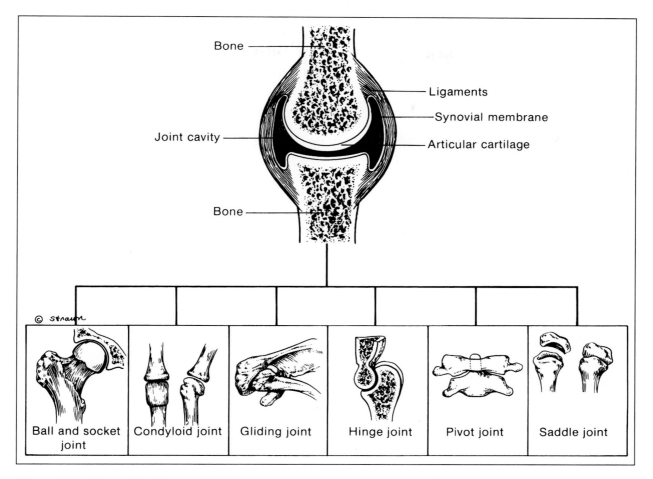

Figure 2-8. Types of freely movable joints

flexible capsuie with an inner membrane that produces thick fluid to lubricate the joint. Joints can be immovable (such as those of the skull), slightly movable (such as those of the spinal column), or freely movable (such as the knee or elbow).

Different **joint** structures include

- **Ball-and-socket** (such as the shoulder and hip)
- **Hinge** (such as the elbow and knee)
- **Pivot** (such as the neck and wrist)
- **Gliding** (such as the hands and feet)
- **Saddle** (such as the ankle)
- **Condyloid,** or modified ball-and-socket (such as the wrist)

The most common emergency involving the skeletal system is **fracture,** a crack or break in the bone. Fracture can not only cause injury to the bone and surrounding muscle, but can damage adjacent nerves, blood vessels, and organs. When blood vessel damage occurs, fracture can also cause potentially serious internal bleeding.

The Muscular System

Learning Objective 4 Describe the main structures and functions of the muscular system.

The muscles give the body its ability to move. Each muscle is composed of long, threadlike cells called fibers, which are bundled in closely packed, overlapping groups bound by connective tissue (see Figure 2-9 on page 22).

ball-and-socket joint The type of joint that permits the widest range of motion
hinge joint A joint that permits a one-way hinge motion
pivot joint A joint that allows a pivotal motion
gliding joint A joint that permits a gliding motion
saddle joint A type of joint that permits up-and-down and side-to-side movement
condyloid joint A modified ball-and-socket joint
fracture A crack or break in the bone

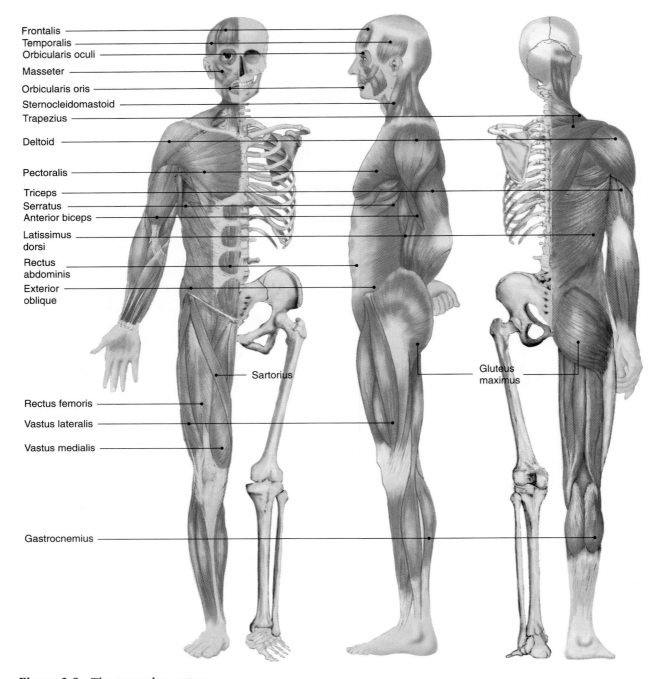

Frontalis
Temporalis
Orbicularis oculi
Masseter
Orbicularis oris
Sternocleidomastoid
Trapezius
Deltoid
Pectoralis
Triceps
Serratus
Anterior biceps
Latissimus dorsi
Rectus abdominis
Exterior oblique
Sartorius
Rectus femoris
Vastus lateralis
Vastus medialis
Gastrocnemius
Gluteus maximus

Figure 2-9. *The muscular system*

There are three basic kinds of muscles in the body (see Figure 2-10):

- **Skeletal muscle,** or **voluntary muscle,** is under a person's conscious control and makes possible actions such as walking, chewing, swallowing, smiling, frowning, talking, and moving the eyeballs. Skeletal muscle helps give the body its shape.

Most skeletal muscles are attached to the bone by tendons, tough cords of fibrous tissue. Skeletal muscle never completely relaxes; some fibers in the muscle are always contracting.

- **Smooth muscle,** or **involuntary muscle,** is muscle over which a person has little or no conscious control. Smooth muscle is found in the walls of

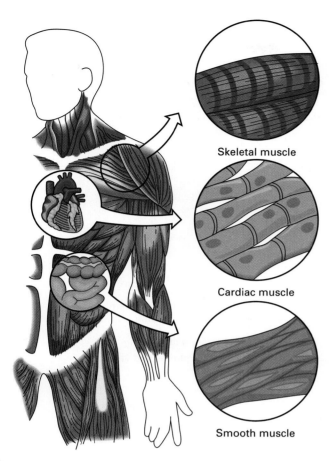

Skeletal muscle

Cardiac muscle

Smooth muscle

***Figure 2-10.** There are three types of muscle. Skeletal muscle, also called voluntary muscle, is found throughout the body. Cardiac muscle is limited to the heart. Smooth muscle, occasionally called involuntary muscle, is found in the intestines, arterioles, and bronchioles.*

tubelike organs, ducts, blood vessels, and the intestines.

- **Cardiac muscle** forms the walls of the heart and is made up of a cellular mesh. Cardiac muscle is able to stimulate itself into contraction without signals from the central nervous system.

Progress Check

1. The adult skeleton has 206 bones that are classified by size and _____ .
   (location/shape/function)

2. The _____ of the joint determines the kind of movement that is possible.
   (location/structure/function)

3. The hip is an example of a _____ joint.
   (hinge/pivot/ball-and-socket)

4. Deliberate acts, such as walking and talking, depend on _____ muscle.
   (skeletal/smooth/cardiac)

5. The movement of the intestines depends on _____ muscle.
   (skeletal/smooth/cardiac)

• Section 3 •
THE BODY'S ORGAN SYSTEMS

The Circulatory System

Learning Objective 5 Describe the main structures and functions of the circulatory system.

The circulatory system (see Figure 2-11 on page 24) is made up of two major transportation systems: The cardiovascular system, which consists of the heart, blood vessels, and blood, carries oxygen and nutrients to body cells and transports waste from body cells and kidneys. The lymphatic system provides drainage for tissue fluid, called lymph.

The heart alternately contracts and relaxes to pump blood through the lungs, where it is oxygenated, and then through the vast network of blood vessels. About the size of a man's fist, the heart is located in the left center of the chest, just behind the sternum (breastbone). The arteries and arterioles carry oxygenated blood from the heart to the cells of the body. The exchange of fluid, oxygen, and carbon dioxide between the blood and the tissue cells takes place through the capillaries. The venules and veins carry oxygen-poor blood back to the heart (see Figure 2-12 on page 25), where the cycle begins again.

skeletal muscle Voluntary muscle

voluntary muscle "Skeletal muscle"; muscle that is under direct voluntary control of the brain

smooth muscle The muscles found in the walls of the internal organs and blood vessels, generally not under voluntary control

involuntary muscle Smooth muscle over which a person has no voluntary or conscious control

cardiac muscle The muscle that makes up the walls of the heart

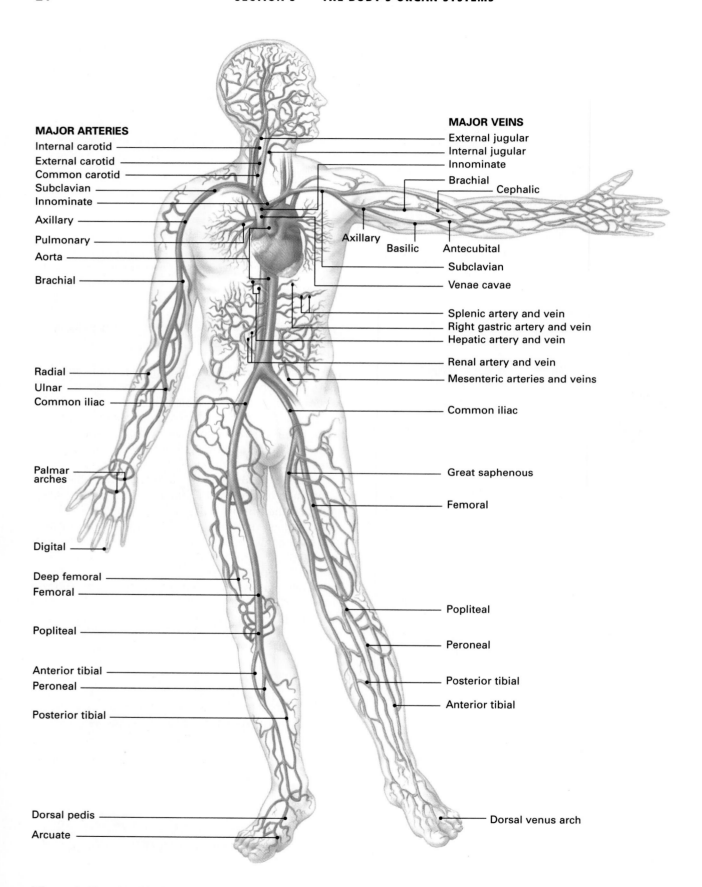

MAJOR ARTERIES

Internal carotid
External carotid
Common carotid
Subclavian
Innominate
Axillary
Pulmonary
Aorta
Brachial

Radial
Ulnar
Common iliac

Palmar arches

Digital

Deep femoral
Femoral

Popliteal

Anterior tibial
Peroneal

Posterior tibial

Dorsal pedis
Arcuate

MAJOR VEINS

External jugular
Internal jugular
Innominate
Brachial
Cephalic
Axillary
Basilic   Antecubital
Subclavian
Venae cavae

Splenic artery and vein
Right gastric artery and vein
Hepatic artery and vein
Renal artery and vein
Mesenteric arteries and veins

Common iliac

Great saphenous

Femoral

Popliteal

Peroneal

Posterior tibial

Anterior tibial

Dorsal venus arch

Figure 2-11. *The circulatory system*

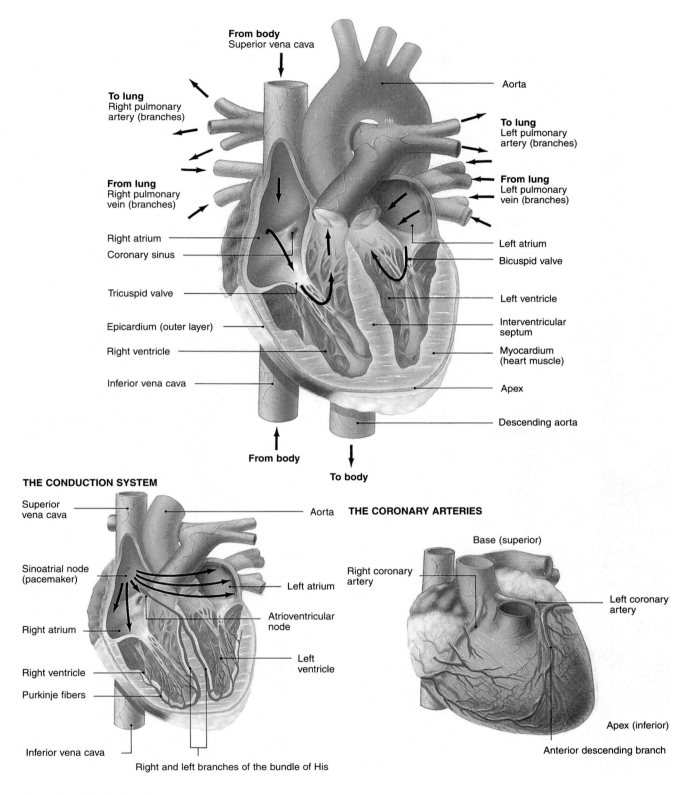

From body
Superior vena cava

Aorta

To lung
Right pulmonary
artery (branches)

To lung
Left pulmonary
artery (branches)

From lung
Right pulmonary
vein (branches)

From lung
Left pulmonary
vein (branches)

Right atrium

Left atrium

Coronary sinus

Bicuspid valve

Tricuspid valve

Left ventricle

Epicardium (outer layer)

Interventricular
septum

Right ventricle

Myocardium
(heart muscle)

Inferior vena cava

Apex

Descending aorta

From body

To body

THE CONDUCTION SYSTEM

Superior
vena cava

Aorta

THE CORONARY ARTERIES

Base (superior)

Sinoatrial node
(pacemaker)

Right coronary
artery

Left atrium

Left coronary
artery

Atrioventricular
node

Right atrium

Left
ventricle

Right ventricle

Purkinje fibers

Inferior vena cava

Apex (inferior)

Right and left branches of the bundle of His

Anterior descending branch

Figure 2-12. *The heart*

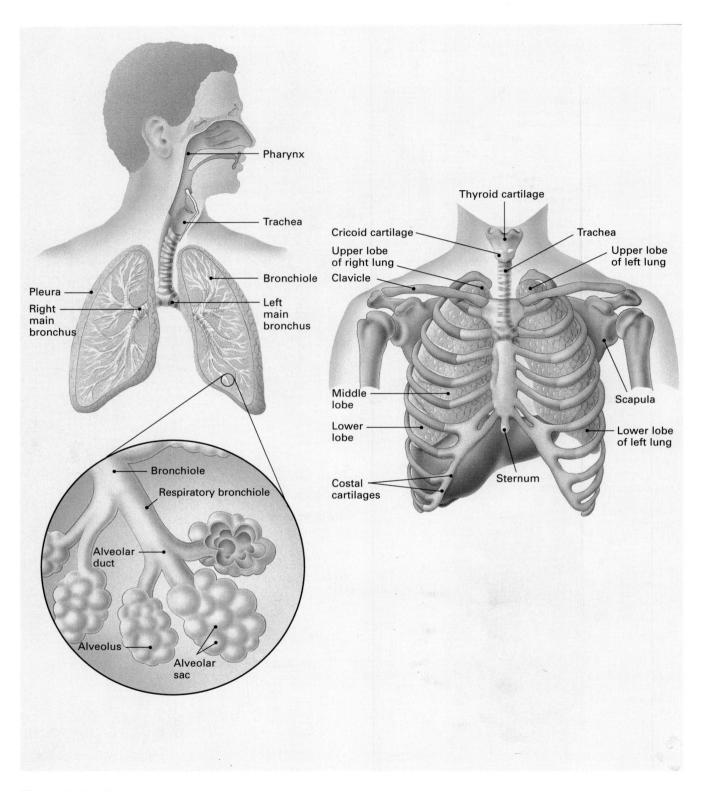

Figure 2-13. The respiratory system

Every time the heart contracts, the current of blood can be felt as a pulse wherever an artery passes over a bone near the surface of the skin. Major pulses can be felt in the wrist, upper arm, thigh, ankle, and neck.

Emergencies involving the circulatory system occur when there is uncontrolled bleeding, when circulation is impaired, or when the heart loses its ability to pump.

The Respiratory System

> **Learning Objective 6** Describe the main structures and functions of the respiratory system.

The body depends on a constant supply of oxygen, which is made available to the blood through the respiratory system (see Figure 2-13), consisting of the nasal passages, pharynx, trachea, and lungs.

The passage of air into and out of the lungs is called **respiration.** During **inhalation** (or **inspiration**), air enters the lungs through the nose, mouth, trachea, and bronchi; the air is warmed, moistened, and filtered before it reaches the lungs. The lungs expand to fill the enlarged chest cavity, and muscles close the larynx to hold the air in. Blood circulating through the lungs is oxygenated.

During **exhalation** (or **expiration**), the muscles of the chest relax and the larynx opens, releasing air from the lungs. The exhaled breath carries with it carbon dioxide and other waste products.

The normal breathing rate at rest is 12 to 20 breaths per minute in adults, 15 to 30 breaths per minute in children, and 25 to 50 breaths per minute in infants.

Emergencies involving the respiratory system include obstruction (choking), difficulty breathing, and respiratory arrest. Airway obstruction is more common among infants and children because their organs are much smaller.

The Digestive System

> **Learning Objective 7** Describe the main structures and functions of the digestive system.

The digestive system (see Figure 2-14) consists of the alimentary tract (the food passageway) and the accessory organs of digestion—the mouth, esophagus, stomach, pancreas, liver, spleen, gallbladder, small intestine, and large intestine. Following are the main functions of the digestive system:

- Ingest and carry food
- Digest food
- Absorb nutrients
- Eliminate wastes

Digestion consists of two processes. The mechanical process includes chewing, swallowing, **peristalsis** (the rhythmic movement of matter through the digestive tract), and defecation (the elimination of digestive wastes). The chemical process consists of breaking food into simple components that can be absorbed and used by the body.

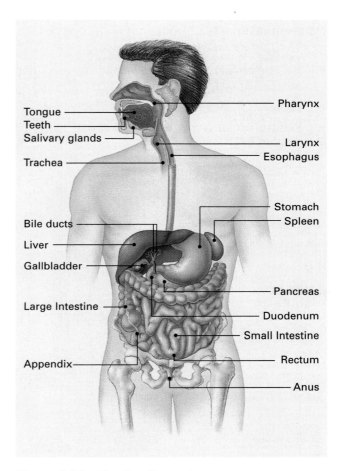

Figure 2-14. *The digestive system*

> **respiration** The act of breathing
> **inhalation** The act of breathing in (inspiration), or the drawing of air or other gases into the lungs
> **inspiration** The act of breathing in (inhalation)
> **exhalation** The act of breathing out (expiration)
> **expiration** The act of breathing out (exhalation)
> **peristalsis** The rhythmic movement of matter through the digestive tract

Emergency care is required for any blunt or penetrating injury to the abdomen.

The Urinary System

Learning Objective 8 Describe the main structures and functions of the urinary system.

The urinary system (see Figure 2-15) filters and excretes waste from the body; it consists of two kidneys, two ureters (which carry urine from the kidneys to the bladder), one urinary bladder, and one urethra (which carries urine from the bladder out of the body).

The urinary system

- Helps maintain the delicate balance of water and other chemicals needed for survival
- Removes wastes from the bloodstream
- Returns useful products to the blood

Emergency care is required for any blunt or penetrating injury to the lower abdomen or genitals, any significant injury to any quadrant of the abdomen, any injury to the external genitals, and any forceful injury to the area of the back below the rib cage.

The Endocrine System

Learning Objective 9 Describe the main structures and functions of the endocrine system.

The **endocrine glands** regulate the body by secreting hormones that affect physical strength, mental ability, stature, maturity, reproduction, and behavior.

Endocrine glands, which have no ducts, secrete hormones directly into the bloodstream; they include the thyroid gland, parathyroid glands, adrenal glands, ovaries, testes, islets of Langerhans, and the pituitary gland.

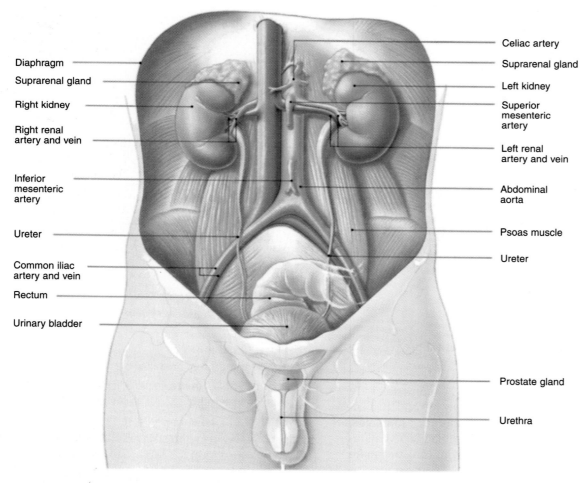

Figure 2-15. The urinary system

Emergency care is required for diabetics who have had too much or too little insulin.

Progress Check

1. The circulatory system has two major fluid transportation systems: the cardiovascular and the _____ .
   (cardiopulmonary/genitourinary/lymphatic)

2. The passage of air into and out of the lungs is called _____ .
   (inspiration/respiration/expiration)

3. The rhythmic movement of matter through the digestive tract is called _____ .
   (extrusion/peristalsis/defecation)

4. The urinary system filters and _____ body wastes.
   (breaks down/metabolizes/eliminates)

5. Endocrine glands, which have no ducts, secrete _____ directly into the bloodstream.
   (hormones/chemicals/fluids)

• Section 4 •
THE NERVES AND SKIN

The Nervous System

Learning Objective 10 Describe the common structures and functions of the nervous system.

The nervous system (see Figure 2-16 on page 30) has two major functions: communication and control. The nervous system

- Enables the person to be aware of the environment
- Enables the person to react to the environment
- Coordinates responses of the body to stimuli
- Keeps body systems working together

The nervous system consists of nerve centers (most of them in the brain and spinal cord) and nerves that branch off from those centers, leading to body tissues and organs.

There are two main structural divisions of the nervous system: The **central nervous system** consists of the brain and spinal cord; the **peripheral nervous system** consists of nerves located outside the brain and spinal cord.

There are also two functional divisions of the nervous system: The **voluntary nervous system** influences voluntary movements throughout the body; the **autonomic nervous system,** a system not directly under the influence of the brain, influences the involuntary muscles and glands.

The autonomic nervous system (see Figure 2-17 on page 31), which regulates unconscious, involuntary body functions, is further divided into two systems:

- The **sympathetic nervous system** regulates heart action, supply of blood to the arteries, secretions of ductless glands, smooth muscle action in the digestive tract, and action of other internal organs. This system responds to stress with the classic "fight or flight" syndrome.

- The **parasympathetic nervous system**—seated in the midportion of the brain, the brain stem, and the lower spinal cord—opposes the sympathetic nervous system by keeping body reactions from becoming extreme.

Emergency care is required for any loss of consciousness, any significant head injury, any brain injury, any spinal injury, and any degree of paralysis.

endocrine glands The ductless glands that regulate the body by secreting hormones

central nervous system The part of the nervous system that consists of the brain and the spinal cord

peripheral nervous system Structures of the nervous system (especially nerve endings) that lie outside the brain and spinal cord

voluntary nervous system The part of the nervous system that influences activity of the voluntary muscles and movements throughout the body

autonomic nervous system The part of the nervous system that influences the activities of involuntary muscles and glands

sympathetic nervous system The part of the autonomic nervous system that causes blood vessels to constrict, stimulates sweating, increases the heart rate, causes the sphincter muscles to contract, and prepares the body to respond to stress

parasympathetic nervous system The part of the autonomic nervous system seated in the midportion of the brain, brain stem, and lower spinal cord

THE BRAIN

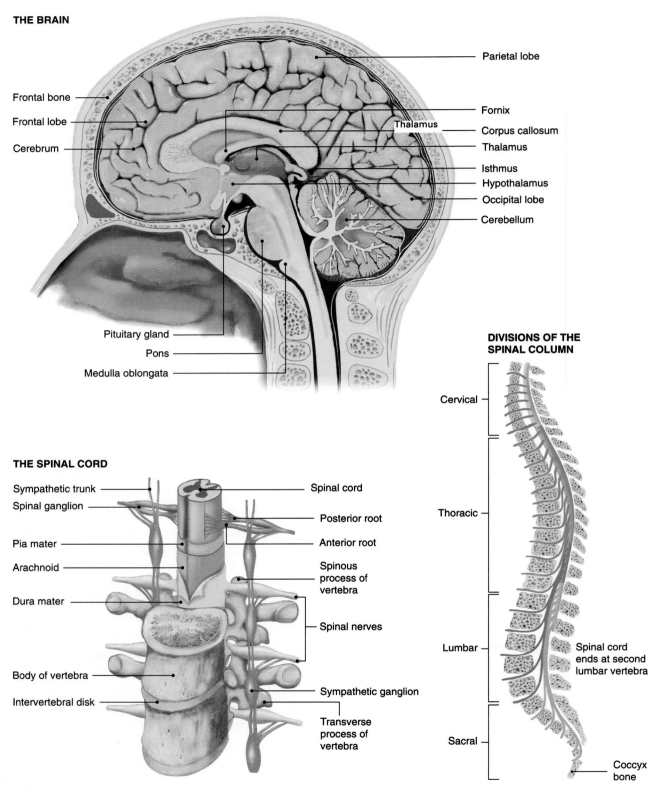

Parietal lobe

Frontal bone

Frontal lobe

Cerebrum

Fornix

Thalamus

Corpus callosum

Thalamus

Isthmus

Hypothalamus

Occipital lobe

Cerebellum

Pituitary gland

Pons

Medulla oblongata

THE SPINAL CORD

Sympathetic trunk

Spinal ganglion

Pia mater

Arachnoid

Dura mater

Body of vertebra

Intervertebral disk

Spinal cord

Posterior root

Anterior root

Spinous process of vertebra

Spinal nerves

Sympathetic ganglion

Transverse process of vertebra

DIVISIONS OF THE SPINAL COLUMN

Cervical

Thoracic

Lumbar

Spinal cord ends at second lumbar vertebra

Sacral

Coccyx bone

Figure 2-16. *The nervous system*

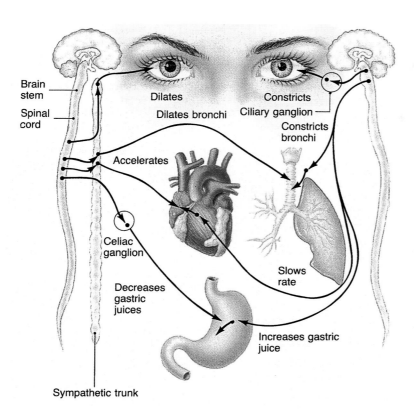

Figure 2-17. *The autonomic nervous system. One way to describe the nervous system is by function. There are two divisions: the voluntary (cerebrospinal) system, which for the most part governs conscious, deliberate bodily actions under the control of the will—plus reflex actions that may or may not be conscious; and the involuntary (autonomic) system, which is automatic and partly independent of the rest of the nervous system. The autonomic nervous system is subdivided into the sympathetic and the parasympathetic nervous systems.*

The Skin

Learning Objective 11 Describe the main structures and functions of the skin.

The skin

- Protects internal organs from injury
- Prevents dehydration
- Protects against invasion by microorganisms
- Regulates body temperature
- Aids in elimination of water and various salts
- Acts as the receptor organ for touch, pain, heat, and cold

The skin consists of three layers (see Figure 2-18 on page 32). The outermost layer, the **epidermis,** contains cells that give the skin its color. The **dermis,** the second layer, contains the vast network of blood vessels, hair follicles, sweat glands, oil glands, and sensory nerves. Just below the dermis is a layer of fatty tissue that varies in thickness, depending on the part of the body it covers.

Progress Check

1. The nervous system has two main functions: communication and _____ .
   (sensation/control/reaction)

2. The brain and spinal cord make up the

   _____ .

   (autonomic nervous system/central nervous system/voluntary nervous system)

3. The peripheral nervous system is nerves located outside the _____ .
   (brain/spinal cord/brain and spinal cord)

4. The "fight-or-flight" syndrome is regulated by the

   _____ .

   (parasympathetic nervous system/sympathetic nervous system/central nervous system)

epidermis The outermost layer of the skin
dermis The second layer of skin

THE SKIN

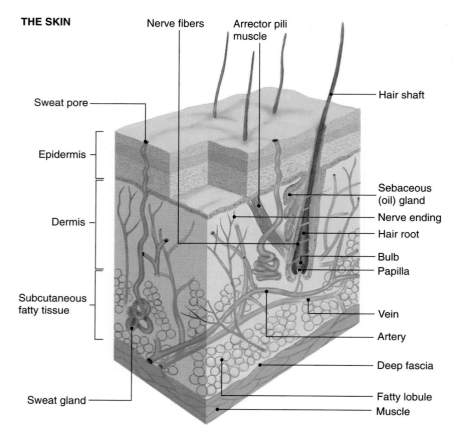

Nerve fibers

Arrector pili muscle

Sweat pore

Epidermis

Dermis

Subcutaneous fatty tissue

Sweat gland

Hair shaft

Sebaceous (oil) gland

Nerve ending

Hair root

Bulb

Papilla

Vein

Artery

Deep fascia

Fatty lobule

Muscle

Figure 2-18. The anatomy of the skin. The skin encloses the entire body and provides watertight protection that is not penetrable by bacteria if it is intact. It protects the deeper tissues from injury, drying out, and invasion from bacteria and other foreign bodies. The skin helps to regulate body temperature, aids in the elimination of water and various salts, and acts as a receptor organ for touch, pain, heat, and cold. The outermost layer, the epidermis, contains cells with pigment granules. The dermis or second layer of skin contains the network of blood vessels, hair follicles, sweat and oil glands, and sensory nerves. The subcutaneous tissue is a layer of fatty tissue that is beneath the skin and serves as a body insulator.

● SUMMARY ●

- Using proper anatomical terms to describe position, direction, and location lets you more accurately communicate the victim's condition and extent of injury.

- The skeletal system serves as the framework of the body, providing support, protection, motion, and flexibility.

- There are three different kinds of muscles: skeletal, which control voluntary movement; smooth, which control involuntary movement; and cardiac, which make up the heart.

- The circulatory system consists of two major fluid transportation systems, one for blood and one for lymphatic fluid.

- The respiratory system provides oxygen to the blood.

- The digestive system ingests food, carries it so it can be digested and absorbed, and eliminates waste.

- The urinary system helps maintain the delicate balance of water and various chemicals in the body and removes wastes from the bloodstream.

- The endocrine glands, which have no ducts, secrete hormones directly into the bloodstream for the regulation of various body functions.

- The nervous system, which provides communication and control, consists mainly of the nerve centers in the brain and spinal cord and the peripheral nerves that branch out to all body tissues and organs.

- The skin, which consists of three layers, protects the internal organs from infection and helps regulate body temperature and aids in elimination.

• KEY TERMS •

Make sure you understand the following key terms:

- anatomical position
- supine position
- prone position
- lateral recumbent position
- superior
- inferior
- anterior
- posterior
- medial
- lateral
- proximal
- distal
- superficial
- deep
- internal
- external
- articulate
- ball-and-socket joint
- hinge joint
- pivot joint
- gliding joint
- saddle joint
- condyloid joint
- fracture
- skeletal muscle
- voluntary muscle
- smooth muscle
- involuntary muscle
- cardiac muscle
- respiration
- inhalation
- inspiration
- exhalation
- expiration
- peristalsis
- endocrine glands
- central nervous system
- peripheral nervous system
- voluntary nervous system
- autonomic nervous system
- sympathetic nervous system
- parasympathetic nervous system
- epidermis
- dermis

Student: _____   Date: _____

Course: _____   Section #: _____

PART 1 • True/False

If you believe the statement is true, circle the T. If you believe the statement is false, circle the F.

T   F   **1.** In the supine position, the victim is lying face down.

T   F   **2.** The location of a joint determines how much it is able to move.

T   F   **3.** Smooth muscle is also known as voluntary muscle.

T   F   **4.** Cardiac muscle can stimulate itself into contraction even when disconnected from the nervous system.

T   F   **5.** An important function of the skin is to regulate body temperature.

PART 2 • Multiple Choice

For each item, circle the correct answer or the phrase that best completes the statement.

1. The adult skeleton has
  a. 409 bones
  b. 147 bones
  c. 311 bones
  d. 206 bones

2. The hip is an example of
  a. a condyloid joint
  b. a ball-and-socket joint
  c. a saddle joint
  d. a synovial joint

3. Which is an example of an involuntary muscle?
  a. the eye muscle
  b. intestinal muscle
  c. heart muscle
  d. leg muscle

4. An example of a hinge joint would be the
  a. hip
  b. knee
  c. head and neck
  d. shoulder

5. Which system permits the body to eliminate certain waste materials filtered from the blood?
  a. endocrine system
  b. lymphatic system
  c. exocrine system
  d. urinary system

6. The peripheral nervous system is made up of
  a. nerves within the spinal cord
  b. special ganglia within the cerebrum
  c. the pons and medulla
  d. nerves located outside the brain and spinal cord

7. Which of the following is *not* a layer of the skin?
  a. dermis
  b. sebaceous gland
  c. endodermis
  d. epidermis

8. A patient lying flat with face up is in which position?
  a. lateral recumbent
  b. anatomical
  c. prone
  d. supine

9. With the head as a point of reference, the feet are
  a. distal
  b. proximal
  c. posterior
  d. lateral

Match the terms on the right with their definitions.

A. Lower
B. Inside
C. Toward the front
D. To the right/left of center
E. Near the surface
F. Near point of reference
G. Toward the back
H. Toward the head
I. Outside
J. Remote from surface
K. Away from point of reference
L. Toward midline
M. Toward the feet
N. Lying face down
O. Lying on left/right side
P. Lying face up

_____ Superior
_____ Inferior
_____ Anterior
_____ Posterior
_____ Medial
_____ Lateral
_____ Proximal
_____ Distal
_____ Superficial
_____ Deep
_____ Internal
_____ External
_____ Inferior
_____ Supine
_____ Prone
_____ Lateral

3

Victim Assessment

Learning Objectives

When you have mastered the material in this chapter, you will be able to

1   Understand how to properly assess a victim

2   Describe how to establish rapport with the victim

3   Explain how to control the scene

4   Describe and conduct a primary survey

5   Know how to conduct a neuro exam

6   Explain how to determine the chief complaint

7   Understand the significance of vital signs (pulse, respiration, and relative skin temperature)

8   Explain how to take a history

9   Understand the sequence and practical application of a secondary survey

SQ3R Plus

- **Survey** to set goals for studying.
- Ask **questions** as you **read.**
- Stop frequently to **recite** and **review.**
- **Write** a summary of key points.
- **Reflect** on the importance of this material and its relevance in your life.

On May 3, 1998, Elaine Smith was preparing the soil in her flowerbeds for a new planting of Martha Washington geraniums. As she rounded the corner of her house, she saw her 82-year-old neighbor, Bessie Johnson, lying on the concrete patio, crying softly.

"Please help me," Bessie whispered. "My leg—oh, it hurts so much! I think I've broken my hip!" As Elaine knelt at her side, she asked what happened. "I don't quite know," Bessie said. "I felt so dizzy. . . ."

As the older woman guarded her hip, Elaine looked at her carefully. Her breathing was labored and there was a slight bluish discoloration around her lips. When Elaine placed the back of her hand against Bessie's pale cheek, she found it to be cool and moist.

Elaine realized that, coupled with her dizziness, Bessie's other symptoms strongly suggested the possibility of a heart attack—even though the woman's chief complaint was the pain in her hip. Elaine called out to a third neighbor who was washing his car to call 9-1-1, then helped Bessie into a more comfortable position and monitored her vital signs while waiting for the ambulance to arrive.

ASSESSING THE VICTIM IS ONE OF THE MOST IMPORTANT and critical parts of first aid: If you can't do at least a rough assessment, you can't know what care to give the victim.

Some injuries are obvious; others are hidden. A conscious victim may be able to guide you to the problem—but an unconscious victim will be of no help at all.

This chapter provides detailed information on assessment and gives you an assessment routine that will help you

- Get the victim's consent for emergency care
- Win the victim's confidence and ease the victim's anxiety
- Rapidly identify the victim's problem(s)
- Quickly determine which problem is a priority for care
- Obtain information that will help emergency personnel

As you assess the victim, your main goals are to

- Protect yourself from injury
- Identify and correct life-threatening problems
- Render proper emergency care
- Stabilize and prepare the victim for transport

• Section 1 •
THE VICTIM ASSESSMENT ROUTINE

Learning Objective 1 Understand how to properly assess a victim.

In most cases, conduct victim assessment in this order:

1. Arrive at the scene.
2. Establish rapport and control.
3. Conduct a primary survey.
4. Conduct a neuro exam.
5. Determine the chief complaint.
6. Assess vital signs.
7. Look for medical information devices.
8. Take a history.
9. Conduct a secondary survey.

You may need to adapt or change the sequence, depending on your experience and the specific emergency situation.

Arriving at the Scene

As you arrive at the scene, quickly assess the environment and the victim. Look for

- Clues to potential problems (police cars, a fire engine)
- Environmental dangers (downed power lines, fuel spills, icy road)
- The mechanism of injury (how the person was injured)

If the police are not present and directing traffic, assign a bystander at the scene to direct traffic, if necessary. Take all appropriate safety precautions to protect yourself, bystanders, and victims at the scene from further injury. Never risk your own safety.

Establishing Rapport and Control

Learning Objective 2 Describe how to establish rapport with the victim.

People who are injured are often frightened, anxious, angry, or in shock. To establish rapport with the victim and get control of the situation, you need to use the three Cs:

- **C**ompetence
- **C**onfidence
- **C**ompassion

Begin by observing any clues at the scene that may help you in assessment, such as damage to a vehicle, the victim's position, pills or food near the victim, or environmental temperature.

Next, approach the victim, ask for the victim's name, and say something like, "I'm [your name], and I'm trained in emergency care. I'd like to help you. Is that all right?" Tell the victim your level of care and what you'd like to do. Through this groundwork, you obtain the victim's consent.

Throughout the assessment and treatment, continue to call the victim by name, maintain eye contact, speak calmly and deliberately, and give orders quietly. People under stress or in medical shock process information more slowly, so speak distinctly and allow time for the victim or bystanders to respond.

Learning Objective 3 Explain how to control the scene.

To establish control:

- Move smoothly and deliberately.
- Position yourself at a comfortable level in relation to the victim. Stay where the victim can see you without twisting his or her neck.
- Keep your eye level above that of the victim.
- Conduct your survey in an unhurried, systematic way.
- Emotions escalate quickly in tense situations, so keep your voice calm and quiet.
- If there is more than one victim, determine which victim(s) needs the most immediate care. **Triage,** a system of sorting victims into treatment priorities, is described in Chapter 28.

Progress Check

1. To establish scene control, use the three Cs—competence, confidence, and _____ .
   (control/charisma/compassion)

2. An important part of introducing yourself to the victim is obtaining _____ .
   (the victim's name/consent for treatment/a history of what happened)

3. To maintain control, keep your voice _____ .
   (calm and deliberate/powerful and authoritative/loud and demanding)

4. Position yourself with your eye level _____ that of the victim.
   (above/even with/below)

---

triage A system of sorting victims into categories by treatment priority

• Section 2 •
CONDUCTING THE PRIMARY SURVEY

Learning Objective 4 Describe and conduct a primary survey.

The major goal of the primary survey is to check for life-threatening problems. Unless you find a life-threatening situation that needs to be treated immediately, you should be able to complete the primary survey in 60 seconds. Figure 3-1 illustrates the order of the primary and secondary surveys. Start with the following three steps:

1. If the victim is conscious, ask, "What happened?" The response will tell you the airway status, the adequacy of ventilation, level of consciousness, and mechanism of injury (see Figure 3-2).

2. Ask, "Where do you hurt?" The response will identify the most likely points of injury.

3. Visually scan the victim for general appearance, **cyanosis** (blueness from lack of oxygen), and sweating.

These steps provide a quick assessment of the victim's overall condition. The rest of the primary survey consists of evaluating the ABCDs—airway and cervical spine, breathing, circulation (hemorrhage), and disability (nervous system disability, or altered responsiveness).

Always assume spinal damage if the victim is unconscious, and do nothing that could aggravate possible spinal injury.

Airway and Cervical Spine

Determine whether the airway is open. If the victim is conscious or talking, the airway is open. If the airway is not open, use either the head-tilt/chin-lift maneuver or the modified jaw thrust maneuver to open it (see Chapter 4).

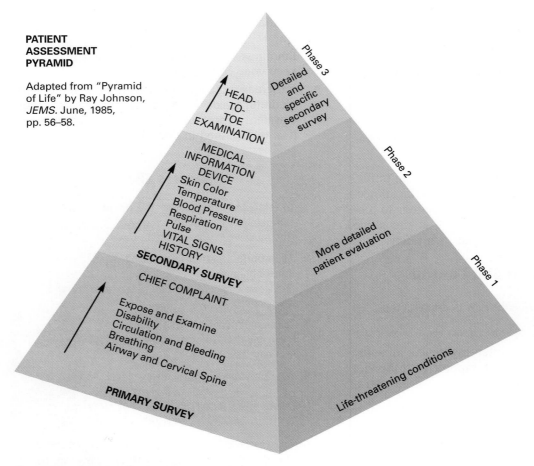

PATIENT ASSESSMENT PYRAMID

Adapted from "Pyramid of Life" by Ray Johnson, *JEMS.* June, 1985, pp. 56–58.

HEAD-TO-TOE EXAMINATION

Detailed and specific secondary survey

Phase 3

MEDICAL INFORMATION DEVICE
Skin Color
Temperature
Blood Pressure
Respiration
Pulse
VITAL SIGNS
HISTORY
SECONDARY SURVEY
CHIEF COMPLAINT

More detailed patient evaluation

Phase 2

Expose and Examine
Disability
Circulation and Bleeding
Breathing
Airway and Cervical Spine
PRIMARY SURVEY

Life-threatening conditions

Phase 1

Figure 3-1. Remember the order of the primary and secondary surveys.

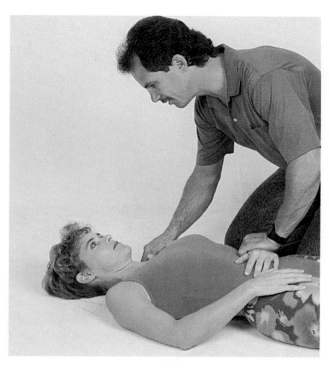

Figure 3-2. If the victim is conscious, ask, "What happened?" "Where do you hurt?"

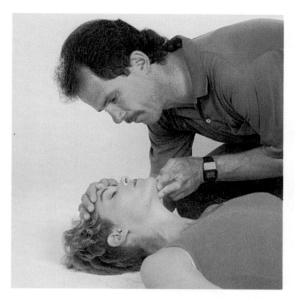

Figure 3-3. If the victim is unconscious, establish an open airway, then check for adequate breathing by the look-listen-feel technique. Assure an adequate open airway by the head tilt/chin lift method.

Check the cervical spine for deformity; pair that finding with the mechanism of injury and what the victim tells you to determine possible cervical spine injury.

Breathing

A responsive person is always breathing. To determine whether an unresponsive victim is breathing

- *Look* for chest movement
- *Listen* for breath sounds at the mouth and nose
- *Feel* on your cheek for air passing in and out of the mouth or nose

If the victim is not breathing spontaneously, begin artificial breathing immediately (see Chapter 4); continue until the victim is breathing spontaneously or until you are relieved by trained emergency personnel (see Figures 3-3 through 3-5).

If the victim is breathing, continue with the primary survey.

Circulation

To determine whether the blood is circulating, check the **radial pulse** (at the wrist) (see Figure 3-6 on page 42). If the victim is unconscious or you can't find the radial pulse, check the **carotid pulse** (in the groove of the neck) (see Figure 3-7 on page 42).

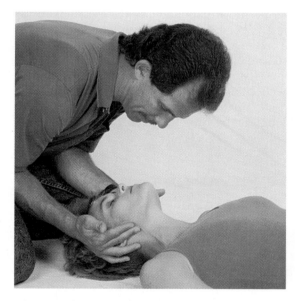

Figure 3-4. If you suspect a cervical spine injury, use a modified jaw thrust to open the victim's airway.

cyanosis Bluish discoloration from lack of oxygen

radial pulse The pulse at the wrist

carotid pulse The pulse at the groove on either side of the neck

Observe the person for 10 to 15 seconds. If the person is breathing, keep the airway open and check for pulses. Absence of respiration calls for rescue breathing.

LOOK   for chest movement
LISTEN   for breath sounds
FEEL   For any exhalation of warm air on your cheek

After opening the airway, observe the patient's chest for respiratory movements

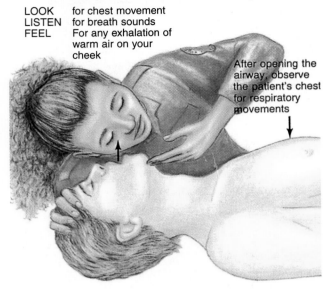

Figure 3-5. Assessing respiration

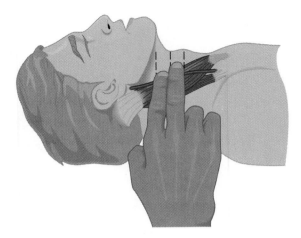

Figure 3-7. Palpate the carotid pulse at either side of the neck.

If the patient is pulseless, not breathing, and unresponsive, begin cardiopulmonary resuscitation (CPR) immediately (see Chapter 5). Continue CPR until circulation resumes or you are relieved by trained emergency personnel.

If the victim is breathing and has a pulse, continue by checking for serious or profuse bleeding (see Figure 3-8). Check for bleeding by thoroughly and quickly, but gently, running your gloved hands over and under the head and neck, arms, chest and abdomen, pelvis and buttocks, and legs. Check your gloves often for blood.

If you find hemorrhage—blood that is spurting or flowing freely—control it by direct pressure, use of pressure points, elevation, or tourniquet. Hemorrhage is the only kind of bleeding that should be treated during the primary survey.

Once you have completed the primary survey, note any signs or symptoms that make you suspect damage to the central nervous system. If you suspect nervous system damage, proceed to the neuro examination. If you have no reason to suspect nervous system damage, determine the chief complaint.

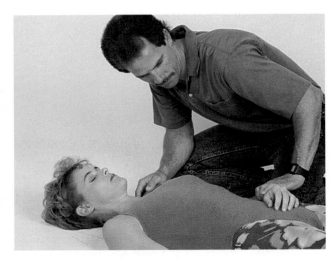

Figure 3-6. Palpate (feel) the radial pulse at the wrist.

Figure 3-8. Perform a quick body sweep for bleeding, checking your gloves often for blood.

Disability

The final step of the primary survey is to determine nervous system disability. Injuries to the nervous system generally result in an altered level of consciousness or responsiveness, which usually indicates decreased oxygen to the brain. There are four general levels of responsiveness:

- Alertness—the victim's eyes are open, and he or she can answer questions clearly and accurately.

- Response to verbal stimulation—the victim seems sleepy, but becomes more alert when spoken to.

- Response to pain—the victim appears to be asleep and does not respond when spoken to, but winces, grimaces, or jerks away when pinched.

- Unresponsiveness—the victim appears to be asleep and does not respond in any way when spoken to or pinched.

The neuro exam which is not strictly part of the primary survey, allows you to assess nervous system disability in greater detail. The neuro exam is described in Section 3.

Progress Check

1. The major goal of the primary survey is to check for

   _____ .
   (breathing/heartbeat/life-threatening problems)

2. You can determine both the level of consciousness and the adequacy of ventilation by _____ .
   (watching for chest movement/checking the pulse/asking if the victim is okay)

3. To conduct the primary survey, check the

   _____ .
   (pulse/breathing/ABCDs)

4. Unless you find life-threatening problems, you should be able to complete the primary survey in

   _____ .
   (1 minute/2 minutes/5 minutes)

5. The only kind of bleeding you should try to control during the primary survey is

   _____ .
   (hemorrhage/bleeding from a chest wound/bleeding from the head)

• Section 3 •

CONDUCTING THE NEURO EXAM

Learning Objective 5 Know how to conduct a neuro exam.

A neuro exam checks

- Level of consciousness
- Motor functions (such as voluntary movement)
- Sensory functions (what the victim can feel)

To conduct the neuro exam

1. Talk to the victim. A person who can't answer general questions is disoriented. If the victim is an infant or young child, estimate alertness by observing voluntary movements and interest in surroundings.

2. Note the victim's speech. Vagueness, slurring of speech, or garbled speech indicates a decreasing level of consciousness.

3. If the victim can't speak, determine whether he or she can understand by assessing his or her response to a simple command, such as "Squeeze my hand" (see Figure 3-9).

4. If the victim is unconscious, determine how easily the victim can be aroused. If the victim doesn't respond to your voice, try a pain stimulus (such as a pinch).

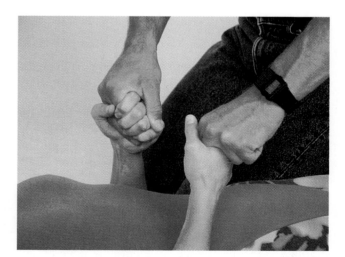

Figure 3-9. Test whether the victim can understand you by stating, "Squeeze my hand" and waiting for a response.

If you even suspect a neck or spinal injury, tell the victim to lie very still; immobilize the neck as well as you can, keep the head and neck in alignment, and activate the EMS system (see Chapter 13).

Progress Check

1. A neuro exam checks both motor and _____ functions.
   (visual/sensory/psychological)

2. Slurring of speech, garbled speech, or vagueness in answering questions indicates deteriorating _____ .
   (level of consciousness/motor control/ speech ability)

3. If a victim can't speak, give a simple _____ to assess level of consciousness.
   (stimulus/test/command)

4. Determine how easily unconscious victims can be aroused by using either verbal or _____ stimuli.
   (touch/pain/sound)

• Section 4 •
CHIEF COMPLAINT AND VITAL SIGNS

Determining the Chief Complaint

Learning Objective 6 Explain how to determine the chief complaint.

Until now, you've concentrated on **signs**—things you can observe yourself (such as a leg deformed by fracture). Now you'll ask specific questions aimed at discovering the **symptoms**—what the victim feels and describes to you (such as abdominal pain) (see Figures 3-10 and 3-11).

Ask, "Tell me where you hurt." The answer is the *chief complaint*. Most chief complaints are characterized by pain or abnormal structure or function and can be pinpointed using observations made by the victim.

Even if injury is obvious, it's important to ask. For example, a victim of a car accident may have an obvious fracture to the leg, but if the chief complaint is "I can't breathe," you may discover an unsuspected chest injury.

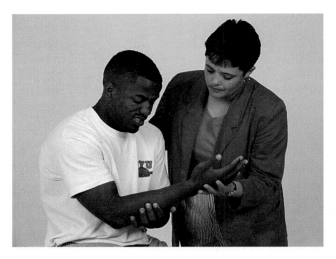

Figure 3-10. A victim exhibiting a sign, such as a deformed wrist

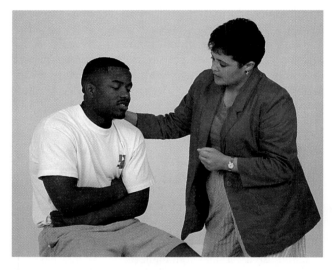

Figure 3-11. A victim describing a symptom, such as stomach pain

Assessing Vital Signs

Learning Objective 7 Understand the significance of vital signs (pulse, respiration, and relative skin temperature).

Vital signs should be taken repeatedly at 2- to 5-minute intervals. Changes in vital signs reflect both changes in the victim's condition and the effectiveness of your emergency care.

Use your senses—sight, hearing, touch, and smell—to determine pulse, respiration, and the temperature and color of the victim's skin.

Pulse

The pulse is the pressure wave generated when the heart beats; it reflects the rhythm, rate, and relative strength of the heart. You can take the pulse at any point where an artery crosses over a bone or lies near the skin, but the best place in a conscious victim is at the wrist (see Figure 3-12). If the victim is unconscious, take the pulse at the carotid artery (in the groove of the neck) (see Figure 3-13).

When you take the pulse, note its

- Rate (normal resting rate is 60 to 100 beats per minute for an adult, 80 to 200 for a child)
- Strength (a normal pulse is full and strong)
- Rhythm (a normal pulse is regular)

To take the pulse, have the victim lie or sit down; use the tips of two or three fingers and examine the pulse gently by touch. Count the number of beats for 15 seconds, then multiply by four to determine the number of beats per minute. Write down the pulse immediately after taking it; don't rely on your memory.

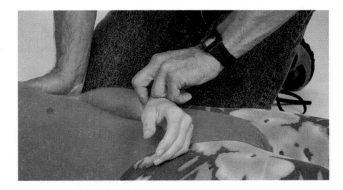

Figure 3-12. Palpate the radial pulse at the wrist.

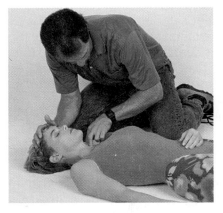

Figure 3-13. If the victim is unconscious, palpate the carotid pulse in the neck.

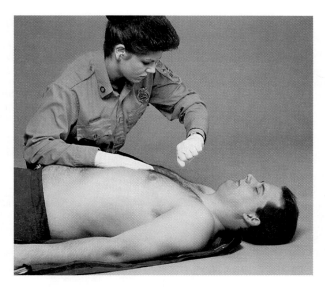

Figure 3-14. Measure respirations by placing your hand on the victim's chest or abdomen. Count the number of times the chest or abdomen rises in 30 seconds. Then multiply that number by two.

Respiration

A respiration consists of one inhalation and one exhalation. Normal respirations are easy and spontaneous, without pain or effort. The average normal rate is 12 to 20 breaths per minute for an adult. Place your hand on the victim's chest and feel for chest movement (see Figure 3-14). The chest should move up at least an inch with each breath.

Cardinal signs of respiratory distress (see Figure 3-15 on page 46) include wheezing, crowing, gurgling, flaring of the nostrils, contracting of the trachea, and use of accessory muscles in the neck and abdomen.

Temperature and Skin Color

Assess relative skin temperature (see Figure 3-16 on page 46) by placing the back of your hand against the skin of the victim's forehead or neck. Normal skin is fairly dry, as well as normal in temperature.

Abnormally high temperature can be caused by fever, heat stroke, or a hot environment. Abnormally low temperature can be caused by shock, spinal injury, heat exhaustion, or exposure to cold.

signs Things you can observe about the victim, such as bleeding

symptoms Things the victim describes to you, such as abdominal pain

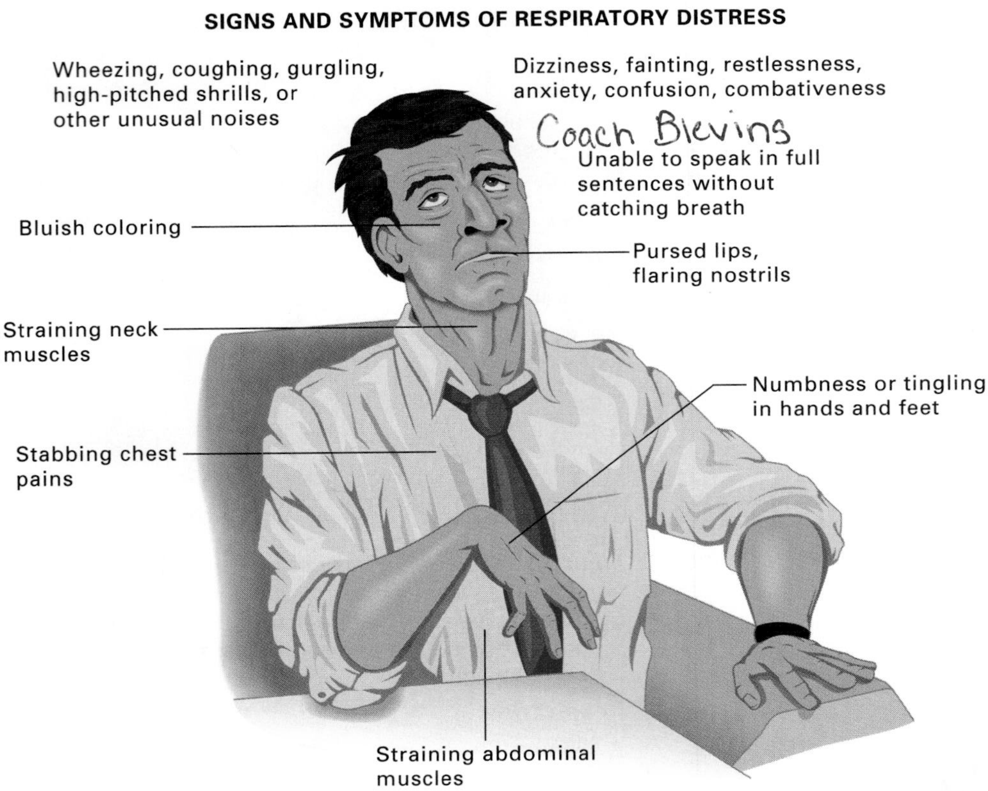

SIGNS AND SYMPTOMS OF RESPIRATORY DISTRESS

Figure 3-15. Look, listen, and feel for signs of respiratory distress.

Wheezing, coughing, gurgling, high-pitched shrills, or other unusual noises

Dizziness, fainting, restlessness, anxiety, confusion, combativeness

Coach Blevins

Unable to speak in full sentences without catching breath

Bluish coloring

Pursed lips, flaring nostrils

Straining neck muscles

Numbness or tingling in hands and feet

Stabbing chest pains

Straining abdominal muscles

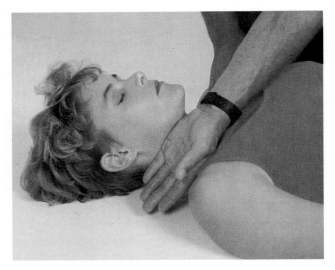

Figure 3-16. For relative skin temperature, touch the victim's skin with the back of your hand.

Skin color can tell you a lot about a victim.

- Paleness may be caused by shock or heart attack.
- Redness may be caused by high blood pressure, the late stages of carbon monoxide poisoning, alcohol abuse, sunburn, heat stroke, fever, or infectious disease.

- Blueness (cyanosis) may be caused by suffocation, lack of oxygen, heart attack, or poisoning. Cyanosis is always a serious problem. It appears first in the fingertips and around the mouth.

Capillary refill is one method of checking for shock. This procedure is performed by squeezing one of the victim's fingernails or toenails. When the nail is squeezed, the tissue under the nail turns white. When the pressure is released, color returns to the tissue. By measuring the time it takes for color to return under the nail, you are obtaining capillary refill. Two seconds or less is considered within normal limits. If refill time is greater than 2 seconds, suspect shock or decreased blood flow to that extremity. Measure capillary refill time by counting "One one-thousand, two two-thousand," and so on.

Looking for Medical Information Devices

While taking vital signs, watch for medical identification devices, such as a Medic Alert tag, necklace, or bracelet (see Figure 3-17). These medical information devices list the victim's medical problem and an emergency 24-hour number you can call for more information.

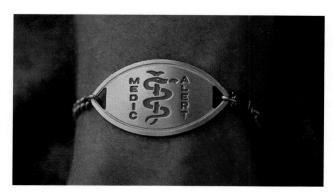

Figure 3-17. Medic Alert bracelet

Medical identification tags are often worn by people with hidden medical conditions, such as heart problems, diabetes, epilepsy, or allergies.

Progress Check

1. The chief complaint is the victim's assessment of where he or she _____ .
(is injured/is compromised/hurts)

2. You can rely on your _____ to assess vital signs; you do not need specialized equipment.
(intuition/senses/wristwatch)

3. Take the pulse of an unconscious victim at the _____ artery.
(carotid/brachial/radial)

4. Take the pulse of a conscious victim at the _____ artery.
(carotid/brachial/radial)

5. Use the back of your hand to check the victim's relative _____ .
(respiration/pulse/temperature)

• Section 5 •
TAKING A HISTORY

Learning Objective 8 Explain how to take a history.

When taking a history:

• Assess the scene. The placement of the victim and objects at the scene can give clues about the injury.

• Ask questions. If the situation is urgent, ask yes-no questions ("Have you eaten today?"); if the situation is less urgent, ask open-ended questions ("Tell me about your last meal"). Whenever possible, ask open-ended questions, because you don't want to suggest answers to the victim.

• Ask about symptoms, allergies, prescribed medications, preexisting medical conditions, last food, events prior to the injury, the duration and intensity of pain, and any positions that ease or relieve the pain.

• If the victim is unresponsive, seems confused, or is a child, get a history by talking to friends or family members.

Progress Check

1. When possible, ask the victim _____ questions.
(yes-no/open-ended)

2. When asking about pain, find out about its duration, intensity, and positions that _____ the pain.
(relieve/intensify/stabilize)

• Section 6 •
CONDUCTING A SECONDARY SURVEY

Learning Objective 9 Understand the sequence and practical application of a secondary survey.

In essence, a secondary survey is a closer look at the victim once life-threatening conditions are controlled and vital signs are recorded. During the secondary survey you conduct a full-body assessment with your hands, checking for swelling, depression, deformity, bleeding, and other problems. Figure 3-18 on page 48 illustrates the order of examination.

Explain to the victim what you are doing, and keep talking calmly throughout the survey. Keep the victim's head and neck in alignment, and don't move the victim unnecessarily until you have finished the survey and ruled out the possibility of neck or spinal injuries.

During the survey, use the following approach:

• *Look for* deformities, wounds, bleeding, discoloration, penetration, openings in the neck, and unusual chest movement.

• *Listen for* unusual breathing sounds, gurgling sounds, or **crepitus** (a sandpaperlike noise made by broken bone ends rubbing against each other).

crepitus A sandpaperlike grating sound made by the ends of broken bones as they rub together

THE SECONDARY SURVEY

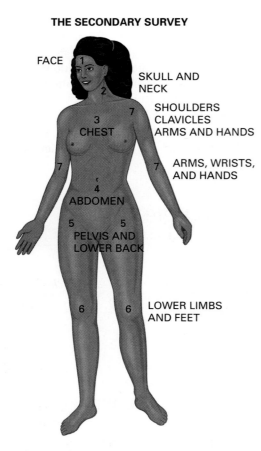

FACE

SKULL AND NECK

SHOULDERS
CLAVICLES
ARMS AND HANDS

CHEST

ARMS, WRISTS,
AND HANDS

ABDOMEN

PELVIS AND
LOWER BACK

LOWER LIMBS
AND FEET

Figure 3-18. The order of examination in the secondary survey

Figure 3-19. Run your fingers over the forehead, orbits of the eyes, and facial structure.

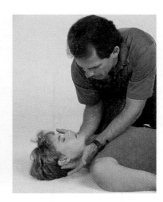

Figure 3-20. Check the nose and ears for blood or clear fluid (cerebrospinal fluid).

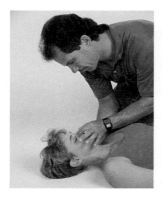

Figure 3-21. Gently check the nose for any possible injury.

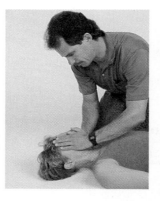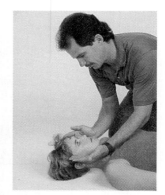

Figure 3-22 and Figure 3-23. Check the eyes for reactive pupils and possible damage.

- *Feel for* unusual masses, swelling, hardness, softness, mushiness, muscle spasms, pulsations, tenderness, deformities, and temperature.
- *Smell for* unusual odors on the victim's breath, body, or clothing.

Make every effort to protect the victim's privacy, but cut away any clothing that interferes with your ability to examine the victim properly.

When you finish the secondary survey, care for any injuries you find as time allows. The extent of the secondary survey and the emergency care you give will depend on how quickly the EMS system arrives on the scene.

Facial Features

Figures 3-19 through 3-25 illustrate the survey of facial features. Check the following:

- Forehead, eye orbits, and facial structures for abnormalities
- Ears and nose for fluid and injury
- Eyes for the ability to track a moving object smoothly and evenly in all four quadrants
- Mouth for internal lacerations, unusual breath odor, and teeth alignment

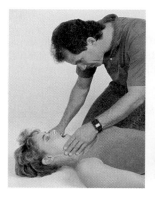 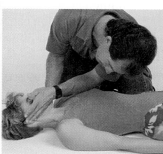

Figure 3-24 and Figure 3-25. Check the mouth for lacerations or obstructions. Is any unusual breath odor present? Check the face for symmetry and the teeth for alignment.

Skull and Neck

Figures 3-26 and 3-27 illustrate the survey of skull and neck. Check the following:

- Scalp for depressions and bruises
- Trachea for position (it should be in the middle of the neck)
- Neck for depressions, bruises, veins (they should not be distended), pulses (equal carotid pulses), pain, and tenderness

The victim should be able to swallow without discomfort, and the voice should not be hoarse.

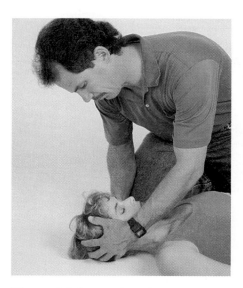

Figure 3-26. Gently palpate the skull for any depressions; bleeding; soft, hard, or mushy lumps; and so forth.

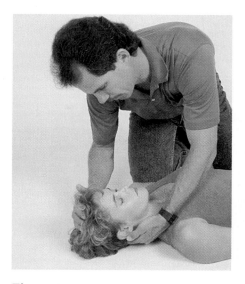

Figure 3-27. Gently palpate the neck to check for any abnormality of the cervical vertebrae.

Chest

Figures 3-28 and 3-29 illustrate the inspection of the chest. Check for the following:

- Soft-tissue injuries, such as cuts, bruises, indentations, impaled objects, or sucking chest wounds
- Abnormalities or signs of fractures
- Breathing abnormalities and symmetry of respiration
- Pain, tenderness, or instability over the ribs

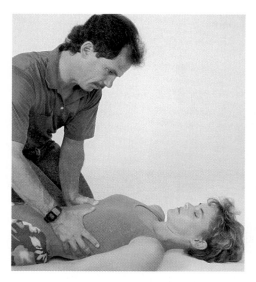

Figure 3-28. Apply compression to the rib cage to discover any rib cage damage. At the same time, visually inspect the chest for deformities, wounds, and equal chest expansion.

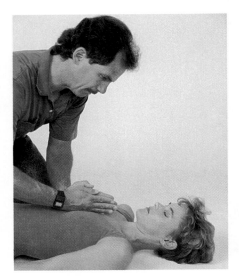

Figure 3-29. Gently press on the sternum for possible chest injury.

Abdomen

To survey the abdomen, have the victim lie down; keep the victim warm (shivering makes the abdominal muscles tense), and use a gentle touch (see Figure 3-30).

- Look for protrusions, soft-tissue wounds, lumps, swelling, or bruising.
- Palpate the four quadrants separately with the pads of your fingers for hardening or abdominal masses. If you suspect injury, feel that quadrant last.
- Ask about pain.

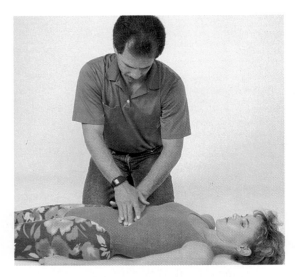

Figure 3-30. Inspect the abdomen visually; then palpate each quadrant for tenderness and deformity.

Pelvic Region

Injury in the pelvic region can cause extreme pain, so be gentle. Examination can also be very embarrassing, so talk to the victim and explain what you are doing (see Figures 3-31 and 3-32).

- Put your hands on each side of the hips and compress inward. Check for tenderness, crepitus, and instability.
- Look for loss of bladder control, bleeding, or erection of the penis (a sign of central nervous system injury).
- Check the strength of the femoral pulse.

Back

If cervical spine injury is a possibility, *do not move the victim.* Without moving the victim, slip your hand beneath the back and feel for possible fractures, dislocations, deformities, pain or tenderness, and bleeding

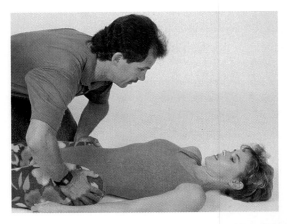

Figure 3-31. Put your hands on each side of the hips and compress inward, checking for tenderness, crepitus, and instability.

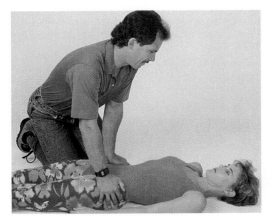

Figure 3-32. Put the base of your hands on the pubic bones, covering the iliac crest and hip bones.

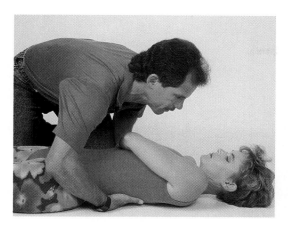

Figure 3-33. *Check the back for point tenderness and deformity. Keep the head and neck in alignment, and be very careful not to move the victim.*

(see Figure 3-33). Check for strength and sensation in all extremities.

Lower Extremities

Figures 3-34 through 3-37 illustrate the survey of the lower extremities.

- Look for bruises, fractures, dislocations, or swelling on the legs and feet.
- Check for abnormal position of the legs (a leg that is turned away, shortened, or rotated).
- Feel for protrusions, depressions, abnormal movement, and tenderness. Check for tenderness in the calves.
- Check each foot for a pulse (on top of the foot), sensation, motion, and warmth.

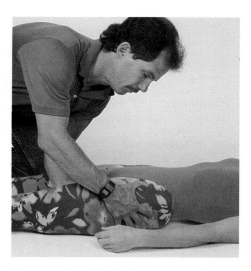

Figure 3-34. *Check the upper leg for pain and deformity.*

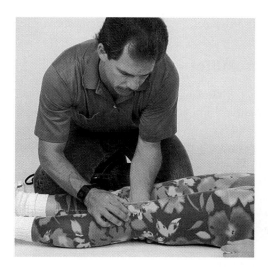

Figure 3-35. *Palpate the knees and feel the patella (kneecap) for any pain or deformity.*

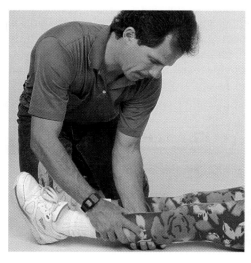

Figure 3-36. *Feel the lower legs; palpate the tibia, ankles, and feet.*

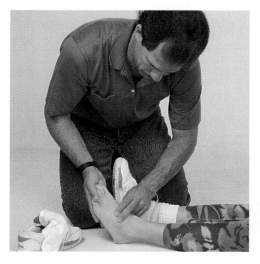

Figure 3-37. *Check for a pulse.*

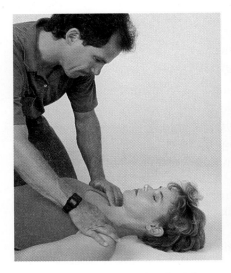

Figure 3-38. *Palpate the clavicles, and ask about any pain.*

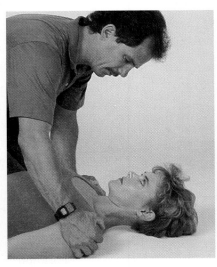

Figure 3-39. *Palpate the complete shoulder girdle.*

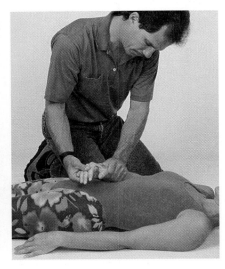

Figure 3-40. *Palpate the length of each arm.*

Upper Extremities

- Feel for fractures or joint dislocations in the clavicles, shoulders, and arms (see Figures 3-38 through 3-40).
- Check for equal grip strength in both hands.

Progress Check

1. During the secondary survey, conduct a full-body assessment with your _____ . *(eyes/hands)*

2. Never move the victim unnecessarily until you are sure _____ . *(emergency personnel are on the way/there are no spinal injuries/the victim is not in pain)*

3. During the secondary survey, keep the head and neck _____ . *(aligned/immobile/comfortable)*

- The only bleeding you should try to control during the primary survey is hemorrhage.
- The neuro examination lets you check level of consciousness, motor functions, and sensory functions.
- The chief complaint—the answer you receive when you ask the victim where it hurts—points you to the most likely area of injury.
- Use your senses—look, listen, feel, and smell—to assess the vital signs, including pulse, respiration, temperature, and skin color.
- When taking a history, ask open-ended questions when possible.
- The secondary survey is a full-body assessment, during which you check for less-obvious injuries and medical problems. Depending on the time you have before emergency personnel arrive, you should provide care for the problems you find during the secondary survey.

• SUMMARY •

- To begin, establish rapport with the victim by introducing yourself and explaining that you are there to help. Obtain consent to treat before assessing the victim.
- During the primary survey, check for and treat life-threatening injuries involving the airway, cervical spine, breathing, circulation, and hemorrhage.

• KEY TERMS •

Make sure you understand the following key terms:

- triage
- cyanosis
- radial pulse
- carotid pulse
- signs
- symptoms
- crepitus

Student: _____   Date: _____

Course: _____   Section #: _____

PART 1 • True/False

If you believe the statement is true, circle the T. If you believe the statement is false, circle the F.

T F **1.** Serious internal injuries are usually very obvious to the First Aider.

T F **2.** It is important for a First Aider to know how an accident took place.

T F **3.** A normal pulse is full and strong.

T F **4.** The "B" in the ABCDs stands for "broken bones."

T F **5.** The number-one first aid priority in every first aid situation is establishing an open airway.

T F **6.** In a secondary survey, begin at the head and work down the body.

T F **7.** The normal breathing rate in the average adult is about 25 breaths per minute.

T F **8.** The normal resting pulse rate in an adult is 60 to 100 beats per minute.

PART 2 • Multiple Choice

For each item, circle the correct answer or the phrase that best completes the statement.

1. In order of priority, which are the three primary first aid measures?
   a. maintain breathing, stop bleeding, manage shock
   b. open the airway, maintain breathing, maintain circulation
   c. prevent shock, stop bleeding, maintain breathing
   d. stop bleeding, prevent shock, avoid infection

2. What should you look for during the survey?
   a. blood in the hair
   b. abdominal spasms and tenderness
   c. paralysis of the extremities
   d. all of the above

3. If you suspect a cervical spinal injury during the course of a secondary survey, what should you do first?
   a. stop the survey and call for assistance
   b. stabilize the head
   c. continue the survey to find other problems
   d. stop the survey completely

4. How long should the First Aider spend on the primary survey?
   a. 10 to 12 minutes
   b. 5 to 10 minutes
   c. 2 to 3 minutes
   d. 1 minute or less

5. Medic Alert tags are worn to
   a. identify allergies
   b. warn of hidden medical conditions, such as diabetes
   c. provide pertinent information about a victim's special medical needs
   d. all of the above

6. The primary survey is conducted in the following order:
   a. check for bleeding, breathing, and pulse
   b. check for airway, breathing, pulse, and bleeding
   c. check for pulse, breathing, and bleeding

7. The most common temperature taken by First Aiders in the field is the
   a. oral temperature
   b. relative skin temperature
   c. rectal temperature
   d. axillary temperature

8. The secondary survey is
   a. a repetition of the primary survey, to detect anything you missed the first time
   b. a full-body assessment, head to toe
   c. an assessment of the extremities
   d. a check for internal injuries

9. Vital signs should be taken
   a. during the primary survey
   b. after all fractures are immobilized
   c. during the secondary survey
   d. only after the primary and secondary survey

10. The artery in the neck where First Aiders most commonly take a pulse on an unconscious victim is called the
   a. cranial
   b. subclavian
   c. brachial
   d. carotid

A young boy falls out of a tree onto a rock pile below. You are the first person to reach the boy, who is unconscious. Rearrange the items in the list below in the correct order under the headings "Primary Survey" and "Secondary Survey."

A. Check the head for lacerations.
B. Check clavicles and arms for fractures.
C. Conduct a neuro exam.
D. Check for an open airway.
E. Check for adequate breathing.
F. Check the chest for movement on both sides and for fractures.
G. Check for a pulse.
H. Check the back for abnormalities.
I. Check the pelvis for fractures.
J. Check for any severely bleeding injuries.
K. Check the legs, ankles, and feet.
L. Check the abdomen for tenderness, spasms, or rigidity.

Primary Survey

1. _____

2. _____

3. _____

4. _____

Secondary Survey

5. _____

6. _____

7. _____

8. _____

9. _____

10. _____

11. _____

12. _____

- You are in a mall where an elderly woman has fallen. She says, "I'm dizzy," and she can't get up. Her lips are bluish and she is breathing in shallow gasps. When you ask her what day it is, she says, "I'm having a heart attack, aren't I?"

  Which are signs and which are symptoms? How would you pursue a victim assessment? When would you decide to phone for an ambulance?

_____ has satisfactorily demonstrated the following practical skills:

    Student's Name

Read the following list of first aid and emergency-care skills; indicate with a checkmark those you feel prepared to perform. At the end of this course, go back over the list to determine your preparedness.

First Aid Skills

	Now	End of Course
Primary victim survey	❏	❏
Survey of vital signs	❏	❏
Secondary victim survey	❏	❏

4

Basic Life Support: Artificial Ventilation

Learning Objectives

When you have mastered the material in this chapter, you will be able to

1 Describe the signs of respiratory distress

2 Explain proper victim assessment for breathing problems

3 Describe how to open the airway of a victim who does not have spinal injury

4 Describe how to open the airway of a victim you suspect has spinal injury

5 Understand the "look, listen, and feel" assessment method of determining breathlessness

6 Explain how to restore breathing through artificial ventilation

7 Adapt ventilation-support procedures to infants and children

8 Identify an obstructed airway

9 Use techniques for dislodging foreign objects that are obstructing the airway of a conscious person

10 Use the technique for dislodging foreign objects that are obstructing the airway of an unconscious person

On February 14, 1998, 58-year-old Richard Quail and his wife joined two other couples at a local steak house to celebrate Valentine's Day. When one woman told about a surprise party her children had planned and executed, all six laughed heartily. When the laughter died down, the others noticed that Richard had a panic-stricken look on his face. His wife put her hand on his arm and asked, hesitantly, "Are you all right?" Richard clutched the table edge with both hands and shook his head briskly; suddenly, clutching his throat as if he was choking, he struggled to his feet, knocking his chair over backward.

Both men at the table leaped toward him; "He's choking!" cried Stan Mortensen. While Stan ran toward the hostess to call for an ambulance, Judith Larsen approached from the next table. Standing behind Richard, she wrapped her arms around his waist. Positioning her fist, thumb side in, just above his navel, she powerfully thrust inward and upward. Still Richard clutched at his throat. After two more powerful thrusts, Richard expelled a large piece of steak, then started coughing. As Judith helped him to a chair, he began to vomit.

By the time EMTs arrived, Richard was shaken, but breathing normally.

THE FIRST PRIORITY IN ANY EMERGENCY IS TO ESTABLISH and maintain an adequate airway. Simply stated, your ability to do so can spell the difference between life and death.

In some instances, airway obstruction itself may be the emergency—a swimmer may stay underwater too long and inhale water, or a business executive at a banquet may choke on a piece of steak. In other cases, the injury process may cause a victim to stop breathing.

By understanding the physiological process of breathing and the methods of care, as outlined in this chapter, you can quickly initiate and maintain an airway adequate enough to save most victims until emergency help arrives.

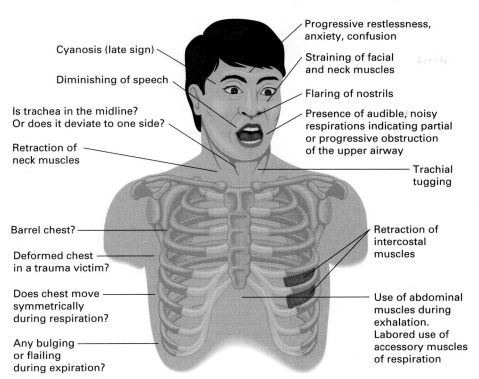

Cyanosis (late sign)

Diminishing of speech

Is trachea in the midline?
Or does it deviate to one side?

Retraction of
neck muscles

Barrel chest?

Deformed chest
in a trauma victim?

Does chest move
symmetrically
during respiration?

Any bulging
or flailing
during expiration?

Progressive restlessness,
anxiety, confusion

Straining of facial
and neck muscles

Flaring of nostrils

Presence of audible, noisy
respirations indicating partial
or progressive obstruction
of the upper airway

Trachial
tugging

Retraction of
intercostal
muscles

Use of abdominal
muscles during
exhalation.
Labored use of
accessory muscles
of respiration

Figure 4-1. Signs and symptoms of respiratory distress

• Section 1 •
RESPIRATORY DISTRESS

Breathing emergencies can be caused by a variety of accidents or medical disorders. The most common type of breathing emergency is respiratory distress. Respiratory distress can be caused by injury, asthma, hyperventilation, and anaphylactic shock. It represents the beginning of a life-threatening emergency.

The most common causes of respiratory arrest are electric shock, drowning, suffocation, toxic gas inhalation, head and chest injuries, heart problems, stroke, drug overdose, and allergic reactions. *Respiratory arrest is a true medical emergency.*

Signs and Symptoms

> **Learning Objective 1** Describe the signs of respiratory distress.

The signs and symptoms of respiratory distress (see Figure 4-1) include the following:

- Abnormal breathing patterns (difficulty catching the breath, gasping for air, or slow or rapid breathing)
- Unusual breathing noises, such as wheezing, snoring, crowing, or gurgling

- Dizziness
- Pain in the chest
- Tingling in the hands and/or feet
- Clammy skin
- Abnormal skin color—paleness, flushed skin (redness), or cyanosis

Basic Life Support

When oxygen is cut off to the lungs—hence, to the brain and heart—the heart continues to pump, and oxygen stored in the lungs and blood will continue to circulate for a short time. Gradually, the heart stops beating, resulting in cardiac arrest.

The body's cells have a residual oxygen supply that keeps them alive for a short time even after breathing and heartbeat stop. The brain cells are the first to die, usually within 4 to 6 minutes after being deprived of oxygenated blood.

Basic life support describes the first aid procedures necessary to sustain life in an emergency situation. The first steps in basic life support are assessing the victim, opening the airway, and providing rescue breathing.

> **basic life support** A term that describes the first aid procedures necessary to sustain life in an emergency situation

• Section 2 •
VICTIM ASSESSMENT

Learning Objective 2 Explain proper victim assessment for breathing problems.

The first crucial step in basic life support is assessment. The American Heart Association has stated that "No victim should undergo any of the more intrusive procedures of cardiopulmonary resuscitation (i.e., positioning, opening the airway, rescue breathing, and external chest compression) until the need for it has been established by the appropriate assessment."

Assessment consists of four steps:

1. Determining unresponsiveness
2. Activating the EMS system
3. Positioning the victim and opening the airway
4. Determining breathlessness

Determining Unresponsiveness

To determine responsiveness, tap the victim gently on the shoulder and ask loudly, "Are you okay?" You are not looking for an answer as much as you are any kind of response—fluttering eyelids, muscle movement, turning to the sound, and so on. If there is no response, the victim is unresponsive.

Activating the EMS System

If the adult victim is unresponsive and you are alone, activate the EMS system immediately. If an infant is unresponsive and you are alone, give emergency care for 1 minute, then activate the EMS system. The person who calls dispatch should give the location of the emergency, the telephone number he or she is calling from, what happened, the number of victims involved, what emergency care is being given to the victim, and any other requested information. *If anyone other than you and the victim is at the scene, ask that person to make the emergency call so you can focus on helping the victim.*

Positioning the Victim and Opening the Airway

Ideally, the victim should be lying on his or her back on a firm, flat surface. Place the victim's arms alongside his or her body, and kneel at the victim's side. If you have to move the victim, roll the victim as a unit so that head, shoulders, and torso move without twisting; maintain neutral alignment of the head and neck.

The most important part of rescue breathing is opening the airway. If the victim is unconscious, the tongue can relax, fall back, and block the airway; the epiglottis can also relax and block the throat. Sometimes, the victim's efforts to breathe can create negative pressure that draws the tongue or the epiglottis, or both, into the airway. In these cases, opening the airway may be all that is needed to restore breathing.

If you see liquids (such as vomitus) in the mouth, wrap your index and middle fingers in cloth and sweep the liquid out. If you can see solid foreign objects (such as broken teeth), quickly hook them out with your index finger.

Use one of the following methods to open the airway.

Head-Tilt/Chin-Lift Maneuver

Learning Objective 3 Describe how to open the airway of a victim who does not have spinal injury.

If you do *not* suspect cervical spine injury

1. Place the tips of the fingers of one hand underneath the lower jaw on the bony part near the chin; put your other hand on the victim's forehead and apply firm, backward pressure (see Figure 4-2).
2. Bring the chin forward, supporting the jaw and tilting the head backward; be careful not to compress the soft tissues underneath the chin. Maintain pressure on the victim's forehead to keep the head tilted backward.
3. Lift the chin so the teeth are nearly brought together; use your thumb to keep the mouth slightly open. Leave dentures in place if you can; the lips are less likely to obstruct breathing if dentures are in place.

Take special precautions with children. Extending a child's head and neck too far can cause the trachea to collapse. Never tilt an infant's head beyond neutral position; in older children, tilt it only slightly beyond

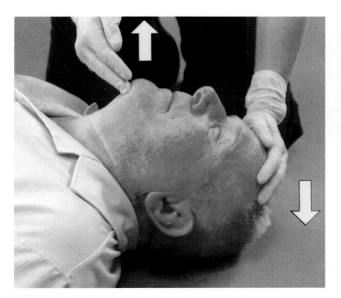

Figure 4-2. Head-tilt/chin-lift maneuver

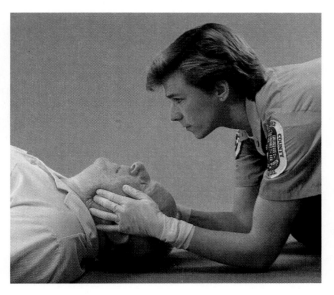

Figure 4-3. Jaw-thrust maneuver

a sniffing position (the nose tilted slightly upward). Placing a rolled towel under the shoulders may adjust the position enough.

Jaw-Thrust Maneuver

Learning Objective 4 Describe how to open the airway of a victim you suspect has spinal injury.

If the head-tilt/chin-lift position is unsuccessful or *if you suspect cervical spine injury*

1. Facing the top of the victim's head, place your elbows on the surface on which the victim is lying, your hands at the sides of the victim's head.

2. Grasp the jawbone on both sides where it angles up toward the victim's ears (see Figure 4-3). Move the jaw forward and upward.

3. Retract the lower lip with your thumb if the lips close.

After you have displaced the jawbone forward, support the head carefully *without* tilting it backward or moving it side to side.

Determining Breathlessness

Learning Objective 5 Understand the "look, listen, and feel" assessment method of determining breathlessness.

With the airway open, check to see whether the victim is breathing. Place your ear close to the victim's mouth and nose for 3 to 5 seconds, and

- *Look* for the chest to rise and fall
- *Listen* for air escaping during exhalation
- *Feel* for the breath against your cheek

If the victim is breathing, maintain an open airway, and place the victim in the recovery position (see Figure 4-4 on page 60). This position helps both conscious and unconscious victims maintain an open airway. If you suspect trauma or cervical spine injury, do not move the victim.

To place the victim in the recovery position, roll her or him onto one side, moving head, shoulders, and torso simultaneously without twisting. Then flex one leg at the knee. Place the bottom arm behind the back. Flex the top arm, placing the hand under the cheek. Continue with your primary survey as described in Chapter 3.

If the victim is not breathing, prepare to perform rescue breathing.

Progress Check

1. The crucial first step in basic life support is

    _____ .

    (opening the airway/assessing the victim/activating the EMS system)

2. Tap the victim on the shoulder and ask if he or she is okay to determine _____ .
    (unresponsiveness/breathlessness/arrest)

    (continued)

Figure 4-4. The recovery position

3. Before you open the airway, the victim should be in a _____ position.
(prone/supine)

4. During the head-tilt/chin-lift maneuver, maintain backward pressure on the victim's _____ .
(chin/forehead)

5. Use the jaw-thrust maneuver if you suspect the victim has a _____ injury.
(head/tracheal/cervical spine)

6. In the jaw-thrust maneuver, you bring the victim's _____ forward instead of tilting the head backward.
(jaw/head)

7. To assess for breathlessness, _____ for the chest to rise and fall.
(feel/look)

8. To assess for breathlessness, _____ for air escaping during exhalation.
(listen/feel)

9. To assess for breathlessness, _____ for breath against your cheek.
(feel/listen)

• **Section 3** •
RESCUE BREATHING

Learning Objective 6 Explain how to restore breathing through artificial ventilation.

If you determine that the victim is not breathing, keep the victim in a supine position and begin providing rescue breathing. The most efficient method, if you can use it, is mouth-to-mouth; you can also use a barrier during mouth-to-mouth to prevent transmission of infectious diseases. Use mouth-to-nose ventilation if the mouth can't be opened, the mouth is seriously injured, or you can't form a tight seal around the mouth. Use mouth-to-stoma ventilation for a victim with a **stoma** (surgical opening) in the neck.

Mouth-to-Mouth Ventilation

Mouth-to-mouth ventilation is the simplest, quickest, and most effective way to perform rescue breathing, and it is preferred whenever possible. Figures 4-5 through 4-9 illustrate mouth-to-mouth ventilation.

Before starting, make sure the victim is properly positioned and the airway is open, as described earlier. Then proceed as follows.

1. Use the thumb and finger of the hand tilting the victim's forehead to pinch the nostrils closed. If you used the jaw-thrust maneuver, continue to hold the lower lip down with your thumb and forefinger, and press your cheek against the victim's nostrils to seal them off.

2. Open your mouth wide, take in a deep breath, and cover the victim's entire mouth with yours, forming an airtight seal. Blow air slowly and evenly into the victim's mouth until you see the chest rise. Then remove your mouth and watch for the chest to fall; feel for the victim's breath against your cheek. While your head is turned away, take in another deep breath.

3. Again cover the victim's mouth with yours, forming an airtight seal, and blow a second breath into the victim's mouth until you see the chest rise. Again remove your mouth and watch for the chest to fall.

4. If you don't see the chest rise and fall on the first attempt, reposition the airway and try again. (The most common cause of difficulty with ventilation is improper positioning of the head and chin.) If the second try also fails, assume the airway is

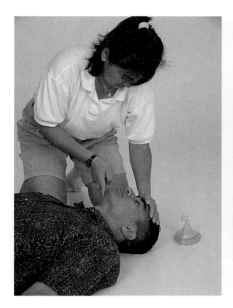

Figure 4-5. *Open the airway using the head-tilt/chin-lift maneuver. If you suspect a spinal injury, use the jaw-thrust.*

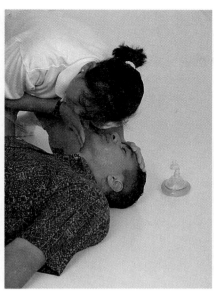

Figure 4-6. *Establish breathlessness with the "look, listen, and feel" assessment method.*

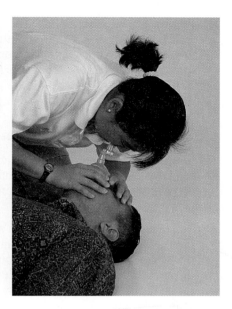

Figure 4-7. *In artificial ventilation, give two initial slow breaths. Allow deflation between breaths.*

Figure 4-8. *Turn to see the chest fall and feel the exhaled breath on your cheek.*

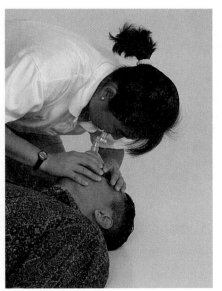

Figure 4-9. *Once you determine that the victim has a pulse, continue mouth-to-mouth ventilation at the rate of one breath every 5 seconds.*

blocked by a foreign object. Follow directions at the end of this chapter under Obstructed Airway Emergencies (see pages 66–67).

5. After the first two breaths, check the victim for a pulse. Using your fingertips, check the carotid pulse (located in the groove of the neck alongside the Adam's apple) on the side closest to you. The carotid pulse is easy to locate and easy to feel and is the last pulse to stop. Check for 5 to 10 seconds (if the victim is hypothermic, check for 30 seconds). If there is no pulse, immediately start ex-

stoma A surgical opening in the neck

ternal chest compressions as described in Chapter 5. If the victim has a pulse, continue ventilation, giving one breath every 5 seconds, or approximately 12 per minute. Continue rescue breathing until the victim begins breathing spontaneously or until you are relieved by emergency personnel.

Mouth-to-Barrier Ventilation

There are two kinds of clear plastic barrier devices that can be used in mouth-to-mouth ventilation to protect you from transmission of infectious diseases during rescue breathing.

- The **face shield** covers the victim's mouth; in some face shields, a short airway extends into the victim's mouth to hold down the tongue. You breath through the face shield to deliver ventilations; because the face shield covers only the mouth, you must still pinch the victim's nose closed.

- The **face mask** covers the victim's nose and mouth, creating an airtight seal; you deliver ventilations through a one-way valve so that the victim's exhaled breath does not enter your mouth. The American Heart Association recommends use of the face mask instead of the face shield, because it is more effective in creating an airtight seal.

If you decide to use a barrier device during mouth-to-mouth ventilation, extend the victim's neck and lift the chin. Place the barrier device over the victim's mouth or mouth and nose, depending on the type of device, and make sure there is an adequate, airtight seal. If you are using a face shield, make sure you pinch the victim's nose closed. Once the barrier device is in place, deliver rescue breaths as described above.

Mouth-to-Nose Ventilation

Use mouth-to-nose ventilation when

- You can't open the victim's mouth
- The victim's mouth is so large that you can't seal it off with your mouth
- The victim has no teeth, which interferes with the formation of a good seal
- The victim has mouth injuries

Proceed as follows.

1. With one hand, tilt the victim's forehead back. With your other hand, lift the lower jaw forward and seal the lips. If you used the jaw-thrust maneuver to open the airway, keep the jaw in place with your hand and seal the victim's mouth with your cheek.

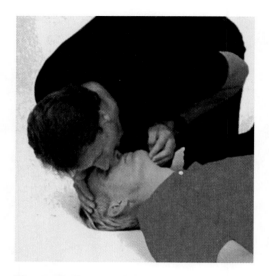

Figure 4-10. *Mouth-to-nose ventilation*

2. Take a deep breath, then place your mouth over the victim's nostrils, forming a tight seal (see Figure 4-10). Blow air slowing and evenly through the victim's nose.

3. If you can, hold the victim's mouth open during exhalation; the victim will exhale more fully, emptying the lungs, if the mouth is open.

Continue rescue breathing as described for mouth-to-mouth ventilation.

Mouth-to-Stoma Ventilation

A *stoma* is a small permanent surgical opening in the neck through which the surgical patient breathes. Figure 4-11 illustrates how a neck breather's airway has been changed by surgery. Proceed with rescue breathing as follows.

1. Remove anything covering the stoma, such as a tie, scarf, or jewelry; clear the stoma of any foreign matter.

2. You don't have to perform a head tilt on a victim with a stoma—simply use one hand to pinch the victim's nose and close the victim's mouth. Pinch off the nose between your third and fourth finger, and seal the lips with the palm of your hand.

3. Take a deep breath, then breathe directly into the stoma, forming a seal around the stoma with your mouth. If there is a tracheostomy tube in the stoma, breathe through the tube.

Continue rescue breathing as described for mouth-to-mouth ventilation. Look, listen and feel for breaths at the victim's stoma.

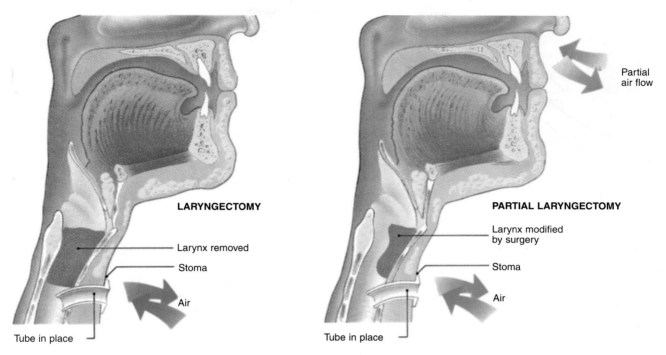

Figure 4-11. The neck breather's airway has been changed by surgery.

Gastric Distention

During artificial ventilation, it is common for air to get into the esophagus and from there, into the stomach. **Gastric distention** (inflation of the stomach with air) occurs most often in children and in airway-obstructed victims when you have breathed too forcefully. To help prevent gastric distention

- Blow only hard enough to make the chest rise.
- Deliver full, slow breaths no faster than two every second.
- Make sure the airway is open.
- Stop rescue breathing if you hear gurgling or bubbling during ventilation.

The American Heart Association recommends *not* pressing on the abdomen to relieve gastric distention. Such pressure could force stomach contents back up into the mouth and down the trachea, causing **aspiration** (breathing foreign matter into the lungs), which interferes with ventilation. You should try to relieve distention only if it is so severe that you cannot ventilate the victim. To decompress

1. Logroll the victim onto one side; guard against twisting the victim's body, which could aggravate spinal injury.
2. With the flat of your hand, exert *moderate* pressure on the victim's abdomen between the navel and rib cage.

 After the victim vomits, quickly wipe the mouth out with gauze pads, wipe off the face, and resume resuscitation.

Ventilating Infants and Children

Learning Objective 7 Adapt ventilation-support procedures to infants and children.

If the victim is an infant or a child under the age of 8

- Position the child on his or her back.
- Tilt the head only to a neutral position in an infant (see Figure 4-12 on page 64); support the head and neck in one hand to maintain a neutral position. Tilt the head only to a sniffing position (the nose tilted slightly upward) in a child. The throat is much more pliable in an infant or child, and tilting the head back too far can actually obstruct the airway.

face shield A barrier device that covers a victim's mouth
face mask A barrier device that covers a victim's mouth and nose
gastric distention Inflation of the stomach with air
aspiration Breathing foreign matter into the lungs

Figure 4-12. Head-tilt/chin-lift for an infant

- With your mouth, cover both the nose and mouth of an infant with a tight seal (see Figure 4-13). Use your mouth to cover the mouth of a child.

- Deliver a slow, small puff of air—just enough to make the chest rise. (A child's smaller air passages provide a greater resistance to airflow, so the pressure will probably need to be greater than you might assume.) Be careful not to overinflate or blow too hard; gastric distention is much more common among infants and children.

- Turn your head to the side and watch for the chest to fall; listen for the child's breath, and feel for exhaled air against your cheek. With your head turned to the side, breathe in another deep breath of air.

- If the first breath did not go in (as indicated by the rise of the child's chest), reposition the airway and deliver a second breath. If the second breath

Figure 4-13. Using the mouth to seal the mouth and nose of an infant

does not go in, treat for an obstructed airway as described at the end of this chapter.

- If the second breath goes in, check for a pulse on the inside upper arm. (An infant's or child's neck is too thick and short to easily find the carotid pulse.) Check for 5 to 10 seconds. If there is no pulse, start external chest compressions immediately, as described in Chapter 5.

- If there is a pulse, continue rescue breathing. For infants up to 1 year old, breathe once every 3 seconds; for children 1 to 8 years old, breathe once every 4 seconds.

Progress Check

1. The most effective form of artificial ventilation is _____ .
   (mouth-to-mouth/mouth-to-barrier/mouth-to-nose)

2. Deliver two full, slow rescue breaths, each one lasting about _____ seconds.
   (2/3/4)

3. Perform rescue breathing at the rate of about _____ breaths per minute.
   (10/12/14)

4. The most common cause of ventilation difficulty is _____ .
   (insufficient air/obstructed airway/improper positioning of the head and chin)

5. Decompress gastric distention only if you cannot _____ because of the inflated stomach.
   (see the chest rise and fall/ventilate the victim)

6. If the victim is an infant or child, ventilations should be faster and more _____ .
   (shallow/forceful)

• Section 4 •
OBSTRUCTED AIRWAY EMERGENCIES

Learning Objective 8 Identify an obstructed airway.

The most common cause of respiratory emergency is upper-airway obstruction—a foreign object blocking the nose, back of the mouth, or area around the larynx. The most common upper-airway obstruction in an unconscious victim is the tongue; the upper airway can also be blocked by food, small objects, or fluids, including saliva, mucus, blood, or vomitus.

Lower-airway obstruction can be caused either by a foreign object or by bronchospasms.

An obstruction can partial or complete. If there is only partial obstruction, the victim will be able to cough; there may be a snoring sound as the victim breathes. If there is fairly good air exchange, encourage the victim to cough and expel the foreign object. Monitor the victim carefully, watching for the following signs of reduced air passage:

- A weak, ineffective cough
- A high-pitched wheeze during inhalation
- Increased strain during breathing
- Clutching at the throat
- Slight cyanosis

Signs of complete airway obstruction are

- Inability to speak, groan, cough, or cry out (the victim of a heart attack or other emergency will be able to at least whisper)

- Absence of breath sounds
- Labored use of muscles required in breathing— flared nostrils, strained neck and facial muscles
- Progressive restlessness, anxiety, and confusion
- Unresponsiveness

You should be prepared to give emergency care in any case of complete airway obstruction; activate the EMS system immediately, before you begin the **Heimlich maneuver** (a system of abdominal thrusts from below the diaphragm). Figures 4-14 through 4-21 illustrate the techniques used to clear a victim's obstructed airway.

> **Heimlich maneuver** A system using abdominal thrusts to remove foreign objects from the airway

Figure 4-14. The universal sign of choking. Ask the victim, "Are you choking?"

Figure 4-15. Position the fist, thumb side in, for the abdominal thrust.

Figure 4-16. Administering the abdominal thrust on a standing victim

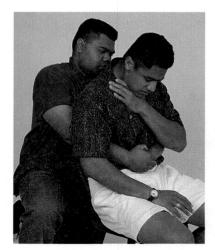

Figure 4-17. Administering the abdominal thrust on a sitting victim

Figure 4-18. Self-administering an abdominal thrust

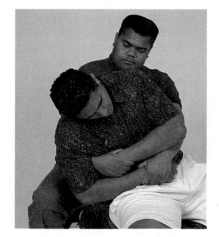

Figure 4-19. Place an unconscious, sitting victim face-up on the floor

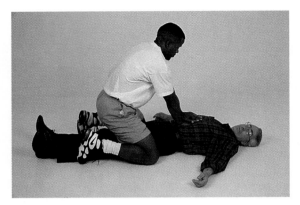

Figure 4-20. Performing abdominal thrusts on an unconscious victim while straddling the victim

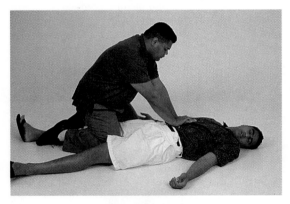

Figure 4-21. Performing abdominal thrusts while kneeling beside the victim

Emergency Care for a Conscious Victim

Learning Objective 9 Use techniques for dislodging foreign objects that are obstructing the airway of a conscious person.

1. Stand behind a standing or sitting victim and wrap your arms around the waist. Keep your elbows out, away from the victim's ribs. Place the thumb of one hand on the midline of the abdomen slightly above the navel and well below the xiphoid process (the tip of the sternum); keeping the thumb positioned, form a fist.

2. Grasp your fist with your other hand, thumbs toward the victim.

3. With a quick inward and upward thrust, press your fist into the victim's abdomen.

4. Give five thrusts, each separate and distinct, then reassess the victim. If the victim's airway is still obstructed, repeat another cycle of five separate, distinct thrusts.

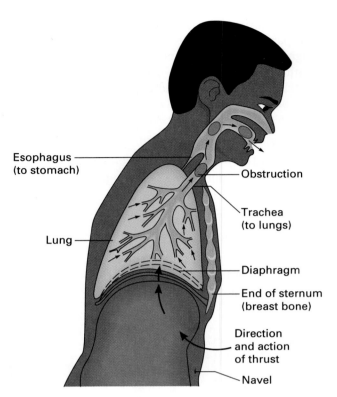

Figure 4-22. The function of abdominal thrusts for a complete airway obstruction victim

5. You may need to do many cycles of thrusts before the object is dislodged; continue until the object is dislodged or the victim becomes unconscious.

  If you are alone and choking, you can perform the Heimlich maneuver on yourself by positioning your hands as described, then delivering quick upward thrusts. You can also lean forward and press your abdomen against a chair back or other similar object.

  Figure 4-22 illustrates the function of abdominal thrusts.

If the Victim Becomes Unconscious or Is Unconscious

Learning Objective 10 Use the technique for dislodging foreign objects that are obstructing the airway of an unconscious person.

1. Lower the victim to the floor and position the victim on his or her back. If the victim was unconscious when you arrived on the scene, open the airway and assess for breathlessness.

2. Open the victim's mouth with one hand by placing your thumb over the victim's tongue, then

After completing the sequences of abdominal thrusts, clear the pharynx of debris.

Perform a jaw lift with one hand, grasping the tongue and the inner aspect of the mandible with the thumb and holding the chin with the other fingers.

- Now, using the index finger of the opposite hand, sweep any foreign material from deep in the throat toward you and up the pharyngeal wall and cheek to the mouth. Grasp foreign material between the fingers carefully, as it may be very slippery.

- Once the airway is cleared, rescue breathing is continued.

- If the airway remains obstructed, repeat the airway maneuvers.

- After two successful ventilations in succession, check the carotid pulse.

Figure 4-23. *Finger sweeps*

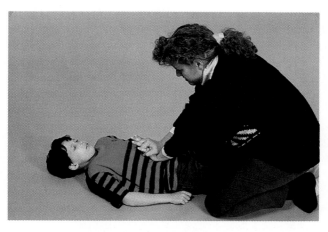

Figure 4-24. *Abdominal thrusts on a child*

grasping the tongue and lower jaw between your thumb and fingers. Lift the victim's chin up.

3. With the index finger of your other hand, sweep along the cheek and deep into the throat to the base of the tongue with a slow, careful hooking motion (see Figure 4-23). Grasp any foreign material firmly between your fingers and remove it. Take extreme care not to force the material deeper into the throat.

4. Position yourself for rescue breathing, and deliver two full breaths. If the victim's chest rises and falls, continue artificial ventilation as described in Section 3. If the victim's chest does not rise and fall, reposition the head and neck and try again.

5. If the breaths are still unsuccessful, kneel astride the victim's thighs or to the victim's side. Place the heel of one hand on the midline of the abdomen between the navel and the xiphoid process; put your second hand directly over the first. Your fingers should be pointing toward the victim's head.

6. Lock your elbows. Exerting pressure from your shoulders, press inward and upward with a quick thrust. Perform as many as five thrusts, making each separate and distinct.

7. Open the victim's mouth and attempt another finger sweep.

8. Reattempt ventilation.

Continue the cycles of thrusts, finger sweeps, and ventilation attempts—delivering one rescue breath, as many as five thrusts, and one finger sweep in each cycle—until the object is dislodged and the victim is breathing spontaneously or until you are relieved by emergency personnel.

If the victim is a child over 1 year, kneel astride the victim and use much less thrust than you would with an adult or use only one hand to deliver the thrusts (see Figure 4-24). If the victim is an infant, follow the guidelines at the end of this section.

If the Victim Is Obese or Pregnant

Figures 4-25 through 4-27 on page 68 illustrate the technique used with an obese victim.

1. Stand behind the victim with your arms directly under the victim's armpits; wrap your arms around the victim's chest.

2. Position the thumb side of your fist on the middle of the breastbone; *if you are near the margins of the rib cage, you are too low.*

3. Seize your fist firmly with your other hand, and thrust backward sharply. Repeat until the object is expelled or the victim becomes unconscious.

4. If the victim is or becomes unconscious, place the victim on his or her back and kneel beside the victim. Place the heel of your hand directly over the lower half of the breastbone and give distinct, separate thrusts downward and toward the head.

Figure 4-25. *Ask the victim, "Are you choking?"*

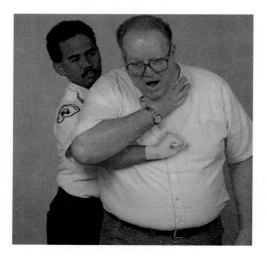

Figure 4-26. *Position the thumb side of your fist at the midline of victim's sternum (breast bone).*

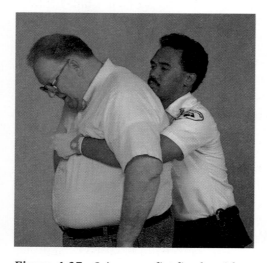

Figure 4-27. *Seize your fist firmly with your other hand and thrust backward sharply.*

If the Victim Is an Infant

Do not use abdominal thrusts on an infant—there is significant risk of injuring the abdominal organs. Instead, do a combination of back blows and chest thrusts (see below). Never do a finger sweep in a conscious infant; perform a finger sweep in an unconscious infant only if you can see the foreign object.

Perform the following procedure only if the obstruction is a foreign body. If obstruction is caused by swelling from infection or disease, the infant should be transported immediately to a medical facility. An infant who is conscious but having difficulty breathing should also be transported.

1. Straddle the infant over one arm with his or her face down and lower than the trunk at about a 60 degree angle. Cradle the infant's head and neck in your hand, and rest your forearm on your thigh for support.

2. Using the heel of your other hand, deliver as many as five back blows rapidly and forcefully between the shoulder blades (see Figure 4-28).

3. While supporting the infant's head, sandwich her or his body between your hands, then turn onto the back, keeping the head lower than the trunk. Lay the infant on your thigh or over your lap.

4. Position the middle and ring fingers of your other hand on the lower third of the infant's sternum,

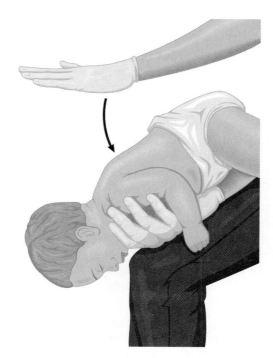

Figure 4-28. *Back blows for an infant*

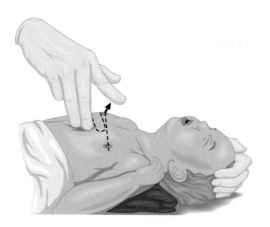

Figure 4-29. *Locating the finger position for chest thrusts in an infant*

approximately one finger's breadth below an imaginary line drawn between the nipples (see Figure 4-29). Deliver as many as five quick chest thrusts, thrusting straight back.

5. Repeat the cycle of back blows and chest thrusts until the object is expelled or the infant becomes unconscious.

6. If the infant is or becomes unconscious, use a gentle tongue-jaw lift to open the mouth. If you can see the obstructing object, sweep it out with your little finger. Attempt rescue breathing. If the infant's chest does not rise and fall, perform back blows and chest thrusts as described above. Continue the sequence of delivering five back blows, delivering five chest thrusts, checking for the object, removing the object if you can see it, and delivering one rescue breath.

Progress Check

1. The most reliable sign of complete airway obstruction is _____ .
(cyanosis/a snoring sound during breathing/complete inability to speak)

2. The Heimlich maneuver is an abdominal thrust delivered just below the _____ .
(sternum/diaphragm/rib cage)

3. During the Heimlich maneuver, your thumb should be positioned slightly above the _____ .
(xiphoid process/diaphragm/navel)

---

4. If the victim with an obstructed airway is unconscious, the victim should be positioned on the

_____ .
(back/side/stomach)

5. If the victim with an obstructed airway is a conscious infant, you should first do _____ .
(back blows/chest thrusts/a finger sweep)

6. If the victim with an obstructed airway is an unconscious infant, you should first do _____ .
(back blows/chest thrusts/a finger sweep)

• SUMMARY •

- Basic life support is a term that describes the first aid procedures necessary to sustain life in an emergency situation.

- The crucial first step of basic life support is assessment—you should perform proper assessment *before* you open the airway, do rescue breathing, or perform chest compressions.

- Activate the EMS system immediately—before you start any rescue procedures.

- Open the airway with the head-tilt/chin-lift maneuver if you do not suspect cervical spine injuries; if you suspect cervical spine injuries, use the jaw-thrust maneuver.

- Assess for breathlessness by looking for the rise and fall of the chest, listening for air escaping, and feeling for breath against your cheek.

- Mouth-to-mouth ventilation is the most effective.

- Do not try to decompress gastric distention unless it makes ventilation impossible.

- If the victim is an infant or small child, seal *both* the mouth and the nose with your mouth, deliver breaths more often, and use less force.

- Perform the Heimlich maneuver only if there is a complete obstruction of the airway, signaled by the victim's inability to speak, groan, cough, or cry out.

• KEY TERMS •

Make sure you understand the following key terms:

- basic life support
- stoma
- face shield
- face mask
- gastric distention
- aspiration
- Heimlich maneuver

Student: _____   Date: _____

Course: _____   Section #: _____

PART 1 • True/False

If you believe the statement is true, circle the T. If you believe the statement is false, circle the F.

T F **1.** If a choking person is unable to speak, you should assume the emergency is life threatening.

T F **2.** When resuscitating infants or small children, use more frequent, less powerful puffs of air into the mouth and nose simultaneously.

T F **3.** To check the effectiveness of artificial ventilation, you should watch to make sure the stomach is bulging.

T F **4.** If you suspect the heart has stopped beating, do not attempt artificial respiration.

T F **5.** An adult victim should be given one breath every 8 to 9 seconds.

T F **6.** You should do artificial ventilation for only as long as 30 minutes; after that, it is no good if the victim has not responded.

T F **7.** Mouth-to-mouth is the most effective method of artificial ventilation.

PART 2 • Multiple Choice

For each item, circle the correct answer or the phrase that best completes the statement.

1. The purpose of artificial ventilation is to
   a. prevent the tongue from being swallowed
   b. provide a method of air exchange
   c. clear an upper-airway obstruction
   d. clear a lower-airway obstruction

2. The first priority in giving emergency care to an unconscious victim is to
   a. establish and maintain an airway
   b. check for a pulse
   c. activate the EMS system
   d. get consent to treat

3. You can tell you are performing mouth-to-mouth ventilation correctly if you can
   a. see the victim's chest rise and fall
   b. feel resistance as you blow air in
   c. feel air escaping from the victim's mouth as he or she exhales
   d. all of the above

4. When you are giving mouth-to-mouth resuscitation, you should
   a. hold the victim's nostrils closed while breathing into the mouth
   b. avoid touching the nostrils unless cardiopulmonary resuscitation is being given at the same time
   c. pinch the nostrils as you lift your mouth from the victim's mouth
   d. keep the nostrils open

5. Without oxygen, brain cells die
   a. within 1 to 2 minutes
   b. within 4 to 6 minutes
   c. within 6 to 8 minutes
   d. after 10 minutes

6. The preferable method of opening the airway is the
   a. jaw thrust
   b. neck-lift/jaw-thrust
   c. head-tilt/jaw-thrust
   d. head-tilt/chin-lift

7. The artificial ventilation rate for an infant is
   a. once every 3 seconds
   b. once every second
   c. once every 5 seconds
   d. about ten breaths per minute

8. The most common source of upper-airway obstruction is
   a. fluid
   b. food
   c. the tongue
   d. swelling

9. The most reliable indication of a blocked airway in a conscious person is
   a. the inability to talk
   b. a compression accident
   c. partially digested food in the mouth
   d. cherry-red skin

PART 3 • Fill in the Blanks

The three major ways you can recognize adequate breathing are to

Look for _____.

Listen for _____.

Feel for _____.

- You are eating at a restaurant. Suddenly a man at the next table stands up, knocks over his chair, and places both hands over his throat. He looks alarmed, and his mouth is open.

  What is the probable cause of this emergency situation? What emergency care would you give in this situation? What would you do if the victim still was not breathing after you provided this emergency care?

5

Basic Life Support: Cardiopulmonary Resuscitation

Learning Objectives

When you have mastered the material in this chapter, you will be able to

1   Identify the signs and symptoms of cardiac arrest

2   List the sequence of basic life support

3   Describe how to assess a victim for breathlessness

4   Describe how to assess a victim for pulselessness

5   Demonstrate proper hand placement for chest compressions

6   Describe how to deliver effective chest compressions

7   Explain the procedures for performing one-rescuer CPR

8   Know when to terminate CPR

9   Explain the procedures for performing two-rescuer CPR

10 Explain how to adapt CPR techniques to infants and children

11 Discuss the most common mistakes made when performing rescue breathing and chest compressions

12 Know when to withhold CPR

SQ3R Plus

- **Survey** to set goals for studying.
- Ask **questions** as you **read.**
- Stop frequently to **recite** and **review.**
- **Write** a summary of key points.
- **Reflect** on the importance of this material and its relevance in your life.

On April 17, 1998, 61-year-old Eileen *Sanders paused on the asphalt track behind the community recreation center. She had felt fine when she started briskly walking a few minutes earlier, but now she felt waves of nausea. As she headed toward a bench at the side of the track, she found it difficult to catch her breath; just before she reached the bench she collapsed, a squeezing pain in her chest suffocating her.*

Just behind Eileen, two employees from the recreation center were taking a break by running a few laps. They rushed for Eileen. Thirty-year-old Madison White probed for a pulse at the side of Eileen's throat. Her skin was pale, cool, and beaded with perspiration; when Madison could find no pulse, she sent her companion back to the office to call an ambulance.

Madison rolled Eileen onto her back, used the head-tilt/chin-lift maneuver to open her airway, and placed her cheek close to Eileen's face. There was no breath. Madison delivered two slow breaths by mouth-to-mouth resuscitation and felt again for a pulse. There was none.

As EMTs ran across the lawn toward them, Madison was alternating between rescue breaths and chest compressions. The EMTs relieved her, performing two-rescuer CPR as a squad from the fire department arrived. Because of Madison's early action, Eileen's heart continued to circulate oxygenated blood, which preserved her life until emergency personnel could transport her to the local hospital. Surgeons later performed bypass surgery to prevent another heart attack.

HEART ATTACKS AND ASSOCIATED HEART DISEASE ARE America's number-one killer: Cardiovascular disease takes the lives of almost 1 million Americans each year. It attacks not only the elderly, but people in their thirties and forties.

Most people who die of a heart attack do so before they ever reach a hospital. Estimates are that many could be saved if immediate, efficient cardiopulmonary resuscitation (CPR), as outlined in this chapter, were provided within 8 to 10 minutes after the attack.

• Section 1 •
CARDIOPULMONARY RESUSCITATION

Learning Objective 1 Identify the signs and symptoms of cardiac arrest.

Cardiac arrest is a condition in which the heart has stopped beating because the heart muscle is not getting the blood—and, therefore, the oxygen and nutrients—it needs.

The signs and symptoms of cardiac arrest can include one or more of the following:

- Chest pain that may radiate to the shoulders and jaw
- Nausea and/or vomiting
- Cool, pale, moist skin
- A fluctuating pulse, gradually becoming absent
- Perspiration
- Breathing difficulties

Cardiopulmonary resuscitation (CPR) itself consists of

- Opening and maintaining the airway
- Providing artificial ventilation through rescue breathing
- Providing artificial circulation through chest compressions

The key objectives of CPR are to oxygenate and circulate the blood until advanced cardiac life support can be provided by trained emergency personnel. The shorter the time between cardiac arrest and the beginning of CPR, the greater the victim's chance of survival. Research has shown that the keys to survival of a cardiac arrest victim are

- Early access to the victim by rescuers (including First Aiders) trained in CPR
- Early CPR
- Early defibrillation by EMTs, paramedics, or other medical personnel

Several studies have shown that CPR technical skills deteriorate rapidly without frequent practice and retraining. Retraining in CPR skills should occur quarterly, and recertification should occur every 1 to 2 years.

Progress Check

1. In cardiac arrest, the heart stops because it is not getting the _____ it needs.
   (electrical stimulation/rest/oxygen)

2. CPR consists of opening the airway, providing rescue breathing, and providing _____ .
   (chest compressions/defibrillation/intrathoracic massage)

3. The key objectives of CPR are to _____ and circulate the blood.
   (provide rescue breathing/defibrillate/oxygenate)

4. A key to survival in cardiac arrest is _____ CPR.
   (early/effective/prolonged)

• Section 2 •
BASIC LIFE SUPPORT SEQUENCE

Learning Objective 2 List the sequence of basic life support.

CPR is only one facet of *basic life support,* a term used to describe the first aid procedures necessary to sustain life in an emergency situation. The major steps in the basic life support sequence (illustrated in Figures 5-1 through 5-9 on page 76) are

- Determine responsiveness
- Activate the EMS system
- Open the airway
- Determine breathlessness
- Provide rescue breathing
- Determine pulselessness
- Deliver chest compressions

Determining Responsiveness

To determine responsiveness, tap the victim gently on the shoulder and ask loudly, "Are you okay?" You are not looking for an answer as much as you are any kind of response—fluttering eyelids, muscle movement, turning to the sound, and so on. If there is no response, the victim is unresponsive.

cardiac arrest The heart stops beating

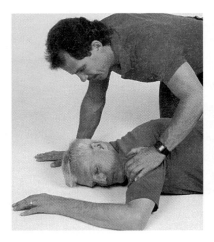

Figure 5-1. *Assess responsiveness and injuries.*

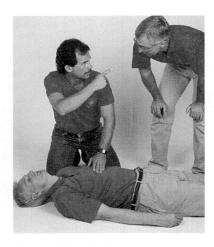

Figure 5-2. *Send someone to activate the Emergency Medical Services system.*

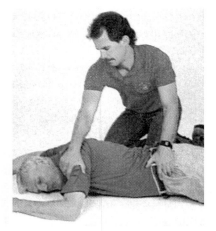

Figure 5-3. *Position the victim on the back on a hard, flat surface.*

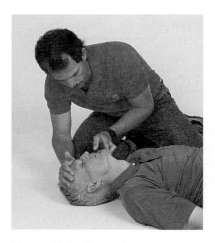

Figure 5-4. *Open the airway with the head-tilt/chin-lift maneuver.*

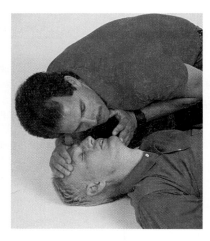

Figure 5-5. *Determine breathlessness with the look-listen-feel method.*

Figure 5-6. *Perform mouth-to-mouth ventilation. Give two slow breaths of air within 5 seconds.*

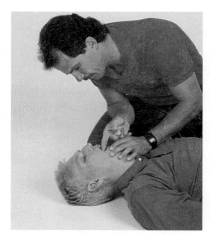

Figure 5-7. *Clear an obstructed airway.*

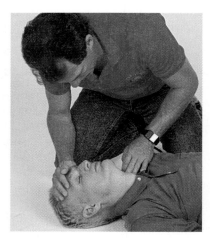

Figure 5-8. *Determine pulselessness by palpating the carotid artery.*

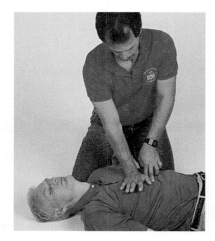

Figure 5-9. *Bare the chest (if necessary), landmark properly, and perform chest compressions.*

Activating the EMS System

If the victim is unresponsive, activate the EMS system immediately. The person who calls dispatch should give the location of the emergency, the telephone number he or she is calling from, what happened, the number of victims involved (if more than one), what emergency care is being given to the victim, and any other requested information.

Opening the Airway

If the victim is unconscious, the tongue can relax, fall back, and block the airway; the epiglottis can also relax and obstruct the larynx. Sometimes, efforts to breathe can create negative pressure that draws the tongue or the epiglottis or both into the airway. In these cases, opening the airway may be all that is needed to restore breathing.

Use one of the techniques described in Chapter 4 to open the airway; your method depends on whether you suspect the victim has cervical spine injury.

Determining Breathlessness

Learning Objective 3 Describe how to assess a victim for breathlessness.

With the airway open, check to see if the victim is breathing. Place your ear close to the victim's mouth and nose for 3 to 5 seconds, and

- *Look* for the chest to rise and fall
- *Listen* for air escaping during exhalation
- *Feel* for the breath against your cheek

If the victim is breathing, maintain an open airway and continue with your primary survey as described in Chapter 3. If the victim is not breathing, prepare to perform rescue breathing.

Providing Rescue Breathing

If the victim is not breathing, provide rescue breathing as described in Chapter 4. Because mouth-to-mouth resuscitation is the most effective method, use it whenever possible. Begin by delivering two slow breaths of 1½ to 2 seconds each; blow with just enough pressure to make the chest rise.

If the victim's chest does not rise and fall with each ventilation, there may be an airway obstruction. Take the necessary steps to remove the obstruction, as described in Chapter 4.

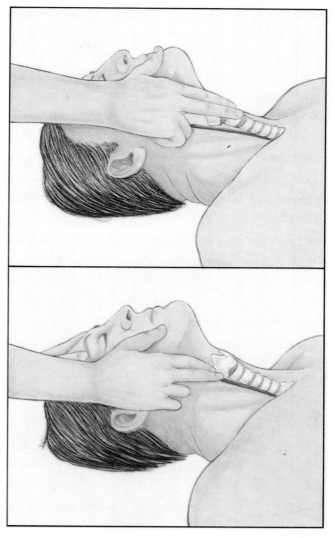

Figure 5-10. *After you have completed ventilation, check the carotid pulse. Palpate the thyroid cartilage in the midline with your index and middle fingers. Slide your fingers laterally to the groove between the trachea and the sternocleidomastoid muscle, and gently feel for the carotid pulse. If you do not feel a pulse, immediately try the opposite side. If you feel no pulse, begin compressions.*

Determining Pulselessness

Learning Objective 4 Describe how to assess a victim for pulselessness.

After you have give the first two breaths of rescue breathing, take the victim's pulse at the carotid artery to determine whether the victim's heart is beating (see Figure 5-10). *Determining pulselessness is a critical step that must be done before delivering chest compressions.* You can seriously injure the victim if you deliver chest compressions while the heart is still beating. Take the pulse at the carotid artery as follows:

1. Maintain the head tilt with one hand on the victim's forehead, and place the first two fingers of your other hand on the victim's **larynx** (voice box).

2. Slide your fingers slightly toward you, into the groove alongside the larynx, to locate the carotid artery.

3. Exert only gentle pressure to avoid compressing the carotid artery, and feel for a pulse for as long as 10 seconds.

If you do not feel a pulse at the carotid artery, you can assume that the patient is pulseless—the carotid pulse is one of the last to cease when the heart stops beating.

Progress Check

1. The first step in the basic life support sequence is to determine _____ .
(responsiveness/breathlessness/pulselessness)

2. If you determine that the victim is unresponsive, you should immediately _____ .
(open the airway/start CPR/activate the EMS system)

3. Before you can determine whether the victim is breathing, you need to _____ .
(open the airway/provide two rescue breaths/start CPR)

4. Before you can determine whether the heart is beating, you need to _____ .
(position the victim/provide two rescue breaths/start CPR)

• Section 3 •
CHEST COMPRESSIONS

If the victim's heart is not beating, as evidenced by a lack of carotid pulse, the next step in the basic life support sequence is to provide chest compressions—rhythmic compressions over the lower half of the sternum that keep the patient's blood circulating.

Chest compressions work on two principles to help circulate the blood: First, they increase pressure in the chest cavity, causing the heart to pump; and second, they provide direct compression to the heart itself. Paired with rescue breathing, chest compressions provide circulation of oxygenated blood until breathing and circulation can be permanently restored by advanced cardiac life support.

For external chest compressions, the victim must be supine (lying on the back) on a firm, flat surface. The victim's head should not be elevated above the position of the heart, but the feet may be elevated to help promote the return of blood from the veins. The victim's clothing doesn't hinder your ability to provide effective chest compressions, but it might keep you from properly positioning your hands; if necessary, pull clothing away.

Kneel next to the victim's shoulders; your knees should be spaced about as wide apart as your shoulders.

Positioning Your Hands

Learning Objective 5 Demonstrate proper hand placement for chest compressions.

Proper hand placement on the victim's chest (see Figures 5-11 and 5-12) is essential to avoid causing internal injury from chest compressions. Your hands *must* be above the **xiphoid process** (the lower tip of the sternum). To position your hands

1. Locate the lower edge of the patient's rib cage on the side of the chest next to where you are kneeling.

2. Using your middle and index fingers, locate the notch where the ribs are attached to the lower end of the sternum in the center of the chest (the **substernal notch**). Place your middle finger on the notch, and put the index finger of the same hand above it (on the lower end of the victim's sternum).

3. Place the heel of your other hand *above* your two fingers (see Figure 5-13 on page 81). At this point, the sternum is flexible—you can compress it without fracturing it.

4. Place the heel of your other hand on top of your first hand, with the fingers of both hands pointing away from you. Interlock your fingers and extend them, keeping them up off the victim's chest (see Figure 5-14 on page 81). If your hands are weak or arthritic, you can grasp the wrist of your first hand with your other hand (see Figure 5-15 on page 81).

Delivering Chest Compressions

Learning Objective 6 Describe how to deliver effective chest compressions.

To deliver chest compressions (see Figure 5-16 on page 81), proceed a follows:

1. With your hands properly placed, straighten your arms, lock your elbows, and position your shoul-

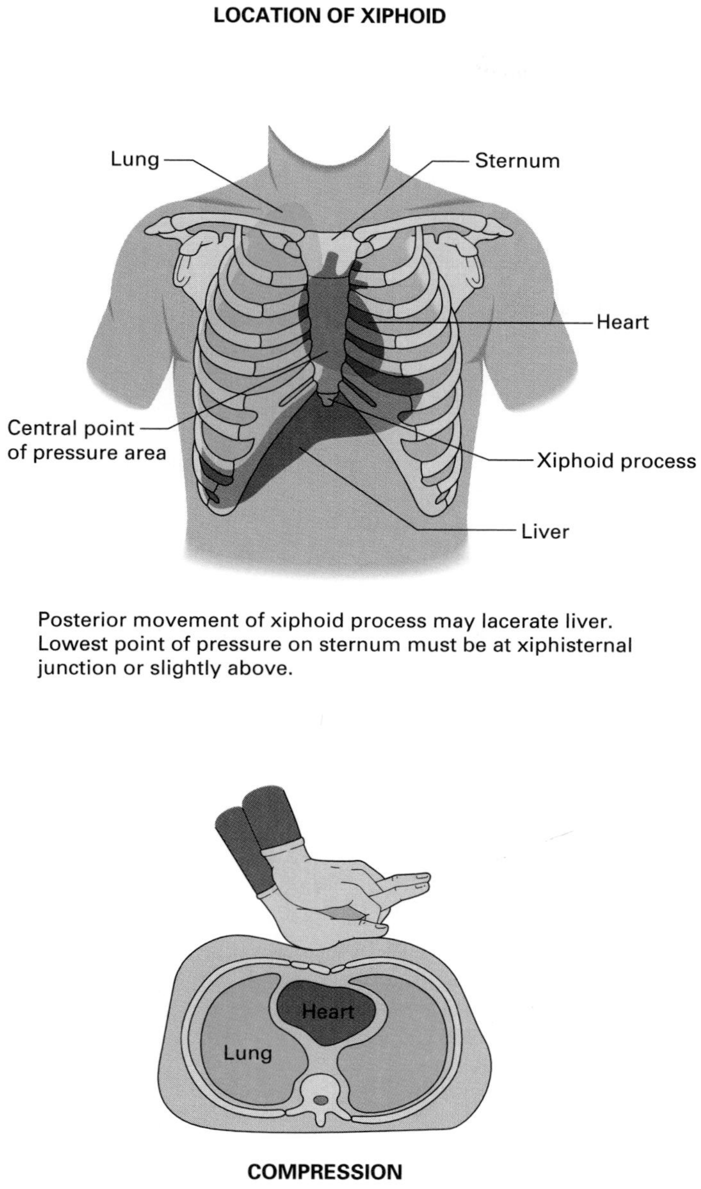
LOCATION OF XIPHOID
Lung
Sternum
Heart
Central point of pressure area
Xiphoid process
Liver
Posterior movement of xiphoid process may lacerate liver. Lowest point of pressure on sternum must be at xiphisternal junction or slightly above.
LOCATING XIPHOID
Heart
Lung
COMPRESSION
Heart
Lung
RELEASE

Figure 5-11. Proper hand placement for CPR

ders directly over your hands. Your nose, shoulders, and navel should be aligned approximately vertically. In this position, each thrust you give will be straight down onto the victim's sternum.

2. Press straight down, using the weight of your upper body to compress the victim's sternum approximately 1½ to 2 inches, which will force blood from the heart. (You may have to compress the chest more in an obese or very muscular person and less in a very thin or small person.)
3. Release the pressure completely to allow blood to flow back into the heart. You should allow the chest to return to its normal position after every compression.
4. Keep your hands on the victim's chest at all times during chest compression—do not lift them or switch their position. Chest compressions should

larynx The voice box
xiphoid process The lower tip of the sternum
substernal notch The notch at the spot where the ribs join the sternum

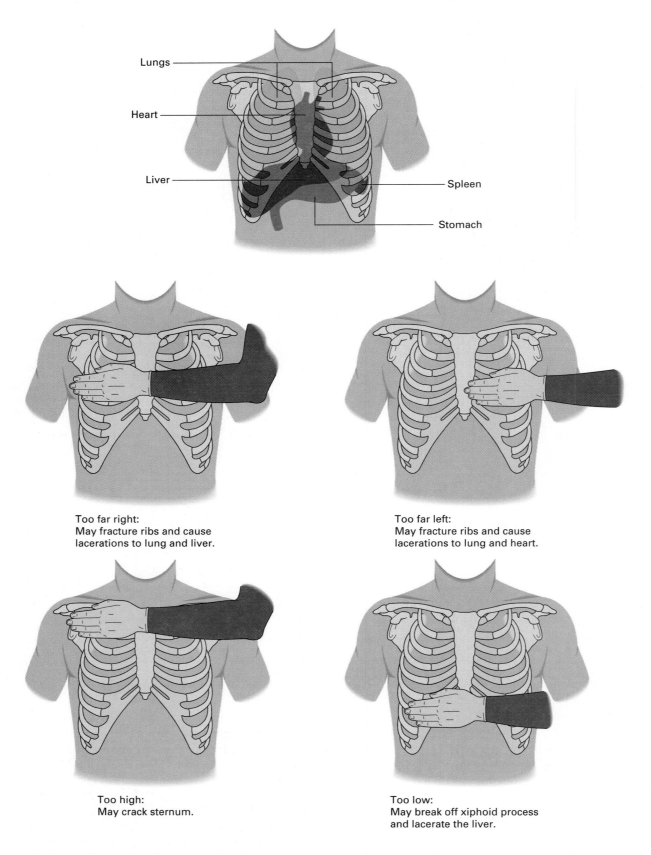

Too far right:
May fracture ribs and cause lacerations to lung and liver.

Too far left:
May fracture ribs and cause lacerations to lung and heart.

Too high:
May crack sternum.

Too low:
May break off xiphoid process and lacerate the liver.

Figure 5-12. *Improper positioning of the hands during CPR can damage the rib cage and underlying organs.*

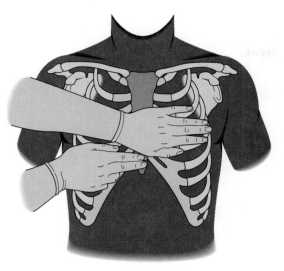

Figure 5-13. *Place heel of hand on sternum.*

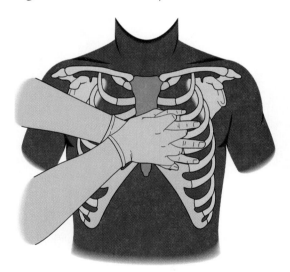

Figure 5-14. *Interlace fingers.*

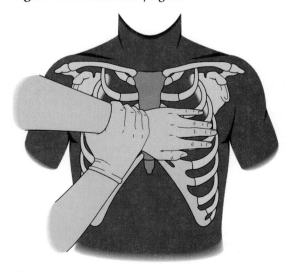

Figure 5-15. *Alternative hand placement for CPR*

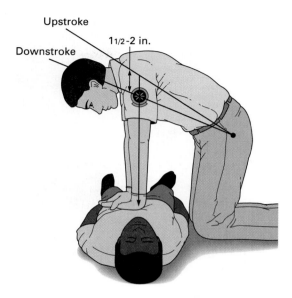

Figure 5-16. *Perform chest compressions properly.*

be smooth and rhythmic; there should be no jerking, jabbing, or starting-stopping movements with each compression.

5. Deliver chest compressions at the rate of 80 to 100 per minute, or slightly more than one per second.

Performing One-Rescuer CPR

Learning Objective 7 Explain the procedures for performing one-rescuer CPR.

If you are alone, determine unresponsiveness, activate the EMS system, open the airway, determine breathlessness, perform rescue breathing, and determine pulselessness as described above (see Figures 5-17 through 5-20 on page 82). To perform CPR

1. Position your hands properly on the victim's chest as described above.

2. Deliver 15 chest compressions at the rate of 80 to 100 per minute. Count aloud to keep track of the compressions.

3. Remove your hands from the victim's chest, open the airway, and deliver two slow rescue breaths of approximately 2 seconds each. Make sure you take a deep breath in between; turn your head to the side while you inhale, and allow the victim's chest to deflate after each breath.

4. Position your hands on the victim's chest again, and deliver 15 more compressions at the rate of 80 to 100 per minute.

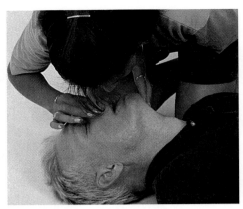

Figure 5-17. Establish breathlessness with the look-listen-feel method, activate the EMS system, open the airway, and perform mouth-to-mouth resuscitation.

Figure 5-18. Establish pulselessness by checking the carotid artery in the neck.

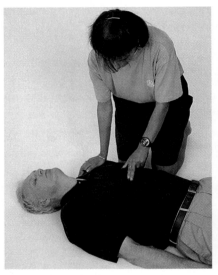

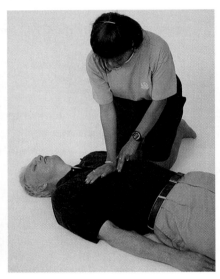

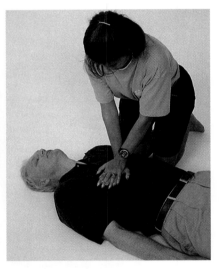

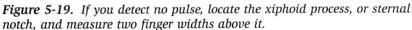

Figure 5-19. If you detect no pulse, locate the xiphoid process, or sternal notch, and measure two finger widths above it.

Figure 5-20. Compress 1½ to 2 inches on an adult at the rate of 80 to 100 compressions per minute.

5. Repeat this cycle, performing four complete cycles of 15 compressions and 2 rescue breaths.

6. After four complete cycles, check again for circulation and breathing. If there is still no pulse, resume CPR. If there is a pulse but the victim is not breathing, perform rescue breathing at the rate of 10 to 12 breaths per minute but *do not* resume chest compressions. Continue to assess the victim every few minutes to determine whether breathing and pulse have returned.

New evidence indicates that chest compression causes increased pressure in the chest cavity, which affects the blood vessels as well as the heart, so make sure the chest compression lasts at least as long as release of the compression.

Terminating CPR

Learning Objective 8 Know when to terminate CPR.

You must continue performing CPR until the victim is breathing and has a pulse or until one of the following occurs:

• Breathing and heartbeat start again spontaneously (this is unusual; most cases of cardiac arrest require advanced life support procedures)

• Another trained rescuer, a physician, or an individual or team directed by a physician assumes responsibility for basic life support

• A physician tells you to stop

- The victim is transferred to an appropriate medical care facility
- You are exhausted and unable to continue life support
- Conditions (such as a fire, noxious fumes, or an unstable building) make it unsafe for you to continue
- Cardiac arrest lasts longer than 30 minutes, even if CPR has been administered the entire time, unless the victim is hypothermic
- The victim is declared dead by a physician

Performing Two-Rescuer CPR

Learning Objective 9 Explain the procedures for performing two-rescuer CPR.

If another person trained in CPR is at the scene, one of you should be positioned at the victim's side, the other at the head. Two-rescuer CPR is the preferred method for several reasons: it delivers more rescue breaths per minute, it results in more effective resuscitation, and it is less exhausting for the rescuers.

The First Aider at the victim's side should deliver five chest compressions, as described above, then pause while the First Aider at the victim's head delivers one breath.

In two-rescuer CPR, the First Aider at the victim's side should not remove his or her hands from the victim's chest. The First Aider at the victim's head should maintain an open airway throughout resuscitation and should monitor the carotid pulse.

When the First Aider delivering chest compressions gets tired, the two First Aiders should rapidly switch positions, then resume resuscitation. Figures 5-21 through 5-27 illustrate two-rescuer CPR.

Performing CPR on Infants and Children

Learning Objective 10 Explain how to adapt CPR techniques to infants and children.

Because children are less likely to require defibrillation, the American Heart Association recommends that, if you are alone, you *perform CPR for 1 minute before activating the EMS system.* As with adults, you should never perform rescue breathing or deliver chest compressions unless you have determined breathlessness and/or pulselessness. (See Figures 5-28 through 5-36 on page 85 for illustrations.)

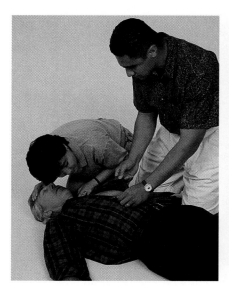

Figure 5-21. After establishing breathlessness, one rescuer gives two breaths while the other rescuer bares the chest (if necessary) and gets into position to perform chest compressions.

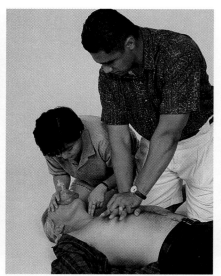

Figure 5-22. After establishing pulselessness, one rescuer gives a ventilation. The other rescuer then begins chest compressions.

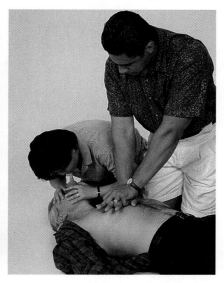

Figure 5-23. CPR continues at a ratio of five compressions to one ventilation. During the ventilation, the rescuer performing the compressions pauses.

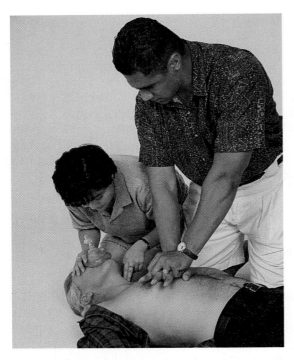

Figure 5-24. *Stop CPR to assess the carotid pulse after the first minute, and every few minutes thereafter.*

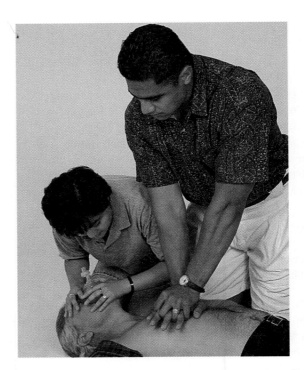

Figure 5-25. *The tired compressor requests a switch.*

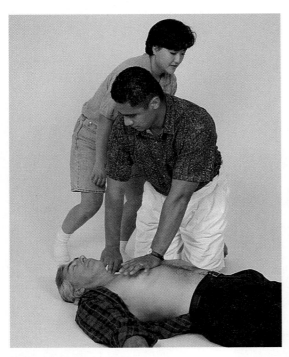

Figure 5-26. *Changing positions in two-rescuer CPR: The rescuer ventilating delivers a breath as usual, then moves into position and positions herself to provide compressions. The rescuer performing the compressions quickly moves to the victim's head and checks the carotid pulse and breathing for 5 seconds. The other rescuer readies for compression.*

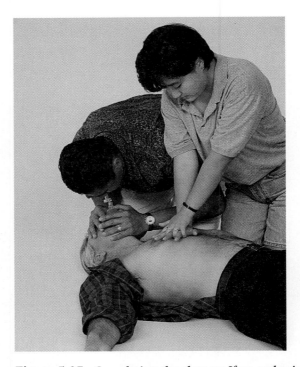

Figure 5-27. *Completing the change: If no pulse is found, the rescuers continue CPR.*

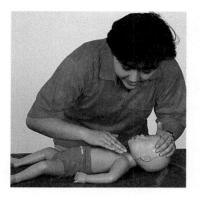

Figure 5-28. *Determine unresponsiveness in the infant by shouting. Do not shake an infant. You may also try flicking the soles of the baby's feet.*

Figure 5-29. *Gently open the airway using the head-tilt/ chin-lift maneuver. Do not tilt the head back very far.*

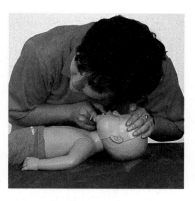

Figure 5-30. *Establish breathlessness by the look-listen-feel method.*

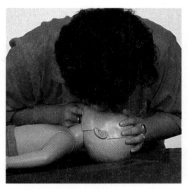

Figure 5-31. *Infant mouth-to-mouth and nose ventilation: The rescuer covers the baby's mouth and nose with a good seal, then gives two ventilations.*

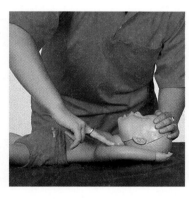

Figure 5-32. *Check the infant for pulselessness by gently palpating the brachial artery.*

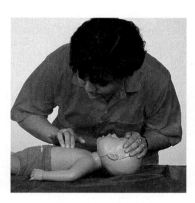

Figure 5-33. *Perform cardiac compressions in an infant by placing two or three fingers on lower half of sternum, one finger's width below nipple line.*

Figure 5-34. *The lower sternum is depressed ½ to 1 inch at a minimum compression rate of 100 per minute.*

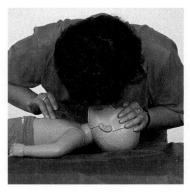

Figure 5-35. *A gentle puff of air is given after each fifth compression. Perform CPR for 1 minute, then activate the EMS system.*

Figure 5-36. *Performing infant CPR while carrying the baby*

In an infant or child, unresponsiveness is characterized by the following signs and symptoms

• No brachial or carotid pulse

• No chest movements

• Blue or pale skin

• No response to gentle shaking or tapping (tap, but do not shake, an infant)

• Gasps, muscular contractions, or seizurelike convulsions

In infants under 1 year of age, determine pulselessness at the pulse on the inner side of the upper arm (the brachial pulse). To perform CPR:

1. Determine proper placement of your fingers on the infant's chest by imagining a line connecting the infant's two nipples, placing your index finger on the line, and placing your middle and ring fingers toward the infant's feet.

2. Place your other hand on the infant's forehead or under the infant's shoulders for support. Lift your index finger off the infant's chest, and use your middle and ring fingers to deliver chest compressions.

3. Depress the infant's sternum ½ inch to 1 inch—a third to a half the depth of the chest—at the rate of at least 100 compressions per minute.

4. Deliver five compressions, then one rescue breath. Continue in cycles of five compressions to one breath; do 20 cycles, then check the infant's pulse to determine whether the heart has started beating.

In children aged 1 to 8 years, determine pulselessness at the carotid artery. To perform CPR:

1. Deliver compressions to the lower half of the sternum.

2. Use the heel of only one hand to depress the sternum; place your second hand on the child's forehead. Never place your second hand on top of the first one.

3. Depress the sternum 1 to 1½ inches.

4. Deliver five compressions, then one rescue breath. Continue in cycles of five to one.

In infants to 1 year, breathe once every 3 seconds; for children 1 to 8 years, deliver rescue breaths at the rate of once every 4 seconds and chest compressions at the rate of 100 per minute. For children over the age of 8, use the same rates as for adults. See Figures 5-37 and 5-38 for a comparison of techniques for adults, children, and infants.

Progress Check

1. You must properly position your _____ during chest compressions, or you can injure the victim.
(shoulders/hands/knees)

2. The xiphoid process is the tip of the _____ .
(rib/clavicle/sternum)

3. The substernal notch is the notch where the _____ meet(s) the sternum.
(ribs/clavicle/xiphoid)

4. During chest compressions, keep your shoulders straight and your elbows _____ .
(bent/locked/aligned)

5. After every two rescue breaths, deliver _____ chest compressions.
(10/15/20)

6. Once you start CPR, you must continue it until breathing and pulse return, someone else takes over, or _____ .
(you are told to stop/you are too tired to continue/you injure the victim)

7. During two-rescuer CPR, the First Aider at the victim's side should never _____ .
(lift hands off the chest/deliver rescue breaths)

8. If delivering chest compressions to an infant, use _____ .
(two fingers/one hand/both hands)

• **Section 4** •

MISTAKES, COMPLICATIONS, AND WHEN TO WITHHOLD

Mistakes in Performing CPR

Learning Objective 11 Discuss the most common mistakes made when performing rescue breathing and chest compressions.

The most common ventilation mistakes are

• Failing to tip the head back far enough in adults

• Failing to maintain an adequate head tilt

• Failing to maintain an adequate seal over the mouth and/or nose, letting air escape

• Not giving full breaths

• Completing a cycle in fewer than 5 seconds

• Failing to watch and listen for exhalation

	Adult	Child Aged 1 to 8	Infant
	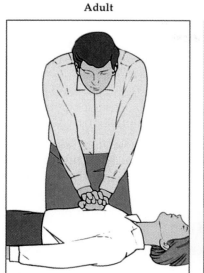		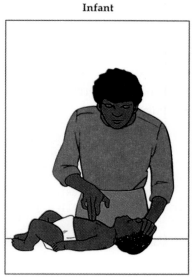
HAND POSITION:	**Two hands** on lower half of sternum	**One hand** on lower half of sternum	**Two fingers** on lower half of sternum (one finger width below nipple line)
COMPRESS:	1½–2"	1–1½"	½–1"
BREATHE:	Slowly until chest rises (1½–2 seconds per breath)	Slowly until chest rises (1–1½ seconds per breath)	Slowly until chest rises (1–1½ seconds per breath)
CYCLE:	15 compressions 2 breaths	5 compressions 1 breath	5 compressions 1 breath
RATE:	15 compressions in about 10 seconds	7 compressions in about 4 seconds	5 compressions in about 3 seconds

Figure 5-37. *The technique for chest compression differs for adults, children, and infants.*

Figure 5-38. *The technique for CPR differs for adults, children, and infants.*

Common chest compression mistakes are

- Bending the elbows
- Not having the shoulders directly over the hands
- Placing the hands on the victim's chest improperly
- Letting the fingers touch the victim's chest during compressions
- Incorrect compression rate
- Jerky rather than smooth compressions
- Lifting or moving the hands between compressions

Complications Caused by CPR

Even properly performed, CPR can cause the following complications

- Fracture of the ribs or sternum
- Separation of rib cartilage (common in the elderly)
- Pneumothorax
- Hemothorax
- Bruising of the lung
- Lacerations of the liver

Even if it causes complications, *effective CPR is necessary;* the alternative is death.

Withholding CPR

Learning Objective 12 Know when to withhold CPR.

If you are on duty or otherwise have a legal duty to act, you are legally required to begin CPR on any victim who needs it—unless there is a legal or medical reason to withhold it:

- There is rigor mortis or other signs of death.
- The victim is decapitated.
- The victim has wounds that will certainly cause death.
- The victim has severe crushing wounds to the chest and/or head.

Progress Check

1. To be effective in CPR, you must _____ the head far enough.
   (lift/tilt/turn)

2. If you think you might be injuring a victim during CPR, you should _____ .
   (continue CPR/stop CPR/assess the injury)

3. If you are on duty, you are legally required to begin CPR on any victim who needs it unless the victim _____ .

   (does not give consent/cannot be properly positioned/has obviously fatal wounds)

- The key objectives of CPR are to oxygenate and circulate the blood of a cardiac arrest victim until advanced cardiac life support can be given.

- The sequence of basic life support is to determine responsiveness, activate the EMS system, open the airway, determine breathlessness, provide rescue breathing, determine pulselessness, and provide chest compressions.

- Determine pulselessness after performing rescue breathing by checking the carotid artery in the neck.

- Chest compressions consist of smooth, regular, rhythmic applications of pressure over the lower half of the sternum.

- A key to effective chest compressions is proper hand placement on the chest.

- Once you start CPR, you should continue it until breathing and pulse start again spontaneously, another trained person takes over, a physician tells you to stop, the victim is transported, you become too exhausted to continue, conditions make it unsafe for you to continue, cardiac arrest lasts longer than 30 minutes (unless the victim is hypothermic), or a physician declares the victim dead.

- In one-rescuer CPR, the First Aider delivers both rescue breaths and chest compressions; in two-rescuer CPR, one First Aider delivers rescue breaths and monitors the carotid pulse while the other performs chest compressions.

- You need to modify your technique if you are performing CPR on an infant or child under the age of 8; children over the age of 8 are treated as adults.

- Even though properly performed CPR can cause complications, such as rib or sternum fracture, you should still perform it—the alternative is death.

- If you are on duty, you are legally required to provide CPR to someone who needs it unless the person is obviously dead (there are signs of lividity), the person has injuries that will certainly cause death, or there are severe crushing injuries to the chest and/or head.

• SUMMARY •

- Cardiac arrest occurs when the heart stops beating.
- Cardiopulmonary resuscitation consists of opening and maintaining the airway, providing rescue breathing, and providing chest compressions.

• KEY TERMS •

Make sure you understand the following key terms:

- cardiac arrest
- larynx
- xiphoid process
- substernal notch

Student: _____   Date: _____

Course: _____   Section #: _____

If you believe the statement is true, circle the T. If you believe the statement is false, circle the F.

T   F   **1.** Chest compressions on an adult man should depress the sternum 4 to 5 inches.

T   F   **2.** The best way to find out if a person has stopped breathing is to check the carotid pulse.

T   F   **3.** You should start chest compressions as soon as you find out the victim is not breathing.

T   F   **4.** For adult CPR, proper hand placement on the chest is two finger widths above the xiphoid process.

T   F   **5.** When performing one-rescuer CPR, deliver compressions at the rate of 60 per minute.

T   F   **6.** The compression rate for infants is at least 100 per minute.

T   F   **7.** Determine heartbeat in an infant by palpating the brachial pulse.

For each item, circle the correct answer or the phrase that best completes the statement.

1. The correct hand position for administering CPR to an infant is
   a. two fingers above the substernal notch
   b. at the base of the sternum
   c. in the lower third of the sternum
   d. two fingers placed one finger width below an imaginary line drawn between the nipples

2. After each chest compression, your hands should
   a. come completely off the chest
   b. apply a small amount of pressure on the chest
   c. rest on the chest in the normal CPR position
   d. none of the above

3. If you are alone and giving CPR, you should give _____ compression(s) after each _____ ventilations.
   a. 2/15
   b. 15/2
   c. 1/2
   d. 1/4

4. Basic life support consists of
   a. recognizing cardiac arrest and providing artificial ventilation and circulation
   b. checking for breathing and applying rescue breathing
   c. checking for heartbeat and applying artificial circulation
   d. checking for heartbeat and applying rescue breathing

5. CPR must begin when a need for it is recognized and must continue until all of the following occurs *except*
   a. the victim is declared dead by the First Aider
   b. the victim is resuscitated
   c. the rescuer can no longer go on
   d. a qualified medical person takes over

6. To check the carotid pulse for circulation
   a. use your thumb
   b. take the pulse on the opposite side of the trachea so that you can feel air exchange in the trachea
   c. check the pulse with your fingertips after you give two full rescue breaths
   d. none of the above

7. You should periodically stop and check to see whether the heartbeat has returned by
   a. checking the pupils
   b. checking the pulse
   c. listening for a heartbeat with a stethoscope
   d. never stop CPR unless the victim is obviously revived

- You are eating at a restaurant with your family when a middle-aged man at another table clutches at his chest and collapses on the floor. You hear the commotion and run to his table. You ask, "Is he choking?" No one can tell you. People are crowded around the body, the man's wife is shaking him and screaming, but no one is in charge.

  What signs and symptoms would tell you that the man is suffering a heart attack? What first aid step would you perform first? Identify the steps you would perform under each category:

  A–Airway, B–Breathing, C–Circulation, and D–Disability.

6

Bleeding and Shock

Learning Objectives

When you have mastered the material in this chapter, you will be able to

1 Describe and demonstrate how to control external bleeding with direct pressure

2 Describe and demonstrate how to control external bleeding with pressure points

3 Describe and demonstrate how to control external bleeding with air splints

4 Describe and demonstrate how to control external bleeding with tourniquets

5 Identify the most common signs and symptoms of internal bleeding

6 Describe and demonstrate the general procedures for controlling internal bleeding

7 Understand the basic physiology of shock

8 Understand the factors that may influence the severity of shock

9 Recognize the various types of shock

10 Identify the signs and symptoms of shock

11 Describe and demonstrate the management of shock

12 Identify the signs and symptoms of anaphylactic shock

13 Describe the management of anaphylactic shock

SQ3R Plus

- **Survey** to set goals for studying.
- Ask **questions** as you **read.**
- Stop frequently to **recite** and **review.**
- **Write** a summary of key points.
- **Reflect** on the importance of this material and its relevance in your life.

On June 5, 1998, 14-year-old Jessica Franklin rounded the curb on her new mountain bike, slid in an area of loose gravel, and flipped up over the handlebars of the bike. A large, jagged laceration on her leg caused by one of the gear handles began bleeding profusely.

Bart Billings, passing on his way to a job interview, stopped to provide aid. His rapid primary assessment showed that the hemorrhaging leg was the only serious injury; he shouted to a woman standing on a neighboring lawn to call 9-1-1.

Because he didn't have gloves, Bart quickly removed his clean shirt, folded it over a number of times, and used it as a thick pad to prevent contact with Jessica's blood. He then elevated the leg, propping it on his knee, and exerted direct pressure on the laceration. When it looked like the bleeding might still be profuse enough to soak through all the layers of his shirt, Bart used his free hand to apply pressure on the femoral artery. Bart maintained both direct pressure and pressure on the artery and monitored Jessica for signs of shock until EMTs arrived 4 minutes later.

THE LIFE PROCESSES DEPEND ON AN ADEQUATE AND uninterrupted supply of blood. The loss of 2 pints of blood in an adult is usually serious; the loss of 3 pints of blood can be fatal if it occurs over the course of a few hours. Hemorrhage in certain parts of the body—such as from the principal blood vessels in the neck—can prove fatal within just a few minutes.

The loss of blood causes a state of physical shock that results because there is insufficient blood flowing through the body to provide tissues with food and oxygen. All the body processes are affected by shock. If the conditions causing shock are not reversed, the victim will die.

This chapter discusses the various ways to control bleeding and outlines the emergency medical care that should be given a victim in shock.

• Section 1 •
HEMORRHAGE AND ITS EFFECTS

The severity of bleeding depends on

- How fast the blood is flowing from the vessel
- The size of the vessel
- Whether the vessel is a vein or an artery
- Whether blood is flowing freely or into a body cavity
- Where the bleeding originated
- The victim's age and weight
- The victim's general physical condition
- Whether the bleeding is a threat to respiration

Bleeding starts a specific chain of events in the body that is designed to compensate for the loss of fluid and for the potential loss of oxygen that circulates to the heart, brain, lungs, and other organs.

Simply, the body starts to manufacture extra red blood cells; excess fluid is reabsorbed into the bloodstream; platelets collect at the wound site to encourage clotting; and white blood cells collect to help control infection.

If the bleeding becomes uncontrolled, as in **hemorrhage,** the body can't compensate quickly enough to maintain the necessary volume of blood, and the hemorrhage becomes a life-threatening emergency (see Figure 6-1). Hemorrhage that goes uncontrolled leads first to moderate shock (loss of 15 percent of blood volume), then severe or fatal shock (loss of 30 percent of blood volume).

The severity of bleeding depends on its source: artery, vein, or capillary (see Table 6-1 above and Figure 6-2 on page 94). Figure 6-3 on page 95 illustrates four stages of hemorrhage.

Figure 6-1. Bleeding from the unconscious victim's mouth or nose can be a serious threat to respiration. Take proper precautions for drainage.

Table 6-1
Sources of Bleeding and Their Effects

Source	Color	Speed	Effect
Artery	Bright red	Rapid (spurting or pulsating)	Too fast to clot, most difficult to control
Vein	Dark red or maroon	Steady flow	Easier to control; large veins may suck in air
Capillary	Red	Slow, even flow or steady drip	Often clots spontaneously, usually causes little blood loss

A **hemophiliac** (sometimes called a "bleeder") is a person whose blood will not clot because of congenital abnormalities in the clotting mechanisms. Even a slight wound that cuts a blood vessel can cause a hemophiliac to bleed to death. When treating a victim who is a hemophiliac, in addition to providing aggressive care, you must activate the EMS system immediately for rapid transport to a hospital.

Progress Check

1. When bleeding is uncontrolled, the body can't compensate quickly enough, and _____ results. *(cardiac arrest/heart failure/shock)*

2. A loss of _____ pints of blood can be fatal if it occurs over a period of a few hours. *(1/2/3)*

3. Blood from an artery is _____ . *(red/bright red/maroon)*

4. Blood from a vein is _____ . *(red/bright red/maroon)*

5. Blood from a capillary is _____ . *(red/dark red)*

6. The most difficult bleeding to control comes from _____ . *(arteries/veins/capillaries)*

hemorrhage Uncontrolled bleeding
hemophiliac A person whose blood will not clot because of congenital abnormalities in the clotting mechanism

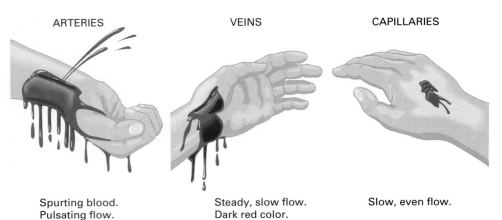

ARTERIES   VEINS   CAPILLARIES

Spurting blood.   Steady, slow flow.   Slow, even flow.
Pulsating flow.   Dark red color.
Bright red color.

Figure 6-2. *Bleeding sources and characteristics*

• Section 2 •
CONTROL OF BLEEDING

Before you take measures to control bleeding

- Determine the cause and source of the bleeding and the general condition of the victim (see Figure 6-4 on page 96); expose the wound to determine where the blood is coming from
- Place the victim in a position in which he or she will be least affected by the loss of blood
- Maintain an open airway

After bleeding is controlled, take measures to prevent or control shock, take vital signs every 5 minutes and repeat victim assessment every 15 minutes, and stay alert for the complications of blood loss.

Taking Infection-Control Precautions

Whenever you help a victim who is bleeding or losing other body fluids, take the following precautions to protect yourself against transmission of bloodborne diseases (see Chapter 1):

- Place a barrier between you and the victim's blood. If you can, wear latex gloves; if not, use plastic wrap, aluminum foil, extra gauze bandages, or a clean, thick, folded cloth. As a last resort, use the victim's own hand.
- Avoid touching your mouth, nose, or eyes or handling food while providing emergency care.
- As soon as you finish treating the victim, wash your hands thoroughly with soap and hot water or an antiseptic cleanser, even if you wore gloves. Use a fingernail brush to clean thoroughly under your fingernails.

- Wash all items that have the victim's blood or body fluids on them in hot, soapy water. Rinse well.

Applying Direct Pressure and Elevation

Learning Objective 1 Describe and demonstrate how to control external bleeding with direct pressure.

The best method of controlling bleeding—and the one you should try first—is applying pressure directly to the wound (see Figures 6-5 through 6-11):

1. Place a sterile dressing over the wound so that it is covered completely. If you do not have a sterile dressing, use the cleanest available material (such as a handkerchief, sanitary napkin, or bed sheet).

2. Press firmly over the dressing with your fingers or the heel of your hand; applying pressure over the dressing ensures that the pressure is evenly distributed. Keep the pressure firm and constant for at least 10 minutes. Wounds on the scalp, face, and hands will bleed more profusely because those areas are so richly supplied with blood.

3. Elevate the bleeding part above heart level *unless* you suspect fracture, dislocation, impaled object, or spinal injury. *Note that elevation alone is not effective in controlling bleeding—it must be used along with direct pressure.*

4. If you want to, use a cold pack over the wound as you apply direct pressure and elevation; cold can discourage blood flow to the area. Make sure you place a layer of gauze or other thin material under the cold pack anywhere it might contact the victim's skin.

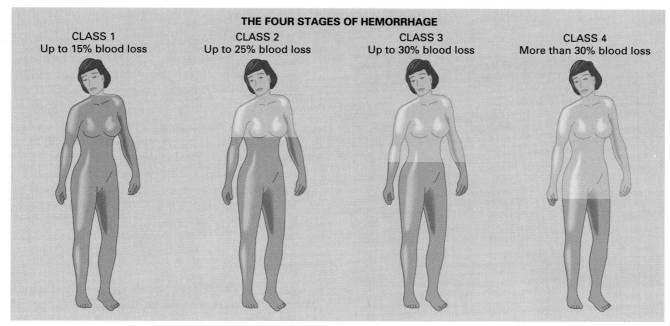

THE FOUR STAGES OF HEMORRHAGE

| CLASS 1
Up to 15% blood loss | CLASS 2
Up to 25% blood loss | CLASS 3
Up to 30% blood loss | CLASS 4
More than 30% blood loss |

HOW THE BODY RESPONDS

The body compensates for blood loss by constricting blood vessels (vasoconstriction) in an effort to maintain blood pressure and delivery of oxygen to all organs of the body.

EFFECT ON PATIENT

- Victim remains alert.
- Blood pressure stays within normal limits.
- Pulse stays within normal limits or increases slightly; pulse quality remains strong.
- Respiratory rate and depth, skin color and temperature all remain normal.

*The average adult has 5 liters (1 liter = approximately 1 quart) of circulating blood; 15% is 750 ml (or about 3 cups). With internal bleeding 750 ml will occupy enough space in a limb to cause swelling and pain. With bleeding into the body cavities, however, the blood will spread throughout the cavity, causing little, if any initial discomfort.

- Vasoconstriction continues to maintain adequate blood pressure, but with some difficulty now.
- Blood flow is shunted to vital organs, with decreased flow to intestines, kidneys, and skin.

EFFECT ON PATIENT

- Victim may become confused and restless.
- Skin turns pale, cool, and dry because of shunting of blood to vital organs.
- Diastolic pressure may rise or fall. It's more likely to rise (because of vasoconstriction) or stay the same in otherwise healthy patients with no underlying cardio-vascular problems.
- Pulse pressure (difference between systolic and diastolic pressures) narrows.
- Sympathetic responses also cause rapid heart rate (over 100 beats per minute). Pulse quality weakens.
- Respiratory rate increases because of sympathetic stimulation.
- Delayed capillary refill.

- Compensatory mechanisms become overtaxed. Vaso-constriction, for example, can no longer sustain blood pressure, which now begins to fall.
- Cardiac output and tissue perfusion continue to decrease, becoming potentially life threatening. (Even at this stage, however, the patient can still recover with prompt treatment.)

EFFECT ON PATIENT

- Victim becomes more confused, restless, and anxious.
- Classic signs of shock appear—rapid heart rate, decreased blood pressure, rapid respiration and cool, clammy extremities.

- Compensatory vasoconstriction now becomes a complicating factor in itself, further impairing tissue perfusion and cellular oxygenation.

EFFECT ON PATIENT

- Victim becomes lethargic, drowsy, or stuporous.
- Signs of shock become more pronounced. Blood pressure continues to fall.
- Lack of blood flow to the brain and other vital organs ultimately leads to organ failure and death.

Figure 6-3. *The four stages of hemorrhage are based on the amount of blood lost.*
Adapted with permission. Copyright © 1989, Springhouse Corporation, 1111 Bethlehem Pike, Springhouse, PA 19477. All rights reserved.

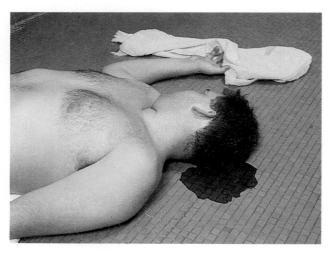

Figure 6-4. Detecting and controlling bleeding are parts of the primary survey.

5. Check the dressing every few minutes. If it soaks through with blood, do not remove it—simply place another dressing on top of it and reapply pressure.

6. *Never apply direct pressure to a wound if there is an object embedded in the wound or if a bone is protruding from the wound.* In these cases, use a doughnut-shaped pad over the wound, then apply moderate pressure to the pad. To make a doughnut-shaped pad, loop a cravat or other narrow bandage around your four fingers several times, then wind the remainder of the bandage in and out around the ring until the entire bandage is wound into the pad.

Leave the dressing in place for at least 10 minutes *after* the bleeding has stopped. Taking it off earlier can disturb the clot and cause the bleeding to start again.

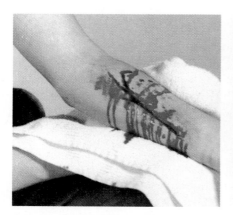

Figure 6-5. Bleeding from a lacerated wound on the forearm

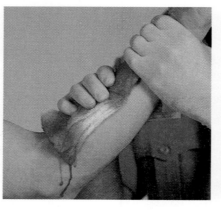

Figure 6-6. Control bleeding with a combination of direct pressure and elevation. If dressings are unavailable, use gloved hand.

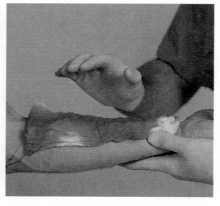

Figure 6-7. If bleeding soaks through the dressing, do not remove it.

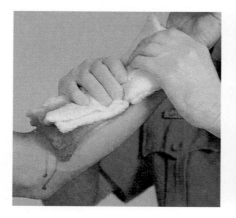

Figure 6-8. Add a new dressing on top of the original. Continue with direct pressure and elevation. After bleeding is under control, bandage the dressing in place.

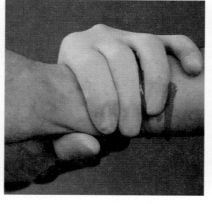

Figure 6-9. In cases of profuse bleeding, do not waste time hunting for a dressing.

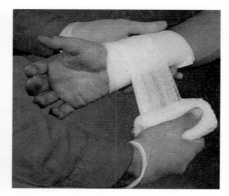

Figure 6-10. Bandage the wound.

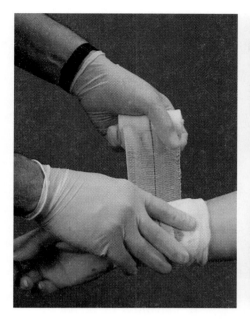

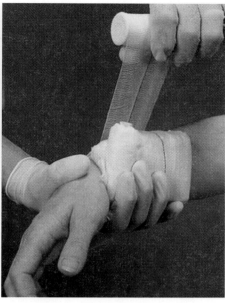

Figure 6-11. *Applying a pressure bandage*

If necessary, you can increase the pressure on the dressing with a pressure bandage, air splint, or blood pressure cuff.

Using a Pressure Bandage

A pressure bandage is used to create pressure over a dressing (see Figure 6-11). To use a pressure bandage:

1. Cover the wound completely with a thick dressing; make sure all edges of the wound are covered.

2. Holding the dressing in place, wrap the pressure bandage around the dressing tightly enough to exert moderate pressure.

3. Periodically check the distal pulses, and frequently check for mottled skin or blanched nails, signs that the pressure bandage is too tight.

Using Indirect Pressure

> **Learning Objective 2** Describe and demonstrate how to control external bleeding with pressure points.

If direct pressure and elevation don't control the bleeding, bleeding from an artery can be controlled by using your thumb or finger to apply pressure on a **pressure point**—a place where the artery is close to a bony structure and also near the skin surface. Pressure points can be difficult to locate and use, but pressure applied at these points can be effective in controlling the flow of blood to the injury site (see Figures 6-12 and 6-13 on page 98).

Never substitute indirect pressure for direct pressure—both should be used simultaneously. Hold the pressure point only as long as necessary to stop the bleeding; reapply indirect pressure if bleeding recurs.

Major arterial pressure (pulse) points (see Figure 6-14 on page 99) include the maxillary, temporal, brachial, radial and ulnar, femoral, posterior tibial, and dorsalis pedis arteries. See Table 6-2 on page 99 for the locations of these pressure points.

Use pressure points with caution, because indirect pressure can cause damage from inadequate blood flow. Never use indirect pressure if you suspect that the bone below the artery might be injured.

The most commonly used pressure points are the brachial and the femoral.

Brachial Artery

Pressure on the brachial artery is used to control severe bleeding from a wound on the upper extremity. The pressure point is located in a groove on the inside of the arm between the armpit and the elbow. To apply pressure

1. Grasp the middle of the victim's arm with the thumb on the outside of the arm and the fingers on the inside.

2. Press the fingers toward the thumb.

3. Use the flat, inside surface of the fingers, not the fingertips. This inward pressure closes the artery by pressing it against the humerus.

> **pressure point** A place where an artery is close to the skin surface and lies over a bone

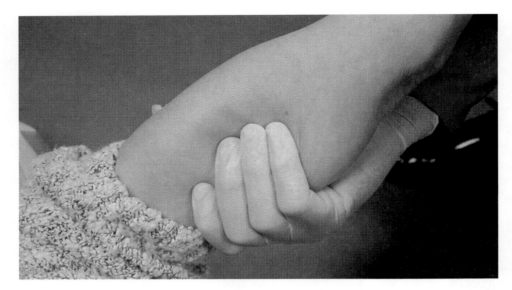

Figure 6-12. Apply pressure to the brachial artery pressure point to control bleeding in the arm.

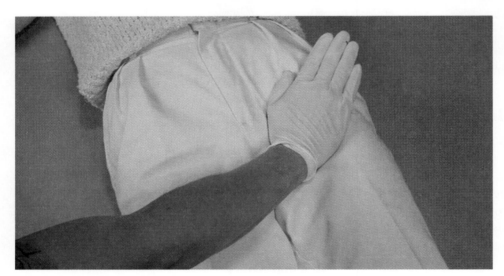

Figure 6-13. Apply pressure to the femoral artery pressure point to control bleeding in the leg.

Femoral Artery

Pressure on the femoral artery is used to control severe bleeding from a wound on the lower extremity. The pressure point is located on the front center part of the crease in the groin area. This is where the artery crosses the pelvic basin on the way into the lower extremity. To apply pressure

1. Place the victim flat on his or her back, if possible.
2. Kneeling on the side opposite the wounded limb, place the heel of one hand directly on the pressure point, and lean forward to apply the small amount of pressure needed to close the artery.
3. If bleeding is not controlled, it may be necessary to press directly over the artery with the flat surface of the fingertips and apply additional pressure on the fingertips with the heel of the other hand.

Using an Air Splint

Learning Objective 3 Describe and demonstrate how to control external bleeding with air splints.

An air splint (see Figure 6-15 on page 100) can be used to create a pressure bandage and control bleeding in an extremity. Using an air splint has one additional benefit: It frees your hands so you can manage other injuries. Use an air splint as follows:

1. Cover the wound with a thick, sterile dressing.
2. Slip the splint over the dressing, taking care not to shift or remove the dressing.
3. Inflate the splint. Take care not to overinflate—you should be able to depress the surface of the splint at least half an inch with your fingertips.

Arterial pulse points are places where an artery lies close to the skin or passes over a bony prominence. When an artery is so located, it can be palpated, or felt with gentle fingertip pressure. Since most body parts are supplied by more than one artery, the use of arterial pressure points alone rarely controls hemorrhage. However, compression of arterial pulse points *in addition to direct pressure* can sometimes help to control severe bleeding. Major arterial pulse points include:

- **Carotid arteries** are located on each side of the neck next to the larynx. These two arteries supply blood to the head. *Do not exert pressure on the carotid pressure points.*

- **Maxillary arteries** supply much of the blood to the face. One can be palpated on each side of the face on the inner surface of the lower jaw.

- **Temporal arteries** supply part of the blood supply to the scalp. One can be palpated on each side of the face just above the upper portion of the ear.

- **Brachial arteries**, located on the inner arms just above the elbows, supply blood to the arms.

- **Radial** and **ulnar arteries**, located in the wrist, also supply blood to the arms and hands.

- **Femoral arteries**, which pass through the groin, supply blood to the legs.

- **Posterior tibial artery**, which passes through the ankle, and the **dorsalis pedis artery**, on the front surface of the foot, can determine circulation to the feet.

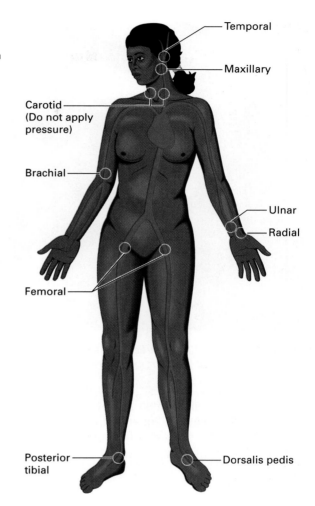

Figure 6-14. *Arterial pulse points*

Table 6-2		
Major Arterial Pressure Points and Their Locations		
Pressure Point	**Location**	**Controls Blood Flow to**
Maxillary	Each side of the face, on the inner surface of the lower jaw	Face
Temporal	Each side of the face, just above the ear	Scalp
Brachial	Inner arm, just above the elbow	Arms
Radial and ulnar	Wrist	Arms and hands
Femoral	Each side of the groin	Legs
Posterior tibial	Inner side of ankle	Foot
Dorsalis pedis	On top of the foot	Foot

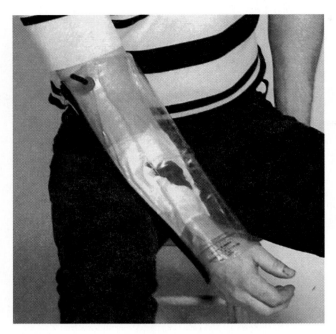

Figure 6-15. Air splints can be used to apply pressure and control bleeding from an extremity.

4. Check distal pulses often if they are not covered by the splint; check frequently for mottled skin or blanched nails, signs that the splint is too tight.

Never deflate an air splint unless a physician is present.

Using a Tourniquet

Learning Objective 4 Describe and demonstrate how to control external bleeding with tourniquets.

A tourniquet should be used rarely and *only as a last resort,* after all other methods of controlling life-threatening hemorrhage have failed. It can be used only on an extremity; using a tourniquet almost guarantees that the extremity below the tourniquet will have to be amputated. As a general rule, consider a tourniquet only when

• A large artery has been severed

• A limb has been partially or totally severed, *and*

• bleeding is uncontrollable

You can improvise a tourniquet from a strap, belt, suspender, handkerchief, towel, necktie, cloth, folded triangular bandage, or other suitable material that is at least 3 inches wide. *Never* use wire, cord, or anything else that could cut into the flesh. *Never* use a clamp on a blood vessel.

To apply a tourniquet (see Figure 6-16)

Figure 6-16. Apply a tourniquet as a last resort.

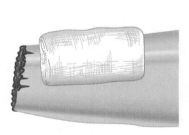

1. Apply pad

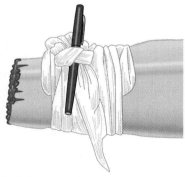

2. Tighten tourniquet

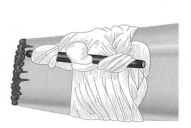

3. Fix in place

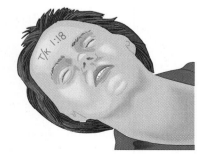

4. Record time

1. Hold the appropriate pressure point to control bleeding temporarily, then place the tourniquet between the heart and the wound, leaving at least 2 inches of uninjured flesh between the tourniquet and the wound.

2. Put a thick pad over the tissue that will be compressed.

3. Wrap the tourniquet material tightly around the limb twice, then tie it in a half-knot on the upper surface of the limb.

4. Place a short stick or other similar object at the half-knot, then tie a square knot.

5. Twist the stick to tighten the tourniquet *only* until the bleeding stops. Secure the stick in place with the ends of the tourniquet or another strip of cloth. Leave the tourniquet uncovered.

6. Write a note detailing the location of the tourniquet, the time it was applied, and the vital signs at the time you applied it. Pin the note to the victim's clothing. Then write *T* or *TK* on the victim's forehead with lipstick or red marker and write the time the tourniquet was applied.

Never loosen or remove a tourniquet except under the direction of a physician.

Using a Blood Pressure Cuff

In some cases, you can use a blood pressure cuff to control bleeding (see Figure 6-17). If you use a cuff,

- Secure it well so the Velcro does not pop open
- Maintain 150 mmHg pressure
- Never deflate the cuff unless a physician is present

A blood pressure cuff can safely remain inflated for as long as 30 minutes.

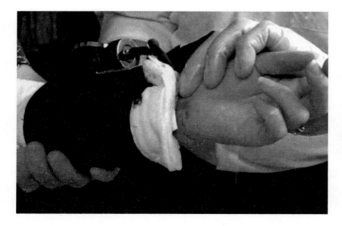

Figure 6-17. A blood pressure cuff can be used to apply pressure and control bleeding in an extremity.

Progress Check

1. Direct pressure is pressure applied directly to the
   _____ .
   (artery/pressure point/wound)

2. If a dressing soaks through with blood, you should
   _____ .
   (remove it/remove and replace it/leave it in place and put another one over it)

3. In addition to direct pressure, _____ the limb and apply cold packs.
   (elevate/compress/ splint)

4. Indirect pressure is applied at _____ .
   (wound sites/pressure points/joints)

5. The pressure point that controls bleeding to the arms is the _____ .
   (femoral/temporal/brachial)

6. The femoral pressure point is located in the
   _____ .
   (neck/inner arm/groin)

7. Material used for a tourniquet should be at least
   _____ inches wide.
   (2/3/4)

8. Release a tourniquet only when _____ .
   (bleeding has stopped/EMTs arrive/a physician is present)

• Section 3 •
INTERNAL BLEEDING

Internal bleeding generally results from blunt trauma or certain fractures (such as pelvic fracture). Though not visible, internal bleeding can be very serious—even fatal—because shock can develop rapidly (see Figure 6-18 on page 102).

You should suspect internal bleeding based on signs and symptoms as well as the mechanism of injury.

Signs and Symptoms

Learning Objective 5 Identify the most common signs and symptoms of internal bleeding.

The signs and symptoms of internal bleeding are similar to those of shock: restlessness and anxiety; cold, clammy skin; weak, rapid pulse; rapid breathing; and, ultimately, a drop in blood pressure. There may be additional signs and symptoms, depending on the

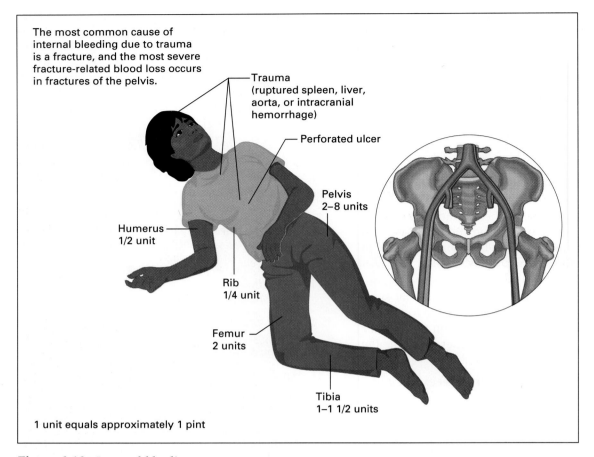

The most common cause of internal bleeding due to trauma is a fracture, and the most severe fracture-related blood loss occurs in fractures of the pelvis.

Trauma
(ruptured spleen, liver, aorta, or intracranial hemorrhage)

Perforated ulcer

Pelvis
2–8 units

Humerus
1/2 unit

Rib
1/4 unit

Femur
2 units

Tibia
1–1 1/2 units

1 unit equals approximately 1 pint

Figure 6-18. Internal bleeding

Table 6-3
Common Causes of Internal Bleeding and Their Signs and Symptoms

Common Causes	Signs and Symptoms
Blunt trauma	Bruising; pain, tenderness, swelling, or discoloration at the site of injury; in blunt trauma to the head, bleeding from the mouth and blood or bloody fluid in the nose or ears; in blunt trauma to the abdomen, bleeding from the rectum or nonmenstrual bleeding from the vagina
Fractured ribs or sternum	Coughing up of bright red, frothy blood; shallow, rapid respiration
Bleeding ulcer or ingestion of a sharp object	Vomiting of bright red blood
Intestinal disease, parasites, blunt trauma to the abdomen	Jet-black, tarry stools; rigidity of the abdomen; spasms of abdominal muscles
Blockage of urethra or pelvic fracture	Blood in the urine or urine that is smoky colored

source of the bleeding (see Table 6-3). Internal bleeding may not cause signs or symptoms for hours or days; realize that internal bleeding may be occurring even if there are no signs or symptoms.

Emergency Care

Learning Objective 6 Describe and demonstrate the general procedures for controlling internal bleeding.

The highest priorities in terms of treatment are internal bleeding into the chest cavity and into the abdominal cavity.

For victims of internal bleeding, activate the EMS system; then:

1. Secure and maintain an open airway, and monitor the ABCDs.

2. Check for fractures; splint if appropriate.

3. Keep the victim quiet. Position and treat the victim for shock by elevating the feet 8 to 12 inches and covering him or her to maintain body heat. (Do not elevate the feet if you suspect leg or spine injuries.) If the victim starts to vomit, position on his or her side with face pointing downward to allow for drainage.

4. Monitor vital signs every 5 minutes until emergency personnel arrive.

If the internal bleeding is in an extremity, use an air splint to control bleeding, then elevate.

Progress Check

1. Internal bleeding is extremely serious because it can cause _____ .
   (massive blood loss/ impaired function/shock)

2. To diagnose internal bleeding, consider both signs and symptoms and _____ .
   (overall appearance/mechanism of injury/pulse)

3. The most common cause of internal bleeding is

   _____ .
   (blunt trauma/perforated ulcer/skull fracture)

4. The signs and symptoms of internal bleeding are much like those of _____ .
   (external bleeding/cardiopulmonary disease/shock)

5. Basic treatment of internal bleeding involves _____ , opening the airway, and positioning the victim to prevent shock.
   (applying pressure/activating the EMS system/ elevating the affected part)

• Section 4 •
NOSEBLEED

Nosebleeds are a relatively common source of bleeding that can result from injury, disease, activity, temperature extremes, or other causes. Severe, uncontrolled nosebleeds can cause enough blood loss to cause shock.

If you suspect the nosebleed was caused by a fractured skull, *do not try to stop the flow of blood;* to do so will increase pressure on the brain. Cover the opening of the nose *loosely* with a dry, sterile dressing to absorb the blood, activate the EMS system, and treat the victim for skull fracture, as outlined in Chapter 13.

If you suspect a nosebleed is caused by something *other* than a fractured skull:

1. Keep the victim quiet and in a sitting position, leaning forward to prevent aspiration of blood (see Figure 6-19). Never have the victim tilt his or her head back.

2. If you do not suspect nasal fracture, pinch the nostrils together (see Figure 6-20) or place rolled gauze between the victim's upper lip and gum and press with your fingers.

3. Apply cold compresses to the nose and face.

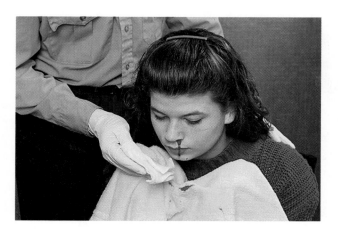

Figure 6-19. For a nosebleed, keep the victim quiet and leaning forward in a sitting position.

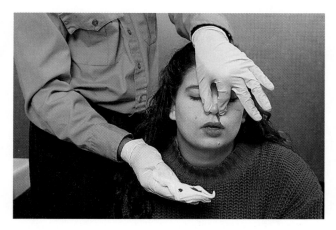

Figure 6-20. Apply pressure by pinching the nostrils and, if necessary, apply cold compresses to the nose and face.

If the above measures don't stop the nosebleed, proceed as follows:

- Insert a small clean gauze pad into the nostril and apply pressure; make sure a free end of gauze extends outside the nostril so you can remove the gauze later.
- If the victim is conscious, apply pressure beneath the nostril, above the upper lip.
- If bleeding continues, activate the EMS system.

Progress Check

1. To control nosebleed, keep the victim _____ .
   (sitting up/lying down/in a position of comfort)

2. Unless you suspect nasal fracture, pinch the nostrils together, then apply _____ .
   (pressure/cold compresses/indirect pressure)

3. If you suspect _____ , do not try to stop a nosebleed.
   (heart attack/elevated blood pressure/skull fracture)

• Section 5 •
SHOCK

In the nineteenth century, **shock** was defined as "a rude unhinging of the machinery of life." Probably no better definition exists to describe what happens during shock. A more recent definition calls shock "the collapse and progressive failure of the cardiovascular system." Left untreated, shock is fatal. Unless you recognize and treat shock immediately, the victim can die.

The Causes of Shock

Learning Objective 7 Understand the basic physiology of shock.

Shock is a step-by-step process that can be either gradual or rapid in onset; throughout the development of shock, the victim's condition constantly changes. Figures 6-21 and 6-22 illustrate the continuous cycle of traumatic shock.

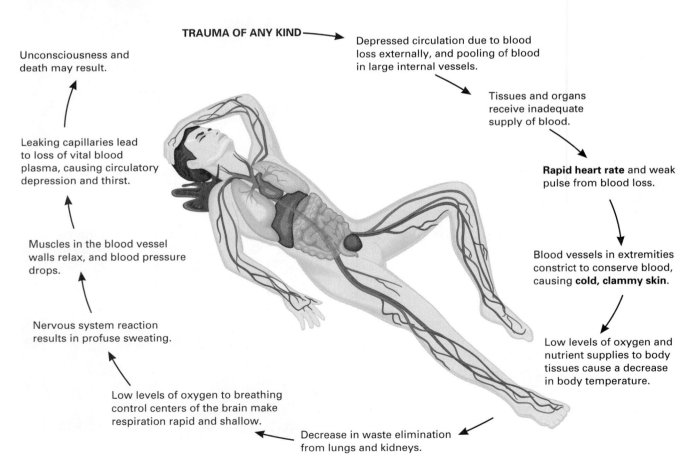

TRAUMA OF ANY KIND

Depressed circulation due to blood loss externally, and pooling of blood in large internal vessels.

Tissues and organs receive inadequate supply of blood.

Rapid heart rate and weak pulse from blood loss.

Blood vessels in extremities constrict to conserve blood, causing **cold, clammy skin**.

Low levels of oxygen and nutrient supplies to body tissues cause a decrease in body temperature.

Decrease in waste elimination from lungs and kidneys.

Low levels of oxygen to breathing control centers of the brain make respiration rapid and shallow.

Nervous system reaction results in profuse sweating.

Muscles in the blood vessel walls relax, and blood pressure drops.

Leaking capillaries lead to loss of vital blood plasma, causing circulatory depression and thirst.

Unconsciousness and death may result.

Figure 6-21. Continuous cycle of traumatic shock

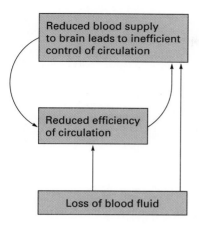

Figure 6-22. *The progressive circle of hemorrhagic shock*

Basically, shock occurs when the heart does not pump enough blood to fill the arteries at great enough pressure to provide oxygen to—or **perfuse**—the organs and tissues. The cells most sensitive to a lack of oxygen are those in the heart, brain, and lungs; they can be irreparably damaged in just 4 to 6 minutes.

There are four basic causes of shock:

1. Fluid is lost from the circulatory system (generally a result of bleeding, burns, or dehydration). See Figure 6-23.

2. The heart fails to pump enough blood.

3. The blood vessels dilate or constrict, causing blood to pool away from vital areas.

4. The body's supply of oxygen is inadequate.

Factors influencing the severity of shock include age (infants and the elderly are at most risk), multiple injuries, myocardial infarction, pregnancy, and physical condition (shock is more severe if there is pain, fatigue, or underlying disease). Shock often progresses rapidly in children.

The Types of Shock

Shock can be caused by conditions that affect the amount of blood in the vessels, the resistance exerted by the vessels, or the amount of oxygen available to the body. Table 6-4 on page 106 lists the types of shock, their descriptions, and causes.

HEMORRHAGIC SHOCK

Watch for shock in all trauma patients. They can lose fluids not only externally through hemorrhage, vomiting, or burns, but also internally through crush injuries and organ punctures.

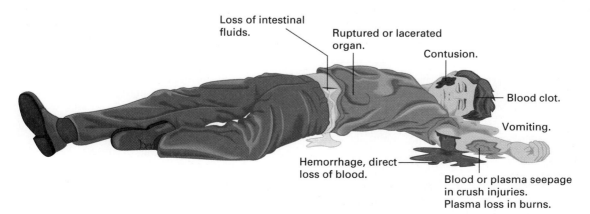

Loss of intestinal fluids.

Ruptured or lacerated organ.

Contusion.

Blood clot.

Vomiting.

Hemorrhage, direct loss of blood.

Blood or plasma seepage in crush injuries. Plasma loss in burns.

Figure 6-23. *Loss of body fluids can be external and internal.*

Table 6-4

Types of Shock

Type	Description and Cause
Hemorrhagic	Loss of blood, usually from multiple trauma and severe burns; there is not enough blood in the system to provide adequate circulation to all parts (see Figures 6-22 and 6-23)
Neurogenic	Spinal or head injury resulting in loss of nerve control; blood vessels dilate, and there is not enough blood to fill them
Psychogenic	Something psychological affects the victim; blood drains from the head and pools in the abdomen, causing fainting
Cardiogenic	The cardiac muscle does not pump effectively enough to circulate blood, usually because of injury, heart attack, or heart disease
Metabolic	Insulin shock, diabetic coma, vomiting, diarrhea, or some other condition causes loss of fluids and change in biochemical balance
Septic	Toxins from severe infection cause dilation of blood vessels, pooling of blood in the small capillaries, and bacterial invasion of blood vessels
Anaphylactic	Severe allergic reaction, usually to insect sting, food, or medicine

The Stages of Shock

Shock is progressive and occurs in three stages: **compensatory, progressive,** and **irreversible shock** (see Table 6-5 and Figure 6-24).

Shock in a child can present a somewhat different picture—generally, it develops early and progresses extremely rapidly. A child may show no signs or symptoms at all, or only very subtle ones, then suddenly exhibit the dramatic signs of irreversible shock. For this reason, *always begin emergency care of a child very early.* Never wait to see if symptoms develop.

Signs and Symptoms of Shock

Learning Objective 10 Identify the signs and symptoms of shock.

Figure 6-25 on page 108 illustrates the signs and symptoms of shock. Signs of shock in a dark-skinned victim may be more subtle (see Figure 6-26 on page 108).

Management of Shock

Learning Objective 11 Describe and demonstrate the management of shock.

Activate the EMS system immediately; then:

1. Secure an open airway. Give extra attention to any victim whose airway is obviously compromised.

2. Place the victim on his or her back *unless* the victim has an advanced pregnancy, a chest injury, difficulty breathing, heart attack symptoms, or a penetrating eye injury. In these cases, position the

Table 6-5

Signs and Symptoms of the Three Stages of Shock

Stage	What Happens	Signs and Symptoms
Compensatory	The body tries to use its normal defense mechanisms to maintain normal function	Minimal—normal blood pressure; increased pulse; cold, clammy skin; dull, chalklike or grayish skin; weakness
Progressive	Body shunts blood away from the extremities and abdomen to the heart, brain, and lungs	Cyanotic or mottled skin; dropping blood pressure; profuse sweating; extreme thirst; nausea and/or vomiting; dizziness; altered levels of consciousness
Irreversible	Blood is shunted from the liver and kidneys to the heart and brain; organs die; blood pools away from vital organs; death occurs	Dull, lusterless eyes; dilated pupils; shallow, irregular breathing; loss of consciousness

RECOGNIZING THE STAGES OF SHOCK

Shock is inadequate perfusion of bodily tissues. It is not a disease in itself but occurs secondary to trauma or illness. Shock may develop when serious injury causes significant blood loss, pump (heart) damage, spinal cord injury, or pulmonary injury, or when serious illness causes peripheral vasodilation or severe dehydration. Remember — in order for blood to circulate properly there must be adequate blood volume, a good working pump, and an intact vascular system.

When the cells of the body are not adequately oxygenated and/or nourished, a sequence of events may occur that, if left uncorrected, will result in death. The body will set in motion a series of complex mechanisms in an attempt to achieve homeostasis and compensate for shock. If the state of shock is severe or prolonged, it may become irreversible. If this occurs, no intervention will save the victim. Recognizing the signs and symptoms of each stage of shock will help you classify the victim's condition according to its severity so you can intervene appropriately.

COMPENSATORY STAGE

- Restlessness, anxiety, irritability, apprehension
- Slightly increased heart rate
- Pale and cool skin in hemorrhagic shock, warm and flushed skin in septic, anaphylactic, and neurogenic shock
- Slightly increased respiratory rate
- Slightly decreased body temperature (except fever in septic shock)

PROGRESSIVE (UNCOMPENSATED) STAGE

- Listlessness, apathy, confusion, slowed speech
- Rapid heart rate
- Slowed, irregular, weak, thready pulse
- Decreased blood pressure
- Cold, clammy, cyanotic skin
- Rapid breathing
- Severely decreased body temperature
- Confusion and incoherent, slurred speech, possibly unconsciousness
- Dilated pupils slow to react
- Slow, shallow, irregular respirations

MAY LEAD TO PROGRESSIVE STAGE

IF APPROPRIATE EMERGENCY CARE IS NOT GIVEN

IRREVERSIBLE SHOCK AND DEATH

Figure 6-24. The stages of shock

victim in a half-sitting position to make breathing easier.

3. Control any obvious bleeding.

4. Elevate the legs *no more than* 8 to 12 inches above heart level. Never elevate the foot of the bed— doing so can impair breathing and slow blood circulation from the brain. *Never elevate the legs of a person with head injury, stroke, or leg injuries* (marked by deformity or swelling); in these cases, elevate the head slightly if there is no sign of spinal injury.

5. Splint any fractures; this can reduce shock by controlling bleeding and relieving pain.

6. Keep the victim warm by conserving body heat, but *do not overheat.*

7. Keep the victim quiet and still; shock is aggravated by rough and/or excessive handling.

8. Give the victim nothing by mouth because of the possible need for surgery, possible injury to the digestive system, and possible vomiting. If the victim complains of intense thirst, moisten his or her lips with a wet towel.

9. Monitor vital signs and state of consciousness at 5-minute intervals until emergency personnel arrive.

compensatory shock The first stage of shock, in which the body attempts to overcome problems with normal defenses

progressive shock The second stage of shock, in which the body shunts blood away from the extremities and abdomen

irreversible shock The final stage of shock, in which body organs start to die

Figure 6-25. Signs and symptoms of shock

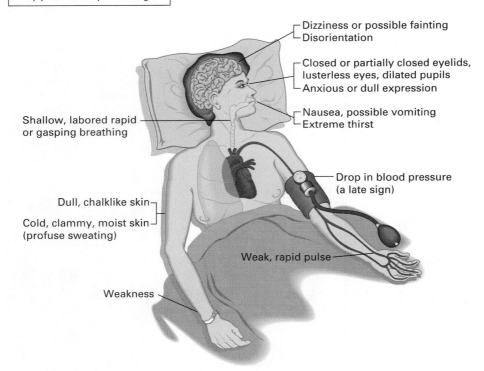

Restlessness, anxiety, and a feeling of impending doom may precede any other signs.

Dizziness or possible fainting
Disorientation

Closed or partially closed eyelids, lusterless eyes, dilated pupils
Anxious or dull expression

Nausea, possible vomiting
Extreme thirst

Shallow, labored rapid or gasping breathing

Drop in blood pressure (a late sign)

Dull, chalklike skin

Cold, clammy, moist skin (profuse sweating)

Weak, rapid pulse

Weakness

Figure 6-26. Look for more subtle signs of shock in a dark-skinned person.

Skin around mouth may be grayish.

Tongue may be blue.

Lips may be blue.

Nail beds may be blue.

Mucous membranes of mouth may be blue or have a pale, grayish, waxy pallor.

A healthy person with dark skin will usually have a red undertone and show a healthy pink color in the nailbeds, lips, mucous membranes of the mouth, and tongue. However, a Black victim in shock from a lack of oxygen does not exhibit marked skin color changes. Rather, the skin around the nose and mouth will have a grayish cast, the mucous membranes of the mouth and tongue will be blue (cyanotic), and the lips and nailbeds will have a blue tinge. If shock is due to bleeding, the mucous membranes in the mouth and tongue will not look blue but will have a pale, graying, waxy pallor. Other landmarks include the tips of the ears, which may be red during fever.

Preventing Shock

Never wait for the signs or symptoms of shock to develop; it is much better to prevent shock. Any victim of injury or illness can develop shock; you can prevent shock by

- Making sure the victim is breathing adequately; if necessary, provide rescue breathing

- Controlling bleeding

- Loosening restrictive clothing

- Reassuring the victim and staying calm and in control yourself

- Splinting and immobilizing fractures

- Taking measures to relieve pain (properly dressing, bandaging, splinting, and positioning the victim)

- Positioning the victim supine with feet elevated approximately 6 inches, if the victim is conscious; if unconscious, on his or her side

- Keeping the victim warm without overheating

Figures 6-27 through 6-34 illustrate body positioning and care for preventing shock.

Progress Check

1. Basically, shock occurs when the heart does not pump adequate amounts of blood to fill the arteries at _____ .
   (the same time/great enough pressure)

2. The loss of blood causes _____ shock.
   (hemorrhagic/cardiogenic/neurogenic)

3. Congestive heart failure could result in _____ shock.
   (hemorrhagic/metabolic/cardiogenic)

4. A victim with sustained vomiting and diarrhea could develop _____ shock.
   (septic/metabolic/neurogenic)

5. Shock is a progressive condition that involves _____ stages.
   (two/three/four)

6. During _____ shock, the body tries to use its normal defenses to maintain normal function.
   (compensatory/progressive)

7. During _____ shock, the body shunts blood away from the extremities and abdomen to the heart, brain, and lungs.
   (compensatory/ progressive)

8. Always begin emergency care for shock very _____ if the victim is a child.
   (early/aggressively/gently)

9. The preferred position for a shock victim is supine with the feet _____ .
   (at heart level/ below heart level/above heart level)

10. You should keep a shock victim warm without _____ .
    (using sources of artificial heat/ overheating the victim/shifting the victim's position)

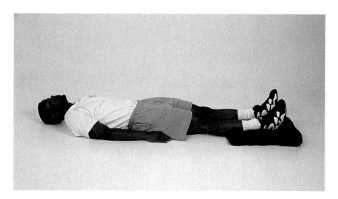

Figure 6-27. Normally, the lower extremities should be elevated. Gravity will reduce the blood in the elevated extremities and may improve the blood supply to the heart. If the victim has leg fractures, the legs should not be elevated unless they are well splinted.

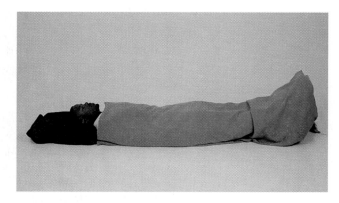

Figure 6-28 Maintain body heat.

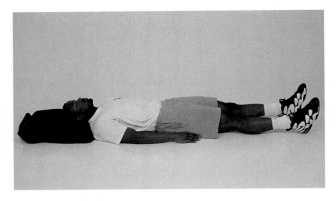

Figure 6-29. If there are indications of head injuries, the head can be raised slightly to reduce pressure on the brain. The feet may also be elevated. The head should not be elevated if there is mucus in the throat.

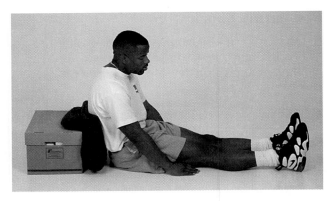

Figure 6-30. If there are breathing difficulties, the victim may be more comfortable with the head and shoulders raised—that is, in a semisitting position.

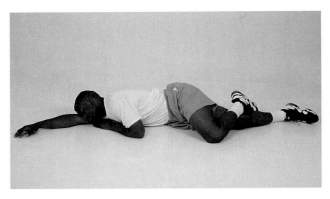

Figure 6-31. If the victim is unconscious, he or she should be placed on his or her side in recovery position.

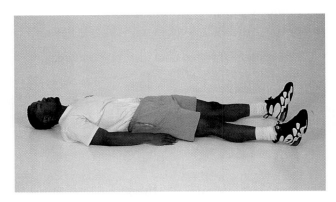

Figure 6-32. If circumstances require it, the individual should be left in the position found.

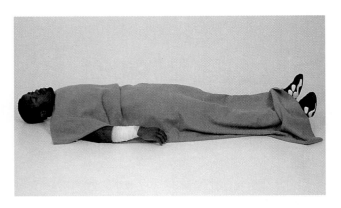

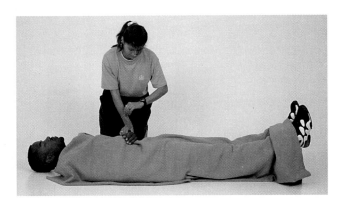

Figure 6-33 and 6-34. Along with proper positioning to prevent shock, it is also important to control bleeding, immobilize fractures, maintain body heat, assure adequate breathing, and reassure the victim.

• Section 6 •

ANAPHYLACTIC SHOCK

Caused by an intense allergic reaction—usually to insect stings, foods, or medicines—anaphylactic shock (see Figure 6-35) is a dire medical emergency. (See the section on insect stings in Chapter 23.) As a rule, anaphylactic reactions occur more frequently and rapidly if the antigen is injected. Untreated, victims can die—often within a few minutes of contacting the antigen.

Of those who die from anaphylactic shock, 60 to 80 percent die because they cannot breathe (because of swollen air passages) and 25 percent die from shock (because not enough blood is circulating through the body).

Anaphylactic shock is a severe allergic reaction of the body to sensitization by a foreign protein, such as insect sting; foods; medicine; ingested, inhaled, or injected substances. It can occur in minutes or even seconds following contact with the substance to which the victim is allergic. This is a grave medical emergency.

Rapidity of onset

As a rule, anaphylactic reactions occur more frequently and rapidly when the antigen in injected (seconds to minutes). By the oral route, they may be delayed (up to hours), although immediate, catastrophic progression is also a possiblity with oral ingestion.

Common early symptoms and signs

—Flushing, itching
—Sneezing, watery eyes and nose
—Skin rash, airway swelling
—"Tickle" or "lump" in the throat that cannot be cleared, cough
—Gastrointestinal complaints

These signs and symptoms may swiftly lead to:

and/or

Acute respiratory obstruction

Anxiety

Sense of throat closing, Coughing, hoarseness, suffocation.

Cyanosis

Wheezing, crowing respirations, difficult expiratory breathing leading to: Altered levels of consciousness, faintness, coma, possible seizures, and cardiac irregularities

Tightness or pain in the chest

Circulatory collapse

Severe headache, pounding in ears, weakness, fainting

Pale skin

Rapid, irregular heartbeat, possible cardiac arrest

Hypotension

Pulse weak or imperceptible

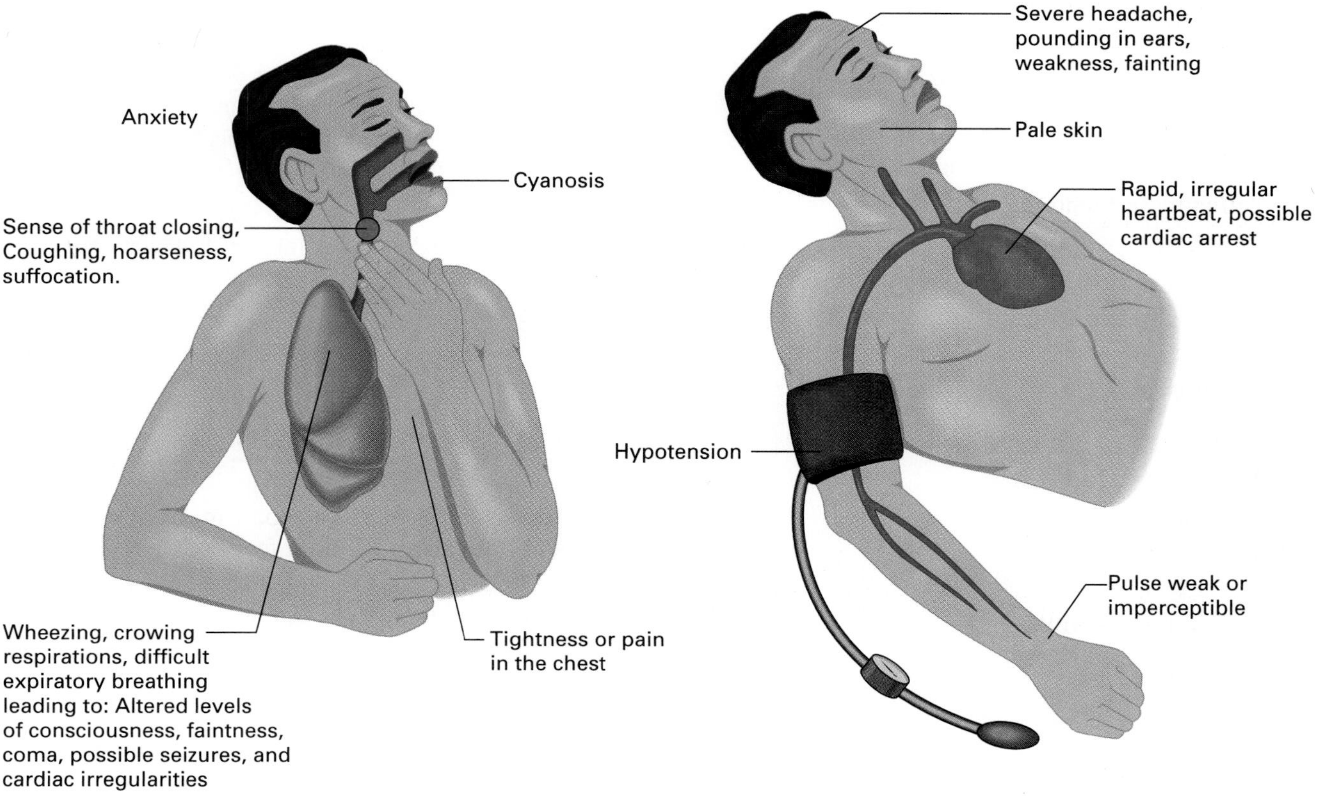

Figure 6-35. Anaphylactic shock

Signs and Symptoms

Learning Objective 12 Identify the signs and symptoms of anaphylactic shock.

The initial signs and symptoms of anaphylactic shock can occur in any combination, affecting the skin, heart and circulation, respiratory tract, gastrointestinal tract, and level of consciousness.

Skin

- Itching and burning, with flushing
- Cyanosis around the lips
- Raised, hivelike patches with severe itching
- Swelling of the face and tongue
- Paleness
- Swelling of the blood vessels just underneath the skin

Heart and Circulation

- Weak, rapid pulse
- Low blood pressure
- Dizziness
- Diminished stroke volume, resulting in less blood being pumped out of the heart

Respiratory Tract

- Spasm of the bronchioles
- A painful, squeezing sensation in the chest
- Difficulty in breathing
- Coughing
- Wheezing
- Swelling of the epiglottis and/or larynx

Gastrointestinal Tract

- Nausea
- Vomiting
- Abdominal cramps
- Diarrhea

Level of Consciousness

- Restlessness
- Faintness
- Convulsions
- Loss of consciousness (occurs very early in anaphylactic shock)

These initial signs and symptoms progress rapidly to either acute respiratory obstruction or circulatory collapse, then death.

Management of Anaphylactic Shock

Learning Objective 13 Describe the management of anaphylactic shock.

Activate the EMS system immediately; the victim will need rapid transport for life-saving treatment. While emergency personnel are en route, proceed as follows:

1. Secure an open airway.
2. If indicated, begin rescue breathing or giving CPR.
3. If the reaction is due to an insect sting, place a constriction band between the sting site and the heart; the band should stop only blood flow through the veins, not the arteries. You should be able to slip your finger between the band and the skin.
4. If the victim has a sting kit or other medication, help the victim use it *if allowed by local protocol.*

Progress Check

1. As a rule, anaphylactic shock occurs most rapidly if the antigen is _____ .
(swallowed/inhaled/injected)

2. Initial signs and symptoms may lead swiftly to _____ or circulatory collapse.
(loss of consciousness/respiratory obstruction/irregular heartbeat)

3. To manage anaphylactic shock, activate the EMS system, then _____ .
(start CPR/ secure an open airway/start rescue breathing)

• SUMMARY •

- The loss of 3 pints of blood in an adult can be fatal if it occurs within a few hours.
- Severity of bleeding depends on how fast the blood is flowing, whether it is flowing from an artery or a vein, where the bleeding originated, and whether the blood is flowing freely or into a body cavity.
- Bleeding from an artery is always more serious than bleeding from a vein or capillary; arterial blood is bright red and spurts or pulsates out.

- You can control bleeding with direct pressure, elevation, indirect pressure, and the use of splints.

- The use of a tourniquet to control bleeding should be a last resort only, when all other methods have failed.

- Internal bleeding can be serious enough to cause shock, and almost always requires surgical intervention.

- Shock occurs when the heart is not circulating enough blood at great enough pressure to oxygenate the body's cells and tissues adequately.

- Shock is a progressive condition that occurs in three stages; left untreated, it causes death.

- Shock in a child develops early and progresses extremely rapidly; never wait for symptoms to occur before beginning treatment.

• KEY TERMS •

Make sure you understand the following key terms:

- hemorrhage
- hemophiliac
- pressure point
- shock
- perfusion
- compensatory shock
- progressive shock
- irreversible shock

Student: _____   Date: _____

Course: _____   Section #: _____

If you believe the statement is true, circle the T. If you believe the statement is false, circle the F.

T   F   **1.** Indirect pressure is a good substitute for direct pressure.

T   F   **2.** Pressure on the arterial pulse points may help slow bleeding when direct pressure is inadequate.

T   F   **3.** Blood from a vein flows in spurts with each heartbeat.

T   F   **4.** Bleeding from capillaries rarely clots spontaneously.

T   F   **5.** A victim of internal bleeding can develop life-threatening shock before the bleeding is apparent.

T   F   **6.** A completely severed artery can sometimes constrict and seal itself off.

T   F   **7.** Internal bleeding usually results from blunt trauma or fractures.

T   F   **8.** Normally, the lower extremities should be elevated for shock.

T   F   **9.** During shock, the oxygen supply is decreased because the heart needs less oxygen.

T   F   **10.** Losing fluid from the circulatory system is one of the primary causes of shock.

T   F   **11.** Give a shock victim fluids if he or she is conscious.

T   F   **12.** If a victim is unconscious, place her or him in a semisitting position.

For each item, circle the correct answer or the phrase that best completes the statement.

1. Which of the following is the best method for controlling severe bleeding and should be applied first?

   a. elevation
   b. pressure point
   c. direct pressure
   d. tourniquet

2. List the four methods of controlling bleeding in order of preference: (1) elevation; (2) direct pressure at the wound; (3) indirect pressure (pressure points); (4) tourniquet.

   a. 2,1,3,4
   b. 2,3,1,4
   c. 1,2,3,4
   d. 3,2,1,4

3. Severe bleeding of the lower arm may be controlled by finger pressure on the

   a. femoral artery
   b. temporal artery
   c. radial artery
   d. brachial artery

4. When a dressing becomes saturated with blood, you should

   a. remove it and apply a new dressing
   b. apply a tourniquet
   c. leave the dressing in place and apply an additional dressing on top of it
   d. tie the knot on the bandage tighter

5. What condition may cause a person to bleed to death from a minor wound?

   a. anemia
   b. leukemia
   c. hypochondria
   d. hemophilia

6. Do *not* try to stop a nosebleed if you suspect

   a. broken nose
   b. fractured skull
   c. fractured jaw
   d. high blood pressure

7. A victim with a nosebleed should

   a. sit quietly and then pinch the nostrils to apply pressure
   b. blow the nose until the bleeding stops
   c. tilt the head back or lie flat while applying pressure to the bridge of the nose
   d. lean forward, pack the nostrils, and apply heat

8. Perfusion is

   a. the process of blood clotting
   b. the manufacture of red blood cells
   c. another word for transfusion
   d. circulation of blood within an organ

9. Which of the following characterizes arterial bleeding?

   a. dark red color and spurting flow
   b. bright red color and spurting flow
   c. dark red color and steady flow
   d. bright red color and steady flow

10. What is a pressure point?

    a. a point where the blood pressure drops low enough to stop bleeding

    b. a place where an artery is protected on all sides by bone and muscle

    c. a place where an artery is close to the skin surface and over a bone

    d. a point where an artery is near the wound

11. Use a tourniquet only if

    a. there is severe hemorrhage

    b. bleeding cannot be controlled by direct pressure

    c. bleeding cannot be controlled by pressure at the appropriate pressure points

    d. all other methods of controlling life-threatening hemorrhage have failed

12. Anaphylactic shock should be considered

    a. a true medical emergency

    b. an emergency only in a sensitized person

    c. an emergency only if the person has been stung on the face or hand

    d. a nonemergency situation

13. Which of the following shock processes occurs first?

    a. the brain loses its ability to function

    b. vital organs and the brain do not receive enough blood

    c. blood rushes to the brain and vital organs, thus depriving other body cells of nutrients

    d. internal organs and brain cells begin to die

14. Which of the following is *not* a means of preventing shock?

    a. keep the victim's body temperature above normal

    b. reassure the victim

    c. loosen constrictive clothing

    d. control hemorrhage

15. Which of the following is *not* a type of shock?

    a. hypothermic

    b. neurogenic

    c. septic

    d. cardiogenic

16. A person may be in anaphylactic shock from

    a. seeing a bloody accident

    b. eating berries

    c. injuring the head

    d. a severe illness

PART 3 • Matching

1. Tourniquets should be used only for severe, life-threatening hemorrhage that cannot be controlled by any other means. Order the following procedures for proper application of a tourniquet:

    _____ Secure the stick in place.

    _____ Wrap the tourniquet around the limb twice and tie in a half-knot on the limb's upper surface.

    _____ Do not cover a tourniquet.

    _____ Twist the stick to tighten the tourniquet only until bleeding stops.

    _____ Place the tourniquet between the heart and the wound.

    _____ Activate the EMS system.

    _____ Place a short stick at the half-knot and tie a square knot.

    _____ Make a written note of the location and time the tourniquet was applied.

2. Match each type of shock with the correct cause:

Type	Definition
_____ Septic	A. Spinal or head injury results in loss of nerve control and integrity of blood vessels
_____ Hemorrhagic	
_____ Cardiogenic	B. Toxins cause pooling of blood in the extremities
_____ Neurogenic	C. Allergic reaction of the body
_____ Anaphylactic	D. Loss of blood
_____ Psychogenic	E. Something psychological affects the victim; blood drains from the head and pools in the abdomen
	F. The heart does not pump efficiently

PART 5 • What Would You Do If?

• You arrive at the scene of an auto/bicycle accident and find a teenager who has a large laceration on the lower leg and is bleeding profusely.

• Your neighbor is stung by a bee and has flushed, itching skin, watery eyes, tightness in the chest, and feels as if his throat is closing.

Soft-Tissue Injuries

Learning Objectives

When you have mastered the material in this chapter, you will be able to

1   List the types of closed soft-tissue injuries

2   Describe the emergency medical care of a victim with a closed soft-tissue injury

3   List the types of open soft-tissue injuries

4   Discuss the threat of infection for a victim of human bites

5   Describe the emergency care of a victim with an open soft-tissue injury

6   Discuss emergency care considerations for a victim with a penetrating chest injury

7   Discuss emergency care considerations for a victim with an open wound to the abdomen

8   Differentiate the care of an open wound to the chest from the care of an open wound to the abdomen

9   Describe the special concerns and cautions necessary in the emergency care of wounds containing impaled objects

10 Outline the special concerns and cautions necessary in the emergency care of clamping injuries

On October 12, 1998, 22-year-old Clay Millett slipped in the mud at a construction site where he was working. In the fall, a large Phillips screwdriver Clay was using plunged into his abdomen, just to the right side of his navel.

Kent Hansen, working nearby, ran to the aid of his co-worker, who was bent over, screaming. Kent rolled Clay over onto his back and helped him lie down; a surprisingly small amount of blood oozed into Clay's clothing around the impaled screwdriver.

Kent sent the supervisor to call for emergency help, elevated Clay's feet by propping them on a toolbox, and took off his own jacket, draping it over Clay's chest and shoulders to help him stay warm. Kent stabilized the impaled screwdriver by spreading out the fingers of one hand and holding his hand still against Clay's abdomen, preventing the screwdriver from moving. When EMTs arrived, they stabilized the screwdriver with dressings, then transported Clay to the hospital, where the screwdriver could be surgically removed and internal injuries repaired.

SOFT TISSUES ARE THE LAYERS OF SKIN, FAT, AND MUSCLES that protect underlying structures and organs. While a soft-tissue injury is often an obvious and dramatic one, it is seldom the most serious type of injury—unless it compromises the airway or causes massive hemorrhage. Because of these possibilities, it is important that you conduct a thorough secondary survey to rule out other, more serious injuries or life-threatening conditions before you take time to treat soft-tissue injuries.

An injury to the skin and underlying musculature is commonly referred to as a **wound.** More specifically, a wound is an injury, caused by trauma, that disrupts the normal continuity of the tissue, organ, or bone affected. Wounds may be generally classified as closed or open, single or multiple.

This chapter outlines the care of both closed and open wounds, including clamping and penetrating injuries, and details the treatment of victims wounded with impaled objects.

• Section 1 •
CLOSED INJURIES

Learning Objective 1 List the types of closed soft-tissue injuries.

In a closed injury, such as a bruise, soft tissues beneath the skin are damaged, but the skin is not broken.

Types of closed injuries include contusions (bruises), hematomas, and crush injuries.

Contusion

In a **contusion** (see Figure 7-1), the **epidermis** (outer layer of the skin) remains intact; in the **dermis** (underlying layer of skin), however, cells are damaged and blood vessels are torn.

Contusions are characterized by local pain and swelling. If small blood vessels beneath the skin have been broken, the area will turn black and blue as blood and fluid leak into the damaged tissue.

Hematoma

If large vessels have been torn beneath a bruised area, a **hematoma**—a collection of blood beneath the skin—develops. Hematomas are characterized by a lump with bluish discoloration. Blood from a deep bruise can actually separate tissue and pool in a pocket. The victim can lose 1 or more liters of blood from a large hematoma.

Crush Injuries

The force of a sudden blow or blunt trauma can cause a crush injury. With a crush injury, underlying layers of skin sustain severe damage; the internal layers of skin can actually rupture. A crush injury that is especially treacherous because the resulting internal in-juries can cause few, if any, external signs. While the injury site may be painful, swollen, or deformed, there is usually little or no external bleeding.

The victim of a crush injury can look fine at first, but his or her condition may quickly deteriorate, resulting in deep shock and/or death. For this reason, always suspect hidden internal damage in victims with crush injuries.

Emergency Care

Learning Objective 2 Describe the emergency care of a victim with a closed soft-tissue injury.

Small bruises generally require no treatment. Larger bruises and crush injuries, however, can cause serious internal injury and blood loss. Treat them as follows:

1. If you suspect internal bleeding or the victim shows the signs and symptoms of shock, treat for shock as outlined in Chapter 6.

2. Apply ice or cold compresses to help relieve pain and reduce swelling. Never apply ice directly to the skin, and do not apply ice for more than 20 minutes at a time. If the bruise is large, apply pressure to control internal bleeding, cover the bruised area with a gauze pad, and wrap with an elastic bandage. Monitor the bandage to make sure it is not too tight.

3. Splint painful, swollen, or deformed extremities to help control pain and swelling and prevent further injury. If large bruised areas are present, assess carefully for fracture, especially if any swelling or deformity is present (see Chapter 11).

wound An injury to the skin and underlying musculature that disrupts the normal continuity of the affected tissue, organ, or bone

contusion A bruise

epidermis The outermost layer of the skin

dermis The second layer of skin, which contains the hair follicles, sweat glands, oil glands, and nerves

hematoma A collection of blood beneath the skin

Progress Check

1. A contusion is a _____ .
    (closed fracture/bruise/laceration)

2. A hematoma is _____ under the skin.
    (blood/swelling/ecchymosis)

continued

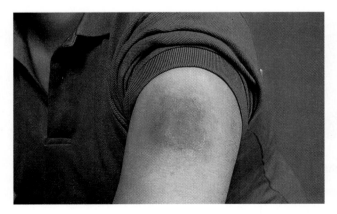

Figure 7-1. Contusions are injuries that cause bleeding beneath the skin but do not break the skin.

3. Crushing injuries don't break the skin but can cause internal injury severe enough to cause

_____ .
(hemorrhage/fracture/shock)

4. Apply _____ to reduce the pain and swelling associated with closed injuries.
(cold compresses/manual pressure/splints)

• Section 2 •
OPEN INJURIES

Learning Objective 3 List the types of open soft-tissue injuries.

In an open wound, the skin is broken and the victim is susceptible to external bleeding and wound contamination. Remember: The wound itself may be only part of the victim's injury—an open wound may be only the surface evidence of a more serious injury, such as a fracture. Figure 7-2 illustrates the classifications of open wounds.

Abrasion

An **abrasion** is a superficial wound caused by rubbing, scraping, or shearing (see Figure 7-3). Part of the skin layer—usually the epidermis and part of the dermis—is lost. All abrasions, regardless of size, are extremely painful because of the nerve endings involved.

Blood may ooze from the abrasion, but bleeding is usually not severe. Abrasions can pose a threat if large areas of skin are involved (as can happen in a motorcycle accident when the rider is thrown against the road). The most serious threat from abrasions is that of contamination and infection.

Laceration

A **laceration** is a break in the skin of varying depth. Lacerations can be either linear (regular) or irregular, and can occur either in isolation or together with other types of soft-tissue injury (see Figures 7-4 through 7-6). Lacerations can cause significant bleeding if the sharp object also cuts the wall of a blood vessel, especially an artery. This is particularly true in areas where major arteries lie close to the skin surface, such as in the wrist.

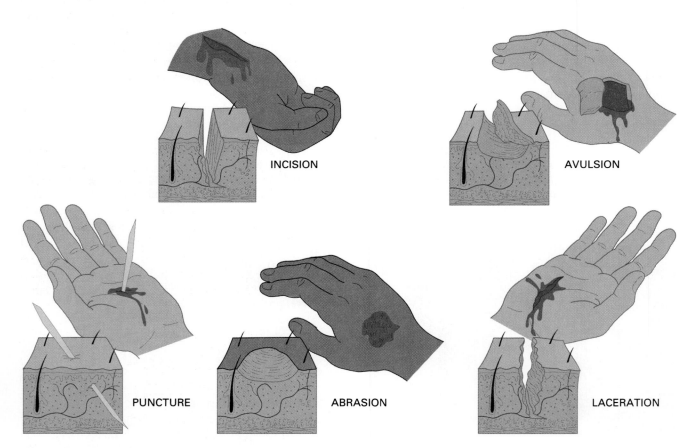

INCISION

AVULSION

PUNCTURE

ABRASION

LACERATION

Figure 7-2. Classification of open wounds

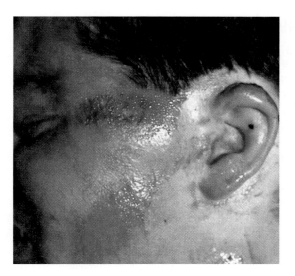

Figure 7-3. An abrasion is an open wound caused by rubbing and scraping off layers of skin.

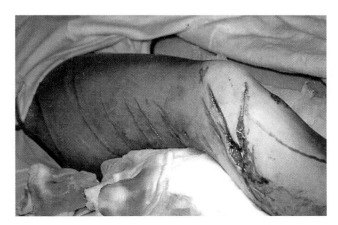

Figure 7-4. Incisions and lacerations

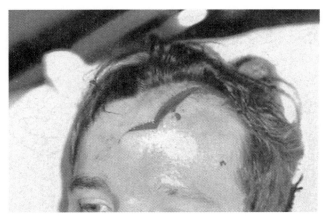

Figure 7-5. Laceration of the forehead and scalp

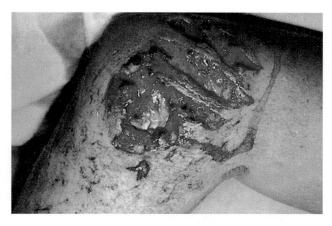

Figure 7-6. Deep abrasions and lacerations

Linear lacerations, also known as *incisions,* are characterized by sharp, even cuts with smooth edges. They are caused by a sharp, cutting object, such as a knife, razor blade, or broken glass. Linear lacerations tend to bleed freely. The greatest dangers with linear lacerations are severe (often profuse) bleeding and damage to tendons and nerves. They usually heal better than irregular lacerations, though, because the edges of the wound are smooth and straight.

A stellate laceration is a tear caused by a sharp, uneven instrument (such as a broken bottle) that produces a ragged incision through the skin surface and underlying tissues.

Avulsion

An **avulsion** is the tearing loose of a flap of skin, which may either remain hanging or be torn off altogether; scarring is often extensive. Avulsions usually bleed profusely; in some cases, however, blood vessels might seal themselves and retreat into surrounding tissue, limiting the amount of blood loss.

If the avulsed tissue is still attached by a flap of skin and is folded back, circulation to the flap can be severely compromised. The seriousness of an avulsion depends on how disrupted circulation is to the flap.

abrasion A superficial wound caused by rubbing, scraping, or shearing

laceration A break in the skin; lacerations can have either smooth or rough edges and can be of varying depth.

avulsion The tearing loose of a flap of skin, which may either remain hanging or be torn off altogether

The most commonly avulsed skin on the body is that on the fingers and toes, hands, forearms, legs, feet, ears, nose, and penis (see Figures 7-7 and 7-8). Avulsions commonly occur in automobile or motorcycle accidents.

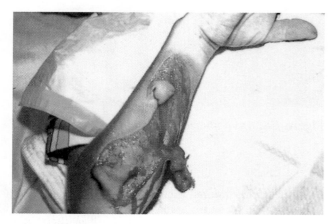

Figure 7-7. *Forearm avulsion*

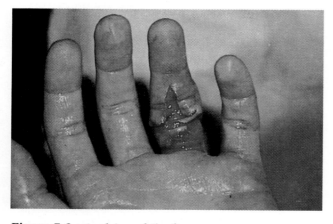

Figure 7-8. *Avulsion of the finger*

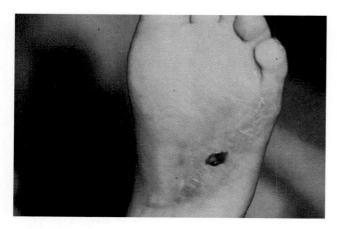

Figure 7-9. *Puncture wound of the foot*

Penetrating and Puncture Wounds

A puncture wound is caused by the penetration of a sharp object (such as a nail) through the skin and underlying structures. The opening in the skin may appear very small, resulting in little external bleeding, but the puncture wound may be extremely deep—causing severe internal bleeding and posing a serious threat of infection (see Figure 7-9).

Internal organs may also be damaged by punctures. In some cases, the object that causes the injury remains embedded in the wound.

Gunshot wounds may cause both entrance and exit wounds. The entrance wound is usually much smaller than the exit wound, which is generally two to three times larger and tends to bleed heavily. Many victims have multiple gunshot wounds; you should look carefully for additional wounds, especially in regions where they may be disguised, such as those covered by pubic hair.

Knife and stab wounds are dangerous—often fatal. Because knife wounds are easy to see, First Aiders too frequently concentrate only on the superficial skin wound and fail to consider the damage to underlying organs. Remember—the superficial skin wound is almost never fatal. The fatalities all relate to the injured organs that lie beneath the skin wound.

Amputations

The ripping, tearing force of industrial and automobile accidents can be great enough to tear away limbs from the body; amputations can also involve other body parts (see Figures 7-10 through 7-12).

Because blood vessels are elastic, they tend to spasm and retract into surrounding tissue in cases of complete amputation; therefore, complete amputations may cause relatively limited bleeding. In partial or degloving amputations, however, lacerated arteries continue to bleed profusely, and blood loss can be massive.

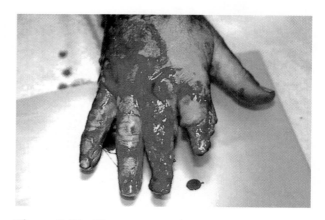

Figure 7-10. *Finger amputation*

Figure 7-11. *Finger amputation*

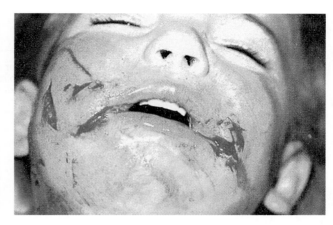

Figure 7-13. *Dog bite*

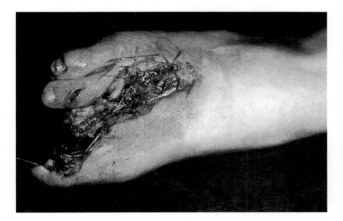

Figure 7-12. *Toe amputation*

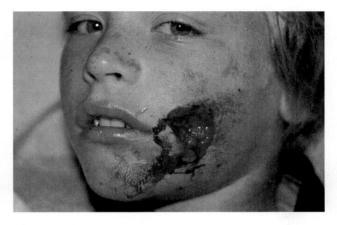

Figure 7-14. *Dog bite*

New techniques in microreconstructive surgery make it possible to save many amputated limbs or digits, so care of the amputated part has become almost as crucial as care of the victim.

Bites

Learning Objective 4 Discuss the threat of infection for a victim of human bites.

More than two million domestic animal bites and more than two thousand snakebites occur in the United States each year. The number of human bites is not recorded, but would probably be staggering if known.

Nine out of ten animal bites are inflicted by dogs; complications can include infection, cellulitis, tetanus, and hepatitis. The worst dog bites are those that leave puncture wounds and those that occur in areas with few blood vessels (see Figures 7-13 through 7-15).

A bite wound is actually a combination of a penetrating injury and a crush injury. A bite wound can

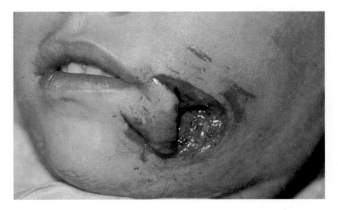

Figure 7-15. *Horse bite*

involve soft tissues, internal organs, and bones, and may include rupturing of tissues or organs. The power of a dog's jaws can cause a severe crush injury; a large breed can bite with the estimated force of 400 pounds per square inch. Figure 7-16 on page 124 details emergency care for dog bites.

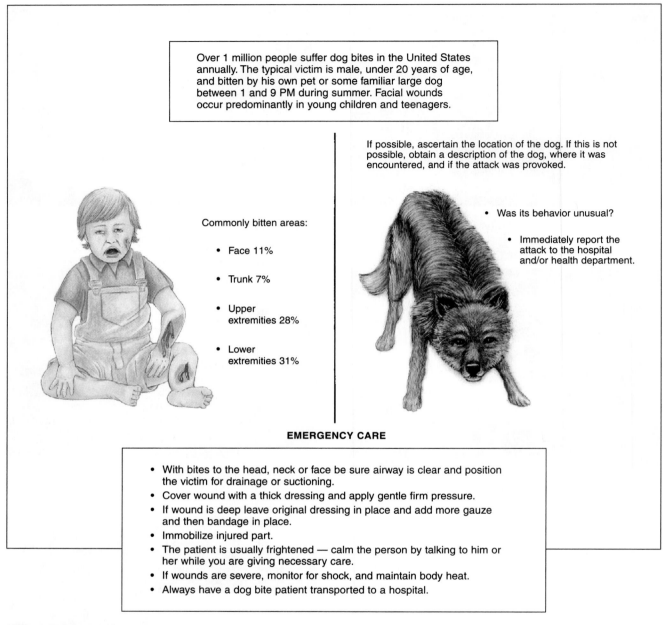

Over 1 million people suffer dog bites in the United States annually. The typical victim is male, under 20 years of age, and bitten by his own pet or some familiar large dog between 1 and 9 PM during summer. Facial wounds occur predominantly in young children and teenagers.

If possible, ascertain the location of the dog. If this is not possible, obtain a description of the dog, where it was encountered, and if the attack was provoked.

Commonly bitten areas:

- Face 11%

- Trunk 7%

- Upper extremities 28%

- Lower extremities 31%

- Was its behavior unusual?

  - Immediately report the attack to the hospital and/or health department.

EMERGENCY CARE

- With bites to the head, neck or face be sure airway is clear and position the victim for drainage or suctioning.
- Cover wound with a thick dressing and apply gentle firm pressure.
- If wound is deep leave original dressing in place and add more gauze and then bandage in place.
- Immobilize injured part.
- The patient is usually frightened — calm the person by talking to him or her while you are giving necessary care.
- If wounds are severe, monitor for shock, and maintain body heat.
- Always have a dog bite patient transported to a hospital.

Figure 7-16. Dog bites

The most difficult bite to manage is a human bite because of the high infection rate associated with it. The human mouth harbors millions of bacteria in a greater variety than found in the mouths of animals, and massive contamination may result from a bite. Human bites on fingers have sometimes resulted in loss of the fingers involved and, in some cases, the entire hand.

Emergency Care

Learning Objective 5 Describe the emergency care of a victim with an open soft-tissue injury.

Always take measures to avoid contact with body substances when caring for a victim of a soft-tissue injury, because there is a high chance of contact with

Control Bleeding

Prevent further contamination: all open wounds will already be contaminated, but a dressing and bandage will prevent further contamination.

Do not remove an impaled object: it may be cut if necessary to move the victim but should remain in place until the victim receives hospital care. The object should be stabilized with bulky dressings.

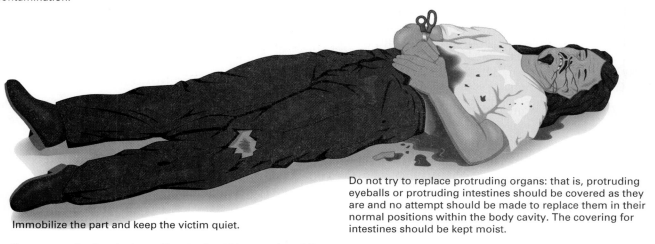

Immobilize the part and keep the victim quiet.

Preserve avulsed parts: torn off parts should be saved, and flaps of skin may be folded back to their normal position before bandaging.

Do not try to replace protruding organs: that is, protruding eyeballs or protruding intestines should be covered as they are and no attempt should be made to replace them in their normal positions within the body cavity. The covering for intestines should be kept moist.

Figure 7-17. Emergency care for open wounds

the victim's blood, body fluids, mucous membranes, traumatic wounds, or sores. If possible, use disposable latex gloves. After caring for the victim, dispose of the gloves and wash your hands thoroughly with soap and hot water.

Before you begin to treat the injury itself, maintain an airway and provide artificial ventilation if necessary. Treat soft-tissue injuries as follows (see Figure 7-17):

1. Expose the wound so you can see it clearly; if necessary, cut the victim's clothing from around the wound. Clean the wound and the area around it with sterile gauze or the cleanest available material (see Figure 7-18).

2. Control bleeding with direct pressure, using your gloved hand and a dry, sterile compression bandage, if possible. (See Chapter 6 for guidelines on controlling bleeding.)

3. Prevent further contamination by keeping the wound as clean as possible. If possible, avoid touching the wound with your hands, clothing, or anything that is not clean. Leave the cleaning of the wound to medical personnel.

4. Apply a dry, sterile dressing to the wound and bandage it securely in place. (See Chapter 10.)

In general, you should activate the EMS system if

- The wound has spurted blood, even if you have controlled the bleeding
- The wound is deeper than the outer layer of skin

- There is uncontrolled bleeding
- There is embedded debris, an embedded object, or extensive contamination
- The wound involves nerves, muscles, or tendons
- The wound involves the mouth, tongue, face, genitals, or any area where a scar would be disfiguring
- The wound is a human or animal bite

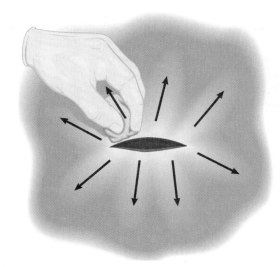

Figure 7-18. Clean the area around a wound using separate small strokes and by wiping away from the edges.

Cleaning Wounds and Preventing Infection

In *most* cases, you should not try to clean a wound yourself. Let an EMT or personnel at the emergency room take care of cleaning wounds, especially those that are large, have embedded debris, are extremely dirty, may require stitches, or are life-threatening.

For a *shallow* wound

- Wash the area around the wound with soap and water.

- Irrigate the wound with clean tap water; the water must flow at moderate pressure and be clean enough to drink. *Never scrub the wound—you can damage the wounded tissues.*

- Gently pat the wound dry with sterile gauze and apply antibiotic ointment (such as Neosporin).

- Cover the wound with a sterile, nonstick dressing, and bandage in place.

Never apply hydrogen peroxide, isopropyl alcohol, Merthiolate, Mercurochrome, or iodine to a wound—these can injure the tissues and delay healing.

Do not close a wound with adhesive tape, Steri-strips, or butterfly strips—these increase the risk of infection.

Removing Slivers

Left embedded in the skin, slivers almost always cause infection, so it is important to remove them. If a sliver is deeply embedded and you cannot see one end of it, take the victim to a physician for removal of the sliver.

If you can see the end of the sliver, use tweezers to remove it. Grasp the sliver firmly and pull at the same angle at which the sliver penetrated the skin. Pull slowly and firmly, and make sure you remove all of the sliver. If you pull too quickly or at the wrong angle, you may break off the sliver and leave part of it behind

If you can see the end of the sliver but can't grasp it with tweezers, use a sterilized needle to gently bring it to the surface; then remove it with tweezers, as described above.

Once you have removed the sliver, clean the area with soap and water, apply antibiotic ointment, and apply an adhesive strip to discourage infection.

Removing a Fishhook

You can safely remove a fishhook if the point *but not the barb* has penetrated the skin. To remove the hook, apply ice to the skin temporarily to numb it, then back the fishhook out. Wash the wound with soap and water, apply antibiotic ointment, and apply an adhesive strip.

If the barb has penetrated the skin, gently tape the fishhook to the skin so it won't move—movement causes pain and increases injury—and wait for a physician to remove the hook.

Removing Cactus Spines

If there are only a few cactus spines embedded in the skin, remove them gently and carefully with tweezers. Cactus spines can be difficult to see, so make sure you have adequate lighting and that you examine the area carefully.

If there are a large number of cactus spines

1. Carefully coat the area with rubber cement or white woodworking glue. *Never* use Super Glue, Scotch tape, electrical tape, duct tape, masking tape, or adhesive tape.

2. While the glue is still tacky, gently press a strip of gauze into the glue.

3. Let the glue dry for at least 30 minutes.

4. When the glue has completely dried, carefully roll it up from the edges, using the gauze to help you roll the glue off the victim's skin.

5. Use tweezers to remove any spines that did not adhere to the glue.

Progress Check

1. The greatest threat from an abrasion is
   _____ .
   (infection/pain/blood loss)

2. Linear lacerations heal better than stellate lacerations because _____ .
   (there is less blood loss/the edges are smooth/infection is less likely)

3. The most dangerous dog bites are those in areas with few _____ .
   (nerve endings/blood vessels/underlying tissues)

4. The greatest danger with an avulsion is compromised _____ in the flap.
   (sensation/circulation/pain reception)

5. The most serious bites are _____ bites.
   (snake/dog/human)

6. Blood loss from an amputation may actually be slight, because the elastic blood vessels may
   _____ .
   (be crushed/retract into surrounding tissue/shut down)

• Section 3 •
SPECIAL TREATMENT CONSIDERATIONS

The preceding emergency guidelines apply to most soft-tissue injuries, but you must be aware of special considerations in the case of chest or abdominal injuries, impaled objects, amputations, and clamping injuries.

Chest Injuries

Learning Objective 6 Discuss emergency care considerations for a victim with a penetrating chest injury.

In the case of penetrating chest injuries, activate the EMS system, then put an **occlusive** (airtight) dressing over the open wound and tape it on three sides. You can use household plastic wrap, aluminum foil, or vaseline gauze. One corner should be left untaped enough to flutter as the victim breathes.

For more information on the emergency medical care of chest injuries, see Chapter 9.

Abdominal Injuries

Learning Objective 7 Discuss emergency medical care considerations for a victim with an open wound to the abdomen.

Learning Objective 8 Differentiate the care of an open wound to the chest from the care of an open wound to the abdomen.

If organs protrude through an open abdominal wound, activate the EMS system; then:

1. Do not touch abdominal organs or try to replace them in the abdomen.

2. Cover protruding abdominal organs with a clean, moist, sterile dressing. Use sterile gauze compresses if available, and moisten them with clear water. *Never use absorbent cotton or any material that clings when wet, such as paper towels or toilet tissue.*

3. Cover the moist dressing with an occlusive material, such as clean aluminum foil or plastic wrap, to retain moisture and warmth.

4. Gently wrap the dressing in place with a bandage or clean sheet (see Chapter 9).

Impaled Objects

Learning Objective 9 Describe the special concerns and cautions necessary in the emergency care of wounds containing impaled objects.

Never remove an impaled object unless it penetrates the cheek or interferes with chest compressions. To treat:

1. Remove the victim's clothing if necessary to expose the wound; cut it away without disturbing the impaled object.

2. Manually secure the impaled object to prevent any motion. Moving the impaled object even slightly can increase bleeding and cause damage to underlying tissues, such as muscles, nerves, blood vessels, bones, and organs.

3. Control bleeding with direct pressure, but do not exert any pressure on the impaled object or on the edges of the skin around the cutting edge of the object.

4. Stabilize the impaled object with bulky dressings and bandage in place. The impaled object itself must be completely surrounded by bulky dressings—the objective in packing dressings around the object and taping them securely in place is to reduce motion to a minimum.

5. Calm and reassure the victim as you monitor for shock.

6. Keep the victim at rest.

7. Do not attempt to cut off, break off, or shorten an impaled object unless transportation is not possible with it in place. If the object must be cut off, stabilize it securely before cutting. Remember—any motion of the impaled object is transmitted to the victim and can cause additional tissue damage and shock. This step should be done by EMS personnel if possible.

8. Activate the EMS system immediately, or, if necessary, promptly but carefully transport the victim to the hospital, avoiding as much movement as possible. *Follow local protocol.*

An object impaled in the cheek should be removed in the field when you are more than 1 hour away from medical help (*follow local protocol*); profuse bleeding into the mouth and throat can impair breathing. To remove an object impaled in the cheek

occlusive Waterproof and airtight

1. Feel inside the victim's mouth to determine whether the object has penetrated completely.
2. Remove the object by pulling it back out the way it entered.
3. Control bleeding on the cheek and dress the wound.
4. If the object penetrated completely, pack the inside of the cheek (between the cheek wall and the teeth) with sterile gauze to control bleeding.
5. Activate the EMS system.

If you encounter too much resistance in trying to remove the object from the cheek, maintain the airway and activate the EMS system immediately. Stabilize the penetrating object while waiting for emergency personnel.

Amputations

A concern in the emergency care of amputations is the appropriate treatment of the amputated part: The way you handle an amputated part can help determine whether it can be reattached later by a surgeon.

Generally, you should not waste time searching for amputated parts or neglect victim care while you look for amputated parts. If you can find the amputated parts quickly or if someone you assign can find them, proceed as follows:

1. If possible, rinse the amputated part with clean water, but *do not scrub*. Wrap the part in a dry sterile gauze dressing secured in place with a self-adherent roller bandage.
2. Place the wrapped part in a plastic bag, plastic wrap, or aluminum foil, in accordance with local protocol. Label the part with the victim's name, date, and time the part was wrapped and bagged; include a statement describing what the part is and the approximate time of amputation.
3. Place the wrapped and bagged part in a cooler or any other available container so that it is on top of a cold pack or a sealed bag of ice (do not use dry ice). The part should be kept as cool as possible, without freezing. Do not cover the part with ice or immerse it in any kind of liquid. Label the container the same way you did the bagged part.
4. When EMTs arrive, give them the amputated part so it can be transported with the victim.

An important consideration in amputation is to preserve as much as possible of the original length of the limb. Even if a limb has been severely mangled and will eventually require amputation, the flap of skin holding the limb together may be used by the surgeon to cover the end of the stump, preserving a significant amount of limb length. In addition, the strands of soft tissue connecting the limb might contain nerves or blood vessels that, with proper surgical management, might allow the limb to survive.

Clamping Injuries

Learning Objective 10 Outline the special concerns and cautions necessary in the emergency care of clamping injuries.

Most clamping injuries involve the hand—more specifically a finger, which can be strangled when it is stuck into a hole and cannot be pulled out. The longer the tissue remains in the clamping object, the harder it will be to remove, because swelling becomes more severe by the minute.

To treat a clamping injury:

1. Remove the clamping object as quickly as possible. If you cannot remove the clamping object, apply a lubricant, such as green soap, and slowly but firmly wiggle the body part until it is loose.
2. If possible, elevate the affected extremity while you remove the clamping object.
3. If you are unable to loosen the body part or remove the clamping object, activate the EMS system.

Progress Check

1. To treat a chest injury, cover the wound with an occlusive dressing and tape it on _____ sides.
   (two/three/all)

2. Cover protruding abdominal contents with a dressing, then _____ material.
   (occlusive/porous/adherent)

3. The goal in treating a wound with an impaled object is to prevent _____ as much as possible.
   (bleeding/pain/motion)

4. If you find an amputated part, wrap it in gauze, then keep it _____ .
   (moist and cool/dry and cool/dry and room temperature)

5. In cases of a clamping injury, activate the EMS system if _____ .
   (the wound bleeds/you cannot remove the clamping object/there is severe pain)

● SUMMARY ●

- Closed wounds are those in which the tissue beneath the skin is damaged, but the skin is not broken; examples are bruises and hematomas.

- Open wounds are those in which the skin is broken; examples are abrasions, incisions, lacerations, punctures, avulsions, bites, and amputations.

- The most serious threat from an abrasion is infection; blood loss is usually minimal.

- Lacerations with smooth edges heal better than those with ragged edges.

- The biggest threat from an avulsion is lack of circulation to the flap; make sure the flap is not bent back.

- If you can find an amputated part, your proper care of it can dramatically improve the odds of the surgeon's successfully reattaching it.

- Even if a limb is severely mangled, you should never complete an amputation; nerves and blood vessels in even small strands of tissue may enable the surgeon to reattach the limb completely.

● KEY TERMS ●

Make sure you understand the following key terms:

- wound
- contusion
- epidermis
- dermis
- hematoma
- abrasion
- laceration
- avulsion
- occlusive

Student: _____ Date: _____

Course: _____ Section #: _____

PART 1 • True/False

If you believe the statement is true, circle the T. If you believe the statement is false, circle the F.

T F **1.** Always thoroughly clean a wound before dressing and bandaging it.

T F **2.** Avulsed parts or flaps of skin should not be folded back into place; this causes more contamination.

T F **3.** Nine out of ten animal bites are inflicted by dogs.

T F **4.** Do not attempt to remove objects embedded in a wound.

T F **5.** Proper handling of a severed body part may allow it to be reattached successfully.

T F **6.** Always break or cut off an impaled object before the victim is transported.

T F **7.** Objects impaled in the neck should be removed.

T F **8.** Objects impaled in the cheek should rarely be removed.

T F **9.** Be patient with clamping injuries of the finger—the longer a finger is stuck, the easier it will be to remove.

PART 2 • Multiple Choice

For each item, circle the correct answer or the phrase that best completes the statement.

1. What type of wound has as its greatest danger severe bleeding and cut tendons and nerves?

 a. an incision
 b. a laceration
 c. a contusion
 d. a puncture

2. An open wound characterized by jagged skin edges and free bleeding is

 a. a laceration
 b. an incision
 c. a contusion
 d. a puncture

3. What type of wound has the greatest danger of infection?

 a. an incision
 b. a laceration
 c. a contusion
 d. a puncture

4. When a puncture wound is caused by an impaled object

 a. remove the object and cover the wound with a sterile dressing
 b. stabilize the object with a bulky dressing
 c. apply slight pressure on the object to control bleeding
 d. always shorten the object so it will be easier to move the victim

5. A serious injury in which large flaps of skin and tissues are torn loose or pulled off is called an

 a. abrasion
 b. amputation
 c. avulsion
 d. incision

6. Proper handling of a severed part includes

 a. cleaning it with an antiseptic solution
 b. wrapping it in gauze or a clean towel
 c. freezing the part as quickly as possible
 d. applying a tourniquet to the severed part to preserve fluids

7. Most clamping injuries involve

 a. the hands
 b. the feet
 c. the arms
 d. the legs

8. Gunshot wounds generally

 a. have no exit wounds
 b. have a smaller exit wound than entrance wound
 c. have identical-sized entrance and exit wounds
 d. have a larger exit wound than entrance wound

- A patron at a local gas station is stabbed in the chest with a large screwdriver. When you arrive, the victim is unconscious and the screwdriver is still in place.
- You hear a gunshot in your apartment building. On investigation, you find a middle-aged man with a gunshot wound to the upper thigh of his right leg. His wife tells you he was cleaning the gun when it accidentally discharged.

Injuries to the Face, Eye, and Throat

Learning Objectives

When you have mastered the material in this chapter, you will be able to

1   Describe how to assess eye injuries

2   Describe general emergency care procedures for eye injuries

3   Demonstrate emergency care for foreign objects in the eye

4   Describe emergency care for injury to the orbits

5   Describe emergency care for eyelid injuries

6   Describe emergency care for injuries to the globe

7   Describe emergency care for chemical burns of the eye

8   Demonstrate emergency care for a victim with an object impaled in the eye

9   Describe emergency care for extruded eyeball

10 Describe how to remove contact lenses

11 Describe general emergency care for injuries to the face

12 Describe emergency care for injuries to the mouth and jaw

13 Describe emergency care for fractures of the face and lower jaw

14 Describe emergency care for injuries of the nose

15 Describe emergency care for injuries of the ear

16 Describe emergency care for injuries of the throat

17 Describe emergency care for common dental injuries

SQ3R Plus

- **Survey** to set goals for studying.
- Ask **questions** as you **read.**
- Stop frequently to **recite** and **review.**
- **Write** a summary of key points.
- **Reflect** on the importance of this material and its relevance in your life.

On August 9, 1998, 10-year-old Cameron Taylor was trying to get an old pair of roller blades from a top shelf in the garage when he knocked over an open container of gasoline. As the can banged against the shelving, gasoline splashed into both of Cameron's eyes. Cameron slapped his hands over his eyes and ran from the garage, screaming.

Next door, Elaine Miller was playing with her two children in the sandbox. She ran toward Cameron, and when he told her what happened, pulled him to the front lawn. Though he was panicked, she forced him to lie down on the grass, then ran and turned on the garden hose. Kneeling next to Cameron, she turned him slightly on his side, then forced one of his eyelids open. Holding the eyelid open with one hand, she directed the gentle stream from the garden hose across the eyeball.

Calling to her 7-year-old daughter, Elaine told her to go get another neighbor. When Diane Park arrived, Elaine had her call 9-1-1, then help her force Cameron's other eye open. When EMTs arrived, Elaine was still irrigating both eyes with the hose.

THE SPECIALIZED STRUCTURES OF THE FACE, PRONE TO injury because of their location, can be permanently and irreversibly damaged. Injuries to the face are quite common: Approximately 75 percent of all victims involved in motor vehicle accidents sustain at least minor facial trauma.

While some injuries to the face are minor, many face and throat injuries are life threatening because they compromise the upper airway, impairing the victim's ability to breathe. In addition, many injuries of the face and throat stem from impacts strong enough to cause cervical spine damage or skull fracture.

In addition to facial injuries, more than 1.5 million eye injuries occur each year in the United States; proper assessment and treatment can be instrumental in saving the victim's eyesight.

This chapter outlines the proper assessment and care of victims with eye injuries as well as injuries to the face, jaw, and throat.

• Section 1 •
INJURIES TO THE EYE

Learning Objective 1 Describe how to assess eye injuries.

Few true **ocular** (eye) emergencies occur, but when they do, they tend to be urgent. The eyes are easily damaged by injury, and injury to the eye probably causes greater anxiety to the victim than any other type of injury. Because of the potential for permanent damage, all eye injuries should receive medical attention immediately.

Nearly half of all serious eye injuries occur in or around the home (see Figure 8-1).

Assessment

Ask the victim when the accident or pain occurred, what the victim first noticed, and how the eyes were affected. Then examine the eyes separately and together with a small penlight to evaluate the following:

- The **orbits** (eye sockets) for ecchymosis (bruising), swelling, laceration, and tenderness
- The lids for ecchymosis, swelling, and laceration

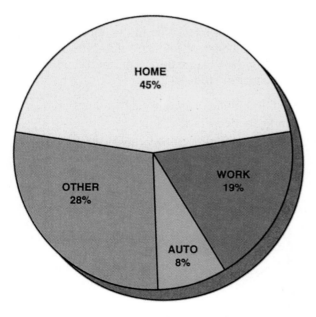

Nearly half of all serious eye injuries occur in or around the home. Most could be prevented by wearing safety glasses while doing chores.

Source: Katherine A. Randall, *Sightsaving*

Figure 8-1. Eye injuries

- The conjunctivae for redness, pus, and foreign bodies
- The **globes** (eyeballs) for redness, abnormal coloring, and laceration
- The pupils for size, shape, equality, and reaction to light; they should be black, round, equal in size, and reactive to light.
- Eye movements in all directions for abnormal gaze, paralysis of gaze, or pain on movement

Suspect significant damage if the victim has loss of vision that does not improve when he or she blinks, loses part of the field of vision, has severe pain in the eye, has double vision, or is unusually sensitive to light.

If the victim is unconscious, gently close the eyes and cover them with moist dressings. An unconscious person loses normal reflexes such as blinking that help protect the eyes.

Basic Treatment Guidelines for Eye Injuries

Learning Objective 2 Describe general emergency care procedures for eye injuries.

Regardless of the eye injury, these basic rules apply:

- Do not irrigate an injured eye except in the case of a chemical burn or if there is a foreign object in the eye.
- Do not put salves or medicine in an injured eye.
- Do not remove blood or blood clots from the eye.
- Do not try to force the eyelid open unless you have to wash out chemicals or a foreign object.
- Have the victim lie down and keep quiet.
- Limit use of the uninjured eye; it is usually best to patch it along with the injured eye.
- Give the victim nothing by mouth in case general anesthesia is required at the hospital.
- Every victim with an eye injury must be evaluated by a physician.

Foreign Objects in the Eye

Foreign objects—such as particles of dirt, sand, cinders, coal dust, or fine pieces of metal—can be blown

ocular Having to do with the eye
orbit The bony socket that holds the eyeball
globe The eyeball

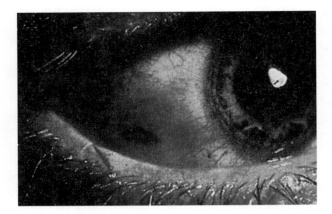

Figure 8-2. Foreign object lodged in the eye

Figure 8-3. Flushing foreign objects from the eye

or driven into the eye and lodged there (see Figure 8-2). If not removed, they may cause inflammation or infection or may scratch the cornea.

You should try to remove only those objects in the **conjunctiva** (the transparent mucous membrane lining the eyelids and covering the outer surface of the eyeball), not those in the cornea.

Emergency Care

Learning Objective 3 Describe emergency care for foreign objects in the eye.

1. Flush the eye with clean water, holding the eyelids apart (see Figure 8-3).
2. Remove an object lodged under the upper eyelid by drawing the upper lid down over the lower lid; as the upper lid returns to its normal position, the undersurfaces will be drawn over the lashes of the lower lid, removing the foreign object.
3. If the foreign object remains in the eye, grasp the eyelashes of the upper lid and turn the lid up over

a cotton swab or similar object. Carefully remove the foreign object from the eyelid with the corner of a piece of sterile gauze (see Figure 8-4).

4. If the foreign object is lodged under the lower lid, pull down the lower lid, exposing the lid's inner surface, and remove the foreign object with the corner of a piece of sterile gauze or cotton swab.
5. If the object becomes lodged in the eyeball, do not disturb it; place a bandage compress over both eyes and activate the EMS system (see Figure 8-5).

Injuries to the Orbits

Trauma to the face may result in the fracture of one or several of the bones of the skull that form the orbits (eye sockets) (see Figure 8-6). Signs and symptoms of orbital fracture include

- Double vision
- Markedly decreased vision
- Loss of sensation above the eyebrow, over the cheek, or in the upper lip due to nerve damage

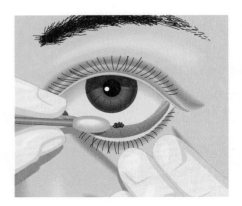

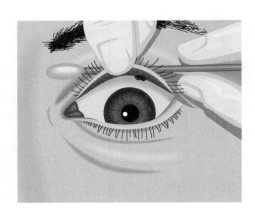

Figure 8-4. To remove particles from the white of the eye, pull down the lower eyelid while the victim looks up or pull up the upper lid as the victim looks down.

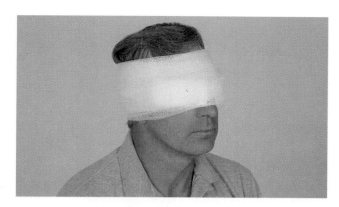

Figure 8-5. If a foreign object becomes lodged in an eye, bandage both eyes to minimize motion.

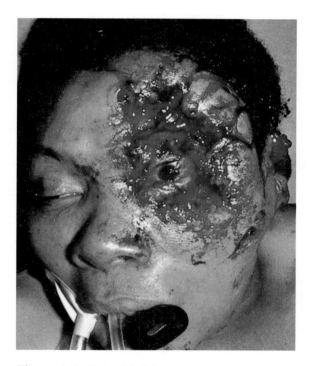

Figure 8-6. Eye orbit injury

- Nasal discharge, which may be profuse
- Paralysis of upward gaze (the victim's eyes will not be able to follow your finger upward)

Whenever the orbit has been fractured, assume there is also head injury.

Emergency Care

Learning Objective 4 Describe emergency care for injury to the orbits.

Orbital fractures require hospitalization and possible surgery. Activate the EMS system; then:

1. If the eyeball has *not* been injured, place ice packs over the injured eye to reduce swelling. Keep the victim in a sitting position until emergency personnel arrive.

2. If you suspect injury to the eyeball, avoid using ice packs. Keep the victim in a supine position until emergency personnel arrive.

Injuries to the Eyelids

Lid injuries include ecchymosis (black eyes), burns, and lacerations (see Figure 8-7). Because the eyelid is richly supplied with blood vessels, lacerations to the lid can cause profuse bleeding.

Anything that lacerates the lid can also cause damage to the eyeball, so assess the injury carefully.

Emergency Care

Learning Objective 5 Describe emergency care for eyelid injuries.

In general, field care consists of controlling bleeding and protecting the injured tissue and underlying structures. *Never try to remove material embedded in the eyeball.* Activate the EMS system; then:

1. Control eyelid bleeding with light pressure from a light dressing; use no pressure at all if the eyeball itself is injured.

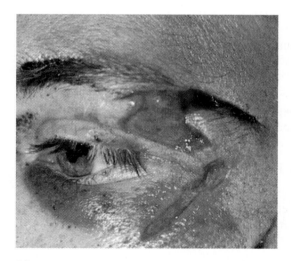

Figure 8-7. Eyelid injury

conjunctiva The transparent mucous membrane lining the eyelids and covering the outer surface of the eyeball

2. Cover the lid with moistened sterile gauze to keep the wound from drying. If the eyelid skin is avulsed, preserve it so it can be transported with the victim for later grafting.

3. If the eyeball is not injured, cover the injured lid with cold compresses to reduce swelling.

4. Cover the uninjured eye with a bandage to decrease movement of the injured eye.

Injuries to the Globe

Injuries to the globe include bruising, lacerations, damage caused by foreign objects, and abrasions. Deep lacerations can cut the cornea, causing the contents of the eyeball to spill out; severe blunt trauma or projectile injury can rupture the eyeball.

Some injuries to the globe—such as lacerations or embedded objects—are immediately apparent. Other signs and symptoms of injury to the globe include

- A pear-shaped or irregularly shaped eyeball
- Blood in the front chamber of the eye

Emergency Care

> **Learning Objective 6** Describe emergency care for injuries to the globe.

Injuries to the globe are best treated in the emergency room, where specialized equipment is available. Activate the EMS system; then:

1. Apply light patches to both eyes. Do not use a patch or any kind of pressure if you suspect a ruptured eyeball, because pressure can force eye contents out.

2. Keep the victim in a supine position until emergency personnel arrive.

Chemical Burns of the Eye

Chemical burns of the eye (see Figure 8-8) represent a dire emergency: Permanent damage to the eye can occur within seconds of the injury, and the first 10 minutes following injury often determine the final outcome. Burning and tissue damage will continue as long as any substance is left in the eye, even if that substance is diluted.

The signs and symptoms of chemical burns include

- Irritated, swollen eyelids
- Redness or red streaks across the surface of the eye
- Blurred or diminished vision

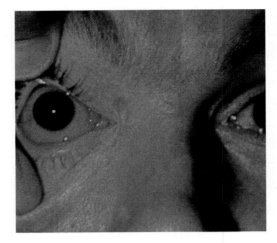

Figure 8-8. Chemical burn of the eye

- Excruciating pain in the eyes
- Irritated, burned skin around the eyes

Emergency Care

> **Learning Objective 7** Describe emergency care for chemical burns of the eye.

Activate the EMS system; then:

1. Holding the eyelids open, continuously irrigate the eye with running water for at least 30 to 60 minutes, beginning as soon as you encounter the victim (see Figure 8-9). Pour from the inside corner, across the eyeball to the outside edge; take care not to contaminate the uninjured eye. Eye wash systems (see Figure 8-10) are often available at

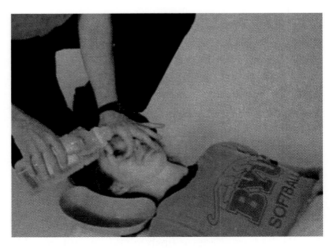

Figure 8-9. Chemical burns of the eye should be irrigated continuously for 30 to 60 minutes.

Figure 8-10. If possible, irrigate chemical burns of the eye in an eye wash system.

work sites. *Do not irrigate the eye with any solutions other than saline or water.* Never use any chemical antidote, including diluted vinegar, sodium bicarbonate, or alcohol.

2. Remove or flush out contact lenses; left in, they will trap chemicals between the contact lens and the cornea. (See Removing Contact Lenses later in this chapter.)

3. Remove any solid particles from the surface of the eye with a moistened cotton swab.

4. Continue irrigation until emergency personnel arrive.

Following irrigation, avoid contaminating your own eyes by washing your hands thoroughly and using a nail brush to clean under your fingernails.

Light Burns of the Eye

Looking at a source of ultraviolet light can burn the eyes, resulting in severe pain as long as 6 hours after exposure. One of the most common sources of light burns to the eyes is sunlight reflected off snow.

A victim of light burns to the eye should be seen by an ophthalmologist, who can determine how extensive the burns are and prescribe necessary treatment or medication. In the meantime

1. Move the victim *out of the sunlight*. If possible, the victim should be in a dark room, away from sources of light.

2. Cover both eyes with gauze pads that have been moistened with cold water.

3. Discourage the victim from rubbing his or her eyes; rubbing will further inflame injured tissues.

Impaled Objects in the Eye and Extruded Eyeball

Objects impaled or embedded in the eye should be removed only by a physician. Field care consists of stabilizing the object to prevent accidental movement or removal until the victim receives medical attention (see Figures 8-11 through 8-14).

During a serious injury, the eyeball may be forced out of the socket, or **extruded** (see Figure 8-15 on page 140). Never attempt to replace the eye in the socket.

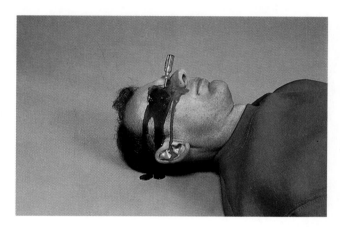

Figure 8-11. Object impaled in eye

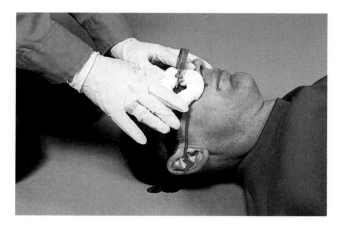

Figure 8-12. Place padding around the object.

extruded Forced out of position; an extruded eyeball has been forced out of the socket.

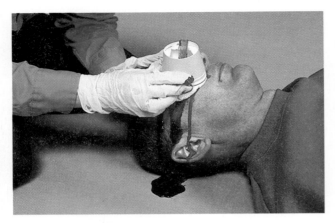

Figure 8-13. Stabilize the impaled object with a cup or other object.

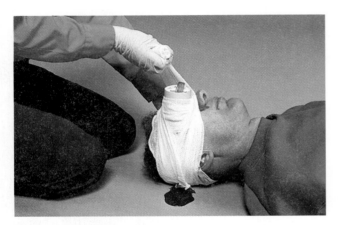

Figure 8-14. Bandage the cup in place.

Emergency Care

Learning Objective 8 Describe emergency care for a victim with an object impaled in the eye.

Learning Objective 9 Describe emergency care for extruded eyeball.

Activate the EMS system; then:

1. With the victim in a supine position, stabilize the head with sandbags or large pads.
2. Gently cover an extruded eyeball with a clean, moist dressing—such as sterile gauze that has been moistened with clean water—to help keep the eyeball moist. Or, encircle the eye and the impaled object with a gauze dressing or other suitable material, such as soft, sterile cloth. Never apply pressure. Cut a hole in a single bulky dressing to accommodate an impaled object.

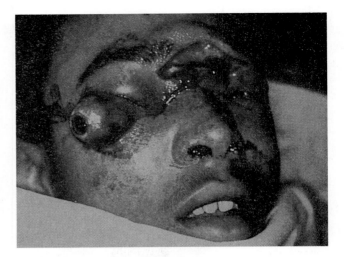

Figure 8-15. Extruded eyeball

3. Place a metal shield, paper cup, or cone over the impaled object or extruded eyeball. Do not use a styrofoam cup, because it can crumble. The impaled object or eyeball should not touch the top or sides of the cup.
4. Hold the cup and dressing in place with a self-adhering bandage compress or roller bandage that covers both eyes; do not wrap the bandage over the cup, because pressure from the bandage can push the cup down onto the impaled object or extruded eyeball. If the victim is unconscious, close the uninjured eye before bandaging to prevent drying of tissues.
5. Treat for shock; give the victim nothing by mouth.

Removing Contact Lenses

Learning Objective 10 Describe how to remove contact lenses.

An estimated 18 million Americans wear contact lenses of some type, some in only one eye; some, especially the elderly, wear both contact lenses and eyeglasses, so don't dismiss the possibility of contact lenses just because the victim is wearing eyeglasses.

To detect lenses, shine a penlight into the eye: A soft lens will show up as a shadow on the outer portion of the eye; a hard lens will show up as a shadow over the iris.

When determining whether to remove contact lenses, follow local protocol. Generally, you should remove contact lenses if there is a chemical burn to the eye or if transport will be delayed; generally, you should not remove contact lenses if the eyeball has any injury other than a chemical burn.

Removing Hard Contact Lenses

About the size of a shirt button, a hard lens fits over the cornea. To remove a hard lens (see Figure 8-16)

1. Separate the eyelids; manipulate them to position the lens over the cornea.

2. Place your thumbs gently on the top and bottom eyelids, and gently press the eyelids down and forward to the edges of the lens.

3. Press the lower eyelid slightly harder, and move it under the bottom edge of the lens.

4. Moving the eyelids toward each other, slide the lens out between them.

Removing Soft Contact Lenses

A soft lens is slightly larger than a dime and covers all of the cornea and some of the **sclera** (the white of the eye). To remove a soft lens (see Figure 8-17)

1. With your middle fingertip on the lower lid, pull the lid down.

2. Place your index fingertip on the lower edge of the lens, then slide the lens down to the sclera.

3. Compress the lens gently between your thumb and index finger, allowing air to get underneath it, and remove it from the eye.

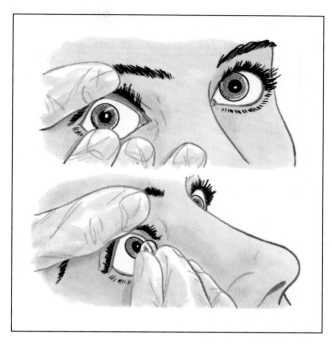

Figure 8-17. *Removing a soft (flexible) contact lens*

If the lens has dehydrated on the eye, run sterile saline across the eye surface, slide the lens off the cornea, and pinch the lens up to remove it.

Store the removed soft contact lenses in water or a saline solution.

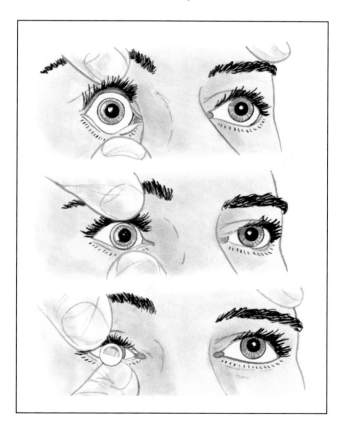

Figure 8-16. *Removing a hard corneal contact lens*

Progress Check

1. All victims of eye injuries require _____ .
   (rapid treatment/evaluation by a physician/surgery)

2. Use ice packs or cold compresses unless the _____ is injured.
   (eyelid/eye socket/eyeball)

3. In case of a chemical burn to the eye, irrigate the eye with clean water for at least _____ minutes.
   (10/20/30)

4. The goal of first aid for an impaled object in the eye is to _____ it.
   (stabilize/remove/shorten)

5. In most eye injuries, you should patch _____ .
   (the injured eye only/both eyes/neither eye)

sclera The white of the eye

• Section 2 •
INJURIES TO THE FACE

> **Learning Objective 11** Describe general emergency care for injuries to the face.

In victims with trauma to the face, mouth, and jaw, you should suspect cervical spine and spinal injuries. Victims of significant facial trauma may also have fractures of the jaw and damage to or loss of teeth (see Figures 8-18 through 8-23).

To treat a victim with facial trauma

1. Establish an airway. Inspect the mouth for small fragments of teeth or broken dentures, bits of bone, pieces of flesh, or fragments of foreign objects on which the victim might choke. Remove them as thoroughly as possible. Pull the tongue forward to open the airway. If you have trouble grasping the tongue, open the throat by pulling the chin forward or grasping the angle of the jaw and pressing it forward.

2. Completely immobilize the neck to prevent aggravation of possible cervical spine injuries.

3. Control hemorrhage—several major arteries run through the face, and they can bleed profusely and rapidly enough to cause death. Apply extremely gentle pressure if you suspect that bones under the wound may be fractured or shattered.

4. If nerves, tendons, or blood vessels have been exposed, cover them with a moist, sterile dressing.

> **Learning Objective 12** Describe emergency care for injuries to the mouth and jaw.

Examine the mouth for broken or missing teeth. If a tooth has been lost, try to find it; a surgeon can reimplant a tooth within 2 hours and can use bone fragments to reconstruct the jaw. For treatment procedures, see Section 3 on pages 147 to 149.

If dentures are in and unbroken, leave them in place—they can help support the structures of the mouth. If dentures are broken, remove them.

Fractures of the Face and Jaw

Maxillofacial fractures may be simple, such as undisplaced nasal fractures, or extensive, involving severe lacerations, bony fractures, and nerve damage (see Figure 8-24 on page 144). Spinal injury, tearing or rupture of an eyeball, and facial burns often accompany facial fracture.

Signs and Symptoms

The signs and symptoms of facial fracture include

- Distortion of facial features
- Numbness or pain
- Severe bruising and swelling
- Bleeding from the nose and mouth
- Limited jaw motion
- Teeth not meeting normally
- Double vision, when bone around the eye is fractured
- Irregularities in the facial bones that can be felt before swelling occurs
- The distance between the eyes appearing too wide

The signs and symptoms of **maxilla** (upper jaw) fracture include

- Movement of the maxilla
- Nosebleed
- Black eyes
- Numbness of the upper lip or cheek
- Eyes that appear unlevel

The signs and symptoms of **mandible** (lower jaw) fracture (see Figure 8-25 on page 145) include

- The mouth is usually open (some victims may be unable to open the mouth)
- Saliva mixed with blood flowing from the corners of the mouth
- Drooling (pain prevents the victim from swallowing)
- Painful and difficult speech
- Missing, loosened, or uneven teeth (even if teeth are not missing, the victim will complain that teeth do not "fit together right")
- Pain around the ears

Emergency Care

> **Learning Objective 13** Describe emergency care for fractures of the face and lower jaw.

The first priority in caring for a victim of maxillofacial fracture is establishing and maintaining the airway,

> **maxilla** The upper jaw
> **mandible** The lower jaw

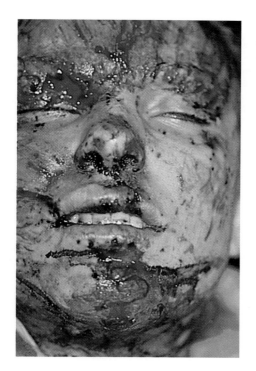

Figure 8-18. *Injury to the face*

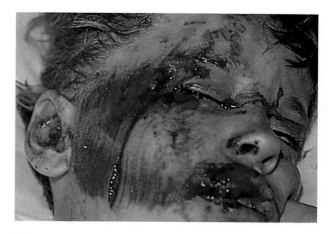

Figure 8-19. *Injury to the face*

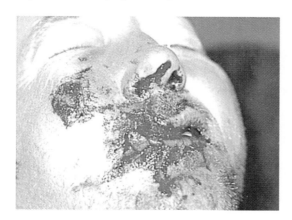

Figure 8-20. *Injury to the mouth*

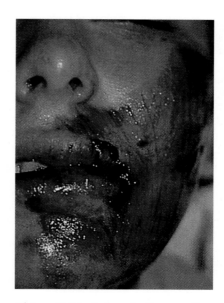

Figure 8-21. *Injury to the mouth*

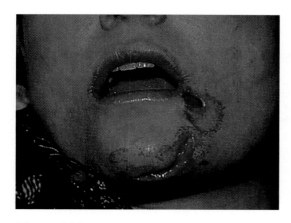

Figure 8-22. *Injury to the chin and jaw*

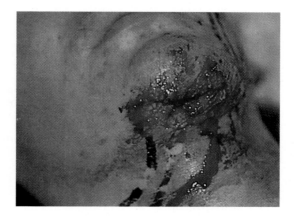

Figure 8-23. *Injury to the chin*

COMMON FRACTURES OF THE FACE AND JAW

Facial fractures often result from impact injuries to the face. The main danger of facial fractures is airway problems. Bone fragments and blood may obstruct the airway. Common signs of a fractured jaw may include irregularity of bite, loss of teeth, bleeding in the mouth, deformity and/or loose bone segments, increased salivation, and the inability to swallow or talk.

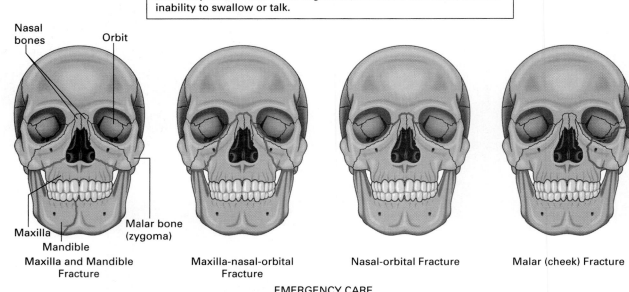

Nasal bones

Orbit

Maxilla

Mandible

Malar bone (zygoma)

Maxilla and Mandible Fracture

Maxilla-nasal-orbital Fracture

Nasal-orbital Fracture

Malar (cheek) Fracture

EMERGENCY CARE

Emergency care is the same as for soft-tissue injuries with special attention to clearing the airway of any obstructing materials, teeth, blood, etc.

■ Maintain open airway, allowing for drainage if neccessary.

■ If necessary, assist ventilation. Control bleeding with as little pressure as is necessary so as not to displace fractures. The use of the temporal and facial pressure points may be necessary.

■ Always suspect and assess for spinal injuries, and take necessary immobil-ization precautions.

■ Dress and bandage open wounds.

■ Continually monitor airway.

■ If necessary, immobilize mandible (lower jaw). However if there is consider-able bleeding in the mouth, it is best to not immobilize because it may com-promise the airway.

■ Keep victim quiet, and be very gentle so fracture areas will not displace or do further damage to other tissues.

■ The victim who is not bleeding should be put in a semi-reclining position unless spinal injuries are suspected. Victims with bleeding facial injuries should be positioned on their sides with head turned down for draining.

■ Assess for other possible injuries.

Figure 8-24. Common fractures of the face and jaw

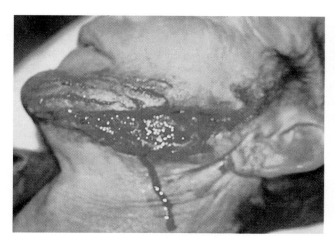

Figure 8-25. *Soft-tissue injuries and fracture of the lower jaw*

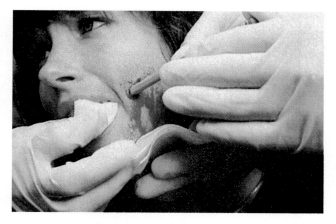

Figure 8-26. *Impaled objects in the cheek may be removed. Dress outside of wound and put dressing on inside of wound between cheek and teeth. Hold dressing in place if necessary.*

which can be compromised by blood, edema, or structural defects. Activate the EMS system; then:

1. Clear the airway; remove any debris from the mouth.
2. Immobilize the neck if you suspect spinal injuries, then position the victim to allow for drainage.
3. Control bleeding; place bandages carefully to allow for vomiting and drainage of blood.
4. If you suspect lower jaw fracture, carefully immobilize the lower jaw with a cervical collar or cravats. Monitor for vomiting.
5. If you suspect a fracture of the nose, control nosebleed as described in Chapter 6. Apply an ice pack to the nose for as long as 20 minutes to reduce swelling and relieve pain. *Never try to straighten the nose.*

Objects Impaled in the Cheek

The only time you should try to remove an impaled object is when it is impaled in the cheek, has penetrated all the way through the cheek, and is loose—threatening to obstruct the airway. To remove, activate the EMS system; then:

1. Pull or push the object out of the cheek in the same direction in which it entered the cheek. Never pull the object through to the inside of the mouth.
2. Pack dressing material between the victim's teeth and the wound; leave some of the dressing outside the mouth and tape it there to prevent the victim from swallowing the dressing (see Figure 8-26).

3. Dress and bandage the outside of the wound to control bleeding.

Injuries of the Nose

> **Learning Objective 14** Describe emergency care for injuries of the nose.

Care for soft-tissue injuries of the nose (see Figures 8-27 and 8-28) as you would other soft-tissue injuries. Take special care to maintain an open airway, and position the victim so that blood does not drain into the throat. For guidelines on nosebleed, see Chapter 6.

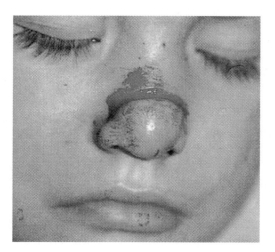

Figure 8-27. *Nose injury*

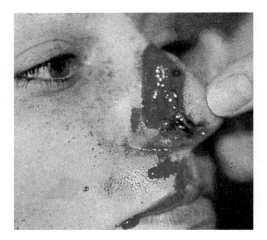

Figure 8-28. Nose injury

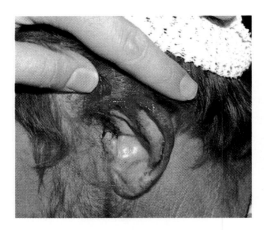

Figure 8-29. Injury to the ear

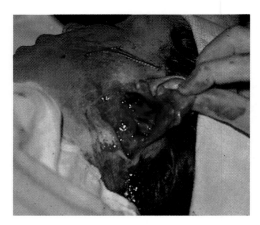

Figure 8-30. Injury to the ear

Foreign objects in the nose usually occur among small children. To treat, reassure and calm the child and parent, then activate the EMS system. Special lighting and instruments available at the hospital minimize the risk of removal.

Nasal fractures are the most common type of facial fracture because of the delicate structure of the nose; the most common signs and symptoms are swelling and deformity. To treat, apply ice compresses to reduce swelling, then activate the EMS system.

Injuries of the Ear

Learning Objective 15 Describe emergency care for injuries of the ear.

Cuts and lacerations of the ear are common (see Figures 8-29 and 8-30); occasionally, a section of the ear may be severed. Treat as for other soft-tissue injuries. Save any avulsed parts; wrap avulsed parts in moistened gauze and save for transport with the victim.

When dressing an injured ear, place part of the dressing between the ear and the side of the head. As a general rule, don't probe into the ear.

Never pack the ear to stop bleeding from the ear canal. Clear or bloody fluid draining from the ear can indicate skull fracture. Place a loose, clean dressing across the opening of the ear to absorb blood, but do not exert pressure to stop the bleeding.

Foreign objects in the external ear are a common problem among children; most common are small, hard objects such as beans and peanuts. If you can see the object and it is at the opening of the ear canal, gently remove the object with tweezers. Otherwise, do not try to remove the object in the field; instead, the victim should be taken to the hospital, where good lighting and appropriate equipment are available. *Never irrigate the ear in an attempt to dislodge a foreign object;* liquid will cause many objects (such as beans) to swell, making removal more difficult.

If the victim has an insect in the ear, never insert anything into the ear canal in an attempt to kill the insect. Remember: Most insects are attracted to light. Gently pull on the earlobe to straighten the ear canal, then shine a flashlight in the ear to attract the insect out.

Injuries of the Throat

The throat can be injured by any crushing blow; common causes include hanging (accidental or intentional), impact with a steering wheel, or running or riding into a stretched wire or clothesline (see Figures 8-31 and 8-32). If the throat is lacerated, bleeding from a major artery or vein can occur, and air bubbles may enter the blood vessels.

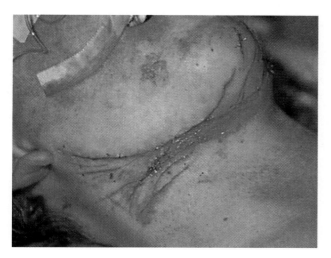

Figure 8-31. Injury to the throat

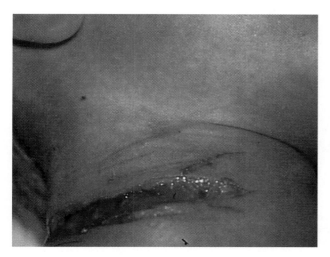

Figure 8-32. Injury to the throat

Signs and Symptoms

Besides obvious lacerations, swelling, or bruising, signs and symptoms of an injured throat include (see Figure 8-33 on page 148)

- Displacement of the trachea to one side
- Difficulty speaking
- Crepitus sounds during speaking or breathing as air escapes from an injured larynx
- Loss of the voice
- Airway obstruction that is not obviously due to other sources (such obstruction is caused by swelling of the throat)

Emergency Care

Learning Objective 16 Describe emergency care for injuries of the throat.

Maintaining an airway is extremely important in throat injuries, because blood clots when it is exposed to air and clots can threaten the airway. Activate the EMS system; then:

1. Open the airway; if necessary, give rescue breathing.

2. Keep the victim lying down to lessen the chance of air entering the blood vessels. Position the victim on the left side with the body tilted downward at a 15-degree angle.

3. Control bleeding with slight to moderate pressure and bulky dressings. If you think the blood is coming from a vein, apply pressure above and below the site to prevent air embolism. Monitor pressure carefully—too much pressure will block the flow of blood to the brain. Never apply pressure to both sides of the neck at the same time.

4. Treat for shock.

Progress Check

1. The priority in treating injuries to the face is to

   _____ .
   (maintain the airway/prevent shock/control bleeding)

2. _____ often accompanies trauma to the mouth and jaw.
   (severe bleeding/spinal injury/severe pain)

• Section 3 •
DENTAL EMERGENCIES

Dental emergencies are rarely life threatening but can be extremely painful and can cause the victim considerable anxiety. Rapid emergency care dramatically improves the prognosis and can make it possible for a dentist to make permanent repairs. A victim with any kind of dental emergency should be referred to a dentist or oral surgeon for treatment as quickly as possible; many injuries can be repaired only within a relatively narrow window of time.

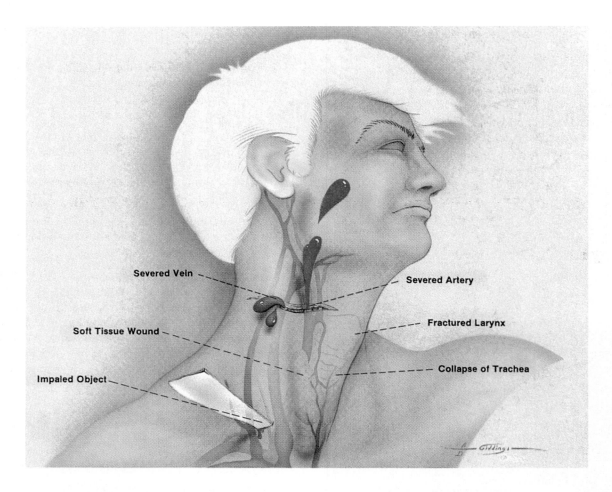

BLUNT OR CRUSHING TRAUMA

- Loss of voice
- Severe airway obstruction even though the mouth and nose are clean and no foreign body is present
- Deformity, contusions, or depressions in the neck
- Swelling in the neck and sometimes the face and chest. When the swollen areas are touched there are crackling sensations under the skin caused by air leakage in the soft tissues.
- If one of the above signs is present, it is an extreme emergency, and the victim needs to be transported to a medical facility immediately.
- Calm and reassure the victim, encouraging him or her to breathe slowly.
- Administer artificial ventilation as needed.
- Be alert for possible cervical-spine injuries, and take appropriate immobilization measures.
- Activate the EMS system immediately.

OPEN INJURIES

- Serious open wounds of the neck can cause profuse bleeding.
- If an **artery** has been severed and there is bright red spurting blood, apply direct pressure with a sterile (if possible) bulky dressing. If blood soaks through the dressing, do not remove it – just add another dressing on the first one. Maintain firm pressure with your hand until you arrive at the hospital. CAUTION: Pressure dressing around the neck can compromise the airway.
- Do not apply pressure over the airway or on both sides of the neck at the same time.
- Keep victim supine with legs slightly elevated, and activate the EMS system immediately.
- If a large **vein** has been severed (profuse, steady flow of dark red to maroon-colored blood), attempt to control bleeding using direct pressure with a bulky dressing. If bleeding is controlled, cover the wound with an occlusive dressing.
- If bleeding is not immediately controlled, apply pressure above and below the point of bleeding. It is imperative that air not be sucked into the vein and carried into the circulatory system. This will create an air embolism, which can be rapidly fatal. This is more likely to occur if the victim is sitting or standing.
- Cover wound with an occlusive dressing or plastic wrap, and tape all edges snugly to form an airtight seal over the severed vein.
- Position the victim on his or her side.
- Activate the EMS system. Administer artificial ventilation as needed.
- Monitor airway.

Figure 8-33. *Common neck and throat injuries*

Loose Tooth

Any trauma to the face can carry enough impact to loosen one or more teeth. To check for a loose tooth, grasp the tooth gently with your fingers and apply slight pressure on both sides of the tooth. The slightest movement indicates that the tooth has been loosened from its socket. To prevent further injury, have the victim bite down firmly, but not too hard, on a piece of gauze. The pressure should be enough to keep the tooth in the socket, but not enough to further loosen it. *Never pull out a loose tooth.*

Broken Tooth

The most common teeth to be broken are the top front teeth; in addition to being broken when the victim suffers head or facial injury, they are often broken in falls, fights, motor vehicle accidents, and sporting events. A broken tooth can be extremely painful, because the nerve may be exposed; immediate dental care is essential. Until the victim can be treated by a dentist

1. Use a clean cloth and warm water to clean blood, dirt, and other debris away from the broken teeth; if there are still tooth fragments in the mouth, remove them to prevent choking.

2. If the jaw is not injured, have the victim gently rinse his or her mouth with warm water to thoroughly clean it.

3. Apply an ice pack or cold compress to the victim's face over the broken teeth to relieve pain and reduce swelling.

Knocked-Out Tooth

An estimated 2 million people have teeth knocked out every year in the United States; as many as 90 percent of those teeth could be saved with proper first aid and *rapid* treatment by a dentist. The ligament fibers necessary for successful reimplantation begin to die soon after the injury, so time is of the essence; a tooth can usually be successfully reimplanted if it is inserted back into the socket within 30 minutes. Keeping the tooth moist until it is placed in the socket dramatically improves the odds of success.

A top priority in the case of a knocked-out tooth is finding the tooth and handling it properly. *Never touch the root of the tooth;* handle it by the crown so you don't damage the ligament fibers necessary for reimplantation. To treat the victim and the tooth properly

1. Have the victim rinse his or her mouth gently with warm water to wash out blood, dirt, and debris.

2. Place a rolled sterile gauze pad against the socket and have the victim bite firmly on it to help control bleeding.

3. Handling the tooth gently and by the crown only, immerse it in the solution found in the commercial Save-a-Tooth™ kit. These kits, available over the counter in drugstores, can improve the chances of successful implantation as long as 24 hours after the injury. If you do not have access to a Save-a-Tooth kit, immerse the tooth in either saliva or cold milk. *Do not put the tooth in water, alcohol, mouthwash, reconstituted powdered milk, skim milk, cottage cheese, or yogurt.*

Saliva is the perfect solution for protecting a tooth, but it is not a good idea to ask an injured person to hold the tooth in his or her mouth—an injured person may become anxious, confused, or upset and may swallow the tooth. If there is nothing else available, ask a family member to hold the tooth *gently* in his or her mouth while the victim is being taken to a dentist or oral surgeon.

Progress Check

1. A knocked-out tooth can almost always be reimplanted if the procedure is done within

   _____ .
   (30 minutes/1 hour/24 hours)

2. To protect a knocked-out tooth, always handle it by

   _____ .
   (the root/the crown)

3. To increase the odds of successful reimplantation, keep a knocked-out tooth _____ .
   (wet/dry/cold/warm)

4. To transport a knocked-out tooth, immerse it in

   _____ .
   (water/mouthwash/milk)

• SUMMARY •

- Use a small penlight or other light to examine the eyes; examine them both separately and together.

- Never try to remove a foreign object that is lodged in the eye.

- All victims of eye injury must be evaluated by a physician.

- Bleeding from the eyelids can be profuse; never apply pressure to the eyelid if you think the eyeball itself might be injured.

- In chemical burns of the eye, irrigate the affected eye for at least 30 minutes or until emergency personnel arrive.

- Remove contact lenses if there has been a chemical burn to the eye or if transport will be lengthy or delayed.

- The amount of force necessary to injure the face will usually also cause spinal injury.

- The top priority in treating victims with maxillofacial injury or fracture is maintaining the airway.

- Rapid emergency treatment of a dental injury dramatically improves long-term prognosis.

• **KEY TERMS** •

Make sure you understand the following key terms:

- ocular
- orbit
- globe
- conjunctiva
- extruded
- sclera
- maxilla
- mandible

Student: _____   Date: _____

Course: _____   Section #: _____

PART 1 • True/False

If you believe the statement is true, circle the T. If you believe the statement is false, circle the F.

T   F   **1.** Both eyes should be bandaged if a foreign object is lodged in just one eye.

T   F   **2.** It is always best to try gently to remove an object lodged in the eyeball.

T   F   **3.** A chemical burn of the eye should be irrigated for approximately 5 minutes.

T   F   **4.** Never force the eyelids open in an attempt to irrigate a chemical burn.

T   F   **5.** Never use cold compresses on injuries to the globe.

T   F   **6.** If the eyelids do not cover the eyeball in a lid injury, use a light, moist dressing to prevent drying.

T   F   **7.** Do not try to remove contact lenses, especially in a chemical burn.

T   F   **8.** Do not remove blood or blood clots from the eye.

T   F   **9.** A victim of trauma to the mouth and face should have the head and neck immobilized.

T   F   **10.** If you find a missing tooth, scrub it thoroughly and pack it in ice.

T   F   **11.** Never apply ice or cold packs to a suspected nasal fracture.

T   F   **12.** A knocked-out tooth should be immersed in cold water.

PART 2 • Multiple Choice

For each item, circle the correct answer or the phrase that best completes the statement.

1. The first priority in treating a chemical burn to the eye is to
   a. irrigate the eye with clean water
   b. irrigate the eye with a chemical antidote
   c. instruct the victim to close the eye
   d. apply a cold compress to the affected eye

2. If a victim has a foreign object embedded in the globe
   a. remove the object, then dress and bandage the eye
   b. place a loose dressing over the object
   c. prepare a thick pressure dressing and secure a protective cone over the impaled object, leaving the uninjured eye unbandaged
   d. prepare a thick dressing and secure a protective cone over the impaled object, bandaging the uninjured eye also

3. If an eyeball is knocked out of the socket, which of the following should you *not* do?
   a. leave the eyeball out of the socket
   b. cover the extruded eyeball with a cup and thick dressing
   c. cover both eyes with a thick dressing
   d. gently replace the eyeball in the socket, then cover with a dressing

4. Eyelid injuries should be
   a. irrigated with cool water
   b. covered with a compress and roller band
   c. treated with antibiotic salve
   d. covered with a light dressing

5. For all chemical burns of the eye
   a. irrigate with water and vinegar solution
   b. have the victim blink repeatedly and wash the eyes
   c. irrigate continuously for at least 30 minutes
   d. irrigate with sodium bicarbonate

6. A whole tooth can sometimes be reimplanted; the key to successful reimplanting is to keep the dislodged tooth
   a. in an airtight bag
   b. moist
   c. warm
   d. covered with baking soda

7. When a victim sustains a possible facial fracture
   a. keep the victim supine with head and neck immobilized
   b. check all possible eye movements
   c. use ice packs over the area
   d. flush the area with clean water

8. The most important aim of emergency care of jaw fractures is to
   a. find teeth that have been knocked out
   b. apply wraps to keep the lower jaw stable
   c. ensure an airway
   d. pack the area in ice to control swelling

*Match the emergency-care procedure in the left-hand column with
the injury in the right-hand column.*

Emergency Care

A. Position a cup or cone over the injured eye, then bandage
B. Check all possible eye movements
C. Cover eyes with a sterile, moist dressing
D. Cover the eyes with a light dressing (moist if necessary)
E. Flush the eyes with clean water
F. Irrigate continuously for at least 30 minutes

Injury

_____ Foreign body in the eye

_____ Injury to the orbits

_____ Lid injuries

_____ Globe injuries

_____ Chemical burns

_____ Object impaled in the eye

PART 4 • What Would You Do If?

•   You are at a construction site where a carpenter is cutting some lumber with a power rip saw. A fragment of wood flies into the carpenter's eye.

•   You are at the scene of a motorcycle accident. The victim was not wearing a helmet and has abrasions and lacerations around the mouth and lower jaw.

9

Injuries to the Chest, Abdomen, and Genitalia

Learning Objectives

When you have mastered the material in this chapter, you will be able to:

1 Identify the three main types of chest injury

2 Identify the general signs and symptoms of chest injury

3 Describe and demonstrate the emergency care principles for chest injuries

4 Recognize flail chest and demonstrate the appropriate emergency care for it

5 Recognize compression injuries of the chest and demonstrate appropriate emergency care for them

6 Recognize broken ribs and demonstrate appropriate emergency care for them

7 Recognize hemothorax, tension pneumothorax, open pneumothorax, and pneumothorax and demonstrate appropriate emergency care for each

8 Describe the differences between open and closed abdominal wounds

9 Describe the assessment of a victim with abdominal injury

10 Describe the common signs and symptoms of abdominal injuries

11 Describe general emergency care for abdominal injuries

12 Demonstrate appropriate emergency care for abdominal eviscerations

13 Describe appropriate emergency care for rupture, or hernia

14 Describe appropriate emergency care for injuries to the male genitalia

15 Describe appropriate emergency care for injuries to the female genitalia

On March 20, 1998, 51-year-old Thomas Meservy was celebrating the arrival of warm weather by playing a spirited game of football with his three sons and five grandsons. As a group struggled to gain control of the football, Thomas took a strong elbow thrust to the heart.

Thomas fell to his knees, holding his hands over a painful area on the right side of his chest. As the group gathered around him, he whispered that it hurt him to move, cough, or even breathe deeply. Examining him more closely, his son Keith saw that there was slight deformity, and heard a grating sound when he gently palpated the chest.

Keith knew from the pain, deformity, and grating sound that his father had broken several ribs—and was in danger of lacerating his lungs or heart. Keith sent his brother in the house to call 9-1-1 and get a pillow. Keith instructed Thomas to hold the pillow against his painful side for support, then draped a coat around his shoulders to help keep him warm. When emergency personnel arrived, they were able to immobilize the ribs with cravats before transporting Thomas to the hospital.

CHEST INJURY IS THE SECOND LEADING CAUSE OF DEATH from trauma—second only to central nervous system injury. *All* chest injury should be considered life threatening until proven otherwise, and you should always assume cardiac damage until it is ruled out. Victims of chest injury can look relatively fine, but can deteriorate suddenly and rapidly.

Injuries to the abdomen can range from severe hemorrhage to rupture of the diaphragm; almost all injuries to the abdomen require surgical repair. You should suspect abdominal injury in any victim involved in fights, falls, or automobile accidents.

This chapter outlines the emergency care procedures for victims with injuries to the chest, abdomen, and genitalia.

• Section 1 •
CHEST INJURIES

> **Learning Objective 1** Identify the three main types of chest injury.

There are two general categories of chest injury: closed and open. In closed (blunt) chest injuries, the skin remains unbroken. Although the skin is not injured, serious underlying damage can occur, especially lacerations to the heart and lungs.

In open (penetrating) chest injury, the skin is broken, either by a penetrating object or the end of a broken rib. Severe internal damage can occur, especially if a bullet mushrooms, tumbles, or fragments or if a knife damages the tissues and organs along the path of penetration. Figure 9-1 illustrates the chest cavity.

Remember: The most visually disturbing or alarming chest injuries are usually not the most life-threatening ones. The main types of chest injury include

- Blunt trauma (caused by a forceful blow to the chest)
- Penetrating injury (a sharp object penetrates the chest wall)
- Compression injury (the chest cavity compresses rapidly, usually during an automobile accident)

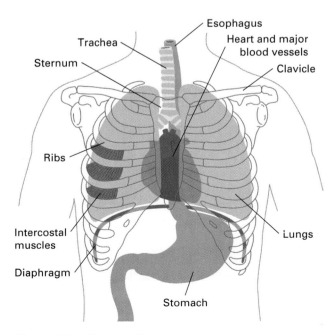

Figure 9-1. Chest cavity

General Signs and Symptoms of Chest Injury

> **Learning Objective 2** Identify the general signs and symptoms of chest injury.

Whether the injury is open or closed, certain signs and symptoms will occur in major chest trauma, many of them simultaneously (see Figure 9-2 on page 156):

- Cyanosis (bluish coloring of the fingernails, fingertips, lips, or skin)
- **Dyspnea** (shortness of breath or difficulty breathing)
- **Tracheal deviation**
- Pain during breathing
- Distended neck veins
- Pain at the injury site, or pain near an injury that is made worse by breathing
- Coughing up of blood (**hemoptysis**), usually bright red and frothy
- Failure of the chest to expand normally during inhalation
- Shock
- Rapid, weak pulse (more than 120 beats per minute)
- Bruising or obvious fracture
- Changing mental status, including confusion, agitation, restlessness, and irrational behavior

Two of the most important signs are the respiratory rate and any change in the normal breathing pattern. If a victim breathes more than 24 times in a minute, experiences pain when breathing, or finds it difficult to take a deep breath, there is probably chest injury.

General Emergency Care Principles for Chest Injuries

> **Learning Objective 3** Describe and demonstrate the emergency care principles for chest injuries.

Activate the EMS system immediately; then:

1. Maintain an open airway; your first priority is to ensure adequate ventilation. If necessary, provide rescue breathing.

> **dyspnea** Shortness of breath or difficulty in breathing
> **tracheal deviation** Displacement of the trachea to one side or the other
> **hemoptysis** Coughing up of blood

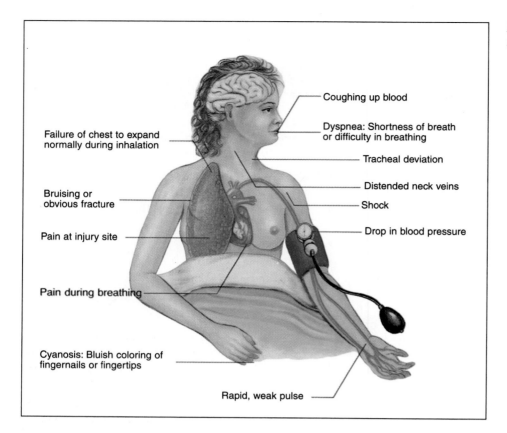

Figure 9-2. Signs and symptoms of chest injury

Coughing up blood

Dyspnea: Shortness of breath or difficulty in breathing

Tracheal deviation

Distended neck veins

Shock

Drop in blood pressure

Failure of chest to expand normally during inhalation

Bruising or obvious fracture

Pain at injury site

Pain during breathing

Cyanosis: Bluish coloring of fingernails or fingertips

Rapid, weak pulse

2. Control external bleeding; dress penetrating chest wounds as described later in this chapter.

3. If there is an object impaled in the chest
   - Cut away clothing to expose the wound.
   - Dress the wound around the impaled object to control bleeding and prevent a sucking chest wound.
   - Stabilize the impaled object with rolls of self-adhering bandages or bulky dressings.
   - Tape bandages in place to stabilize the impaled object.

4. Never try to remove an impaled object; stabilize it to prevent movement until the victim can receive medical help.

Progress Check

1. One of the two most important signs of chest injury is a change in _____ .
(skin color/mental status/normal breathing pattern)

2. One of the two most important signs of chest injury is the _____ rate.
(respiratory/heart)

3. The first priority in caring for a victim of chest injury is to _____ .
(control bleeding/ensure adequate ventilation/prevent further injury)

4. You should _____ an impaled object in the chest.
(remove/stabilize, then remove/immobilize and leave in place)

• **Section 2** •

SPECIFIC CHEST INJURIES

Flail Chest

Learning Objective 4 Recognize flail chest and demonstrate the appropriate emergency care for it.

Flail chest occurs when the chest wall becomes unstable because of fractures of the sternum, the cartilage connecting the ribs to the sternum, and/or the ribs. It

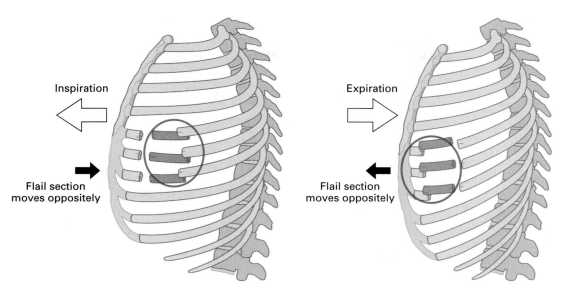

Figure 9-3. Flail chest

can affect the front, back, or sides of the rib cage (see Figure 9-3). Because it usually involves bruising of the lung tissues and inadequate oxygenation of the heart, flail chest is a life-threatening injury.

Most often, multiple ribs are fractured in multiple places; the segment of chest wall over them becomes free-floating. When the victim inhales, the area does not expand; when the victim exhales, the flail section protrudes—a pattern called **paradoxical breathing.**

Signs and symptoms of flail chest include

- Shortness of breath
- Paradoxical breathing accompanied by severe pain
- Swelling over the injured area
- Signs of shock
- Increasing airway resistance
- Victim's attempt to support the chest wall with arms and hands

If the heart has also been injured, there will be bluish discoloration of the head, neck, shoulders, lips, and tongue; bulging neck veins; bulging, bloodshot eyes; and obvious deformity of the chest.

To check for flail chest, have the victim lie in the supine position; watch for a see-saw motion as the victim breathes.

Emergency Care

Immediately activate the EMS system; then:

1. Maintain an open airway and administer artificial ventilation if needed.

2. Use *gentle* palpation to locate the edges of the flail section; stabilize with a pad of dressings or a pillow weighing less than 5 pounds (see Figure 9-4 on page 158). Secure with wide cravats, straps, or tape.

3. Position the victim with the flail segment against an external support in a semisitting position or lying on the injured side; monitor vital signs and care for shock.

Compression Injuries and Traumatic Asphyxia

Learning Objective 5 Recognize compression injuries of the chest and demonstrate appropriate emergency care for them.

A life-threatening emergency, severe and sudden compression of a victim's chest (such as when a person is thrown against a steering wheel) causes a rapid increase in pressure inside the chest. Most serious, the sternum exerts sudden and severe pressure on the heart.

Traumatic asphyxia occurs from a sudden compression of the chest wall that forces blood the wrong way out of the heart.

flail chest Instability of a section of chest wall
paradoxical breathing A condition in which the injured area of the chest moves opposite the rest of the chest during breathing
traumatic asphyxia Sudden compression of the chest wall that forces blood the wrong way out of the heart

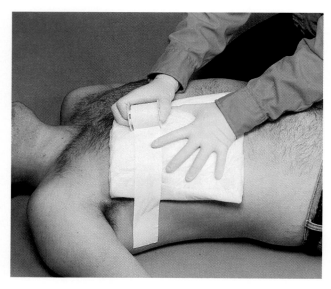

Figure 9-4. *Stabilize flail chest by applying a pillow or bulky dressing.*

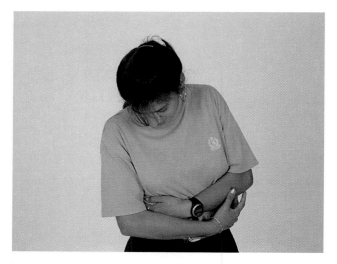

Figure 9-5. *Typical "guarded" position of victim with rib fracture*

Signs and symptoms include

- Severe shock
- Distended neck veins
- Bloodshot, protruding eyes
- Cyanotic tongue and lips
- Coughing or vomiting blood
- Swollen, cyanotic appearance of the head, neck, and shoulders

Emergency Care

Activate the EMS system immediately; then:

1. Maintain an open airway and administer artificial ventilation as needed.

2. Control any bleeding that results from the trauma.

3. Monitor the victim closely; position the victim in a semi-reclining position on the injured side if breathing is easier or you suspect internal bleeding.

Broken Ribs

Learning Objective 6 Recognize broken ribs and demonstrate appropriate emergency care for them.

While broken ribs themselves are not life threatening, they can cause injuries that *are*, such as injury to the heart, lungs, or great blood vessels.

The most common symptom of rib fracture is pain at the fracture site; it usually hurts the victim to move, cough, or breathe deeply (see Figure 9-5). Other signs and symptoms (see Figure 9-6) can include

- Grating sound upon palpation (**crepitus**)
- Chest deformity
- Shallow, uncoordinated breathing
- Crackling sensation near the fracture site
- Bruising or lacerations at the suspected fracture site
- Frothy blood at the nose or mouth (indicating lung laceration)

Emergency Care

The top priority in emergency care is making sure the victim can breathe adequately by splinting the chest as needed. Activate the EMS system, then give the victim a pillow or blanket to hold against the chest for support (see Figure 9-7). If the victim can't hold a pillow

1. Apply three cravat bandages around the chest to support the ribs. The first should be centered immediately below the site of the pain; the second should be positioned above the painful area; and the third bandage should be positioned just below the first. Have the victim exhale, then tie the ban-

crepitus A sandpaperlike grating sound made by the ends of a broken bone as they rub together

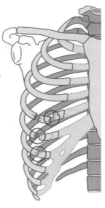

Pain at fracture site.
Pain on moving, coughing, or breathing deeply.
Shallow, uncoordinated breathing.
Chest deformity.
Bruising or lacerations.
Grating sound upon palpation.
Crackling sensation near site.
Frothy blood at nose or mouth (lung puncture).

Figure 9-6. The most common symptom of rib fracture is pain. Other signs and symptoms may not be present.

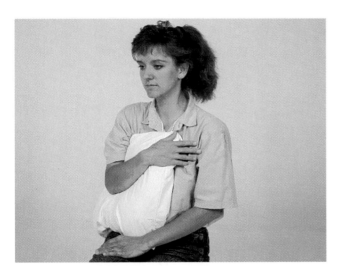

Figure 9-7. Place a pad between arm and chest

dages over a pad on the *uninjured side* before allowing the victim to inhale again (see Figure 9-8); or

2. Use a sling and swathe to utilize the victim's arm as a splint and support; the forearm of the injured side positioned across the chest (see Figures 9-9 and 9-10).

3. Position the victim in a semiprone position, injured side down.

4. Monitor the victim's ABCDs, watching for signs of internal bleeding that could lead to shock.

Do not
• Tape the ribs
• Use continuous strapping
• Wrap the victim's chest if the ribs are depressed or there is frothy blood coming from the mouth

Figure 9-8. Immobilizing fractured ribs with cravats or roller bandage and pad

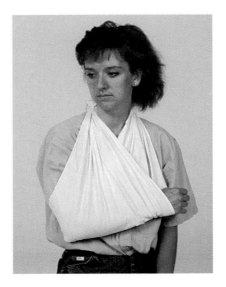

Figure 9-9. Supporting with a sling

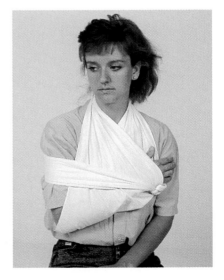

Figure 9-10. Immobilizing the arm and sling with a swathe, a bandage that stabilizes the sling, as shown

Hemothorax, Tension Pneumothorax, Open Pneumothorax, and Pneumothorax

> **Learning Objective 7** Recognize hemothorax, tension pneumothorax, open pneumothorax, and pneumothorax and demonstrate appropriate emergency care for each.

In four conditions—**hemothorax, tension pneumothorax,** open pneumothorax, and **pneumothorax** (see Figure 9-11)—pressure against the lungs and/or heart interferes with breathing and circulation; all four are life threatening (see Table 9-1). For each condition, activate the EMS system immediately; *tension pneumothorax is one of the few emergencies in which seconds count.* Fig-

ures 9-13 through 9-16 on page 162 illustrate emergency care of a victim with possible pneumothorax.

> **hemothorax** An accumulation of blood in the chest cavity
>
> **tension pneumothorax** A situation in which air enters the pleural space through a one-way defect in the lung, resulting in a progressive increase in pressure in the pleural cavity that causes the lung to collapse and that impairs circulation
>
> **pneumothorax** A condition in which air from a lung or from the outside fills the chest cavity, but does not fill the lung

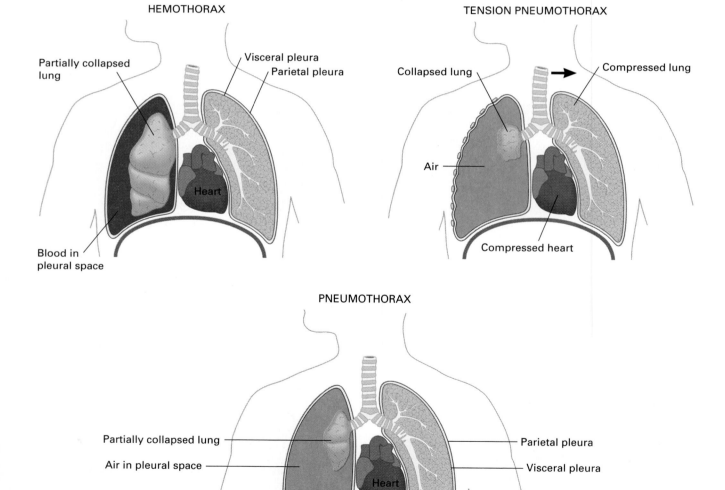

Figure 9-11. Complications of chest injury

Progress Check

1. In flail chest, the chest wall _____ when the victim exhales.
(collapses/moves/protrudes)

2. Flail chest most often occurs when multiple _____ are fractured.
(bones/ribs/joints)

3. To check for flail chest, have the victim lie on his or her back and check for _____ as the victim breathes.
(crepitus/pain/a see-saw motion)

4. Traumatic asphyxia occurs from sudden _____ of the chest wall.
(compression/collapse/penetration)

5. The most common symptom of rib fracture is

_____ .
(deformity/pain/bruising)

6. The greatest priority in treating rib fracture is to splint the chest so the victim _____ .
(can breathe adequately/is not in pain/will not be further injured by broken bone ends)

7. In treating rib fracture, you can either use cravats or

_____ .
(tape/continuous strapping/sling and swathe)

8. In hemothorax, _____ enters the chest cavity.
(air/blood/pressure)

9. To help prevent tension pneumothorax, you should always leave one corner of a chest bandage

_____ .

(over the wound/untaped/ at least 2 inches beyond the wound)

Table 9-1
Life-Threatening Conditions of the Chest Cavity

Condition	Cause	Signs and Symptoms	Emergency Care
Hemothorax	Blood fills the chest cavity	• Shock • Rapid heartbeat • Rapid breathing • Weak pulse • Hemoptysis • Frothy or bloody sputum	Administer artificial ventilation; control bleeding from external wounds; treat for shock
Tension pneumothorax	Air leaks out of the lung continuously; the lung becomes a small ball and presses against the heart	• Obvious and increasing difficulty in breathing • Bulging of neck veins • Tracheal deviation • Uneven chest movements	Administer artificial ventilation; if the chest is bandaged, leave one corner of the bandage untaped, creating a flutter valve (see Figure 9-12); treat for shock
Open pneumothorax (sucking chest wound)	Open chest wound allows air into the chest cavity	• Moist sucking or bubbling sound as air passes in and out of the wound	Apply an occlusive dressing over the wound to create a flutter valve, leaving one corner untaped; administer artificial ventilation
Pneumothorax	Air enters the chest cavity, but not the lung	• Sudden, sharp chest pain • Failure of the lung to expand during inhalation	Maintain open airway; administer artificial ventilation; apply occlusive dressing to any chest wounds and leave one corner untaped

On inspiration, dressing seals
wound, preventing air entry

Expiration allows trapped air to escape
through untaped section of dressing

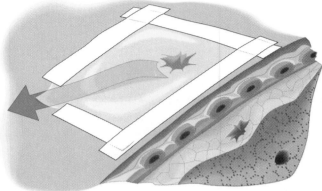

Collapsed
lung

Figure 9-12. *Creating a flutter valve to relieve tension pneumothorax*

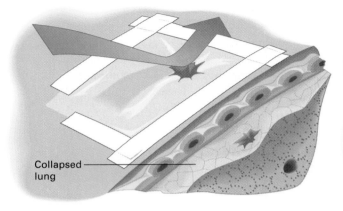

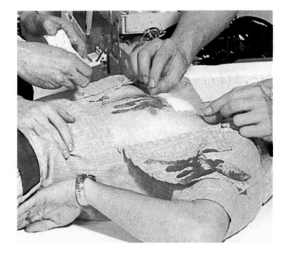

Figure 9-13. *Sucking chest wound and possible pneumothorax*

Figure 9-14. *Tape dressing in place.*

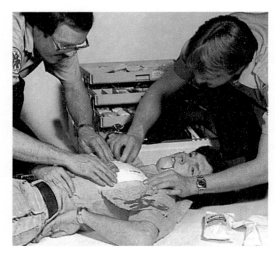

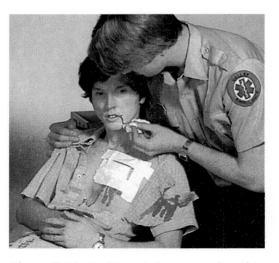

Figure 9-15. *Position occlusive covering, which should contact the chest wall directly.*

Figure 9-16. *Position victim to ease breathing.*

• Section 3 •
ABDOMINAL INJURIES

Learning Objective 8 Describe the differences between open and closed abdominal wounds.

A wide range of accidents, from motor vehicle accidents to shootings, affect the organs of the abdomen; because the abdominal cavity contains not only vital organs but a rich supply of blood vessels, major abdominal injuries are life threatening and demand prompt and proper treatment. Figure 9-17 illustrates injuries to the abdomen, chest, and pelvic cavity.

If a victim has suffered abdominal trauma, assume that he or she has also suffered chest trauma until proven otherwise.

An open wound that penetrates the abdominal cavity is extremely dangerous because of possible damage to internal organs. The stomach or intestine may

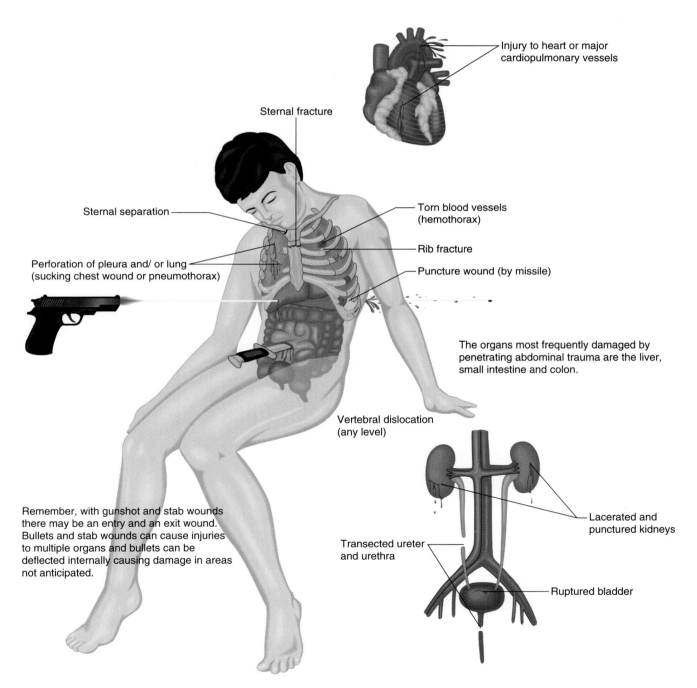

Injury to heart or major cardiopulmonary vessels

Sternal fracture

Sternal separation

Torn blood vessels (hemothorax)

Rib fracture

Perforation of pleura and/ or lung (sucking chest wound or pneumothorax)

Puncture wound (by missile)

The organs most frequently damaged by penetrating abdominal trauma are the liver, small intestine and colon.

Vertebral dislocation (any level)

Remember, with gunshot and stab wounds there may be an entry and an exit wound. Bullets and stab wounds can cause injuries to multiple organs and bullets can be deflected internally causing damage in areas not anticipated.

Lacerated and punctured kidneys

Transected ureter and urethra

Ruptured bladder

Figure 9-17. Injuries to the chest, abdomen, and pelvic cavity

be perforated, internal bleeding may occur, and infection may develop. Bacteria may be introduced into the peritoneal cavity from the outside or from a perforated intestine.

In closed abdominal wounds, the abdomen is damaged by a severe blow or crushing injury, but the skin remains unbroken. Such wounds may be extremely dangerous—they can cause serious injury to the internal organs, internal hemorrhage, and shock.

Assessment of Abdominal Injuries

Learning Objective 9 Describe the assessment of a victim with abdominal injury.

To assess a victim for abdominal injury

1. Have the victim lie supine with knees flexed and supported; remove or loosen clothing over the abdomen.
2. Inspect for lacerations, open wounds, bruising, impaled objects, or protruding abdominal organs.
3. Watch abdominal movement as the victim breathes.
4. Gently palpate all four quadrants; watch for guarding, rigidity, pain, and tenderness.

Signs and Symptoms of Abdominal Injuries

Learning Objective 10 Describe the common signs and symptoms of abdominal injuries.

The amount of blood you can see is not necessarily indicative of the severity of injury: Deep underlying damage may occur with only little external hemorrhage. Abdominal injuries may cause any of several signs and symptoms (see Figure 9-18):

• Distended or irregularly shaped abdomen

• Bruising of the abdomen or back

• Abdominal rigidity and tenderness

• Pain, ranging from mild discomfort to intense, intolerable pain

• Pain other than at the injury site

• Pain radiating to either shoulder

• "Guarding" (positioning the body to protect the abdomen) (see Figure 9-19)

• Abdominal cramping

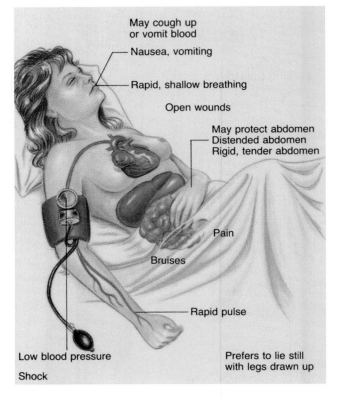

Figure 9-18. Common signs and symptoms of abdominal injuries

Figure 9-19. Victims with abdominal injuries often lie with their legs drawn up in the fetal position.

• Nausea and/or vomiting; the victim may vomit blood

• Rapid, shallow breathing

• Rapid pulse with low blood pressure

• Open wounds and penetrations

• Organs protruding through open wounds

- Blood in the urine
- Extreme weakness
- Thirst

General Emergency Care

Learning Objective 11 Describe general emergency care for abdominal injuries.

As with all injured victims, top priorities are airway, breathing, and circulation. Additionally, activate the EMS system; then:

1. Take measures to prevent shock; keep the victim warm, but do not overheat.

2. Control bleeding and dress all open wounds with a dry, sterile dressing. If organs are protruding, follow the guidelines under Abdominal Evisceration, below.

3. If any object has penetrated or impaled the victim
   - Cut clothing away from the object.
   - Dress the wounds around the object to control bleeding.
   - Stabilize the object with bulky dressings.
   - Bandage the object in place to prevent movement.

4. Position the victim for greatest comfort; most victims will want to lie on the back with the knees flexed. If possible, elevate the feet.

5. Be alert for vomiting; position the victim for adequate drainage. Constantly monitor vital signs and abdominal condition.

6. Do not give the victim anything by mouth.

Abdominal Evisceration

Learning Objective 12 Demonstrate appropriate emergency care for abdominal eviscerations.

If abdominal contents are protruding through a wound (**evisceration**), activate the EMS system; then:

1. Cover protruding abdominal organs with a clean dressing moistened with clear water that is clean enough to drink. Never use absorbent cotton or any material that clings or disintegrates when wet, such as paper towels or toilet tissue.

2. Cover the moist dressing with an occlusive material, such as clean aluminum foil or plastic wrap, to retain moisture and warmth. Gently wrap the dressing in place with a bandage or clean sheet. Keep the bandage and dressing loose enough so that they do not exert pressure on the abdominal organs or cause injury.

3. Prevent shock, and constantly monitor the victim's vital signs.

Never touch abdominal organs or try to replace them in the abdominal cavity. See Figures 9-20 through 9-24 on page 166.

Rupture or Hernia

Learning Objective 13 Describe appropriate emergency care for rupture, or hernia.

The most common kind of rupture, or **hernia,** occurs when part of an internal organ protrudes through the wall of the abdomen. Most, but not all, ruptures occur in or just above the groin, and result from a combination of abdominal wall weakness and muscle strain. Signs and symptoms include

- Sharp, stinging pain
- Feeling of something giving way at the site of the rupture
- Swelling
- Possible nausea and vomiting

Emergency Care

Activate the EMS system; then:

1. Position the victim on his or her back with the knees well drawn up, and place a blanket or other padding under the knees (see Figure 9-25 on page 166).

2. Cover the victim with a blanket to preserve body warmth.

Never try to force a protrusion back into the abdominal cavity.

evisceration The protrusion of abdominal contents through a laceration or other wound

hernia Protrusion of an internal organ through the abdominal wall or into another body cavity

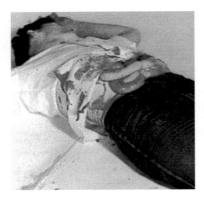

Figure 9-20. *Abdominal evisceration—an open wound resulting in protrusion of intestines*

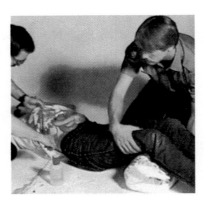

Figure 9-21. *Cut away clothing from wound and support knees in a flexed position.*

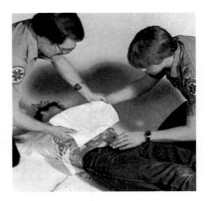

Figure 9-22. *Place dressing over wound. Do not attempt to replace intestines within abdomen.*

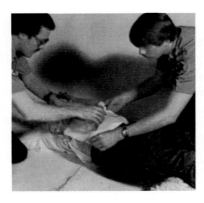

Figure 9-23. *Moisten dressing with clean water. (Note that under ideal conditions you will premoisten the dressing before application. Also, in some areas, dry dressings are recommended. Follow local protocol.)*

Figure 9-24. *Gently and loosely tape the dressing in place, then apply an occlusive material such as aluminum foil or plastic wrap. Tape loosely over dressing to keep dressing moist.*

Progress Check

1. The amount of _____ does not necessarily indicate how serious abdominal injury is.
   (pain/blood/deformity)

2. Most abdominal injury victims are most comfortable on their back with the _____ .
   (feet elevated/head elevated/knees drawn up)

3. If abdominal organs protrude through a wound, you should _____ them.
   (cover/replace/ moisten)

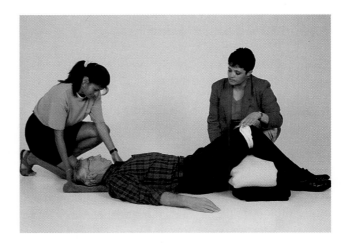

Figure 9-25. *Emergency care for a rupture or hernia*

• Section 4 •
INJURIES TO THE GENITALIA

In treating injuries to the genitalia, act in a calm, professional way; protect victims from onlookers and help protect their privacy by using sheets, towels, or other material as a drape over the genital area.

Male Genitalia

Learning Objective 14 Describe appropriate emergency care for injuries to the male genitalia.

While injuries to the external male genitalia—lacerations, avulsions, abrasions, penetrations, and contusions—are excruciatingly painful, they are not necessarily life threatening. However, the amount of pain involved and the nature of the injury can cause great concern to the victim.

To treat, activate the EMS system; then:

1. Wrap the penis or scrotum in a soft, sterile dressing moistened with clean water. If there is external bleeding, control it with direct pressure.

2. If there is a penetrating or impaled object, do not remove it; stabilize it with a bulky dressing to prevent movement.

3. If part of the penis or scrotum is caught in a zipper, cut off the zipper fastener and separate the teeth; if a long section of skin is caught, cut the zipper out of the pants to make the victim more comfortable.

4. Apply an ice bag or cold compresses to relieve pain and reduce swelling.

5. If there are avulsed parts, wrap in sterile gauze moistened with clean water and send them with the victim.

Female Genitalia

Learning Objective 15 Describe appropriate emergency care for injuries to the female genitalia.

Injuries to the external female genitalia are rare but can occur with straddle injuries, sexual assault, blows to the perineum, or abortion attempts; following childbirth; or when foreign objects are inserted into the vagina. Because the area is richly supplied with blood vessels and nerves, the injury can cause blinding pain and considerable bleeding.

To treat, activate the EMS system; then:

1. Control bleeding with direct pressure, using moist compresses.

2. Dress the wounds, keeping the dressing in place with a diaper-type bandage. Stabilize any impaled objects or foreign bodies.

3. Use ice packs or cold compresses to relieve pain and reduce swelling.

If the woman was a victim of sexual assault, preserve the chain of evidence:

- Do not allow her to bathe or douche.

- Do not allow her to wash her hair or clean under her fingernails.

- If possible, do not clean wounds.

- Handle her clothing as little as possible.

- Put all items of clothing and other items in separate bags; if there is blood on any object, do not use plastic bags.

Progress Check

1. In both male and female victims with injuries to the genitalia, apply _____ to relieve pain and reduce swelling.
   (direct pressure/an ice bag/sterile gauze)

2. Always try to _____ avulsed skin.
   (preserve/finish detaching/clean)

3. If a woman was the victim of sexual assault, try to _____.
   (comfort her/find the assailant/preserve the chain of evidence)

• SUMMARY •

- All injuries to the chest are life threatening.

- Two of the most important signs of chest injury are the respiratory rate and any change in the normal breathing pattern.

- The first priority in treating chest injuries is to ensure adequate ventilation.

- Flail chest usually occurs when multiple ribs are fractured in multiple places, resulting in a section of chest that is unstable.

- Broken ribs are rarely life threatening, but they can cause injuries that *are;* stabilize them with cravats or a sling and swathe.

- In hemothorax, blood fills the chest cavity and creates pressure on the lungs and heart, interfering with respiration and circulation.

- Tension pneumothorax, in which air continuously leaks out of the lung into the chest cavity, is one of the few emergencies in which seconds count.

- To prevent pneumothorax, cover any open chest wound with an occlusive material, creating a flutter valve; leave one corner untaped so air can escape on expiration.

- Never try to remove a penetrating or impaled object from the chest or abdomen; stabilize the object to prevent movement.

- The amount of blood is not necessarily indicative of the severity of abdominal injury; severe internal damage can result from blunt, closed trauma.

- Never touch abdominal organs that protrude through a wound, and never try to replace them in the abdomen; cover them with a moist dressing, then with an occlusive material such as clean aluminum foil to retain warmth.

- Most victims of abdominal injury are most comfortable on the back with the knees drawn up.

- Few injuries to the external genitalia are life threatening, but the amount of pain and the nature of the injury can cause the victim great concern.

- In injuries to the genitalia, control bleeding, dress wounds, and apply ice packs or cold compresses to relieve pain and reduce swelling.

- If a woman is a victim of sexual assault, preserve the chain of evidence during treatment.

● KEY TERMS ●

Make sure you understand the following key terms:

- dyspnea
- tracheal deviation
- hemoptysis
- flail chest
- paradoxical breathing
- traumatic asphyxia
- crepitus
- hemothorax
- tension pneumothorax
- pneumothorax
- evisceration
- hernia

Student: _____ Date: _____

Course: _____ Section #: _____

PART 1 • True/False

If you believe the statement is true, circle the T. If you believe the statement is false, circle the F.

T F **1.** Traumatic asphyxia occurs from sudden compression of the chest wall.

T F **2.** Flail chest most often occurs when two or more adjacent ribs are broken in two or more places.

T F **3.** In paradoxical breathing, the injured chest wall moves in and the uninjured chest wall moves out.

T F **4.** Stabilize a flail chest with pads or a pillow.

T F **5.** Position a flail chest victim so the flail segment is not against any external support.

T F **6.** Do not tape the ribs or use continuous strapping on a flail chest victim.

T F **7.** Common signs and symptoms of abdominal injury include slow, shallow breathing and rapid pulse.

T F **8.** Do not remove penetrating or impaled objects from the abdomen.

T F **9.** Most hernias occur in or just below the groin.

T F **10.** A dull, pulsating pain is the most common symptom of a hernia.

T F **11.** Bleeding from an injury to the genitalia should always be controlled at the femoral pressure point.

PART 2 • Multiple Choice

For each item, circle the correct answer or the phrase that best completes the statement.

1. In what position should you place a victim with broken ribs?

   a. semisitting
   b. upright
   c. semiprone, injured side down
   d. flat on the back

2. Where should cravat bandages be applied to an uncomplicated rib fracture?

   a. have the victim inhale, then tie the bandages on the injured side
   b. have the victim exhale, then tie the bandages on the injured side
   c. have the victim inhale, then tie the bandages on the uninjured side
   d. have the victim exhale, then tie the bandages on the uninjured side

3. Which of the following is *not* a sign of a chest injury?

   a. coughing blood
   b. shock
   c. strong, bounding pulse
   d. distended neck veins

4. The leakage of blood into the chest cavity from lacerated vessels or from the lung, causing the lung to compress, is called

   a. pneumothorax
   b. flail chest
   c. traumatic asphyxia
   d. hemothorax

5. Paradoxical breathing occurs when

   a. compression injuries cause gasping breaths interspersed with extremely shallow breathing
   b. a compressed lung lacks oxygen
   c. air remains in the chest cavity outside the lungs
   d. the motion of the injured chest area is opposite the motion of the remainder of the chest

6. The two general categories of chest wounds are

   a. open and closed
   b. simple and compound
   c. fracture and puncture
   d. lung related and heart related

7. Pneumothorax occurs when

   a. air enters the chest cavity but does not enter the lung from a wound site
   b. the descending aorta is lacerated
   c. blood fills up the chest cavity
   d. three or more ribs break and the chest wall that lies over the break area collapses

8. Which of the following is *not* appropriate care for abdominal injuries?

   a. carefully remove impaled objects
   b. do not give the victim anything by mouth
   c. work to prevent shock
   d. have the victim lie on the back with knees flexed

9. Eviscerated organs should be
   a. replaced within the abdomen
   b. covered with a dry dressing
   c. covered with a moist sterile dressing and an occlusive dressing
   d. rinsed thoroughly with copious amounts of water

10. The most common form of rupture or hernia occurs when
   a. a portion of an internal organ protrudes through the abdominal wall
   b. a portion of a thoracic organ protrudes through the thoracic wall
   c. veins or arteries become weak and bulge or rupture
   d. any of the above

PART 3 • Matching

Match the definitions in the left column with the conditions in the right column.

_____ Air enters the chest cavity through a sucking wound

_____ Blood leaks into the chest cavity

_____ Air continuously leaks out of the lung and the lung collapses

_____ Sudden compression of the chest wall

A. Traumatic asphyxia
B. Hemothorax
C. Tension pneumothorax
D. Pneumothorax

PART 4 • What Would You Do If?

- A victim has been stabbed in the chest with a large kitchen knife. When you arrive, the knife has been removed. When the victim breathes, there is a bubbling produced at the wound site.
- You are at a construction site where a worker has fallen on some reinforcing rods. He is lying on his back and has an obvious abdominal evisceration.
- You are at the home of a victim who has been lifting and moving heavy boxes. He complains of nausea and sharp, stinging pain just above the groin. There is swelling and protrusion in the area of pain.

Bandaging

Learning Objectives

When you have mastered the material in this chapter, you will be able to

1 Identify the various types of dressings

2 Identify the various types of bandages

3 Demonstrate how to apply triangular bandages to different parts of the body

4 Demonstrate how to apply cravat bandages to different parts of the body

5 Demonstrate how to apply roller bandages to different parts of the body

6 Describe the basic principles of dressing and bandaging wounds

7 Demonstrate how to apply a pressure dressing

8 Demonstrate how to use a sling

SQ3R Plus

- **Survey** to set goals for studying.
- Ask **questions** as you **read.**
- Stop frequently to **recite** and **review.**
- **Write** a summary of key points.
- **Reflect** on the importance of this material and its relevance in your life.

*O*n May 2, 1998, 16-year-old Chris Jamison was hurrying to school on his brother's motorcycle when a motorist coming through an intersection on a yellow light nearly struck the motorcycle. Swerving to avoid a collision, Chris "laid the bike down" and skidded along the roadway. Although his helmet protected him from head injury, he sustained severe abrasions on his shoulder and upper arm.

Margaret Grayson, following Chris through the intersection in her van, stopped to give assistance. Although blood was only oozing slightly from the abrasions, Margaret could quickly see that a large area was involved; gravel and other road debris were embedded in the wound.

A quick primary and secondary survey showed that Chris didn't require help from emergency personnel, but Margaret knew that a physician needed to clean the wound. While a bystander helped wheel Chris's motorcycle to the curb, Margaret helped Chris to the edge of a nearby lawn. Grabbing the first-aid kit from the back of her van, Margaret applied three large petroleum gauze dressings to the abrasion. She then used a triangular bandage and a cravat to secure the dressings to Chris's shoulder and upper arm.

Before leaving the scene, Margaret arranged for Chris to use a telephone to call his mother, who soon arrived to take him to a physician for advanced treatment of the wound.

ONCE HEAVY HEMORRHAGE FROM A WOUND HAS BEEN controlled, the wound should be dressed and bandaged. Proper wound care enhances healing, adds to the comfort of the victim, and promotes more rapid recovery. Improper wound care can delay healing, cause infection, cause severe discomfort to the victim, and—in rare cases—result in the loss of a limb.

The basic purposes of dressings and bandages are to

- Control bleeding
- Prevent further contamination and injury
- Keep the wound dry
- Immobilize the wound site

This chapter outlines the principles of dressing and bandaging and includes a discussion of specific types of dressings and bandages that can be used in wound care.

• Section 1 •
DRESSINGS

Learning Objective 1 Identify the various types of dressings.

A **dressing** is a sterile covering for a wound. It should be

- **Sterile,** meaning that any microorganisms and spores on the dressing have been killed
- **Aseptic,** meaning that it is free of bacteria
- Held in place with a bandage tightly enough to control bleeding but not so tightly that it stops blood circulation

The ideal dressing is layered, consists of coarse mesh gauze, is bulky enough to immobilize tissues and protect the wound, is larger than the wound, and is soft, thick, and pliable. In an emergency, you can use *clean* handkerchiefs, towels, sheets, cloth, or sanitary napkins as dressings. Never use elastic bandages, paper towels, toilet tissue, or any other material that could shred, disintegrate, or cling to the wound. A dressing is always placed against the wound, and the dressing is held in place with a bandage; the bandage is never placed directly against the wound

There are several types of dressings (see Figures 10-1 through 10-4):

- Aseptic—a sterile dressing
- Wet—a moist dressing that is not necessarily sterile
- Dry sterile—a sterile dressing free from moisture

dressing A sterile covering for a wound
sterile Free of all microorganisms and spores
aseptic Free of bacteria

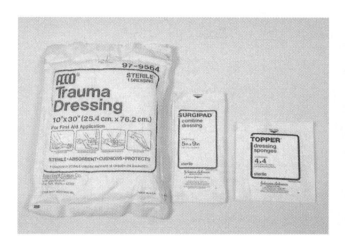

Figure 10-1. Sterile gauze pads

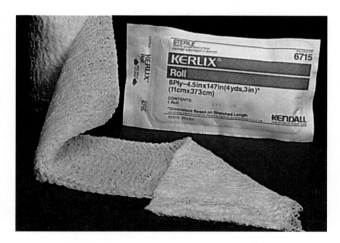

Figure 10-2. Nonelastic, self-adhering dressing and roller bandage

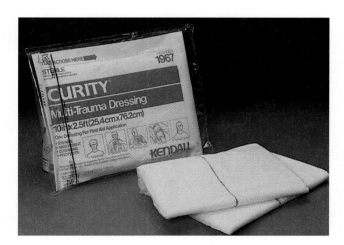

Figure 10-3. Multitrauma dressing

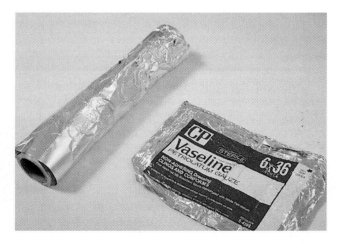

Figure 10-4. Occlusive and petroleum gauze dressings

- Petroleum gauze—sterile gauze saturated with petroleum jelly to keep it from sticking to a wound
- **Occlusive**—plastic wrap, aluminum foil, petroleum gauze, or other dressing that forms an airtight seal
- Compress—a bulky, usually sterile dressing intended to stop or control bleeding
- Universal—a dressing made from a 9-by-36-inch piece of thick, absorbent material
- Adhesive strips—a combination of a sterile dressing and a bandage, individually packaged and used for small wounds (often called Band-Aids)

Gauze Pads

Gauze is used several ways in dressings; plain gauze can be used in place of a bandage compress to cover large wounds. Plain gauze of various sizes is sterilized and sold commercially in individually wrapped packages. Make sure you don't touch the part of the gauze that will contact the wound.

The most popular sizes of sterile **gauze pads** are 2-by-2s, 4-by-4s, and 4-by-8s. In cases of major multiple trauma, nonsterile bulk packages of 4-by-4 dressings are often used.

Some gauze pads are impregnated with ointment or have a plasticlike coating to prevent them from sticking to the wound. You can improvise by applying a small amount of antibiotic ointment, such as Neosporin, to the gauze pad before placing it against the wound. Be careful to hold the gauze pad by its corner and touch it only with ointment to avoid contaminating it.

Special Pads

Large, thickly layered bulky pads, some with waterproof outer surfaces, are available in several sizes for quick application to an extremity or to a large area of the trunk. They are used where bulk is required to stop profuse bleeding and to stabilize impaled objects. Such **special pads** are also referred to as multitrauma dressings, trauma packs, general-purpose dressings, burn pads, or ABD dressings.

You can use individually wrapped sanitary napkins in place of special pads when necessary; however, even individually wrapped sanitary napkins are not sterile and can introduce infection to the wound.

Bandage Compresses

A bandage compress (see Figure 10-5) is a special dressing designed to cover open wounds. It consists of a pad made of several thicknesses of gauze attached to the middle of a strip of bandaging material. The pad sizes range from 1 to 4 inches. Unless other-

Figure 10-5. *Already prepared bandage compresses are available in individual packages.*

wise specified, all bandage compresses and all gauze dressings should be covered with open triangular, cravat, or roller bandages.

Progress Check

1. A sterile dressing is one on which there are no _____ .
   (bacteria/microorganisms/viruses)

2. An aseptic dressing is free of _____ .
   (bacteria/microorganisms/viruses)

3. Use petroleum gauze when you don't want the dressing to _____ .
   (get wet/shred/stick to the wound)

4. An occlusive dressing is _____ .
   (dry/moist/airtight)

5. A compress dressing is used to _____ .
   (control bleeding/prevent infection/absorb fluids oozing from the wound)

6. A 9-x-36-inch piece of thick, absorbent material is called a _____ dressing.
   (occlusive/universal/compress)

• Section 2 •
<u>BANDAGES</u>

Learning Objective 2 Identify the various types of bandages.

A **bandage**

- Holds a dressing in place over a wound
- Creates pressure that controls bleeding

- Helps keep the edges of the wound closed

- Secures a splint to an injured part of the body

- Provides support for an injured part of the body

Properly applied, bandages promote healing, prevent severe complications, and help the victim stay comfortable. Bandages should be properly applied and well secured; if a bandage becomes loose, wounds may bleed or become infected and broken bones can further displace.

The two most common mistakes in bandaging are bandaging too loosely and bandaging too tightly. Bandages should be firm enough to hold the dressing in place, but not so tight that they restrict circulation. You should immediately loosen any bandage that is too tight. The following are signs that a bandage is too tight:

- The skin around the bandage becomes pale or cyanotic.

- The victim complains of pain, usually only a few minutes after you apply the bandage.

- The skin below the bandage (distal) is cold.

- The skin below the bandage (distal) is tingling or numb.

- The victim cannot move his or her fingers or toes.

Triangular Bandages

Learning Objective 3 Demonstrate how to apply triangular bandages to different parts of the body.

A standard **triangular bandage** (see Figure 10-6) is made from a piece of unbleached cotton cloth approximately 40 inches square; the square is folded diagonally, then cut along the fold. A triangular bandage is easy to apply and can be handled so the part over the dressing won't be soiled. When applied correctly, a triangular bandage does not slip off.

A triangular bandage can be used fully opened or folded into a cravat; it is most commonly used to

- Support fractures and dislocations

- Apply splints

- Form slings

- Make improvised tourniquets

In an emergency, you can make a triangular bandage from a clean handkerchief, a cotton towel, or a clean piece of shirt. If a regular-sized bandage is too short, tie a second bandage to one end.

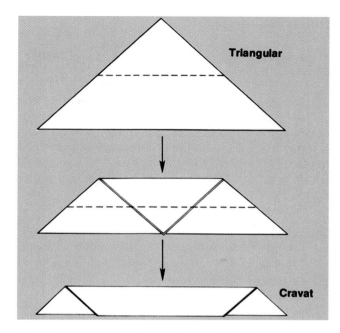

Figure 10-6. Triangular and cravat bandages

Cravat Bandages

Learning Objective 4 Demonstrate how to apply cravat bandages to different parts of the body.

Folded, a triangular bandage becomes a **cravat.** To make a cravat (see Figure 10-6), make a 1-inch fold along the base of the triangular bandage. Then

- *To make a wide cravat,* bring the point to the center of the folded base, then place the point underneath the fold.

- *To make a medium cravat,* make a wide cravat, then fold lengthwise along a line midway between the base and the new top of the bandage.

- *To make a narrow cravat,* make a medium cravat, then repeat the lengthwise fold one more time.

occlusive Waterproof and airtight

gauze pads Commercially manufactured, individually wrapped sterile pads made of gauze

special pads Large, thickly layered bulky pads used to control bleeding and stabilize impaled objects

bandage Material used to hold a dressing in place

triangular bandage Triangle-shaped piece of cloth used to apply splints and form slings

cravat A folded triangular bandage

Roller Bandages

The most popular and easy-to-use roller bandage is a self-adhering (nonelastic), form-fitting **roller bandage,** which can be secured easily with several overlapping wraps and can then be cut and tied or taped in place (see Figures 10-7 through 10-15). Examples of commercial self-adhering roller bandages are Kerlix and Kling.

To apply a roller bandage over a dressing

1. Place the end of the roller bandage on the dressing, then wrap it around the body part in a circular fashion.
2. Crisscross the bandage over itself as you circle until the complete wound area is covered.
3. Fasten the bandage in place with an adhesive strip. Make sure the adhesive strip is adhered to the skin; if it is used simply to fasten one part of the bandage to another, the bandage will slip.

You can also use two gauze rolls, wrapping alternately around and across the wound until it is wrapped completely. Do *not* use elastic roller bandages except in cases of profuse bleeding, because they can create a tourniquet effect.

Progress Check

1. Bandages are applied on top of a _____ .
   (wound/dressing/splint)

2. A bandage should normally not contact a

   _____ .
   (wound/dressing/splint)

3. Cold, numb, or tingling skin distal to a bandage indicates the bandage is _____ .
   (too tight/too loose/controlling bleeding)

4. A folded triangular bandage is a _____ bandage.
   (roller/compress/cravat)

5. The easiest roller bandages to use are

   _____ .
   (gauze/elastic/self-adhering)

6. You should use an elastic roller bandage only in cases of _____ .
   (shock/profuse bleeding/fracture)

roller bandage A form-fitting bandage designed to be wrapped around a wound site

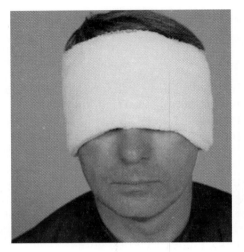

Figure 10-7. Head and/or eye bandage

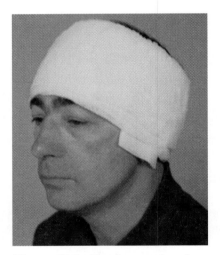

Figure 10-8. Head or ear bandage

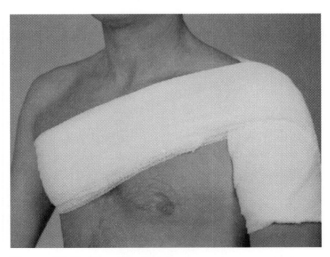

Figure 10-9. Shoulder bandage

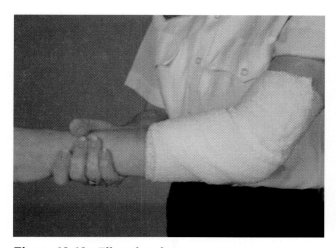

Figure 10-10. Elbow bandage

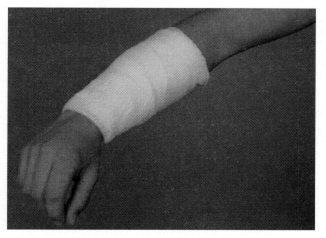

Figure 10-11. Lower arm bandage

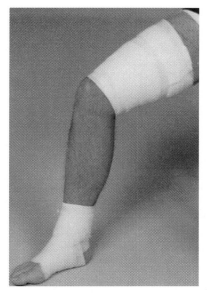

Figure 10-12. Thigh and ankle bandages

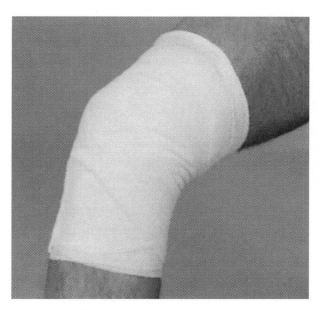

Figure 10-13. Knee bandage

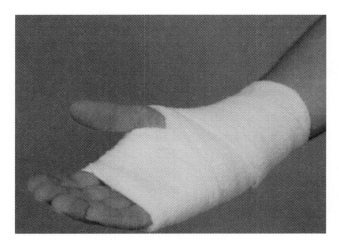

Figure 10-14. Hand bandage

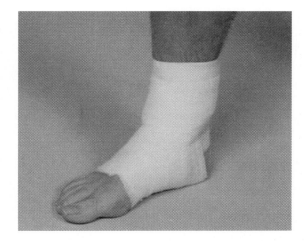

Figure 10-15. Foot or ankle bandage

• **Section 3** •
PRINCIPLES OF DRESSING AND BANDAGING

Learning Objective 6 Describe the basic principles of dressing and bandaging wounds.

There are no hard-and-fast rules for dressing and bandaging wounds; often, adaptability and creativity are far more important than even the best-intentioned rules. In dressing and bandaging, use the materials you have on hand and the methods to which you can best adapt, as long as you meet the following conditions:

- Material used for dressings should be as clean as possible (sterile, if you can get it).
- Bleeding is controlled; generally, you should not bandage any wound with anything other than a pressure bandage until bleeding has stopped.
- The dressing is opened carefully and handled in an aseptic manner.
- The original dressing is not removed; if blood soaks through, add another dressing on top of the original.
- The dressing adequately covers the entire wound.
- Wounds are bandaged snugly, but not too tightly.
- Bandages are not too loose; neither the dressing nor the bandage should shift or slip.
- There are no loose ends of cloth, gauze, or tape that could get caught; when possible, you should tie bandage ends in a square knot (see Figure 10-16), then tuck them under.
- The bandage covers all edges of the dressing.
- Tips of the fingers and toes are left exposed when arms and legs are bandaged so you can check for impaired circulation.
- A small bandage on an extremity is covered with a larger bandage to more evenly distribute the pressure and to avoid creating a pressure point.
- The body part is bandaged in the position in which it is to remain; you can bandage over a joint, but don't try bending the joint after you apply the bandage.
- Ask the victim how the bandage feels; if it is too tight, loosen it and make it comfortable but snug.

Applying Special Dressings and Bandages

Pressure Dressings

Learning Objective 7 Demonstrate how to apply a pressure dressing.

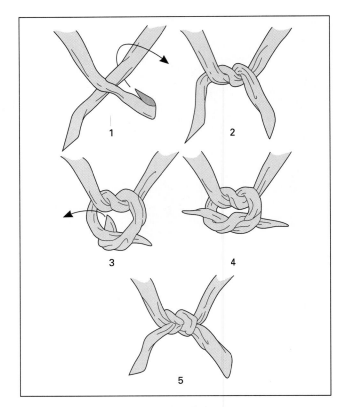

Figure 10-16. Tying a square knot

Use a pressure dressing to control profuse bleeding.

1. Cover the wound with a bulky, sterile dressing.
2. Apply direct pressure with your hand over the dressing until bleeding stops.
3. Apply a firm roller bandage (preferably self-adhering) and monitor continuously for signs that the bandage is too tight. You can also use an air splint or a blood pressure cuff to hold a pressure dressing in place (see Chapter 6). Use an elastic roller bandage only in cases of difficult-to-control, profuse bleeding.
4. If blood soaks through the original dressing and bandage, do not remove them; leave them in place and apply another dressing and roller bandage over the originals.

Slings

Learning Objective 8 Demonstrate how to use a sling.

Slings are used to support injuries of the shoulder, upper extremities, or ribs. If available, use a commercial triangular bandage as a sling; in an emergency, you can use a belt, necktie, scarf, or similar article.

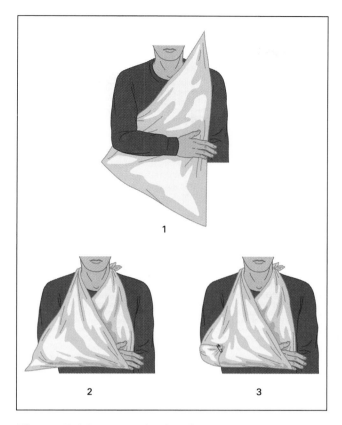

Figure 10-17. Triangular bandage as an arm sling

To tie a triangular sling that will support an injured arm (see Figure 10-17)

1. Place one end of the base of an open triangular bandage over the shoulder of the uninjured side.

2. Allow the bandage to hang down in front of the chest so its apex will be behind the elbow of the injured arm.

3. Bend the arm at the elbow with the hand slightly elevated (four to five inches). When possible, the fingertips should be exposed so you can monitor for impaired circulation.

4. Bring the forearm across the chest and over the bandage.

5. Carry the lower end of the bandage over the shoulder of the injured side, and tie a square knot at the uninjured side of the neck; make sure the knot is at the *side* of the neck.

6. Twist the apex of the bandage and tuck it in or pin it at the elbow. Figures 10-18 through 10-31 illustrate how to apply triangular bandages and cravats to the forehead or scalp, jaw or face, eye, ear, chest or back, shoulder, elbow, hand, hip, leg, knee, ankle, and foot.

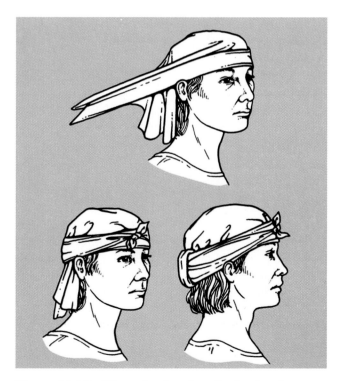

Figure 10-18. Triangular bandage for forehead or scalp

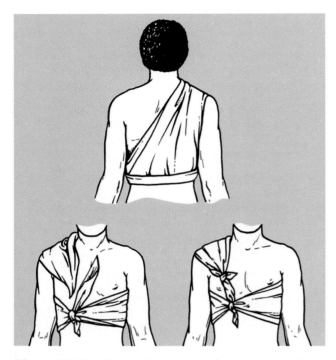

Figure 10-19. *Triangular bandage for chest or back*

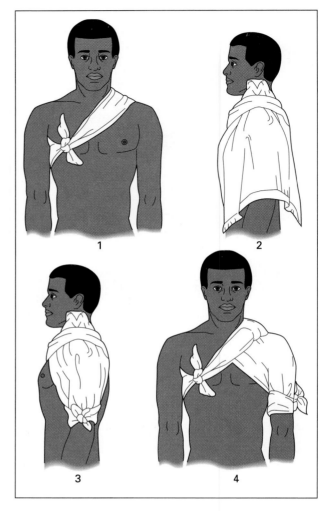

Figure 10-20. *Triangular bandage for the shoulder*

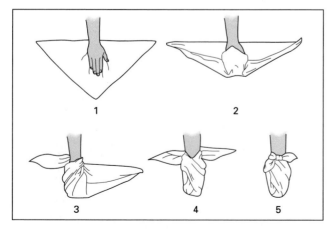

Figure 10-21. *Triangular bandage for the hand*

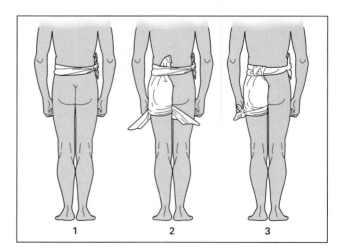

Figure 10-22. *Triangular bandage for the hip*

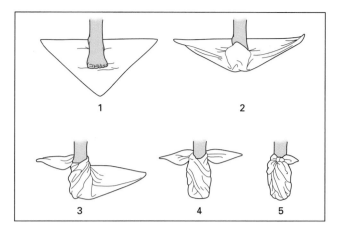

Figure 10-23. Triangular bandage for the foot

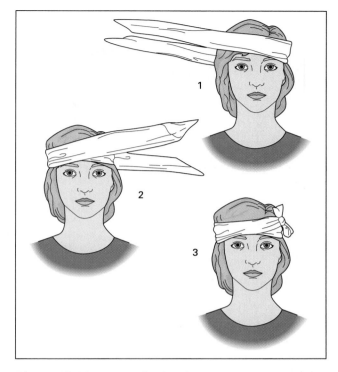

Figure 10-24. Cravat for head or ear

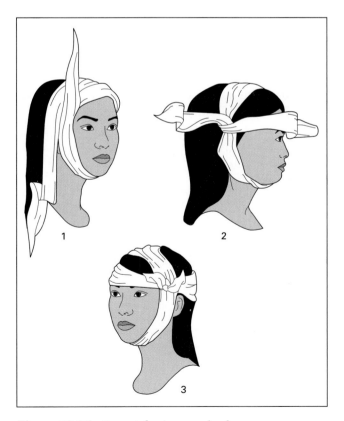

Figure 10-25. Cravat for jaw or cheek

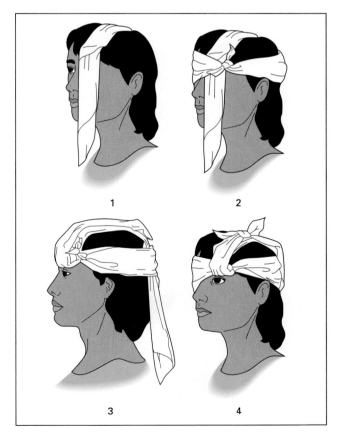

Figure 10-26. Cravat for eye

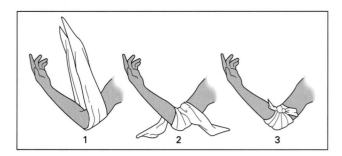

Figure 10-27. *Cravat for elbow*

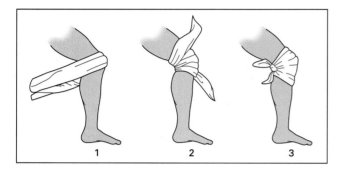

Figure 10-28. *Cravat for knee*

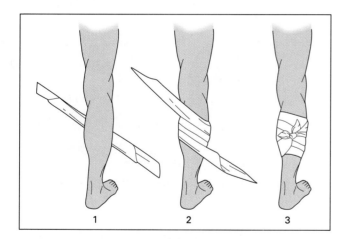

Figure 10-29. *Cravat for leg*

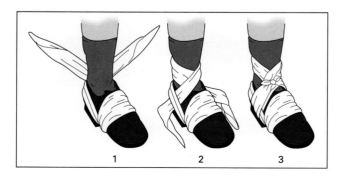

Figure 10-30. *Cravat ankle wrap*

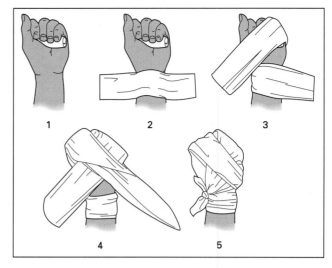

Figure 10-31. *Cravat pressure bandage—palm of hand*

• SUMMARY •

- A dressing is a sterile covering for a wound; the ideal dressing is layered and consists of coarse gauze.

- Never use as a dressing paper towels, toilet tissue, or other material that could shred or cling to the wound.

- A bandage holds a dressing in place and does not touch the wound.

- An occlusive, or airtight, dressing can be improvised from plastic wrap, aluminum foil, or petroleum gauze.

- Signs that a bandage is too tight include paleness or cyanosis of the skin around the bandage and cold, tingling, or numb skin distal to the bandage.

- Triangular, cravat, and roller bandages are special kinds of bandages.

• KEY TERMS •

Make sure you understand the following key terms:
- dressing
- sterile
- aseptic
- occlusive
- gauze pads
- special pads
- bandage
- triangular bandage
- cravat
- roller bandage

Student: _____ Date: _____

Course: _____ Section #: _____

PART 1 • True/False

If you believe the statement is true, circle the T. If you believe the statement is false, circle the F.

T F **1.** A bandage should normally contact a wound.

T F **2.** Bandages should be applied firmly and fastened securely.

T F **3.** The most popular and adaptable bandage is the cravat.

T F **4.** Never use an air splint to hold a dressing in place.

T F **5.** A bandage compress is a special dressing for creating a tourniquet effect.

T F **6.** Triangular bandages are made from cloth that is approximately 20 inches square.

T F **7.** You should always bandage a dressing in place before the bleeding has been controlled.

T F **8.** Do not attempt to bandage an area any larger than the wound site.

T F **9.** If blood soaks through the original dressing, remove it and apply a new dressing.

T F **10.** Elastic roller bandages should not be used except in cases of profuse bleeding.

PART 2 • Multiple Choice

For each item, circle the correct answer or the phrase that best completes the statement.

1. If the fingers or toes of an injured limb become cold, swollen, blue, or numb, you should

   a. immediately loosen the bandage
   b. elevate the affected limb
   c. cover the limb with a warm blanket
   d. treat the victim for shock

2. The primary reason elastic roller bandages are not recommended for use in emergency care is

   a. they are difficult to remove
   b. they tend to stretch after a period of time
   c. they may seriously constrict blood flow
   d. they do not absorb moisture

3. Which type of knot is most frequently used in bandaging?

   a. square knot
   b. slip knot
   c. half hitch
   d. claw hitch

4. Which of the following is an example of an occlusive dressing?

   a. adhering roller gauze
   b. petroleum gauze
   c. butterfly bandage
   d. gauze roller

5. Bandages should never

   a. be applied directly over the wound without a dressing
   b. be applied tightly enough to hinder circulation
   c. be applied loosely
   d. all of the above

6. Which of the following is *not* a principle of bandaging?

   a. when bandaging the arm, leave the fingers uncovered
   b. place the body part to be bandaged in the position in which it is to remain
   c. leave no loose ends that could get caught
   d. if in doubt, leave a bandage tied loosely

7. Which of the following is *not* a guideline for use of an arm sling?

   a. it should cover the entire hand
   b. the knot should not be tied in the middle of the back of the neck
   c. bend the arm at the elbow and elevate the hand 4 to 5 inches
   d. the apex of the bandage should be behind the elbow of the injured arm

8. Which of the following is *not* a recognized type of wound dressing?

   a. bacteriostatic dressing
   b. aseptic dressing
   c. petroleum gauze
   d. dry sterile dressing

Match the type of wound dressing with its description.

A. Aseptic
B. Compress
C. Wet
D. Dry sterile
E. Petroleum gauze
F. Occlusive

_____ A dressing that may not be sterile

_____ A dressing that forms an airtight seal

_____ A sterile dressing

_____ Sterile gauze saturated with a substance to prevent the dressing from sticking to an open wound

_____ A dressing that is free of moisture

_____ A bulky, usually sterile dressing

• A pedestrian is hit by a car and sustains a large avulsion on the left thigh.

Musculoskeletal Injuries

Learning Objectives

When you have mastered the material in this chapter, you will be able to

1 Describe the common signs of sprains, strains, cramps, and dislocations

2 Describe and demonstrate emergency care for a sprain

3 Describe and demonstrate emergency care for a strain

4 Describe and demonstrate emergency care for a cramp

5 Describe and demonstrate emergency care for a dislocation

6 Differentiate between an open and a closed injury to a bone (fracture)

7 Describe how to assess a painful, swollen, deformed extremity

8 Describe and demonstrate emergency care for a victim with a fracture

9 State the reasons for splinting

10 List the general rules of splinting

11 List the complications of splinting

O n April 3, 1998, 7-year-old Nicholas Rose was walking along the top of a brick retaining wall when he lost his balance and fell; reflexively, he thrust out his arm to break the fall, landing with his full weight on the heel of his hand. Both bones of his forearm—the ulna and the radius—snapped from the force of the fall.

Nicholas ran toward home, screaming loudly from the pain. As his mother met him in the street in front of their home, she immediately saw that the arm was severely deformed. Because they lived only 5 minutes by car from the medical clinic, she led Nicholas to the car, helped him sit down, and calmed him. Helping him hold his arm against his chest for support, she placed a pillow against the arm as an improvised splint, then placed an ice bag against the arm over a cotton towel.

When they arrived at the medical center, Nicholas was taken for X-rays; his badly fractured arm was professionally splinted for almost a week until the swelling subsided enough for a cast to be formed around the arm. After 7 weeks in a cast, the arm healed without complication.

INJURIES TO MUSCLES, JOINTS, AND BONES ARE SOME OF the most common situations encountered by First Aiders. These injuries can range from simple and not life threatening ones (such as a broken finger or sprained ankle) to critical, life-threatening ones (such as a fracture of the femur or spine). Regardless of whether the injury is mild or severe, your ability to provide emergency care efficiently and quickly may prevent further painful and damaging injury and may even keep the victim from suffering permanent disability or death.

This chapter covers assessment skills and care guidelines for sprains, strains, and fractures, including splinting.

THE MUSCULOSKELETAL SYSTEM

The human musculoskeletal system is composed of 206 bones, 6 types of joints, and more than 600 muscles. The skeletal system itself has four major functions:

1. It gives shape or form to the body.
2. It supports the body, allowing it to stand erect.
3. It provides the basis for locomotion, or movement, by giving muscles a place to attach, and it contains joints (where bones are joined together by ligaments) that allow movement.
4. It forms protection for major body organs, such as the brain (skull), the heart and lungs (rib cage), pelvic organs, and the spinal cord (vertebrae).

Muscle

Muscle is a special type of tissue that contracts, or shortens, when stimulated. All body movement results from muscles contracting and relaxing. The voluntary (skeletal) muscles are under conscious control. Voluntary muscles make up the arms, legs, upper back, and hips and cover the ribs and the abdomen. Skeletal muscles are attached to the bones either directly or by tendons (tough, fibrous, connective tissue). When a voluntary muscle is stimulated to contract, it shortens and pulls on a part of the skeletal system, causing movement.

Tendons

Tendons are highly specialized connective tissue. They allow for maximum strength because they are oriented in the direction of muscle pull. Tendons form a shiny white band that attaches to the muscles and, through a network of tiny fibers, connects with a bone. If sharp, sudden force is applied, the tendon may pull loose from the bone and may even pull a small piece of bone with it.

Ligaments

Ligaments connect bone to bone. When a ligament is injured, sections of it give way at different places along the entire ligament length. Skin lacerations are rarely involved. Ligaments may be injured without any external tissue damage.

   Most joints of the body have ligaments at the side farthest from the center plane of motion. More complex joints (like the knee) feature ligaments that are attached to the joint capsule. The ligament is often injured simultaneously with the joint; consequent internal bleeding causes early joint swelling.

• Section 1 •
SPRAINS, STRAINS, CRAMPS, AND DISLOCATIONS

Learning Objective 1 Describe the common signs of sprains, strains, cramps, and dislocations.

A **sprain** is an injury to a joint, in which ligaments are stretched and partially or completely torn, usually from the sudden twisting of the joint beyond its normal range of motion. A **strain** is a soft-tissue injury or a muscle spasm around a joint. A **cramp** is an uncontrolled spasm of a muscle. A **dislocation** is the separation of a bone end from a joint, leaving the bone end out of alignment with the joint. See Figure 11-1 on page 188.

Sprains

The signs of a severe sprain are similar to those of a fracture. The most common signs and symptoms are

- Pain
- Swelling
- Deformity
- Discoloration of the skin
- Inability to use the affected part normally

The joints most often sprained are the knee and ankle. Severe sprains may rupture ligaments or dislocate or fracture the bones that form the joint. Mild sprains, which only stretch ligament fibers, generally heal quickly.

Learning Objective 2 Describe and demonstrate emergency care for a sprain.

In most cases, you should care for a sprain as if it were a fracture, and immobilize it accordingly. The goal of first aid treatment is to prevent further injury to the ligament. To treat, do not allow the victim to

sprain An injury in which ligaments are stretched and partially or completely torn
strain A soft-tissue injury or muscle spasm around a joint
cramp Uncontrolled spasm of a muscle
dislocation The displacement of a bone end from a joint

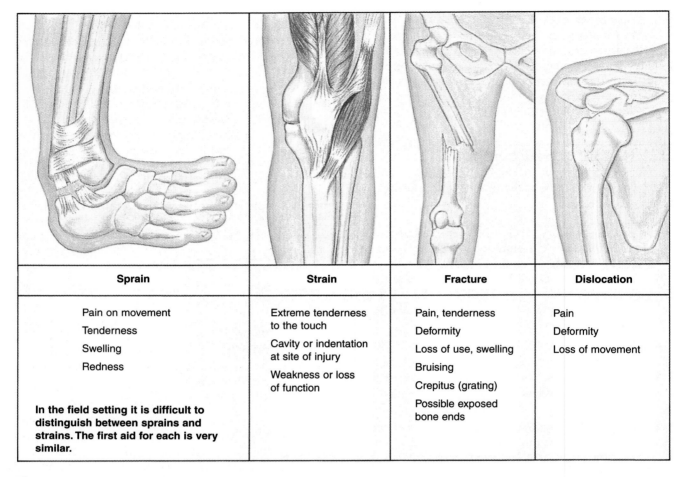

Sprain	Strain	Fracture	Dislocation
Pain on movement Tenderness Swelling Redness **In the field setting it is difficult to distinguish between sprains and strains. The first aid for each is very similar.**	Extreme tenderness to the touch Cavity or indentation at site of injury Weakness or loss of function	Pain, tenderness Deformity Loss of use, swelling Bruising Crepitus (grating) Possible exposed bone ends	Pain Deformity Loss of movement

Figure 11-1. Signs and symptoms of common orthopedic injuries

use the sprained joint; provide care based on the acronym RICE:[1]

1. **R**est—have the victim stay off the injured part completely and not use the joint at all. Splint the sprained joint to give it complete rest. Any movement increases blood circulation to the joint, which increases swelling.

2. **I**ce—cold relieves pain and prevents swelling and inflammation. Immediately put cold packs, crushed ice, or cold towels on the injured area, or immerse it in ice water for 20 to 30 minutes at a time every 2 to 3 hours. Protect the skin from frostbite by putting a wet cloth between the ice pack and the skin. *Never* put an ice pack behind the knee, however; doing so can cause nerve damage. Make an ice pack by putting crushed ice or ice cubes in a towel or plastic bag. If you use a commercially manufactured chemical cold pack, follow manufacturer's directions; in most cases, you will snap or squeeze the pack to activate it. Use each chemical cold pack only once, and take extra care not to rupture or puncture the bag—leaks can cause chemical burns.

3. **C**ompression—to limit internal bleeding and compress fluid from the injury site, wrap a compression bandage (usually an elastic one) in an overlapping spiral that supports the entire injured area. The victim should wear the bandage continuously for 18 to 24 hours, except when applying a cold pack. The bandage should exert even pressure without being too tight; leave fingers and toes exposed so you can make sure the bandage is not too tight. Pale skin, pain, tingling, and numbness are signs that the bandage is too tight.

4. **E**levation—limits circulation and reduces swelling. Elevate the injured area to heart level or just above *if* you do not suspect fracture.

[1]Alton L. Thygerson, "Muscle Injuries," *Emergency* (July 1985): 50–51; Susanna Levin, "Sprains Are a Pain," *Walking Magazine* (June/July 1987): 75.

For maximum effect, start the RICE treatment within 10 to 60 minutes of the injury; follow up by activating the EMS system or transporting the victim to a medical facility.

Strains

Often the result of overexertion, strains are a stretching and tearing of muscle fibers. They occur when muscles are stretched beyond their normal range or when cold or tight muscles are suddenly exerted. Neglected, they often recur. Strains are usually marked by rapid and pronounced swelling.

> **Learning Objective 3** Describe and demonstrate emergency care for a strain.

Assume that the injury may be a fracture, and immobilize accordingly; then

1. Place the victim in a comfortable position that takes pressure off the strained muscles.
2. Apply cold directly to the strained area, as described in step 2 of the RICE system.
3. Activate the EMS system or transport the victim to a medical facility.

Cramps

It's not known exactly what causes cramps—uncontrolled spasms of a muscle—but they are associated with certain illnesses, can follow physical activity, are a sign of dehydration, may occur when a victim loses too many electrolytes (usually through heavy perspiration), and sometimes occur during sleep.

> **Learning Objective 4** Describe and demonstrate emergency care for a cramp.

Though it may seem natural to massage a cramp, massage can actually increase the pain and rarely helps relieve the cramping. Instead, treat a cramp as follows:

1. Have the victim gently stretch the cramping muscle. Because cramps are extremely painful, the victim may need you to gently pull the affected area to stretch out the muscle. If the muscle is in the calf of the leg, standing on the affected leg will lengthen the muscle and relieve the cramp.
2. Apply steady, firm pressure to the cramping muscle with the heel of your hand.
3. Apply an ice pack over the cramped muscle.
4. If the cramp occurs during or after heavy physical activity, have the victim drink a commercial electrolyte drink or lightly salted water (¼ teaspoon of salt dissolved in a quart of water).

Dislocations

A dislocation is a displacement or separation of a bone from its normal position at a joint, usually caused by severe force. The joints most frequently dislocated are the hip, knee, ankle, shoulder, elbow, and finger.

Signs and symptoms of a dislocation are similar to those of a fracture. The principal symptoms are pain or a feeling of pressure over the involved joint and a loss of motion in the joint. The principal sign is deformity. If the dislocated bone end is pressing on a nerve, numbness or paralysis may occur below the dislocation; if it presses on a blood vessel, loss of pulse may occur below the dislocation.

> **Learning Objective 5** Describe and demonstrate emergency care for a dislocation.

Immediately assess blood flow by checking distal pulses and assess nerve function by checking for loss of sensation, numbness, or paralysis. Absence of a pulse means the extremity is not receiving enough blood; activate the EMS system *immediately*. Because dislocations are often accompanied by fractures, you should

1. Immobilize all dislocations *in the position found*. Splint above and below the dislocated joint with an appropriate splint that will keep the joint immobile. (See Figure 11-2 on page 190 for an example.) *Do not try to straighten (**reduce**) the dislocation.* Check the distal pulse again after you have applied the splint.
2. Elevate the affected limb, and place a cold compress or ice pack on the dislocation.
3. Treat for shock; keep the victim warm and quiet and in the position most comfortable.

> ## Progress Check
>
> 1. An injury in which ligaments are stretched and partially or completely torn is a _____ .
>   *(sprain/strain/dislocation)*
>
> 2. A soft-tissue injury or muscle spasm around a joint is a _____ .
>   *(sprain/strain/dislocation)*
>
> 3. You should care for sprains and dislocations as if they were _____ .
>   *(life threatening/fractures/strains)*
>
> 4. Treat a cramp with _____ .
>   *(gentle massage/firm massage/stretching)*

reduce To straighten

Figure 11-2. Use of cravat with pad and sling to immobilize dislocated shoulder

● Section 2 ●
INJURIES TO BONES

Learning Objective 6 Differentiate between an open and a closed injury to a bone (fracture).

A fracture is a break in the continuity of a bone (see Figure 11-3). A bone or joint injury can be one of two kinds (see Figure 11-4):

● Closed (simple), in which the overlying skin is intact and no wound is nearby

● Open (compound), in which the skin over the fracture site has been damaged or broken; the bone may or may not protrude through the wound, and you may or may not be able to see the bone through the wound

In assessing and treating injuries to the bones and joints, it is important to determine the mechanism of injury as well as the signs and symptoms of the injury itself (see Figures 11-5 through 11-7).

Mechanisms of Injury

The force that injures a bone or joint may also cause injuries to the surrounding soft tissues (such as nerves and arteries), or even to body areas distant from the bone injury site. You can get a good idea of how much damage may have occurred by determining the mechanism of injury.

Figure 11-3. Types of fractures

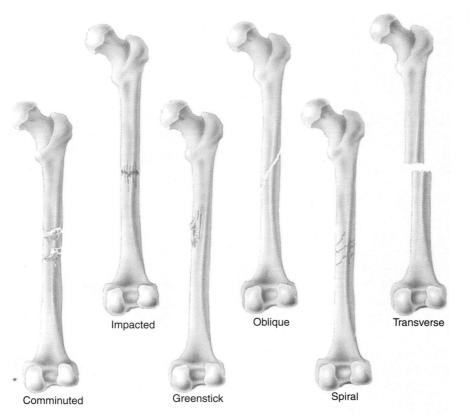

Comminuted

Impacted

Greenstick

Oblique

Spiral

Transverse

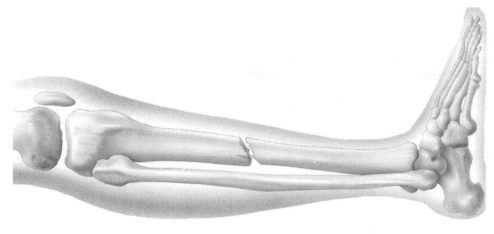

CLOSED
Skin is intact.

OPEN
Bone is protruding or has
protruded through the skin

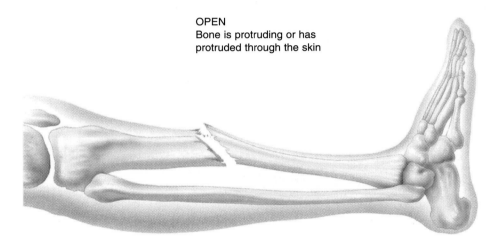

*Figure 11-4. Closed and
open fractures*

As you approach the accident scene and talk with the victim or bystanders, try to imagine the forces the victim's body was subjected to and the direction in which those forces propelled the body. The forces that may cause bone and joint injury (see Figure 11-8 on page 192) include the following.

Direct Force

The fracture from direct force, or a direct blow, occurs at the point of impact. For example, a victim in an automobile accident who is not wearing a seatbelt may be thrust forward, the knees hitting the dashboard; as a result, the patella (kneecap) is fractured.

Indirect Force

Indirect force affects one end of a limb, causing injury to the limb some distance away from the point of impact. For example, a woman riding a horse may be thrown from the horse and may land on two outstretched hands. One arm sustains a fractured wrist, and the clavicle (collarbone) at the end of the other arm is fractured.

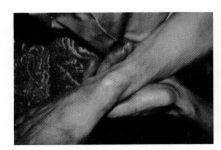

Figure 11-5. Closed fracture of the radius

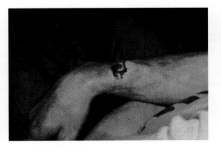

Figure 11-6. Open fracture of the radius

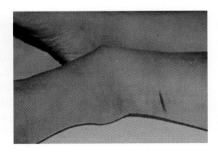

Figure 11-7. Closed fracture; observe the deformity

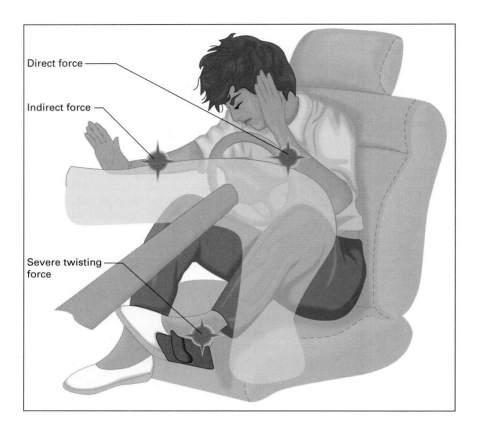

Figure 11-8. *Different types of force can cause different types of injuries.*

Direct force

Indirect force

Severe twisting force

Twisting Force

When a bone is fractured by twisting force, one part of the bone remains stationary while the rest of the bone twists. For example, a child running across a field may step into a hole. The foot is rammed snugly into the hole and stays stationary, while the rest of the lower leg twists and is fractured. Bone and joint injuries from twisting force commonly occur in football or skiing accidents.

Signs and Symptoms

Learning Objective 7 Describe how to assess a painful, swollen, deformed extremity.

With rare exceptions, fractures and other bone injuries are not life threatening. And although they are often the most obvious and dramatic injuries a victim suffers, fractures may not necessarily be the most serious. Therefore, it is important that you complete the primary survey and manage any life-threatening conditions *before* you look for the signs and symptoms of bone and joint injury (see Figure 11-9):

• Deformity, shortening, or angulation; deformity is not always obvious, but when the normal and the injured extremity are compared, there is a difference in the size, length, shape, or position of the injured one.

• Pain and tenderness, usually only at the site of injury

• Crepitus, a grating noise that can be heard or sensation that can be felt as broken fragments of bone grind against each other

• Rapid swelling

• Bruising (discoloration)

• Open wound, with or without exposed bone ends; it may be a puncture wound

• Joint locked into position

• Guarding (victim tries to hold the injured area in a comfortable position and avoids moving it)

• Possible loss of function; in some cases, the victim can use or move the bone with little or no pain, even when there is a fracture

Children's bones are much more flexible than those of adults, and fractures are often incomplete (called *greenstick fractures*). Localized pain and swelling in a child often indicates fracture, not a sprain.

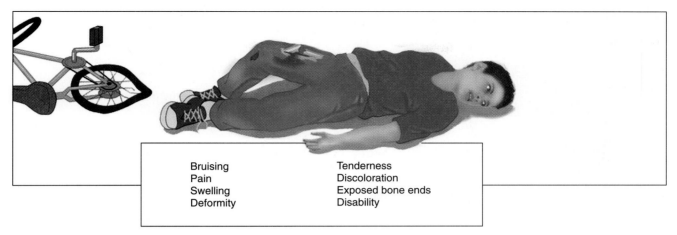

Bruising	Tenderness
Pain	Discoloration
Swelling	Exposed bone ends
Deformity	Disability

Figure 11-9. Signs and symptoms of fractures

Emergency Care

> **Learning Objective 8** Describe and demonstrate emergency care for a victim with a fracture.

It is difficult to tell whether a bone is broken, so when in doubt, always treat the injury as a fracture. Fractures should be treated in priority order, as follows:

- Spinal fractures
- Fractures of the head and rib cage
- Pelvic fractures
- Fractures of the lower limbs
- Fractures of the upper limbs

Remember—if there was enough force to damage the pelvis or to cause severe head or facial injuries, assume there are also injuries to the spine.

The most important emergency care is immobilization of any suspected fracture or extensive soft-tissue injury. You should immobilize before you apply ice or elevate the injured part; doing so

- Minimizes damage to soft tissue, muscle, or bone sheathing that may become wedged between fracture fragments
- Prevents a closed fracture from becoming an open one
- Prevents more damage to surrounding nerves, blood vessels, and other tissues from the broken bone ends
- Minimizes bleeding and swelling
- Diminishes pain, which helps control shock
- Prevents restriction of blood flow by bone ends compressing blood vessels

Any fracture of the spine is always a first priority for treatment; for guidelines in managing spine frac-

tures, see Chapter 13. Treat a fracture as follows (see Figures 11-10 and 11-11 on page 194):

1. Support the injured part; gently remove clothing and jewelry around the injury site without moving the injured area.

2. Cover any open wounds with sterile dressings to control bleeding and prevent infection. Gently wipe away dirt and debris, and irrigate the exposed bone end with clean water.

3. Assess blood flow and nerve function; this step is essential, since the most serious complication of fracture is reduced blood flow and subsequent tissue death. Check the distal pulse of the suspected fracture site—the wrist for an arm fracture, the ankle for a leg fracture. *Lack of a pulse indicates a dire medical emergency.* Gently manipulate the limb once in an attempt to restore circulation. To assess nerve function, gently squeeze the victim's fingers or toes; if the victim can't feel the squeeze, there may be nerve damage.

4. If there is severe deformity or angulation, apply minimal traction—a firm, steady pull to bring the limb into more normal alignment—except for crushing injuries; immobilize joints above and below the fracture. When applying traction, grasp an arm with one hand on either side of the injury, and pull gently and steadily in line with the bone. For a fractured leg, position both your hands below the fracture and pull gently and steadily downward. *Do not attempt to push bone ends back underneath the skin, and avoid excessive pressure on the wound.* Remember that traction is not used to completely correct a deformity—something that can be done only in a hospital—but to *reduce* the amount of angulation. *As a general rule, never straighten a wrist, elbow, knee, or shoulder.* Except

Figure 11-10. *An open tibia fracture*

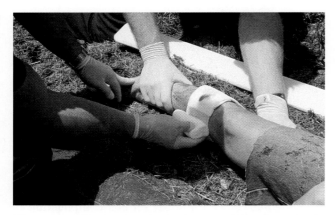

Figure 11-11. *Support the limb, control bleeding, apply traction, locate a distal pulse, and splint. Brace the fracture with your hand under the fracture site.*

for the wrist and shoulder, make one attempt to straighten closed, angulated fractures *if no distal pulse is found.* If pain, resistance, or crepitus increases, stop. Wrap from the distal end of the splint to the proximal end; splint firmly enough to immobilize but not tightly enough to stop blood circulation. Follow specific guidelines for splinting listed in the next section.

5. Check distal pulses after the splint is in place to make sure circulation is still adequate.

6. Use cold compresses and elevation to relieve pain and reduce swelling.

Progress Check

1. In assessing for fractures, it is important to consider the _____ as well as the signs and symptoms.
   (history/mechanism of injury/pain)

2. Though fractures may be the most obvious and dramatic injuries suffered by a victim, they are often not the most _____ ones.
   (life-threatening/easy-to-manage/painful)

3. Before you try to identify fractures, you should complete _____ .
   (artificial ventilation/chest compressions/the primary survey)

4. The most important emergency care for suspected fracture is _____ .
   (control of bleeding/immobilization/replacing bone ends)

5. _____ helps minimize damage to soft tissue, surrounding nerves, and blood vessels by broken bone ends.
   (Immobilization/Splinting/Compression)

6. If the forearm is fractured, you should also immobilize the _____ .
   (upper arm/shoulder/wrist and elbow)

7. You _____ try to straighten the wrist, elbow, knee, or shoulder.
   (should/should not)

• Section 3 •
SPLINTING

Learning Objective 9 State the reasons for splinting.

Any device used to immobilize (prevent movement of) a fracture or dislocation is a *splint.* A splint can be soft or rigid, commercially manufactured or improvised from virtually any object that can provide stability.

Splints are used to support and immobilize suspected fractures, dislocations, or severe sprains; to help control bleeding; to reduce swelling; to help control pain; and to prevent further damage to tissues from the movement of bone ends. Any victim with suspected fracture, dislocation, or severe sprain should be splinted before being moved.

Rules for Splinting

Learning Objective 10 List the general rules of splinting.

Regardless of where you apply the splint (see Figure 11-12), follow these general rules:

- Do not splint if it will cause more pain for the victim.

- Both before and after you apply the splint, assess the pulse and sensation below the injury. You should evaluate these signs every 15 minutes after

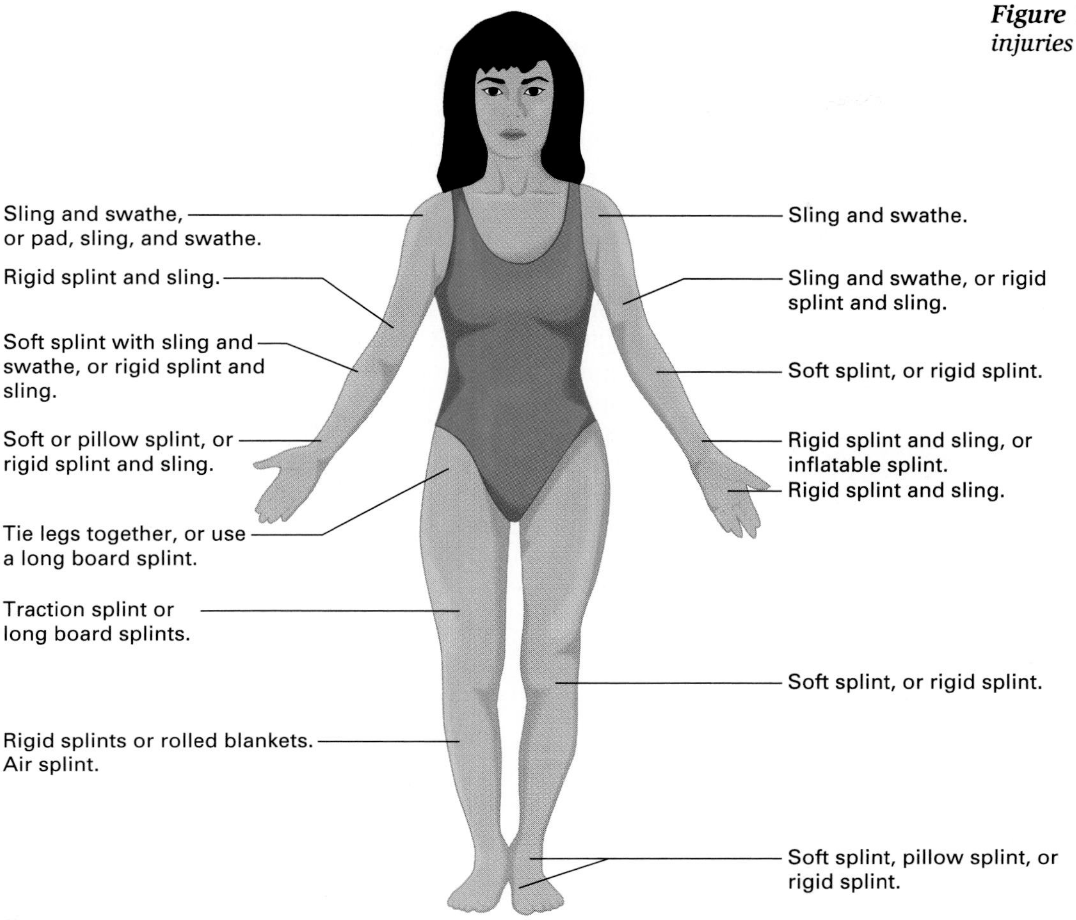

Figure 11-12. Care for injuries to the extremities.

Sling and swathe, or pad, sling, and swathe.

Rigid splint and sling.

Soft splint with sling and swathe, or rigid splint and sling.

Soft or pillow splint, or rigid splint and sling.

Tie legs together, or use a long board splint.

Traction splint or long board splints.

Rigid splints or rolled blankets. Air splint.

Sling and swathe.

Sling and swathe, or rigid splint and sling.

Soft splint, or rigid splint.

Rigid splint and sling, or inflatable splint.
Rigid splint and sling.

Soft splint, or rigid splint.

Soft splint, pillow splint, or rigid splint.

applying the splint to make sure the splint is not impairing circulation.

- Immobilize the joints both above and below the injury.
- Splint an injury in the position you found it. If there is no distal pulse or movement, you may attempt to return the bone to its normal alignment by placing one hand above the injury and another below. Then pull with gentle traction while moving the injury back toward the correct anatomical position.
- Remove or cut away all clothing around the injury site with a pair of bandage scissors so you won't accidentally move the fractured bone ends and complicate the injury. Remove all jewelry around the fracture site.
- Cover all wounds, including open fractures, with sterile dressing before applying a splint (see Figure 11-13 on page 196), then gently bandage. Avoid excessive pressure on the wound.
- If there is a severe deformity or the distal extremity is cyanotic or lacks pulses, align the injured

limb with gentle traction before splinting, following the guidelines above.
- Never intentionally replace protruding bone ends.
- Pad the splint to prevent pressure and discomfort to the victim.
- Apply the splint before trying to move the victim.
- When in doubt, splint the injury.
- If the victim shows signs of shock, align the victim in the normal anatomical position and arrange for immediate transport without taking the time to apply a splint.

Types of Splints

There are four general types of splints:

Rigid Splints

Rigid splints are commercially manufactured splints (see Figure 11-14 on page 196) made of wood, aluminum, wire, plastic, cardboard, or compressed wood fibers. Some are designed in specific shapes for arms

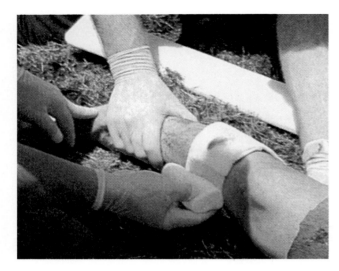

Figure 11-13. Splinting immobilizes fractures and dislocations.

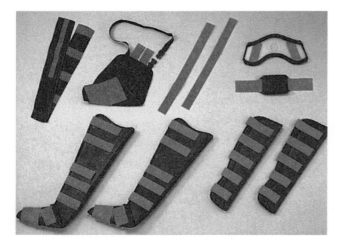

Figure 11-14. A set of commercial splints

mizing further injury. Traction splints are not intended to reduce the fracture, but simply to immobilize the bone ends and prevent further injury. A traction splint should be used only for a broken thigh, and should be applied only by EMTs or those who have had special training in applying traction splints.

Pneumatic (Air) Splints

Air splints (see Figure 11-15) are soft and pliable before being inflated but rigid once they are applied and filled with air. A similar type of splint is the vacuum splint, which works on the principle of a vacuum. Air splints are used mainly on the forearm and lower leg. Air and vacuum splints cannot be sized, may impair circulation, may interfere with the ability to assess pulses, and may lose pressure with temperature and altitude changes.

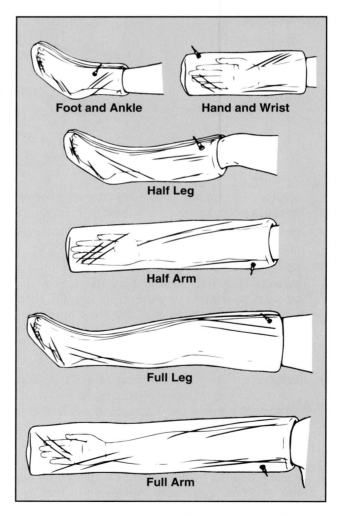

Figure 11-15. Examples of inflatable splints (air, or pneumatic, splints)

and legs and are equipped with Velcro closures; others are pliable enough to be molded to fit any appendage. One of the most popular commercial splints is the SAM splint, a lightweight splint made of pliable aluminum sandwiched between layers of foam; it can be molded to fit any body part. Some commercial splints come with washable pads, but others must be padded before being applied. The splint must be long enough to extend both above and below the fracture.

Traction Splints

Traction splints gently pull in the direction opposite the injury, alleviating pain, reducing blood loss, and mini-

Improvised Splints

You may have access to a commercial splint, but it is much more likely that you will need to improvise at the scene. A splint can be improvised from a cardboard box, cane, ironing board, rolled-up magazine, umbrella, broom handle, catcher's shin guard, or any other similar object (see Figure 11-16).

You can also use a *self-splint* (also called an *anatomical splint*) by tying or taping an injured part to an adjacent uninjured part; for example, splint a finger to a finger, a toe to a toe, a leg to the other leg, or an arm to the chest (see Figure 11-17). An effective improvised splint must be

- Light in weight, but firm and rigid
- Long enough to extend past the joints and prevent movement on either side of the fracture
- As wide as the thickest part of the fractured limb
- Padded well so the inner surfaces are not in contact with the skin

An ordinary bed pillow can be an effective improvised splint when wrapped around the area and secured with several cravats.

Hazards of Improper Splinting

Learning Objective 11 List the complications of splinting.

Improper splinting can

- Compress the nerves, tissues, and blood vessels under the splint, aggravating the existing injury and causing new injury

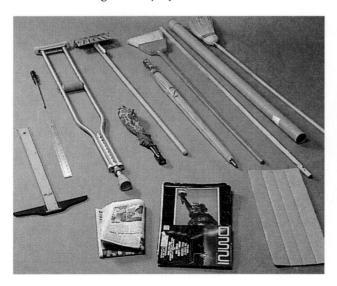

Figure 11-16. *You must know how to make emergency splints from whatever materials are available.*

- Delay the transport of a victim who has a life-threatening injury
- Reduce distal circulation, threatening the extremity
- Aggravate the bone or joint injury by allowing movement of the bone fragments or bone ends or by forcing bone ends beneath the skin surface
- Cause or aggravate damage to the tissues, nerves, blood vessels, or muscles as a result of excessive bone or joint movement

Special Considerations in Splinting

There are certain special techniques to remember when splinting long bones or joints or when using a traction splint.

Splinting a Long Bone

Splint a long bone as follows:

1. Gently grasp the limb and apply gentle, steady pressure to stabilize the bone.
2. Assess the pulse and sensory function below the injury site. Look for **paresthesia** (a pricking or tingling sensation that indicates loss of circulation) or paralysis. If the injury involves an upper

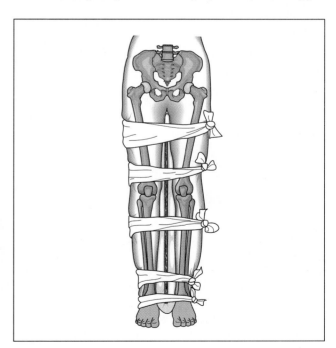

Figure 11-17. *Improvised self-splint*

paresthesia Pricking or tingling sensation that indicates loss of circulation

extremity, nerve function is intact if the victim can make a fist, undo the fist, spread the fingers, and make a hitchhiking sign with the thumb. If the injury involves a lower extremity, nerve function is intact if the victim can tighten the kneecap and move the foot up and down as if pumping an automobile accelerator.

3. If the limb is severely deformed, is cyanotic, or lacks distal pulses, align it by providing steady, gentle pressure along with traction (see Figure 11-18); if pain or crepitus increases, stop.

4. Measure the splint to make sure it is the right size. The splint should be long enough to immobilize the entire bone plus the joints on both sides (see Figure 11-19). If you are immobilizing the leg, ideally, the outside splint should be long enough to reach from the victim's armpit to below the heel; the inner splint should be long enough to reach from the groin to below the heel.

5. Apply the splint, immobilizing the bone and the joint both above and below the injury (see Figures 11-20 through 11-23).

6. Secure the entire injured extremity; you can use the straps or Velcro closures that come with commercial splints, or wrap roller bandages around improvised splints and secure them with cravats.

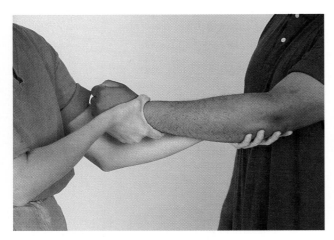

Figure 11-18. Applying traction

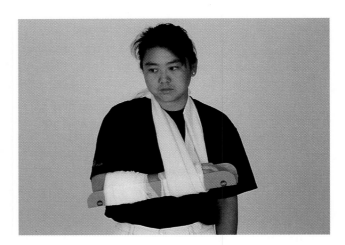

Figure 11-19. Cardboard splint of the lower arm

A pad is between the fractured arm and the body. A padded splint is tied to the outer arm.

The arm is supported by a wide cravat. The knot is to the side, not pressed against the neck.

A swathe binds the arm to the chest.

Figure 11-20. A fracture of the humerus immobilized by a splint

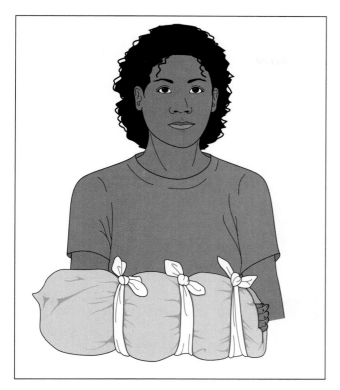

Figure 11-21. *Pillow splint for fractures of the forearm, wrist, and hand*

7. Immobilize the hand or foot in the normal position of function. Make sure you can still see and feel the hand or foot so you can assess pulse and sensation.

Splinting a Joint

Splint a joint as follows:

1. Stabilize the joint manually; one First Aider should apply firm but gentle stabilization while a second readies the splint.

2. Assess the pulse and sensory function below the injury site; check for paresthesia or paralysis.

3. If the distal extremity is cyanotic (bluish) or lacks pulses, align the joint with gentle traction. If pain or crepitus increases, stop.

4. Immobilize the site of the injury with a splint.

5. Immobilize the bones both above and below the injured joint to help prevent accidental movement of the joint (see Figures 11-24 through 11-27 on pages 200–201).

6. After applying the splint, reassess pulse and sensation; reassess every few minutes throughout care.

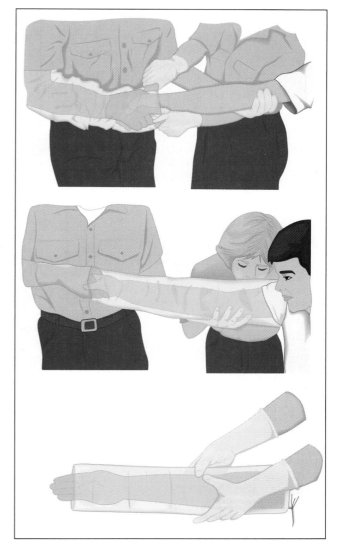

Figure 11-22. *Applying an air splint*

Progress Check

1. You should not apply a splint if it will cause more _____ for the victim.
   (pain/disability/deformity)

2. You should assess the victim's _____ both before and after you apply a splint.
   (breathing/pulses/level of consciousness)

3. You should immobilize _____ both above and below the injury.
   (bones/joints/tissues)

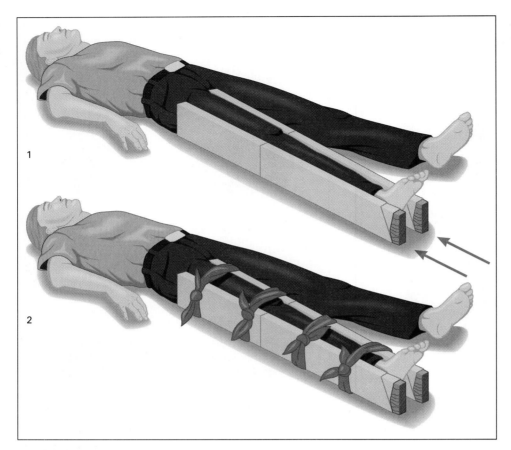

Figure 11-23. Fixation splint of the tibia/fibula, using padded boards

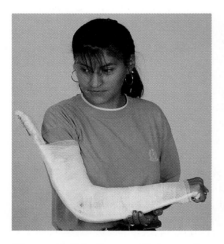

Figure 11-24. Some splints can be formed to the injured limb, but they should be well padded, and secured with gauze rolls.

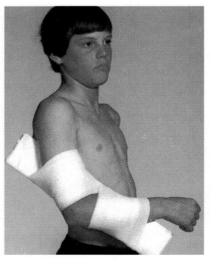

Figure 11-25. Fractured elbow immobilized with a board splint

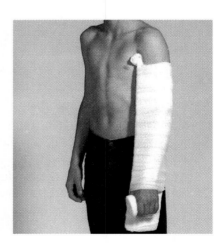

Figure 11-26. Splint a dislocated or fractured elbow in the position found.

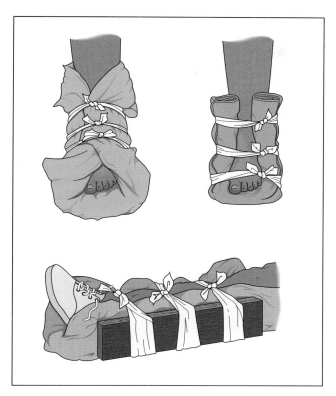

Figure 11-27. Immobilizing a fracture of the ankle and foot; always untie laces if a shoe is left on the foot

over the fracture site is broken) or closed (in which the skin over the fracture site is intact).

- Injuries to bones can be caused by direct force, indirect force, or twisting force.

- A fracture may often be the most obvious or dramatic injury the victim has, but few are life threatening; therefore, it is critical that you complete the primary survey and manage life-threatening conditions before attempting to identify fractures.

- Fractures should be treated in priority order: spinal fractures, fractures of the head and rib cage, pelvic fractures, fractures of the lower limbs, and fractures of the upper limbs.

- The most important emergency care for fractures is immobilization; you should always immobilize before you apply ice or elevate the injured part.

- As a general rule, never straighten a wrist, elbow, knee, or shoulder.

- Always immobilize the joints just above and below a fractured bone; always immobilize the bones just above and below an injured joint.

- Always check pulses both before and after you splint.

- Any device used to immobilize a fracture or dislocation is a splint; splints are used to support, immobilize, and protect injured parts. You can use a rigid splint, traction splint, pneumatic splint, or improvised splint.

- Improvised splints must be light in weight but firm and rigid; long enough to extend past the joints and prevent movement on either side of the fracture; as wide as the thickest part of the fractured limb; and padded well so the inner surfaces are not in contact with the victim's skin.

- Improper splinting can compress nerves, tissues, and blood vessels and can reduce circulation to the limb.

● SUMMARY ●

- A sprain is an injury in which ligaments are stretched and partially or completely torn.

- A strain is a soft-tissue injury or muscle spasm around a joint.

- Use gentle stretching to care for a cramp; never massage a cramping muscle.

- A dislocation is the displacement of a bone end from a joint.

- Emergency care for sprains consists of the RICE treatment—rest, ice, compression, and elevation.

- You should always assume that strains and dislocations are fractures, and treat accordingly.

- Never try to straighten a dislocation.

- A fracture is a break in the continuity of a bone; fractures can be either open (in which the skin

● KEY TERMS ●

Make sure you understand the following key terms:

- sprain
- strain
- cramp
- dislocation
- reduce
- paresthesia

Student: _____   Date: _____

Course: _____   Section #: _____

If you believe the statement is true, circle the T. If you believe the statement is false, circle the F.

T F **1.** It is usually impossible to tell the difference between a sprain and a closed fracture without an x-ray.

T F **2.** To test for fracture, ask the victim to try to move the injured part or walk on the injured leg.

T F **3.** In cases of suspected dislocation, correct the deformity before splinting it.

T F **4.** Permanent nerve damage can result from a splint that is too tight; you should carefully monitor for signs of discoloration and swelling.

T F **5.** Apply heat to a sprained joint for the first 24 hours.

T F **6.** A fracture is a crack or splinter in a bone that is not broken.

T F **7.** A closed fracture can become an open fracture through mishandling.

T F **8.** A splint should be placed directly against the skin without padding or dressings for maximum effectiveness.

T F **9.** A splint should not extend beyond the joints above and below the suspected fracture.

T F **10.** A fractured elbow should always be immobilized in the position in which it is found.

For each item, circle the correct answer or the phrase that best completes the statement.

1. The primary objective in first aid care for a fracture is to

   a. set the bone
   b. immobilize the fracture
   c. push a protruding bone end back into its original position
   d. all of the above

2. In cases of fracture, the purpose of a splint is to

   a. reduce the chance of shock
   b. decrease pain
   c. prevent motion of the injured limb
   d. all of the above

3. What is a sign or symptom of a strain?

   a. immediate swelling
   b. inability to move
   c. sharp pain that lasts for prolonged periods
   d. a sudden burning sensation

4. An injury in which ligaments are partially torn is

   a. a sprain
   b. a strain
   c. tendinitis
   d. a dislocation

5. Displacement of a bone end from a joint with associated ligament damage is called a

   a. strain
   b. sprain
   c. dislocation
   d. fracture

6. To treat an open fracture

   a. wash the wound thoroughly with either disinfectant or clear running water
   b. control bleeding with pressure through a dressing
   c. if the bone is protruding, do not cover the wound
   d. replace bone fragments before covering the wound with a dressing

7. If you suspect a fracture of the upper arm, you should immobilize

   a. the elbow
   b. the upper arm
   c. the shoulder
   d. all of the above

8. If you have been trained to do so, you should apply traction with a traction splint until

   a. the limb is noticeably stretched
   b. the victim feels relief
   c. the bone ends realign
   d. the fracture is reduced

Match each of the four conditions with both its definition and its care.

A. Overstraining of muscles and/or tendons, causing muscles and tendons to stretch and/or rupture

B. Displacement of bone ends that form the joint

C. Crack or break in the continuity of the bone

D. Injury to ligaments around the joint, producing undue stretching or tearing of tissues

E. Heat if there is no swelling; plenty of rest

F. Control any bleeding and immobilize

G. Rest, ice, compression, and elevation

H. Don't try to reduce; splint, apply cold, and treat for shock

_____ Strain

_____ Sprain

_____ Dislocation

_____ Fracture

PART 4 • What Would You Do If?

- At the scene of an automobile accident, you diagnose a young man as having a closed fracture of the femur about midthigh. He also has a fracture of the pelvis on the opposite side of the leg injury.

  What first aid would you administer if an ambulance will reach you within 10 minutes? How would you splint the fractures if no ambulance will respond and you will have to transport the victim to a medical facility?

Common Sport and Recreational Injuries

Learning Objectives

When you have mastered the material in this chapter, you will be able to

1 Describe and demonstrate emergency care of a fractured clavicle

2 Describe and demonstrate emergency care of a shoulder separation

3 Describe the usual mechanism of injury that causes a shoulder dislocation

4 Describe the usual mechanism of injury that causes a dislocated elbow

5 Describe the signs and symptoms of a fractured radial head

6 Define Colles's and Smith's fractures and describe the usual mechanism of injury for each

7 Describe the mechanisms of injury that cause fractures to the carpal and metacarpal bones, dislocations of the carpal bones, and fractured or dislocated fingers

8 Describe emergency care for injuries to the hip

9 Describe emergency care for injuries to the hamstring and knee ligaments

10 Describe the signs and symptoms of a dislocated kneecap (patella)

11 Describe the emergency care of an achilles tendon rupture

12 Describe the emergency care of sprains or fractures of the ankle and foot

This chapter was written by David O. Draper, Ed.D., A.T.C.

On April 19, 1998, 16-year-old Shauna Randall was playing volleyball on a field behind the high school where two coaches had set up a series of nets. When a player from the opposing team spiked the ball just over the net, Shauna dived to reach it; instead, her outstretched hand slammed into the turf.

Coach Linda Ames ran to Shauna, who was complaining of pain in the shoulder and holding her elbow up into her side. Coach Ames sent another player into the gym to call for emergency help, then assessed Shauna. There was an obvious lump over the tip of Shauna's shoulder that was extremely painful to the touch; Coach Ames suspected a second- or third-degree separation of the acromioclavicular joint—more simply stated, shoulder separation.

Helping Shauna to her office, Coach Ames used both vertical and horizontal swathes and a sling to support Shauna's arm. When emergency personnel arrived, Coach Ames was holding a cold compress against the injured shoulder joint, to help control pain and swelling.

BECAUSE OF THE NATURE OF SPORT AND RECREATIONAL activities, injuries are common; first aid on the scene can prevent additional pain and injury and can dramatically improve the victim's eventual outcome.

Each section in this chapter discusses the likely mechanisms of injury, the most likely signs and symptoms you will find during assessment, and the immediate first aid care you should give at the scene. All victims of the injuries described in this chapter need medical and/or surgical care; either activate the EMS system or transport the victim yourself to a medical facility after providing appropriate emergency care.

• Section 1 •
INJURIES TO THE SHOULDER, ELBOW, WRIST, AND HAND

Fractured Clavicle

A fractured clavicle (collarbone) occurs from blunt trauma, such as when two rugby players collide. The most common mechanism of injury is a fall—such as when a gymnast falls off the beam headfirst or a rider falls off a horse. As the athlete attempts to break the fall with the hand, the force goes up the arm, and the clavicle is actually pinched between the humerus and the sternum. The clavicle usually breaks in the middle, which is its weakest point.

Signs and Symptoms

Signs and symptoms are similar to those of other fractures, as described in Chapter 11. You might be able to see and feel a lump over the fracture sight; the lump will be tender, swollen, and deformed. The athlete typically supports the arm and holds it near his or her chest.

Emergency Care

> **Learning Objective 1** Describe and demonstrate emergency care of a fractured clavicle.

1. Don't move the victim until you have splinted the fracture with one of the following three methods:
   - *Sling and swathe*
   - *Figure-eight bandage* (see Figure 12-1) *or butterfly sling*, which provides slight traction on the fracture site, stabilizing the area and relieving some pain
   - *Improvised immobilization* using cravats tied together, a roller bandage, or elastic wrap

2. Gently apply an ice pack or cold compresses to the fracture site to alleviate pain.
3. Allow the victim to stay in the most comfortable position, usually sitting.

Shoulder Separation

A shoulder separation involves the **acromioclavicular joint,** the most freely movable joint in the body and the joint where the clavicle, scapula, and humerus meet. Three major ligaments support this joint, and the severity of the injury is measured by the number of ligaments damaged and the extent of the damage. The shoulder is one of the most commonly dislocated joints, second only to the joints in the fingers.

The most common mechanism of injury in shoulder separation (see Figure 12-2 on page 208) is falling directly on the tip of the shoulder—such as when a wrestler is thrown to the mat or a hurdler trips and lands shoulder-first on the track. A second mechanism of injury is falling on an outstretched hand. In either situation, the ligaments supporting the joint are stretched or torn.

Signs and Symptoms

With a slight (first-degree) separation, there is little swelling or deformity over the joint. A second- or third-degree separation causes

- An obvious and **palpable** lump over the tip of the shoulder; the lump is the tip of the clavicle that has dislodged from the scapula
- Extreme pain at the site of the separation

> **acromioclavicular joint** The joint in the shoulder where the clavicle, scapula, and humerus join
>
> **palpable** Able to be felt by the First Aider

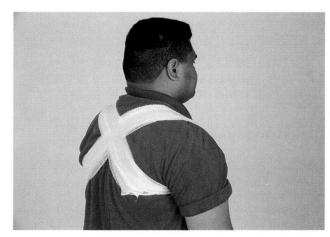

Figure 12-1. A figure-eight bandage seen from the front and the back

Figure 12-2. Acromioclavicular joint separation—mechanism of injury is falling on the point of the shoulder.

- "Guarding" (support of the injured arm by holding the elbow up and the upper arm away from the body)
- Inability to hold the arm across the chest (as it would be positioned in a sling)

Emergency Care

Learning Objective 2 Describe and demonstrate emergency care of a shoulder separation.

To care for a mild (first-degree) separation, immobilize the shoulder with a roller or elastic bandage and apply an ice pack or cold compress. If there is deformity, suspect a second- or third-degree separation; to treat:

1. Immobilize the shoulder with both horizontal and vertical swathes and a sling.

2. Apply an ice pack or cold compress to the shoulder joint if the victim can tolerate it.

Dislocated Shoulder

Learning Objective 3 Describe the usual mechanism of injury that causes a shoulder dislocation.

A shoulder dislocation is a more severe injury than a separation, because the dislocation involves the artic-

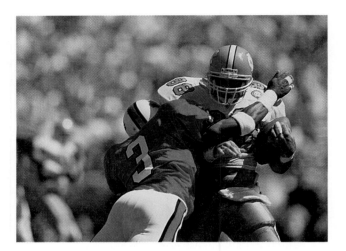

Figure 12-3. Mechanism of an anterior dislocation. The arm is forced into extension, abduction, and external rotation.

ulating surface of the shoulder (the glenohumeral joint). Many nerves and arteries pass through the area of the joint and can be involved in the injury.

The most common mechanism of injury causing shoulder dislocation is when the athlete's arm is held out from the side with the palm at shoulder height, then pulled backward; a classic example is a football player reaching out to tackle an oncoming opponent (see Figure 12-3). The force of the opposing player causes the head of the humerus to dislocate from its attachment on the scapula. Figure 12-4 illustrates a dislocated shoulder.

Signs and Symptoms

Signs and symptoms of a dislocated shoulder include

- The usually rounded part of the shoulder is flattened.
- The injured arm appears longer than the opposite arm.
- The victim exhibits a guarding of the shoulder and an inability to lift the arm.
- You may be able to feel the head of the humerus in the victim's armpit.

Emergency Care

1. Check for a pulse in the wrist and sensation in the hand; if either is missing, activate the EMS system immediately.

2. Immobilize the shoulder in the position found; *never attempt to straighten a dislocated shoulder.*

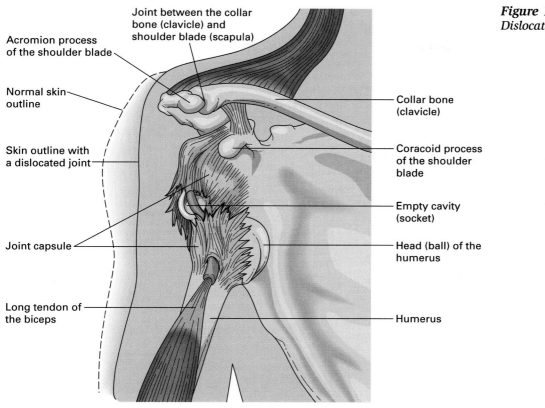

Joint between the collar
bone (clavicle) and
shoulder blade (scapula)

Acromion process
of the shoulder blade

Normal skin
outline

Skin outline with
a dislocated joint

Joint capsule

Long tendon of
the biceps

Collar bone
(clavicle)

Coracoid process
of the shoulder
blade

Empty cavity
(socket)

Head (ball) of the
humerus

Humerus

Figure 12-4.
Dislocated shoulder

Dislocated Elbow

> **Learning Objective 4** Describe the usual mechanism of
> injury that causes a dislocated elbow.

Although not a common injury in sports and recreation, gymnasts and wrestlers occasionally suffer a
dislocated elbow (see Figure 12-5) because their sport
involves supporting their weight on their hands. A
typical mechanism of injury is having one's wrestling
opponent fall on the back of the arm that is supporting one's weight. Occasionally a gymnastics coach or
spotter dislocates an elbow trying to catch an off-
balance athlete.

A dislocated elbow is not the same as **tennis
elbow,** an injury that causes inflammation on the outside bony protrusion of the elbow. Tennis elbow actually involves the tendons of the wrist, and results from
quick snapping twists of the wrist in any activity, not
just tennis. The tendon in the elbow is attached to the

> **tennis elbow** Inflammation of the bony protrusion of
> the elbow

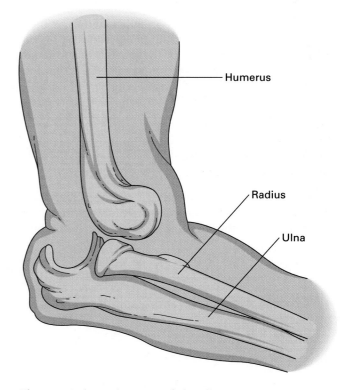

Humerus

Radius

Ulna

Figure 12-5. Dislocation of the elbow joint

muscle that controls wrist and finger movement, so the tennis player experiences extreme pain when using either the wrist or the elbow.

As with a dislocated shoulder, a dislocation of the elbow carries the risk of injuring the numerous nerves and blood vessels that pass through the elbow. Accompanying fractures are common.

Signs and Symptoms

The signs and symptoms of a dislocated elbow include

- Gross deformity of the elbow
- A golf-ball-sized lump on the back of the elbow
- A shortened forearm on the injured side
- Inability to bend the elbow

Emergency Care

1. Immobilize the injury in the position found; *never try to straighten a dislocated elbow.* If possible, use a ladder splint, Sam splint, or vacuum splint; do not use an air splint, because it forces the bones into the shape of the splint.
2. Apply an ice pack or cold compress.

Fracture of the Radial Head

The head of the radius is on the thumb side of the elbow; typically, it is fractured when a victim falls on an outstretched hand, such as when hiking or bicycling. Though the elbow itself usually doesn't hit the ground, energy travels from the ground to the hand, then up the arm, causing the humerus to compress the radial head.

Signs and Symptoms

> **Learning Objective 5** Describe the signs and symptoms of a fractured radial head.

The most common symptom of radial head fracture is pain while rotating the forearm. To assess, have the victim hold out the arm with the elbow slightly bent and the hand cupped. Then have the victim turn the palm down, as if pouring water from the palm. If that kind of rotation causes significant pain, suspect radial head fracture.

Other signs and symptoms include

- Mild deformity, if any
- Slight swelling over the lateral side of the elbow
- Head of the radius painful to the touch
- Guarding (the victim will try to hold the elbow slightly bent)

Emergency Care

1. Splint the injured arm in a flexed position; if possible, use a vacuum splint, ladder splint, or board splint.
2. Use a sling and swathe to support the injured arm.
3. Apply an ice bag or cold compress to the injury site.

Colles's and Smith's Fractures

> **Learning Objective 6** Define Colles's and Smith's fractures and describe the usual mechanism of injury for each.

Both Colles's and Smith's fractures are displaced fractures of the forearm just above the wrist. While they cause the same signs and symptoms, they differ in the mechanism of injury.

- **Colles's fracture** (see Figure 12-6) occurs when the victim falls on the palm of the hand with the wrist extended.

- **Smith's fracture** occurs when the victim falls on the back of the hand with the wrist flexed.

Both injuries are most common in children and adolescents—usually from falls on the playground or during in-line skating or surfboarding—because the growth plate just above the wrist does not fully mature until around the age of 18 and is more prone to fracture.

Figure 12-6. Colles's fracture

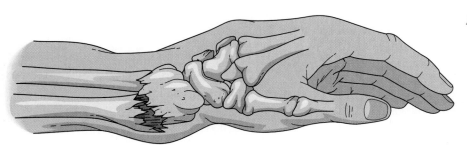

Signs and Symptoms

Both Colles's and Smith's fractures cause

- A classic "silver fork deformity"—a hollow or depression in the lower third of the forearm and a prominence and swelling at the wrist

- Extreme pain

Emergency Care

1. Splint the forearm; if possible, use a Sam splint, ladder splint, or vacuum splint. Immobilize both the wrist and the elbow, but leave the fingers exposed.

2. Because a number of blood vessels pass through the area, check circulation by monitoring the capillary refill in the fingernails.

3. Apply an ice pack or cold compress to the injury site to reduce swelling and pain.

> **Learning Objective 7** Describe the mechanisms of injury that cause fractures to the carpal and metacarpal bones, dislocations of the carpal bones, and fractured or dislocated fingers.

Fracture and Dislocation of the Carpal Bones

In sports and recreation, carpal fracture and dislocation most commonly result from falling on an outstretched, extended hand. The most commonly fractured carpal bone—the navicular—has a limited blood supply and heals very poorly unless promptly and properly treated. Thus, you should never dismiss wrist injury as a simple sprain.

Signs and Symptoms

Both fracture and dislocation may cause swelling, deformity, and tenderness on the back of the wrist. In addition, navicular fracture causes pain and a throbbing sensation in the **anatomical snuffbox** (the area of the wrist through which the radial artery passes) (see Figure 12-7).

Emergency Care

1. If there is no deformity, splint the wrist and hand with an air splint or other appropriate splint.

2. If there is deformity, splint the wrist and hand with a Sam splint, ladder splint, vacuum splint, or other splint that will conform to the shape of the deformity; do not use an air splint if there is deformity.

3. Use an ice pack or cold compress to reduce pain and swelling.

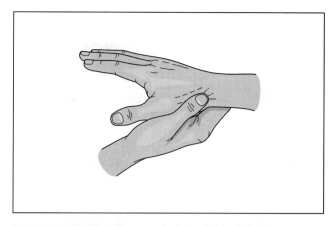

Figure 12-7. The "anatomical snuffbox." Tenderness on palpation is highly suggestive of a fractured navicular.

Metacarpal Fractures

Fractures of the metacarpal bones can occur to the base, neck, or shaft. A "boxer's fracture," or compacted fracture, typically results from a mistimed punch with a closed fist. Other fractures occur from severe twisting or severe hyperextension, such as when a basketball player catches a finger in an opposing player's jersey (see Figure 12-8 on page 212).

Signs and Symptoms

Typical signs and symptoms include

- Pain in the hand (often so mild that the victim insists the injury is only a sprain)

- Swelling of the hand

- Possible twisting of the finger so the nailbed is turned to one side

Emergency Care

1. If there is no gross deformity, splint the hand with an air splint, Sam splint, ladder splint, or vacuum splint; if there is deformity, do not use an air splint. Keep the fingertips exposed.

> **Colles's fracture** A displaced fracture of the forearm caused when the victim falls on the palm of the hand with the wrist extended
>
> **Smith's fracture** A displaced fracture of the forearm caused when the victim falls on the back of the hand with the wrist flexed
>
> **anatomical snuffbox** The area of the wrist through which the radial artery passes

Figure 12-8. Fracture due to hyperextension of a finger

2. Assess for circulation by checking capillary refill every few minutes while you take the patient to a medical facility.

Fractured or Dislocated Fingers

Both fractures and dislocations of the fingers are common; the fingers are the most commonly broken bones in the body. Finger fractures and dislocations occur most often in football and gymnastics when the athlete lands on the hand in an awkward position or when the ball hits the tips of the fingers.

Signs and Symptoms

While dislocations and severe fractures are usually obvious, nondisplaced fractures can cause very little deformity; swelling may or may not occur. Whether or not the victim experiences deformity and swelling, pain is usually severe. The finger may hurt even when it is not being moved. Loss of function doesn't always occur; the victim may be able to move fingers that are broken.

Emergency Care

1. Splint the fingers; if there is little deformity, splint the injured finger to an adjacent uninjured finger (see Figure 12-9).

2. *Never* try to reduce a dislocated finger.

3. Apply an ice pack or cold compress to reduce pain and swelling.

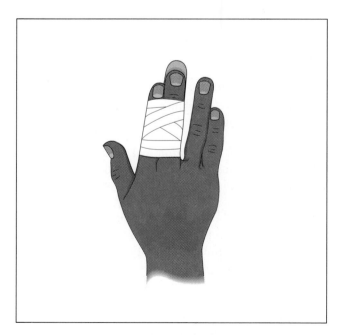

Figure 12-9. Finger splinted to an adjacent uninjured finger

Progress Check

1. If the arm on the injured side appears longer than the one on the other side, suspect _____ of the shoulder.
   (fracture/dislocation/separation)

2. In shoulder fracture or separation, there is generally a lump at the tip of the shoulder; with dislocation, the tip of the shoulder is typically _____.
   (swollen/prominent/flattened)

3. Use slight traction or pulling to immobilize all shoulder injuries other than _____.
   (separation/dislocation/fracture)

4. You should splint an elbow dislocation _____.
   (with the arm straightened/in the position found/with the elbow bent)

5. Do not use a _____ splint on a dislocated elbow.
   (air/Sam/ladder)

6. To assess fractured radial head, have the victim _____.
   (bend the elbow/straighten the elbow/rotate the forearm)

7. In all splints of the forearm, wrist, and/or hand, leave the _____ exposed.
   (elbow/wrist/fingertips)

8. The general emergency care procedure for all injuries to the shoulder, elbow, wrist, and hand is to _____.
   (apply traction/use a sling/immobilize, usually by splinting)

• Section 2 •
INJURIES TO THE HIP, LEG, KNEE, ANKLE, AND FOOT

"Hip Pointer"

A "hip pointer," or bruising of the area over the iliac crest of the pelvis, results from blunt trauma—typically from two athletes colliding or an athlete landing on the hip while diving for a ball.

Signs and Symptoms

Signs and symptoms include

- Inability to bear full weight on the injured side, causing limping
- Tenderness to the touch
- Red discoloration, later turning purple

Emergency Care

Because a fracture needs to be ruled out, the victim should be transported to a medical facility. To relieve pain and reduce swelling until a physician can evaluate the injury, apply an ice pack or cold compress held in place with a roller bandage.

Ischial Tuberosity Fracture

During a sprint or other activity in which the hip is flexed and the leg extended—such as running, jumping, and hurdling—an athlete can suffer an **ischial tuberosity** fracture (an avulsion fracture of the hamstring attachment). This kind of injury is most common in children and adolescents because of the soft growth plate in the hip.

Signs and Symptoms

Ischial tuberosity fracture causes

- Pain in the buttocks where the ischial tuberosity attaches
- Swelling in the buttocks on the affected side
- A lump in the buttocks on the affected side

Emergency Care

1. Use a roller bandage to support the affected buttocks.
2. Apply an ice pack or cold compress to relieve pain and reduce swelling.
3. Because this injury makes it extremely difficult to walk, provide crutches, a stretcher, or other way to transport the victim.

Hamstring Strain

An athlete who flexes the hip and extends the knee can also strain the hamstring (see Figure 12-10 on page 214); unlike an ischial tuberosity fracture, hamstring strain occurs among people of all ages, not just the young.

There are varying degrees of injury; however, a common symptom is tenderness over the injured aspect of the muscle. The more severe the muscle tear, the greater the deformity and the greater the difficulty

ischial tuberosity The spot where the top of the hamstring attaches

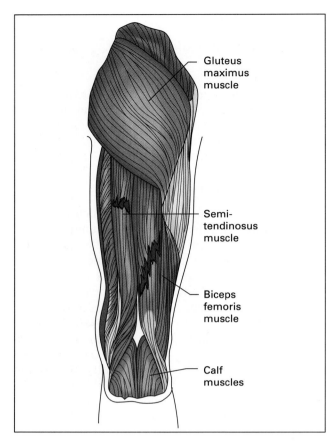

Figure 12-10. Hamstring strain

in bending the leg. Within a few days to a week, the area becomes discolored.

Treat as for ischial tuberosity fracture.

Sprained Knee Ligaments

Any external or internal force that causes the leg to go beyond the normal range of motion can tear a knee ligament (see Figure 12-11). These forces include hyperextension, twisting, and forces that either bow the legs or knock the knees. Depending on the ligament involved, surgical reconstruction may be necessary.

Signs and Symptoms

Signs and symptoms include pain and possible swelling. In some cases, there is an audible "pop" when the injury occurs.

Emergency Care

Learning Objective 9 Describe emergency care for injuries to the hamstring and knee ligaments.

1. Wrap the knee in the most comfortable position with a pillow splint, or immobilize the knee and the bones above and below it with an air splint, vacuum splint, or padded splint.

2. Apply an ice pack or cold compress to relieve pain and reduce swelling.

Dislocated Patella

Learning Objective 10 Describe the signs and symptoms of a dislocated kneecap (patella).

A twisting, hyperextension, or "knock-knee" force can dislocate the **patella** (kneecap), generally to the lat-

Figure 12-11. Valgus knee injury. If a valgus force is applied to the knee while the foot is fixed, a tear of the medial ligamentous structures will occur. If the force is great enough, the anterior cruciate ligament may also be torn as well as the medial meniscus.

eral side of the leg. For example, a tennis player who plants a foot, then twists to reach the ball might suffer this kind of injury. A kneecap that is dislocated can be clearly felt laterally.

In some cases, the knee itself is dislocated, which is considered to be a severe injury. Because of the similarity in signs and symptoms, it can be difficult to tell the difference between a dislocated kneecap and a dislocated knee.

Signs and Symptoms

Signs and symptoms include

- An audible "pop" as the injury occurs

- Extreme pain

- Inability to straighten or extend the injured leg

- Severe swelling

- Lateral dislocation of the kneecap that can be palpated

Emergency Care

A dislocated kneecap or knee needs immediate medical attention; if the injury is untreated for more than 8 hours, the athlete could lose his or her leg. The greatest concern during first aid is for the major artery that runs behind the knee joint: It can be compressed by the patella, cutting off blood flow to the lower leg. To treat:

1. Check the ankle pulse. If it is absent, try once to straighten the knee. *Never try to straighten or extend the knee for any other reason.*

2. Splint the injured leg in the position in which it was found; use a pillow splint, Sam splint, or vacuum splint to immobilize the knee and the bones above and below it, taking care not to push against the patella.

3. Apply an ice pack or cold compress to relieve pain and reduce swelling.

Achilles Tendon Rupture

Learning Objective 11 Describe the emergency care of an achilles tendon rupture.

Most frequently seen in people in their thirties, achilles tendon rupture results from jumping and cutting maneuvers, such as those that typically occur in basketball and tennis.

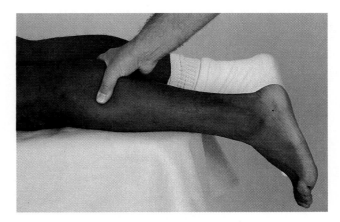

Figure 12-12. Thompsen's test

Signs and Symptoms

The victim may hear an audible "pop" during the injury itself, and may feel as though he or she has been shot in the leg. A partial tear causes only pain and limited range of motion. If the tear is complete, the victim will also have extreme deformity; the tendon may roll up in a ball, or there may be a divot in the muscle. If you squeeze the victim's calf muscle and the foot does not flex (Thompsen's test), the tear is complete (see Figure 12-12).

Emergency Care

1. Splint the affected leg with a lower leg splint.

2. Apply an ice pack or cold compress to the area, and secure it with a roller bandage.

Learning Objective 12 Describe the emergency care of sprains or fractures of the ankle and foot.

Ankle Sprain

Most ankle sprains result from the foot rolling inward (see Figure 12-13 on page 216)—such as when a basketball player comes down on another player's foot. Sprains can also result from the foot rolling outward.

Depending on which way the foot rolled, there will be swelling and pain on one side of the ankle.

To treat, follow the guidelines in Chapter 11 under Sprains.

patella The kneecap

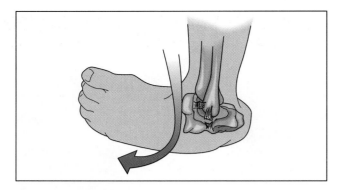

Figure 12-13. Ankle sprain

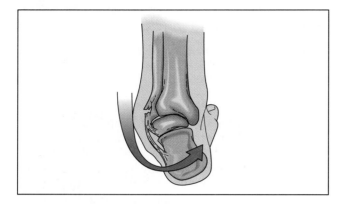

Figure 12-14. Fibula fracture

Fractured Tibia or Fibula

The bones of the lower leg—the tibia and fibula—can be fractured by a direct blow to the leg and by the forces that cause sprained ankle. If the foot rolls outward, the tibia may fracture; if the foot rolls inward, the fibula may fracture (see Figure 12-14).

Signs and Symptoms

Signs and symptoms include

- Swelling, almost always on both sides of the ankle (swelling is usually on one side only if the ankle is sprained instead of fractured)

- Possible deformity over the injured area

- Pain when the bottom of the foot is tapped

Emergency Care

1. If there is no displacement or deformity, immobilize the leg with an air splint; otherwise, use a Sam splint, ladder splint, vacuum splint, or similar splint to immobilize the leg.

2. Apply an ice pack or cold compress to relieve pain and reduce swelling.

• SUMMARY •

- Because it can be difficult to distinguish between fractures and other injuries, victims of the sports injuries discussed in this chapter should always be evaluated by a physician.

- Applying a sling and swathe or an elastic bandage that supplies slight traction is appropriate for a fracture or separation of the shoulder; you should not apply pressure or traction if the shoulder is dislocated.

- Always splint a dislocated joint in the position found.

- Never use an air splint for an injury in which there is deformity, because the air splint forces the limb to conform to its shape. Instead, use a splint that will conform to the deformity.

- Apply ice packs or cold compresses to injuries involving fractures, strains, sprains, dislocations, and separations to relieve pain and reduce swelling. Use a roller bandage to hold the ice pack in place unless there is a dislocation.

- Whenever you splint an arm or leg, leave the tips of the fingers or toes exposed so you can assess circulation by checking capillary refill.

• KEY TERMS •

Make sure you understand the following key terms:

- acromioclavicular joint
- palpable
- tennis elbow
- Colles's fracture
- Smith's fracture
- anatomical snuffbox
- ischial tuberosity
- patella

Student: _____   Date: _____

Course: _____   Section #: _____

PART 1 • True/False

If you believe the statement is true, circle the T. If you believe the statement is false, circle the F.

T   F   **1.** You should provide slight traction or pressure for a dislocated shoulder.

T   F   **2.** The most common victims of dislocated elbow are those who support their weight on their hands, such as wrestlers or gymnasts.

T   F   **3.** The best way to assess fracture of the radial head is to have the victim rotate the forearm.

T   F   **4.** Ischial tuberosity fracture carries with it the classic "silver fork deformity."

T   F   **5.** Dislocation of the carpal bones causes deformity and swelling on the back of the wrist; to treat, immobilize with an air splint.

T   F   **6.** A twisted finger with the nailbed turned to one side is typically the result of metacarpal fracture.

T   F   **7.** You should assess for dislocated elbow by having the victim straighten the arm.

T   F   **8.** A victim may hear an audible "pop" during several different injuries, including dislocated patella and achilles tendon rupture.

T   F   **9.** The force that causes a sprained ankle can also fracture the bones of the lower leg.

PART 2 • Multiple Choice

For each item, circle the correct answer or the phrase that best completes the statement.

1. A shoulder that appears almost flattened is an indication of
   a. fracture
   b. dislocation
   c. separation
   d. strain

2. A classic sign of a dislocated elbow is
   a. a shortened forearm
   b. pain while rotating the forearm
   c. compromised pulse at the wrist
   d. lack of swelling

3. The classic sign of Colles's fracture is
   a. compromised pulse at the wrist
   b. a golf-ball-sized lump on the back of the elbow
   c. the "silver fork deformity"
   d. inability to straighten the leg

4. Care for dislocated carpal bones by
   a. immobilizing with a ladder or vacuum splint
   b. immobilizing with an air splint
   c. reducing the dislocation
   d. none of the above

5. Swelling, pain, and a lump in the buttocks of a sprinter would probably indicate
   a. hamstring strain
   b. gluteus maximus strain
   c. contusion of the iliac crest
   d. ischial tuberosity fracture

6. To treat a dislocated patella
   a. splint in the position in which the leg was found
   b. use a pillow splint or vacuum splint
   c. apply ice packs or cold compresses
   d. all of the above

7. Splint a victim of a sprained knee ligament
   a. in the position in which the leg was found
   b. with the leg straightened
   c. with the knee flexed
   d. in the most comfortable position

8. To assess whether achilles tendon rupture is complete, squeeze the victim's calf muscle; if the rupture is complete,
   a. squeezing the muscle will cause severe pain
   b. you will hear a "pop"
   c. the foot will not flex
   d. there will be limited range of motion

Match the injury with the appropriate treatment.

Emergency Care

A. Immobilize in the position found
B. Use immobilization that provides slight traction on the injury site
C. Splint against the adjacent one
D. Use a combination of a splint and a sling

Injury

_____ Fractured clavicle
_____ Finger fracture with little deformity
_____ Radial head fracture
_____ Shoulder dislocation

- During an attempted tackle, a defensive lineman rams his helmet into the quarterback's hip. The quarterback limps from the field, but insists his leg is not broken.
- A 20-year-old woman competing in a triathalon skids in the gravel rounding a curve and catapults over the handlebars of her bicycle, falling on her outstretched hand. There is only mild deformity and slight swelling over the lateral side of the elbow.

    What injury would you suspect? How would you assess it? If your hunch proved right, how would you care for the woman?

Head and Spine Injuries

Learning Objectives

When you have mastered the material in this chapter, you will be able to

1 Describe the appropriate emergency care for injury to the scalp

2 Describe the physiology of injury to the brain

3 List the four types of skull fracture

4 Describe appropriate assessment for victims of head injury

5 List the signs and symptoms of skull fracture

6 Distinguish between open and closed head injury

7 Discuss the signs and symptoms of both open and closed head injury

8 Describe and demonstrate the appropriate emergency care for head injury

9 Describe the common mechanisms of spinal injury

10 Describe the assessment of spinal injury victims

11 List the signs and symptoms of spinal injury

12 Describe and demonstrate the appropriate emergency care for spinal injury

13 Describe the technique for removing a helmet from a head- or spinal-injured victim

SQ3R Plus

- **Survey** to set goals for studying.
- Ask **questions** as you **read.**
- Stop frequently to **recite** and **review.**
- **Write** a summary of key points.
- **Reflect** on the importance of this material and its relevance in your life.

*O*n June 30, 1998, Fred Hansen and two of his colleagues from a local software company stopped by the community swimming pool to discuss some software needs with the city's recreation director. As they got out of the car, they saw a group of people gathered around an adolescent boy, who was lying still at the pool edge.

Fred and the other two men ran toward the group and asked what happened. "My friend was doing some dives off that board," said 13-year-old Mark Welling. "I think he hit his head on the bottom of the pool. Jake and I pulled him out."

Fourteen-year-old Lance Colledge was unconscious, but he was breathing and had a pulse. Fred immediately suspected cervical spine injury. The lifeguard on duty had already called for an ambulance.

Fred grabbed a beach towel from a bystander; rolling it, he improvised a "collar" that would stabilize Lance's neck. As his colleague placed both hands on Lance's head and maintained it in a neutral position, Fred tucked the towel gently around Lance's neck, placing it firmly against both his chin and his collarbone.

By the time EMTs arrived, Fred had immobilized Lance's neck with the rolled towel and had covered him with a thick terrycloth robe to preserve his body heat and prevent shock.

HALF A MILLION AMERICANS SUFFER HEAD INJURIES every year (see Figure 13-1); head injury is second only to stroke as a cause of major neurological trauma. While head injury constitutes only a small percentage of all injuries, it causes more than half of all fatalities from injuries.

Any trauma severe enough to cause injury to the head—including a simple fall—can also cause injury to the spine. Spinal injury can also result from any force that pushes the spine beyond its normal weight-bearing ability or its normal limits of motion. Spinal cord injuries are some of the most formidable and traumatic injuries you will face: spinal cord injury affects most other organ systems, and improper handling may kill the victim.

This chapter outlines the specific assessment skills needed to evaluate victims of suspected head and spinal injuries and details the emergency care procedures that will enable you to prevent further injury for such victims.

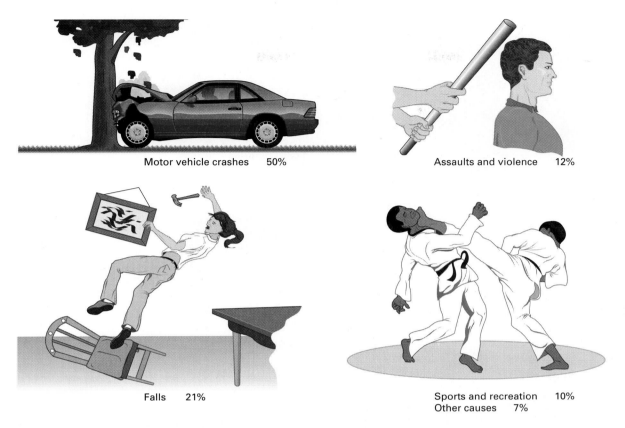

Motor vehicle crashes   50%

Assaults and violence   12%

Falls   21%

Sports and recreation   10%
Other causes   7%

Figure 13-1. Causes of head injuries

• Section 1 •
TYPES OF HEAD INJURY

The brain is enclosed in the skull—a rigid, unyielding case. If the brain tissue swells or bleeding occurs within the skull following injury, resulting pressure on the brain compromises brain function. Unrelieved, the pressure can cause death.

Head injuries can involve either injury to the scalp or injury to the brain itself.

Injury to the Scalp

Learning Objective 1 Describe the appropriate emergency care for injury to the scalp.

The scalp may be injured in the same way as any other soft tissue—it may be contused, lacerated, abraded, or avulsed.

Because of the rich supply of blood vessels to the scalp, injuries of the scalp tend to bleed very heavily. In addition, the underlying fascia may be torn even when the skin stays intact; bleeding then occurs under the skin and may be confusing at first as you try to as-

sess the victim. (The presence of blood under intact skin can mimic a depressed skull fracture.)

To control bleeding of a scalp injury, slightly elevate the head and shoulders and apply gentle direct pressure with a dry sterile dressing, as with other soft-tissue injuries. Do not apply pressure directly over the area if you suspect skull fracture; doing so can drive bone fragments into the brain tissue. Instead, apply pressure over a broad area or around the edges of the wound. If an object is impaled in the scalp, do not remove the impaled object; stabilize it with bulky dressings as described in Chapter 8.

Injury to the Brain

Learning Objective 2 Describe the physiology of injury to the brain.

Most brain injury (see Figure 13-2 on page 222) is caused by trauma, most often in a motor vehicle accident or fall. Brain injury may also be secondary—the brain can be injured as a result of an injury to another body system (changes in blood pressure, for example, can affect perfusion of the brain). Because of the relatively large size of their heads and weakness

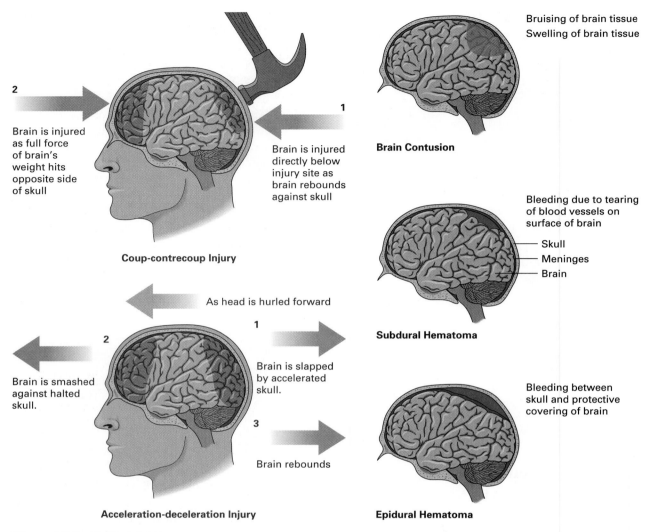

Figure 13-2. Brain injuries

of their necks, children are especially vulnerable to brain injury. One of the most common types of injury is **coup-contrecoup,** a type of acceleration-deceleration injury—the head comes to a sudden stop, but the brain continues to move back and forth inside the skull, resulting in massive injury. There are actually two sites of injury: the point of impact, and the point on the opposite side where the brain hits the skull.

When the brain is injured, blood vessels in the brain dilate so that more blood can flow to the injured area. If that fails, the blood vessels undergo further changes that cause fluid to leak into the affected area. As a result, the brain is diluted with water, which lowers the level of carbon dioxide in the brain.

When such leakage occurs, swelling results; there is less space inside the skull for the blood and cerebrospinal fluid. At first, the brain compensates—it stops producing cerebrospinal fluid, absorbs existing fluid

more rapidly, and decreases the amount of blood it receives from the circulatory system. However, that process can only go so far. Eventually, pressure within the skull rises, and blood flow throughout the brain becomes inadequate. The brain stem can become compressed by swelling of the rest of the brain, affecting heart and lung function. When heart and lung functions are diminished, the brain cannot function normally.

Some brain injury occurs in the absence of trauma. Clots or hemorrhaging (such as the bleeding that occurs with stroke) can cause brain injury through much the same process described above.

coup-contrecoup A mechanism of brain injury in which the head comes to a sudden stop but the brain continues to move back and forth inside the skull

Signs and Symptoms of Brain Injury

Signs and symptoms may not occur immediately following brain injury; they become obvious as the brain swells inside the skull, which may take as long as 18 hours (see Figure 13-3 on page 224). Signs of increased pressure inside the skull include

- Altered responsiveness; the victim is no longer alert, and may respond only to verbal stimuli or pain.
- Combativeness and erratic behavior
- Nausea and/or vomiting
- Pupils that are not equal or reactive to light; "doll's eyes" (eyes do not move together when the victim turns his or her head to the side)
- Double vision or other visual disturbances
- Headache, sometimes severe
- Loss of memory, confusion, or disorientation
- Weakness or loss of balance
- Seizures

Emergency Care for Brain Injury

Any victim with suspected brain injury needs *immediate* medical attention; as mentioned above, continued swelling of the brain can compress the brain stem, affecting breathing and heart function. First Aiders really can't do anything to stop the swelling or to treat brain injury; the goal of first aid is to support the victim until medical help arrives. To treat:

1. Suspect spine injury in any victim with suspected brain injury; stabilize the head and neck as described later in this chapter.
2. Monitor the victim's ABCDs; the victim may need help breathing.
3. Anticipate vomiting; be prepared to keep the victim's head and neck stabilized as you roll the victim on his or her side to prevent aspiration.
4. Treat the victim for shock; keep the victim warm, but *do not elevate the legs.*

Injury to the Skull (Skull Fracture)

Learning Objective 3 List the four types of skull fracture.

Because of the skull's shape (spherical) and its thickness (approximately ¼ inch), it is generally fractured only if the trauma is extreme. Skull fracture itself presents no danger unless accompanied by brain injury, hematoma, cerebrospinal fluid leakage, or subsequent infection.

There are four basic types of skull fracture (see Figure 13-4 on page 225):

1. Depressed—An object strikes the skull, leaving an obvious depression or deformity; bone fragments are often driven into the membranes or the brain itself by the force of the impact.
2. Linear—The most common type of skull fracture, linear causes a thin-line crack in the skull. Linear fractures are the least serious and the most difficult to detect.
3. Comminuted—A comminuted fracture appears at the point of impact, with multiple cracks radiating from the center (it looks like a cracked eggshell).
4. Basal—A basal skull fracture occurs when there is a break in the bed of the skull; it is often the result of a linear fracture that extends to the floor of the skull. Difficult to detect even by X-ray, a basal skull fracture often causes extensive damage.

Progress Check

1. Bleeding from a scalp laceration, as from any other soft-tissue injury, is best controlled with _____ . *(direct pressure/indirect pressure/compression bandages)*
2. Coup-contrecoup injury occurs when the head suddenly stops but the brain _____ . *(begins bleeding/keeps moving/leaks fluid)*
3. The basic physiology of brain injury occurs when brain tissue _____ . *(bleeds/leaks fluid/swells)*
4. _____ skull fracture occurs when an object strikes the skull and leaves an obvious deformity. *(Depressed/Linear/Comminuted)*
5. _____ skull fracture resembles a cracked egg. *(Linear/Comminuted/Depressed)*
6. _____ skull fracture is the most common. *(Comminuted/Linear/Basal)*

• Section 2 •
ASSESSMENT, SIGNS, AND SYMPTOMS OF HEAD INJURY

Victim Assessment

Learning Objective 4 Describe appropriate assessment for victims of head injury.

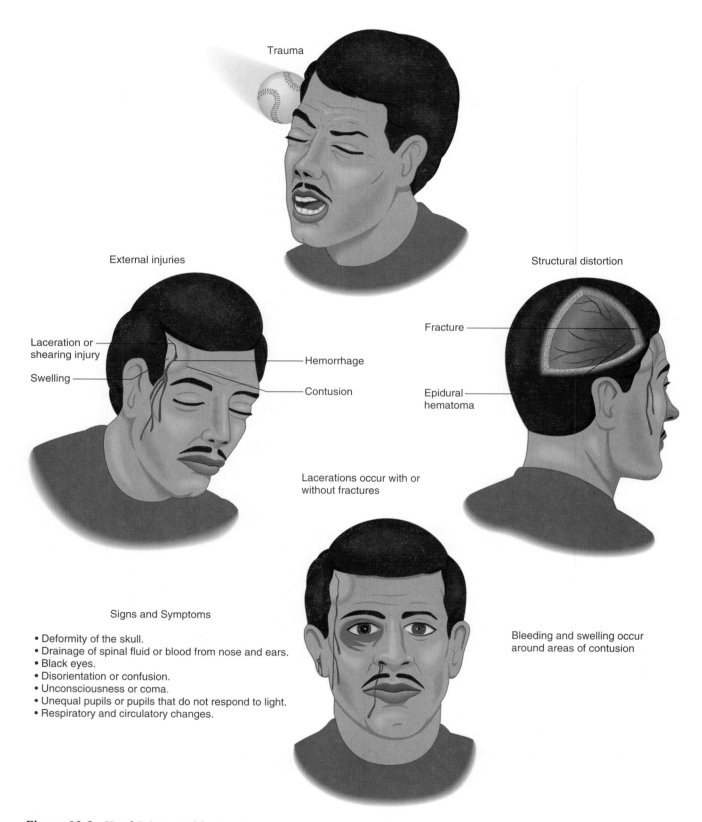

Trauma

External injuries

Laceration or shearing injury

Swelling

Hemorrhage

Contusion

Structural distortion

Fracture

Epidural hematoma

Lacerations occur with or without fractures

Signs and Symptoms

- Deformity of the skull.
- Drainage of spinal fluid or blood from nose and ears.
- Black eyes.
- Disorientation or confusion.
- Unconsciousness or coma.
- Unequal pupils or pupils that do not respond to light.
- Respiratory and circulatory changes.

Bleeding and swelling occur around areas of contusion

Figure 13-3. *Head injury and brain trauma*

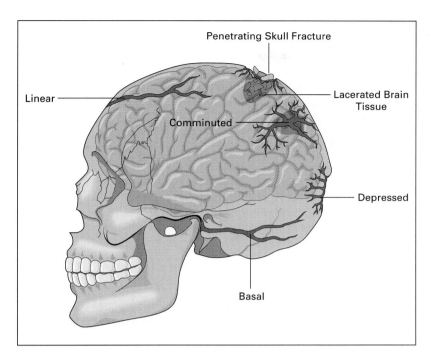

Figure 13-4. Types of skull fracture

To assess a victim of head injury:

1. Obtain a history that includes the mechanism of injury, whether the victim's level of conscious-ness has changed, and whether the victim has been moved.

2. Complete a primary survey to detect and correct any life-threatening problems. Use the modified jaw-thrust maneuver to open the airway and pro-vide artificial ventilation if needed; the most seri-ous complication of head injury is lack of oxygen to the brain. Immobilization of a spinal injury can wait, *but there must be absolutely no movement of the victim until the victim is immobilized.*

3. Check the head (see Figure 13-5); look for depres-sions, fractures, lacerations, deformities, bruising, and other obvious problems. Determine whether the pupils are equal and react to light, whether the face is symmetrical on both sides, and whether blood or fluid is dripping from the nose, ears, or mouth. *Never palpate a wound, probe a wound to determine its depth, separate the edges of a wound to explore it, or remove impaled objects.*

4. Maintaining light in-line stabilization, check the neck and spine for lacerations, bruises, swelling, protrusions, spaces, or other obvious deformities; ask the victim if there is tenderness, pain, or mus-cle spasm.

5. Check the arms and legs for paralysis or loss of sensation.

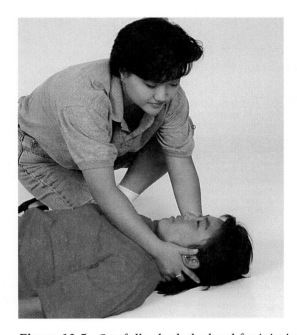

Figure 13-5. Carefully check the head for injuries.

Signs and Symptoms of Skull Fracture

Learning Objective 5 List the signs and symptoms of skull fracture.

You should suspect skull fracture with any significant trauma to the head; the mechanism of injury will tell

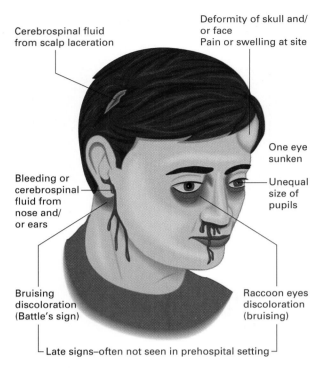

Cerebrospinal fluid from scalp laceration

Deformity of skull and/ or face
Pain or swelling at site

One eye sunken

Unequal size of pupils

Bleeding or cerebrospinal fluid from nose and/ or ears

Bruising discoloration (Battle's sign)

Raccoon eyes discoloration (bruising)

Late signs–often not seen in prehospital setting

Figure 13-6. Signs and symptoms of skull fracture

how much force was exerted. Skull fracture can cause the following signs and symptoms (see Figure 13-6)

- Contusions, lacerations, or hematomas to the scalp
- Deformity of the skull
- Blood or cerebrospinal fluid (clear, pinkish fluid) leaking from the ears, nose, mouth, or a wound in the scalp
- Bruising around the eyes in the absence of trauma to the eyes (**raccoon eyes**)
- Bruising behind the ears, or mastoid process (**Battle's sign**)
- Damage to the skull visible through lacerations in the scalp
- Pain, tenderness, or swelling at the site of injury

Cerebrospinal fluid in blood can, but does not always, form a characteristic "targeting" pattern when the blood drips onto a sheet, pillowcase, or sponge; a double ring may rapidly form as the fluid migrates out of the blood.

Closed and Open Head Injuries

Learning Objective 6 Distinguish between open and closed head injury.

Injuries to the head can be open or closed. In closed head injuries, the scalp may be lacerated, but the skull is not exposed and there is no opening to the brain. Brain damage, however, can nonetheless be extensive. In general, brain tissue is susceptible to the same kinds of injury as any soft tissue—contusion, laceration, and puncture wounds—even when the skull is not exposed.

An open head injury is accompanied by a break in the skull, such as that caused by fracture or an impaled object. It involves direct local damage to the involved tissue, but can also cause brain damage due to infection, laceration of the brain tissue, or puncture of the brain by objects that penetrate the skull.

Signs and Symptoms of Closed and Open Head Injuries

Learning Objective 7 Discuss the signs and symptoms of both open and closed head injury.

The following are general signs and symptoms of closed head injury:

- Altered or decreasing mental status—the best indicator of a brain injury; a conscious victim may be confused, disoriented, or suffering from deteriorating mental status.
- Unresponsiveness
- Irregular breathing pattern
- Obvious signs of a mechanism of injury—contusions, lacerations, or hematomas to the scalp or deformity to the skull
- Blood or cerebrospinal fluid leaking from the ears or nose
- Bruising around the eyes in the absence of trauma to the eyes (raccoon eyes)
- Bruising behind the ears, or mastoid process (Battle's sign)
- Neurologic disability
- Nausea and/or vomiting; vomiting may be forceful or repeated
- Unequal pupil size with altered mental status
- Possible seizures

The following are general signs and symptoms of open head injury (see Figure 13-7):

- Obvious results of the mechanism of injury—contusions, lacerations, or hematomas to the scalp; deformity to the skull; or obvious penetrating injury
- A soft area or depression detected during palpation
- Brain tissue exposed through an open wound

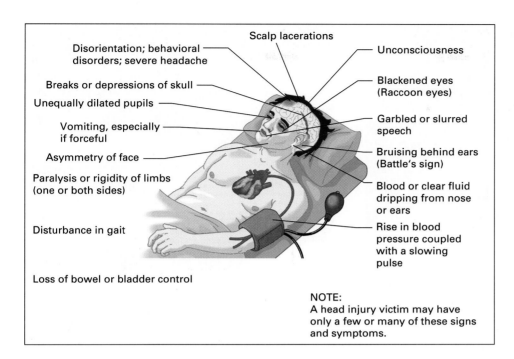

Disorientation; behavioral disorders; severe headache

Scalp lacerations

Unconsciousness

Breaks or depressions of skull

Blackened eyes (Raccoon eyes)

Unequally dilated pupils

Garbled or slurred speech

Vomiting, especially if forceful

Bruising behind ears (Battle's sign)

Asymmetry of face

Blood or clear fluid dripping from nose or ears

Paralysis or rigidity of limbs (one or both sides)

Rise in blood pressure coupled with a slowing pulse

Disturbance in gait

Loss of bowel or bladder control

NOTE:
A head injury victim may have only a few or many of these signs and symptoms.

Figure 13-7. Signs and symptoms of head injury

- Bleeding from an open bone injury
- Blood or cerebrospinal fluid leaking from the ears, nose, mouth, or a scalp wound
- Bruising around the eyes in the absence of trauma to the eyes (raccoon eyes)
- Bruising behind the ears, or the mastoid process (Battle's sign)
- Nausea and/or vomiting, often forceful or repeated

Progress Check

1. The most serious complication of head injury is _____ to the brain.
   (contusion/laceration/lack of oxygen)

2. During assessment, check for scalp and skull wounds by _____ .
   (visually examining/probing/separating the edges of the wound)

3. During assessment, check the arms and legs for paralysis and _____ .
   (pulse/fractures/loss of sensation)

4. In closed head injury, the _____ is not broken.
   (scalp/skull/fascia)

5. Raccoon eyes, a classic sign of skull fracture, involves bruising around the _____ .
   (ears/eyes/mastoid process)

6. Head injury is indicated by blood or _____ dripping from the ears, nose, or mouth.
   (lymph fluid/cerebrospinal fluid/mucus)

• Section 3 •
EMERGENCY CARE FOR HEAD INJURY

Learning Objective 8 Describe and demonstrate the appropriate emergency care for head injury.

Before beginning any emergency care for head injury, assess the victim's level of consciousness. Any victim who loses consciousness, even briefly, must be evaluated at an emergency room. A victim who worsens needs immediate transport and continuous monitoring during transport.

Whenever you care for a victim of head injury (see Figures 13-8 and 13-9 on page 228), always as-

raccoon eyes Bruising around the eyes in the absence of trauma to the eyes; a sign of skull fracture

Battle's sign Bruising behind the ears (mastoid process); a sign of skull fracture

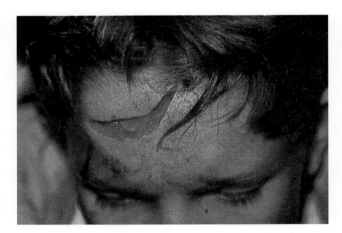

Figure 13-8. Always suspect and assess for spinal injury in a head-injured victim.

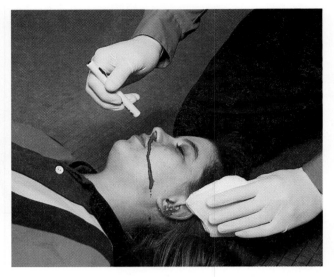

Figure 13-10. Blood and/or cerebrospinal fluid may come from the ears and/or nose of a victim of head injury. Cover lightly with dressing. Do not block drainage.

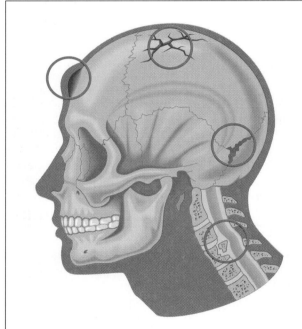

REMEMBER: Take spinal injury precautions in all cases of head trauma, as well as all cases of multiple trauma involving unconsciousness, particularly if resuscitative measures are required at the accident site.

Figure 13-9. Always take spinal injury precautions in case of injury to the head.

sume that neck and/or spinal injury also exist. Activate the EMS system; then:

1. The top priority is establishing and maintaining an open airway with adequate oxygenation. Use the modified jaw-thrust technique to open the airway, maintain neutral positioning of the head and neck, remove any foreign bodies from the mouth, and provide rescue breathing if needed.

    Closely monitor the airway, breathing, pulse, and mental status for deterioration; *any victim who worsens must be transported immediately.* A victim of head injury usually vomits, so position the victim to keep the airway clear.

2. Control bleeding; face and scalp wounds may bleed heavily, but such bleeding is usually easy to control with pressure.

    • Do not apply pressure to an open or depressed skull injury.

    • Dress and bandage open head wounds as indicated in the discussion of treatment of soft-tissue injuries (see Chapter 7).

    • Keep the victim's head and shoulders slightly elevated to control bleeding and pressure.

    • Do not attempt to stop the flow of blood or cerebrospinal fluid from the ears or nose (see Figure 13-10); instead, cover loosely with a completely sterile gauze dressing to absorb, but not stop, the flow.

3. Never try to remove a penetrating object; instead:

    • Immobilize it with soft, bulky dressings and dress the wound with sterile dressings.

    • If the object is too long to allow for victim transport, it will need to be stabilized and cut; wait for the arrival of emergency personnel.

4. If the victim sustained a medical or nontraumatic injury, place the victim on the left side; keep the victim warm, but avoid overheating.

5. If the victim gets too warm, sponge the victim with cool water or place a cool compress on the forehead.

6. While waiting for emergency personnel to arrive:

   • Dress any facial and scalp wounds that have not been dressed.

   • Continue to monitor vital signs.

   • Stay alert to the possibility of vomiting or seizures; work quickly to prevent aspiration.

   • Continually monitor the airway and the victim's neurological status.

Progress Check

1. The top priority in treating victims of head injury is establishing and maintaining _____ .
   (an open airway/circulation/hemorrhage control)

2. Use the modified _____ technique to open the airway.
   (head-tilt/chin-lift/jaw-thrust)

3. If there is blood or fluid dripping from the ear,

   _____ .
   (control it with pressure/pack the ear with gauze/cover the ear loosely with gauze to absorb the flow)

4. If you suspect fracture beneath a bleeding scalp wound, _____ .
   (do not apply pressure/apply pressure/use a compression bandage)

5. _____ any object protruding from the head.
   (Remove/Cut off/Stabilize and leave in place)

• **Section 4** •

INJURIES TO THE SPINE

The spine consists of a column of hollow vertebrae; the spinal cord, which controls many of the nervous functions of the body, passes through the channel formed by the hollow spaces. Injury to the spine can pinch or sever the spinal cord, resulting in permanent damage and disability.

The four top causes of spinal cord injury, in order, are car accidents, shallow-water swimming/diving accidents, motorcycle accidents, and other injuries and falls. Many sports—including diving/swimming, skiing, sledding, and football—cause accidents that lead to spinal damage.

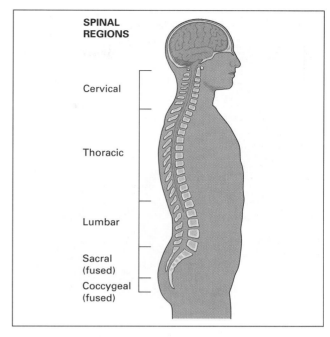

Figure 13-11. *Regions of the spine*

Some parts of the spine are far more susceptible to injury than others (see Figure 13-11 for spinal regions). Half of all spinal injuries occur in the neck, and half of those result in complete paralysis. Fewer injuries involve the thoracic vertebrae or the sacral and coccygeal vertebrae, which have little movement but are designed to bear weight (see Chapter 2).

Mechanisms of Injury

Learning Objective 9 Describe the common mechanisms of spinal injury.

The basic mechanisms that cause spinal injury (see Figure 13-12 on page 230) include

• Compression (the weight of the body is driven against the head, as in falls)

• Excessive flexion, extension, or rotation

• Lateral bending

• **Distraction** (a sudden "pulling apart" of the spine that stretches and tears the spinal cord, as in hangings)

---

distraction The sudden pulling apart of the spine that stretches and tears the cord, as in hanging

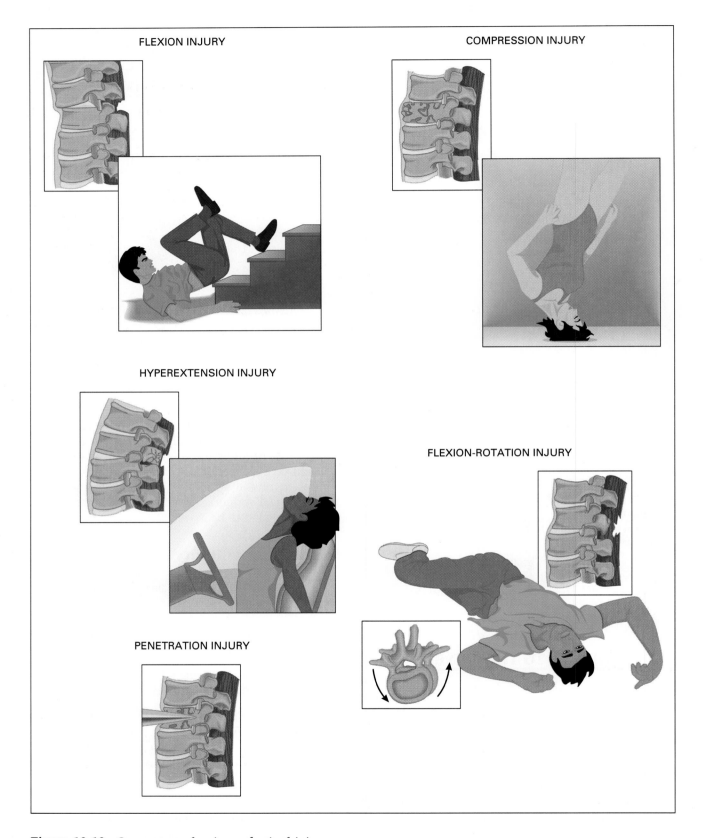

Figure 13-12. *Common mechanisms of spinal injury*

In addition, bony spinal injuries occur when fragments of bone or pieces of disc injure the spinal cord. Spinal cord injuries in the absence of fractures are always a possibility in cases involving penetrating objects and in any instance of sudden, unexplained loss of consciousness.

You should suspect spinal injury in the following situations:

- Motor vehicle accidents
- Pedestrian-vehicle accidents
- Falls (even from a standing position to the ground)
- Blunt trauma
- Penetrating trauma to the head, neck, or torso
- Motorcycle accidents
- Hangings
- Diving accidents (especially in shallow water)
- Unwitnessed near-drownings
- Sports injury accidents that cause damage to helmets

- Violent injuries, assaults, and shootings
- Unconscious accident victims

Complications of Spinal Injury

There are two major complications of spinal injury (see Figure 13-13):

Inadequate breathing effort. Respiratory paralysis may occur with cervical spine injury, and death may occur rapidly if respiratory assistance is delayed. The diaphragm may continue to function even if the chest wall muscles are paralyzed; a victim who is breathing with the diaphragm alone will have shallow breathing with little movement of the chest or abdomen.

Paralysis. There is usually weakness, loss of sensation, or paralysis below the level of injury. In the conscious victim, paralysis of the arms or legs is considered the most reliable sign of spinal injury.

NOTE:
Persons with neck injuries may have paralyzed chest muscles and damage to nerves affecting size of blood vessels. Breathing can then be accomplished only by the diaphragm. Inadequate breathing and shock may occur.

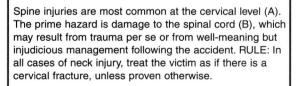

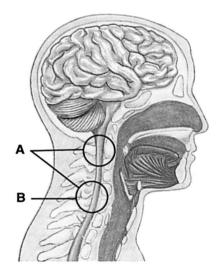 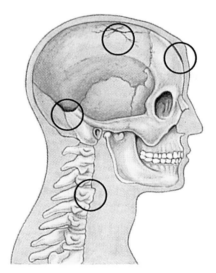

Spine injuries are most common at the cervical level (A). The prime hazard is damage to the spinal cord (B), which may result from trauma per se or from well-meaning but injudicious management following the accident. RULE: In all cases of neck injury, treat the victim as if there is a cervical fracture, unless proven otherwise.

REMEMBER: Take spinal injury precautions in all cases of head trauma, as well as all cases of multiple trauma involving unconsciousness, particularly if resuscitative measures are required at the accident site.

Figure 13-13. Considerations in cervical spine injury

Victim Assessment

Learning Objective 10 Describe the assessment of spinal injury victims.

Caution: The extent of assessment should be based on the level of training the First Aider has had under the direction of a qualified and certified instructor.

To assess a responsive victim:

1. Note the mechanism of injury—especially the type of movement and amount of force that was involved in the injury. Even if a victim can move or walk around, spinal injury may exist—so always suspect spinal injury if the mechanism of injury suggests it.

2. Ask:
   - Does your neck or back hurt? Pain from a spinal injury often radiates from the neck to the arms, from the upper back to the ribs, and from the lower back to the legs—so pain may not be confined to the neck or back.
   - What happened?
   - Where does it hurt?
   - Can you move your hands and feet?
   - Can you feel me touching your fingers?
   - Can you feel me touching your toes?

3. Inspect the back for contusions, deformities, lacerations, punctures, penetrations, and swelling. If necessary, cut clothing away so you can see the area clearly (see Figures 13-14 through 13-22).

4. Palpate gently for areas of tenderness or deformity.

5. Assess equality of strength in the victim's extremities:
   - Have the victim grip and squeeze both your hands; note differences in strength.
   - Have the victim gently push his or her feet against your hands; note strength and equality.

To assess an unresponsive victim:

1. Note the mechanism of injury. If the mechanism of injury suggests spinal injury and the victim is unconscious, assume spinal injury has occurred.

2. Inspect for contusions, deformities, lacerations, punctures, penetrations, or swelling; palpate for areas of deformity.

3. Ask others at the scene about the mechanism of injury and the victim's mental status before you arrived on the scene.

Progress Check

1. The vertebrae most likely to be injured are the

   _____ .
   (thoracic/lumbar/cervical)

2. One mechanism of spinal injury is distraction, or _____ of the vertebrae.
   (compression/pulling apart/rotation)

3. The first step in assessment of spinal injury victims is to note the _____ .
   (level of consciousness/loss of motor function/mechanism of injury)

4. If the victim is _____ and the mechanism of injury suggests it, suspect spinal injury.
   (paralyzed/unconscious/in pain)

• **Section 5** •

SIGNS AND SYMPTOMS
OF SPINAL INJURY

Learning Objective 11 List the signs and symptoms of spinal injury.

Suspect spinal injury with any serious injury, even injuries to the arms and legs; spinal injury often accompanies head, neck, and back injuries.

Remember that a fracture of one spot on the spine is usually associated with a fracture in other areas of the spine. Remember, too, that the ability to walk, move the arms and legs, feel sensation, or the lack of pain to the spinal column does not rule out the possibility of spinal column or spinal cord damage.

The general signs and symptoms of spinal injury include the following (see Figure 13-23 on page 234):

- Tenderness in the area of the injury; lacerations, cuts, punctures, or bruises over or around the spine indicate forceful injury.

- Pain associated with movement; suspect spinal injury if the victim complains of pain when moving an apparently uninjured neck, shoulder, or leg. Pain from spinal injury may be localized, and the victim may be able to indicate exactly where it hurts. *Never ask the victim to move, never allow the victim to move, and never move the victim yourself to test for pain*; base your assessment on any movement that occurred before you arrived on the scene.

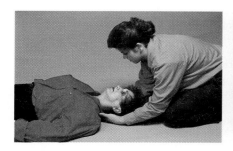

Figure 13-14. *Assess for cervical tenderness and deformity.*

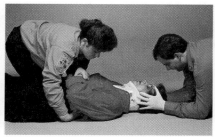

Figure 13-15. *Assess for spinal column tenderness and deformity.*

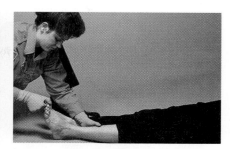

Figure 13-16. *Use the toe touch to assess for sensation.*

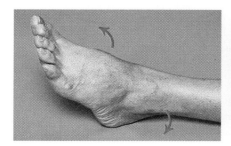

Figure 13-17. *Use the foot wave to see if the feet and toes move.*

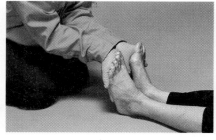

Figure 13-18. *Use the foot push to assess for strength.*

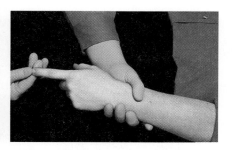

Figure 13-19. *Use the finger touch to assess for sensation.*

Figure 13-20. *Use the hand wave to see if the hands and fingers move.*

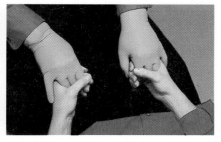

Figure 13-21. *Use the hand squeeze to assess for strength.*

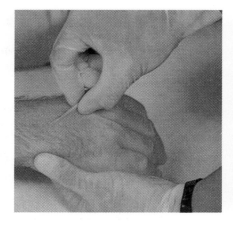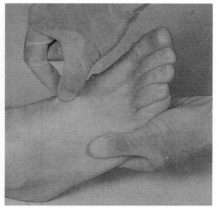

Figure 13-22. *An unconscious patient may respond to painful stimuli.*

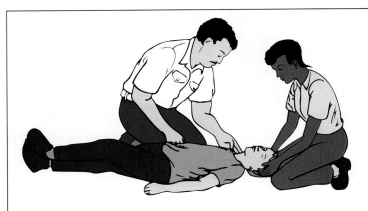

STEPS FOR CHECKING SIGNS AND SYMPTOMS

PAIN. The victim may be aware of unprovoked pain in the area of injury.

TENDERNESS. Gently touching the suspected area may result in increased pain.

DEFORMITY. Deformity is rare although there may be an abnormal bend or bony prominence.

CUTS AND BRUISES. Victims with neck fractures may have cuts and bruises on the head, or face. Victims with injuries in other areas of the spine will have bruises on the shoulders, back, or abdomen.

PARALYSIS. If the victim is unable to move or feels no sensation in some part of his body, he may have a spinal fracture, with cord injury.

PAINFUL MOVEMENT. If the victim tries to move, the pain may increase – never try to move the injured area for the victim.

CONSCIOUS VICTIMS	UNCONSCIOUS VICTIMS
■ Ask: What happened? Where does it hurt? Can you move your hands and feet? Can you feel me touching your hands (feet)? Can you raise your legs and arms?	■ Assess for breathing.
■ Look: for bruises, cuts, deformities.	■ Look: for cuts, bruises, deformities.
■ Feel: for areas of tenderness, deformity, abnormal sensation.	■ Feel: for deformities, sensation.
■ The victim's strength can be determined by having him squeeze the rescuer's hand or by checking pressure against the foot.	■ Ask others: What happened?
	■ Probe the soles of the feet, then the palms of the hands with a sharp object to check for response.

Figure 13-23. *Signs of possible spinal cord injury*

- Pain independent of movement or palpation along the spinal column or in the lower legs. Such pain is generally intermittent instead of constant, and it may occur anywhere along the spine between the top of the head and the tops of the legs. If the lower spinal column or cord is injured, the victim may feel pain in the legs.

- Obvious deformity of the spine upon palpation (not a usual sign). Never have the victim remove clothing so you can examine the back, because the movement may aggravate any existing injury. If necessary, cut clothing away.

- Soft-tissue injuries associated with trauma in the head and neck (causing cervical spine injury); shoulders, back, or abdomen (causing thoracic or lumbar injury); or the legs (causing lumbar or sacral injury)

- Numbness, weakness, or tingling in the arms or legs

- Loss of sensation or paralysis in the arms or legs. (Paralysis of the arms or legs is considered the most reliable sign of spinal injury.)

- Urinary or fecal incontinence

- Impaired breathing, especially breathing that involves little or no chest movement and only slight abdominal movement (an indication that the victim is breathing with the diaphragm alone)

Progress Check

1. The ability to walk or move the arms and legs does not rule out _____ .
   (priapism/deformity/spinal injury)

2. The most reliable sign of spinal injury in a conscious victim is _____ .
   (priapism/incontinence/paralysis of the extremities)

3. Breathing that involves little or no chest movement indicates that the victim is breathing with only the _____ .
   (abdomen/diaphragm/mouth)

Always activate the EMS system first. Take every precaution against converting a spinal injury into cord damage. In vehicular accidents immobilize cervical spine (using spine board, cervical collar, rolled blanket, etc.) before removing victim. Advise the conscious victim not to move the head. A helmet should be removed unless there is difficulty in removing it. *Follow local protocol.* In such cases, immobilize victim on spine board with helmet in place.

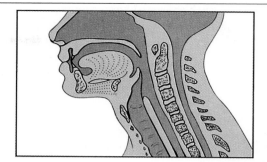

Is the victim experiencing respiratory difficulty? Remember that the airway has first priority. If resuscitative measures are indicated, support the head, immobilize the neck, and get help to move the victim to a flat surface. Check the mouth for obstruction (dentures, tongue, etc.), and ventilate, taking care to minimize motion of the neck. Control severe bleeding by direct pressure. If necessary, initiate CPR.

Keep in mind that respiratory paralysis may occur with cervical spine injury and that death may occur rapidly if respiratory assistance is delayed. Unless it is necessary to change a victim's position to maintain an open airway or for some other compelling reason, it is best to splint the neck or back in the original position of deformity.

Be alert for shock and vomiting. If necessary, administer artificial ventilation.

Immobilize victim before moving. As soon as possible, transfer to a firm stretcher or spine board and restrict head movement with tape, sandbags, collar, rolled towels, and/or blankets.

Provide emotional support.

Always support the head in neutral alignment with body. Avoid flexion, extension, lateral movement, rotation, and traction.

Figure 13-24. *Emergency care for suspected spinal injury*

• Section 6 •
EMERGENCY CARE FOR SPINAL INJURY

> **Learning Objective 12** Describe and demonstrate the appropriate emergency care for spinal injury.

Caution: The emergency care (first aid) procedures discussed in this chapter should not be attempted unless you have adequate classroom and practical training under the direction of an authorized instructor.

The general rule for management of spinal injury is to support and immobilize the spine, the head, the torso, and the pelvis. Your goal is to end up with a victim who is properly immobilized on a backboard. It is

better to overtreat than to risk further injury (see Figure 13-24).

Activate the EMS system; then:

1. The first priority is to ensure an adequate air supply by maintaining an open airway and adequate ventilation. Use the modified jaw-thrust technique to open the airway and provide rescue breathing if needed.

2. Establish and maintain in-line immobilization.
   • Place the head in a neutral in-line position unless the victim complains of pain or the head is not easily moved into position.
   • If you encounter resistance, stabilize the neck in the position in which you found it.
   • Place the head in alignment with the spine.

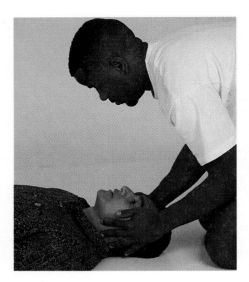

Figure 13-25. *Maintaining neutral in-line stabilization of the head and neck*

- Maintain a constant manual in-line immobilization (see Figure 13-25) until the victim is properly secured to a backboard with the head immobilized.

Prevent movement of the victim's head by one of the following methods:

- Place a heavy object on either side of the victim's head.
- Kneel with the victim's head held firmly between your knees.
- Grasp the victim's shoulders and hold his or her head firmly between your forearms (this can be exhausting; use this method only if medical help will arrive within a few minutes).

3. Perform the initial assessment; check pulse and circulation; perform CPR if necessary, but do not move the victim. Control hemorrhage, but never try to stop the flow of blood or fluid from the ears, nose, or mouth. Never apply pressure to a bleeding head wound if you suspect skull fracture.

Helmet Removal

Learning Objective 13 Describe the technique for removing a helmet from a head- or spinal-injured victim.

Caution: Never attempt to remove a helmet unless you have been trained in these advanced techniques by a certified instructor.

Thorough assessment of any victim is difficult, and that especially applies to a victim who is wearing a helmet. You need to assess the fit of the helmet and movement of the victim's head within the helmet, and determine your ability to gain access to airway and breathing.

You should leave the helmet in place if

- The helmet fits well, and there is little or no movement of the victim's head inside the helmet.
- There are no impending airway or breathing problems.
- Removal of the helmet would cause further injury to the victim.
- You can properly immobilize the spine with the helmet in place.
- The helmet doesn't interfere with your ability to assess and reassess airway and breathing.

You should remove the helmet if

- The helmet interferes with your ability to assess or reassess airway and breathing.
- The helmet interferes with your ability to manage the airway or breathing adequately.
- The helmet does not fit well and allows excessive movement of the head inside the helmet.
- The helmet interferes with proper spinal immobilization.
- The victim is in cardiac arrest.

There are two general types of helmets: sports helmets (such as those worn for football) and motorcycle helmets. Generally, sports helmets have an opening in the front and allow much easier access to the airway. Motorcycle helmets, on the other hand, generally cover the full face and have a shield that prevents access to the airway.

The technique for removal of a helmet depends on the type of helmet the victim is wearing. The following are general rules for removal of a helmet (see Figures 13-26 through 13-29)

1. Take the victim's eyeglasses off before you attempt to remove the helmet.

2. One First Aider should stabilize the helmet by placing hands on each side of the helmet, fingers on the mandible (lower jaw) to prevent movement.

3. A second First Aider should loosen the chin strap.

4. The second First Aider should place one hand on the mandible at the angle of the jaw, and the other hand at the back of the head.

5. The First Aider holding the helmet should pull the sides of the helmet apart (to provide clearance for

the ears), gently slip the helmet halfway off the victim's head, then stop.

6. The First Aider who is maintaining stabilization of the neck should reposition, sliding the hand under the victim's head to secure the head from falling back after the helmet is completely removed.

7. The first First Aider should remove the helmet completely.

8. The victim should then be immobilized as described on pages 235–236.

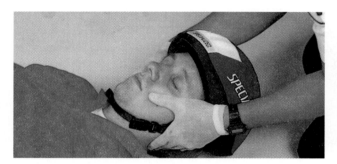

Figure 13-26. The first First Aider takes a position above or behind the victim and places hands on each side of the neck at the base of the skull and applies steady stabilization with the neck in a neutral position. The First Aider may use the thumbs to perform a jaw-thrust while doing this.

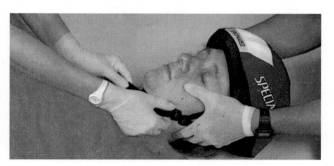

Figure 13-27. The second First Aider takes a position over or to the side of the patient and removes or cuts the chin strap.

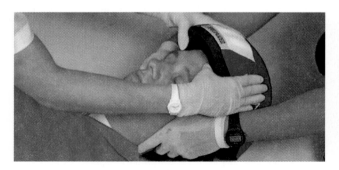

Figure 13-28. The second First Aider now removes the helmet by pulling out laterally on each side to clear the ears and then up to remove. Full face helmets will have to be tilted back to clear the nose (tilt the helmet, not the head). If the victim has glasses on, the second First Aider should remove them through the visual opening before removing the full face helmet. The first First Aider maintains steady stabilization during this procedure.

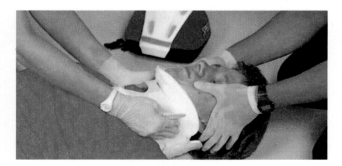

Figure 13-29. The second First Aider now applies a suitable cervical immobilization device, and the victim is secured to a long board.

• SUMMARY •

- In open head injury, the skull is fractured, causing exposure of the brain; in closed head injury, the scalp may be lacerated but the skull is intact.

- Skull fracture itself does not cause disability and death; the underlying damage is what leads to serious consequences.

- There are four types of skull fracture—depressed, linear, comminuted, and basal.

- You should suspect skull fracture with any significant trauma to the head.

- Never attempt to stop the flow of blood or fluid from the nose, ears, or mouth; cover loosely with a piece of gauze that will absorb, but not block, the flow.

- The top priority in treating head injuries is to establish and maintain an open airway with adequate oxygenation; the most common cause of death following head injury is oxygen deficiency in the brain.

- Head and scalp wounds may bleed heavily; don't apply direct pressure on a wound if you suspect underlying damage to the skull.

- The cervical vertebrae are most prone to injury; the lumbar are least.

- The basic mechanisms of spinal injury are compression, distraction, rotation, flexion, and extension.

- Paralysis in a conscious victim is the most reliable sign of spinal injury.

- The general rule for management of spinal injury is to support and immobilize the spine, head, torso, and pelvis.

- The first priority in treating spinal injury is to ensure an adequate air supply.

• KEY TERMS •

Make sure you understand the following key terms:

- coup-contrecoup
- raccoon eyes
- Battle's sign
- distraction

Student: _____   Date: _____

Course: _____   Section #: _____

If you believe the statement is true, circle the T. If you believe the statement is false, circle the F.

T F **1.** In a head-injured victim, use the head-tilt/chin-lift maneuver to open the airway.

T F **2.** Forceful vomiting may be a sign of head injury.

T F **3.** A basal skull fracture is the most common and least serious.

T F **4.** Face and scalp wounds may bleed heavily but are usually easy to control.

T F **5.** It is not possible for a spine-injured victim to walk around.

T F **6.** Spinal-injury precautions should be taken in all cases of head trauma.

T F **7.** The airway is the first priority in a spine-injured victim.

T F **8.** Always pad behind the neck of the victim on a rigid support.

T F **9.** Any trauma severe enough to cause injury to the brain can also cause injury to the spine.

T F **10.** With proper precautions, one First Aider can safely remove a victim's helmet.

For each item, circle the correct answer or the phrase that best completes the statement.

1. If a victim has blood or cerebrospinal fluid draining from the ears but shows no indication of spinal injury, the first step in emergency care is to
   a. stabilize the neck
   b. stop the flow of blood and cerebrospinal fluid
   c. complete the primary survey
   d. establish and maintain an open airway

2. Which of the following methods of maintaining an open airway should be used on an unconscious victim with a head injury?
   a. chin-lift only
   b. head-tilt/chin-lift
   c. modified jaw-thrust
   d. head-tilt/neck-lift

3. When a foreign object is impaled in the skull
   a. do not remove the object, but carefully stabilize it
   b. remove the object and apply a loose sterile dressing
   c. do not remove the object unless it will hinder transport
   d. remove the object and pack the wound with sterile pads

4. With a comminuted skull fracture
   a. the fracture is not in the area of impact or injury
   b. the skull is depressed
   c. scalp laceration and brain laceration are also present
   d. multiple cracks radiate from the center of impact

5. What is the most common characteristic of Battle's sign?
   a. unequal dilation of the pupils
   b. discoloration of the soft tissue under the eyes
   c. a bruise-like mark behind either ear
   d. one eye that appears sunken

6. Which of the following occurs in coup-contrecoup injury to the brain?
   a. the brain is slapped against the skull as the head is hurled forward
   b. the brain rebounds against the opposite side of the skull
   c. the skull stops suddenly and the brain is smashed against it
   d. all of the above

7. Which of the following is *not* a sign of spinal injury?
   a. numbness and tingling in the arms and/or legs
   b. loss of response to pain
   c. loss of bowel and bladder control
   d. position of the legs

8. Check for spinal-cord damage in a conscious victim by
   a. asking the victim to wiggle fingers and toes
   b. asking the victim to speak
   c. asking the victim to read
   d. checking reflexes at the knees or elbows

- A 5-year-old child falls off a high fence, hitting his head on a concrete driveway. He has an open wound on the forehead, he is unconscious, and he has blood-tinged fluid draining from his left ear.
- You are at a park where a teenaged boy has been hit in the head with a baseball. He is in a prone position and has a large swelling on the side of his head. Bystanders say that he was unconscious, but he is conscious now. He seems confused, restless, and irritable and is vomiting.
- You are at the scene of an automobile accident and find a woman who was thrown out of one of the vehicles. She is in a sitting position, has a large forehead laceration, and is complaining of neck pain.

14

Poisoning Emergencies

Learning Objectives

When you have mastered the material in this chapter, you will be able to

1   Identify the ways in which poisons can enter the body

2   List the signs and symptoms of ingestion of poison

3   Describe and demonstrate emergency care for victims of ingested poisons

4   Discuss the guidelines for use of activated charcoal

5   List the signs and symptoms of inhalation of poison

6   List the signs and symptoms of carbon monoxide poisoning

7   Describe and demonstrate emergency care for victims of inhaled poisons

8   List the signs and symptoms of injection of poison

9   Describe and demonstrate emergency care for victims of injected poisons

10 List the signs and symptoms of absorption of poison

11 Describe and demonstrate emergency care for victims of absorbed poisons

SQ3R Plus

- **Survey** to set goals for studying.
- Ask **questions** as you **read.**
- Stop frequently to **recite** and **review.**
- **Write** a summary of key points.
- **Reflect** on the importance of this material and its relevance in your life.

O n October 9, 1998, 29-year-old Cliff
Harding was raking leaves in his front
yard when he heard 2-year-old Joshua
Bandley screaming in the garage next door. Running
to the garage, Cliff found the toddler wiping frantically at his mouth. Next to him on the garage floor
was a soda pop bottle; sniffing at the mouth of the
bottle, Cliff knew some kind of insecticide had been
stored inside.

As Cliff assessed the situation, Joshua began
vomiting. Cliff realized the toddler's breathing rate
was slowing and that he was showing signs of
shock. When Joshua's mother ran into the garage in
response to her child's screams, Cliff sent her to call
for emergency personnel.

Cliff positioned Joshua on his side, covered him
with a jacket, and—still wearing garden gloves—
wiped the remaining vomitus from Joshua's mouth
to keep his airway clear. Cliff monitored Joshua's
breathing and kept him on his side with his face
pointed downward until emergency personnel arrived a few minutes later.

EACH YEAR IN THE UNITED STATES, THOUSANDS OF
people die from suicidal or accidental poisonings.
Poisoning is the third most common cause of accidental death in the United States, and is a leading
cause of deaths among children. In addition to the fatalities, approximately one million cases of nonfatal
poisoning occur because of exposure to substances
such as industrial chemicals, cleaning agents, plant
and insect sprays, and medications—in fact, two-
thirds of all poisonings in all age groups involve
drugs.

A poison is any substance—liquid, solid, or
gas—that impairs health or causes death by its chemical action when it enters the body or comes into contact with the surface of the skin. Some substances
that are otherwise harmless become deadly if used
incorrectly.

Learning Objective 1 Identify the ways in which poisons can enter the body.

Poisons may enter the body in four ways (see
Figure 14-1):

- Ingestion of substances such as medications,
  household cleaners, or chemicals

- Inhalation of noxious dusts, gases, fumes, or mists

- Injection with hypodermic needles or by animal,
  snake, or insect bites

- Absorption through the skin (as with poisonous
  liquids) or contact with the skin (as with poisonous plants)

This chapter discusses the challenges involved in
treating victims who have ingested, inhaled, injected,
or absorbed poisons; outlines emergency care; and
provides the latest guidelines on the use of activated
charcoal.

Poisons May Enter the Body Through

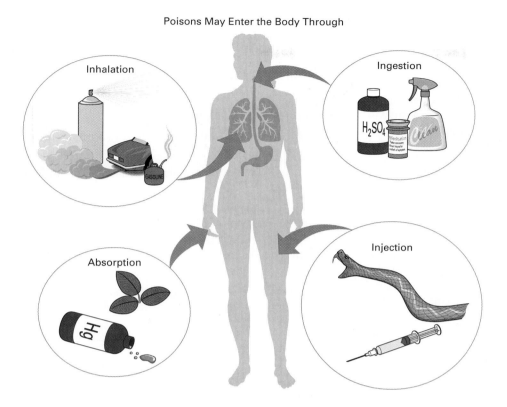

Figure 14-1. Poisons may enter the body by ingestion, inhalation, absorption, and injection.

• Section 1 •
INGESTED POISONS

The most common ingested agents are aspirin, acetaminophen, alcohol, detergents/soaps, and petroleum distillates. Children are frequently poisoned (see Figure 14-2) by household products or by **ingestion** of (eating) houseplants or outdoor plants; half of all plant poisonings are caused by mushrooms. Poisonous plants are not necessarily exotic—they include common household and backyard plants, such as morning glory, rhubarb leaves, buttercup, daisy, daffodil, lily of the valley, narcissus, tulip, azalea, English ivy, mistletoe berries, iris, hyacinth, laurel, philodendron, rhododendron, wisteria, and certain parts of the tomato, potato, and petunia plants.

Ingested poisons usually remain in the stomach only a short time; most absorption takes place after the poison has passed into the small intestine. Management of ingestion poisoning, then, is aimed at ridding the body of poison before it enters the intestinal tract.

Poison Control Centers

Poison control centers have been set up across the United States and Canada to assist in the treatment of poison victims. Officials at the center can help you set

Figure 14-2. Poisoning is the number-one cause of accidental death among children.

ingestion Taking a substance into the body through the mouth

priorities and formulate an effective care plan and can provide information about any available antidote that may be appropriate.

Calls to poison control centers are toll-free, and most centers are staffed 24 hours a day by experienced professionals. Each center is also connected to a network of nationwide consultants who can answer questions about almost any toxin. In addition, information on the poison center's computer is updated every 90 days to provide the latest information on treatment options and antidotes. Finally, centers provide follow-up telephone calls, monitoring the victim's progress and making treatment suggestions until the victim is either hospitalized or asymptomatic.

Be prepared to tell poison center officials the victim's approximate age and weight. Summarize the victim's condition, including level of consciousness, level of activity, skin color, vomiting, and so on. Give as many specifics about the poison as you can.

The Importance of Taking a History

Getting a history from a poisoning victim can be difficult, and the history you do get may not be accurate—the victim may be misinformed, may be subject to a drug-induced confusion, or may be deliberately trying to deceive you. To manage a poisoning victim correctly, however, you need a relevant history.

If the victim is a child, other children in the house may have also eaten the poison, so assess all children carefully. Interview family members and witnesses. Look for clues at the scene—overturned or empty medicine bottles, scattered pills or capsules, recently emptied containers, spilled chemicals, spilled cleaning solvents, an overturned plant or pieces of plant, the remains of food or drink, or vomitus.

Ask the victim or bystanders the following questions:

- What was ingested?
- When was the substance taken?
- How much was taken?
- Has anyone tried to induce vomiting? Has anything been given as an antidote?
- Does the victim have a psychiatric history that suggests a possible suicide attempt?
- Does the victim have an underlying medical illness, allergy, chronic drug use, or addiction?

Signs and Symptoms

Learning Objective 2 List the signs and symptoms of ingestion of poison.

The signs and symptoms of poisoning by ingestion vary, depending on what was ingested (see Figure 14-3); following are the most common:

- A history of ingestion
- Nausea, vomiting, and diarrhea
- Excessive salivation
- Altered mental status, including varying levels of unconsciousness
- Abdominal pain, tenderness, distension, and/or cramps
- Burns or stains around the mouth (see Figure 14-4), pain in the mouth or throat, and/or pain during swallowing (corrosive poisons may corrode, burn, or destroy the tissues of the mouth, throat, and stomach)
- Unusual breath or body odors; characteristic chemical odors (such as turpentine) on the breath

Emergency Care

Learning Objective 3 Describe and demonstrate emergency care for victims of ingested poisons.

Activate the EMS system; then:

1. Maintain the airway and monitor the victim's ABCDs. Protect yourself from injury by wearing gloves to remove any remaining pills, tablets, capsules, or other fragments from the victim's mouth. Secretions may be profuse following the ingestion of certain poisons, so keep the victim's face pointed downward to facilitate drainage.

2. If the poison was a corrosive (acid) or caustic (alkali), immediately give the victim one or two 8-ounce glasses of *cold* water or milk to dilute the poison.

3. Place the victim on his or her left side to delay the poison from entering the small intestine, where most substances are absorbed into the bloodstream.

4. Consult Poison Control; don't simply follow a container's label, which may be outdated or incorrect. In most areas, you will be instructed to administer activated charcoal to absorb the poison; details on activated charcoal are found later in this chapter.

5. *Never induce vomiting unless you are told to do so by Poison Control.* If Poison Control tells you to induce vomiting, carefully follow all instructions.

6. Send suspected poisons, containers, plant parts, or other specimens with the victim to the receiv-

POSSIBLE INDICATORS OF CHILDHOOD POISONING

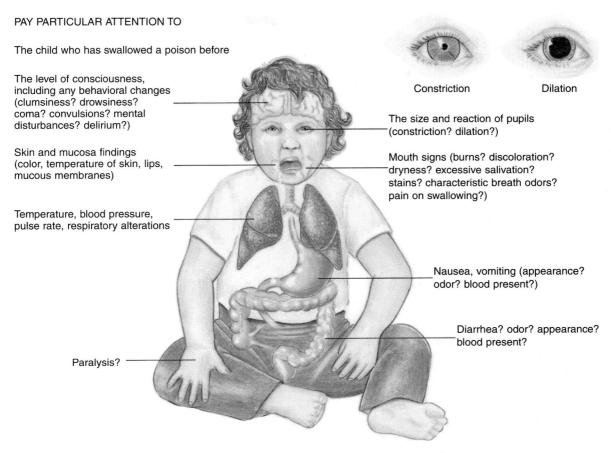

PAY PARTICULAR ATTENTION TO

The child who has swallowed a poison before

The level of consciousness, including any behavioral changes (clumsiness? drowsiness? coma? convulsions? mental disturbances? delirium?)

Skin and mucosa findings (color, temperature of skin, lips, mucous membranes)

Temperature, blood pressure, pulse rate, respiratory alterations

Paralysis?

Constriction   Dilation

The size and reaction of pupils (constriction? dilation?)

Mouth signs (burns? discoloration? dryness? excessive salivation? stains? characteristic breath odors? pain on swallowing?)

Nausea, vomiting (appearance? odor? blood present?)

Diarrhea? odor? appearance? blood present?

Figure 14-3. Thousands of U.S. children require some treatment for poisoning annually.

ing facility. If the victim has vomited, send a sample of the vomitus in a clean, closed container to the receiving facility.

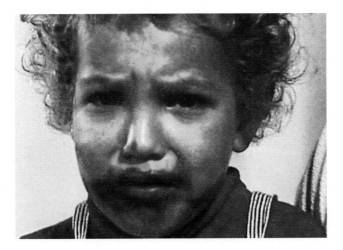

Figure 14-4. Skin discoloration—possible poisoning

All poisoned victims need to see a physician, even if it appears that all signs and symptoms have been controlled and the emergency is over.

Food Poisoning

A specific kind of ingestion poisoning is "food poisoning"—ingestion of food that contains bacteria or the toxins that bacteria produce. The incidence of food poisoning is increasing dramatically; each year, some 33 million Americans develop gastrointestinal disease as a result of food poisoning.

Because the signs and symptoms vary greatly, food poisoning can be difficult to detect. General signs and symptoms include abdominal pain, nausea and vomiting, gas, diarrhea, and loud or frequent bowel sounds.

To care for a victim of food poisoning, follow the general guidelines for any ingested poison. Do not give the victim anything by mouth; the victim needs medical help as soon as possible.

Progress Check

1. One of the most common agents involved in poisoning by ingestion is _____ .
   (Tabasco sauce/motor oil/aspirin)

2. While the signs and symptoms of ingestion poisoning vary, it often causes _____ .
   (nausea/cyanosis/paralysis)

3. The top priority in managing ingestion poisoning is maintaining the _____ .
   (airway/circulation/level of consciousness)

4. Food poisoning should be treated like any other case of _____ .
   (gastrointestinal disease/ingestion poisoning/acute abdomen)

• Section 2 •
ACTIVATED CHARCOAL

The medication of choice in the emergency care of ingestion poisoning is **activated charcoal,** a special distilled charcoal treated with superheated steam that can absorb many times its weight in contaminants because of its porous surface. (See Figure 14-5.) Activated charcoal is an odorless, tasteless, insoluble black powder that works best when used promptly, but it can still be effective after several hours—as long as 4 hours after ingestion for some poisons.

Simply, activated charcoal binds to poisons in the stomach, prevents their absorption into the body, and enhances their elimination from the body. Some commercially available activated charcoal products also contain a laxative agent that helps speed the charcoal through the intestinal tract, further limiting any absorption into the body. Activated charcoal does not bind to alcohol, kerosene, gasoline, caustics, or metals, such as iron.

Some of the more well-known trade names of activated charcoal are SuperChar, InstaChar, Actidose, and LiquiChar.

Activated charcoal should be used for victims who have ingested poisons by mouth. Do *not* give activated charcoal to a victim who

- Is not fully conscious (has an altered mental status)
- Has swallowed acids or alkalies
- Is unable to swallow

Dosage

Learning Objective 4 Discuss the guidelines for the use of activated charcoal.

For first aid, use activated charcoal that has been premixed with water instead of charcoal in a powder form; the most common brands contain 12.5 grams of activated charcoal mixed with water in a plastic bottle.

Unless directed otherwise by Poison Control, give both adults and children 1 gram of activated charcoal per kilogram of body weight. The usual adult dose is 25 to 50 grams. The usual dose for infants and children is 12.5 to 25 grams.

Administration

Directions that follow are general. Consult Poison Control for direction before administering activated charcoal to any victim. To administer activated charcoal (see Figure 14-6):

1. Shake the container of activated charcoal thoroughly; if it is too thick to shake well, remove the

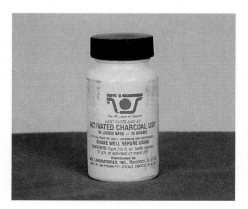

Figure 14-5. *Activated charcoal should be used only for victims who have ingested poison by mouth.*

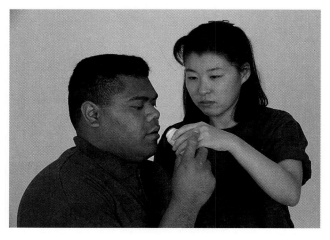

Figure 14-6. *Administering activated charcoal to a victim who has ingested a poison by mouth*

cap and stir it until well mixed. The activated charcoal settles to the bottom of the bottle, and needs to be evenly distributed.

2. Activated charcoal looks like mud; you may have an easier time persuading the victim to drink it if you use a straw and a covered, opaque container so the victim can't see it. Don't mix the activated charcoal with anything else in an effort to make it more acceptable to the victim; you could make it less absorbent.

3. If the victim takes a long time to drink the activated charcoal, it will settle. Make sure you shake or stir it again before letting the victim finish the dose.

4. Record the time the victim took the activated charcoal and the specifics about the dose.

5. If the victim vomits, repeat the dose once.

Once you have given a victim activated charcoal, don't let the victim have milk, ice cream, or sherbet; all decrease the effectiveness of the activated charcoal.

Progress Check

1. Activated charcoal absorbs poison because of its _____ .
   (chemical composition/additives/porous surface)

2. Activated charcoal works by _____ poisons.
   (absorbing/binding/neutralizing)

3. You should not use activated charcoal for a victim who ingested _____ .
   (morning glory/detergent/gasoline)

4. Don't give activated charcoal to someone who is not fully _____ .
   (alert/compromised/able to consent)

5. Use the _____ form of activated charcoal whenever possible.
   (powdered/premixed/premeasured)

• Section 3 •
INHALED POISONS

Almost 8,000 people die each year in the United States from inhaling poisonous vapors and fumes, some of which are present without any sign. Most toxic **inhalation** (taking toxins into the body through the lungs) occurs as a result of fire; other common inhaled poisons include chemicals at industrial sites,

fumes from liquid chemicals, ammonia, solvents used in dry cleaning, sewer gas, and carbon monoxide generated by the incomplete combustion of natural gas.

Immediate care is critical, because the body absorbs inhaled poisons rapidly. The longer the exposure without treatment, the poorer the prognosis.

Carbon Monoxide Poisoning

Of special concern is **carbon monoxide** poisoning: Carbon monoxide causes half of all poisoning deaths in the United States each year and is the leading cause of death among people who inhale the smoke from fires.

Carbon monoxide—formed by the incomplete combustion of gasoline, coal, kerosene, plastic, wood, and natural gas—is common in the environment and is completely nonirritating, tasteless, colorless, and odorless. It causes a life-threatening lack of oxygen in two ways. First, it reduces the amount of oxygen carried to the bloodstream by the red blood cells; instead of binding to oxygen in the bloodstream, they are two hundred times more likely to bind to any carbon monoxide in the bloodstream. Second, it inhibits the ability of body cells to utilize what little oxygen is delivered. The brain and heart sustain the greatest damage.

The primary sources of carbon monoxide are home-heating devices (including furnaces and wood-burning fireplaces) and automobile exhaust fumes (which often enter the car through rust holes in the exhaust system). Because of exhaust fumes, it is extremely dangerous to ride in the back of an enclosed pickup truck. Other common sources of carbon monoxide are tobacco smoke, barbecue grills and charcoal briquettes, kitchen stoves, gas lamps, recreational fires, propane-powered industrial equipment, and faulty water heaters, kerosene heaters, and space heaters.

It takes only a few minutes to die from carbon monoxide poisoning. Death is so certain, in fact, that more than half of all suicides in the United States each year are committed with automobile exhaust, which is 7 percent carbon monoxide.

activated charcoal A special steam-distilled charcoal that can absorb many times its weight in contaminants because of its porous surface

inhalation The act of breathing in (inspiration), or the drawing of air or other gases into the lungs

carbon monoxide An odorless, tasteless, colorless toxic gas that results from incomplete combustion

Signs and Symptoms

General signs and symptoms of inhalation poisoning include the following:

• A history of inhaling a toxic substance

• Difficulty breathing or shortness of breath

• Chest pain or tightness; a burning sensation in the chest or throat

• Cough, stridor, wheezing, or rales

• Hoarseness

• Dizziness

• Headache, often severe

• Seizures

• Altered mental status or confusion

• Signs of respiratory tract burns, such as singed nasal hairs, soot in the sputum, or soot in the throat

The signs and symptoms of carbon monoxide poisoning (see Figure 14-7) change with length of exposure and intensity of poisoning. They also change in certain situations (diminishing when you go outside, for example), during certain times of the day (worse when the furnace is running, or when meals are being prepared on a gas stove), and so on. A characteristic sign is that pets in the household also become ill. Carbon monoxide poisoning can initially produce flu-like symptoms, but there are several important differences: carbon monoxide poisoning does not cause a fever, generalized body aches, or swollen lymph glands. One of the things that makes carbon monoxide poisoning—especially from chronic exposure—so dangerous is that it may easily be mistaken for something else.

Low levels of carbon monoxide cause throbbing headache, shortness of breath, nausea, irritability, confusion, loss of judgment, and difficulty concentrating.

Moderate levels of carbon monoxide cause severe headache, severe nausea and vomiting, dizziness, yawning, visual disturbances, and difficulty thinking.

High levels of carbon monoxide cause lethargy and stupor, fainting on exertion, chest pain, heart arrhythmias, temporary loss of vision, convulsions, and coma.

Skin color is normal at first, but becomes pale and then cyanotic as poisoning progresses. At very high

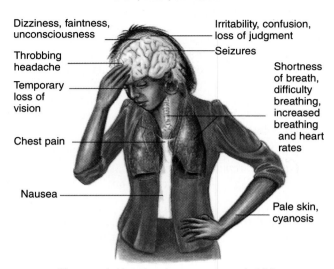

Greatest effects are on the brain, heart, and fetus.

Dizziness, faintness, unconsciousness

Throbbing headache

Temporary loss of vision

Chest pain

Nausea

Irritability, confusion, loss of judgment

Seizures

Shortness of breath, difficulty breathing, increased breathing and heart rates

Pale skin, cyanosis

Cherry red skin color also may appear, but it is not a reliable indicator. It usually occurs at high levels of exposure at late stages only.

Figure 14-7. Signs and symptoms of carbon monoxide poisoning

levels, the mucous membranes and skin become bright cherry-red in color; cherry-red lips are not commonly seen.

You should consider carbon monoxide poisoning whenever you encounter unexplained flu symptoms (such as headache, nausea, vomiting, and confusion)—especially if the symptoms are shared by other people and pets in the same environment.

Emergency Care

Activate the EMS system *immediately;* then:

1. Get the victim into fresh air as quickly as possible. Protect yourself—a trained First Aider should remove the victim from the poisonous environment. Never enter an area that might be contaminated. If you suspect that someone has suffered carbon monoxide poisoning, evacuate everyone from the enclosed space—even people who apparently have no symptoms. Ideally, victims should be moved at least 150 feet from the suspected source of the carbon monoxide into open air.

2. Monitor the ABCDs. If there are no contraindicating injuries and the victim is conscious, have the

victim lie down with head elevated; loosen all tight-fitting clothing, especially around the neck and over the chest. If the victim is unresponsive, place the victim on his or her left side.

3. If the victim is not breathing, start artificial ventilation immediately; do not interrupt it for any reason. Continue until the victim is breathing spontaneously or you are relieved by emergency personnel.

All victims of carbon monoxide poisoning must receive medical care; 45 percent develop delayed neurological complications after initial recovery. A carbon monoxide victim needs medical treatment immediately, even if the victim seems to have recovered. (Remember that awakening or seeming alertness can be false signs of recovery.)

Progress Check

1. Most cases of toxic inhalation occur as a result of _____ .
   (automobile exhaust/carbon monoxide/fire)

2. The most common gas that causes poisoning is _____ .
   (sulphur dioxide/nitrous oxide/carbon monoxide)

3. Carbon monoxide is difficult to detect because it is completely colorless and _____ .
   (pervasive/odorless/combustible)

4. Carbon monoxide poisoning causes symptoms similar to _____ symptoms.
   (flu/emphysema/respiratory arrest)

5. _____ victims of carbon monoxide poisoning need medical care, even if they seem to have recovered.
   (No/About half/All)

● Section 4 ●
INJECTED POISONS

"Injected" poisons are those that enter the body through a break in the skin—sometimes by the intentional injection of illicit drugs, other times by the bites or stings of animals and insects.

Illicit drugs may be injected under the skin, into the muscle, or directly into the bloodstream. More detailed information on specific drug-related emergencies is found in Chapter 15.

The most common sources of injected poisons are animal and insect bites and stings. Most common are stings from bees, wasps, hornets, yellow jackets, and ants; others include the bites of spiders, ticks, snakes, and the stings of marine animals (such as jellyfish, coral, anemones, and stingrays). (See Chapter 23.)

Injected poisons generally cause an immediate reaction at the injection site followed by a delayed systemic reaction. Of special note is the threat of anaphylactic shock following the allergic reaction to an insect bite or sting (see Chapter 6).

Signs and Symptoms

Learning Objective 8 List the signs and symptoms of injection of poison.

General signs and symptoms of toxic injection include

- Weakness
- Dizziness
- Chills and fever
- Nausea and/or vomiting

Specific signs and symptoms of anaphylactic shock are listed in Chapter 6.

Emergency Care

Learning Objective 9 Describe and demonstrate emergency care for victims of injected poisons.

Activate the EMS system; then:

1. Maintain the victim's airway.
2. Be alert for vomiting; keep the victim sitting if possible to prevent aspiration.
3. In the case of an animal or insect bite or sting, protect yourself from injury and protect the victim from repeated injection. Bees can sting only once, then lose their stinger, but wasps, hornets, and yellow jackets can sting repeatedly. (See Chapter 23.)
4. If the victim was bitten or stung, identify the insect, reptile, or animal that caused the injury, if possible; if you killed it, send it to the receiving facility with the victim.

Progress Check

1. The most common source of injected poison is _____ .
   (illicit drugs/marine animals/insect stings)

continued

2. Injected poisons cause a reaction at the injection site followed by a delayed _____ reaction.
(systemic/respiratory/circulatory)

3. The greatest danger from insect stings is

_____ .
(systemic poisoning/lack of antitoxins/anaphylactic shock)

4. The highest priority in caring for a victim of injected poison is _____ .
(removing the stinger/protecting the airway/placement of a constricting band)

• **Section 5** •

ABSORBED POISONS

Absorption of poisons—usually chemicals or poisons from plants that enter through the skin—generally causes burns, lesions, and inflammation. Chemicals that are splashed into the eyes cause extreme burning pain, excessive tearing, and the inability to open the eye.

Skin reactions range from mild irritation to severe chemical burns. Absorbed poisons often cause both local and systemic reactions, which can be severe—exposure of as little as 2.5 percent of the body surface to 100 percent hydrofluoric acid, for example, can cause death.

A fairly common type of absorbed poisoning comes from skin contact with a poisonous plant (see Figures 14-8 through 14-11)—usually poison ivy, poison sumac, or poison oak. You don't need direct contact with poison ivy in order to have a reaction from it: the poisonous element, **urushiol,** can be carried on animal fur, tools, and clothing. If poison ivy is burned, molecules of urushiol are emitted in the smoke and can be breathed in or absorbed through the skin.

Figure 14-8. Poison ivy

Figure 14-9. Poison sumac

Figure 14-10. Poison oak

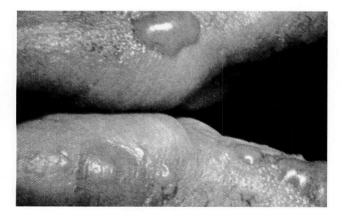

Figure 14-11. Blisters from contact with a poisonous plant

The stems and leaves of the stinging nettle are covered with fine, hollow stinging "hairs." Unlike poison ivy, which generally causes an allergic response, the effect of stinging nettle is due to its irritating sap, which is injected into the skin by the hairs. An allergic reaction to stinging nettle is rare. The primary symptom of contact with stinging nettle is immediate, intense, burning or stinging pain; depending on how sensitive the victim is, the stinging nettle may also cause redness and itching that can last for several hours.

Other plants that can cause mild to severe dermatitis include crown of thorns, buttercup, mayapple, marsh marigold, candelabra cactus, brown-eyed Susan, shasta daisy, and chrysanthemum.

Signs and Symptoms

> **Learning Objective 10** List the signs and symptoms of absorption of poison.

Signs and symptoms of absorbed poison include

- A history of exposure to a poisonous substance
- Traces of liquid or powder on the skin
- Burns
- Itching and/or irritation
- Redness

Signs and symptoms of contact with a poisonous plant include

- Fluid-filled, oozing blisters
- Itching and burning
- Swelling
- Possible pain
- A rash lasting from 1 to 3 weeks
- Secondary infections from an irritated rash

Emergency Care

> **Learning Objective 11** Describe and demonstrate emergency care for victims of absorbed poisons.

The more skin that is affected by poison, the greater the need for medical attention. If a victim has absorbed poison through the skin:

1. Protecting your hands with gloves, move the victim from the source of the poison and remove the victim's contaminated clothing.
2. Brush any dry chemicals or solid toxins from the skin, taking extreme care not to abrade the skin.

3. If the poison is liquid, irrigate the body with clean water for at least 20 minutes. (A shower or garden hose is ideal.) Carefully check "hidden" areas, such as the nailbeds, skin creases, areas between the fingers and toes, and any hair.

4. If the victim has been in contact with a poisonous plant, clean the skin well with soap and water, and rinse well. For a mild reaction, have the victim soak in a lukewarm bath sprinkled with 2 cups of colloidal oatmeal (available in commercial preparations to relieve itching), apply calamine lotion, or apply a paste of water and baking soda. For a moderate reaction, soak the affected areas in hot water; heat will cause intense itching for a few minutes, followed by as many as 8 hours of relief.

5. To relieve the reaction from stinging nettle, wash the area well with soap and water, rinse thoroughly, and apply cold, wet compresses to relieve pain and itching.

6. If any reaction is severe, activate the EMS system or transport the victim to a medical facility.

If there are any chemicals on the skin or in the eye, activate the EMS system immediately. If poison has been splashed into the eye, follow the guidelines listed in Chapter 8 for treatment of chemical burns to the eye.

Progress Check

1. Absorbed poisons enter the body through the
   _____ .
   (alveoli/skin/small intestine)

2. The poisonous element in poison _____ can be breathed in from smoke or carried on an animal's fur.
   (oak/ivy/sumac)

3. If there is a liquid poison on the victim's skin, _____ for at least 20 minutes.
   (keep the victim quiet/irrigate with running water/monitor the victim's status)

absorption Taking a substance into the body through the skin

urushiol The toxic element of poison ivy, which can be carried on animal fur, tools, clothing, and, when the plant is burned, in the air

• SUMMARY •

- Poisons can enter the body through ingestion, inhalation, injection, or absorption.

- Ingested poisons usually only remain in the stomach a short time; most absorption takes place after the poison passes into the small intestine. Therefore, care is aimed at getting the substance out of the body as quickly as possible.

- Activated charcoal is the treatment of choice for victims of ingested poison; it works by absorbing many times its weight in contaminants.

- You should not administer activated charcoal to a victim who has ingested alcohol, kerosene, gasoline, acids, or alkalies or a victim who is not fully alert.

- If possible, use the premixed form of activated charcoal.

- Poison Control centers are professionally staffed, 24-hour-a-day referral centers that can provide information on care and antidotes.

- Most toxic inhalation occurs as a result of fire; the most common gas that causes poisoning is carbon monoxide.

- Because carbon monoxide is completely colorless, odorless, and tasteless, it is difficult to detect.

- Symptoms of carbon monoxide poisoning are similar to those caused by the flu, except there is no fever, body ache, and swollen glands; suspect carbon monoxide poisoning in cases where there are unexplained flu symptoms.

- The greatest danger from injected poison is anaphylactic shock.

- You do not actually have to contact poison ivy to have a reaction; urushiol, the poisonous element, can be carried on animal fur, tools, clothing—and, if the poison ivy is burned, in smoke.

• KEY TERMS •

Make sure you understand the following key terms:

- ingestion
- activated charcoal
- inhalation
- carbon monoxide
- absorption
- urushiol

Student: _____   Date: _____

Course: _____   Section #: _____

If you believe the statement is true, circle the T. If you believe the statement is false, circle the F.

T   F   **1.** Ingestion of poisonous plants is a common poisoning emergency in children.

T   F   **2.** A victim of inhaled poison should be given activated charcoal.

T   F   **3.** Cherry-red lips are a common early sign of carbon monoxide poisoning.

T   F   **4.** A throbbing headache is a symptom of low-level carbon monoxide poisoning.

T   F   **5.** Activated charcoal should be used only if the victim vomits.

T   F   **6.** A victim of poisoning should be kept in a sitting position.

T   F   **7.** Initial symptoms of carbon monoxide poisoning include headache, weakness, agitation, confusion, and dizziness.

T   F   **8.** For first aid, you should use powdered activated charcoal so you can determine the strength of dosage.

T   F   **9.** Activated charcoal will not bind to alcohol, kerosene, or gasoline.

T   F   **10.** Activated charcoal should be used in cases of ingested poisoning because of its ability to neutralize poisons.

For each item, circle the correct answer or the phrase that best completes the statement.

1. Poisoning is the _____ common cause of accidental death in the United States.

  a. most
  b. third most
  c. fifth most
  d. second most

2. Which of the following is *not* a way that poisons may enter the body?

  a. absorption
  b. emesis
  c. inhalation
  d. injection

3. The common signs and symptoms of poisoning by ingestion are

  a. nausea, vomiting, diarrhea
  b. severe abdominal pain or cramps
  c. excessive salivation
  d. all of the above

4. It is critical that care be given immediately to the person who has inhaled poison because

  a. inhaled poisons are more toxic than ingested poisons
  b. the body absorbs inhaled poisons rapidly
  c. inhaled poisons remain in the system longer than ingested poisons
  d. the victim may experience convulsions, which makes treatment difficult

5. Which of the following is a characteristic symptom of carbon monoxide poisoning?

  a. headache
  b. cool, pale skin
  c. complaints of a strange taste in the mouth
  d. stains around the mouth

6. What is the initial emergency care procedure for inhalation poisonings?

  a. remove the victim to fresh air
  b. begin mouth-to-mouth resuscitation
  c. treat the victim for shock
  d. seek medical care immediately

7. The First Aider's primary responsibility in the emergency care of poisoning is to

  a. maintain the airway and prevent aspiration of vomitus
  b. determine what substance caused the poisoning
  c. assess the level of consciousness
  d. assess respirations

8. After a poisoning victim vomits, give the victim

  a. activated charcoal
  b. lemon juice in a glass of water
  c. raw egg to coat the stomach
  d. syrup of ipecac and water

For each poisoning situation, indicate whether activated charcoal should be used.

Poisoning Situation

1. _____ A stuporous or comatose victim
2. _____ A victim who swallowed silver nitrate
3. _____ A victim who swallowed strychnine
4. _____ A victim who swallowed acid
5. _____ A victim who swallowed kerosene
6. _____ A victim who swallowed insecticide
7. _____ A victim who swallowed gasoline

Emergency Care

A. Give activated charcoal.
B. Do not give activated charcoal.

• A teenaged boy is found in his garage with the car running and the doors closed. When you arrive, he has been removed from the garage. He is unconscious, has a rapid heart and breathing rate, and is cyanotic.

Drug and Alcohol Emergencies

Early in the morning of January 27, 1998, Connor Wilson answered his apartment door to find his distraught neighbor. "My roommate passed out!" she cried. "I think she took something!"

When he arrived at the apartment, Connor found 23-year-old Anne Rhodes unconscious in the hallway next to the bathroom. Placing his hand on her wrist to determine a pulse, he found that she was feverish; her pulse was irregular, and her breathing was weak and shallow.

Instructing the roommate to call 9-1-1, Connor used a head-tilt/chin-lift maneuver to open Anne's airway and check for foreign objects; there were none. He then gently turned Anne on her side and positioned her face downward in case she vomited. Monitoring Anne's breathing constantly in case she needed rescue breathing, Connor had her roommate rinse several washcloths in cool water and sponge Anne off in an effort to bring her temperature down.

By the time ambulance personnel arrived, Connor had started rescue breathing. EMTs took over, stabilizing Anne and transporting her to a nearby hospital for treatment of an accidental drug overdose.

DRUGS AND ALCOHOL ARE MISUSED AND ABUSED BY A variety of people. Alcoholism—which is treatable but not curable, and fatal if not treated—strikes all classes and almost every age group. In the United States alone, there are an estimated ten million alcoholics. Alcohol is the most abused drug in the United States: two-thirds of all adults are "social drinkers," and there are more than 100 million drinkers, 20 percent of whom are alcoholics.

Each year, alcohol is directly involved in thousands of automobile accidents that result in death and injury. It is a factor in 40 percent of all motor vehicle accidents and in 78 percent of all fatal injuries of drivers over the age of 25. It is a factor in half of all arrests for criminal activity. Because of its deleterious effects on the liver, pancreas, central nervous system, and other body organs, alcohol reduces the average life span of an alcoholic by 10 to 12 years.

Drug abusers are more prone to certain injuries, illnesses, and infectious diseases. Most prominent among these are AIDS, hepatitis, endocarditis, phlebitis, paranoia, depression, and injuries from falls. In addition, drug abusers are often the victims of homicide, and they may be the victims of accidental or intentional suicide.

This chapter helps you determine when an emergency is drug or alcohol related and details the steps you should take to deal with both drug and alcohol emergencies.

• Section 1 •

THE NATURE OF DRUG AND ALCOHOL EMERGENCIES

Many emergencies involve drug overdose—poisoning by a drug. Most drug overdoses involve habitual drug users, but drug overdose can also be accidental (the result of miscalculation, confusion, or using more than one drug) or intentional (usually a suicide attempt). Drug and alcohol abuse can have both immediate and long-term effects (see Figures 15-1 through 15-9).

It is usually not possible to determine in the field which drug a victim has taken. Many users take a combination of drugs (sometimes without knowing it), and many drugs purchased on the street are adulterated with white, powdery substances such as starch, talc, sugar, or sawdust. (Some estimate that cocaine sold on the street is often diluted up to 75 percent with sucrose, talc, or starch.)

Even if the victim can tell you what he or she took, that self-assessment might not be accurate—the victim may have been misled by the person who sold the drug. For example, only about 3 to 4 percent of all

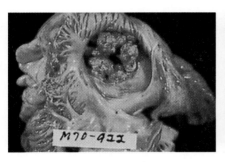

Figure 15-1. *Heart damage caused by fungus introduced during drug injection*

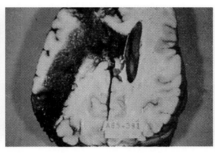

Figure 15-2. *Bullet wound to brain, alcohol related*

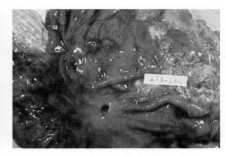

Figure 15-3. *Chronic gastric ulcer from alcohol use*

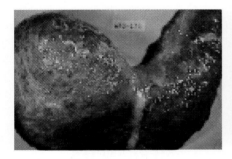

Figure 15-4. *Alcoholic cirrhosis of liver*

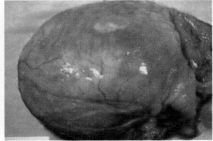

Figure 15-5. *Enlarged, weak heart, alcohol induced*

Figure 15-6. *Ruptured vein in esophagus, causing severe internal bleeding, alcohol induced*

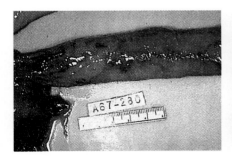

Figure 15-7. *Dilated esophageal veins from chronic alcohol use*

Figure 15-8. *Internal bleeding from an ulcer caused by chronic alcohol use*

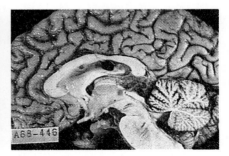

Figure 15-9. *Brain damage (cerebellum) from chronic alcohol use*

the drugs that contain PCP are actually sold on the street as PCP.

Determining Whether an Emergency Is Drug- or Alcohol-Related

Learning Objective 1 Determine if an emergency is drug or alcohol related

Because drugs and alcohol produce signs that mimic a number of system disorders or diseases, it can be difficult to assess a drug or alcohol emergency properly, especially if the victim is unconscious.

If you suspect an unconscious victim might be experiencing a drug or alcohol emergency, do the following:

* Inspect the area immediately around the victim for evidence of drug or alcohol use—empty or partially filled pill bottles, syringes, empty liquor bottles, and so on. Be sure to check the victim's pockets.

* Check the victim's mouth for signs of partially dissolved pills or tablets; if you find any, remove them.

* Smell the victim's breath for traces of alcohol. (Do not confuse a musky, fruity, or acetone odor for alcohol—all three can indicate diabetic coma.)

* Ask the victim's friends or family members or any witnesses what they know about the incident.

If the victim is conscious, watch for an unsteady, staggering gait or a pronounced lack of coordination. Remember that many serious diseases (such as diabetes and epilepsy) resemble drug overdose or abuse. Don't assume that ingested drugs are the only reason a person is stuporous or has slurred speech. *Never jump to conclusions.*

Determining if a Drug- or Alcohol-Related Emergency Is Life Threatening

Learning Objective 2 Determine if a drug- or alcohol-related emergency is life threatening.

The following six signs and symptoms indicate a life-threatening emergency (see Figure 15-10):

1. Unconsciousness—the victim cannot be awakened or, if awakened, lapses back into unconsciousness almost immediately.

2. Breathing difficulties—the victim's breathing may have stopped, may be weak and shallow, or may be weak and strong in cycles. The victim's exhalations may be raspy, rattling, or noisy. The victim's skin may be cyanotic, indicating lack of oxygen.

3. Fever—any temperature above 100 degrees F (38 degrees C) may indicate a dangerous situation when drugs and/or alcohol are involved.

4. Abnormal or irregular pulse—any pulse less than 60 or more than 100 beats per minute may indicate danger, as does a pulse that is irregular (not rhythmical).

5. Vomiting while not fully conscious

6. Convulsions—an impending convulsion may be indicated by twitching of the face, trunk, arms, or legs; muscle rigidity; or muscle spasm.

Progress Check

1. Alcohol on the breath does not smell musky, fruity, or acetone; those odors are caused by

    _____ .
    (insulin shock/hypoglycemia/diabetic coma)

2. A life-threatening emergency is indicated by a pulse lower than _____ beats per minute.
    (50/60/70)

3. A fever higher than _____ degrees F indicates a life-threatening emergency if drugs are involved.
    (99/100/101)

• Section 2 •
ALCOHOL EMERGENCIES

Alcohol is a central nervous system depressant that in moderate doses causes stupor, and in large doses can cause coma or death.

Alcohol is completely absorbed from the stomach and intestinal tract within 2 hours of the time it is ingested—and sometimes as quickly as within 30 minutes. Once absorbed from the stomach, it is distributed to all body tissues relatively quickly. It is concentrated, however, in the blood and brain, with brain concentrations rapidly approaching those found in the blood.

The alcoholic syndrome usually consists of problem drinking—during which alcohol is used frequently to relieve tensions or other emotional difficulties—and true addiction, in which abstinence from drinking

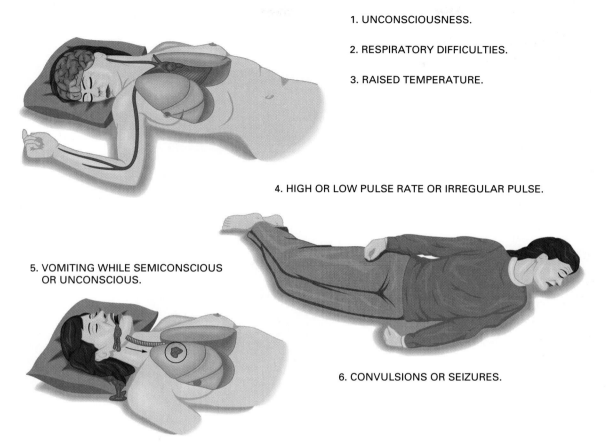

DRUG AND ALCOHOL EMERGENCY INDICATORS

1. UNCONSCIOUSNESS.

2. RESPIRATORY DIFFICULTIES.

3. RAISED TEMPERATURE.

4. HIGH OR LOW PULSE RATE OR IRREGULAR PULSE.

5. VOMITING WHILE SEMICONSCIOUS OR UNCONSCIOUS.

6. CONVULSIONS OR SEIZURES.

Figure 15-10. Emergency care and medical assistance are needed immediately if any of the six danger signs are present—no matter what the cause.

causes major withdrawal symptoms. Alcoholics use alcohol in all its forms: Sterno, moonshine, grain alcohol, antifreeze, and rubbing alcohol, to name a few. Frequently, alcoholics are dependent on other drugs as well, especially those in the sedative, barbiturate, and tranquilizer categories.

Many alcoholics have underlying psychiatric disorders (especially schizophrenia). The alcoholic usually begins drinking early in the day, is more prone to drink alone or secretly, and may periodically go on prolonged binges characterized by loss of memory ("blackout periods"). Abstinence from alcohol is likely to produce withdrawal symptoms, such as tremulousness, anxiety, or delirium tremens (DTs).

As the alcoholic becomes more dependent on alcohol, performance at work and relationships with friends and family are likely to deteriorate. Absences from work, emotional disturbances, and automobile accidents become more frequent.

Acute Intoxication

Learning Objective 3 List the signs and symptoms of acute alcohol intoxication.

The degree of acute intoxication depends on the amount of alcohol consumed. Signs and symptoms (see Figure 15-11 on page 260) include

- Drowsiness
- Disordered speech and gait
- Violence
- Destructive or erratic behavior

Note: Acute intoxication often mimics insulin shock. Always suspect diabetes; when in doubt, give sugar.

Also be alert to the possibility that the victim may have taken a combination of alcohol and sedative

ALCOHOL EMERGENCIES

CAUTION: Do not immediately decide that a patient with apparent alcohol on the breath is drunk. The signs may indicate an illness or injury such as epilepsy, diabetes, or head injury.

SIGNS OF INTOXICATION
• Odor of alcohol on the breath.
• Swaying and unsteadiness.
• Slurred speech.
• Nausea and vomiting.
• Flushed face.
• Drowsiness.
• Violent, destructive, or erratic behavior.
• Self-injury, usually without realizing it.

EFFECTS
• Alcohol is a depressant. It affects judgment, vision, reaction time, and coordination.
• When taken with other depressants, the result can be greater than the combined effects of the two drugs.
• In very large quantities, alcohol can paralyze the respiratory center of the brain and cause death.

MANAGEMENT
• Give the same attention as you would to any patient with an illness or injury.
• Monitor the patient's vital signs constantly. Provide life support when necessary.
• Position the patient to avoid aspiration of vomit.
• Protect the patient from hurting him or herself.

Figure 15-11. The signs, effects, and management of alcohol emergencies

drugs. Check the victim's pockets and surroundings for evidence of medications, which may significantly complicate the picture.

Withdrawal Syndrome

Learning Objective 4 List the signs and symptoms of withdrawal syndrome.

Withdrawal syndrome occurs after a cutback in the amount of alcohol a person is used to; it does not require that the alcoholic stop drinking completely. Withdrawal syndrome can also occur when blood alcohol levels begin to fall after severe intoxication. Withdrawal syndrome is dose dependent: the more the alcoholic was drinking, the more severe the syndrome will be.

There are four general stages of alcohol withdrawal (see Figure 15-12)

1. Stage 1, which occurs within about 8 hours of a cutback in alcohol, is characterized by nausea, insomnia, sweating, and tremors.

2. Stage 2, which occurs within 8 to 72 hours, is characterized by a worsening of Stage 1 symptoms plus vomiting and illusions or hallucinations.

3. Stage 3, which usually occurs within 48 hours, is characterized by major seizures.

4. Stage 4 is characterized by delirium tremens.

Withdrawal syndrome, which can mimic a number of psychiatric disorders, is characterized by the following signs and symptoms:

• Insomnia

• Muscular weakness

• Fever

• Seizures

• Disorientation, confusion, and thought-process disorders

• Hallucinations

• Anorexia

• Nausea and vomiting

withdrawal syndrome A four-stage syndrome that occurs after a cutback in the amount of alcohol a person is used to or when blood alcohol levels start to fall after severe intoxication

Delirium tremens constitutes the most extreme form of alcohol withdrawal syndrome. Less severe forms include alcoholic tremulousness, alcoholic hallucinosis, and withdrawal seizures, which generally (but not always) precede delirium tremens.

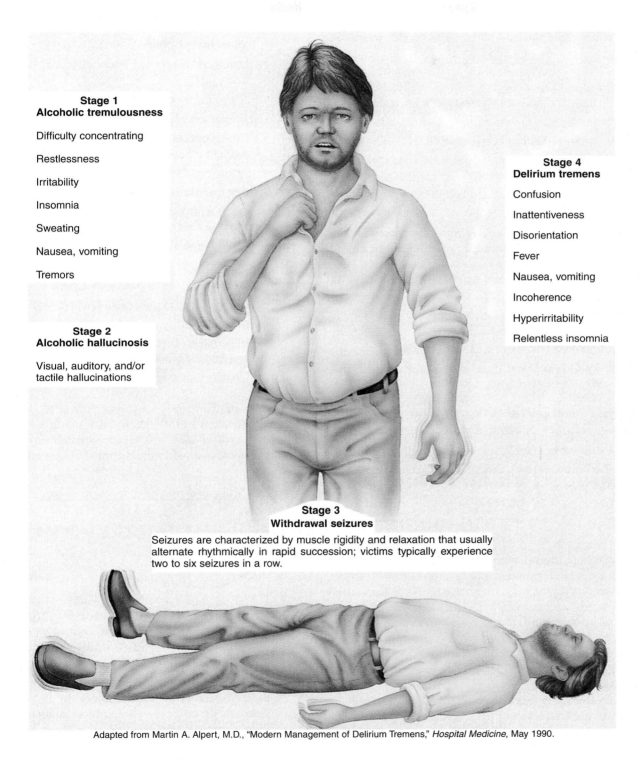

**Stage 1
Alcoholic tremulousness**

Difficulty concentrating

Restlessness

Irritability

Insomnia

Sweating

Nausea, vomiting

Tremors

**Stage 2
Alcoholic hallucinosis**

Visual, auditory, and/or tactile hallucinations

**Stage 4
Delirium tremens**

Confusion

Inattentiveness

Disorientation

Fever

Nausea, vomiting

Incoherence

Hyperirritability

Relentless insomnia

**Stage 3
Withdrawal seizures**

Seizures are characterized by muscle rigidity and relaxation that usually alternate rhythmically in rapid succession; victims typically experience two to six seizures in a row.

Adapted from Martin A. Alpert, M.D., "Modern Management of Delirium Tremens," *Hospital Medicine,* May 1990.

Figure 15-12. Stages of withdrawal

- Sweating
- Rapid heartbeat

Delirium Tremens

Delirium tremens (DTs)—a severe, life-threatening condition with a mortality rate of approximately 15 percent—can occur between 1 and 14 days after the victim's last drink, most commonly within 2 to 5 days. A single episode of DTs lasts between 1 and 3 days; multiple episodes can last as long as a month. DTs should be suspected in any victim with delirium of unknown cause.

Signs and symptoms of DTs include:

- Severe confusion
- Loss of memory
- Tremors
- Restlessness
- Extremely high fever
- Dilated pupils
- Profuse sweating
- Insomnia
- Nausea
- Diarrhea
- Hallucinations, mostly of a frightening nature (such as delusions of snakes, spiders, or rats)

Seizures are very common in alcoholic withdrawal, but not in DTs. However, approximately one-third of all those who have seizures in early withdrawal will progress to DTs if left untreated or if treated inadequately.

Progress Check

1. Alcohol is completely absorbed from the stomach and intestines within _____ hours.
   (2/3/4)

2. Alcohol is concentrated in the blood and the _____ .
   (liver/brain/spleen)

3. Acute intoxication mimics _____ .
   (epilepsy/cerebral hemorrhage/insulin shock)

4. _____ syndrome occurs when blood alcohol levels start to fall after intoxication.
   (Withdrawal/Habituation/Metabolic acidosis)

5. Delirium tremens are characterized by confusion and _____ , usually of a frightening nature.
   (seizures/hallucinations/thought process disorders)

6. _____ is fatal in about 15 percent of the cases.
   (Alcoholism/Delirium tremens/Withdrawal syndrome)

• Section 3 •
ASSESSMENT AND MANAGEMENT

Observation and Assessment

Learning Objective 5 Identify assessment techniques to use in drug and alcohol emergencies.

The most important information to be gathered during assessment of the drug/alcohol victim is severity of intoxication and level of consciousness.

Severity of Intoxication

Determine the severity of intoxication by observing

- Whether the victim is awake and will answer questions
- Whether the victim withdraws from painful stimuli
- Whether respirations are adequate
- Whether the circulatory system is functioning properly (as indicated by pulse and skin color)

Level of Consciousness

Typically, victims fall into one of three categories:

- Awake, claiming to have ingested a medicine—the victim answers questions and is alert and aware.
- Semicomatose—the victim will respond appropriately to verbal or noxious stimuli but will fall asleep when the stimuli are removed.
- Comatose—the victim cannot be aroused to consciousness by verbal or noxious stimuli.

If the victim took a drug that was adulterated with starch, talc, sugar, sawdust, or other white, powdery substance, the emergency can be further complicated by the introduction of bacteria.

Obtaining a History

Obtain a history by asking the following questions:

- What was taken? If you can, find the drug container and its contents so it can be transported with the victim.

- When was it taken?

- How much was taken?

- Was anything else taken (other drugs or alcohol)?

- What has been done to try to correct the situation? Has vomiting been induced? (Street resuscitation procedures are frequently as dangerous as the overdose itself, so it is important to find out exactly what has been done for the victim.)

Signs That Immediate Medical Attention Is Needed

The following signs and symptoms indicate that medical attention is needed immediately:

- Nervous system depression (sleepiness, coma, lethargy, and decreased response to pain)

- Tremors (especially if the victim is suffering withdrawal)

- Withdrawal accompanied by pain

- Digestive problems that include gastritis, vomiting, bleeding, and dehydration

- Excessively slow or absent breathing

- Grand mal seizures

- Delirium tremens

- Disturbances of vision, mental confusion, and muscular incoordination

- Disinterested behavior and loss of memory

General Guidelines for Managing a Drug/Alcohol Crisis

Learning Objective 6 Describe and demonstrate the general guidelines for managing a drug- or alcohol-related emergency.

Crisis intervention is by definition short term. It involves alleviating the pain and confusion of victims in a specific event or circumstance. The goal of crisis intervention is to establish and maintain rapport, create trust, and build a short-term working relationship that will lower anxiety, produce a clearer understanding of the problem at hand, and identify the resources necessary to cope with it (see Figure 15-13).

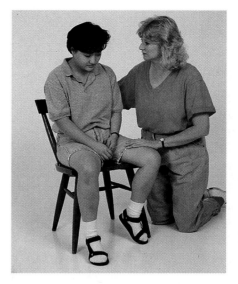

Figure 15-13. Reassure the victim. Explain who you are and that you are trying to help.

Follow these guidelines:

1. Provide a reality base.
   - Identify yourself and your position.
   - Use the victim's name.
   - Anticipate the concerns of the victim, family, and friends.
   - Based on the victim's response, introduce as much familiarity as possible—persons, objects, newspapers, or TV programs.
   - Be calm and self-assured.

2. Provide appropriate nonverbal support.
   - Maintain eye contact.
   - Maintain a relaxed body posture.
   - Be quiet, calm, and gentle.
   - Touch the victim if it seems appropriate.

3. Encourage communication.
   - Communicate directly with the victim, not through others.
   - Ask clear, simple questions.
   - Ask questions slowly, one at a time.

delirium tremens A life-threatening condition causing delirium that usually occurs within 5 days of an alcoholic's last drink

- Try not to ask questions that require a simple "yes" or "no."
- Tolerate repetition; do not become impatient.

4. Foster confidence.
   - Be nonjudgmental; don't accuse the victim.
   - Help the victim gain confidence in you.
   - Listen carefully.
   - Respond to feelings; let the victim know that you understand his or her feelings.
   - Identify and reinforce progress.

Managing a Violent Drug/Alcohol Victim

Learning Objective 7 Describe and demonstrate the guidelines for managing a violent victim of drug overdose.

The following indicate that a victim is about to lose control and become violent (see Figure 15-14)

- Extreme agitation
- Sweating
- Excessive talking while struggling with violent impulses

Be alert to such signals and take evasive action—such as leaving the room or calling in other people—before the victim gets violent.

If a drug or alcohol user becomes violent:

1. Do not approach a potentially violent victim alone. Make sure there are enough First Aiders and other rescuers to overpower the victim. If possible, have law enforcement personnel help.

Figure 15-14. Agitation, perspiration, and excessive talking may indicate that a victim is about to lose control.

2. Avoid aggressive actions unless there is the immediate possibility of serious injury. In all other circumstances, use only defensive techniques, such as holding the victim's arms or legs or wrapping the victim in a blanket.

3. Let the victim sit near the door of the room; do not place any obstacle (person or furniture) between the victim and the door. In other words, don't block the victim's route of escape. A person who feels trapped will likely become more anxious, which will exaggerate hostility and violence. *Make absolutely certain to protect your own route of escape as well.*

4. If the victim is armed, call the police.

5. Protect the victim while in the emergency setting by placing objects such as needles, sharp instruments, and drugs out of reach.

For information on how to restrain a violent victim, see Chapter 28.

Emergency Care

The immediate objective in emergency care of the drug or alcohol victim is to assess cardiopulmonary functioning and to stabilize basic life support functions. The primary concern in acute intoxication is maintaining an airway.

A drug or alcohol victim in a coma or with cardiac complications should be given the same emergency care as any other comatose victim.

Hyperventilation, common in drug-abuse victims, can indicate metabolic acidosis, severe pain, drug withdrawal, or aspirin poisoning. In a drug emergency, treat hyperventilation as a medical disorder, not as anxiety hyperventilation. (See Chapter 17.) Do not have the victim breathe into a paper bag.

Emergency Care for Overdose

Learning Objective 8 Describe and demonstrate the guidelines for managing an overdose.

An increasing overdose problem has grown out of the practice of using individuals as **"mules"** or "body packers." These people swallow latex containers filled with pure cocaine and try to smuggle the cocaine across international borders. They commonly use surgical gloves, latex balloons, or condoms; the package of cocaine may be as large as a golf ball.

In most cases, the package passes through the intestinal system and out of the body without causing damage, but sometimes it breaks. If it ruptures, the carrier's system is flooded with a massive dose of pure cocaine. The ensuing toxic emergency requires aggressive life support measures and rapid transport.

The general goals in handling a victim of overdose are to protect both victim and First Aiders, to calm the victim, and to prevent physical injury, aspiration, and hyperthermia. Activate the EMS system; then:

1. Be prepared for cardiac arrest. Constantly monitor vital signs; your primary priority is to maintain an open airway.

2. Do not panic; treat the victim calmly. Move a victim who is inhaling a harmful substance or who is in immediate danger from surroundings.

3. If the person is conscious, try to get the victim to sit or lie down. Do not use restraints unless the victim poses a risk to safety.

4. Establish and maintain a clear airway. Remove anything from the mouth or throat that might pose a breathing hazard, including false teeth, blood, mucus, or vomitus. Administer artificial ventilation if needed.

5. Turn the victim's head to the side or toward the ground in case of vomiting. Report any blood in the vomitus; bright red blood in the vomitus can be a sign of ruptured blood vessels in the stomach or esophagus.

6. Monitor the victim's vital signs frequently; overdose victims can be conscious one minute and lapse into a coma the next. In case of respiratory or cardiac complications, treat life-threatening situations immediately.

7. Try to maintain proper body temperature. If the temperature goes over 104 degrees F, sponge the victim with tepid water.

8. Take measures to correct or prevent shock, which can result from vomiting, profuse sweating, or inadequate fluid intake. Be alert for allergic reactions.

9. Reduce stimuli as much as possible; lower the lights if you can, and let the victim rest in a calm, quiet atmosphere. If the victim is agitated, move the victim to a quiet place for observation.

10. Carefully explain each step of care so that you can help reduce paranoia.

If there is time before the victim is transported, search the area around the victim for tablets, capsules, pill bottles or boxes (especially empty ones), syringes, other drug paraphernalia, ampules, prescriptions, hospital attendance cards, or physician's notes that might help you identify what drug the victim has taken. Any such evidence should be transported with the victim.

The Talk-Down Technique

Learning Objective 9 Describe and demonstrate the talk-down technique.

The dangers associated with the use of hallucinogens and marijuana are primarily psychological in nature. These may be evident as intense anxiety or panic states (bad trips), depressive or paranoid reactions, mood changes, disorientation, and an inability to distinguish between reality and fantasy. Some prolonged psychotic reactions to psychedelic drugs have been reported, particularly in persons who are already psychologically disturbed.

The talk-down technique is the preferred method for handling bad trips. This technique involves nonmoralizing, comforting, personal support from an experienced individual. It is aided by limiting external stimulation, such as intense light or loud sounds, and having the person lie down and relax. The goal of talking down is to reduce the victim's anxiety, panic, depression, or confusion.

Never use the talk-down technique for victims who have used PCP, because it may further aggravate them. To use the technique in other situations, follow these steps (see Figure 15-15):

1. Make the victim feel welcome. Remain relaxed and sympathetic. Because a victim can become suddenly hostile, have a companion with you. Be calm, but be authoritative.

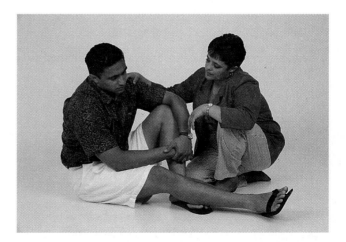

Figure 15-15. Using the talk-down technique to help calm an anxious victim

"mules" Individuals who swallow latex containers filled with cocaine in an attempt to smuggle the drug

2. Reassure the victim that his or her strange mental condition is caused by the drug and will not last forever. Help the victim realize he or she is not mentally ill.

3. Identify yourself clearly. Tell the victim who you are and what you are doing to help. Be careful not to invade the victim's "personal space" until you have established rapport; try to stay approximately 8 to 10 feet away until you sense that the victim has some trust in you. Never touch the victim until he or she gives you permission or unless the victim suddenly poses a threat to safety (his or her own or someone else's).

4. Help the victim verbalize what is happening. Review for the victim what is going on; ask questions. Outline the probable schedule of events, if appropriate.

5. Reiterate simple and concrete statements; repeat and confirm what the victim says. Orient the victim to time and place: be absolutely clear in letting the victim know where he or she is, what is happening, and who is present. Help the victim identify surrounding objects that should be familiar—a process that helps with self-identification. Listen for clues that will let you know whether the victim is anxious; if so, discuss those anxieties. Help the victim work through them and to conquer guilt feelings.

6. Forewarn the victim about what will happen as the drug begins to wear off. There may be confusion one minute, mental clarity the next. Again, help the victim understand that these changes are due to the drug, not to mental illness.

Once the victim is calm, transport the person to a medical facility.

Progress Check

1. A victim who is _____ will respond to verbal or noxious stimuli but will fall asleep when the stimulus is removed.
(awake/semicomatose/comatose)

2. _____ is a sign that medical attention is needed immediately.
(Grand mal seizure/Vomiting/Rapid heartbeat)

3. One way to provide a reality base is to

_____ .
(maintain eye contact/listen carefully/use the victim's name)

4. You can provide nonverbal support by _____ .
(touching the victim/letting the victim watch TV/listening carefully)

5. You can encourage communication by

_____ .
(responding to feelings/maintaining a relaxed body posture/asking questions slowly)

6. The primary goals of care are to monitor vital signs and _____ .
(prevent shock/provide basic life support/prevent aspiration)

7. The top priority in caring for victims of drug/alcohol emergencies is to _____ .
(maintain the airway/maintain circulation/maintain consciousness)

8. The talk-down technique should not be used if the victim took _____ .
(cocaine/PCP/alcohol)

• Section 4 •
SPECIAL CONSIDERATIONS

Because of the unique effects of some drugs, treating users requires special considerations in the field.

Phencyclidine (PCP)

Learning Objective 10 Describe the signs and symptoms of PCP use.

One of the most dangerous hallucinogens is phencyclidine (**PCP**). Among at least 46 names for the drug are angel dust, killer weed, supergrass, crystal cyclone, hog, elephant tranquilizer, PeaCe Pill, embalming fluid, horse tranquilizer, mintweed, mist, monkey dust, rocket fuel, goon, surfer, KW, and scuffle.

Nothing has so bewildered and amazed researchers as phencyclidine—a drug that is cheap, easy to make, easy to take, and is related to horrible psychological effects (some of which can last for years).

PCP is stored in body fat. If a user suddenly loses weight, the drug can be released into the bloodstream and can cause a reaction even if the person has not recently taken the drug.

Physical signs and symptoms of moderate PCP intoxication include

• Extreme agitation

• Involuntary horizontal and vertical movement of the eyes

• Unresponsiveness to pain

- Severe muscular rigidity
- Excessive bronchial and oral secretions (leading to choking in some cases)

Signs and symptoms of moderate intoxication tend to come in spurts—a victim may seem to have no reaction, then may suddenly flare into frantic physical and mental activity. Behavioral manifestations of PCP use include violence, agitation, and bizarre behavior.

All the physical and psychological signs and symptoms of a moderate dose will be exaggerated with a high dose. Other signs and symptoms of a high dose are

- Disruptions in heart rhythm
- Decreased urinary output
- Convulsions
- Respiratory arrest or decrease in respiration
- Vivid visual hallucinations
- Coma (A user may be intermittently in and out of a coma for weeks and months following severe intoxication.)
- Acute muscle rigidity
- Eyes fixated open with a blank stare
- Spasm of the throat muscles
- Excessive sweating, drooling, and vomiting

Three of the most severe reactions stemming from high doses of PCP are psychological ones: schizophrenia, paranoia, and memory loss (amnesia)—in some cases, permanent. A high dose of phencyclidine—10 to 20 milligrams—can cause death.

Learning Objective 11 Describe and demonstrate special care considerations for victims who have taken PCP.

Talking down, a method recommended for other victims of hallucinogenic drugs, should not be used with PCP victims. To give emergency care, activate the EMS system; then:

1. The PCP victim may be combative and require restraint. Your first priority is to protect yourself.
2. Most victims will be confused and upset; keep the lights in the room as dim as you can.
3. Because PCP is an anesthetic, the victim will probably be unaware of any injuries. Check quickly to determine whether there are any injuries that need attention; administer emergency care for those injuries before continuing with psychological care.
4. Monitor vital signs regularly until EMTs arrive.

Cocaine

Learning Objective 12 Describe and demonstrate special care considerations for victims who have taken cocaine.

Another drug that deserves special mention is cocaine, partly because of its widespread use, and partly because of the devastating medical complications of its use. Cocaine is now the drug whose use most often leads to emergency room visits.

Cocaine has become known as the "equal opportunity drug" because of its widespread use and acceptance in all age, racial, ethnic, and socioeconomic groups. It is inhaled through the nose, injected into the veins, and injected into the muscles; in its "freebase" form, it is also smoked. Cocaine is highly addictive and dangerous; cocaine overdose can be fatal.

Before treating any suspected victim of cocaine intoxication, make certain you take measures to prevent the spread of hepatitis, AIDS, and other infectious diseases. These are becoming prominent among cocaine users as intravenous use gains popularity.

To treat, activate the EMS system; then:

1. Immediately monitor vital signs; cocaine intoxication can cause rapidly progressing cardiac and respiratory complications that can lead to cardiac or respiratory arrest.
2. Maintain heartbeat and respirations, using rescue breathing and chest compressions as necessary.
3. If the victim begins to experience seizures, treat as you would any other convulsing victim. Move any obstacles that might cause injury, and monitor vital signs after the seizure has stopped.
4. Cocaine intoxication causes disturbances in body temperature, so monitor core body temperature and initiate cooling measures if temperature increases.
5. Remember that victims of cocaine intoxication may become psychotic, agitated, or suicidal; protect yourself and others at the scene from injury.
6. Limit the amount of stimulation to which the victim is exposed; keep the victim in a quiet place with lights dimmed, and talk in a quiet, reassuring way.

PCP Phencyclidine, a hallucinogenic drug that acts as an anesthetic

Progress Check

1. The most severe reactions from PCP use are
_____ ones.
(physical/emotional/psychological)

2. Do not use _____ with a PCP victim.
(rescue breathing/dim lights/the talk-down technique)

3. Because PCP is an anesthetic, victims may be
unaware of _____ .
(injuries/respiratory problems/time orientation)

4. The first priority in care of a PCP victim is to

_____ .
(maintain an airway/protect yourself/dim the lights)

5. The drug that most often leads to emergency room
visits is _____ .
(PCP/cocaine/LSD)

6. Cocaine intoxication can rapidly lead to

_____ .
(respiratory arrest/metabolic acidosis/coma)

• SUMMARY •

- Because many serious diseases resemble drug and
alcohol overdose, it is important to assess the situation carefully to determine whether an emergency is drug or alcohol related.

- A musky, fruity, or acetone odor on the breath is
a sign of diabetic coma, not alcohol intoxication.

- Six signs and symptoms indicate that a drug/al-
cohol emergency is life-threatening: unconsciousness, breathing difficulties, fever, abnormal or
irregular pulse, vomiting while not fully conscious, and seizures.

- Acute alcohol intoxication has many of the same
signs and symptoms of insulin shock; when in
doubt, give sugar.

- Withdrawal syndrome occurs after a cutback in
the amount of alcohol a person is used to, or
when blood alcohol levels start to fall after
severe intoxication; it can progress to delirium
tremens.

- Delirium tremens, characterized by severe confusion and often frightening hallucinations, are a
life-threatening condition.

- The general guidelines for managing a drug/alcohol
crisis are to provide a reality base, provide appropriate nonverbal support, encourage communication, and foster confidence.

- To manage a violent victim of drug overdose,
watch for the signs that a person is about to lose
control—high degrees of agitation, sweating, and
excessive talking while struggling with violent impulses.

- Handle a victim of drug or alcohol overdose much
as you would a victim with any other medical
problem; top priorities are breathing and circulation.

- The talk-down technique involves nonmoralizing,
comforting, personal support from an experienced
individual and is recommended for handling bad
trips caused by any drug other than PCP.

• KEY TERMS •

Make sure you understand the following key terms:

- withdrawal syndrome
- delirium tremens
- "mules"
- PCP

Student: _____ Date: _____

Course: _____ Section #: _____

If you believe the statement is true, circle the T. If you believe the statement is false, circle the F.

T   F   **1.** The most important information about a drug overdose is what kind of drug was used.

T   F   **2.** Seizures are rare in alcoholic withdrawal.

T   F   **3.** The most severe reactions from PCP use include paranoia and memory loss.

T   F   **4.** Hyperventilating drug-emergency victims should be encouraged to breathe into a paper bag.

T   F   **5.** DTs that occur more than 1 day after the last drink are rarely life threatening.

For each item, circle the correct answer or the phrase that best completes the statement.

1. A common emergency among drug-abuse victims is
   a. hyperventilation
   b. cardiac arrhythmias
   c. convulsions
   d. tremors

2. Hyperventilation in a drug emergency should be treated by
   a. removing the victim from the crisis situation as soon as possible
   b. quieting the victim and leaving the victim alone to calm down
   c. encouraging the victim to place the head lower than the knees
   d. having the victim breathe into a paper bag

3. A pulse rate _____ may indicate danger in a drug/alcohol emergency in an adult.
   a. below 60 or above 100
   b. below 60 or above 130
   c. below 60 or above 120
   d. below 80 or above 100

4. Which of the following may indicate that a drug/alcohol emergency is life threatening?
   a. pancreatitis
   b. impaired coordination
   c. vomiting while not fully conscious
   d. disturbance of vision

5. Which of the following is *not* a guideline for dealing with an overdose victim?
   a. induce vomiting
   b. throw a little cold water on a semiconscious victim
   c. be alert for allergic reactions
   d. be firm but friendly

6. What is the preferred method for handling a victim experiencing a bad trip?
   a. throw cold water on the victim
   b. use the talk-down technique
   c. get the victim to walk around
   d. put the victim in an isolated room

7. The signs of acute intoxication may be mimicked by a victim of
   a. diabetic coma
   b. insulin shock
   c. epilepsy
   d. violence

8. Which of the following indicate that medical attention is needed immediately for an alcohol-abuse victim?
   a. grand mal seizure
   b. high blood pressure
   c. hypoglycemia
   d. increased breathing rate

9. Delirium tremens occur as a result of
   a. alcohol overdose
   b. alcohol taken with tranquilizers
   c. high alcohol concentrations ingested very quickly
   d. alcohol withdrawal

10. Which of the following is *not* a symptom of delirium tremens?
   a. confusion
   b. hallucinations
   c. shaking hands
   d. deep, comatose sleep

- You find an older man unconscious in an alley. He smells of alcohol and exhibits respiratory depression and signs of shock.

16

Cardiovascular and Stroke Emergencies

Learning Objectives

When you have mastered the material in this chapter, you will be able to:

1 Identify the two types of coronary artery disease

2 Describe the physiological process involved in angina pectoris

3 List the signs and symptoms of angina pectoris

4 Describe the physiological process involved in congestive heart failure

5 List the signs and symptoms of congestive heart failure

6 Describe the physiological process involved in myocardial infarction

7 List the signs and symptoms of myocardial infarction

8 Describe and demonstrate the emergency care of a victim who does not have a pulse

9 Describe and demonstrate the emergency care of a victim who is responsive

10 Explain the guidelines for use of nitroglycerin

11 Describe and demonstrate how to help a victim use physician-prescribed nitroglycerin

12 Describe the physiological processes in the brain that cause stroke

13 List the signs and symptoms of stroke

14 Describe and demonstrate the emergency care of a stroke victim

O n October 27, 1998, 70-year-old Harold Hawker was raking leaves under a stand of maples when he suddenly felt nauseous and light-headed. As he walked toward a garden bench at the edge of his yard, he began to feel a squeezing, burning, heavy sensation on the left side of his chest. As he slumped onto the bench, he called out to his neighbor, Phyllis Gibb, who was raking leaves in her own yard.

When Phyllis reached Harold, the pain in his chest had become intense. He was still complaining of nausea, and his skin was cool and moist. He was struggling with shortness of breath, and he told Phyllis he felt extremely weak. She noticed that his brow was covered with profuse perspiration, despite the cool weather.

Phyllis told Harold to keep still, ran back to her own yard, and asked her teenage son to call for paramedics. She returned to Harold and verified that he was still breathing and had a pulse. Reassuring him, she helped him to a sitting position, which enabled him to breathe a little more easily. Phyllis unbuttoned Harold's top two shirt buttons, then draped her own sweater across his shoulders to help him keep warm. Phyllis continued to reassure and calm Harold and to monitor his vital signs while they both waited for emergency personnel to arrive. EMTs verified that Harold had suffered a minor heart attack, stabilized him, and transported him to a nearby hospital while Phyllis waited for Harold's wife to return from the grocery store.

HEART ATTACKS AND ASSOCIATED HEART DISEASE ARE the number-one killer in the United States today. Almost half a million Americans die each year of cardiovascular disease, and nearly 29 million more Americans suffer from some form of the disease. The most common problem is coronary artery disease, which usually causes angina pectoris and, left untreated, may eventually lead to acute myocardial infarction (heart attack).

Because of the critical nature of heart disease emergencies, you should treat every adult with chest pain as a heart attack victim until proven otherwise.

This chapter lists the signs and symptoms associated with cardiovascular emergencies and outlines life-sustaining care you can provide until emergency personnel arrive at the scene.

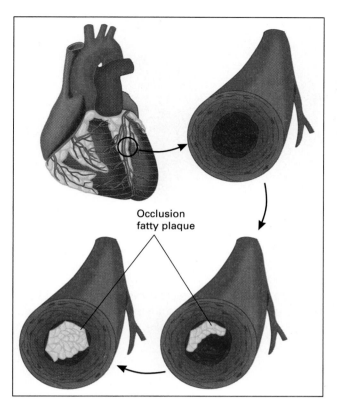

Figure 16-1. *Fatty deposits build up in arteries, depriving the heart muscle of blood and oxygen.*

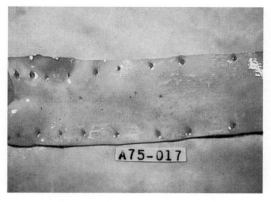

Figure 16-2. *Inside surface of a normal artery*

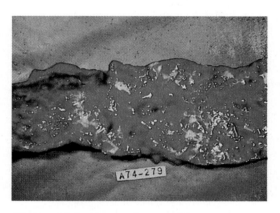

Figure 16-3. *Artery damaged by coronary artery disease*

• Section 1 •
CORONARY ARTERY DISEASE

Learning Objective 1 Identify the two types of coronary artery disease.

As the name implies, **coronary artery disease** affects the arteries that supply the heart with blood by injuring the inner lining of the arterial walls. The two types of coronary artery disease are **atherosclerosis** and **arteriosclerosis;** atherosclerosis is a form of arteriosclerosis, and victims commonly have both kinds. In coronary artery disease, the opening of the coronary artery is narrowed, restricting the amount of blood that can reach and nourish the heart muscle (see Figures 16-1 through 16-5). Roughened interior surfaces on the artery cause buildup of additional debris, further narrowing the artery. At some point, the victim may experience angina pectoris or a heart attack, because the coronary artery eventually becomes blocked. Figure 16-6 on page 274 outlines cardiac risk factors.

Atherosclerosis

Atherosclerosis results when fatty substances—called **plaque**—and other debris are deposited on the inner lining of the arterial wall. As a result, the opening of the artery is narrowed, reducing the flow of blood through the affected artery.

Arteriosclerosis

Arteriosclerosis occurs when calcium is deposited in the walls of the arteries, resulting in loss of arterial

coronary artery disease A condition in which a coronary artery has been damaged

atherosclerosis A condition in which fatty substances and other debris are deposited on the arterial walls

arteriosclerosis A disease condition in which the arteries lose their elasticity

plaque Fatty deposits on the arterial walls

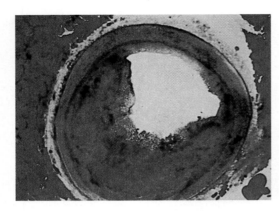

Figure 16-4. *Severe atherosclerosis (inside surface of artery)*

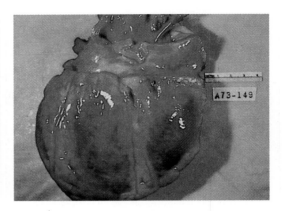

Figure 16-5. *Atherosclerosis (cross-section of artery)*

elasticity and an increase in blood pressure. The plaque deposits of atherosclerosis can also cause arteriosclerosis, or "hardening of the arteries." Arte-

riosclerosis generally affects other arteries in addition to the coronary arteries, and may lead to hypertension, kidney disease, or stroke.

CARDIAC RISK FACTORS

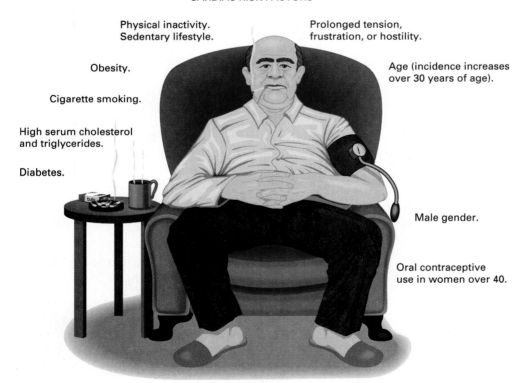

Physical inactivity.
Sedentary lifestyle.

Obesity.

Cigarette smoking.

High serum cholesterol
and triglycerides.

Diabetes.

Prolonged tension,
frustration, or hostility.

Age (incidence increases
over 30 years of age).

Male gender.

Oral contraceptive
use in women over 40.

Family history of premature coronary heart disease (usually under age 60).

Figure 16-6. *Each additional risk factor increases the likelihood of premature myocardial infarction. The risk for a victim who has high cholesterol levels and high blood pressure and who is a heavy smoker is ten times that of someone without those risk factors.*

Progress Check

1. _____ results when fatty substances are deposited on the inner lining of the arterial walls. *(Arteriosclerosis/Atherosclerosis/Angina pectoris)*

2. _____ occurs when arteries lose their elasticity. *(Arteriosclerosis/Atherosclerosis/Angina pectoris)*

3. Coronary artery disease affects the arteries that supply the _____ . *(heart/lungs/brain)*

4. Heart attack occurs when the coronary artery becomes _____ . *(constricted/dilated/blocked)*

• Section 2 •
ANGINA PECTORIS, CONGESTIVE HEART FAILURE, AND MYOCARDIAL INFARCTION

Angina Pectoris

Learning Objective 2 Describe the physiological process involved in angina pectoris.

Angina pectoris literally means "pain in the chest" and is actually a set of signs and symptoms that can occur in a victim with serious coronary artery disease. Angina occurs when the heart's demand for oxygen is temporarily greater than what it is receiving. Because of the disease, the coronary arteries are narrowed, and only a limited supply of oxygen-rich blood can be delivered to the heart.

Like any muscle, the heart relies on a constant supply of oxygen to function. When the demand for oxygenated blood is greater than the diseased or constricted arteries can provide, the victim experiences angina pectoris—a brief feeling of pain or discomfort that signals the heart's need for oxygen.

Most often angina pectoris occurs because the victim has increased the heart's workload and thus its demand for oxygen, usually by physical activity or emotional excitement, and most often in cold weather. When the heart's workload is increased, it needs greater amounts of blood, which the diseased arteries are unable to deliver.

Angina is reversible and produces no permanent damage to the heart. Pain is generally relieved by rest, usually within a few minutes after the victim stops the

activity, calms down, moves indoors, or takes nitroglycerin as prescribed by a physician.

Many cases of chest pain are actually unrelated to the heart. Chest pain can be caused by a respiratory infection (such as bronchitis or pneumonia), pleuritis (which causes the lining of the lung to separate), overexertion, injuries to the ribs, strained muscles in the chest or back, or indigestion.

Signs and Symptoms

Learning Objective 3 List the signs and symptoms of angina pectoris.

The most common symptom of angina is chest pain; it may range from a mild ache to a severe crushing pain. It appears suddenly, but is usually associated with physical exertion. The pain is located under the sternum, but may also radiate to the jaw, neck, left shoulder, left arm, and left hand.

Other common signs and symptoms include (see Figure 16-7 on page 276):

- Dyspnea (shortness of breath)
- Profuse perspiration
- Light-headedness
- Palpitations
- Nausea and/or vomiting
- Pale, cool, moist skin

Remember: It is impossible for a First Aider to tell the difference between the pain of angina pectoris and that of heart attack. All victims with chest pain should be treated for heart attack and should be transported to a medical facility for evaluation.

Congestive Heart Failure

Learning Objective 4 Describe the physiological process involved in congestive heart failure.

Congestive heart failure results when the heart's output of oxygenated blood does not meet the needs of the body's tissues. As a result, the tissues are not adequately perfused with oxygen. While there are a number of causes, the most common include heart attack, high blood pressure, chronic obstructive pulmonary disease, coronary artery disease, and heart valve damage.

angina pectoris Chest pain caused when the heart's need for oxygen is not met

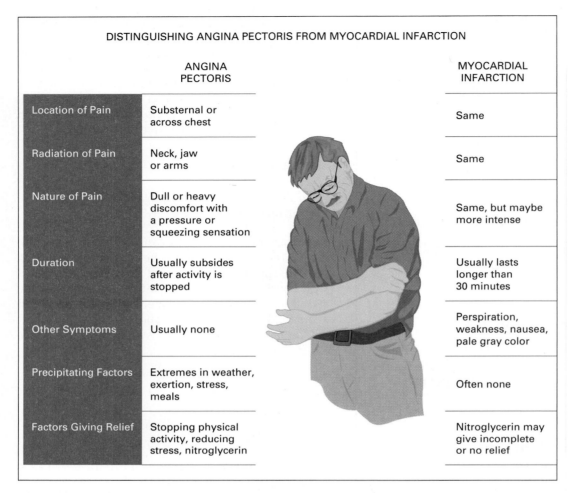

DISTINGUISHING ANGINA PECTORIS FROM MYOCARDIAL INFARCTION

	ANGINA PECTORIS	MYOCARDIAL INFARCTION
Location of Pain	Substernal or across chest	Same
Radiation of Pain	Neck, jaw or arms	Same
Nature of Pain	Dull or heavy discomfort with a pressure or squeezing sensation	Same, but maybe more intense
Duration	Usually subsides after activity is stopped	Usually lasts longer than 30 minutes
Other Symptoms	Usually none	Perspiration, weakness, nausea, pale gray color
Precipitating Factors	Extremes in weather, exertion, stress, meals	Often none
Factors Giving Relief	Stopping physical activity, reducing stress, nitroglycerin	Nitroglycerin may give incomplete or no relief

Figure 16-7. *If in doubt as to which condition the victim has, always treat as if it is an acute myocardial infarction.*

As congestive heart failure progresses, fluid builds up behind the failing left side of the heart. This increases pressure in the pulmonary capillaries, causing plasma to seep out of the capillaries and into the surrounding lung tissue, a condition called **pulmonary edema.** If pulmonary edema is not corrected, severe respiratory distress follows. Congestive heart failure gradually reduces the lungs' oxygen capacity, and death occurs.

The symptoms of congestive heart failure can be treated, but the underlying condition is almost never curable. Congestive heart failure is a true medical emergency—a stable victim can suddenly and rapidly deteriorate without warning.

Signs and Symptoms

Learning Objective 5 List the signs and symptoms of congestive heart failure.

Pain may or may not occur with congestive heart failure, usually depending on whether heart attack has also occurred. The most dramatic sign of congestive heart failure is pulmonary edema, resulting in severe shortness of breath and, sometimes, spasmodic coughing that produces pink frothy sputum. Other signs and symptoms include (see Figure 16-8):

• Wheezing

• Profuse sweating

• Rapid heart rate

• Increased respiratory rate with fast, labored breathing

• Paleness or cyanosis

• Difficulty breathing while lying flat

• Swelling of the feet and lower legs

• Anxiety

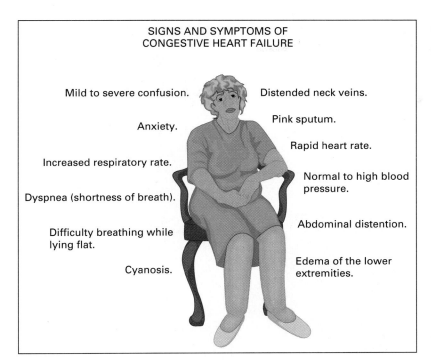

SIGNS AND SYMPTOMS OF
CONGESTIVE HEART FAILURE

Mild to severe confusion.

Anxiety.

Increased respiratory rate.

Dyspnea (shortness of breath).

Difficulty breathing while
lying flat.

Cyanosis.

Distended neck veins.

Pink sputum.

Rapid heart rate.

Normal to high blood
pressure.

Abdominal distention.

Edema of the lower
extremities.

*Figure 16-8. While
these signs and symptoms
are most common, the
victim of congestive heart
failure may have any
combination of symptoms
or only one or two.*

- Mild to severe confusion

- A desire to sit upright

- Abdominal distension

- Distended neck veins

- Apprehension or agitation coupled with the feeling of being smothered

Remember: While these signs and symptoms are the most common, the victim may have any combination of them, and some victims have only one or two.

Myocardial Infarction

Learning Objective 6 Describe the physiological process involved in myocardial infarction.

Most often called a "heart attack," **myocardial infarction** means the death of the **myocardium,** or heart muscle. When blood supply to part of the heart is significantly reduced or is stopped completely, the affected part dies (see Figure 16-9 on page 278).

Myocardial infarction is most often associated with coronary artery disease—most frequently, with a thrombus or clot in a coronary artery already diseased by atherosclerosis. It can also result from a spasm in the coronary artery or when the heart's need for oxygen exceeds its supply for an extended period of time.

Signs and Symptoms

Learning Objective 7 List the signs and symptoms of myocardial infarction.

The signs and symptoms of myocardial infarction vary, depending on the amount of heart damage and how the autonomic nervous system responds to the damage.

It can be very difficult to determine whether someone has suffered a heart attack without sophisticated diagnostic equipment. The major symptom of myocardial infarction is chest pain (see Figure 16-10 on page 279) that may range from mild discomfort to severe crushing pain; it can also be an uncomfortable squeezing, pressure, or sensation of fullness. *Note that 25 percent of all myocardial infarction victims have no chest pain at all.* A heart attack without pain is called a **silent myocardial infarction.**

pulmonary edema A condition in which plasma seeps out of the capillaries into the lungs as a result of pressure from a failing heart
myocardial infarction Heart attack, caused when the blood supply to the heart is restricted or cut off
myocardium The heart muscle
silent myocardial infarction A heart attack that does not cause chest pain

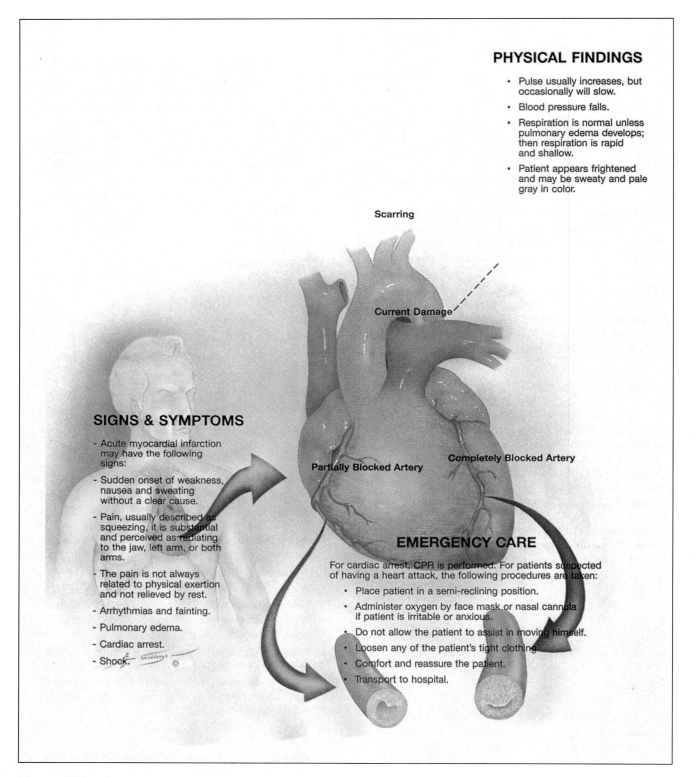

PHYSICAL FINDINGS

- Pulse usually increases, but occasionally will slow.
- Blood pressure falls.
- Respiration is normal unless pulmonary edema develops; then respiration is rapid and shallow.
- Patient appears frightened and may be sweaty and pale gray in color.

Scarring

Current Damage

SIGNS & SYMPTOMS

- Acute myocardial infarction may have the following signs:
- Sudden onset of weakness, nausea and sweating without a clear cause.
- Pain, usually described as squeezing, it is substantial and perceived as radiating to the jaw, left arm, or both arms.
- The pain is not always related to physical exertion and not relieved by rest.
- Arrhythmias and fainting.
- Pulmonary edema.
- Cardiac arrest.
- Shock.

Partially Blocked Artery   Completely Blocked Artery

EMERGENCY CARE

For cardiac arrest, CPR is performed. For patients suspected of having a heart attack, the following procedures are taken:

- Place patient in a semi-reclining position.
- Administer oxygen by face mask or nasal cannula if patient is irritable or anxious.
- Do not allow the patient to assist in moving himself.
- Loosen any of the patient's tight clothing.
- Comfort and reassure the patient.
- Transport to hospital.

Figure 16-9. Myocardial infarction (heart attack)

When present, the pain lasts for longer than a few minutes. The classic location of the pain is the center of the chest; it often radiates to the neck, jaw, left shoulder, and left arm (see Figure 16-11). *Any adult with chest pain should be suspected of suffering myocardial infarction unless proven otherwise.*

Figure 16-10. *The major symptom of myocardial infarction is chest pain.*

Not all signs and symptoms listed occur with every heart attack, but the most common signs and symptoms of myocardial infarction include

- Shortness of breath
- Profuse sweating
- Cool, pale, moist skin
- Cyanosis
- Nausea and/or vomiting
- Weakness
- Light-headedness
- Anxiety
- Feeling of impending doom
- Pulse exceeding 100 beats per minute
- A pulse of less than 60 beats per minute
- Fainting

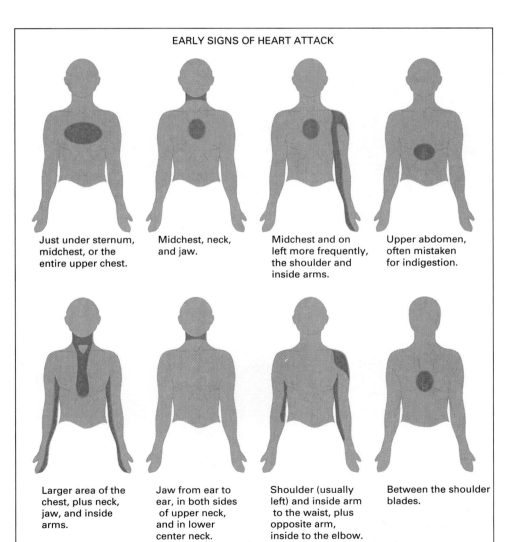

EARLY SIGNS OF HEART ATTACK

Just under sternum, midchest, or the entire upper chest.

Midchest, neck, and jaw.

Midchest and on left more frequently, the shoulder and inside arms.

Upper abdomen, often mistaken for indigestion.

Larger area of the chest, plus neck, jaw, and inside arms.

Jaw from ear to ear, in both sides of upper neck, and in lower center neck.

Shoulder (usually left) and inside arm to the waist, plus opposite arm, inside to the elbow.

Between the shoulder blades.

Figure 16-11. *Pain or discomfort can occur in any one location or any combination of locations.*

Progress Check

1. Angina pectoris occurs when the heart's demand for _____ exceeds its supply.
   (blood/oxygen/rest)

2. The most common symptom of angina pectoris is
   _____ .
   (light-headedness/profuse perspiration/chest pain)

3. Congestive heart failure occurs when the heart's ability to _____ does not meet the demands of the body.
   (pump blood/oxygenate blood/circulate blood to the lungs)

4. The most common cause of congestive heart failure is _____ .
   (diabetes/stroke/heart attack)

5. The most dramatic sign of congestive heart failure is
   _____ .
   (pulmonary edema/swollen ankles/distended neck veins)

6. Myocardial infarction literally means death of the
   _____ .
   (pericardium/myocardium/epicardium)

7. The major symptom of myocardial infarction is
   _____ .
   (dyspnea/nausea/chest pain)

8. Approximately _____ percent of all myocardial infarction victims do not experience chest pain.
   (10/25/50)

• Section 3 •
EMERGENCY CARE

Time is critical in the treatment of cardiac emergencies—the first few minutes after cardiac compromise begins are critical to survival. If CPR is started within 4 minutes, there is a dramatic difference in the survival of the victim. Most of the permanent damage done to the heart occurs within the first hour.

Treatment varies depending on whether the victim has absent circulation or the victim is responsive with a known history of cardiac problems. Regardless of the situation, *immediately* access the EMS system.

Emergency Care—Pulse Is Absent

Learning Objective 8 Describe and demonstrate the emergency care of a victim who does not have a pulse.

If circulation and pulse are absent, activate the EMS system, then initiate CPR. For details on CPR, see Chapter 5.

Emergency Care—Responsive Victim

Learning Objective 9 Describe and demonstrate the emergency care of a victim who is responsive.

To treat a responsive victim, activate the EMS system; then:

1. Perform an initial assessment. Note the type, location, and intensity of any pain and the presence of other signs and symptoms characteristic of cardiac compromise.

2. If the victim complains of chest pain or discomfort, monitor vital signs continuously; provide rescue breathing if it becomes appropriate (see Figure 16-12).

3. If the victim has physician-prescribed **nitroglycerin,** help the victim take one dose of the medication *if you are allowed to do so in your area and if the victim has not already taken it.*
   - Repeat the dose in 3 to 5 minutes if pain is not relieved.
   - Give as many as three doses, each 3 to 5 minutes apart. Reassess vital signs and chest pain after each dose.

4. Don't let the victim move on his or her own; reassure and comfort the victim, and place the victim in the position of greatest comfort (usually semisitting, with legs up and bent at the knees).

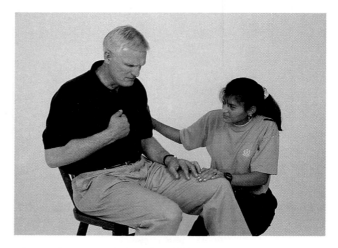

Figure 16-12. Assessing a victim with chest pain

5. Loosen restrictive clothing at the neck and midriff, and keep the victim warm, but do not overheat.

6. Monitor vital signs continuously, and be prepared to start CPR if needed.

Cautions about Nitroglycerin

Learning Objective 10 Explain the guidelines for the use of nitroglycerin.

The most commonly prescribed medication for those with a history of cardiac compromise is nitroglycerin, known by the trade names of Nitro-bid, Nitrong, and Nitro-stat.

If allowed to do so in your area, you can help the victim take the nitroglycerin if all of the following criteria exist:

- The victim has chest pain.
- The nitroglycerin was prescribed for the victim by a physician.
- You have specific authorization to assist the victim in taking the nitroglycerin.

You should not allow the victim to take nitroglycerin if any of the following exist:

- The victim has low blood pressure (systolic pressure below 100 mmHg).
- You suspect or know that the victim has a head injury.
- The victim is an infant or child.
- The victim already took the maximum prescribed dose before you arrived on the scene.

Learning Objective 11 Describe and demonstrate how to help a victim use physician-prescribed nitroglycerin.

Nitroglycerin is available in two different forms, tablets and spray, both of which are administered under the tongue. If you are authorized to help the victim:

1. Take the victim's blood pressure; the systolic pressure must be more than 100 mmHg if you are to use nitroglycerin.

2. Verify that you have the right victim, the right medication (nitroglycerin), the right form of medication (tablets or spray), and that the victim is alert and responsive.

3. Check the expiration date on the victim's prescription to verify that the medication is still potent.

4. Ask the victim to lift his or her tongue; wearing latex gloves, place the tablet or spray under the tongue, or have the victim place the tablet or spray under the tongue.

5. Have the victim keep his or her mouth closed (without swallowing) until the tablet has dissolved and been absorbed by the tissues under the tongue.

6. Within 2 minutes, check the victim's blood pressure; perform a reassessment.

Progress Check

1. If the victim does not have a pulse, immediately begin _____ .
(monitoring vital signs/CPR/rescue breathing)

2. If the victim is responsive, keep the victim in a _____ position.
(comfortable/supine/prone)

3. Do not let the victim _____ .
(eat/drink/move around)

4. If the victim has physician-prescribed _____ , help the victim use it.
(pain medication/high blood pressure medication/nitroglycerin)

• Section 4 •
STROKE

Stroke (cerebrovascular accident, or CVA) is defined as any disease process that impairs circulation to the brain. Without adequate blood circulation, brain cells are deprived of oxygen and die within minutes; dead brain cells are never replaced and do not regenerate. The third most common cause of death in this country, stroke affects more than half a million Americans each year. More than half of those die, and many others suffer permanent physiological damage.

The characteristics of stroke depend on the extent of the stroke, the site of the stroke, and the amount of brain damage that results. The outcome depends on the age of the victim, the location and function of

nitroglycerin Medication prescribed to ease the pain of angina pectoris

stroke Any disease process that impairs circulation to the brain

brain cells that were damaged, the extent of the damage, and how rapidly other areas of brain tissue are able to take over the work of the damaged cells.

Causes of Stroke

Learning Objective 12 Describe the physiological processes in the brain that cause stroke.

Stroke, also known as cerebrovascular accident (CVA), occurs when blood flow to the brain is interrupted long enough to cause damage, resulting in the sudden onset of brain dysfunction. There are four general causes of stroke (Figure 16-13):

- Thrombus
- Embolus
- Hemorrhage
- Compression

Thrombus

Approximately 75 to 85 percent of all strokes occur when a cerebral artery is blocked by a clot **(thrombus)** that forms inside the brain. A thrombus stroke is also called an **ischemic stroke.** Most occur in those over the age of 50, and the incidence increases with age. Clots generally do not form in healthy arteries, but rather around the hardened, thickened walls of arteries damaged by atherosclerosis.

As many as 75 percent of all thrombus strokes are preceded by one or more **transient ischemic attacks** (TIAs), brief spells similar to strokes that occur when the blockage is partial or lasts only a few minutes. TIAs often occur in a series over a period of days, usually getting worse with time; brain cells are injured, but they do not die.

The symptoms of a TIA last for less than 24 hours and usually for less than 1 hour; TIAs do *not* cause nausea or vomiting, and headache is not often present. The most common signs and symptoms of TIAs are the

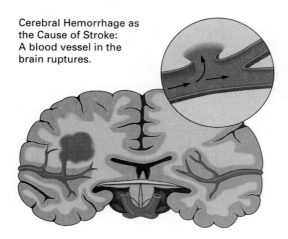

Cerebral Hemorrhage as the Cause of Stroke: A blood vessel in the brain ruptures.

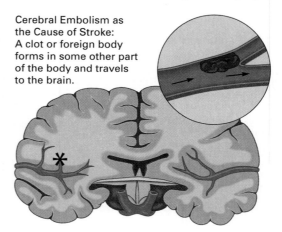

Cerebral Embolism as the Cause of Stroke: A clot or foreign body forms in some other part of the body and travels to the brain.

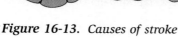

STROKE

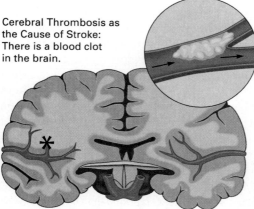

Cerebral Thrombosis as the Cause of Stroke: There is a blood clot in the brain.

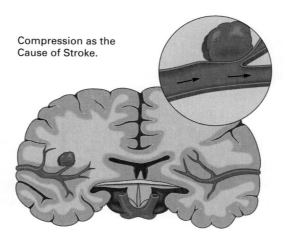

Compression as the Cause of Stroke.

Figure 16-13. Causes of stroke

same as those of stroke, and include

- Blindness in one eye
- Dizziness
- Light-headedness
- Fainting
- Difficulty performing familiar acts
- Temporary paralysis of the face
- Temporary paralysis of one side of the body
- Difficulty pronouncing or understanding words
- Inability to recognize familiar objects

Embolus

A stroke may also result when a clot develops elsewhere in the body, travels through the bloodstream, and becomes lodged in one of the cerebral arteries—a condition called **cerebral embolism.** Of all strokes, these have the most rapid onset; they often occur in young or middle-aged adults and are most common among people with existing heart disease.

Hemorrhage

In 15 to 25 percent of all strokes, a diseased blood vessel in the brain bursts, flooding the surrounding brain tissue with blood (Figure 16-14). Bleeding can either be into the brain tissue itself or into the spinal fluid that surrounds the brain. Hemorrhage is the most dramatic form of stroke, and 80 percent of its victims die. Onset is abrupt.

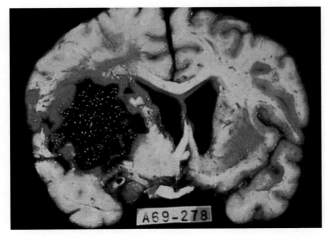

Figure 16-14. Brain of a victim of cerebrovascular accident (stroke) from cerebral hemorrhage

Compression

A small percentage of strokes occur when extreme pressure is applied to a cerebral artery, cutting off blood supply to adjacent brain tissue and nerves. Pressure can be caused by a brain tumor, displaced brain tissue following hemorrhage somewhere else in the brain, or a clot that forms outside the artery from blood leakage.

Signs and Symptoms

> **Learning Objective 13** List the signs and symptoms of stroke.

The signs and symptoms of stroke depend on the cause, location, and severity of the stroke. A stroke caused by thrombus results in lessening of bodily functions without accompanying pain or seizures; onset is gradual and progresses in a step-like way. A stroke caused by cerebral hemorrhage produces sudden, excruciating headache followed by a rapid loss of consciousness, neck rigidity, and coma. A stroke caused by an embolus may be marked by sudden seizures, paralysis, and abrupt loss of consciousness; an explosive headache may occur.

The general signs and symptoms of stroke occur suddenly and may include the following (Figure 16-15 on page 284):

- Altered level of consciousness—dizziness, confusion, unsteadiness, change in personality, change in the level of mental ability, seizures, decreased consciousness, or coma

- Motor function problems—weakness of the arms, legs, or face; numbness or paralysis of the face, arms, or legs, often on only one side; one-sided weakness or numbness that gradually spreads; mouth drawn to one side or drooping; paralysis of facial muscles

thrombus A clot that forms in a cerebral artery

ischemic stroke A stroke caused by a clot inside the brain

transient ischemic attack Brief attacks similar to strokes that occur when arterial blockage is partial or brief

cerebral embolism A clot that forms elsewhere in the body, travels through the bloodstream, and lodges in a cerebral artery

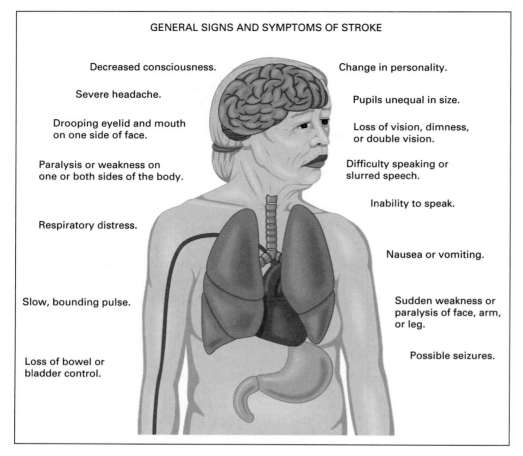

GENERAL SIGNS AND SYMPTOMS OF STROKE

Decreased consciousness.

Severe headache.

Drooping eyelid and mouth on one side of face.

Paralysis or weakness on one or both sides of the body.

Respiratory distress.

Slow, bounding pulse.

Loss of bowel or bladder control.

Change in personality.

Pupils unequal in size.

Loss of vision, dimness, or double vision.

Difficulty speaking or slurred speech.

Inability to speak.

Nausea or vomiting.

Sudden weakness or paralysis of face, arm, or leg.

Possible seizures.

Figure 16-15. One or more signs or symptoms may be sufficient reason to begin emergency care.

- Sensory function problems—loss of vision, temporary dimness of vision, or double vision
- Altered communication abilities—inability to speak, trouble speaking or understanding speech, or stuttering
- Headache that is sudden, severe, or accompanied by a stiff neck
- Flushed or pale face
- Respiratory distress
- Constricted pupils, or pupils unequal in size or reaction
- Loss of bowel or bladder control
- Nausea and/or vomiting

It is important to note the victim's state of consciousness. Only massive strokes or those involving the brain stem render the victim completely unconscious. The most critical stroke victim is the one who loses consciousness completely and becomes limp on one side; these signs indicate major brain injury.

Emergency Care for Stroke

Learning Objective 14 Describe and demonstrate the emergency care of a stroke victim.

Remember: It is not important to determine at the scene the kind of stroke that occurred. Emergency care is the same, regardless of what caused the stroke, and is limited to support of the victim.

To treat a victim of stroke, activate the EMS system; then:

1. Handle the victim calmly and carefully; be particularly gentle with paralyzed parts. Say nothing to increase the victim's anxiety (remember that a victim who can't communicate can still hear you); anxiety can considerably worsen a stroke.

2. If the victim is conscious, position him or her on the back with the head and shoulders slightly raised; keep the head in a neutral, forward-facing position. If the victim is unconscious, place him or her on the left side with the chin extended.

3. Assess airway and respiration.
4. If the victim develops difficulty breathing or becomes unconscious, turn him or her on the side with the paralyzed side down and well cushioned. If the victim vomits, clear the airway and allow drainage.
5. If the eyelid is affected, gently close the eye and loosely tape it closed to prevent it from drying.
6. Keep the victim warm, but don't overheat.
7. Keep the victim absolutely quiet and shielded from onlookers.
8. Never give the victim anything to eat or drink.

Progress Check

1. Stroke occurs when _____ to the brain is impaired.
   (blood pressure/blood circulation/nerve impulse)

2. Most strokes are caused by _____ .
   (embolus/thrombus/hemorrhage)

3. The most serious strokes are characterized by _____ .
   (paralysis/loss of vision/total loss of consciousness)

4. Position a stroke victim _____ .
   (on the side/flat on the back/on the back with head and shoulders elevated)

• SUMMARY •

- Coronary artery disease affects the artery that supplies the heart with blood; when the blood supply is compromised, angina pectoris or myocardial infarction can result.

- Angina pectoris occurs when the heart's need for oxygen exceeds its supply; it is reversible and is usually relieved by rest.

- Congestive heart failure is a true medical emergency, because its victims can deteriorate rapidly; while symptoms can be treated, the underlying cause usually cannot be corrected.

- Myocardial infarction, or heart attack, causes death of the myocardium (the heart muscle); it occurs when the blood supply to the heart is restricted or cut off completely.

- All victims of chest pain should be suspected of having suffered myocardial infarction.

- The most classic symptom of both angina pectoris and myocardial infarction is chest pain; the most dramatic symptom of congestive heart failure is pulmonary edema.

- To care for a cardiac victim without a pulse, initiate CPR as described in Chapter 5.

- To care for a responsive cardiac victim, keep the victim still, monitor vital signs continuously, place the victim in a position of comfort, and keep the victim warm.

- Stroke occurs when blood circulation to the brain is impaired; it can be caused by a clot that forms in a cerebral artery, a clot that forms elsewhere and gets lodged in a cerebral artery, a cerebral vessel that bursts and bleeds into brain tissue, or severe compression of a cerebral artery.

- The signs and symptoms of stroke depend on the cause, location, and severity of the stroke; the most critical stroke victim is the one who completely loses consciousness and becomes limp on one side of the body.

• KEY TERMS •

Make sure you understand the following key terms:

- coronary artery disease
- atherosclerosis
- arteriosclerosis
- plaque
- angina pectoris
- pulmonary edema
- myocardial infarction
- myocardium
- silent myocardial infarction
- nitroglycerin
- stroke
- thrombus
- ischemic stroke
- transient ischemic attack
- cerebral embolism

Student: _____ Date: _____

Course: _____ Section #: _____

PART 1 • True/False

If you believe the statement is true, circle the T. If you believe the statement is false, circle the F.

T F **1.** Atherosclerosis results when fatty substances and other debris are deposited on the inner lining of the arterial wall.

T F **2.** Angina does not always cause pain.

T F **3.** Angina pain is usually relieved by rest.

T F **4.** Angina pain is usually on the left side.

T F **5.** It is quite easy to differentiate between the pain of angina pectoris and myocardial infarction.

T F **6.** About 25 percent of all myocardial infarction victims have no chest pain.

T F **7.** The pain of myocardial infarction lasts longer than 30 minutes and is usually under the sternum, radiating to the neck, jaw, left shoulder, and left arm.

T F **8.** Congestive heart failure with respiratory difficulty is life threatening and requires immediate care.

T F **9.** The major symptom of myocardial infarction is cyanosis.

T F **10.** Victims of heart disease emergencies should be put in a prone position.

PART 2 • Multiple Choice

For each item, circle the correct answer or the phrase that best completes the statement.

1. The signs and symptoms of myocardial infarction include all of the following except
   a. pale skin color
   b. shortness of breath
   c. a pulse rate of 70–80 beats per minute
   d. feeling of impending doom

2. Most acute heart attacks are caused by blockage of the _____ artery.
   a. cephalic
   b. coronary
   c. coronal
   d. carotid

3. The buildup of fatty deposits in the arteries is called
   a. atherosclerosis
   b. angina pectoris
   c. coronary thrombosis
   d. cholesterol

4. Angina pectoris
   a. is often accompanied by weakness and nausea
   b. is a term that describes any kind of chest pain
   c. usually lasts longer than 30 minutes
   d. is pain in the heart caused by insufficient oxygen

5. Which of the following heart conditions would probably develop over a period of several months?
   a. acute myocardial infarction
   b. heart attack
   c. cardiogenic shock
   d. congestive heart failure

6. Which of the following is *not* an emergency care measure for a cardiac victim?
   a. loosen restrictive clothing
   b. place the victim in a sitting position
   c. have the victim cease all movement
   d. do not help the victim administer medication until a physician has evaluated the victim

7. Dyspnea means
   a. shortness of breath while lying down
   b. profuse sweating
   c. lack of oxygen
   d. shortness of breath

8. A victim with swelling in the lower legs and frothy, pink sputum would be manifesting symptoms of
   a. angina pectoris
   b. cardiac arrest
   c. congestive heart failure
   d. none of the above

9. Which of the following is *not* a cause of stroke?
   a. a blood clot in a cerebral artery
   b. a blood clot that forms elsewhere, then gets lodged in a cerebral artery
   c. a blood clot in the heart
   d. bleeding into brain tissue

10. A victim of stroke should be positioned
   a. flat on the back
   b. on the back with the feet raised
   c. on the back with the head and shoulders elevated
   d. on the side

- You are called to the home of a middle-aged woman who is experiencing severe dyspnea and a rapid heart rate. She has lower-extremity edema and distended neck veins, and seems confused.

Respiratory Emergencies

Learning Objectives

When you have mastered the material in this chapter, you will be able to

1   Understand the physiology of dyspnea

2   Describe the emergency care of dyspnea

3   Understand the physiology of emphysema

4   Understand the physiology of chronic bronchitis

5   Describe and demonstrate the emergency care for a victim with chronic obstructive pulmonary disease

6   List the signs and symptoms of asthma

7   Describe and demonstrate the emergency care for a victim with asthma

8   List the signs and symptoms of pneumonia

9   Describe and demonstrate the emergency care for a victim with pneumonia

10 List the signs and symptoms of hyperventilation

11 Describe and demonstrate the emergency care for a victim with hyperventilation

SQ3R Plus

- **Survey** to set goals for studying.
- Ask **questions** as you **read.**
- Stop frequently to **recite** and **review.**
- **Write** a summary of key points.
- **Reflect** on the importance of this material and its relevance in your life.

On May 13, 1998, Bess Adams was hosting a birthday party for her 9-year-old son. A friend of the family had come in cowboy garb and had brought a horse so the children could take turns riding around the block.

About 15 minutes after Cody Reese finished his ride, Bess noticed that he was struggling to breathe. He was making a whistling, high-pitched wheezing sound as he tried to exhale and using the muscles of his neck and shoulders to assist his breathing. Even with all his effort to breathe, he was moving very little air in and out.

Recognizing the signs of asthma, Bess called Cody's mother, who confirmed that Cody had both asthma and an allergy to horse hair. Cody's mother knew from the description of his symptoms that his attack was severe; she told Bess to call for help while she drove over with Cody's inhaler. Bess called 9-1-1, then asked her teenage daughter to take the other children to the backyard and supervise the other party activities. Bess led Cody to the couch and tried to calm him where it was quiet. Because his airway was clear, though constricted, and he was still able to move some air, Bess helped him into the most comfortable position on the couch—sitting upright and leaning forward. Bess coaxed Cody to drink a large glass of water, to help loosen bronchial secretions, and monitored his breathing carefully until emergency personnel arrived.

VITAL TO SURVIVAL IS THE BODY'S ABILITY TO DELIVER sufficient amounts of freshly oxygenated blood to all cells. Without enough oxygen, some cells—such as those in the heart and brain—can die within minutes.

A variety of diseases and injuries can interfere with the body's ability to get enough oxygen. Rapid medical attention in these cases is essential to saving life and preventing cell death from oxygen starvation.

This chapter explains some of the major diseases that cause respiratory emergencies and outlines appropriate emergency care for each.

• Section 1 •
DYSPNEA

Learning Objective 1 Understand the physiology of dyspnea.

Dyspnea, one of the most common medical complaints, is defined as a sensation of shortness of breath—a feeling of air hunger accompanied by labored breathing. Two major sets of circumstances generally accompany dyspnea: in one, air cannot pass easily into the lungs; in the other, air cannot pass easily out of the lungs. Most commonly, the victim experiences resistance either in the airway or in expansion of the lungs.

Dyspnea is not a disease in itself but is a symptom of a number of diseases. Breathing will generally be rapid and shallow, but victims may feel short of breath whether they are breathing rapidly or slowly. Remember, shortness of breath is normal following exercise, fatigue, coughing, or the production of excess sputum. In these cases, the condition is not considered true dyspnea.

Emergency Care

Learning Objective 2 Describe the emergency care of dyspnea.

Activate the EMS system immediately; then:

1. Maintain an open airway. Dyspnea may be caused by aspiration of a foreign body, so immediately check for aspiration and clear the airway if necessary.

2. Treat for shock.

Progress Check

1. Dyspnea is defined as _____ .
    (labored breathing/air hunger/shortness of breath)

2. Victims of dyspnea may be breathing rapidly or slowly, but always feel _____ .
    (dizzy/short of breath/faint)

3. Dyspnea is not a _____ , but is a symptom of a number of diseases.
    (disease itself/medical emergency/respiratory syndrome)

4. Because dyspnea can be caused by _____ , always check the airway.
    (aspiration/internal bleeding/bronchitis)

• Section 2 •
CHRONIC OBSTRUCTIVE PULMONARY DISEASE

More than 90 percent of those with **chronic obstructive pulmonary disease** (COPD) have emphysema, chronic bronchitis, or both. COPD can also be caused by asthma. The most important known factor in COPD is cigarette smoking; most COPD victims are also prone to allergies and a variety of infections.

Emphysema and chronic bronchitis (Figure 17-1 on page 292) represent two extremes of a whole spectrum of problems. Most victims fall somewhere in between the two extremes, manifesting signs and symptoms of both disorders.

Emphysema

Learning Objective 3 Understand the physiology of emphysema.

Emphysema is characterized by distension of the air sacs (groups of alveoli) beyond the bronchioles, with destructive changes in their walls. Basically, the alveoli lose their elasticity, become distended with trapped air, and stop functioning. When air is trapped in the alveoli, the walls eventually break down and the total number of alveoli decreases, making it more difficult for the victim to breathe.

Signs and Symptoms

Because victims of emphysema are usually not cyanotic, they are referred to as **"pink puffers."** Signs and symptoms may include

*   Evidence of weight loss
*   History of increasing dyspnea on exertion
*   Progressive limitation of activity
*   Production of only small amounts of mucus with coughing
*   Prolonged and difficult exhalation
*   Lungs remain expanded even after exhalation
*   Barrel-shaped chest (see Figure 17-2 on page 293)

dyspnea Shortness of breath or difficulty in breathing
chronic obstructive pulmonary disease A range of diseases including emphysema, chronic bronchitis, and asthma
emphysema A respiratory disease characterized by overinflated alveoli
"pink puffer" A victim of emphysema

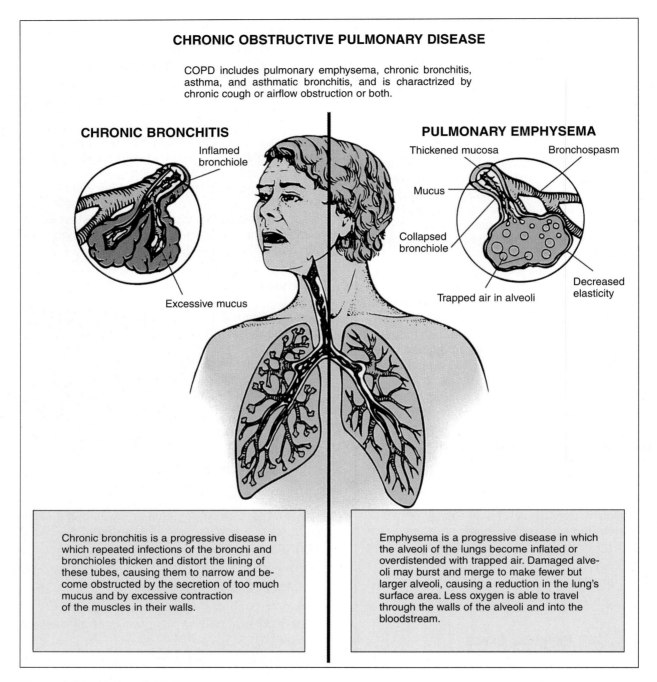

CHRONIC OBSTRUCTIVE PULMONARY DISEASE

COPD includes pulmonary emphysema, chronic bronchitis, asthma, and asthmatic bronchitis, and is charactrized by chronic cough or airflow obstruction or both.

CHRONIC BRONCHITIS

Inflamed bronchiole

Excessive mucus

PULMONARY EMPHYSEMA

Thickened mucosa

Bronchospasm

Mucus

Collapsed bronchiole

Trapped air in alveoli

Decreased elasticity

Chronic bronchitis is a progressive disease in which repeated infections of the bronchi and bronchioles thicken and distort the lining of these tubes, causing them to narrow and become obstructed by the secretion of too much mucus and by excessive contraction of the muscles in their walls.

Emphysema is a progressive disease in which the alveoli of the lungs become inflated or overdistended with trapped air. Damaged alveoli may burst and merge to make fewer but larger alveoli, causing a reduction in the lung's surface area. Less oxygen is able to travel through the walls of the alveoli and into the bloodstream.

Figure 17-1. Forms of COPD

Chronic Bronchitis

Learning Objective 4 Understand the physiology of chronic bronchitis.

Chronic bronchitis is characterized by inflammation, edema, and excessive mucus production in the bronchial tree. By definition, chronic bronchitis features a productive cough that has persisted for at least 3 months out of the year over the past 2 years.

The typical victim with chronic bronchitis has invariably been a heavy cigarette smoker with many respiratory infections. There is a tendency toward associated heart disease and right-heart failure.

Figure 17-2. Victims of emphysema and chronic bronchitis often lean forward in an attempt to breathe.

Signs and Symptoms

Because victims of chronic bronchitis are often cyanotic, they are called **"blue bloaters."** Signs and symptoms include

- Coughing that produces thick mucus
- Use of neck and chest muscles to assist breathing
- Cyanosis
- Swelling of the hands, feet, and ankles
- Distended neck veins
- High-pitched wheezing during both inhalation and exhalation
- Low-pitched snoring sounds during both inhalation and exhalation

Emergency Care for COPD

Learning Objective 5 Describe and demonstrate the emergency care for a victim with chronic obstructive pulmonary disease.

The number-one goal of emergency care for COPD is to enhance oxygenation; without it, the victim may die. The major threat to life in COPD is a lack of oxygen. To care for COPD, activate the EMS system; then:

1. Establish an airway.
2. Help the victim into the most comfortable position—usually sitting or semisitting.
3. If the victim is unconscious, administer artificial ventilation if necessary.
4. Monitor the victim's respiratory rate and depth, and assist ventilations if respiration becomes de-

pressed. *Watch the victim closely for changes in rate and depth.*
5. Maintain the victim's body temperature.
6. Loosen restrictive clothing, comfort and reassure the victim, and encourage the victim to cough up secretions.

Progress Check

1. Victims of emphysema are sometimes called
   _____.
   (blue bloaters/pink puffers)

2. The condition in which repeated infections thicken and distort the lining of the bronchial tree is
   _____.
   (emphysema/chronic bronchitis/status asthmaticus)

3. Because the walls of the alveoli have broken down in victims of emphysema, air is _____ in the lungs.
   (trapped/concentrated/leaking)

4. The number-one goal of care for COPD is to
   _____.
   (prevent aspiration/enhance oxygenation/assist ventilation)

• Section 3 •
ASTHMA

Asthma, which affects more than 10 million people in the United States, is characterized by an increased sensitivity of the trachea, bronchi, and bronchioles to various stimuli, with widespread reversible narrowing of the airways. It is a chronic inflammatory disease, and occurs in two general degrees:

- Acute asthma, consisting of periodic attacks and symptom-free periods between attacks
- Status asthmaticus, consisting of a prolonged and life-threatening attack

There are also generally two different kinds of asthma. Extrinsic asthma, or "allergic" asthma, is usually a reaction to dust, pollen, or other irritants. It is often seasonal, occurs most often in children, and often clears up after adolescence. Intrinsic, or "nonallergic," asthma is most common in adults and occurs most often in response to emotion, industrial or

---

"blue bloater" A victim of chronic bronchitis

other fumes, strong odors, strong perfumes, viral infections, aspirin and other medications, cold air, air pollution, or some other irritant.

The acute asthma attack varies in duration, intensity, and frequency and reflects airway obstruction due to one of the following:

- **Bronchospasm** (generalized spasm of the bronchi)
- Swelling of the mucous membranes in the bronchial walls
- Plugging of the bronchi by thick mucus secretions

Signs and Symptoms

> **Learning Objective 6** List the signs and symptoms of asthma.

The signs and symptoms of asthma can range from mild to severe, and can be life-threatening. A typical acute attack may feature the following signs and symptoms:

- Victim sits upright, often leaning forward with nostrils flared, fighting to breathe.
- Spasmodic, unproductive cough
- Whistling, high-pitched wheezing, usually during exhalation
- Very little movement of air during breathing, even when the victim is at rest
- Hyperinflated chest with air trapped in the lungs because of increased obstruction during exhalation
- Rapid, shallow respirations
- Rapid pulse (usually more than 120 beats per minute)
- Fatigue
- Use of accessory muscles in the neck and shoulders to aid breathing

Emergency Care

> **Learning Objective 7** Describe and demonstrate the emergency care for a victim with asthma.

The three goals of emergency care for an acute asthma attack are to improve oxygenation, relieve bronchospasm, and improve the victim's ventilation. Activate the EMS system; then:

1. Establish an airway and assist ventilations if necessary.
2. Stay calm and keep the victim as calm as possible; stress and emotional intensity worsen the asthma attack. Keep the victim in a position of comfort, usually sitting up.

3. *If you are allowed to do so in your area,* help the victim use any asthma medication he or she may have (often an inhaler).
4. If you do not anticipate vomiting, give the victim as much fluid by mouth as possible; fluids help loosen secretions. *Follow local protocol.*

Status Asthmaticus

Status asthmaticus is a severe, prolonged asthma attack that does not respond to aggressive treatment and that represents a *dire medical emergency.*

Signs and Symptoms

Wheezing is not a reliable sign of status asthmaticus: *There may be no wheezing at all.* In fact, breath sounds may be almost absent. Other signs and symptoms may include (see Figure 17-3):

- Severe inflation of the chest due to continued trapping of air in the lungs
- Bluish discoloration of the skin
- Walking and talking only with the greatest effort
- Extremely labored breathing, with the victim fighting to move air and using accessory muscles to breathe
- Inaudible breath sounds
- Exhaustion
- Dehydration

Don't be fooled by a victim who seems to be suffering from status asthmaticus but who then seems to begin to recover; *the victim could still be in grave danger.*

Emergency Care

To care for the victim of status asthmaticus, follow the same general guidelines as for acute asthma, *but increase your urgency in establishing care and activating the EMS system.*

One note of caution: All that wheezes is not asthma. Many other diseases and injuries—such as left heart failure, pneumonia, smoke inhalation, partial airway obstruction, cystic fibrosis, upper-airway inflammation, and anaphylactic shock—cause wheezing.

---

bronchospasm Generalized spasm of the bronchi

status asthmaticus A severe, prolonged asthma attack that represents a dire medical emergency

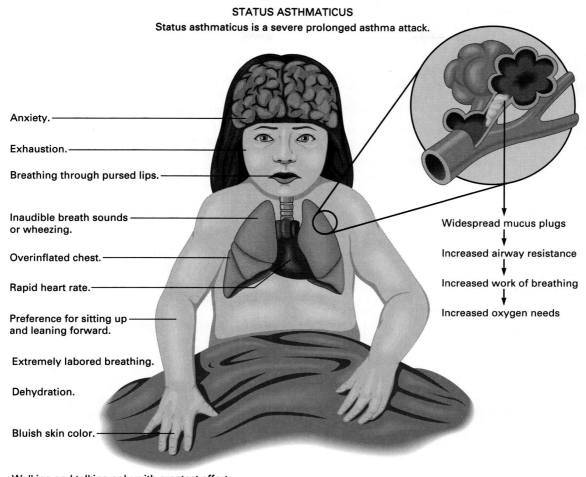

STATUS ASTHMATICUS
Status asthmaticus is a severe prolonged asthma attack.

Anxiety.

Exhaustion.

Breathing through pursed lips.

Inaudible breath sounds
or wheezing.

Overinflated chest.

Rapid heart rate.

Preference for sitting up
and leaning forward.

Extremely labored breathing.

Dehydration.

Bluish skin color.

Walking and talking only with greatest effort.

Widespread mucus plugs

Increased airway resistance

Increased work of breathing

Increased oxygen needs

Figure 17-3. Status asthmaticus is a dire medical emergency.

Progress Check

1. The main physiological event in asthma is _____ of the airway.
   (obstruction/narrowing/complete blockage)

2. A prolonged, life-threatening asthma attack is called _____ .
   (acute asthma/bronchial asthma/status asthmaticus)

3. There are two different kinds of asthma—one most often caused by infection or emotion and the other most often caused by _____ .
   (allergy/aspirin/cold air)

4. In a typical attack, the victim's cough is _____ .
   (productive/unproductive/intermittent)

5. The three goals of emergency care for asthma are to improve oxygenation, relieve bronchospasm, and improve _____ .
   (circulation/metabolism/ventilation)

6. Status asthmaticus is usually characterized by _____ .
   (severe wheezing/low-pitched snoring/absent breath sounds)

• Section 4 •
PNEUMONIA

Pneumonia is a medical term used to describe a group of illnesses characterized by lung inflammation and fluid- or pus-filled alveoli, leading to inadequately oxygenated blood. Pneumonia is most frequently caused by a bacterial or viral infection, but can also be caused by inhaled irritants or aspirated materials.

Signs and Symptoms

Learning Objective 8 List the signs and symptoms of pneumonia.

Victims of pneumonia generally appear very ill; most complain of fever and chills that "shake the bed"; fever usually exceeds 101 degrees F. Signs and symptoms depend on the lobe of the lung that is affected, and may include

- Chest pain, usually worse when breathing
- Dyspnea
- Rapid respiration
- Respiratory distress
- Noisy breathing
- Productive cough, usually with yellow sputum or mucus that is sometimes streaked with blood
- Hot, dry skin

Emergency Care

Learning Objective 9 Describe and demonstrate the emergency care for a victim with pneumonia.

1. Place the victim in a position of comfort that enables the victim to breathe with the least distress; most prefer an upright or semisitting position.
2. Maintain an open airway.
3. Administer plenty of fluids unless there are contraindications; fluids help loosen mucus and prevent dehydration.
4. Transport the victim to a physician.

Progress Check

1. Pneumonia describes a group of illnesses characterized by _____ .
   (fever and chills/productive cough/lung inflammation)

2. Pneumonia is most often caused by _____ .
   (infection/immune suppression/injury)

3. A characteristic sign of pneumonia is _____ .
   (wheezing/fatigue/fever and chills)

4. Unless there are contraindications, give the pneumonia victim plenty of _____ .
   (fluids/pain reliever/ventilations)

• Section 5 •
HYPERVENTILATION

Hyperventilation is a condition characterized by "overbreathing," or breathing too rapidly and too deeply. It is normal under a variety of conditions (such as following exercise), as long as breathing quickly returns to a normal rate.

Hyperventilation syndrome, on the other hand, is an abnormal state in which rapid breathing persists. The causes of hyperventilation syndrome are varied, but usually involve anxiety or emotional stress.

If caused by anxiety or stress, hyperventilation syndrome is relatively benign. If caused by an underlying medical condition—such as diabetic coma, asthma, pulmonary embolism, or increased pressure in the skull—the outcome can be catastrophic.

Signs and Symptoms

Learning Objective 10 List the signs and symptoms of hyperventilation.

Hyperventilation involves breathing at a rate faster than 40 breaths per minute. Overbreathing lowers the carbon dioxide in the blood to an abnormal level, causing the following signs and symptoms:

- Marked anxiety, leading to panic
- Air hunger
- Giddiness or unusual behavior
- Fatigue
- Abdominal discomfort or bloating
- Drawing up of the hands at the wrists and knuckles with flexed fingers (**carpopedal spasm**)
- Dyspnea
- Dizziness or light-headedness
- Blurring of vision
- Dryness or bitter taste in the mouth
- Numbness and/or tingling of the hands and feet or the area around the mouth
- Tightness or a "lump" in the throat

hyperventilation A condition characterized by overbreathing or breathing too rapidly

hyperventilation syndrome An abnormal state in which rapid breathing persists

carpopedal spasm Drawing up of the hands at the wrists and knuckles with flexed fingers

- Pounding of the heart with stabbing pains in the chest
- Great weakness
- A feeling of impending doom
- Fainting
- Deep, sighing, rapid respirations with a rapid pulse

Emergency Care

Learning Objective 11 Describe and demonstrate the emergency care for a victim with hyperventilation.

Before starting any emergency care, rule out any medical causes for rapid breathing, such as diabetic coma, trauma, or asthma. If they exist, care for them appropriately. If you are certain the hyperventilation has no medical causes:

1. Remain calm and reassuring; listen carefully, show understanding and consideration, and try to calm the victim down.
2. Try to talk the victim into slowing the breathing rate. Have the victim breathe with his or her abdominal muscles as much as possible; instruct the victim to breathe in through the nose, hold the breath for a few seconds, then breathe out as slowly as possible through pursed lips.
3. Explain to the victim what happened, and reassure the victim that it is not serious.
4. Transport the victim to an emergency room or activate the EMS system.

Do not have the victim breathe into a paper bag; doing so does not balance blood gases, and can seriously stress the heart and lungs.

Progress Check

1. Hyperventilation syndrome is an abnormal state in which rapid breathing _____ .
   (occurs periodically/comes in cycles/persists)

2. Hyperventilation is fairly benign unless caused by _____ .
   (anxiety/severe fright/an underlying medical condition)

3. Hyperventilation is characterized by _____ during breathing.
   (deep sighs/wheezing/rales)

4. To care for hyperventilation not caused by a medical condition, _____ .
   (have the victim breathe into a paper bag/calm the victim/give artificial ventilation)

• SUMMARY •

- Dyspnea, one of the most common medical complaints, is characterized by shortness of breath; make sure you rule out airway obstruction.
- Chronic obstructive pulmonary disease encompasses emphysema, chronic bronchitis, and asthma; more than 90 percent of its victims have both emphysema and chronic bronchitis.
- In emphysema, damaged alveoli break down and fill with trapped air; in chronic bronchitis, repeated infections thicken and distort the lining of the bronchioles.
- In asthma, there is a generalized spasm of the bronchi, swelling of the mucous membranes in the bronchial walls, and plugging of the bronchi by thick mucus secretions.
- The three goals of emergency care for asthma are to improve oxygenation, relieve bronchospasm, and improve the victim's ventilation.
- Status asthmaticus, a prolonged, severe asthma attack, represents a dire medical emergency.
- Pneumonia is a group of illnesses that cause lung inflammation; the most characteristic sign is high fever and chills.
- Hyperventilation is fairly benign unless it is caused by an underlying medical condition.
- Never treat hyperventilation by having a victim breathe into a paper bag.

• KEY TERMS •

Make sure you understand the following key terms:

- dyspnea
- chronic obstructive pulmonary disease
- emphysema
- "pink puffers"
- "blue bloaters"
- bronchospasm
- status asthmaticus
- hyperventilation
- hyperventilation syndrome
- carpopedal spasm

Student: _____   Date: _____

Course: _____   Section #: _____

PART 1 • True/False

If you believe the statement is true, circle the T. If you believe the statement is false, circle the F.

T F **1.** Dyspnea is not a disease itself, but a symptom of a number of other diseases.

T F **2.** Dyspnea is a feeling of air hunger accompanied by labored breathing.

T F **3.** Victims with emphysema are usually cyanotic.

T F **4.** The victim with emphysema usually appears thin and wasted with a barrel-shaped chest.

T F **5.** The chronic bronchitis victim uses the neck and chest muscles to assist in breathing.

T F **6.** The number-one goal of emergency care for COPD is to enhance oxygenation.

T F **7.** Never give asthma victims fluids by mouth.

T F **8.** One of the three main goals of emergency care for asthma is to treat for shock.

T F **9.** Have a hyperventilation victim breathe into a paper bag.

T F **10.** The major threat to life for a COPD victim is a lack of oxygen.

PART 2 • Multiple Choice

For each item, circle the correct answer or the phrase that best completes the statement.

1. Dyspnea means

   a. painful, rapid breathing
   b. excess sputum production
   c. shortness of breath
   d. fatigue

2. Which of the following is not a category of COPD?

   a. emphysema
   b. asthma
   c. chronic bronchitis
   d. atherosclerosis

3. Initial care for a person who is hyperventilating includes

   a. establishing an airway
   b. encouraging the victim to take rapid, shallow breaths
   c. loosening tight clothing
   d. calming and reassuring the victim

4. In status asthmaticus

   a. the victim is not in much danger
   b. the chest is sunken
   c. wheezing is very audible
   d. the victim uses accessory muscles of respiration

5. Which of the following is *not* a symptom of hyperventilation?

   a. slow heart rate
   b. fainting
   c. tingling in the hands and feet
   d. a feeling of weakness

6. Emergency care for COPD victims is aimed primarily at

   a. causing expectoration of sputum
   b. enhancing oxygenation
   c. humidifying the air
   d. transporting the victim as soon as possible

7. "Pink puffers" and "blue bloaters" are

   a. newborns with breathing difficulties
   b. victims of heart disease
   c. victims with COPD
   d. all of the above

Match the definitions on the right with the correct term on the left.

A. Dyspnea
B. COPD
C. Emphysema
D. Chronic bronchitis
E. Asthma
F. Status asthmaticus
G. Pneumonia
H. Hyperventilation

_____ "Pink puffers"

_____ Represents a dire medical emergency

_____ Sensation of shortness of breath

_____ Most frequently caused by a bacterial or viral infection

_____ Rapid, deep, abnormal breathing

_____ Characterized by chronic cough, airflow obstruction, or both

_____ Usually brought on by allergic reaction, respiratory infection, or emotional stress

_____ "Blue bloater"

- You are at the home of a middle-aged man and find him sitting on the edge of his bed, gasping for air. He has distended neck veins and audible wheezes, and is cyanotic.
- You are at a college dormitory where you find a woman having an asthma attack. She is fighting to breathe and has audible wheezes. The attack has been severe and prolonged, and the victim is exhausted.

Diabetic Emergencies

Learning Objectives

When you have mastered the material in this chapter, you will be able to

1 Understand the basic physiology of diabetes

2 Differentiate between diabetic coma and insulin shock

3 List the signs and symptoms of diabetic coma

4 List the signs and symptoms of insulin shock

5 Describe and demonstrate the emergency care of a victim in diabetic coma

6 Describe and demonstrate the emergency care of a victim with insulin shock

SQ3R Plus

- **Survey** to set goals for studying.
- Ask **questions** as you **read.**
- Stop frequently to **recite** and **review.**
- **Write** a summary of key points.
- **Reflect** on the importance of this material and its relevance in your life.

*O*n November 12, 1998, 29-year-old Steve Cox returned to his desk at the university advisement center after playing an especially fast-paced game of handball during his lunch hour. About half an hour later, when co-worker Julia Gallagher entered his office to discuss a meeting scheduled for that afternoon, Steve snarled angrily at her and ordered her from his office.

Knowing he was an insulin-dependent diabetic, Julia took as close a look at Steve as she could from across his desk. Though his office was almost cool, he was perspiring heavily; his breathing was shallow, his hands were trembling, and his pupils were dilated.

"Steve, have you eaten today?" she asked. "Breakfast," he replied coolly. "What about lunch?" she asked again. "Nope. Played handball." The brusque replies were unusual for Steve, who was normally a warm, talkative person. "Have you taken your insulin today?" she coaxed. "Yup."

Suspecting Steve was going into insulin shock, Julia stepped into the doorway and sent a co-worker to the vending machine for a chocolate candy bar. She asked another co-worker to call the university's emergency services personnel.

With some coaxing, she persuaded Steve to eat the candy bar while she monitored his vital signs. By the time emergency personnel arrived a few minutes later, his symptoms were easing and his mental status was returning to normal.

CONSERVATIVELY ESTIMATED, THERE ARE MORE THAN 14 million diabetics in the United States. In approximately half of these cases, diabetes has not been diagnosed or recognized, so the victims are completely unaware of the disease. Unfortunately, the first indication of the disease may be a life-threatening medical emergency, such as diabetic coma or insulin shock.

This chapter gives basic background information about diabetes, differentiates between diabetic coma and insulin shock, and details how to care for each.

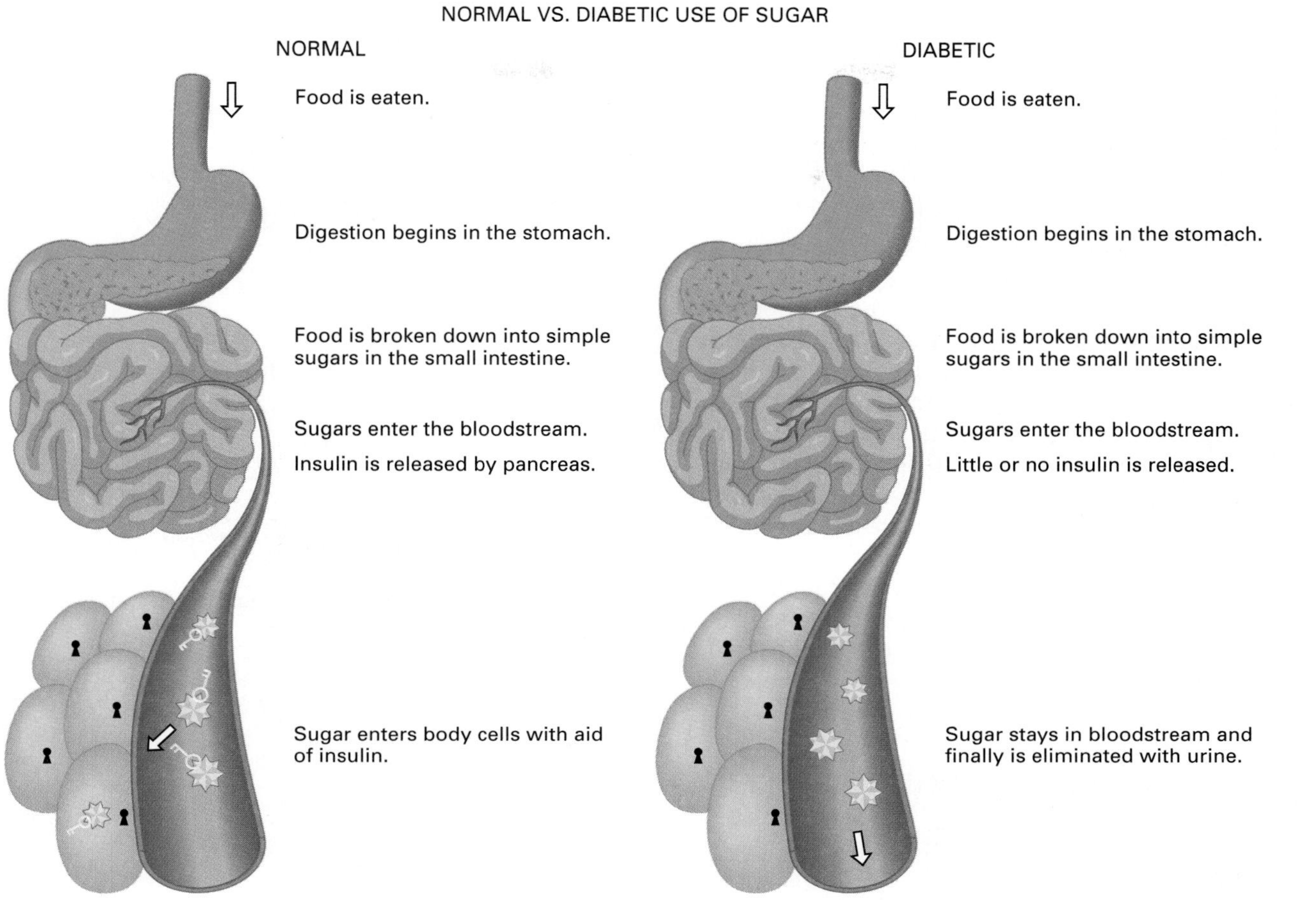

NORMAL VS. DIABETIC USE OF SUGAR

NORMAL

Food is eaten.

Digestion begins in the stomach.

Food is broken down into simple sugars in the small intestine.

Sugars enter the bloodstream.

Insulin is released by pancreas.

Sugar enters body cells with aid of insulin.

DIABETIC

Food is eaten.

Digestion begins in the stomach.

Food is broken down into simple sugars in the small intestine.

Sugars enter the bloodstream.

Little or no insulin is released.

Sugar stays in bloodstream and finally is eliminated with urine.

Figure 18-1. Diabetes has long been recognized as a serious metabolic disorder.

• Section 1 •
<u>DIABETES</u>

Learning Objective 1 Understand the basic physiology of diabetes.

Insulin is a hormone needed to facilitate the movement of **glucose** (sugar) out of the bloodstream, across cell membranes, and into the cells. Without glucose, cells are not able to meet their energy needs.

In people with diabetes, sugar accumulates in the bloodstream because insulin does not move it into the body cells (see Figure 18-1). It is a paradoxical situation: The diabetic has extremely elevated levels of sugar in the blood, but a severely depleted supply of sugar in the cells, where it is critically needed. All organ systems are affected.

When glucose does not get delivered to the cells, the cells resort to using proteins as fuel, eventually robbing the muscles and vital organs of their mass. The sugar builds up in the blood. The kidneys start spilling sugar into the urine, then start eliminating massive amounts of water to wash the sugar away.

Diabetes can cause complications in a number of body systems. Common complications include circulatory problems, blindness (due to degeneration of the small blood vessels in the retina), and central nervous system problems, including lack of sensation in the hands and feet, delayed emptying of the stomach, and sexual dysfunction and impotence.

There are two basic types of diabetes:

- **Type I diabetes,** or insulin-dependent diabetes, in which the victim has little or no ability to produce

insulin A hormone needed to facilitate movement of glucose out of the bloodstream, across the cell membranes, and into the cells

glucose Sugar

Type I diabetes Diabetes that results when the body produces little or no insulin

insulin. Type I usually begins in childhood ("juvenile-onset"), and victims require daily insulin injections.

- **Type II diabetes,** often called "adult-onset diabetes," in which the victim produces enough insulin but cannot utilize it. Type II diabetes is generally controlled by diet and/or oral medication.

Another type of diabetes, which is not permanent, is **gestational diabetes.** Gestational diabetes develops during pregnancy and occurs when the hormones in the placenta cause the body to resist the action of insulin. It is almost always treated with diet, though some women require medication to control gestational diabetes. Women with gestational diabetes tend to deliver very large babies. Gestational diabetes ends when the baby is born, and may or may not occur in subsequent pregnancies. It does increase a woman's risk of developing Type II diabetes later in life.

Diabetics face a grave physical situation when their blood glucose level is too high or too low: Either condition can cause coma, and both can be life threatening if not treated promptly.

Progress Check

1. Insulin is needed to move _____ out of the bloodstream.
   (oxygen/glucose/carbon dioxide)

2. Cells need glucose to meet their _____ needs.
   (energy/metabolic/elimination)

3. In diabetes, sugars accumulate in the _____ .
   (kidneys/liver/bloodstream)

4. _____ diabetes usually starts later in life and occurs because the body cannot utilize insulin.
   (Type I/Type II)

5. _____ diabetes results when the body produces little or no insulin.
   (Type I/Type II)

• **Section 2** •

UNDERSTANDING THE DIFFERENCES BETWEEN DIABETIC COMA AND INSULIN SHOCK

Learning Objective 2 Differentiate between diabetic coma and insulin shock.

Both **diabetic coma,** also known as hyperglycemia, and **insulin shock,** also known as hypoglycemia, are grave medical emergencies that can be life threatening if not treated promptly. However, there are significant differences in the causes, onset, and signs and symptoms of each condition.

Learning Objective 3 List the signs and symptoms of diabetic coma.

Learning Objective 4 List the signs and symptoms of insulin shock.

Figures 18-2 through 18-4 illustrate the signs and symptoms of diabetic coma and insulin shock.

Progress Check

1. _____ is caused by too little insulin and too much blood sugar.
   (Diabetic coma/Insulin shock)

2. _____ is caused by too much insulin and too little blood sugar.
   (Diabetic coma/Insulin shock)

3. You would suspect _____ in a diabetic who has a viral respiratory infection and a fever.
   (diabetic coma/insulin shock)

4. You would suspect _____ in a diabetic who skipped lunch for an exercise session, but who took prescribed insulin anyway.
   (diabetic coma/insulin shock)

5. Diabetic coma causes _____ breath odor.
   (fruity/alcohol/no)

6. Insulin shock causes _____ breath odor.
   (acetone/fruity/no)

7. The onset of insulin shock is _____ .
   (gradual/rapid)

• **Section 3** •

EMERGENCY CARE

If you encounter a person who is unconscious, always look for signs of diabetes—a Medic Alert tag, bracelet, or card; signs of insulin injection (needle marks in the thigh or abdomen); signs of oral diabetic medication (bottles in the house); signs of poor circulation or amputation of the toes, feet, or lower leg; or other telltale signs of diabetes.

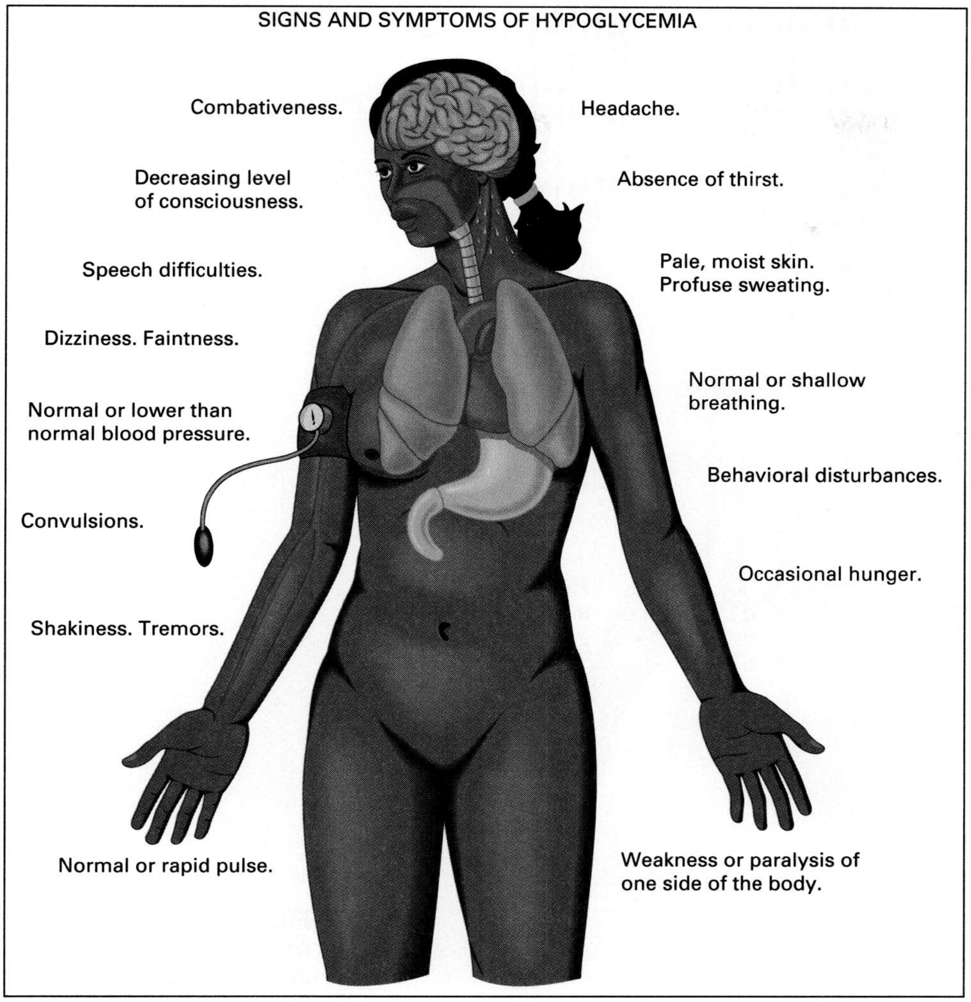

SIGNS AND SYMPTOMS OF HYPOGLYCEMIA

Combativeness.

Decreasing level of consciousness.

Speech difficulties.

Dizziness. Faintness.

Normal or lower than normal blood pressure.

Convulsions.

Shakiness. Tremors.

Normal or rapid pulse.

Headache.

Absence of thirst.

Pale, moist skin. Profuse sweating.

Normal or shallow breathing.

Behavioral disturbances.

Occasional hunger.

Weakness or paralysis of one side of the body.

Figure 18-2. Insulin shock is also known as hypoglycemia.

The general rule to remember about emergency care for diabetics is simple: *When in doubt, give sugar.* You will not harm a diabetic coma victim by giving sugar; the amount administered is trivial compared to what the diabetic already has in the bloodstream. However, *you may save the life of a victim in insulin shock by administering sugar.* Figure 18-5 on page 307 compares the causes, emergency care, and signs and symptoms of diabetic coma and insulin shock.

Emergency Care of Diabetic Coma

Learning Objective 5 Describe and demonstrate the emergency care of a victim in diabetic coma.

Activate the EMS system; then:

1. Monitor vital signs carefully every few minutes; rule out heart attack, stroke, or other cardiac emergencies as the cause of the coma.

2. Check for signs of head or neck injury that may have occurred if the victim fell when losing con-

sciousness; if any injuries are present, administer appropriate care.

3. Provide airway maintenance and artificial ventilation; give CPR if needed.

4. Be alert for vomiting; be prepared to position the victim on the side with the face pointed downward to prevent aspiration and allow drainage.

5. Treat for shock; keep the victim warm.

6. Continue careful monitoring of vital signs until emergency personnel arrive.

Type II diabetes Diabetes that results when the body cannot utilize the insulin it produces

gestational diabetes Temporary diabetes that develops in a pregnant woman

diabetic coma A condition that results from too little insulin and too much sugar

insulin shock A condition that results from too much insulin and too little food

305

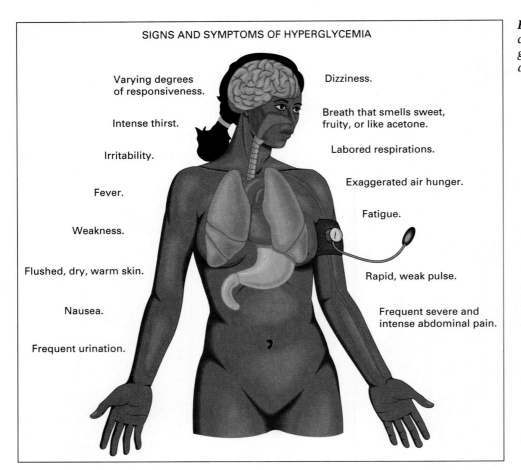

SIGNS AND SYMPTOMS OF HYPERGLYCEMIA

Varying degrees of responsiveness.

Dizziness.

Intense thirst.

Breath that smells sweet, fruity, or like acetone.

Irritability.

Labored respirations.

Fever.

Exaggerated air hunger.

Fatigue.

Weakness.

Flushed, dry, warm skin.

Rapid, weak pulse.

Nausea.

Frequent severe and intense abdominal pain.

Frequent urination.

Figure 18-3. *Diabetic coma, or severe hyperglycemia, is also known as diabetic ketoacidosis.*

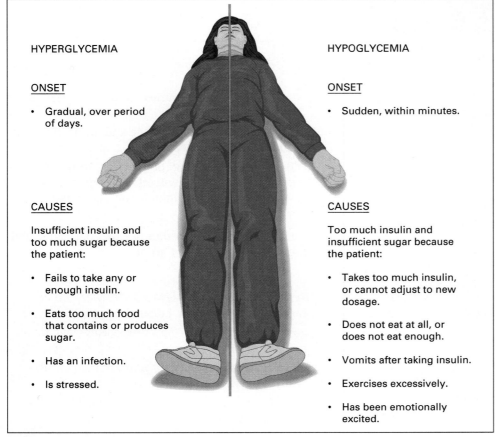

HYPERGLYCEMIA

ONSET

• Gradual, over period of days.

CAUSES

Insufficient insulin and too much sugar because the patient:

• Fails to take any or enough insulin.

• Eats too much food that contains or produces sugar.

• Has an infection.

• Is stressed.

HYPOGLYCEMIA

ONSET

• Sudden, within minutes.

CAUSES

Too much insulin and insufficient sugar because the patient:

• Takes too much insulin, or cannot adjust to new dosage.

• Does not eat at all, or does not eat enough.

• Vomits after taking insulin.

• Exercises excessively.

• Has been emotionally excited.

Figure 18-4. *If you cannot distinguish between diabetic coma and insulin shock, give sugar. You will not harm a diabetic coma victim by doing so, and you will probably save the life of an insulin shock victim.* Follow local protocol.

DIABETIC COMA (Hyperglycemia)

INSULIN SHOCK (Hypoglycemia)

CAUSES:

- The diabetic's condition has not been diagnosed and/or treated.
- The diabetic has not taken his insulin.
- The diabetic has overeaten, flooding the body with a sudden excess of carbohydrates.
- The diabetic suffers an infection that disrupts his glucose/insulin balance.

EMERGENCY CARE:

- Open airway, monitor vital signs and rule out heart attack, stroke, or other emergency.
- Immediately activate the EMS system.

SYMPTOMS AND SIGNS:

- Gradual onset of symptoms and signs, over a period of days.
- Victim complains of dry mouth and intense thirst.
- Abdominal pain and vomitting common.
- Gradually increasing restlessness, confusion, followed by stupor.
- Coma, with these signs:
  · Signs of air hunger—deep, sighing respirations
  · Weak, rapid pulse.
  · Dry, red, warm skin.
  · Eyes that appear sunken.
  · Normal or slightly low blood pressure.
  · Breath smells of acetone—sickly sweet, like nail polish remover.

CAUSES:

- The diabetic has taken too much insulin.
- The diabetic has not eaten enough to provide his normal sugar intake.
- The diabetic has overexercised or overexerted himself, thus reducing his blood glucose level.
- The diabetic has vomited a meal.

EMERGENCY CARE:

- Conscious victim—activate the EMS system and administer sugar. Granular sugar, honey, lifesaver or other candy placed under the tongue, orange juice, or glucose.
- Avoid giving liquids to the unconscious victim; provide "sprinkle" of granular sugar under tongue.
- Turn head to side or place in lateral recumbent position.

SYMPTOMS AND SIGNS:

- Rapid onset or symptoms and signs, over a period of minutes.
- Dizziness and headache.
- Abnormal hostile or aggressive behavior, which may be diagnosed as acute alcoholic intoxication.
- Fainting, convulsions, and occasionally coma.
- Normal blood pressure.
- Full rapid pulse.
- Patient intensely hungry.
- Skin pale, cold, and clammy; perspiration may be profuse.
- Copious saliva, drooling.

SPECIAL NOTES: DIABETIC COMA AND INSULIN SHOCK

When faced with a victim who may be suffering from one of these conditions:
- Determine if the victim is diabetic. Look for medical alert medallions or information cards; interview victim and family members.
- If the victim is a known or suspected diabetic, and insulin shock cannot be ruled out, assume that it is insulin shock, activate the EMS system and administer sugar.

Often a victim suffering from either of these conditions may simply appear drunk. Always check for other underlying conditions—such as diabetic complications—when giving emergency care to someone who appears intoxicated.

Figure 18-5. *Comparison of diabetic coma and insulin shock*

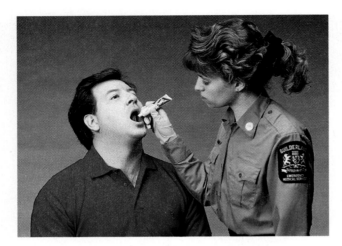

Figure 18-6. Administering concentrated glucose to a conscious diabetic victim

Emergency Care of Insulin Shock

Learning Objective 6 Describe and demonstrate the emergency care of a victim with insulin shock.

Insulin shock is a grave medical emergency that can cause death within a few minutes. Activate the EMS system immediately; then:

1. If the victim is conscious, give orange juice with 1 or 2 teaspoons of sugar; concentrated glucose; soft drinks that contain sugar; corn syrup, honey, or jelly; lifesavers, gumdrops, sugar cubes, or candy to help increase the blood sugar level. (See Figure 18-6.)

2. If the victim is unconscious, establish an airway and administer artificial ventilation if necessary.

3. If the victim is unconscious and *you are allowed to do so in your area*, place instant glucose between the victim's cheek and gums or under the tongue; position the victim on the side with the face pointed downward to prevent aspiration. *Follow local protocol.*

4. Watch for complications and treat them appropriately.

5. Continue to monitor vital signs until emergency personnel arrive.

Progress Check

1. For a diabetic victim, when in doubt, give
   _____ .
   (artificial ventilation/CPR/sugar)

2. Treat a victim of _____ for shock.
   (diabetic coma/insulin shock)

3. If a victim of _____ is conscious, immediately give the victim orange juice, candy, or soft drinks that contain sugar.
   (diabetic coma/insulin shock)

• SUMMARY •

• Diabetes is a disease in which too little insulin is produced by the body or in which the body cannot utilize the insulin that is produced.

• Type I diabetes, or juvenile-onset diabetes, generally starts during childhood and occurs because the body produces little or no insulin. Victims need insulin injections daily.

• Type II diabetes, or adult-onset diabetes, generally starts later in life because the body cannot utilize the insulin that is produced. It is usually controlled by diet and/or medication.

• Diabetic coma occurs gradually and is the result of too little insulin and too much blood sugar; it often results from infection, failure of the victim to take prescribed insulin, eating too much food that contains too much sugar, or stress.

• Insulin shock occurs rapidly and is the result of too much insulin and too little sugar; it often results when the victim takes too much insulin, does not eat enough food, or exercises strenuously.

• A victim of diabetic coma may appear intoxicated; never automatically assume someone is drunk without ruling out diabetic coma.

• A victim of insulin shock may be hostile or belligerent, or may appear to be intoxicated; never make assumptions about the causes of a victim's behavior without ruling out insulin shock.

• Diabetic coma causes flushed, warm, dry skin; sunken eyes; a fruity or acetone odor on the breath; extreme thirst; and lack of appetite. Insulin shock, on the other hand, causes pale, moist skin; dilated pupils; no unusual odor on the breath; lack of thirst; and extreme hunger.

• Both diabetic coma and insulin shock represent grave life-threatening emergencies; when in doubt, give sugar.

• KEY TERMS •

Make sure you understand the following key terms:

• insulin
• glucose
• Type I diabetes
• Type II diabetes
• gestational diabetes
• diabetic coma
• insulin shock

Student: _____   Date: _____

Course: _____   Section #: _____

PART 1 • True/False

If you believe the statement is true, circle the T. If you believe the statement is false, circle the F.

T   F   **1.** There are two basic types of diabetes: insulin-dependent diabetes and adult-onset diabetes.

T   F   **2.** Diabetic coma is a condition of too little insulin and too much blood sugar in the body.

T   F   **3.** The diabetic coma victim has intense abdominal pain and a rapid, weak pulse.

T   F   **4.** The victim in insulin shock appears extremely weak and has profuse sweating.

T   F   **5.** If a diabetic has taken insulin but has not eaten, he or she may go into insulin shock.

T   F   **6.** If in doubt about whether a victim is in insulin shock or diabetic coma, give sugar.

PART 2 • Multiple Choice

For each item, circle the correct answer or the phrase that best completes the statement.

1. A fruity odor on the breath is often a characteristic of
   a. stroke
   b. insulin shock
   c. diabetic coma
   d. an ulcer

2. Which symptom is the characteristic clue of diabetic coma?
   a. bluish lips
   b. moist, clammy skin
   c. involuntary muscular twitching
   d. fruity, sweet breath odor

3. The onset of diabetic coma generally occurs
   a. suddenly, in 5 to 20 minutes
   b. in 1 to 2 hours
   c. in 12 to 48 hours
   d. gradually, over a period of days

4. The major emergency care procedure for a victim in diabetic coma is to
   a. monitor vital signs and rule out other possible emergencies
   b. administer insulin
   c. give a glass of orange juice
   d. try to keep the victim awake

5. A diabetic who exhibits rapid, bounding pulse; cold, clammy skin; and tremors probably has
   a. insulin shock
   b. diabetic coma
   c. insulin coma
   d. diabetic shock

6. If you cannot distinguish between diabetic coma and insulin shock, you should
   a. do nothing—the wrong treatment can be deadly
   b. treat for shock and activate the EMS system
   c. give a shot of insulin or put an insulin tablet in the mouth
   d. help the victim take some kind of sugar

7. Which of the following is *not* true of diabetic coma?
   a. it is the result of too little insulin or too much sugar
   b. it occurs gradually, usually over several days
   c. it is a less serious condition than insulin shock
   d. it can be caused by excessive exercise

8. Which of the following is *not* true of insulin shock?
   a. it may be caused by eating too much food
   b. it should always be treated by giving sugar
   c. it can be caused by excessive exercise
   d. it always requires immediate transport

9. Insulin
   a. absorbs excess sugar that has been eaten
   b. converts sugar into glucose in the digestive tract
   c. permits sugar to pass from the blood into body cells
   d. all of the above

10. An excess of insulin causes
   a. diabetic coma
   b. diabetic shock
   c. insulin coma
   d. insulin shock

Match the condition on the right with the description on the left.

Description

1. _____ Too little insulin and too much blood sugar

2. _____ A dire medical emergency

3. _____ Hunger, headache, and muscle weakness

4. _____ Gradual onset

5. _____ Result of excessive exercise

6. _____ High blood sugar

7. _____ Rapid onset

8. _____ Result of eating too much food that contains sugar

9. _____ Pale, moist skin

10. _____ Labored respirations and an acetone odor on the breath

11. _____ Need for sugar

12. _____ Red, dry, warm skin

13. _____ Low blood sugar

Condition

A. Diabetic coma
B. Insulin shock

• In response to a frantic call for help from her husband, you find a middle-aged woman unconscious on her bedroom floor. The husband tells you that she has not been very responsive since the previous day and that she complained of abdominal pain. You find that she has flushed, warm, dry skin, an acetone breath odor, and a rapid, weak pulse.

• You respond to a call of a neighbor and find a 12-year-old child who appears extremely weak. Her skin is pale and moist, she feels faint, has a headache, and is having trouble focusing her eyes. The only other person at home is her brother, who tells you that several hours ago she was fine—she had run some foot races and had not yet eaten today.

Acute Abdominal Distress and Related Emergencies

Learning Objectives

When you have mastered the material in this chapter, you will be able to

1 Describe the special assessment procedures used for a victim of abdominal distress

2 List the signs and symptoms of abdominal distress

3 Describe and demonstrate general emergency care for acute abdominal distress

4 List the signs and symptoms of ruptured esophageal varices

5 Describe and demonstrate the emergency care of a victim with ruptured esophageal varices

6 List the signs and symptoms of ruptured abdominal aortic aneurysm

7 Describe and demonstrate the emergency care of a victim with ruptured abdominal aortic aneurysm

SQ3R Plus

- **Survey** to set goals for studying.
- Ask **questions** as you **read.**
- Stop frequently to **recite** and **review.**
- **Write** a summary of key points.
- **Reflect** on the importance of this material and its relevance in your life.

On December 28, 1998, John Simons was just arriving home from a company party when his neighbor ran out to the driveway. "Quick!" she cried. "Burt is inside, and he's throwing up. There's blood everywhere!"

John followed his neighbor inside to find Burt, a middle-aged man known for his heavy drinking, propping himself against the kitchen sink. He had vomited profuse amounts of bright red blood. Burt was starting to have breathing problems; he was pale, but had no pain in the stomach. The signs and symptoms coupled with Burt's drinking history led John to suspect ruptured esophageal varices—and he knew that seconds counted.

John called 9-1-1 and talked to a dispatcher while he positioned Burt on the floor on his left side, his face pointed downward to let the blood drain out. Burt continued to vomit blood, and John continued to maintain an open airway by letting blood and saliva drain out until paramedics arrived.

ACUTE ABDOMINAL DISTRESS FEATURES PAIN THAT MAY stem from the cardiac, gastrointestinal, genitourinary, reproductive, or other systems—or even pain that may be referred from elsewhere. According to medical reference guides, there are approximately 100 different causes of abdominal pain. In most cases, it is not appropriate to try to isolate the cause of abdominal distress in the field; instead, priorities are to assess for injury or illness, render appropriate emergency care, and transport.

Abdominal distress in every victim should be considered life threatening until proven otherwise. Abdominal pain should be considered especially serious if the pain is associated with lowered blood pressure, fainting, or an extremely ill appearance.

This chapter outlines appropriate assessment techniques and provides general guidelines for care regardless of the cause of the abdominal pain. It also discusses several specific conditions that are dire medical emergencies requiring rapid emergency medical attention.

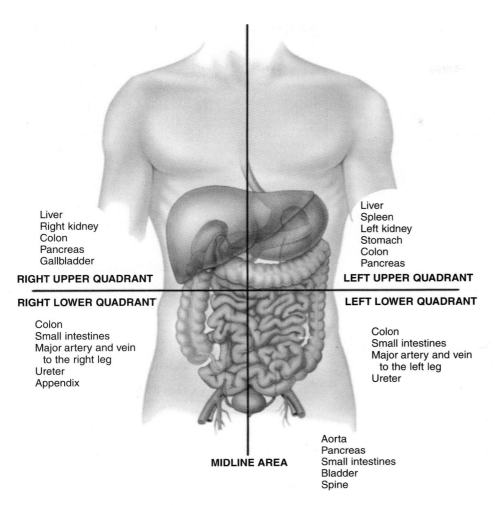

Figure 19-1. The abdominal area in quadrants

Liver
Right kidney
Colon
Pancreas
Gallbladder

RIGHT UPPER QUADRANT

RIGHT LOWER QUADRANT

Colon
Small intestines
Major artery and vein
 to the right leg
Ureter
Appendix

Liver
Spleen
Left kidney
Stomach
Colon
Pancreas

LEFT UPPER QUADRANT

LEFT LOWER QUADRANT

Colon
Small intestines
Major artery and vein
 to the left leg
Ureter

MIDLINE AREA

Aorta
Pancreas
Small intestines
Bladder
Spine

• Section 1 •
ASSESSMENT

Learning Objective 1 Describe the special assessment procedures used for a victim of abdominal distress.

Abdominal distress can be caused by a wide range of conditions, from mild to life-threatening; diagnosis must be confirmed by a physician using medical equipment. The goal of first aid is to stabilize the victim and get medical help. First aid for abdominal distress is generally the same, regardless of the cause.

In assessing a victim with acute abdominal distress, your number-one priority should be to look for signs of shock—rapid, thready pulse; restlessness; cold, clammy skin; and falling blood pressure. Irritation of the thin membrane that lines the abdomen is called **peritonitis;** in addition to causing shock, it is a grave life-threatening condition. Shock is also common with internal bleeding or diarrhea, both of which cause substantial fluid loss.

The **abdomen** is the entire area between the nipples and the groin. For ease in assessment, the abdomen is divided into four **quadrants,** or sections (see Figure 19-1). Pain above the navel is said to be in the upper right or upper left quadrant; pain below the navel is considered in the lower right or lower left quadrant. The location, direction, and characteristics of abdominal pain are important indicators that you should note when activating the EMS system; use the quadrant name to describe where the pain occurs.

Because the abdomen may be very tender, the victim will be guarded (see Figure 19-2 on page 314), and

peritonitis Inflammation of the lining of the abdomen

abdomen The area of the body between the nipples and the groin

quadrants Sections; the abdomen is divided into four quadrants

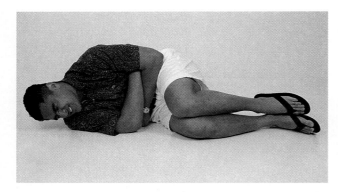

Figure 19-2. Typical guarded position for victim with acute abdominal distress

because even slight palpation can aggravate existing pain, follow these general assessment guidelines:

- Determine whether the victim is restless or quiet, and whether movement causes pain.

- Look to see whether the abdomen is distended.

- Confirm the abnormal contour with the victim.

- Feel the abdomen very gently to determine whether it is tense or soft (see Figure 19-3) and whether any masses are present. If you know that a specific quadrant is causing the pain or the majority of the pain, examine that quadrant last.

- Determine whether the abdomen is tender when touched and whether the victim can relax the abdominal wall upon request. Note any abdominal guarding.

- Determine the location and quadrant of the pain.

Do not waste time with extensive palpation of the abdomen—it can worsen the pain and aggravate the medical condition that causes it.

Note: If the victim is a child, suspect the need for surgery if there is tenderness or guarding on palpation.

Progress Check

1. For assessment purposes, the abdomen is divided into four _____ .
   (sections/quadrants/areas)

2. In assessing a victim with abdominal distress, your number-one priority is to look for signs of
   _____ .
   (appendicitis/internal bleeding/shock)

3. If you know what section of the abdomen is causing pain, feel that section _____ .
   (first/last/gently)

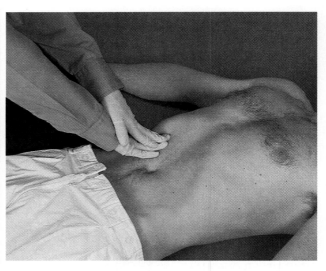

Figure 19-3. Gently determine if the abdomen is tense or soft.

• Section 2 •

SIGNS AND SYMPTOMS

Learning Objective 2 List the signs and symptoms of abdominal distress.

Any severe abdominal pain should be considered an emergency.

A victim with an acute abdomen appears very ill; general signs and symptoms of acute abdominal distress include

- Abdominal pain (local or diffuse)

- **Colicky pain** (cramplike pain that occurs in waves)

- Local or diffuse abdominal tenderness

- Anxiety and reluctance to move

- Rapid, shallow breathing

- Rapid pulse

- Nausea and/or vomiting

- Low blood pressure

- Tense, often distended abdomen

- Signs of shock

- Signs of internal bleeding: vomiting blood (bright red or coffee-grounds) or passing blood in the stool (bright red or tarry black)

A victim with acute abdominal distress often adopts a position on his or her side with knees drawn up toward the abdomen.

Progress Check

1. Any severe abdominal pain should be considered
_____ .
(after the primary survey/an emergency/a treatment priority)

2. A victim of abdominal distress usually appears very
_____ .
(anxious/fatigued/ill)

3. Colicky pain is a cramplike pain that occurs in
_____ .
(waves/infants/liver disease victims)

4. A victim of acute abdominal distress often positions himself or herself on the _____ .
(back/stomach/side)

• Section 3 •

EMERGENCY CARE

Learning Objective 3 Describe and demonstrate general emergency care for acute abdominal distress.

The goals of first aid care for acute abdominal distress are to prevent any possible life-threatening complications (such as hemorrhage or shock), to make the victim comfortable, and to activate the EMS system so the victim can be transported as quickly as possible for diagnostic care by a physician. A victim with acute abdominal distress must always be transported, because many need surgery; the sooner the victim is transported and evaluated by a physician, the better the outcome.

Activate the EMS system; then:

1. Secure and maintain the airway; be alert for vomiting and possible aspiration. If the victim is nauseated, position him or her on the left side if it does not cause too much pain; if the victim vomits, save some of the vomitus so it can be transported with the victim and tested at the hospital.

2. Position the victim as comfortably as possible, and take steps to prevent shock. If there are signs of shock, place the victim on his or her back with the legs slightly elevated. If there are no signs of shock, let the victim determine the most comfortable position unless it interferes with emergency care. Most victims prefer to lie on their sides or backs with their knees drawn up toward the abdomen.

3. Comfort and reassure the victim (see Figure 19-4).

4. *Never give anything by mouth.* Never give the victim medications of any kind, and do not let the

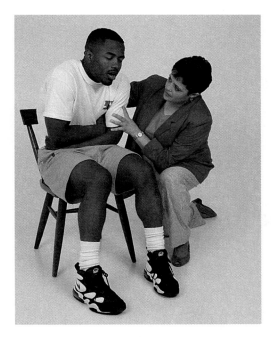

Figure 19-4. Reassure and monitor the victim of abdominal distress while waiting for emergency personnel to arrive.

victim take them on his or her own. Never give the victim an enema.

5. Record signs and symptoms, including the victim's description of the condition, and continue to monitor until emergency help arrives.

Figure 19-5 on page 316 illustrates several causes of acute abdominal distress.

Progress Check

1. A goal of emergency care for acute abdominal distress is to _____ .
(prevent shock/predict the need for surgery/prevent vomiting)

2. Let the victim choose the most comfortable position unless there are signs of _____ .
(internal bleeding/appendicitis/shock)

3. If the victim is nauseated, position the victim on
_____ .
(the back/the left side/the stomach)

colicky pain Cramplike pain that occurs in waves

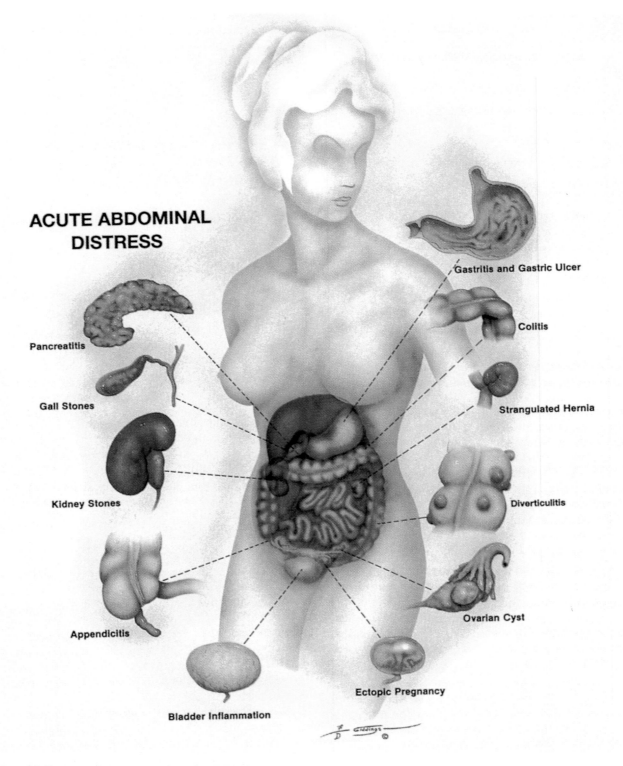

ACUTE ABDOMINAL DISTRESS

Gastritis and Gastric Ulcer

Colitis

Pancreatitis

Strangulated Hernia

Gall Stones

Diverticulitis

Kidney Stones

Ovarian Cyst

Appendicitis

Ectopic Pregnancy

Bladder Inflammation

Figure 19-5. *Potential sources of acute abdominal distress*

• Section 4 •
SPECIAL CONSIDERATIONS

Ruptured Esophageal Varices

Esophageal varices are bulging, engorged, and weakened blood vessels lining the wall of the lower one-third of the esophagus. Varices can potentially develop in anyone, but they are most common in certain types of victims:

- Heavy alcohol drinkers
- Victims of liver disease (such as cirrhosis or hepatitis)
- Victims with chronic liver dysfunction
- Victims with an enlarged liver
- Victims of jaundice

Varices usually lead to painless gastrointestinal bleeding. When one or more of these varices rupture, bleeding is profuse and severe and can be fatal within minutes unless the victim has prompt treatment.

Signs and Symptoms

Learning Objective 4 List the signs and symptoms of ruptured esophageal varices.

Ruptured esophageal varices cause the following signs and symptoms:

- Vomiting of profuse amounts of bright red blood
- Blood welling up in the back of the throat, with or without vomiting
- Absence of pain or tenderness in the stomach
- Rapid pulse (usually more than 120 beats per minute)
- Respiratory distress
- **Pallor** (paleness)

Because esophageal varices are most common among victims with liver disease, additional signs and symptoms of ruptured varices may include those of liver disease—jaundice, an enlarged liver, or dilated veins just below the skin's surface.

Emergency Care

Learning Objective 5 Describe and demonstrate the emergency care of a victim with ruptured esophageal varices.

The victim of ruptured esophageal varices needs rapid blood replacement and surgical procedures aimed at

stopping the bleeding. First aid priorities are to activate the EMS system *immediately,* secure and maintain the airway, prevent aspiration, and treat or prevent shock.

Activate the EMS system, explaining the need for urgency; then:

1. Immediately secure an open airway.
2. Position the victim on his or her left side with the face pointed downward to allow drainage of blood and saliva. Maintaining a clear airway is critical to the victim's survival.
3. Treat for shock.

Abdominal Aortic Aneurysm

Learning Objective 6 List the signs and symptoms of ruptured abdominal aortic aneurysm.

An **abdominal aortic aneurysm** occurs when the wall of the aorta in the abdomen weakens, dilates, and eventually ruptures. One of the most lethal conditions that causes abdominal pain, it is most common in those with atherosclerosis. It is estimated that approximately 20 percent of all men over the age of 50 have abdominal aortic aneurysms.

Signs and Symptoms

The pain from a ruptured abdominal aortic aneurysm is very sudden in onset. Signs and symptoms include

- Sudden, severe, constant pain in the abdomen or back; the pain tends to radiate to the lower back, flank, or pelvis
- Possible nausea and vomiting
- Mottled abdominal skin
- Pale legs
- Decreased or absent pulses in the groin (femoral) and foot (pedal)

esophageal varices Bulging, engorged, weakened blood vessels in the lining of the wall of the lower one-third of the esophagus

pallor Paleness

abdominal aortic aneurysm A section of the wall of the aorta in the abdomen that weakens, dilates, and eventually ruptures

If the abdomen is soft, you will be able to detect a pulsating abdominal mass that is palpable; if the aneurysm has burst, the abdomen will likely be hard and rigid.

Emergency Care

Learning Objective 7 Describe and demonstrate the emergency care of a victim with ruptured abdominal aortic aneurysm.

Activate the EMS system without delay, explaining the need for great urgency; then:

1. Palpate the abdomen very gently; pressure or firm palpation can aggravate the emergency and cause further dissection of the artery.

2. Treat the victim for shock and monitor vital signs until emergency personnel arrive.

Progress Check

1. Esophageal varices are bulging, engorged _____ in the lower esophagus.
   (cysts/blood vessels/ulcerated sores)

2. Esophageal varices are most common among heavy drinkers or people with _____ .
   (liver disease/heart disease/diverticulitis)

3. The key sign of ruptured esophageal varices is vomiting of _____ blood.
   (black/tarry/bright red)

4. The first priority in treating a victim of ruptured esophageal varices is to _____ .
   (maintain the airway/prevent shock/relieve pain)

5. An abdominal aortic aneurysm that _____ represents a dire emergency.
   (increases in size/ruptures/blocks the intestine)

6. The goal in treating ruptured abdominal aortic aneurysm is to _____ .
   (maintain an airway/prevent shock/relieve pain)

• SUMMARY •

- It is extremely difficult to determine which of the more than 100 possible causes of abdominal pain may be present in a given situation, so your primary goal is emergency care, not assessment.

- The special assessment procedure for acute abdominal distress is to proceed gently, determining as much as possible by sight. If you know which quadrant is the site of the victim's distress, feel that one last.

- Any severe abdominal pain should be considered an emergency. Any abdominal pain that lasts more than 6 hours, regardless of intensity, should be considered an emergency.

- The goals of emergency care for acute abdominal distress are to prevent any possible life-threatening complications (such as shock), make the victim comfortable, and arrange for transport as soon as possible.

- Unless there are signs of shock, let the victim determine the position that is most comfortable—usually on the side or back with knees drawn up toward the abdomen. If there are signs of shock, place the victim on his or her back with legs elevated.

- When bulging, engorged, and weakened blood vessels in the esophagus rupture, the victim will vomit profuse amounts of bright red blood; your primary goal is to secure and maintain the airway.

- When an abdominal aortic aneurysm ruptures, your primary goal is to prevent shock and to arrange for rapid transport.

• KEY TERMS •

Make sure you understand the following key terms:

- peritonitis
- abdomen
- quadrants
- colicky pain
- esophageal varices
- pallor
- abdominal aortic aneurysm

Student: _____   Date: _____

Course: _____   Section #: _____

PART 1 • True/False

If you believe the statement is true, circle the T. If you believe the statement is false, circle the F.

T   F   **1.** In assessing a victim with acute abdominal distress, your number-one priority should be to assess pain.

T   F   **2.** The blood vomited with ruptured esophageal varices is the consistency of coffee grounds.

T   F   **3.** A victim with acute abdomen rarely appears ill.

T   F   **4.** There is usually absence of pain or tenderness in the stomach with ruptured esophageal varices.

T   F   **5.** If you know that the pain is originating in a certain quadrant, palpate that one first.

T   F   **6.** Adequate assessment of an acute abdomen requires firm and steady palpation.

T   F   **7.** You should never give a victim of acute abdominal distress anything by mouth.

T   F   **8.** Severe abdominal pain should be considered an emergency.

T   F   **9.** The primary goal of first aid for acute abdominal distress is to make a diagnosis.

T   F   **10.** The primary goal in caring for ruptured abdominal aortic aneurysm is to prevent shock.

PART 2 • Multiple Choice

For each item, circle the correct answer or the phrase that best completes the statement.

1. A victim lying on one side with knees drawn up; with rapid, shallow breathing; with a rapid pulse; and who is quiet, anxious, and reluctant to move is likely to be suffering from

   a. stroke
   b. insulin shock
   c. acute abdominal distress
   d. myocardial infarction

2. Victims suffering from acute abdominal distress should be allowed to

   a. determine the most comfortable position
   b. drink liquids
   c. take personal medication
   d. all of the above

3. Pain from acute abdominal distress is often

   a. colicky
   b. shifting
   c. radiating
   d. all of the above

4. Which of the following is *not* appropriate emergency care for ruptured esophageal varices?

   a. position the victim to allow drainage from the mouth and throat
   b. treat the victim for shock
   c. put the victim in a supine position
   d. activate the EMS system without delay

5. Any abdominal pain that lasts longer than _____ should be considered an emergency.

   a. 30 minutes
   b. 6 hours
   c. 2 hours
   d. 24 hours

- A victim you are assisting complains of lower abdominal pain on the right side that has increased in intensity for the last 6 hours. The victim is nauseated and nervous.
- You are at a social gathering when a middle-aged man starts vomiting large amounts of bright red blood. The man's wife tells you that he has a history of a drinking problem. He has pale skin and a rapid pulse and is experiencing some respiratory distress.

20

Epilepsy, Dizziness, and Fainting

Learning Objectives

When you have mastered the material in this chapter, you will be able to

1 Explain the physiology of seizures

2 List the various causes of seizures

3 List the types of seizures

4 List the signs and symptoms of grand mal seizures

5 Define status epilepticus

6 Describe assessment priorities for a seizure victim

7 Describe and demonstrate emergency care for a victim of a seizure

8 Explain the types of dizziness

9 Describe and demonstrate emergency care for a victim of fainting

A pproaching a city transit stop on a windy day in March, Steve Broadbent saw a crowd of people gathered around a man on the ground. Walking closer, Steve saw that the man appeared to be in his late twenties and was suffering a seizure.

Steve asked a bystander to call 9-1-1 from a nearby pay phone, then asked other people in the crowd to go back to the bus loading area, hoping to protect the man's privacy. Steve quickly determined that the man was breathing, then removed the man's eyeglasses and loosened the first few buttons of his shirt. Steve then covered the man with his own coat to help keep him warm. A quick scan of the area showed that there were no dangerous objects in reach.

Steve continued to monitor the victim; just before emergency personnel arrived, the seizure stopped. Because it was the victim's first seizure, he was transported to the hospital for evaluation.

NEUROLOGICAL EMERGENCIES INVOLVING A DISTURBANCE in the chemical or electrical activity of the brain are generally more frightening than life threatening. With quick recognition of the condition and vigorous airway management to prevent oxygen deprivation, you can generally prevent a major medical emergency.

A victim who passes from one seizure to another without first regaining consciousness, however, *is* experiencing a life-threatening medical emergency.

This chapter explains the physiology of seizures, explains the causes and types of seizures, outlines general emergency care for seizures, and gives guidelines for managing dizziness and fainting.

• Section 1 •
CAUSES AND TYPES OF SEIZURES

Learning Objective 1 Explain the physiology of seizures.

A **seizure** is an involuntary, sudden change in sensation, behavior, muscle activity, or level of consciousness that results from irritation or overactivity of brain cells (see Figure 20-1). In general, seizures are caused by an abnormal discharge of electrical energy in the brain; they are sudden in onset, usually occurring after only very brief warning, if any.

Any condition that affects the structural cells of the brain or alters its chemical metabolic balance may trigger seizures.

Causes of Seizures

Learning Objective 2 List the various causes of seizures.

A significant cause of seizures is **epilepsy,** a chronic brain disorder characterized by recurrent seizures not caused by acute problems (such as head trauma, fever, or hypoglycemia). Epilepsy is a general term for approximately 20 different seizure disorders.

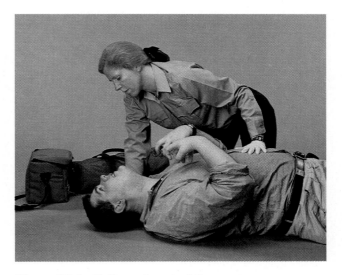

Figure 20-1. Epilepsy is one of the most common causes of seizures.

Seizures can also occur in anyone as a result of an acute injury to the brain or a more long-lasting condition involving the brain. Other causes include (see Figure 20-2)

• Allergic reactions to drugs or other chemicals

• Withdrawal from addictive substances

Causes of Seizures

Seizures can occur in anyone as a result of an acute injury to the brain, or a more long-lasting condition involving the brain.

• **Toxic**—Seizures can occur as a direct consequence of allergic reactions to drugs, using drugs or other chemicals, or withdrawal from addicting substances, especially alcohol.

• **Metabolic**—Derangements in the body's chemistry may be accompanied by a seizure; this accounts for 10 to 15 percent of all seizures.

• **Trauma**—A previous injury to the brain could result in formation of a scar, which can serve as a seizure focus. Head trauma is the leading cause of seizures, and seizures occur in the first year following head trauma in 75 percent of the cases.

• **Vascular**—Any condition that reduces cerebral blood flow can cause seizures. Seizure potential varies with the severity of reduced blood flow, and most often is the result of arteriosclerosis or cerebral infarction.

• **Infection**—An inflammation of the brain such as that caused by encephalitis; the infection can be bacterial, viral, or parasitic.

• **Febrile**—Most commonly seen in children ages 6 months to 3 years, these seizures occur in conjunction with a fever. Fever is the most common cause of seizures in children under the age of 5; most often it is the rapid rise in temperature, and not the degree of the fever itself, that causes the seizure. Only in rare cases does this condition cause seizures later in life.

• **Idiopathic**—By definition, this type of seizure arises spontaneously from an unknown cause.

• **Degenerative**—Disorders causing degeneration of the central nervous system, including multiple sclerosis and certain dementias, can cause seizures.

• **Congenital defects of the brain**—Particularly in infants and young children

• **Brain tumor**—Uncommon as a cause of seizures in children. Seizures—especially local seizures—can be a first sign of brain tumor in adults.

• **Other**—Other causes of seizures include hypertension, eclampsia, severe burns, endocrine changes during pregnancy and menstruation, spurts in growth, childhood illnesses, extreme variations in sleep habits (including sleep deprivation), and swelling of brain tissue (regardless of cause).

(Adapted in part from *Mayo Clinic Health Letter*, November 1988, with permission of Mayo Foundation for Medical Education and Research, Rochester, Minnesota.)

Figure 20-2. The various causes of seizures

- Derangements in the body's chemistry

- Trauma or other injury to the brain that causes scar formation

- Reduced blood flow to the brain

- Inflammation of the brain, usually caused by bacterial, viral, or parasitic infection

- Fever, usually in children 6 months to 3 years old

- Degeneration of the central nervous system, such as from multiple sclerosis

- Congenital brain defects

- Brain tumor

- Severe burns

- Endocrine changes during pregnancy or menstruation

Some seizures occur spontaneously with no known cause.

Types of Seizures

Learning Objective 3 List the types of seizures.

Learning Objective 4 List the signs and symptoms of grand mal seizures.

Table 20-1 lists the seven general types of seizures and their signs and symptoms.

Table 20-1
Seizure Symptoms

Type of Seizure	What Happens	What It Is Often Mistaken For
Grand mal	• Sudden cry or moan • Rigidity • Muscle jerks • Frothy saliva • Shallow breathing • Bluish skin • Usually lasts 2–5 minutes; normal breathing then starts again	• Heart attack • Stroke
Petit mal	• Blank stare • Rapid blinking • Chewing movements • Lasts only a few seconds	• Daydreaming • Inattention • In children, deliberately ignoring adult instructions
Jacksonian	• Jerking in fingers and toes • Victim stays awake, aware • Jerking may progress up hand, arm, then to whole body and becomes a convulsive seizure	• Acting out • Bizarre behavior
Psychomotor	• Starts with blank stare, followed by chewing and random activity • Victim appears dazed • Mumbling • Victim picks at self, may remove clothing • Victim struggles or flails if restrained • Post-seizure confusion	• Drunkenness • Drug intoxication • Mental illness • Indecent exposure • Disorderly conduct • Shoplifting
Myoclonic	• Sudden, brief, massive muscle jerking that can involve part or all of body	• Clumsiness • Poor coordination
Atonic	• Child's legs suddenly collapse, causing child to fall • Lasts less than a minute	• Clumsiness • Lack of walking skills • Normal childhood "stage"
Infantile	• Head falls forward • Arms flex forward • Knees are drawn up • Occurs between the ages of 3 months and 2 years	• Normal infant movements

Status Epilepticus

Learning Objective 5 Define status epilepticus.

Most seizures stop within 5 minutes (even though the victim may remain unconscious for several minutes longer). In contrast, **status epilepticus** is a single seizure that lasts 5 to 10 minutes *or* a series of seizures that occur without the victim's regaining consciousness between them. *Status epilepticus is a dire medical emergency;* approximately half of all victims die. Because of the length of the prolonged or recurrent seizures, the brain is deprived of oxygen. Irreversible brain damage can result, as well as complications of the cardiac, respiratory, and renal systems.

Status epilepticus may result from a worsening of whatever caused the seizures in the first place, or it may be the result of a new condition. It is often the result of improper drug therapy for an epilepsy victim.

Progress Check

1. Seizures are caused by _____ brain cells.
   (irritation of/damage to/lack of oxygen in)

2. One of the most common causes of seizures is
   _____ .
   (trauma/brain tumor/epilepsy)

3. A seizure that causes a sudden cry or moan followed by muscle jerks and frothy saliva is a
   _____ seizure.
   (petit mal/grand mal/Jacksonian)

4. A petit mal seizure is often mistaken for
   _____ .
   (daydreaming/stroke/mental illness)

5. Status epilepticus means the seizure has lasted
   _____ minutes.
   (5/5–10/more than 10)

6. Status epilepticus represents a dire medical emergency because the brain is deprived of _____ .
   (blood/glucose/oxygen)

• Section 2 •
ASSESSMENT AND EMERGENCY CARE

Most seizures—other than status epilepticus—are self-limiting and last at most 5 minutes, although the victim may experience residual drowsiness for several hours. Seizures stop and start spontaneously; you cannot reduce their duration.

Grand Mal Stages

A grand mal seizure (see Figure 20-3 on page 326) occurs in stages, ranging from the warning phase to a period of recovery, and includes the following:

- The **aura,** a peculiar "warning" sensation that lasts only a few seconds (it may be visual or auditory hallucinations, a peculiar taste in the mouth, or a painful sensation, for example)
- The **tonic phase** lasts 15 to 20 seconds; the victim loses consciousness, the eyes roll upward, there

seizure An involuntary, sudden change in sensation, behavior, muscle activity, or level of consciousness that results from irritation or overactivity of brain cells

epilepsy A chronic brain disorder characterized by recurrent seizures not caused by acute problems, with or without loss of consciousness

grand mal seizure A convulsive seizure characterized by alternating muscle rigidity and jerking, temporarily suspended breathing, and unconsciousness

petit mal seizure A seizure characterized by a blank stare that lasts only a few seconds, most common in children; a petit mal seizure does not involve convulsions

Jacksonian seizure A simple, partial seizure characterized by jerking in the fingers and toes; the jerking may spread to involve the entire arm or leg, or even the entire body, but the victim stays awake and aware

psychomotor seizure A seizure that starts with a blank stare, then progresses into chewing and random activity; the victim seems dazed

myoclonic seizure A seizure characterized by sudden, brief, massive muscle jerks that involve part or all of the body

atonic seizure Also called a "drop attack," a seizure in which the legs of a child suddenly and temporarily collapse

infantile seizure A seizure in an infant characterized by falling forward of the head and flexing forward of the arms

status epilepticus A severe, prolonged seizure or a series of seizures that occur without the victim's regaining consciousness between them

aura The first phase of a seizure that lasts only a few seconds and involves a peculiar sensation that may be psychic or sensory in nature

tonic phase The early stage of a seizure during which the victim loses consciousness, the eyes roll upward, and the body is completely rigid with continuous muscular contraction

STAGES OF GRAND MAL SEIZURES

A grand mal seizure is a sign of an abnormal release of impulses in the brain. It is a physical, not a psychological, disorder.

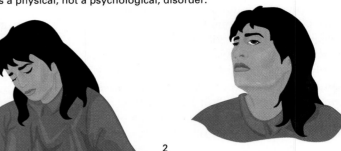

1
The victim may have an "aura" or premonition, which is part of the seizure. An aura is often described as an odd or unpleasant sensation that rises from the stomach toward the chest and throat.

For some victims the aura is always the same, such as numbness or motor activity (such as turning of head and eyes, spasm of a limb) or it may consist of a peculiar sound or taste.

2
Loss of consciousness follows the aura. The forced expulsion of air caused by contraction of the skeletal muscles may cause a high-pitched cry sound. The victim may be pale at this point with possible spasms of various muscle groups causing the tongue to be bitten.

3
The victim will usually fall with seizures and lose consciousness. Cyanosis may accompany the seizure because breathing stops during the phase of prolonged muscle contraction. Within seconds the victim will manifest an arched back and alternating contraction and relaxation of movements in all extremities (clonic convulsive movements). The attack usually lasts from about 30 seconds to 5 minutes. The victim may lose bladder and bowel control.

4
Gradually the clonic phase (seizure) subsides. It is followed by a postictal state, characterized by a deep sleep with gradual recovery to a state of transient confusion, fatigue, muscular soreness, and headache. The victim should be encouraged to rest since activity could precipitate another attack.

EMERGENCY CARE

- If the victim seems to stop breathing, monitor airway and assist ventilation if necessary. The situation becomes life-threatening if the victim passes from seizure to seizure without regaining consciousness (status epilepticus). This situation requires transport and medical attention.
- The major requirements of the First Aider are the ABCDs and to protect the victim from hurting herself during a seizure.
- The victim should not be physically restrained in any way unless she is endangering her own welfare.
- Move objects, not the victim.
- Position the victim to allow for drainage and suctioning.
- Loosen tight clothing.
- If status epilepticus occurs or breathing ceases, assist breathing as necessary and transport immediately.
- Keep victim from being a spectacle
- Reassure and reorient victim following the seizure.
- Allow her to rest.
- An ambulance is often called for a grand mal seizure, but if the victim responds normally she may not need transport. If in doubt, always transport to a medical facility. Follow local protocol.

Figure. 20-3. Grand mal seizures

is continuous muscular contraction, and the victim stops breathing.

- The **hypertonic phase** lasts 5 to 15 seconds; there is extreme muscular rigidity.

- The **clonic phase** lasts 30 to 60 seconds; muscular rigidity and relaxation alternate rhythmically and in rapid succession, there is frothy saliva, and the victim may lose bowel and bladder control.

- **Autonomic discharge** lasts for a few seconds; there is hyperventilation, salivation, and rapid heartbeat.

- During the **postseizure phase,** the victim lapses into a coma.

- The **postictal stupor** usually lasts 5 to 30 minutes, but occasionally several hours; all muscles relax and the victim falls into a deep sleep.

Assessment Considerations

Learning Objective 6 Describe assessment priorities for a seizure victim.

Because a victim will rarely remember the seizure, you need to get a history from bystanders unless you witnessed the seizure yourself. Try to find out the following:

- What the seizure was like
- Whether the victim has a history of seizures
- Whether the victim takes medication for seizures
- How the seizure progressed
- Whether the victim has suffered a head injury
- Whether the victim uses drugs or alcohol
- Whether the victim has diabetes

In performing a physical assessment, pay particular attention to the following:

- Signs of injury to the head, tongue, or elsewhere on the body
- Signs of drug or alcohol abuse (such as alcohol on the breath or needle tracks)
- The victim's level of consciousness
- Fever
- Presence of a Medic Alert tag or other identifying medal or bracelet

Emergency Care for Seizures

Learning Objective 7 Describe and demonstrate emergency care for a victim of a seizure.

Although seizures are generally not life threatening, anyone who experiences a seizure for the first time should be evaluated by a physician. You should also send for medical help if the seizure lasts longer than 5 minutes; if you are uncertain of the cause; if the victim has more than one seizure; if the victim appears to be injured; if the victim has trouble breathing after the seizure; if the victim is diabetic; or if the victim is an infant, child, or pregnant woman.

The general goal of first aid is to support the victim, prevent injury, and refer the victim to medical care if appropriate.

Activate the EMS system if appropriate; then:

1. Help the victim lie on the floor to avoid a fall and subsequent injury; do not move the victim unless he or she is near a dangerous object that cannot be moved (such as a hot radiator). Otherwise, move objects away from the victim (see Figure 20-4 on page 328). Place padding (such as a rolled towel) under the victim's head to prevent injury.

2. Maintain an open airway.

3. Stay calm; if the victim is conscious, reassure him or her; reassure others who are with the victim.

4. Stay with the victim until the seizure has passed; if you need to get help, send someone else.

5. Never try to force anything between the victim's teeth, and never give the victim anything by mouth.

hypertonic phase The phase in a seizure that signals the end of continuous muscle contractions, characterized by extreme muscle rigidity and hypertension

clonic phase The phase of a seizure characterized by muscular rigidity and relaxation that alternate rhythmically in rapid succession

autonomic discharge A stage in a grand mal seizure that lasts for a few seconds and includes hyperventilation, salivation, and rapid heartbeat

postseizure phase One of the final phases of a seizure, during which the victim progresses into a coma

postictal stupor The phase following a seizure, during which all muscles relax and the victim falls into a deep sleep

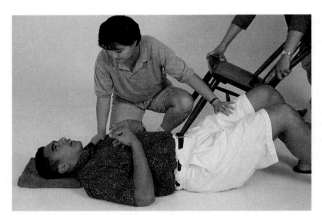

Figure 20-4. Move objects away from the seizure victim rather than trying to move the victim.

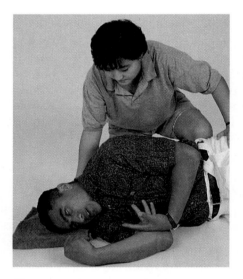

Figure 20-5. Position the seizure victim to allow drainage of saliva and vomit.

6. Remove or loosen any tight clothing, especially around the neck; remove eyeglasses.

7. Turn the victim on his or her left side with the face pointed downward (see Figure 20-5) so secretions and vomitus can drain quickly out of the mouth and so the tongue will not fall back and block the throat.

8. If the victim stops breathing, open the airway, remove anything that might impair breathing, and give artificial ventilation.

9. Do not try to restrain the victim unless he or she is in danger from objects that cannot be moved.

10. Cover the victim with a blanket to preserve warmth.

11. Keep the victim from becoming a spectacle; ask bystanders to leave.

12. Following the seizure, reassure and reorient the victim; speak slowly and calmly in a normal tone of voice. Allow the victim to rest; help the victim be as comfortable as possible.

Emergency Care for Status Epilepticus

If the victim experiences status epilepticus, *you are faced with a dire medical emergency.* The number-one goal is oxygenation. Activate the EMS system immediately; then:

1. Place the victim on the floor or bed, away from other furniture. Do not try to restrain the victim.

2. Clear and maintain the airway; turn the victim's head sideways to prevent aspiration.

3. Administer artificial ventilation as needed; even though it can be extremely difficult to administer artificial ventilation to a seizing person, you must do it—lack of oxygen during seizure activity is the most serious threat to life.

4. Carefully monitor vital signs until emergency personnel arrive.

Progress Check

1. An aura may involve a _____ .
   (hallucination/muscle contraction/coma)

2. The period in which a seizure victim loses consciousness is the _____ phase.
   (clonic/tonic/hypertonic)

3. During the _____ , the victim falls into a deep sleep.
   (clonic phase/autonomic discharge/postictal stupor)

4. During assessment of a seizure victim, pay particular attention to signs of injury to the _____ .
   (throat/head/back)

5. You should activate the EMS system if the victim has more than _____ seizure(s).
   (one/two/three)

6. The primary goal in caring for the victim of status epilepticus is _____ .
   (preventing injury/maintaining airway/oxygenation)

• Section 3 •
DIZZINESS AND FAINTING

Two of the most common medical complaints are dizziness and syncope, or fainting. Actually, dizziness and fainting are not medical conditions at all, but are symptoms that can result from a wide variety of diseases and injuries.

Dizziness

Learning Objective 8 Explain the types of dizziness.

Most victims are not experiencing true dizziness, or **vertigo.** Instead, they may feel woozy, light-headed, or as though they are in a dream.

True vertigo involves a hallucination of motion—the victim feels as though he or she is spinning around, or, more commonly, that the room is whirling in circles. Some feel they are being pulled to the ground; others feel the room has tilted so much that they can no longer stand up.

Signs and Symptoms

There are two different types of vertigo, and each causes very different signs and symptoms.

Central vertigo, the less common and most serious, signifies a dramatic medical problem involving the central nervous system and causes the following signs and symptoms:

- Dysfunction of the eye muscles
- Unequal pupil size
- Facial droop

Victims of central vertigo do not experience nausea, vomiting, hearing loss, or a whirling sensation.

Labyrinthine vertigo, which is much more common, occurs as a disturbance in the inner ear and causes the following signs and symptoms:

- Nausea
- Vomiting
- Rapid, involuntary twitching of the eyeball
- A whirling sensation
- Pale, moist skin
- Rapid heartbeat

All symptoms of labyrinthine vertigo are made worse when the victim moves; episodes can last for hours and recur over a period of many years.

Emergency Care

1. Reassure the victim; help the victim get in a comfortable position and to move as little as possible.
2. Conduct a thorough assessment to rule out any immediate life-threatening conditions.
3. Encourage the victim to see a physician.

Fainting

Fainting, or **syncope,** is a sudden and brief loss of consciousness that results when the brain is temporarily deprived of adequate oxygen. Some victims feel as though everything is going dark; then they suddenly lose consciousness. A death-like collapse follows that puts the body in a horizontal position, which improves blood circulation to the brain. As a result, the victim rapidly regains consciousness.

Fainting itself is not a disease, but can be a symptom of a wide range of conditions and diseases—most commonly, severe emotion, fright, heat, use of certain drugs, profound pain, standing or sitting too long without moving, low blood sugar, or irregular heart rhythm.

Signs and Symptoms

Some victims have the following warning signs that they are about to faint:

- Nausea
- Light-headedness
- Weakness
- Shakiness
- Deep abdominal pain
- A pounding pain in the head

Emergency Care

Learning Objective 9 Describe and demonstrate emergency care for a victim of fainting.

If appropriate, activate the EMS system; then:

1. If the victim has not yet fainted, prevent him or her from falling by having the victim sit down (see Figure 20-6 on page 330) with head between the knees or have the victim lie on the floor with legs elevated 8 to 12 inches.

vertigo Dizziness

central vertigo The least common type of vertigo (dizziness), which mimics a transient ischemic attack or stroke; victims do not experience nausea, vomiting, hearing loss, or a whirling sensation

labyrinthine vertigo The most common kind of dizziness, caused by a disturbance in the inner ear and characterized by nausea, vomiting, and a whirling sensation

syncope Fainting

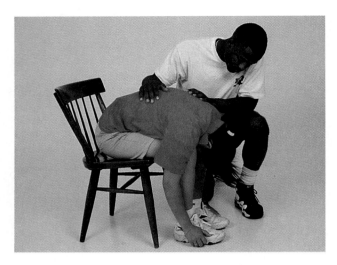

Figure 20-6. Seat the victim who feels faint. Put the head between the legs.

2. If the victim has already fainted, keep the victim in a supine position; elevate the legs 8 to 12 inches (see Figure 20-7).

3. Until proven otherwise, assume the brain has been deprived of oxygen; establish an airway and provide artificial ventilation if necessary.

4. Monitor for possible vomiting; loosen clothing that might restrict free breathing.

5. Make a rapid assessment for any life-threatening condition that may have caused the fainting; initiate appropriate care.

6. Check for any injuries that may have occurred during the fall; treat appropriately.

7. Do not allow a person who has fainted to sit up immediately; doing so could cause a stroke. Instead, have the victim sit up slowly and gradually.

8. Help the victim feel better by moving him or her to fresh air or by putting a cool, damp cloth on the face.

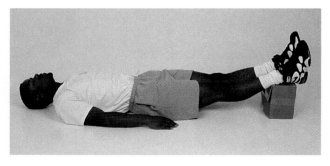

Figure 20-7. Elevate the legs of a victim who has fainted.

Progress Check

1. The medical term for dizziness is _____ .
   (syncope/acidosis/vertigo)

2. The medical term for fainting is _____ .
   (syncope/acidosis/vertigo)

3. The most serious kind of vertigo, _____ vertigo, causes symptoms like those of a stroke.
   (central/positional/labyrinthine)

4. _____ vertigo is caused by a disturbance in the inner ear.
   (Central/Positional/Labyrinthine)

5. Fainting occurs when the _____ is temporarily deprived of oxygen.
   (heart/brain/liver)

6. You can prevent someone from fainting by placing the head _____ .
   (at heart level/between the knees/lower than the feet)

● SUMMARY ●

- A seizure is an involuntary, sudden change in sensation that is caused by irritation or overactivity of brain cells; the most common cause of seizure is epilepsy.

- In addition to epilepsy, other causes of seizures are fever, infection, head injury, brain tumor, lack of blood flow to the brain, and derangements in the body's chemistry.

- The type of seizure that involves jerking and frothing at the mouth is only one kind of seizure; others cause apparent daydreaming or erratic behavior similar to that seen with mental illness.

- You cannot lessen the duration of a seizure.

- Anyone who experiences a first-time seizure should see a physician; you should also get medical help if the seizure lasts more than a few minutes; if you are uncertain about the cause of the seizure; or if the victim has more than one seizure, appears to be injured, or is an infant, child, diabetic, or pregnant woman.

- To care for a seizing victim, do whatever you can to prevent the victim from injuring himself or herself.

- Status epilepticus is a prolonged seizure or a series of seizures that occur without the victim's regaining consciousness.

- The number-one goal in treating status epilepticus is oxygenation.

- Most victims of dizziness are not experiencing true vertigo, which is a hallucination of motion.

- Fainting is a loss of consciousness that occurs when the brain is temporarily deprived of enough oxygen; if placed in a supine position, the victim almost always rapidly regains consciousness.

• KEY TERMS •

Make sure you understand the following key terms:

- seizure
- epilepsy
- grand mal seizure
- petit mal seizure
- Jacksonian seizure
- psychomotor seizure
- myoclonic seizure
- atonic seizure
- infantile seizure
- status epilepticus
- aura
- tonic phase
- hypertonic phase
- clonic phase
- autonomic discharge
- postseizure phase
- postictal stupor
- vertigo
- central vertigo
- labyrinthine vertigo
- syncope

Student: _____   Date: _____

Course: _____   Section #: _____

PART 1 • True/False

If you believe the statement is true, circle the T. If you believe the statement is false, circle the F.

T   F   **1.** A seizure is a voluntary, sudden change in behavior, sensation, muscular activity, and level of consciousness.

T   F   **2.** Epilepsy is a chronic brain disorder.

T   F   **3.** Seizures are always life threatening.

T   F   **4.** Grand mal seizures always produce a loss of consciousness.

T   F   **5.** Jacksonian seizures always produce a loss of consciousness.

T   F   **6.** Irreversible brain damage can occur from status epilepticus.

T   F   **7.** Most seizures are self-limiting and last less than 5 minutes.

T   F   **8.** In a postictal stupor, the victim falls into a deep sleep.

T   F   **9.** Do not attempt to restrain a seizure victim unless he or she is in immediate danger.

T   F   **10.** Dizziness and fainting are not medical conditions, but are symptoms.

T   F   **11.** True vertigo involves a hallucination of motion.

T   F   **12.** Fainting is a temporary loss of consciousness due to an inadequate supply of oxygen to the brain.

T   F   **13.** True vertigo is an actual disturbance of the victim's sense of balance.

T   F   **14.** The number-one goal in a status epilepticus emergency is oxygenation.

PART 2 • Multiple Choice

For each item, circle the correct answer or the phrase that best completes the statement.

1. A characteristic of petit mal seizures is
   a. convulsive movements of one part of the body
   b. brief periods where the victim appears to be daydreaming
   c. loss of consciousness
   d. repetition of inappropriate actions

2. Which of the following is *not* a stage of epilepsy?
   a. clonic phase
   b. tonic phase
   c. aura
   d. catatonic phase

3. The most serious threat in status epilepticus is
   a. lack of oxygen due to impaired breathing
   b. fractures
   c. swallowing the tongue
   d. dehydration

4. Status epilepticus in adults is
   a. a dire medical emergency
   b. a single seizure that lasts 5 to 10 minutes
   c. a series of seizures in an unconscious victim
   d. all of the above

5. Which of the following is *not* an emergency care procedure for seizure?
   a. stay calm and reassure the victim
   b. put a padded object between the victim's teeth
   c. do not attempt to restrain the victim unless the person is in danger
   d. stay with the victim until the seizure has passed

- You are at a large public gathering and a person suddenly cries out, falls, becomes rigid, and has muscular jerks. He has frothy saliva on the lips and very shallow breathing. In about 5 minutes the symptoms subside, and within the next 30 minutes the symptoms reappear and subside numerous times.
- At the same gathering, a person complains of dizziness and nausea. She is shaky, has cool skin, and tells you that she feels faint.

Childbirth and Related Emergencies

Learning Objectives

When you have mastered the material in this chapter, you will be able to

1 Understand basic reproductive anatomy

2 Describe the recommended first aid kit equipment for childbirth emergencies

3 List the signs and symptoms of miscarriage

4 Describe and demonstrate how to manage a seizure during pregnancy

5 Describe and demonstrate how to care for vaginal bleeding during pregnancy

6 Describe and demonstrate how to care for ectopic pregnancy

7 List the signs and symptoms of toxemia

8 Describe and demonstrate how to care for ruptured uterus

9 Explain the situations in which you would *not* try to take a pregnant woman to the hospital for delivery

10 List the signs and symptoms indicating that delivery is imminent

11 Describe how to transport a woman who is in labor to the hospital

12 Describe and demonstrate normal delivery procedures

13 Describe and demonstrate how to care for vaginal bleeding following delivery

14 Describe and demonstrate care of the newborn

15 Describe and demonstrate resuscitation of the newborn

16 Describe and demonstrate how to manage abnormal deliveries

---

SQ3R Plus

- **Survey** to set goals for studying.
- Ask **questions** as you **read.**
- Stop frequently to **recite** and **review.**
- **Write** a summary of key points.
- **Reflect** on the importance of this material and its relevance in your life.

*O*n November 2, 1998, Cynthia Hobbs had just pulled into her driveway after picking her children up from school when her neighbor's 9-year-old daughter ran toward the car. She had come home from school to find her mother curled up on the living room sofa in excruciating pain. Cynthia, a trained First Aider, sent her own children into the house and went to check on 36-year-old Susan Brienholt.

Susan was sitting at the end of the sofa, her arms wrapped around her knees, rocking back and forth as she moaned with pain. The pain had started about an hour earlier, she said; it was sharp and stabbing and localized on the left side. Cynthia convinced Susan to lie flat on the sofa; during a brief assessment, Cynthia could feel a mass on the left side in the area Susan described as most painful. Cynthia noticed that Susan's pulse was rapid and that she showed other signs of shock.

Taking a quick history, Cynthia learned that Susan had missed her last two menstrual periods and suspected she was pregnant; she was about to schedule an appointment with the doctor, but had started spotting a day earlier.

Cynthia was convinced Susan had an ectopic pregnancy—a serious medical emergency. Cynthia quickly called for emergency help. She kept Susan on the sofa on her back and elevated her knees; she covered Susan with an afghan to keep her warm and slipped a pillow under her knees to keep her comfortable. When EMTs arrived, they confirmed Cynthia's assessment and radioed ahead so a surgical team could be waiting at the hospital.

FIRST AIDERS ARE OFTEN CALLED ON TO HELP PREGNANT women, and too often a woman is taken to a hospital in great haste because a First Aider is afraid the mother will give birth before reaching the hospital.

Although some babies *are* born at home or in vehicles, there is no need to hurry in most circumstances. Childbirth is a normal, natural process—in only a few situations involving complications do victims need to be transported rapidly.

In order to determine whether rapid transport is necessary, you should be familiar with the nature, signs, symptoms, and emergency care of both normal childbirth and obstetric complications. This chapter provides that information and outlines the care required for both normal birth and childbirth-related emergencies.

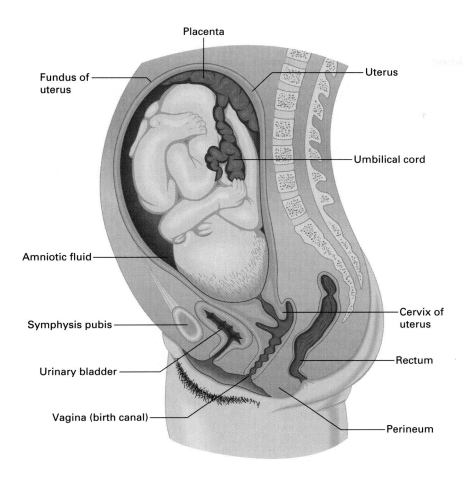

Fundus of uterus

Placenta

Uterus

Amniotic fluid

Umbilical cord

Symphysis pubis

Cervix of uterus

Urinary bladder

Rectum

Vagina (birth canal)

Perineum

Figure 21-1. Anatomy of pregnancy

• Section 1 •
REPRODUCTIVE ANATOMY

Learning Objective 1 Understand basic reproductive anatomy.

The term **fetus** refers to the developing unborn baby. Other terms related to the anatomy and physiology of reproduction include the following (see Figure 21-1):

- *The uterus.* The **uterus,** the organ in which the fetus grows, is responsible for labor and expulsion of the infant. During pregnancy, the walls of the uterus become thin, and its muscle fibers stretch and thicken. The special arrangement of smooth muscle and blood vessels in the uterus allows for great expansion during pregnancy, for forcible contractions during labor and delivery, and for rapid contraction after delivery to constrict the blood vessels and prevent hemorrhage.

- *The birth canal.* The vagina and lower part of the uterus are known as the **birth canal.**

- *The placenta.* The **placenta** is a disk-shaped inner lining attached at one surface to the uterus and at the other to the umbilical cord. Rich in blood vessels, the placenta provides the fetus with nourishment and oxygen from the mother's blood and absorbs fetal waste products into the mother's bloodstream. The exchange of nutrients and wastes occurs through a special sievelike mechanism in the placenta; the baby's and mother's

fetus The developing unborn baby

uterus The organ in which the baby grows

birth canal The vagina and lower part of the uterus

placenta Structure on the inner lining of the uterus that provides the fetus with nourishment

blood do not mix. The placenta also produces hormones, such as estrogen and progesterone, that sustain the pregnancy.

At full term, the placenta is about 8 inches wide, 1 inch thick, and weighs about one-sixth of the baby's weight. After the birth, the placenta separates from the uterine wall and is delivered as the afterbirth.

- *The umbilical cord.* The **umbilical cord** is an extension of the placenta through which the fetus receives nourishment while in the uterus. The cord contains one vein and two arteries arranged in a spiral and enclosed in a protective, gelatinlike substance. When the baby is born, the nerveless cord resembles a sturdy rope; it is about 22 inches long and about 1 inch in diameter.

- *The amniotic sac.* Sometimes called the "bag of waters," the **amniotic sac** is filled with the amniotic fluid in which the baby floats; the plasticlike sac of fluid insulates and protects the baby during pregnancy.

- *The vagina.* Extending from the neck of the uterus to the outside of the body, the **vagina** is the lower part of the birth canal and provides a passage for both menstrual flow and childbirth. The smooth muscle layer of the vagina allows it to stretch gently to accommodate the infant during delivery.

- *The perineum.* The **perineum** is the area of skin between the vagina and the anus. As the baby's head comes down the birth canal, the perineum bulges significantly—a sign of impending birth. The perineum is sometimes incised during hospital births to prevent tearing, which commonly occurs during emergency delivery.

- *Crowning.* As the head or presenting part of the baby presses against the vagina, the vagina bulges outward—a sign that delivery is imminent. **Crowning** occurs when the baby's head (or other body part) emerges at the vaginal opening.

- *"Bloody show."* During pregnancy, the **cervix** (neck of the uterus) contains a mucous plug that is discharged during labor. The expulsion of this mucous plug signals the first stage of labor and is known as the **bloody show.** The bloody show appears as pink-tinged mucus in the vaginal discharge as labor begins.

- *Presenting part.* The **presenting part** is the part of the infant that appears first from the birth canal. In a normal birth, it is the head. In some cases (known as breech births), it may be the buttocks or an arm or leg.

- *Miscarriage.* Delivery of the products of conception early in pregnancy is called a **miscarriage.** Generally, miscarriage refers to the spontaneous delivery of the fetus and placenta before the 28th week of pregnancy—before the baby can survive on its own.

Labor

Labor—the process that begins with the first uterine contraction and ends with delivery of the baby—consists of three distinct stages (see Figure 21-2).

Dilation

During the first and longest stage, **dilation,** the cervix becomes fully dilated to allow the baby's head to pass from the body of the uterus to the birth canal. Uterine contractions cause the cervix to stretch and thin gradually until the opening is large enough to allow the baby to pass. These contractions usually begin as an aching sensation in the small of the back; within a short time, they become cramplike pains in the lower abdomen that occur at regular intervals. At first, contractions are 10 to 20 minutes apart and are not very painful; they may even stop completely and start again later.

The first stage of labor may last as long as 18 hours or more for a woman having her first baby; women who have had a baby before may have only 2 or 3 hours of early labor.

Crowning and Delivery

During the second stage of labor, the baby moves through the birth canal. Contractions are closer together and last longer, usually 45 to 90 seconds. As the baby moves down the birth canal, the mother experiences considerable pressure in her rectum, much like the feeling of a bowel movement. That sensation is a sign that the baby is moving through the birth canal.

As the tightening and bearing-down sensations become stronger and more frequent, the mother will have an uncontrollable urge to push down. Bloody discharge from the vagina usually increases at this point. Soon after the baby's head appears at the opening of the birth canal, the shoulders and the rest of the body follow.

Delivery of the Placenta

During the third stage of labor, the placenta separates from the uterine wall, and the placenta and its attached fetal membranes are expelled from the uterus.

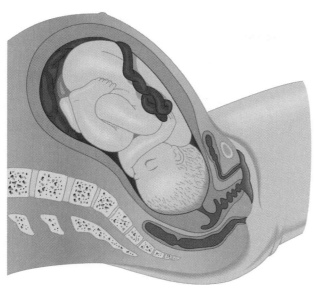

FIRST STAGE:
First uterine contraction to dilation of cervix

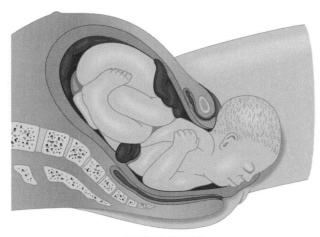

SECOND STAGE:
Birth of baby or expulsion

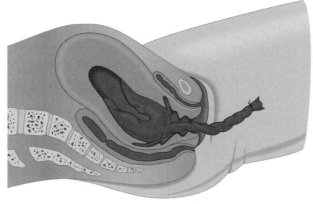

THIRD STAGE
Delivery of placenta

Figure 21-2. *Three stages of labor*

First Aid Supplies for Delivery

> **Learning Objective 2** Describe the recommended first aid kit equipment for childbirth emergencies.

A basic sterile obstetric pack can be included as part of a comprehensive first aid kit, although most simple first aid kits do not include these materials. Recommended equipment for an obstetric pack includes

- Surgical scissors (for cutting the cord)
- Cord clamps
- Umbilical tape or sterilized cord
- Bulb syringe
- Five towels
- 2 × 10 gauze sponges
- Sterile gloves
- One baby receiving blanket
- Two to three sanitary napkins, individually wrapped
- Two large plastic bags
- Foil-wrapped germicidal wipes

---

umbilical cord An extension of the placenta that resembles a sturdy rope, through which the fetus is nourished

amniotic sac A plasticlike sac of fluid in which the baby floats

vagina The passage for childbirth

perineum The area of skin between the vagina and the anus

crowning The emergence of the baby's head at the vaginal opening

cervix The neck of the uterus

bloody show Pink-tinged mucus in the vaginal discharge that is evident as labor begins

presenting part The part of the baby that emerges first through the birth canal; in a normal birth it is the head.

miscarriage Loss of pregnancy before the baby is able to survive, usually before 28 weeks of gestation; also called "spontaneous abortion"

labor The process that begins with the first uterine contraction and ends with delivery of the baby and placenta

dilation The stage of labor during which the cervix dilates and contractions occur

Progress Check

1. The organ that houses a fetus during its development is the _____ .
   (vagina/perineum/uterus)

2. The _____ carries nutrients and oxygen to the fetus and waste away from the fetus.
   (placenta/cervix/amniotic sac)

3. The _____ often tears during emergency childbirth.
   (placenta/perineum/vagina)

4. One of the earliest indications of imminent delivery is the _____ .
   (presenting part/crowning/"bloody show")

5. Spontaneous delivery of a fetus before it can sustain life is called _____ .
   (abortion/miscarriage/breech birth)

6. The first stage of labor is called _____ .
   (crowning/dilation/presentation)

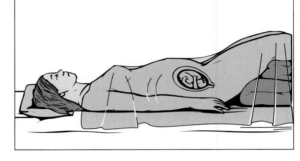

SIGNS AND SYMPTOMS OF SPONTANEOUS ABORTION

- Passage of tissue
- Heavy vaginal bleeding
- Inability to feel the uterus
- Cramplike pains in lower abdomen
- Uterus located below woman's navel

Figure 21-3. Diagram depicts the appropriate treatment of a victim who is cramping and bleeding, threatening miscarriage.

• Section 2 •

PREDELIVERY EMERGENCIES

Emergencies that occur before delivery of the baby include miscarriage, seizures, vaginal bleeding not associated with the birth, ectopic pregnancy, toxemia, and ruptured uterus.

Miscarriage

Learning Objective 3 List the signs and symptoms of miscarriage.

A miscarriage (sometimes called a spontaneous abortion) occurs for any number of reasons and involves delivery of the fetus and placenta before the fetus is able to survive on its own. Signs and symptoms of miscarriage (see Figure 21-3) include

- Cramplike abdominal pain similar to labor
- Moderate to severe vaginal bleeding
- Passage of tissue
- Inability to feel the uterus
- Uterus located below the woman's navel

If a woman has attempted a nonmedical abortion, there may also be high fever due to infection.

Activate the EMS system; then:

1. Ask the woman when her last menstrual period began. If the last period began more than 24 weeks earlier, be prepared for potential delivery of a premature baby.

2. Conduct an initial assessment; monitor vital signs.

3. Provide emergency care based on the woman's symptoms. Help control vaginal bleeding by placing a sanitary napkin over the vaginal opening; never pack the vagina in an attempt to control bleeding. If the pad becomes soaked with blood, replace it.

4. Save any passed tissue or evidence of blood loss, such as bloody sheets, towels, or underwear. These should be taken to the hospital with the woman.

5. Provide emotional support to the mother and the members of her family; intense grief is normal and to be expected of both parents.

Seizure during Pregnancy

Learning Objective 4 Describe and demonstrate how to manage a seizure during pregnancy.

Seizures during pregnancy often signal toxemia, discussed in greater detail later in this chapter. Women with certain medical conditions, such as diabetes or heart disease, are also more prone to seizures during pregnancy.

Activate the EMS system; assess as you would for any seizure victim; then:

1. Treat the woman based on the signs and symptoms, providing the same treatment as you would for any seizure victim. Take care to protect the woman from harming herself.

2. Position the woman on her left side to allow for drainage and to keep her tongue from blocking breathing; keep her warm, but do not overheat.

Note: Bright lights and loud noises can trigger seizures in a toxemia victim; dim the lights if possible and avoid making loud sounds.

Vaginal Bleeding in Late Pregnancy

Learning Objective 5 Describe and demonstrate how to care for vaginal bleeding during pregnancy.

Vaginal bleeding can sometimes occur late in the pregnancy; excessive vaginal bleeding can constitute a life-threatening emergency for either the mother or the fetus.

Possible causes of excessive bleeding late in the pregnancy include

- **Placenta previa,** in which the placenta is positioned abnormally, so that it partially or completely covers the opening between the uterus and the vagina

- **Abruptio placenta,** in which the normally positioned placenta separates from the uterine wall sometime during the last 3 months of pregnancy

Activate the EMS system; assess the victim; then:

1. Treat the victim according to signs and symptoms, which will usually include shock. Place the victim on her left side (to prevent the baby from pressing on the woman's vena cava) with her legs and feet elevated. Keep her warm, but don't overheat.

2. Place a sanitary napkin over the vaginal opening, but do not pack the vagina. Save all soaked pads and other evidence of blood loss, as well as any tissue that is passed, for evaluation by a physician.

3. If the bleeding is caused by trauma, control any external bleeding with direct pressure. Control internal bleeding as described in step 2 above.

Ectopic Pregnancy

Learning Objective 6 Describe and demonstrate how to care for ectopic pregnancy.

In a normal pregnancy the egg is implanted in the uterus. In an **ectopic pregnancy,** the egg is implanted outside the uterus—in the abdominal cavity, in the fallopian tube, on the outside wall of the uterus, on the ovary, or on the outside of the cervix.

The placenta eventually invades surrounding tissue, causing rupture of a blood vessel and life-threatening bleeding. Ectopic pregnancy is the leading cause of first-trimester maternal deaths and occurs in one of every 200 pregnancies.

Signs and symptoms of ectopic pregnancy include

- Sudden, sharp abdominal pain, localized on one side

- Vaginal spotting

- Missed menstrual period

- Pain under the diaphragm

- Pain radiating to one or both shoulders

- Tender, bloated abdomen

- A palpable mass in the abdomen (either the embryo or a blood clot)

- Weakness when in a sitting position

- Increased pulse

- Shock

Remember: External bleeding through the vagina is usually slight with ectopic pregnancy. Suspect ectopic pregnancy in any woman of childbearing age, especially if any of the above-listed signs and symptoms are present.

Activate the EMS system; then place the victim on her back with her knees elevated; keep her warm and treat for shock.

Toxemia

Learning Objective 7 List the signs and symptoms of toxemia.

A common condition affecting about one in 20 pregnant women is **toxemia,** or "poisoning" of the blood during pregnancy. Toxemia occurs most frequently in

placenta previa A condition in which the placenta is positioned abnormally

abruptio placenta A condition in which a normally positioned placenta separates from the uterine wall during the last 3 months of pregnancy

ectopic pregnancy A pregnancy in which the fertilized egg is implanted outside the uterus

toxemia Poisoning of the blood during pregnancy

the last 3 months of pregnancy and is most likely to affect women in their twenties who are pregnant for the first time.

Toxemia is characterized by high blood pressure and swelling in the extremities. Any of the following signs and symptoms may occur:

- Sudden weight gain (2 pounds a week or more)
- Blurred vision or spots before the eyes
- Pronounced swelling of the face, fingers, legs, or feet (some swelling of the feet and legs is normal)
- Decreased urine
- Severe, persistent headache
- Persistent vomiting
- Mental confusion or disorientation
- Abdominal pain

During the first stage of toxemia, called **preeclampsia,** a previously normal pregnant woman develops high blood pressure, swelling, headaches, and visual disturbances. During the second stage, **eclampsia,** life-threatening convulsions occur.

Activate the EMS system immediately; then:

1. Position the victim on her left side to prevent obstruction of the major blood vessels, allowing better oxygen supply to the fetus.
2. Keep the victim calm and quiet; while waiting for emergency help, keep the lights dimmed and avoid making loud noises.

Ruptured Uterus

Learning Objective 8 Describe and demonstrate how to care for ruptured uterus.

As the uterus enlarges during pregnancy, the uterine wall becomes extremely thin, especially around the bottom. The uterus may rupture if

- The victim has a weak uterine scar from a previous cesarean section or surgical operation
- The victim has had many previous pregnancies
- The baby is too large for the pelvis
- Labor is extended and forceful (extended, forceful labor may force a large baby out through the uterine wall)

As many as 20 percent of the mothers who experience it, and 50 percent of the babies involved, die from ruptured uterus.

Signs and symptoms of a ruptured uterus include

- A tearing sensation in the abdomen
- Constant and severe pain
- Nausea
- Shock
- Minimal vaginal bleeding in most cases
- Cessation of noticeable uterine contractions (the uterus relaxes during the contraction)
- Ability to feel the baby in the abdominal cavity
- Uterus located below the woman's navel

Immediately activate the EMS system; treat the victim for shock, and do not allow her to have anything by mouth, because surgery will be required.

Progress Check

1. To care for vaginal bleeding, you should _____ . (pack the vagina/apply pressure on the abdomen/place a sanitary napkin over the opening)
2. Seizures caused by toxemia can be aggravated by _____ . (bright lights/movement/pain)
3. The leading cause of first-trimester maternal deaths is _____ . (ruptured uterus/abortion/ectopic pregnancy)
4. An ectopic pregnancy is one in which the fertilized egg implants _____ . (near the cervix/outside the uterus/at an angle)
5. Toxemia is literally _____ of the bloodstream. (perfusion/infusion/poisoning)
6. A characteristic sign of toxemia is _____ . (swelling of the extremities/cyanosis/rash)
7. As many as _____ percent of the babies of women who suffer ruptured uterus die. (25/50/75)

• Section 3 •
NORMAL DELIVERY

Learning Objective 9 Explain the situations in which you would *not* try to take a pregnant woman to the hospital for delivery.

It is best to take a pregnant woman to a doctor's office, medical clinic, or hospital for delivery of the baby. As a general guideline, there are three cases in which you should *not* try to transport the mother for delivery:

- When you have no suitable transportation
- When the hospital or doctor cannot be reached because of bad weather, a natural disaster, or some other kind of catastrophe
- When delivery is expected within 5 minutes

Imminent Delivery

> **Learning Objective 10** List the signs and symptoms indicating that delivery is imminent.

The following signs and symptoms indicate that delivery is imminent, especially if the woman has had more than one pregnancy:

- The amniotic sac has ruptured
- Crowning occurs during contractions
- Contractions are closer than 2 minutes apart
- Contractions are intense and last from 45 to 90 seconds
- The woman feels as if she needs to have a bowel movement (a sensation caused by the baby's head in the birth canal pressing against the rectum)
- The woman's abdomen is rock hard

Transporting a Woman in Labor

> **Learning Objective 11** Describe how to transport a woman who is in labor to the hospital.

If you think time will permit, follow these guidelines in transporting a woman in labor:

1. Keep the woman lying down during transport; remove any underclothing that could interfere with delivery.
2. Place a folded blanket, sheet, or other clean object under the woman's buttocks and lower back.
3. Have the woman bend her knees and spread her thighs apart so you can watch for the crown of the baby's head in the birth canal.
4. Never ask the woman to cross her legs or ankles; never hold the woman's legs together; and never try to delay or restrain delivery in any way—the pressure can result in permanent injury or the death of the baby.
5. If the woman vomits, turn her head to one side and clean out her mouth.

Assisting with Delivery

> **Learning Objective 12** Describe and demonstrate normal delivery procedures.

If you determine that birth is imminent or that you cannot attempt transport for some other reason, you need to assist in delivery of the baby. Take the following precautions:

- Make sure you use appropriate protection against exposure to body substances, including latex gloves, a mask, a gown, and eye protection.
- Do not touch the woman's vagina at *any* time; touch the vaginal area only during delivery and in the presence of another First Aider.
- Do not let the woman use the bathroom, even if she feels as if she needs to move her bowels (in reality, the baby's head is moving down the birth canal and pressing against the rectum).
- Do not hold the mother's legs together or do anything else to delay delivery.
- Recognize your own limitations; if you get into a situation you cannot handle, take the mother to a physician, even if delivery must occur during transport.
- If you prepare for delivery and it does not occur within 10 minutes, transport.

Delivery Procedures

As you assist in delivery, stay calm; reassure the mother that you are there to help; and protect the mother's comfort, modesty, and peace of mind. Try for as few distractions as possible.

If possible, use a sterile obstetrics kit packed specifically for childbirth. If your first aid kit does not have one, use materials that are as sterile or clean as possible under the circumstances.

Activate the EMS system; then:

1. Take infection control precautions; exposure to blood and body fluids during delivery is usually significant. Handle blood- and body-fluid-soaked dressings, pads, and linens carefully and bag them in moisture-proof bags to prevent leakage. Wash your hands thoroughly, and wear latex gloves. If they are available, you should also wear a mask and gown.

> **preeclampsia** The first stage of toxemia
> **eclampsia** The second stage of toxemia

2. Have the woman lie on a firm surface with her knees drawn up and spread apart. Her feet should be flat on the surface beneath her, and she should be positioned several feet from the edge of the bed or other surface. Place your equipment close enough to reach, but far enough from the birth canal so it will not be contaminated by a gush of blood.

3. Elevate the woman's buttocks several inches with a folded blanket, sheet, towels, or other clean object. Support the mother's head, neck, and shoulders with pillows or folded blankets so she does not feel like she is slipping "downhill."

4. Remove clothing or push it above the mother's waist. Place one sterile sheet under the woman's hips, unfolding it toward her feet, and another sheet over her abdomen and legs. Have the woman take short, quick breaths during each contraction, and long, deep breaths between contractions.

5. As the infant's head appears in the birth canal (see Figures 21-4 through 21-12), place your fingers on the bony part of the infant's skull and exert *very* gentle pressure to prevent explosive delivery. Take extra caution to avoid touching the fontanel (soft spot on the top of the baby's head). Apply gentle pressure to the perineum to reduce the risk of tearing; allowing the head to deliver between contractions can also help reduce the risk of perineal tearing.

6. If the amniotic sac has not broken, tear the sac with your fingers, then push it away from the baby's head and mouth as they appear.

7. As the infant's head is delivered, determine whether the umbilical cord is around the infant's neck. If it is, use two fingers to slip the cord over the baby's shoulder. If you can't move the cord, clamp and cut it, then unwrap it from around the neck.

8. When the head is delivered, support the head with one hand and suction the mouth and nostrils two

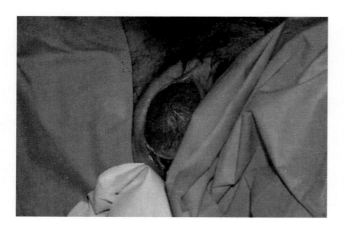

Figure 21-4. Crowning

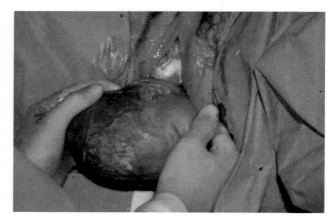

Figure 21-5. Head delivers and turns.

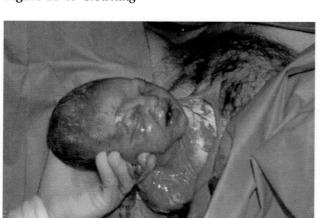

Figure 21-6. Shoulders deliver.

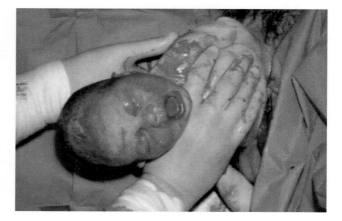

Figure 21-7. Chest delivers.

to three times with a bulb syringe. Make sure you compress a bulb syringe before you bring it to the baby's face. Insert the tip of the compressed bulb 1 to 1½ inches into the baby's mouth; slowly release the bulb to allow mucus and other fluid to be drawn into the syringe. Avoid touching the back of the mouth. Remove the syringe, then discharge the contents onto a towel. Repeat. Use the same procedure to suction each nostril. (Babies breathe through their noses, so the nostrils must be clear.)

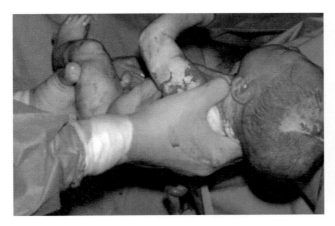

Figure 21-8. Infant is fully delivered.

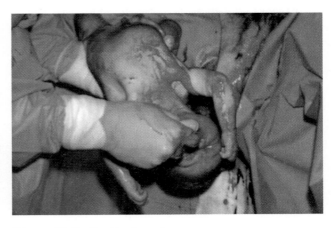

Figure 21-9. Suctioning airway

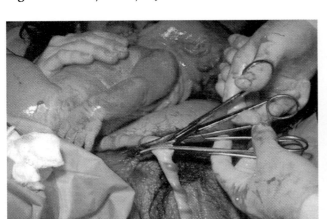

Figure 21-10. Cutting the cord

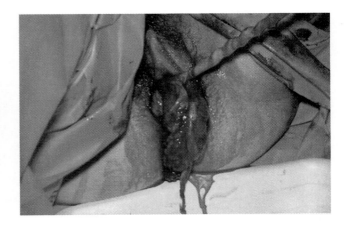

Figure 21-11. Placenta begins delivery.

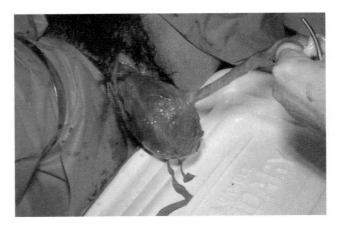

Figure 21-12. Placenta delivers.

9. As the torso and full body are born, support the baby with both hands (see Figure 21-13). Never pull the baby from the vagina. Do not put your finger in the baby's armpit, because pressure on the nerve centers there can cause paralysis. The baby will be slippery, covered with a whitish, cheeselike substance known as the **vernix caseosa**. Receive the baby in a clean or sterile towel, which will help you hold on to the baby.

10. As the feet are born, grasp the feet. Take caution not to pull on the cord as you lift or deliver the baby.

11. Wipe blood and mucus from the baby's mouth and nose with sterile gauze, then suction the mouth and nose again. The baby will probably cry almost immediately. Soon after this cry, the cord will become limp and will no longer pulsate, because the blood flow through the cord ceases at birth.

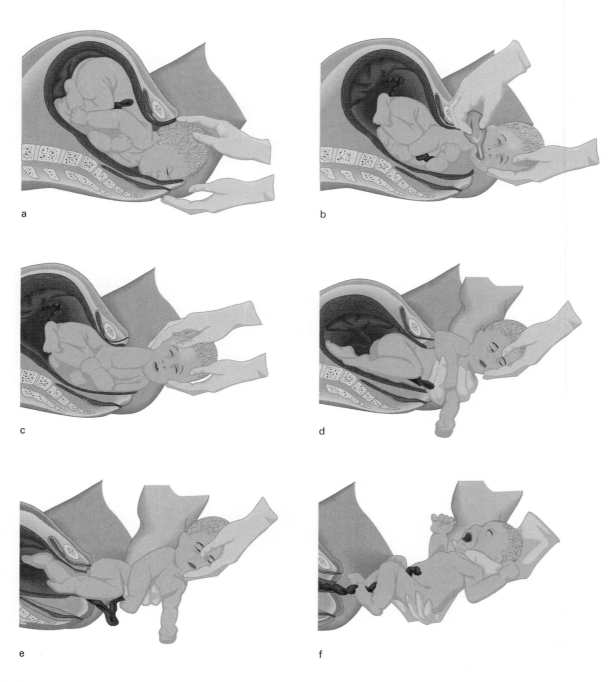

Figure 21-13. *Normal delivery*

12. Wrap the infant in a warm blanket and place on its side, its head slightly lower than its trunk. Keep the infant level with the mother's vagina until the cord is cut. If possible, assign another First Aider to monitor and care for the newborn while you finish caring for the mother.

13. Clamp, tie, and cut the umbilical cord when pulsations cease in the cord. Place two clamps or tapes on the cord about 3 inches apart; the first clamp should be approximately four finger-widths from the infant. Use sterile surgical scissors to cut the cord between the two clamps. Periodically check the end of the cord for bleeding, and control any bleeding that may occur.

14. While preparing the mother and infant for transport, watch for delivery of the placenta. The placenta is usually delivered within 10 minutes—and almost always within 20 minutes—after the baby. Never pull on the cord to check whether the placenta has separated from the uterus. When the placenta appears at the vagina, grasp it gently and rotate it. Do not pull; instead, slowly and gently guide the placenta and the attached membranes from the vagina.

15. When the placenta is delivered, wrap in it a towel, then place it in a plastic bag for transport to the hospital. A physician needs to examine the placenta and confirm that delivery was complete.

16. Place one or two sterile sanitary napkins over the vaginal opening, lower the victim's legs, and help her hold her legs together. Elevate her feet if necessary.

17. Record the time of delivery. If emergency personnel are not en route, transport the mother, infant, and placenta, keeping both the mother and the infant warm.

Vaginal Bleeding following Delivery

Learning Objective 13 Describe and demonstrate how to care for vaginal bleeding following delivery.

Vaginal loss of as much as 2 cups of blood is considered normal following delivery. If there is excessive blood loss, massage the uterus as follows:

1. Place your hand on the woman's lower abdomen above the pubis.

2. Using the palm of your hand, your fingers fully extended, the flat of your four fingers cupped around the uterus, massage in a circular motion until you feel the uterus firm up. It should feel like a hard grapefruit.

3. If bleeding continues, check your massage technique, continue massage, and transport the woman immediately.

If the mother appears to be in shock, treat for shock and take her to a hospital before you begin uterine massage. Perform uterine massage during transport.

Progress Check

1. You should not try to get a woman in labor to a hospital if _____ .
   (her husband is not present/you have no suitable transportation/the mother wants a home delivery)

2. _____ indicates that delivery is imminent.
   (Contractions more frequent than every 2 minutes/Severe cramplike pains/Shortness of breath)

3. To prevent explosive delivery, exert gentle pressure on the _____ .
   (pubis/vaginal opening/bony part of the baby's skull)

4. Cut the cord _____ .
   (before the baby starts breathing/as the baby starts breathing/after the cord goes limp)

5. Before you cut the cord, it should be clamped or taped in _____ places.
   (two/three/four)

6. It is normal for a woman to lose as much as _____ of blood following birth.
   (1 cup/2 cups/1 pint)

• Section 4 •
CARE AND RESUSCITATION OF THE NEWBORN

Learning Objective 14 Describe and demonstrate care of the newborn.

The body surface area of an infant is proportionately greater than that of older children or adults, so infants are likely to lose more heat more quickly. Protecting

vernix caseosa The white, cheeselike covering on a newborn's skin

newborn infants against heat loss preserves their energy and avoids the complex problem that hospitals face in trying to warm a cold infant.

A normal baby should be crying. The baby's heartbeat should be at least 100 beats per minute, and the baby's respiratory rate should be at least 40 breaths per minute.

Care of a Newborn

To care for a newborn:

1. Immediately dry the infant, paying particular attention to the head, which has a large surface area. Wrap the newborn in a blanket or a plastic bubble bag swaddle and cover the infant's head.

2. Repeat suctioning with the bulb syringe, making sure the infant's nostrils and mouth are clear.

3. Assess the infant, evaluating the infant's color, pulse, grimace (does the infant cry when you flick the soles of its feet?), activity, and ease of breathing. (These are the standard signs used in the Apgar scoring system, which physicians use to evaluate a newborn's condition.) Distress is indicated by bluish discoloration, irregular or sluggish pulse, lack of grimace, limpness, and irregular, shallow, gasping, or absent respirations.

4. Stimulate the newborn if it is not breathing. You may simply need to encourage the infant to breathe by flicking the soles of its feet or rubbing its back in a circular motion with three fingers (see Figure 21-14).

Resuscitating a Newborn

Learning Objectives 15 Describe and demonstrate resuscitation of the newborn.

If the infant requires either rescue breathing or CPR, activate the EMS system; then:

1. If the infant's breathing is shallow, slow, gasping, or absent, provide artificial ventilations at the rate of one breath every 3 seconds. Assess again after 1 minute

2. If the infant's heart rate is less than 100 beats per minute, provide artificial ventilations at the rate of 60 per minute. Reassess every 30 seconds.

3. If the infant's heart rate is less than 80 beats per minute and the infant is not responding to the artificial ventilation, start chest compression. If the infant's heart rate is less than 60 beats per minute, start both chest compression and artificial ventilation.

Progress Check

1. The first step in caring for the newborn is to _____ it.
    (measure/dry/assess)

2. To assess an infant, use the same factors used in the _____ scoring system.
    (Apgar/Andrews/Smithson)

3. To encourage an infant to breathe, _____ the soles of its feet.
    (pinch/slap/flick)

4. To resuscitate an infant with a low heart rate, deliver artificial ventilation at the rate of _____ breaths per minute.
    (30/60/100)

5. If an infant's pulse rate is less than _____ beats per minute, deliver chest compressions.
    (80/100/110)

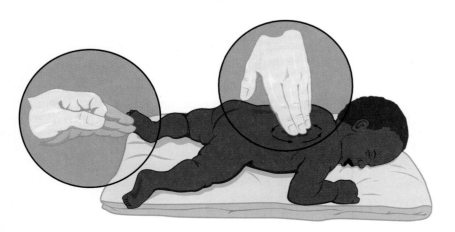

Figure 21-14. It may be necessary to encourage the newborn to breathe.

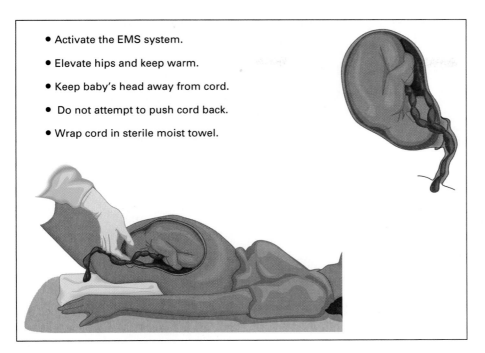

- Activate the EMS system.
- Elevate hips and keep warm.
- Keep baby's head away from cord.
- Do not attempt to push cord back.
- Wrap cord in sterile moist towel.

Figure 21-15. Management of a prolapsed cord

• Section 5 •
ABNORMAL DELIVERIES

Learning Objective 16 Describe and demonstrate how to manage abnormal deliveries.

In the case of abnormal delivery—such as prolapsed cord, breech birth, limb presentation, multiple births, presence of meconium, or premature birth—you will need to take more aggressive measures in assisting delivery.

Prolapsed Cord

A **prolapsed cord** is an umbilical cord that presents through the birth canal before delivery of the infant's head (see Figure 21-15). Because the cord is compressed against the birth canal by the baby's head, the baby's supply of oxygenated blood is cut off, and the baby is in great danger of suffocation.

Activate the EMS system; then:

1. Position the mother with her head down or her buttocks raised, allowing gravity to reduce the pressure on the cord in the birth canal.

2. Insert a sterile, gloved hand into the vagina and push the presenting part of the fetus away from the pulsating cord. *Follow local protocol.*

3. Do not try to push the cord back into the vagina. Cover the cord with a sterile, moist towel.

4. Maintain pressure on the presenting part and monitor pulsations in the cord until emergency personnel arrive.

Breech Birth

With a **breech birth,** the buttocks or lower extremities of the baby are the first part presented through the birth canal. The newborn is at great risk for trauma during delivery (see Figure 21-16 on page 350), and prolapsed cord is common with breech presentation.

In a breech birth, delivery will generally not occur within 10 minutes. If the buttocks emerge first, support the emerging baby. Do *not* pull. Place one hand in the vagina, your palm toward the baby's face. Form a V with two of your fingers on either side of the baby's nose, then push away the vaginal wall from the baby's nose. Maintain that position until the baby's head is delivered. If the baby does not emerge, activate the EMS system or transport immediately. Get the mother to the hospital as rapidly as you can; throughout transport, keep the mother in a head-down posi-

prolapsed cord The presentation of the umbilical cord at the vaginal opening before the baby

breech birth A situation in which the buttocks of the baby present first through the birth canal

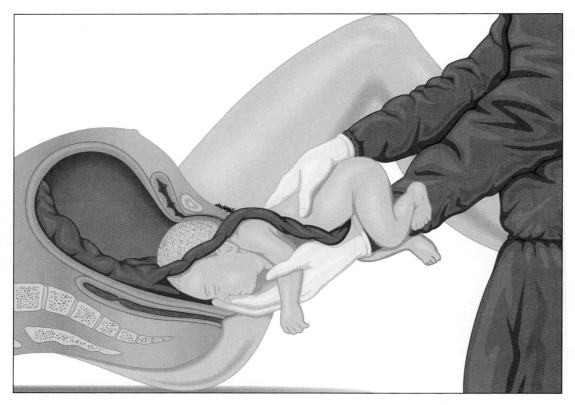

Figure 21-16. *Provide and maintain an airway during a breech birth.*

tion with her pelvis elevated so gravity will discourage the baby's progress into the birth canal.

Limb Presentation

Limb presentation occurs when one of the infant's arms or legs protrudes first from the birth canal. The most common limb presentation is a foot, which commonly accompanies breech presentation. Manage as you would a breech birth; never pull the baby by its arm or leg, and never try to force the limb back into the vagina.

Multiple Births

With nonidentical, or fraternal, twins, each twin has its own placenta; identical twins share one placenta. Even if the mother is unaware that she is carrying more than one baby, you should suspect a multiple birth if any of the following signs are present:

- The abdomen is still very large after one baby is delivered.
- Uterine contractions continue to be extremely strong.

- Uterine contractions begin again about 10 minutes after one baby has been delivered.
- The baby's size is out of proportion with the size of the mother's abdomen.

In case of multiple births, activate the EMS system; then:

1. Be prepared for complications; about one-third of second twins have a breech presentation. Expect and handle hemorrhage following the second birth.

2. If there are no complications, deliver the second baby as you did the first.

3. If the second baby has not delivered within 10 minutes of the first, take the mother and the first baby to the hospital for delivery of the second baby.

Passage of Meconium

Meconium—the newborn's first feces—in the amniotic fluid makes the fluid greenish or brownish-yellow rather than clear. The presence of meconium indicates that the fetus has been distressed and has had a bowel movement inside the amniotic sac. If the baby breathes in any of the meconium-stained fluid, infection and aspiration pneumonia can result. Meconium passage is common in breech births.

Activate the EMS system *immediately;* then:

1. Suction the baby's nose and mouth *before* you stimulate the baby. The most critical aspect of treatment for meconium passage is to clear the nose and mouth before the baby takes its first breath.

2. Maintain the baby's airway.

Premature Birth

A **premature baby** may weigh less than 5½ pounds and/or is born before 36 weeks of gestation. Premature babies are more susceptible to respiratory diseases and infection, and must be given special care.

You can generally tell by appearance whether a baby is premature: premature babies are thinner, smaller, and redder than full-term babies and have larger heads in proportion to their bodies.

Premature babies generally require resuscitation; you should resuscitate unless it is physically impossible. Then take these additional steps to care for a premature baby:

1. Keep the baby warm; use warmed blankets or plastic bubble bag swaddle, then wrap in aluminum foil for extra insulation if you lack other supplies. If you take the baby to the hospital, heat your vehicle.

2. Use gentle suction with a bulb syringe to keep the baby's mouth and nose clear of fluid. Perform resuscitation if necessary.

3. Prevent bleeding from the umbilical cord; a premature infant cannot tolerate losing even minute amounts of blood.

4. Premature babies are highly susceptible to infection. Prevent contamination and do not let anyone breathe into the baby's face.

Progress Check

1. A _____ cord is an umbilical cord that presents through the birth canal before the baby.
   (pulsating/prolapsed/inverted)

2. A _____ birth occurs when the baby's buttocks or lower extremities present first.
   (breech/premature/multiple)

3. During a breech or limb presentation, take advantage of _____ .
   (suction/gravity/force)

4. Meconium indicates that the baby has had a _____ in the amniotic sac.
   (seizure/hemorrhage/bowel movement)

5. The primary goal if you see meconium is to _____ the baby before it takes its first breath.
   (stimulate/suction/resuscitate)

6. Suspect a multiple birth if _____ begin after delivery of a baby.
   (strong contractions/fluid leaks/cyanosis)

7. A premature baby is smaller and _____ than a full-term baby.
   (hairier/redder/bluer)

• SUMMARY •

- Predelivery emergencies can include miscarriage, seizure, vaginal bleeding, ectopic pregnancy, toxemia, and ruptured uterus. Because some of these require surgery, never let the victim eat or drink.

- Do not try to take a woman who is in labor to the hospital if you have no suitable transportation, the hospital is unreachable for some reason, or you expect delivery within 5 minutes.

- When transporting a woman in labor to the hospital, allow her to lie on her back; remove her underwear and have her separate her legs so you can monitor for crowning.

- When assisting delivery, take precautions against exposure to body substances; exposure to blood and body fluids is significant during delivery.

- Never touch the vagina; touch the area around the vagina only during delivery and only with another First Aider present.

meconium The feces of the newborn; greenish or brownish-yellow amniotic fluid indicates that the baby had a bowel movement in the uterus before delivery.

premature baby A baby that weighs less than 5½ pounds and/or is born after less than 36 weeks' gestation

- It is normal for a woman to lose as much as 2 cups of blood following delivery; if bleeding is significant, massage the uterus to help it contract.

- Flick the soles of a newborn's feet or massage its back gently to encourage it to take its first breath.

- Always be prepared for complications in a multiple birth.

- If the amniotic fluid is stained with meconium, suction the baby's nose and mouth before it takes its first breath.

- A premature baby is smaller and redder than a full-term baby, with a head that is larger in proportion to the rest of its body.

- A priority in caring for a premature baby is to keep it warm.

• KEY TERMS •

Make sure you understand the following key terms:

- fetus
- uterus
- birth canal
- placenta
- umbilical cord
- amniotic sac
- vagina
- perineum
- crowning
- cervix
- bloody show
- presenting part
- miscarriage
- labor
- dilation
- placenta previa
- abruptio placenta
- ectopic pregnancy
- toxemia
- preeclampsia
- eclampsia
- vernix caseosa
- prolapsed cord
- breech birth
- meconium
- premature baby

Student: _____ Date: _____

Course: _____ Section #: _____

PART 1 • True/False

If you believe the statement is true, circle the T. If you believe the statement is false, circle the F.

T F **1.** Emergency childbirth is just that—measures that should be taken when it is impossible for the mother to reach a hospital or physician.

T F **2.** If you are close to a medical facility and the birth begins, tell the mother to clamp her legs tightly together and try to keep the baby's head inside the birth canal.

T F **3.** It is important to take the placenta to the hospital with the mother and the baby.

T F **4.** A gentle pull on the baby as it is being born will give a more efficient delivery.

T F **5.** An umbilical cord that is wrapped around the baby's neck must be quickly, but gently, removed.

T F **6.** After delivery, gentle massage of the uterus helps control the mother's bleeding.

T F **7.** You should always try to reach a hospital, no matter how soon delivery is likely to be.

T F **8.** When taking a mother in labor to the hospital, keep her seated with a seatbelt on; keeping her seated discourages the birth.

T F **9.** It is normal for a woman to lose as much as 2 cups of blood following birth.

T F **10.** In case of prolapsed cord, grasp the cord and tuck it back into the vagina.

PART 2 • Multiple Choice

For each item, circle the correct answer or the phrase that best completes the statement.

1. If the baby's head emerges from the birth canal and the amniotic sac is still unbroken, you should

a. wait for the baby to emerge completely
b. tear the bag with your fingers so the fluid can drain
c. carefully puncture the bag
d. wait for EMS team to arrive

2. A woman should be given immediate help instead of being transported when her labor contractions are

a. 5 minutes apart
b. 3 minutes apart
c. 2 minutes or less apart
d. 10 minutes apart

3. To decide whether to transport the mother prior to delivery

a. ask the mother if she is having her first baby
b. examine the mother for signs of crowning
c. ask the mother if she needs to move her bowels
d. all of the above

4. As the baby's head emerges, you should

a. push gently on the bony part of the head
b. pull gently on the top of the head
c. apply downward pressure
d. guide and support the head

5. If the baby does not begin to breathe by itself, you should

a. start artificial ventilation and infant CPR if necessary
b. hyperextend its neck
c. use the Holgar-Nielson method of resuscitation
d. turn the baby upside down and gently shake it

6. The longest stage of labor will probably be

a. the dilation stage
b. the expulsion stage
c. the placental stage
d. none of the above; all stages are about equal in length

7. The developing baby is attached by the umbilical cord to the

a. cervix
b. placenta
c. amniotic sac
d. perineum

8. If you think you have time to transport the mother to the hospital, *do not*

a. keep the mother lying down
b. allow the mother to go to the toilet immediately before you leave
c. keep the mother relaxed
d. have the mother bend her knees and spread her thighs apart so you can watch for crowning

9. Crowning is when

a. the position of the baby is incorrect for delivery
b. the baby's head can be seen at the opening of the birth canal
c. the bag of waters is not broken
d. the baby is suffering a lack of oxygen

10. Ectopic pregnancy occurs when

a. more than one egg is fertilized
b. the fertilized egg implants outside the uterus
c. the placenta separates from the uterus
d. the uterus ruptures

11. Victims of ectopic pregnancy and ruptured uterus require immediate
    a. CPR
    b. transport to the hospital
    c. placement in the prone position
    d. neurological assessment

12. To help control bleeding after delivery
    a. massage the uterus
    b. pack the vagina with sterile pads
    c. place sterile pads over the vaginal opening
    d. apply direct pressure to the abdomen

13. Encourage a baby to breathe following delivery by
    a. slapping the soles of its feet
    b. flicking the soles of its feet
    c. pinching the soles of its feet
    d. spanking it

14. You should suspect a multiple birth if
    a. the size of the baby does not correspond to the size of the mother's abdomen
    b. strong contractions begin after the baby is born
    c. uterine contractions continue after the baby is born
    d. all of the above

15. Meconium in the amniotic sac means the baby was distressed and is indicated by
    a. blood in the amniotic fluid
    b. black, tarry material in the amniotic fluid
    c. greenish or brownish-yellow fluid
    d. clear fluid

PART 3 • Matching

Match each stage of childbirth with its description.

Stage of Labor

A. Dilation
B. Expulsion
C. Placental

Description

1. _____ The placenta is "born."

2. _____ Contractions occur and the "bag of waters" breaks.

3. _____ The baby is born.

PART 4 • What Would You Do If?

- You are at a neighboring apartment where a woman is in labor. The hospital is 30 minutes away. She suddenly says, "The baby's coming—now!" This is her sixth child.

  What questions would you ask the mother? What preparations would you make for childbirth? How would you assist the childbirth?

22

Pediatric and Geriatric Emergencies

Learning Objectives

When you have mastered the material in this chapter, you will be able to

1　Explain special assessment techniques to use with children

2　Explain how children's vital signs differ from those of adults

3　List special emergency situations involving children

4　Distinguish between croup and epiglottitis

5　Distinguish between asthma and bronchiolitis

6　Discuss other common emergencies among children

7　Describe how to manage a case of sudden infant death syndrome

8　Explain how to identify child abuse and neglect

9　Explain how body systems change with age

10　Explain special issues to consider in assessing the elderly

11　Discuss special issues to consider in caring for trauma in the elderly

SQ3R Plus

- **Survey** to set goals for studying.
- Ask **questions** as you **read.**
- Stop frequently to **recite** and **review.**
- **Write** a summary of key points.
- **Reflect** on the importance of this material and its relevance in your life.

Shortly after settling four of the children she cared for down for story time, day-care provider Becky Christensen noticed that 6-year-old Chelsea Weist had stayed on a chair in the family room instead of joining the others. As she approached the little girl, Becky saw that she was obviously quite ill.

Chelsea was sitting awkwardly in the overstuffed chair, leaning forward, breathing through her mouth, her chin thrust outward. Though Chelsea was not struggling to breathe, Becky noticed a short, crouplike "croak" as she inhaled. Most significantly, Chelsea was drooling profusely. Becky placed her hand on Chelsea's arm and found the little girl to be running what felt like a high fever.

When Becky began asking Chelsea questions, the child had a very difficult time answering. Alarmed, Becky immediately suspected epiglottitis—a bacterial infection that causes the epiglottis to swell and that can cause death if left untreated.

Becky quietly excused herself, called for an ambulance, then returned to Chelsea. She kept the little girl sitting up in the chair and knelt next to her, reassuring and calming her gently until paramedics arrived a few minutes later. As they prepared Chelsea for transport, Becky called the child's mother so they could meet at the emergency room. Becky's calmness and reassuring manner helped prevent Chelsea from becoming anxious, which could have caused her larynx to spasm—completely blocking her airway.

AS A FIRST AIDER, YOU WILL OFTEN HAVE TO CARE FOR people at two extremes of the age spectrum—children (infants, children between 1 and 12, and adolescents) and the elderly (those over 65). Each group presents special physical and emotional challenges that need to be considered each time you give care.

This chapter explains the special assessment considerations you need to make, summarizes special emergency situations for each age group, and outlines emergency care for those emergency situations.

• Section 1 •
ASSESSING THE CHILD

Children are not simply small adults; rather, there are important psychological and physical differences between adults and children (see Figure 22-1). Although a breathing problem is always a breathing problem, and a bleeding wound is always a bleeding wound, the way you approach them in a 5-year-old child can differ from the way you approach them in an adult.

That is not all: When you deal with a child in distress, you also deal with parents or caregivers in distress. It is natural for parents to be upset, to cry, to blame themselves, or to blame someone else. Let par-

ents feel they are participants in their child's care; calm and cooperative parents will help reassure the child.

Special Assessment Techniques

Learning Objective 1 Explain special assessment techniques to use with children.

It is difficult to assess pain in children because they lack both the body awareness to describe the exact location of the pain and the vocabulary to describe it.

During your first look at the child, ask yourself

* Does the child look sick?
* Is the child in shock?

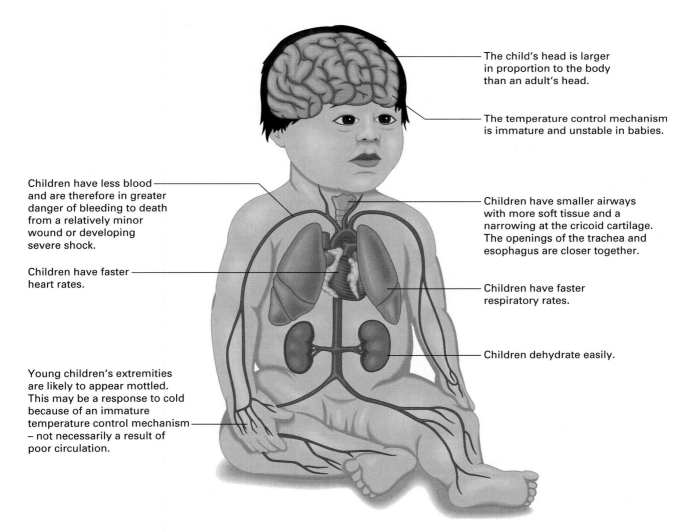

The child's head is larger in proportion to the body than an adult's head.

The temperature control mechanism is immature and unstable in babies.

Children have less blood and are therefore in greater danger of bleeding to death from a relatively minor wound or developing severe shock.

Children have faster heart rates.

Young children's extremities are likely to appear mottled. This may be a response to cold because of an immature temperature control mechanism – not necessarily a result of poor circulation.

Children have smaller airways with more soft tissue and a narrowing at the cricoid cartilage. The openings of the trachea and esophagus are closer together.

Children have faster respiratory rates.

Children dehydrate easily.

Figure 22-1. Differences between children and adults

Figure 22-2. Establish gentle contact and examine the child visually.

- Is the child in extreme pain?
- How is the child breathing?

Regardless of the child's age, follow these general procedures when assessing a child (see Figure 22-2):

- Prepare yourself psychologically so you can radiate confidence, competence, and friendliness.
- If you are a stranger to the child, remember that children between 1 and 6 seldom like strangers, especially if their parents are not there.
- Get as close to the child's eye level as possible.
- Explain what you are doing in terms the child can understand; speak in a calm, quiet voice and avoid "baby talk."
- Save the most painful parts of the assessment for last.
- Involve the parents as much as possible.
- Be honest. "It will hurt when I touch your leg, but it will only last a minute. If you feel like crying, that's okay."
- Be gentle; do everything you can to reduce the child's pain, and use restraint only when absolutely necessary—and then use minimal restraint.

Obtaining a History

If the situation is life threatening, take the primary survey quickly and manage serious conditions promptly. If you have more time, use the following guidelines in obtaining a history:

- Do not let upset parents and a screaming child unnerve you; take the time you need to get the information you need.
- Get information from parents or other witnesses, not the child.
- Ask when symptoms developed, how they progressed, and what care has already been given.
- If there was an accident, determine the details of the accident, the mechanism of injury, and what emergency care has already been given.

Taking Vital Signs

Learning Objective 2 Explain how children's vital signs differ from those of adults.

You need to check a child's vital signs more frequently than you would an adult's. Your overall impressions of how the child looks and acts are more important and can tell you more about the child's status than any one vital sign.

Keep these considerations in mind:

- *Respirations.* Children breathe faster than adults—the average for an infant is 40 breaths per minute, and for an 8-year-old it is 25 breaths per minute. Take respiratory rates frequently by placing your hand on the child's stomach; increases are significant, as is the quality of breathing (inadequate, noisy, and so on).
- *Pulse.* To take a pulse quickly, use the radial pulse in a child, the brachial pulse in an infant. Rapid pulse can be normal in a scared or overly excited child, but a slow pulse is a worrisome sign that can be caused by pressure in the skull, depressant drugs, or several comparatively rare medical conditions.
- *Temperature.* A child's temperature is a much more important warning sign than an adult's because it can change so quickly; young children can develop high fevers rapidly, so monitor the temperature frequently.
- *Neurological assessment.* Assessing possible neurological damage in a child is similar to assessment of an adult, but the stimuli must be more simple. For example, in testing response to painful stimuli, pinch the skin between the child's thumb and forefinger. Watch for other simple things, such as the child's ability to recognize familiar objects and people and the ability to move the arms and legs purposely.

● Section 2 ●
EMERGENCIES INVOLVING CHILDREN

Most emergencies involving children are managed in the same way as those involving adults. However, the different size and psychological development of a child means that you must treat some emergencies differently. Use the following considerations:

- Because the head of an infant or small child is large in proportion to the body, head injury is more likely. Assume cervical spine injury if the child has any injury above the clavicles or is unconscious.

- Because the liver, spleen, and kidneys of children are not as well protected as those of adults, and because they constitute a larger proportion of the abdominal cavity, they are more susceptible to blunt trauma.

- Because a child's skin surface is large compared to body mass, children are more susceptible to hypothermia, hyperthermia, and dehydration.

- Injuries of the extremities can also damage the growth plates.

- Infants have proportionally large tongues, and a relaxed tongue can block the airway.

- Most children involved in trauma will have enlarged stomachs, which can press against the diaphragm and make breathing difficult.

- It is especially important to stop bleeding in a child quickly; what is comparatively minor blood loss in an adult can constitute major bleeding in a child.

Common Emergencies in Children

Learning Objective 3 List special emergency situations involving children.

Some of the most common emergencies in children involve respiratory distress or obstructed airway (see Figure 22-3). Children are more susceptible than adults to respiratory distress because they have smaller air passages and less reserve air capacity.

Learning Objective 4 Distinguish between croup and epiglottitis.

Two emergencies that may be difficult to distinguish are infectious **croup** and **epiglottitis** (see Figure 22-4 on page 360). Use the guidelines in Table 22-1 on page 360 to distinguish the two.

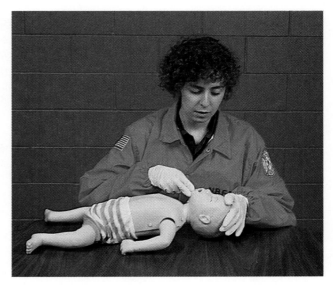

Figure 22-3. Airway obstruction in an infant or child may be relieved by keeping the head in a neutral or slightly extended position.

croup A viral infection that causes swelling beneath the glottis and progressive narrowing of the airway

epiglottitis A bacterial infection that causes swelling of the epiglottis and blocking of the airway

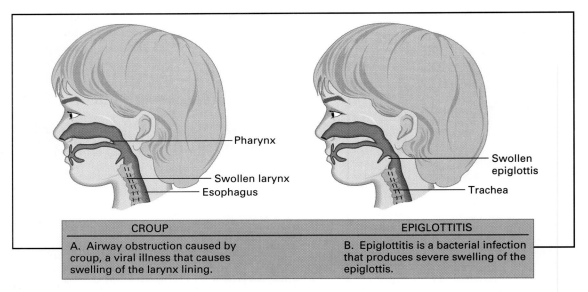

Figure 22-4. Croup and epiglottitis

	Croup	Epiglottitis
Cause	Viral infection of the upper airway	Bacterial infection
Physiology	Swelling beneath the glottis that progressively narrows the airway	Inflammation and swelling of the epiglottis
Signs and Symptoms	Peculiar whooping sound; high-pitched squeaking sounds; hoarseness; coughing with a harsh "seal bark" *Severe attacks are dangerous*	Pain on swallowing; high fever; drooling; difficulty speaking, but no hoarseness; mouth breathing; insistence on sitting up and leaning forward with chin thrust outward *Epiglottitis is life threatening*
Emergency Care	Keep the child in a comfortable position, usually propped up; activate the EMS system or take the child to the hospital	Keep the child calm and relaxed; *do not let the child lie down;* do not examine the child's throat; activate the EMS system

Table 22-1
Croup and Epiglottitis

Learning Objective 5 Distinguish between asthma and bronchiolitis.

Two other respiratory conditions in children that can be difficult to distinguish are asthma and **bronchiolitis.** Asthma is very common in children, especially among those with allergies. Both conditions can cause wheezing, an overly inflated chest, increasingly impaired breathing, exhaustion, sleepiness, rapid pulse, and cyanosis. Both conditions should be regarded as serious medical emergencies. To distinguish between the two, follow the guidelines in Table 22-2.

The care for both conditions is the same:

1. Allow the child to assume the position of greatest comfort—almost always sitting or semisitting. Additionally, give an asthma victim plenty of fluids, which help loosen and thin mucus in the air passages.

2. Be calm and reassuring.

3. Activate the EMS system or take the child to a medical facility.

Learning Objective 6 Discuss other common emergencies among children.

	Table 22-2	
	Asthma and Bronchiolitis	
	Asthma	**Bronchiolitis**
Cause	Usually allergies or emotional distress	Viral infection
Physiology	The bronchioles spasm and constrict, causing the bronchial membranes to swell and congest; thick mucus blocks the airways	The bronchioles become inflamed in response to infection
Age of Victim	Almost always over the age of 1	Almost always under the age of 2

Cardiac Arrest

Ninety-five percent of cardiac arrests in children result from airway obstruction and respiratory arrest; the other 5 percent are caused by shock. As when treating an adult, the goal is to keep the brain oxygenated and to begin care rapidly.

The signs and symptoms of cardiac arrest in a child (see Figure 22-5) include

- Unresponsiveness
- Seizure
- Gasping or absent respiratory sounds
- No audible heart sounds
- Absence of chest movement
- Pale or blue skin
- Absent brachial pulse

For guidelines on CPR in infants and children, see Chapter 6.

Seizures

Seizures in a child can be caused by any condition that would cause them in adults—head injury, meningitis, oxygen deficiency, drug overdose, and hypoglycemia,

among others. While adults rarely have seizures caused by fever, children under the age of 6 do.

To treat a seizure in a child, activate the EMS system; then:

1. Turn the child onto his or her side to prevent the tongue from relaxing and shifting backward, blocking the air passage.
2. Do not hold the child down, but place the child where he or she will not fall or strike something. A rug on the floor is excellent; so is a crib with padded sides.
3. Loosen tight or restrictive clothing.
4. Sponge a feverish child with lukewarm water.

Shock

The major causes of shock in children are blood loss, acute infection, and heart failure. Loss of body heat will cause newborns to go into shock, because they cannot shiver or warm themselves by moving around

bronchiolitis A viral infection that inflames the bronchioles

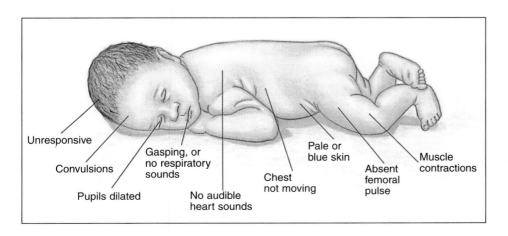

Figure 22-5. Signs of cardiac arrest in a child

Unresponsive

Convulsions

Pupils dilated

Gasping, or no respiratory sounds

No audible heart sounds

Chest not moving

Pale or blue skin

Absent femoral pulse

Muscle contractions

and because their surface area is large in relation to their body weight.

The signs and symptoms of shock in a child (see Figure 22-6) include

- Paleness
- Cold, moist skin
- Low blood pressure
- A rapid, thready pulse
- Lack of vitality
- Extreme anxiety
- Unconsciousness

To care for shock, activate the EMS system, have the child lie flat, keep the child warm and as calm as possible, and monitor vital signs frequently.

Progress Check

1. Injuries of the extremities in a child can also damage the _____ .
   (bone marrow/growth plates/large ball-and-socket joints)

2. An infant has a proportionally large _____ , which can block the airway.
   (tongue/epiglottis/larynx)

3. Most children involved in trauma have an enlarged _____ , which can interfere with breathing.
   (tongue/larynx/stomach)

4. A characteristic "seal bark" cough is a sign of _____ .
   (asthma/croup/epiglottitis)

5. A child who is drooling, having difficulty speaking, and having difficulty swallowing probably has _____ .
   (asthma/croup/epiglottitis)

6. Seizures in a child can be caused by _____ , which rarely causes seizures in an adult.
   (head injury/oxygen deficiency/fever)

7. _____ , which does not usually cause shock in older victims, can cause shock in an infant.
   (Blood loss/Loss of body heat/Major trauma)

• Section 3 •

SUDDEN INFANT DEATH SYNDROME AND CHILD ABUSE

Sudden Infant Death Syndrome

Learning Objective 7 Describe how to manage a case of sudden infant death syndrome.

Sudden infant death syndrome (SIDS), more commonly known as "crib death," is the number-one cause of death among infants between 1 month and 1 year of age. It cannot be predicted or prevented, and almost always occurs while the baby is sleeping.

The typical SIDS case involves an apparently healthy infant, frequently born prematurely, and usually between the ages of 4 weeks and 7 months, who suddenly dies overnight in his or her crib. There is usually no indication of a struggle, though some infants

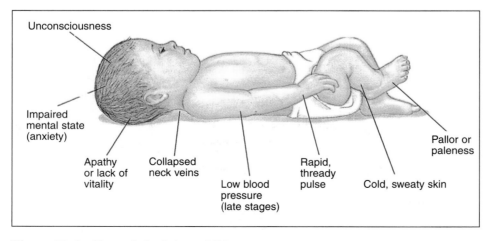

Figure 22-6. Signs of shock in a child

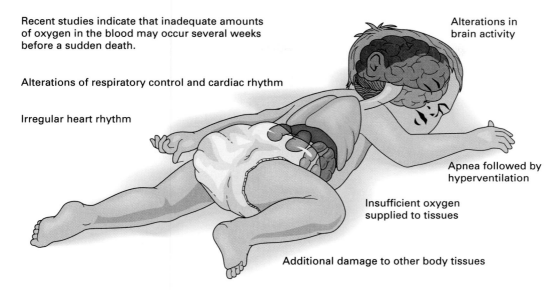

Recent studies indicate that inadequate amounts of oxygen in the blood may occur several weeks before a sudden death.

Alterations of respiratory control and cardiac rhythm

Irregular heart rhythm

Alterations in brain activity

Apnea followed by hyperventilation

Insufficient oxygen supplied to tissues

Additional damage to other body tissues

Figure 22-7. Causes of sudden infant death

have obviously changed position at the time of death. A red blotchiness of the skin is usually apparent.

While researchers are not sure of the cause (see Figure 22-7), recent studies indicate that inadequate amounts of oxygen in the blood may occur several weeks before a sudden death. Other causes may be alterations in brain activity, alterations of respiratory control and cardiac rhythm, and apnea followed by hyperventilation.

The guidelines for managing a SIDS case vary by location; *follow local protocol,* keeping these general guidelines in mind:

1. *Even if the child is obviously dead, have someone activate the EMS system and immediately begin infant CPR.*

2. Be aware of the parents' extreme distress; the best first aid is to make them feel that everything possible has been done for their child. Leave no room for "ifs" and "maybes."

3. After the ambulance arrives, encourage the parents to accompany their baby in the ambulance and arrange for someone to stay with other children at the home.

Child Abuse and Neglect

Learning Objective 8 Explain how to identify child abuse and neglect.

Thousands of cases of child abuse and neglect are reported annually in the United States—and because they occur chiefly in the privacy of the home, no one knows how many more cases go unreported.

Identifying Abuse

The abusing adult—usually a parent—often behaves in an evasive manner when confronted, volunteering little information or giving contradictory versions of what happened to the child. The parent may show outright hostility toward the child or toward the other parent, and rarely shows any guilt.

Abuse can be physical, emotional, or sexual, or may fall into the category of neglect. Each type of abuse has distinct characteristics that may allow you to identify the child as an abuse victim (see Figure 22-8 on page 364); in general, look for the following signs (see Figures 22-9 through 22-14 on page 365):

- The child is fretful, frightened of parents, afraid to go home, wary of adults, or apathetic (a child who does not cry, despite injuries)

- Abrasions, lacerations, incisions, bruises, broken bones, or multiple injuries in various stages of healing

- Injuries on both the front and the back or on both sides

- Unusual wounds, such as circular burns

- Injuries to the head, back, and abdomen, including the genitals

- Pain, itching, bruises, or bleeding in the genital, vaginal, or anal areas

- Injuries that do not match the mechanisms of injury described by the parents or caregivers

sudden infant death syndrome Sudden death of an apparently healthy infant, usually while asleep

Type of Abuse/ Neglect	Physical Indicators	Behavioral Indicators
Physical Abuse	Unexplained bruises and welts • on face, lips, mouth • on torso, back, buttocks, thighs • in various stages of healing • clustered, forming regular patterns • reflecting shape of article used to inflict them (electric cord, belt buckle) • on several different surface areas • regularly appear after absence, weekend, or vacation • especially about the trunk and buttocks Be particularly suspicious if there are old bruises in addition to fresh ones Unexplained burns • cigar, cigarette burns, especially on soles, palms, back, or buttocks • immersion burns (occur when a child is immersed in scalding water; when hands are immersed, burns look like reddened gloves; when feet are immersed, burns look like socks. Doughnut-shaped burns may appear on buttocks and genitalia.) • showing the pattern of electric stove burner, iron, etc. • rope burns on arms, legs, neck, or torso Unexplained fractures (particularly if multiple) • to skull, nose, facial structures • in various stages of healing • multiple or spiral fractures Unexplained lacerations or abrasions • to mouth, lips, gums, eyes • to external genitalia	Wary of adult contacts Apprehensive when other children cry Behavioral extremes: • aggressiveness • withdrawal Frightened of parents Afraid to go home Reports injury by parents The child is apathetic and *may not* cry despite his or her injuries The child has been seen by emergency personnel recently for related complaints The child's injury occurred several days before you were called
Sexual Abuse	Difficulty in walking or sitting Torn, stained, or bloody underclothing Pain or itching in genital area Bruises or bleeding in external genitalia, vaginal or anal areas Venereal disease, especially in preteens Pregnancy	Unwilling to change for gym or participate in physical education classes Withdrawal, fantasizing, or infantile behavior Bizarre, sophisticated, or unusual sexual behavior or knowledge Poor peer relationships Delinquent or run-away Reports sexual assault by caretaker
Emotional Abuse	Speech disorders Lags in physical development Failure to thrive	Habit disorders (sucking thumb, biting, rocking, etc.) Conduct disorders (antisocial, destructive, etc.) Neurotic traits (sleep disorders, inhibition of play) Psychoneurotic reactions (hysteria, obsession, compulsion, phobias, hypochondria) Behavioral extremes: • complaisant, passive • aggressive, demanding Overly adaptive behavior: • inappropriately adult • inappropriately infantile Developmental lags (mental, emotional) Attempted suicide
Neglect	Consistent hunger, poor hygiene, inappropriate dress Consistent lack of supervision, especially in dangerous activities or for long periods Physical problems or medical needs that indicate lack of a caregiver Abandonment	Begging, stealing food Extended stays at school (early arrival and late departure) Constant fatigue, listlessness, or falling asleep in class Alcohol or drug use Delinquency (e.g., thefts) States there is no caretaker

Figure 22-8 Physical and behavioral indicators of child abuse and neglect. (*Note:* Much of the above will not be obvious in the field—but the information can help you understand what may have precipitated the emergency.)

Emergency Care

1. Calm the parents; let them know by your actions that you are there to help and render emergency care. Speak in a low, firm voice.

2. Focus attention on the child; speak softly to the child, using the first name. Never ask the child to recreate the situation while in the crisis environment or with the suspected abuser still present.

3. Conduct a thorough, head-to-toe exam; care for injuries appropriately.

4. It is not your responsibility to confront any adult with the charge of child abuse; be supportive and nonjudgmental while at the scene.

5. *Always* report your suspicions of child abuse to the proper authorities, and maintain total confidentiality with others regarding the incident.

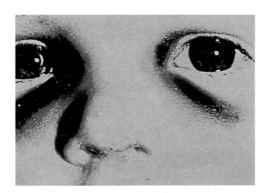

Figure 22-9. Signs of physical child abuse

Figure 22-10. Signs of physical child abuse

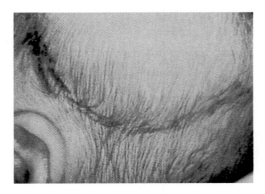

Figure 22-11. Signs of child neglect from lack of appropriate medical care

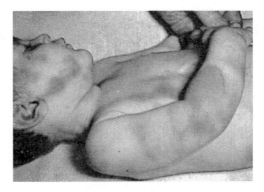

Figure 22-12. Abused child dead from multiple injuries

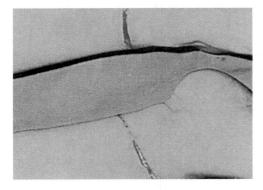

Figure 22-13. Signs of physical abuse— restraining by tying

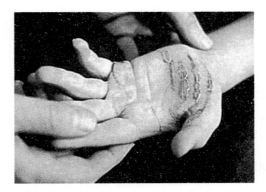

Figure 22-14. Signs of physical abuse— burns from hand held on an electric stove

Caring for Yourself

Almost half of the children in the United States who die from accidents are pronounced dead either at the scene or as they arrive at the hospital. The sudden and/or violent death of a child, either before you arrive or while you are giving first aid, is emotionally wrenching. The possibility of child abuse or neglect can be especially difficult to deal with emotionally.

If you are faced with such a situation, control your emotions while at the scene so you can render the best possible care and so you can support other victims. After the case is over, however, it is important to talk about your feelings and sort through your emotions. If you do not, you may well develop worry about your own children or disturbing nightmares. If necessary, seek professional help or participate in stress debriefing.

Progress Check

1. Sudden infant death syndrome occurs when an apparently _____ infant dies while sleeping.
   (distressed/healthy/ill)

2. Even if a victim of SIDS is obviously dead, you should _____ .
   (begin infant CPR/treat for shock/do a primary survey)

3. An abusing adult often shows _____ to the child.
   (compassion/guilt/hostility)

4. Suspect child abuse if the child is _____ .
   (frightened of parents/clinging to parents/affectionate to parents)

5. If you suspect child abuse, you should _____ .
   (confront the parents at the scene/report your suspicions to authorities/ask the child to confirm your suspicions)

• Section 4 •
GERIATRIC EMERGENCIES

People over the age of 65 present special challenges to the First Aider. While the elderly represent only about 10 percent of the population, they take 30 percent of all prescription drugs and account for 25 percent of all fatal injuries. They have an average of three coexisting chronic diseases, take three times as many medications as the general population, and are affected by the physiology of aging.

How Body Systems Change with Age

Learning Objective 9 Explain how body systems change with age.

Body systems change with age (see Figure 22-15), affecting the signs and symptoms manifested in common medical emergencies. To complicate matters, many elderly people suffer from malnutrition and have a combination of different disease processes in varying stages of development. To give effective first aid, you need to recognize these changes (see Table 22-3 on page 368).

Differing Signs and Symptoms

While many medical problems present a standard set of signs and symptoms in the general population, the changes involved in the aging process can cause the following altered signs and symptoms in the elderly.

In myocardial infarction:
- Pain is less common.
- Aching shoulders and indigestion are common.
- The most common symptoms are shortness of breath, fainting, severe confusion, and stroke.

In congestive heart failure:
- Little or no dyspnea is present.

In pneumonia:
- Fever is usually absent (it is a classic sign of pneumonia in other age groups).
- Chest pain is much less common.
- Cough is much less common.
- Most cases are due to aspiration, not infection.

Special Assessment Considerations

Learning Objective 10 Explain special issues to consider in assessing the elderly.

Assessment of the elderly victim can be difficult; the following factors can complicate evaluation (see Figure 22-16 on page 368):
- The elderly become debilitated much more rapidly; a minor problem can become major within a few hours.
- The victim may be taking a number of medications.
- As many as one in four elderly have psychiatric disorders, which can be the cause of some symptoms (such as clouding of consciousness).

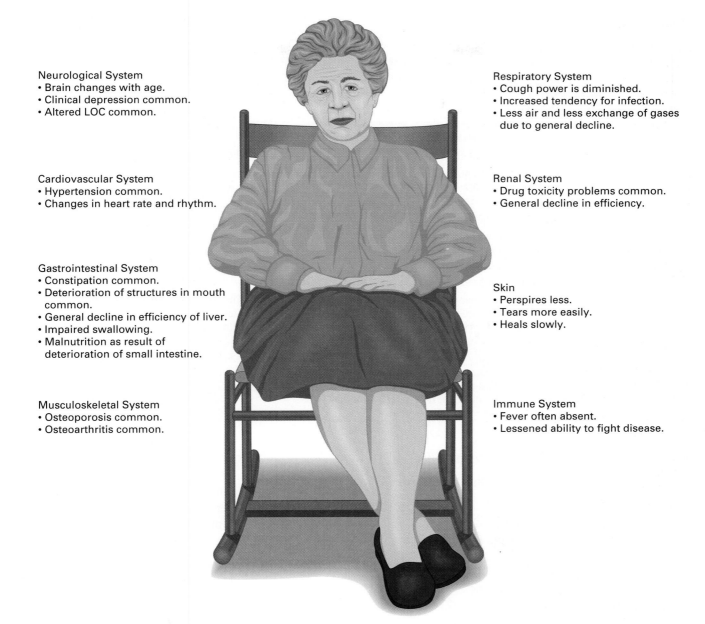

Neurological System
• Brain changes with age.
• Clinical depression common.
• Altered LOC common.

Cardiovascular System
• Hypertension common.
• Changes in heart rate and rhythm.

Gastrointestinal System
• Constipation common.
• Deterioration of structures in mouth common.
• General decline in efficiency of liver.
• Impaired swallowing.
• Malnutrition as result of deterioration of small intestine.

Musculoskeletal System
• Osteoporosis common.
• Osteoarthritis common.

Respiratory System
• Cough power is diminished.
• Increased tendency for infection.
• Less air and less exchange of gases due to general decline.

Renal System
• Drug toxicity problems common.
• General decline in efficiency.

Skin
• Perspires less.
• Tears more easily.
• Heals slowly.

Immune System
• Fever often absent.
• Lessened ability to fight disease.

Figure 22-15. Physical changes in the elderly

• It can be difficult to separate the effects of aging from the consequences of disease.

• The victim's chief complaint may seem trivial.

• The victim may fail to report important symptoms.

• The geriatric victim is likely to suffer from more than one disease at a time.

• Aging may change the victim's response to illness and injury, causing you to underestimate the severity of the victim's condition.

• The elderly person's temperature-regulating mechanism may be depressed, leading to absent fever even with severe infection.

• Communication problems are common because the senses diminish, especially sight and hearing.

• Common complaints of geriatric victims that may not be specific to any one disorder include fatigue and weakness, dizziness/vertigo/syncope, falls, headache, insomnia, loss of appetite, inability to void, and constipation/diarrhea.

Table 22-3

Physical Changes in the Elderly

The System	How It Changes	What the Changes Mean
Cardiovascular	Calcium is deposited in areas of wear and tear; fibrous tissue thickens; vessels lose elasticity; the heart pumps less volume	Blood pressure increases; the heart rate may not increase, even with infection, shock, or stress
Musculoskeletal	Osteoporosis makes bones less dense	Susceptibility to fractures; delayed healing
Immune	Changes in the components of the immune system, weakening	Little or no fever in response to infection, recurrence of disease
Neurological	Conditions that accompany aging can aggravate dementia	Confusion; lack of accurate victim history
Gastrointestinal	Reduced salivary flow, deterioration of mouth structures	Susceptibility to various medical conditions and malnutrition
Renal	Kidneys become smaller; arteries that supply them become hard and brittle	Susceptibility to infection and disease
Skin	Becomes thin, tears easily; less attachment between layers; cells are produced less rapidly; less perspiration; dulled sense of touch	Susceptibility to injury; delayed healing; loss of protective barrier; inability to describe pain accurately
Respiratory	Calcium deposits in rib cage make it difficult for lungs to expand; less air enters lungs; less gas exchange; tissues degenerate; lungs lose elasticity; cilia are no longer as mobile	Susceptibility to infection; delayed recovery

Special Examination Considerations

Be alert to the following when examining an elderly victim:

- The victim may be fatigued easily.
- The victim may be wearing several layers of clothing.

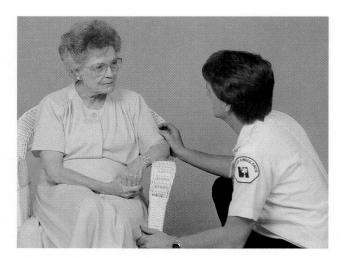

Figure 22-16. It is often necessary to consider special issues when assessing an elderly victim.

- You need to explain actions clearly before assessing the elderly victim.
- The victim may minimize or deny symptoms out of fear of being bedridden or institutionalized or of losing a sense of self-sufficiency.

Special Trauma Considerations

Learning Objective 11 Discuss special issues to consider in caring for trauma in the elderly.

Situations that would call for basic care with victims in other age groups call for aggressive care in the elderly, and the elderly are at greater risk for sustaining traumatic injury because of the following factors:

- They may have slower reflexes, failing eyesight and hearing, arthritis, less elastic blood vessels, and fragile tissues and bones.
- They are at higher risk for trauma from criminal assault.
- They are prone to head injury, even from relatively minor trauma; signs and symptoms of brain compression develop more slowly, sometimes over days or weeks.

- They often have a significant degree of degenerative disease of the cervical vertebrae, which can gradually compress the roots of nerves to the arms or possibly to the spinal cord itself. Sudden neck movement, with or without fracture, can cause spinal cord injury.

Progress Check

1. _____ is less common in elderly victims of myocardial infarction.
(Pain/Indigestion/Shortness of breath)

2. There is usually little or no _____ in elderly victims of congestive heart failure.
(edema/cyanosis/dyspnea)

3. _____ , a classic sign of pneumonia, is usually absent in the elderly.
(Weakness/Pain/Fever)

4. Signs or symptoms may be masked in elderly victims because they usually _____ .
(take multiple medications/are immobile/have failing eyesight)

• SUMMARY •

- When assessing a child, try to stay at the child's eye level, speak in a calm and quiet voice, avoid "baby talk," involve the parents, and save the most painful part of the assessment for last.

- Check a child's vital signs more frequently than you would an adult's; remember, too, that your overall impression of how the child looks and acts can be more important than any one vital sign.

- Children are more susceptible to head injury; blunt trauma of the liver, spleen, and kidneys; hypothermia, hyperthermia, and dehydration; and blocking of the airway by a relaxed tongue.

- A comparatively small blood loss in an adult can constitute major bleeding in a child.

- Respiratory problems—such as croup, epiglottitis, asthma, and bronchiolitis—are serious medical emergencies in children. Epiglottitis can cause death if untreated.

- Always initiate infant CPR in cases of sudden infant death syndrome, even when the baby is obviously dead.

- Never confront parents about child abuse at the scene; always report your suspicions to appropriate authorities later.

- The physiological changes of aging can make the elderly more susceptible to disease and can alter usual signs and symptoms as well.

- When assessing the elderly, remember that they often fail to report important symptoms, often take a combination of medications, and often have several coexisting chronic diseases.

• KEY TERMS •

Make sure you understand the following key terms:

- croup
- epiglottitis
- bronchiolitis
- sudden infant death syndrome

Student: _____ Date: _____

Course: _____ Section #: _____

PART 1 • True/False

If you believe the statement is true, circle the T. If you believe the statement is false, circle the F.

T F **1.** Do not allow a child victim to have any contact with his or her parents.

T F **2.** Get as close as you can to the child's eye level during assessment.

T F **3.** Children between the ages of 1 and 6 enjoy strangers and are usually easy to assess.

T F **4.** Never tell a child the truth about his or her pain.

T F **5.** Children are more susceptible than adults to respiratory problems.

T F **6.** The special needs of elderly people may require some modification of first aid techniques.

T F **7.** Elderly victims have more pain with myocardial infarction than younger victims.

T F **8.** The elderly are often taking several regular medications, which can mask signs and symptoms.

PART 2 • Multiple Choice

For each item, circle the correct answer or the phrase that best completes the statement.

1. When assessing children, you should

  a. avoid "baby talk"
  b. perform the most painful part of the assessment first
  c. stay above the child's eye level
  d. keep the child and parents separated

2. In assessing infants or small children, you will be less effective if you

  a. are gentle
  b. talk quietly and calmly
  c. separate the child and parent
  d. allow the child to remain with a parent

3. In caring for a suspected victim of child abuse, you should *not*

  a. focus attention on the child while you give emergency care
  b. question the child about abuse in front of the parents
  c. make efforts to calm the parents
  d. report your suspicions of child abuse to proper authorities

4. When managing a SIDS situation, you should *not*

  a. immediately initiate infant CPR
  b. encourage parents to accompany their baby in the ambulance
  c. discuss a SIDS case with colleagues
  d. talk out your feelings after a SIDS emergency

5. In children up to age 2, seizures are often due to

  a. epilepsy
  b. fever
  c. hyperglycemia
  d. drowning

6. The major causes of shock in children are

  a. blood loss, fever, head injury
  b. near-drowning, respiratory distress, seizures
  c. blood loss, acute infection, heart failure
  d. fever, head injury, epiglottitis

7. SIDS most often occurs

  a. among twins or triplets
  b. in low-income families
  c. among very sick children
  d. while the baby is sleeping

8. Which of the following is *not* true of child abuse and neglect?

  a. abuse may be physical, emotional, or sexual
  b. the adult who abuses a child typically shows remorse
  c. signs of child abuse include abrasions, lacerations, and broken bones
  d. we do not really know how many children are abused

9. What changes take place in the immune system of the elderly as a result of infection?

  a. stress on the immune system is more likely to lead to fever
  b. the salivary glands degenerate
  c. the white cell count does not increase normally
  d. the cilia lose mobility

10. Which of the following factors tend to make assessment of the elderly more difficult?

  a. they may have multiple disorders
  b. they rarely take medications
  c. they usually report symptoms
  d. all of the above

- At a motor-vehicle accident, one of the victims is a 3-year-old in a safety seat. He is screaming at the top of his lungs, and he has a shallow gash in his thigh from which blood is oozing. His older sister has been thrown from the car and is unconscious. The driver is staggering up and down the road sobbing.

  Who would you attend to first, and why? How would you approach the child in the car seat for a physical assessment? What would you do to try to calm the child in the car seat?

Bites and Stings

Learning Objectives

When you have mastered the material in this chapter, you will be able to

1 Distinguish between poisonous and nonpoisonous snakes

2 List the factors that determine the severity of pit viper bite

3 List the signs and symptoms of pit viper bite

4 List the signs and symptoms of coral snake bite

5 Determine when medical help is needed for insect bite

6 List the signs and symptoms of black widow spider bite

7 Explain why the bite of the brown recluse spider is so serious

8 List the signs and symptoms of scorpion sting

9 List the signs and symptoms of anaphylactic shock

10 Identify the two important differences between the bites and stings of marine animals and those of land animals

11 Describe and demonstrate emergency care for bites and stings

12 Describe and demonstrate emergency care for marine life poisoning

13 Describe and demonstrate how to remove a tick

O n October 6, 1998, 28-year-old Andrew Wyatt was cleaning out a corner of his garage to make room for firewood. As he reached into a dark area behind some tools, he felt a definite pinprick on the back of his hand. Jerking his hand into the light, he examined it closely; he could not tell whether he had been bitten or had merely brushed his hand against the sharp edge of a tool. Dismissing the incident, Andrew went back to work.

Within about half an hour, Andrew realized his hand was aching. He also started having intense pain and spasms in his shoulders, back, and abdomen—far greater than the mild muscle stress he should have felt from the work he was doing. Alarmed, he walked next door and described his symptoms to Nate Ford, a trained First Aider and Scoutmaster.

Andrew was grimacing and his face was flushed. Placing the back of his hand against Andrew's skin, Nate found that Andrew was feverish. By then, Andrew was also complaining of headache and nausea. Nate suspected the bite of a black widow spider—a suspicion that was confirmed when the two of them returned to Andrew's garage and carefully moved a few tools in the corner to reveal the spider.

Nate reassured Andrew, then got him into the car. Nate draped his jacket over Andrew's chest to help preserve body warmth and placed a cold compress on his hand over the bite site. Nate then drove Andrew the 6 miles to a local medical center, where physicians took over care of the bite.

INSECT BITES AND STINGS ARE COMMON, AND MOST ARE considered minor. It is only when the insect is poisonous or when the victim has an allergic reaction and runs the risk of developing anaphylactic shock that the situation becomes an emergency.

Proper first aid care for insect bites and stings and for snakebite can save lives and prevent permanent tissue damage. This chapter outlines the kinds of bites and stings that are of special concern, lists signs and symptoms, and provides basic guidelines for emergency care.

Figure 23-1. Rattlesnake

Figure 23-2. Water moccasin or cottonmouth

Figure 23-3. Coral snake

Figure 23-4. Copperhead

• Section 1 •
SNAKEBITE

Learning Objective 1 Distinguish between poisonous and nonpoisonous snakes.

Approximately 50,000 people are bitten by snakes every year in the United States; of those, 8,000 are bitten by poisonous snakes. There are only four kinds of poisonous snakes in the United States: rattlesnakes, coral snakes, water moccasins (also known as cottonmouths), and copperheads. Fewer than 12 people die each year in the United States from snakebite, almost all from rattlesnake bite. (Though coral snakes are actually more poisonous, their teeth are small and slanted backward, making it difficult for them to inject very much venom.)

Nonpoisonous snakebites are not considered serious and are generally treated as minor wounds; only poisonous snakebites are considered medical emergencies. Symptoms generally occur immediately, but only occur in about one-third of all poisonous snakebites; the majority of people do not have symptoms, usually because no venom was injected into the victim.

Most poisonous snakes (Figures 23-1 through 23-4) have the following characteristics:

- Large fangs; nonpoisonous snakes have small teeth. The exception is the **coral snake,** a poisonous snake that has small teeth rather than fangs.

- **Elliptical pupils** (vertical slits, much like those of a cat); nonvenomous snakes have round pupils.

- A pit between the eye and the mouth, which identifies the snake as a **pit viper.**

- A variety of differently shaped blotches on a background of pink, yellow, olive, tan, gray, or brown

coral snake A type of poisonous snake that does not have a pit or fangs

elliptical pupils Pupils that are vertical slits, like those of a cat

pit viper snake A type of poisonous snake, such as a rattlesnake, characterized by a pit between the eyes and mouth

skin. The exception is the coral snake, which is ringed with red, yellow, and black.

- A triangular head that is larger than the neck

Severity of Snakebite

> **Learning Objective 2** List the factors that determine the severity of pit viper bite.

The severity of a pit viper bite is gauged by how rapidly symptoms develop, which depends on how much poison was injected. Other factors that determine the severity of a snakebite include the following:

- The location of the bite (fatty tissue absorbs the venom more slowly than muscle tissue)
- Whether disease-causing organisms are in the venom
- The size and weight of the victim
- The general health and condition of the victim
- How much physical activity the victim engaged in immediately following the bite (physical activity helps spread venom)

As a general rule, you can safely assume that the victim has not been poisoned if the burning pain characteristic of pit viper bite does not develop within 1 hour of the bite.

Signs and Symptoms of Snakebite

> **Learning Objective 3** List the signs and symptoms of pit viper bite.

The signs and symptoms of pit viper bite (see Figures 23-5 through 23-7) include

- Two distinct fang marks at the bite site
- Immediate and severe burning pain and swelling around the fang marks, usually within 5 minutes
- Purplish discoloration around the bite, usually within 2 to 3 hours
- Numbness and possible blistering around the bite
- Nausea and vomiting
- Rapid heartbeat
- Low blood pressure
- Weakness and fainting
- Numbness and tingling of the tongue and mouth
- Excessive sweating
- Fever and chills
- Muscular twitching
- Convulsions

- Dimmed vision
- Headache
- A minty, metallic, or rubbery taste in the mouth

> **Learning Objective 4** List the signs and symptoms of coral snake bite.

The signs and symptoms of coral snake bite include

- One or more tiny scratch marks in the area of the bite (a coral snake "chews" its victim)
- Little or no pain and swelling
- Little or no discoloration
- Blurred vision and drooping eyelids
- Slurred speech
- Increased salivation and sweating
- Drowsiness
- Difficulty in breathing
- Nausea and vomiting
- Shock
- Paralysis
- Coma

The signs and symptoms of a pit viper bite generally occur immediately; those of a coral snake bite are usually delayed by at least 1 and as many as 8 hours.

Progress Check

1. Most poisonous snakes have _____ .
   (large fangs/small, irregular fangs/rows of small teeth)

2. The pupils of most poisonous snakes are
   _____ .
   (round/elliptical/oval)

3. Pit vipers are so named because of a pit between the _____ .
   (eyes/eyes and mouth)

4. The poisonous snake that does not share typical characteristics of poisonous snakes is the
   _____ .
   (copperhead/water moccasin/coral snake)

5. Pain from a pit viper bite is _____ .
   (sharp/burning/dull)

6. Pain from a coral snake bite is usually
   _____ .
   (absent/sharp/dull)

7. Signs and symptoms of pit viper bites are generally
   _____
   (immediate/slightly delayed/delayed by as many as 8 hours)

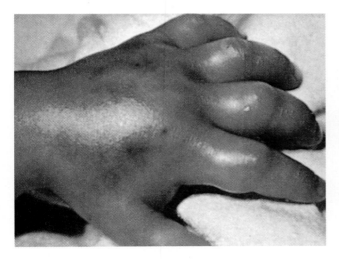

Figure 23-5. Snakebite to the hand

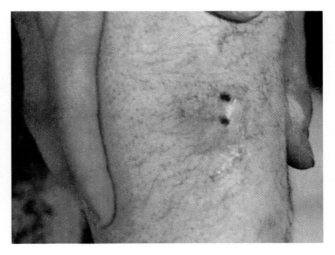

Figure 23-6. Rattlesnake bite

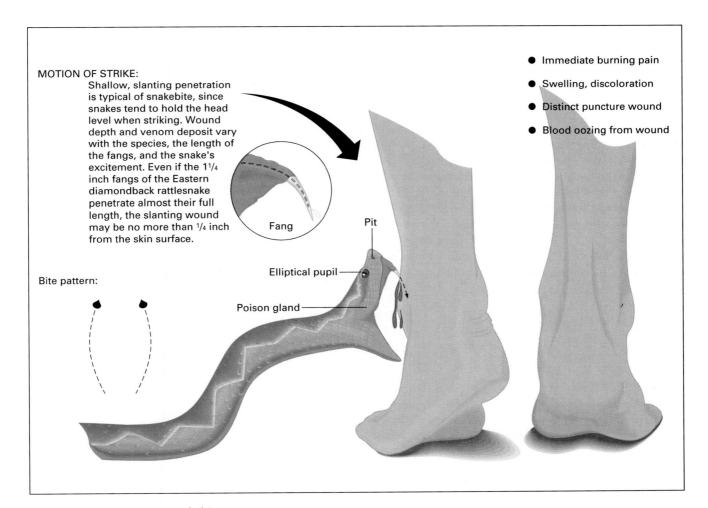

MOTION OF STRIKE:
Shallow, slanting penetration is typical of snakebite, since snakes tend to hold the head level when striking. Wound depth and venom deposit vary with the species, the length of the fangs, and the snake's excitement. Even if the 1¼ inch fangs of the Eastern diamondback rattlesnake penetrate almost their full length, the slanting wound may be no more than ¼ inch from the skin surface.

Fang

Bite pattern:

Pit

Elliptical pupil

Poison gland

● Immediate burning pain
● Swelling, discoloration
● Distinct puncture wound
● Blood oozing from wound

Figure 23-7. Poisonous snakebites

• Section 2 •

INSECT BITES AND STINGS

Learning Objective 5 Determine when medical help is needed for insect bite.

Most insect bites are treated like any other wound. Generally, medical help is necessary only if

- Itching lasts longer than 2 days
- Signs of infection develop
- Signs of an allergic reaction develop
- The insect is poisonous

Black Widow Spider

Learning Objective 6 List the signs and symptoms of black widow spider bite.

The **black widow spider** (see Figure 23-8) is characterized by a shiny black body, thin legs, and a crimson red marking on its abdomen, usually in the shape of an hourglass or two triangles. Note: Of the five species in the United States, only three are black, and not all have the characteristic red marking. Black widow spiders are usually found in dry, secluded, dimly lit areas; they have extremely strong, funnel-shaped webs.

Black widow spider bites are the leading cause of death from spider bites in the United States. Those at highest risk for developing severe reactions to bites are children under the age of 16, adults over the age of 60, people with chronic illness, and anyone with hypertension.

In addition to the general signs and symptoms of bites and stings, black widow spider bites cause

- Small red fang marks
- Severe muscle spasms, especially in the shoulders, back, chest, and abdomen, starting within 1 to 4 hours of the bite
- Fever and chills
- Profuse sweating
- Headache and dizziness
- Nausea and vomiting

Brown Recluse Spider

Learning Objective 7 Explain why the bite of the brown recluse spider is so serious.

The **brown recluse spider** (see Figure 23-9) is generally brown but can range in color from yellow to

Figure 23-8. Black widow spider

Figure 23-9. Brown recluse spider

dark chocolate brown. The characteristic marking is a brown, violin-shaped marking on the upper back. In the United States, brown recluse spiders are found mostly in the southern and midwestern states; there are none in the Pacific northwest.

The bite of the brown recluse spider creates a serious medical condition: the bite does not heal, and requires surgical repair (see Figure 23-10).

The brown recluse spider bites only when it is trapped against the skin. Unfortunately, most victims are unaware that they have been bitten, because the bite is often painless at first. Initial signs and symptoms include redness with moderate itching and swelling at the site of the bite. Several hours after the bite, the site becomes bluish surrounded by a white periphery, then a red halo (a bull's-eye pattern). Within 7 to 10 days, the bite becomes a large ulcer. It continues to scab over; then the scab falls off to reveal an even larger ulcer.

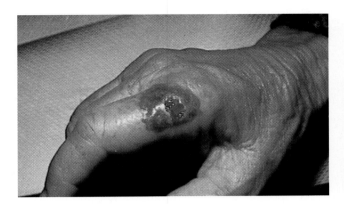

Figure 23-10. Brown recluse spider bite

Scorpion

Figure 23-11. Scorpion

Learning Objective 8 List the signs and symptoms of scorpion sting.

In the United States, scorpions (Figure 23-11) are found in the desert southwest, in Utah, and in Nevada. Of the three species of scorpion in the United States that sting and inject poisonous venom, only the venom of one is generally fatal. The severity of the sting depends on the amount of venom injected. Ninety percent of all scorpion stings occur on the hands.

In addition to the general signs and symptoms of bites and stings, scorpion stings cause sharp pain at the sting site that is followed by numbness or tingling. In cases of severe reaction, the victim will experience drooling, poor coordination, incontinence, and seizures.

Fire Ants

Most common in the southeastern United States, fire ants get their name not from their color (which may range from red to black), but from the intense, fiery, burning pain their bite causes.

Fire ants bite down into the skin, then pivot, using their tail stingers repeatedly; the result is a characteristic circular pattern of stings (see Figure 23-12). Fire ant stings produce extremely painful vesicles that are filled with fluid. At first the fluid is clear; later it becomes cloudy. Fire ant stings can also cause a large local reaction, characterized by swelling, pain, and redness that affect the entire area.

Ticks

Tick bites are serious because ticks can carry tick fever, Rocky Mountain spotted fever, and other bacterial diseases. The deer tick can transmit Lyme disease, which can cause long-term neurologic complications.

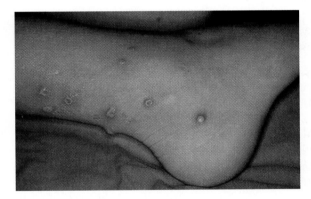

Figure 23-12. Fire ant bites

Ticks (see Figure 23-13 on page 380) are visible after they have attached themselves to the skin; they often choose warm, moist areas, such as the scalp, other hairy areas such as the armpits or the groin, and skin creases. Tick bites are generally painless; many victims are unaware that they have been bitten. As the tick becomes engorged with blood, it can become as much as 50 times larger.

The only appropriate prehospital treatment for tick bite is prompt removal of the tick, which can help prevent infection. Never pluck an embedded tick out of the skin; you may force infected blood into the victim. For information about safe tick removal, see Removing a Tick later in this chapter.

black widow spider A poisonous spider identified by a red mark shaped like an hourglass on its underside

brown recluse spider A brown poisonous spider identified by a violin-shaped mark on its back; brown recluse spider bites do not heal and require surgical grafting

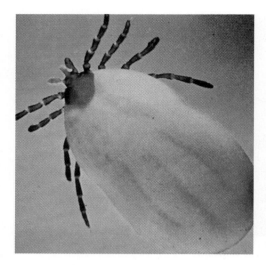

Figure 23-13. Engorged tick

Insect Stings

The stinging insects include the honeybee, bumblebee, wasp, hornet, and yellow jacket. Most are aggressive only when their hives or nests are disturbed, or when they feel threatened, though a new breed of "Africanized" bees (a cross between African bees and more placid European bees) are much more aggressive. Though swarms are rare, any of the stinging insects may sting in swarms. Honeybees leave the stinger and venom sac behind, embedded in the skin, so they can sting only once; hornets and wasps do not lose their stingers, so they can sting repeatedly.

The normal reaction to an insect sting is a sharp, stinging pain followed by an itchy, swollen, painful wheal. Redness, tenderness, and swelling at or around the sting site—even if severe—is considered to be a local reaction in the absence of other symptoms. Local reactions are rarely serious or life threatening and can be treated successfully with cold compresses. Stings on the face, especially the mouth or eyes, are considered more serious, even if the reaction is local. Most serious are stings inside the mouth or throat, which usually occur when the insect is accidentally swallowed. Figure 23-14 describes wasps, bees, and fire ants that commonly attack humans.

> **Learning Objective 9** List the signs and symptoms of anaphylactic shock.

Allergic reactions, which cause anaphylactic shock, are much more serious than local reactions. Thousands of people are allergic to the stings of bees, wasps, hornets, and yellow jackets. For such people, a single sting may cause death—on the average, within 10 minutes of the sting, but almost always within the first hour. The sooner the symptoms occur, the more serious the reaction and the greater the threat of death. More than a hundred people in the United States are killed every year by insect stings; most deaths are caused when swelling of the airway obstructs the breathing.

The range of signs and symptoms of allergic reaction and anaphylactic shock include

- Nausea and vomiting
- Itching of the throat
- Faintness
- Dizziness
- Generalized itching
- Hives
- Flushing
- Generalized swelling, including the eyelids, lips, and tongue
- Upper airway obstruction
- Difficulty swallowing
- Shortness of breath, wheezing, or stridor
- Labored breathing
- Abdominal cramps
- Confusion
- Loss of consciousness
- Convulsions
- Low blood pressure

Progress Check

1. In addition to general signs of insect bite, a sign of black widow bite is _____ .
   (cramps/ulcerated skin/fluid-filled blisters)

2. A brown recluse spider bite is especially serious because it _____ .
   (causes neurological damage/does not heal/goes unnoticed)

3. Fire ants sting in a characteristic _____ pattern.
   (circular/parallel/random)

4. Ticks can cause a serious problem because they carry _____ .
   (meningitis/encephalitis/Rocky Mountain spotted fever)

5. Anaphylactic shock is a severe _____ that can cause death within a few minutes.
   (sting/allergic reaction/venom)

6. _____ leave the stinger behind, so they can sting only once.
   (Wasps/Hornets/Bees)

The following members of this group can attack humans, causing local pain, redness, swelling, and subsequent itching. Always consider the possibility of anaphylaxis.

HONEYBEE: Found throughout the United States at any time of the year, except in colder temperatures when they remain in their hives. In the Northeast and Midwest, they are the insects most likely to cause sting reactions. Hives are usually found in hollowed out areas such as dead tree trunks. Honeybees principally ingest nectar of plants, so they are often seen in the vicinity of flowers. The honeybee loses its barbed stinger after a sting, leaving the venom sac and stinger in place in the wound.

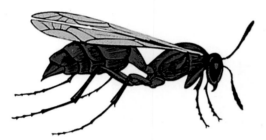

WASPS: The most likely insect to cause sting reactions in the Southeast and Southwest. Wasps tend to nest in small numbers under the eaves of houses and buildings. They are carnivores that are found in picnic areas, garbage cans, and food stands. Can deliver multiple stings at one time.

FIRE ANT: Fire ants can range from red to black and live in loose dirt mounds. They are found throughout the southern states as far west as New Mexico. Fire ants may cause serious illness and/or anaphylaxis. The ant attaches itself to the skin with its strong jaws and swivels its tail stinger about, inflicting repeated stings.

Figure 23-14. Wasps, bees, and fire ants

YELLOW JACKET: A principal insect causing sting reactions in the Northeast and Midwest. Yellow jackets tend to be prevalent in late summer and fall. Nests are located in the ground. Often seen in picnic areas and garbage cans, yellow jackets are ill-tempered and aggressive and can deliver multiple stings at one time. They often sting without being provoked.

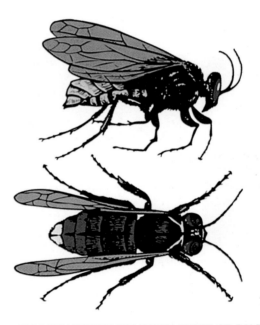

YELLOW HORNET AND WHITE-FACED OR BALD-FACED HORNET: Seen mainly in the spring and early summer. Nests usually found in branches and bushes above ground. They are carnivores that are seen in picnic areas, garbage cans, and food stands. Can deliver multiple stings at one time.

Adapted with permission from: John W. Georgitis. "Insect Stings—Responding to the Gamut of Allergic Reactions," *Modern Medicine*

• Section 3 •
MARINE LIFE BITES AND STINGS

Learning Objective 10 Identify the two important differences between the bites and stings of marine animals and those of land animals.

There are approximately 2,000 poisonous marine animals. While most live in temperate or tropical waters, they can be found in virtually all waters. Most are not aggressive; in fact, most marine life poisoning occurs when a victim swims into or steps on an animal.

Some marine animals—such as eels or sharks—inflict injury by biting or ripping the soft tissues. Others—such as the stingray—cause puncture wounds. And still other marine animals—including the coral, anemone, and jellyfish, among others—sting their victims.

There are two important differences between the bites and stings of marine animals and those of land animals. First, the venom of marine life may cause more extensive tissue damage than that of land animals. Second, venoms of aquatic organisms are destroyed by heat, so heat—not ice—should be applied to marine bites and stings.

In cases of bites and stings by marine life, try to identify the animal—some very effective antivenins are available. Figures 23-15 through 23-25 illustrate several types of marine life. Figures 23-26 and 23-27 show the stings of jellyfish and stingray.

Progress Check

1. Poisonous forms of marine life are found in
   _____ waters.
   (temperate/tropical/all)

2. The venom of marine animals causes _____ tissue damage than that of poisonous land animals.
   (less extensive/more extensive/more varied)

3. The venom of marine animals is destroyed by
   _____ .
   (cold/heat/antiseptics)

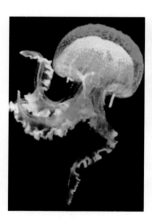

Figure 23-15. Jellyfish

Figure 23-16. Stingray

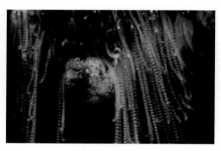

Figure 23-17. Tentacles of the Portuguese man-of-war

Figure 23-18. Lionfish

Figure 23-19. Feather hydroid

Figure 23-20. Sea anemone and clownfish

Figure 23-21. Fire coral

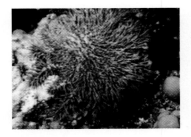

Figure 23-22. *Crown-of-thorns starfish*

Figure 23-23. *Sea urchin*

Figure 23-24. *Scorpion fish*

Figure 23-25. *Moray eel*

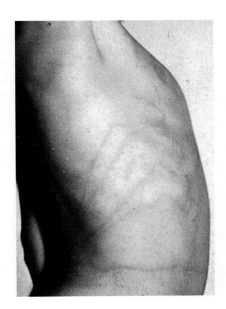

Figure 23-26. *Jellyfish sting*

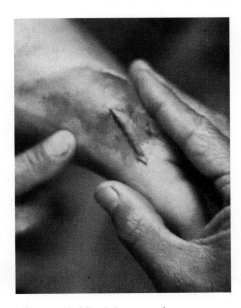

Figure 23-27. *Stingray sting*

• Section 4 •

GENERAL SIGNS AND SYMPTOMS AND EMERGENCY CARE

Signs and Symptoms

General signs and symptoms of bites and stings include

- History of a bite (from a spider or snake) or a sting (from an insect, scorpion, or marine animal)
- Pain, often immediate and severe or burning; within several hours, the area around the bite or sting may become numb
- Redness or other discoloration around the bite
- Swelling around the bite, sometimes spreading gradually
- Weakness or faintness
- Dizziness
- Chills
- Fever
- Nausea and vomiting
- Bite marks or a stinger

Learning Objective 11 Describe and demonstrate emergency care for bites and stings.

General Emergency Care

For general emergency care, activate the EMS system if the victim's condition warrants it; then:

1. If the stinger is still present, remove it by gently scraping against it with the edge of a credit card (see Figure 23-28 on page 384), the edge of a knife, or your fingernail. Be careful not to squeeze the stinger with tweezers, forceps, or your fingers; doing so can force additional venom from the venom sac into the wound. (Make sure you remove the venom sac—it can continue to secrete venom even though the stinger is detached from the insect.)

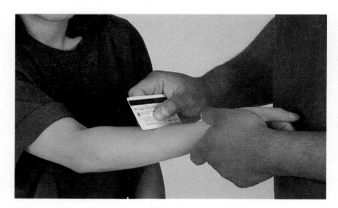

Figure 23-28. Scraping a honeybee stinger away with the edge of a credit card

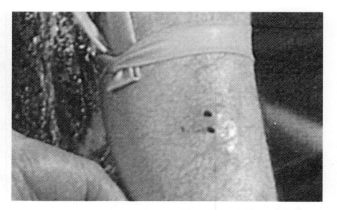

Figure 23-29. For poisonous snakebite (bites of pit vipers), apply a constricting band above the bite. The band should be tight enough to slow surface circulation, but should not interfere with arterial blood flow. It should be loose enough so that the fingers can be inserted under the band.

2. Wash the area around the bite or sting gently with a soap solution; if necessary, irrigate the area with a large amount of clean water. Never scrub the area; venom makes the tissues fragile. Make sure that the liquids flow away from the body to prevent further contamination.

3. Remove any jewelry or other constricting objects as soon as possible—ideally, before any swelling begins.

4. Lower the site of the bite or sting slightly below the level of the victim's heart.

5. Apply a cold compress to the site of an insect bite to relieve pain and swelling. Do not apply cold to snakebites; apply heat to injuries inflicted by marine animals.

6. Some experts advise the use of a constricting band in the treatment of snakebite (see Figure 23-29). *Follow local protocol.*

7. Observe the victim carefully for at least 30 minutes to determine whether he or she is developing the signs and symptoms of an allergic reaction (see Figure 23-30); treat as needed. For guidelines on the treatment of anaphylactic shock, see Chapter 6.

8. Keep the victim calm, limit physical activity, and keep the victim warm; arrange for transport as soon as possible. If the victim shows any signs of allergic reaction, the victim needs to be transported immediately.

9. Assist victim who carries an insect sting kit (see Figures 23-31 and 23-32).

Emergency Care for Snakebite

Specific treatment for snakebite varies, depending on the kind of snake involved.

1. Treat a *nonpoisonous snakebite* as you would any minor wound; clean with soap and water, cover with a dry sterile dressing, and seek medical advice.

2. For *rattlesnake bite,* keep the victim calm and quiet; if possible, the victim should not walk. Seek medical attention *immediately;* antivenin is available only in hospitals (partly because of its short shelf life) and must be administered within 4 hours.

3. For *coral snake bite,* gently wash the bite with soap and water and wrap the entire extremity with elastic bandages, exerting moderate pressure to slow the spread of venom. Seek medical attention immediately; an effective antivenin is available.

Emergency Care for Insect Stings

If the victim does not have any signs of allergic reaction:

1. Apply a paste of baking soda and water to a honeybee or bumblebee sting; rinse a wasp sting with lemon juice or vinegar.

2. Apply a topical steroid cream to reduce swelling and relieve itching.

Emergency Care for Marine Life Poisoning

Learning Objective 12 Describe and demonstrate emergency care of marine life poisoning.

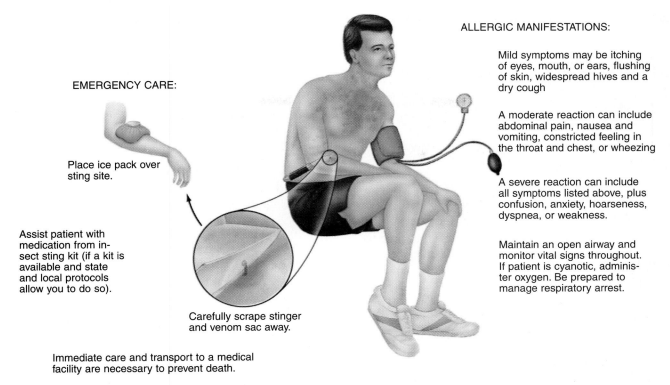

EMERGENCY CARE:

Place ice pack over sting site.

Assist patient with medication from insect sting kit (if a kit is available and state and local protocols allow you to do so).

Carefully scrape stinger and venom sac away.

Immediate care and transport to a medical facility are necessary to prevent death.

ALLERGIC MANIFESTATIONS:

Mild symptoms may be itching of eyes, mouth, or ears, flushing of skin, widespread hives and a dry cough

A moderate reaction can include abdominal pain, nausea and vomiting, constricted feeling in the throat and chest, or wheezing

A severe reaction can include all symptoms listed above, plus confusion, anxiety, hoarseness, dyspnea, or weakness.

Maintain an open airway and monitor vital signs throughout. If patient is cyanotic, administer oxygen. Be prepared to manage respiratory arrest.

Figure 23-30. *Allergic reaction to insect venom*

In general, bites and stings inflicted by marine life should be treated the same as soft-tissue injuries. However, follow these specific guidelines as needed:

- If the victim was stung by a jellyfish, coral, hydra, or anemone, carefully remove dried tentacles; do not rub the tentacles or touch them with your bare hands. Pour vinegar on the affected area to denature the toxin. Never rinse the site with fresh water; fresh water can cause the stinging mechanism to fire.

- Use tweezers to remove any material that sticks to the sting site on the surface of the flesh, then irrigate the wound with hot water.

- Never try to remove spines that are embedded in joints, deeply embedded in skin, or embedded in areas richly supplied by nerves or blood vessels.

- Apply heat or soak the affected area in hot water for at least 30 minutes.

Figure 23-31. *Assist the victim who has a history of allergic reactions to insect stings and carries a sting kit.*

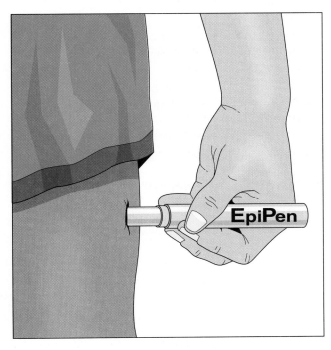

Figure 23-32. *Administering an EpiPen for anaphylactic shock caused by insect sting*

385

Removing a Tick

Learning Objective 13 Describe and demonstrate how to remove a tick.

A tick's mouth has a barb that helps it attach to its victim. To remove a tick:

1. Using tweezers, grasp the tick as close as possible to the point where it is attached to the skin.

2. Pull firmly and steadily until the tick is dislodged. Do not twist or jerk the tick, because that may result in incomplete removal. Avoid squashing an engorged tick during removal, because infected blood may spread contamination.

3. Wash the bite area thoroughly with soap and water and apply an antiseptic to the area.

4. Apply a cold pack to relieve any pain and swelling.

Never use a hot match, gasoline, rubbing alcohol, petroleum jelly, or fingernail polish to remove a tick. All have been shown to be ineffective and using them could injure the victim.

Progress Check

1. To remove a stinger, _____ it.
(*squeeze/twist/scrape*)

2. Apply _____ to all bites except snakebite and those of marine animals.
(*antiseptic/heat/cold*)

3. Monitor the victim continuously for signs of _____ .
(*anaphylactic shock/dyspnea/rapid pulse*)

4. Pour _____ on marine life stings to denature the toxin.
(*rubbing alcohol/vinegar/hydrogen peroxide*)

5. Remove the barbs of marine life unless they are embedded in _____ .
(*the chest/a joint/the abdomen*)

6. When you remove a tick, be careful not to _____ it.
(*squeeze/break/twist*)

SUMMARY

- Most poisonous snakes have large fangs, elliptical pupils, and a characteristic pit between the eyes and the mouth. The exception is the coral snake, which has small teeth and round pupils.

- The signs and symptoms of pit viper bite occur almost immediately; those of coral snake bite may be delayed by as long as 8 hours.

- Pit viper bites cause severe, burning pain and marked swelling; coral snake bites cause little or no pain or swelling.

- Generally, medical help is not needed for insect bites unless itching persists for longer than 2 days, infection develops, there are signs of allergic reaction, or the insect is poisonous. Otherwise, insect bites are cared for the same as other wounds.

- The bite of a black widow spider causes pain and spasms in the shoulders, back, chest, and abdomen and a rigid, boardlike abdomen.

- The bite of the brown recluse spider is especially serious because it does not heal; surgical grafting is necessary.

- Tick bites are especially serious because ticks carry disease, such as Lyme disease and Rocky Mountain spotted fever.

- Marine life venom causes more widespread tissue damage than venom from land animals, and it is destroyed by heat rather than cold.

KEY TERMS

Make sure you understand the following key terms:

- coral snake
- elliptical pupils
- pit viper
- black widow spider
- brown recluse spider

Student: _____ Date: _____

Course: _____ Section #: _____

PART 1 • True/False

If you believe the statement is true, circle the T. If you believe the statement is false, circle the F.

T   F   **1.** Two of the most common signs and symptoms of pit viper bite are immediate and severe burning pain and swelling.

T   F   **2.** Ice should be applied to pit viper bites.

T   F   **3.** Coral snake bites leave the same distinct fang marks as a pit viper bite.

T   F   **4.** Venoms of most aquatic animals are destroyed by heat.

T   F   **5.** Tentacle stings from a jellyfish should be cleansed with rubbing alcohol.

PART 2 • Multiple Choice

For each item, circle the correct answer or the phrase that best completes the statement.

1. Most poisonous snakes have
  a. multicolored rings around the body
  b. elliptical pupils
  c. small teeth
  d. flat heads

2. Venoms of aquatic organisms
  a. may cause severe vomiting
  b. can cause anaphylactic shock
  c. are destroyed by heat
  d. are activated by cold

3. Which of the following is *not* a symptom of coral snake bite?
  a. blurred vision
  b. paralysis
  c. black and blue discoloration
  d. drowsiness and slurred speech

4. Coral snakes inject poison through
  a. long fangs in the forward part of the upper jaw
  b. long fangs in both the upper and lower jaw
  c. a chewing motion
  d. long fangs in the lower jaw

5. The first step in providing emergency care for a honeybee sting is to
  a. grasp the stinger with a pair of tweezers and gently pull it out
  b. apply wet mud to the sting area; let it dry
  c. apply baking soda to the affected area
  d. remove the stinger by scraping it gently

6. Which of the following is *not* recommended in the care of marine life poisoning?
  a. pour vinegar on the site of the sting
  b. apply heat
  c. carefully remove tentacles or other material on the surface of the skin
  d. irrigate the wound with water

7. Which of the following is *not* a sign or symptom of a poisonous snakebite?
  a. severe pain and burning
  b. swelling of the wound
  c. discoloration of the wound
  d. a series of small, shallow puncture wounds

8. Characteristics of the majority of poisonous snakes include
  a. irregularly shaped blotches on the skin
  b. fangs
  c. elliptical pupils
  d. all of the above

Match each characteristic with the type of snake.

Snake

A. Poisonous
B. Nonpoisonous

Characteristic

_____ Bite is a series of small, shallow puncture wounds

_____ Wound begins to swell and discolor

_____ Differently shaped blotches on background of pink, yellow, olive, tan, gray, or brown skin

_____ Elliptical pupils

_____ Large, triangular head

_____ Round pupils

_____ Large, hollow fangs

_____ Immediate pain and burning from a bite

_____ Pit between the eyes and mouth

- You are hiking in the foothills just outside your community, about 20 minutes from town. You find a teenage boy in shorts who has been bitten by a snake on the lower leg. There are two distinct puncture wounds. The boy is experiencing severe pain and burning; is nauseated and sweating; and feels weak. His heartbeat is rapid.
- A young woman who was just stung by a bee is dizzy, is short of breath, has difficulty swallowing, and has generalized itching and swelling.

24

Burn Emergencies

Learning Objectives

When you have mastered the material in this chapter, you will be able to

1 Understand the various burn classifications and how they relate to the anatomy of the skin

2 Identify the characteristics of first-, second-, and third-degree burns

3 Calculate the extent of burns using the Rule of Nines

4 Explain how to assess the severity of burns

5 Describe appropriate burn management for thermal and radiant burns

6 Identify the signs and symptoms of inhalation injuries

7 Describe appropriate emergency care for inhalation injuries

8 Describe appropriate emergency care for chemical burns

9 Understand how electrical energy and lightning can injure the body

10 Describe appropriate emergency care for electrical shock

11 Describe appropriate emergency care for injuries inflicted by lightning

SQ3R Plus

- **Survey** to set goals for studying.
- Ask **questions** as you **read.**
- Stop frequently to **recite** and **review.**
- **Write** a summary of key points.
- **Reflect** on the importance of this material and its relevance in your life.

On July 17, 1998, 11-year-old Kevin Thompson took a can of lighter fluid from his family's garage to a friend's house, where he and three other children planned to make a "fire ball" to settle a neighborhood quarrel. Huddled at the side of the house, Jonathan Parker crumpled up a section of the morning newspaper, and Kevin doused the wad with fluid. Twelve-year-old Quinn Merritt struck a large wooden kitchen match and dropped it on the damp papers. Flames exploded from the paper; neighbor Steve Harding, hearing their screams, ran to the boys. Jonathan's shirt was ablaze; his left hand was blistered, his right hand and forearm charred. Steve ripped off his jacket and used it to smother first the shirt, then the burning newspapers. Steve noticed that Jonathan's nasal hair was singed, but knew from his screams that he was still breathing. Steve sent Kevin into the house to call 9-1-1 and told him to bring a clean sheet from the linen closet. Steve then helped Jonathan lie down on the grass, covered Jonathan's arms and chest with the sheet Kevin had found, and continued to watch the boy's breathing while waiting for the ambulance to arrive. Steve's quick action helped confine the injury and prevent contamination and infection.

MORE THAN TWO MILLION BURN ACCIDENTS OCCUR EACH year in the United States. Most burns occur at home, and most deaths from burns are a result of house fires. Of those who are burned—in fires, by chemicals, by the sun, in automobile accidents, or in other kinds of accidents—more than 12,000 die as a result of their burns and almost one million require long-term hospitalization. Burns are a leading cause of accidental death in the United States; the number of productive years lost to burns is greater than those lost to cancer, heart disease, and strokes.

Burns can be complex injuries. In addition to the damage to tissues caused by the burn itself, a burn injury can impair the body's normal fluid/electrolyte balance, temperature, thermal regulation, joint function, manual dexterity, and physical appearance. There is also often associated trauma—most often internal injury, blunt trauma, head injury, multiple fractures, and serious lacerations.

This chapter teaches how to determine the seriousness of a burn, gives guidelines for the management of a burn, and discusses the care of victims who have sustained inhalation injuries, chemical burns, and electrical burns, including injuries from lightning.

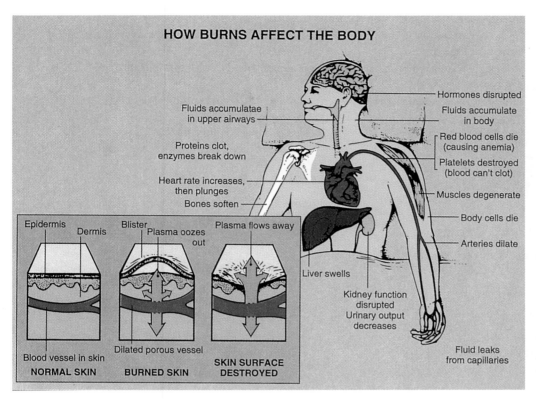

Figure 24-1. Burns may cause shock by damaging surface tissue and dilating underlying blood vessels, which may lead to extensive loss of plasma.

• Section 1 •
ASSESSMENT OF BURNS

The seriousness of a burn is determined by the following factors:

- Degree of the burn
- Percentage of the body burned
- Severity of the burn
- Location of the burn
- Accompanying complications (such as preexisting physical or mental conditions)
- Age of the victim

Figure 24-1 illustrates how burns affect the body.

Degree of the Burn

Learning Objective 1 Understand the various burn classifications and how they relate to the anatomy of the skin.

Learning Objective 2 Identify the characteristics of first-, second-, and third-degree burns.

Burns are classified by degree of damage to the skin and underlying tissues (see Figures 24-2 through 24-11 on pages 392 and 393) as **first-, second-,** or **third-degree** (see Table 24-1 on page 393). Most burns represent a combination of classifications (see Figure 24-12 on page 394). Part of the skin may be burned to the first degree, part to the second degree, and part may be burned to the third degree.

first-degree burn A burn that involves only the epidermis, or outer layer of skin, characterized by pain and redness

second-degree burn A burn that involves both the epidermal and dermal layers of the skin, characterized by blistering, swelling, and pain

third-degree burn A full-thickness burn, involving all layers of the skin as well as fat, muscle, and bone; a third-degree burn is characterized by dry, leathery, charred skin

Figure 24-2. *Scalds are the most common causes of burns in children under 8 years old.*

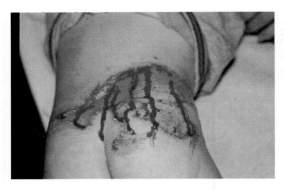

Figure 24-3. *Contact burn from a steam iron*

Figure 24-4. *Second- and third-degree burns*

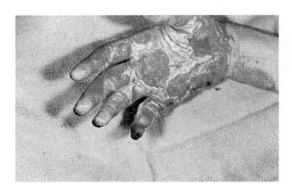

Figure 24-5. *Third-degree burns*

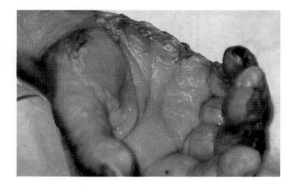

Figure 24-6. *Second- and third-degree burns*

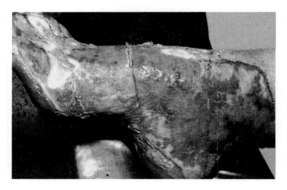

Figure 24-7. *Second- and third-degree burns*

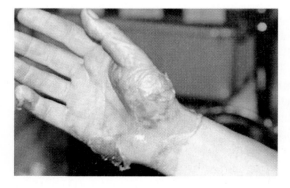

Figure 24-8. *Second-degree burn*

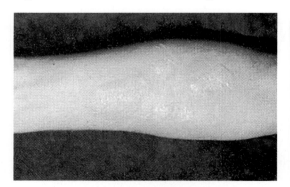

Figure 24-9. *Second-degree burn*

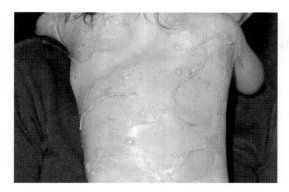

Figure 24-10. Second-degree burn

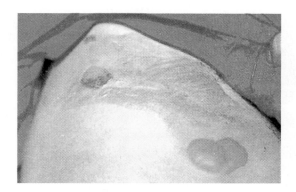

Figure 24-11. Second-degree burn

Table 24-1
Classifications of Burns

	First Degree	Second Degree	Third Degree
Causes	Flash of electricity, flame, scald, the sun	Contact with hot liquids or solids, flash of electricity, flame, chemicals, the sun	Contact with hot liquids or solids, flames, chemicals, or electricity
Layers of Skin Affected	Epidermal layer only	Epidermis and dermis	All dermal layers and subcutaneous tissues
Appearance	Skin surface is dry and reddened; no blisters or swelling	Skin is moist and mottled, ranging from white to cherry red; blistered	Skin is dry and leathery; charred blood vessels are often visible; skin is a mixture of white, dark, and charred
Symptoms	Extremely painful	Extremely painful	Victim may feel no pain because nerve endings have been destroyed
Healing Time	2 to 5 days	5 to 21 days	Weeks to years
Prognosis	No scarring; temporary discoloration	Some scarring	Usually requires surgery and skin grafting

Percentage of Body Burned

Learning Objective 3 Calculate the extent of burns using the Rule of Nines.

There are two methods you can use to determine quickly the percentage of the body that has been burned: the **Rule of Nines** and the **palmar surface method**.

The Rule of Nines (see Figure 24-13 on page 394) divides the body into regions: head and neck (9 percent), posterior trunk (18 percent), anterior trunk (18 percent), each upper extremity (9 percent), each lower extremity (18 percent), and external genitalia (1 percent). In an infant, the head and neck are considered to be 18 percent and the lower extremities are each considered to be 14 percent of the body surface.

Rule of Nines A method of estimating how much body surface was burned by mentally dividing the body into regions, each representing 9 percent (or a multiple of 9 percent) of the body surface

palmar surface method A method of using the size of the victim's palm to estimate the percentage of body surface that has been burned

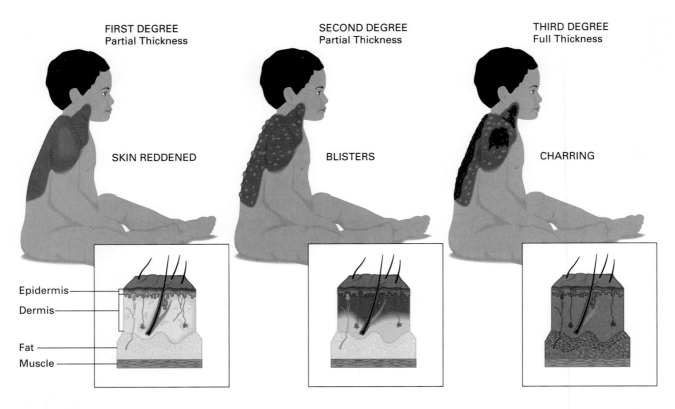

FIRST DEGREE
Partial Thickness

SKIN REDDENED

SECOND DEGREE
Partial Thickness

BLISTERS

THIRD DEGREE
Full Thickness

CHARRING

Epidermis
Dermis

Fat
Muscle

Figure 24-12. *Classification of burns*

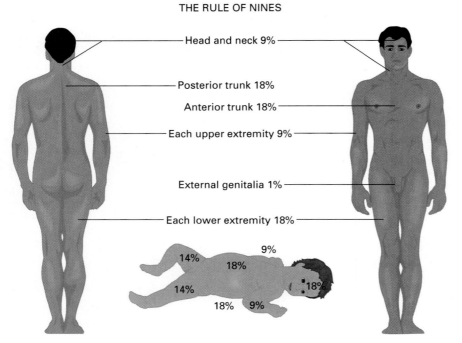

THE RULE OF NINES

Head and neck 9%

Posterior trunk 18%

Anterior trunk 18%

Each upper extremity 9%

External genitalia 1%

Each lower extremity 18%

9%
14%   18%
14%
18%
18%   9%

*Figure 24-13. The Rule of
Nines is a quick method of
estimating how much body
surface is burned.*

An alternative method is the palmar surface method. The palm of the victim's hand is equal to approximately 1 percent of the body surface, regardless of the victim's age. You can estimate the burned surface by comparing its size to the size of the victim's palm.

Severity of the Burn

Learning Objective 4 Explain how to assess the severity of burns.

You should assess the depth of the burn as soon as you have determined the extent of the body surface affected. A full-thickness burn (third-degree burn) is one that extends through all layers of skin into the subcutaneous tissues; first- and second-degree burns, which involve only part of the skin layers, are referred to as partial-thickness burns.

As a very rough rule, use the following guide to guess the depth of a burn:

- If the burn is a scald on bare skin and the victim is an adolescent or adult, the burn is probably superficial, involving only the outer layer of skin, because the heat from such a burn dissipates rapidly. If the victim is an infant or an elderly person, the burn may involve additional skin layers.

- A thermal burn (a burn caused by flames) is usually partial- or full-thickness.

- If the burn was caused by hot grease, it is probably a full-thickness burn. Grease cools slowly and is difficult to remove; therefore, it may cause extensive damage before it can be removed.

- Burns caused by electricity or chemicals are almost always full-thickness burns because of the extensive, unseen damage that accompanies even apparently minor skin injuries. Victims with such burns are almost always hospitalized so physicians can monitor vital signs and functioning of major organs.

Use Table 24-2 to gauge the severity of a burn (and see Figure 24-14 on page 396).

Remember—victims with even *minor* burns of the face, eyes, ears, hands, feet, or genital area need immediate transport to a hospital.

Location of the Burn

Certain areas of the body are more critically damaged by burns than others. Burns on the face or neck should be seen by a physician immediately because of possible burns to the eyes or possible respiratory complications.

Other locations that are particularly critical in burn injuries are the hands, feet, and external genitalia. Any burn to the upper body is more serious than a burn of similar extent and degree on the lower body. Victims with burns in any of these areas should be taken to a hospital or burn center immediately.

Accompanying Complications and Age of the Victim

People who have major diseases, such as heart disease or diabetes, or who have other injuries will always react more severely to a burn, even a minor one.

The age of the victim may also be a complicating factor. Children under the age of 5 and adults over the age of 60 tolerate burns very poorly. In an elderly patient, a burn covering only 20 percent of the body can often be fatal. Because the elderly and the young have extremely thin skin, they will sustain much deeper burns from a much less severe source.

Table 24-2
Severity of Burns

	Critical Burn	Moderate Burn	Minor Burn
First Degree	More than 75% of an adult's body surface	50–75% of an adult's body surface	Less than 20% of an adult's or child's body surface
Second Degree	More than 30% of body surface in adults, more than 20% in a child	15–30% of body surface in adults, 10–20% in a child	Less than 15% of body surface in adults, less than 10% in a child
Third Degree	More than 10% of the body surface in adults, more than 2–3% in a child; burns that involve the face, hands, feet, or genital area	2–10% of the body surface, excluding the face, hands, feet, and genital area	Less than 2% of the body surface
Other Types	Burns complicated by respiratory tract injuries, other major injuries, or fractures; burns of any degree in victims with serious underlying medical conditions; most chemical burns; all electrical burns	Otherwise critical burns that do not have complicating factors	

Critical burns include:

- All inhalation injuries.

- Electrical burns.

- Deep acid burns.

- Burns in patients with underlying physical or medical conditions.

- First-degree burns that cover more than 75% of the body surface.

- Second-degree burns covering more than 30% of the body surface in an adult, 20% or more in a child.

- Third-degree burns covering more than 10% of body surface in an adult and 2% to 3% in a child.

- Third-degree burns involving the face, eyes, ears, hands, feet, or genitalia.

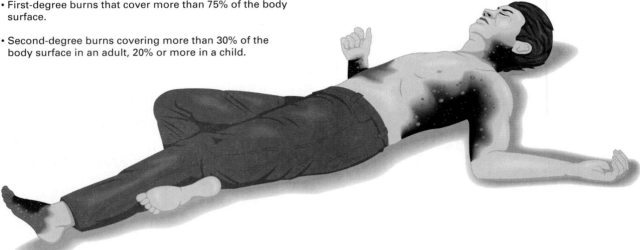

Figure 24-14. Critical burns are burns complicated by respiratory tract injury and other major injuries.

The young and elderly also have a disproportionate fluid-to-surface-area ratio, so even a small fluid loss can result in serious problems. An additional problem is immunity: The immune system is incompletely developed in the young child and is usually compromised in the elderly.

Progress Check

1. In a first-degree burn, the skin is _____ and extremely painful.
   (mottled/reddened/moist)

2. A second-degree burn affects both the epidermal and dermal layers of skin and is characterized by _____ .
   (blistering/oozing/redness)

3. A full-thickness, or third-degree, burn can extend to the bone and may cause the victim little or no pain because _____ .
   (the victim is in shock/the nerve endings are destroyed/the victim is usually unconscious)

4. You can quickly assess the amount of body surface involved by using the Rule of Nines, which divides the body into _____ .
   (regions that each represent 9 percent of the body surface/ nine regions/nine areas most critical if burned)

5. The most serious burn in an adult is _____ .
   (a third-degree burn covering 10 percent of the body/a second-degree burn covering 30 percent of the body/an electrical burn)

6. Burns on the face are considered especially serious because of possible _____ .
   (disfigurement/injury to the mouth/damage to the eyes)

• Section 2 •
BURN MANAGEMENT

The first priority in emergency care is to prevent further injury. The problems most often associated with burns are

- Airway or respiratory difficulties

- Related musculoskeletal injuries

- Loss of body fluids, contributing to shock

- Pain, contributing to shock
- Anxiety, contributing to shock
- Swelling
- Infection due to destruction of skin tissue

General Care of Thermal and Radiant Burns

The most common burns are thermal burns (caused by flame) and radiant burns (caused by radiant heat, such as the sun). Critical to the success of first aid is establishing an accurate history and assessing the extent of injury. Ask when the burn occurred, what has been done to care for the burn, whether the victim was trapped in an area with steam or smoke, whether the victim lost consciousness, what caused the burn, and whether the victim has any history of significant heart disease, diabetes, or other serious illness.

Emergency Care

Learning Objective 5 Describe appropriate burn management for thermal and radiant burns.

Care of a thermal or radiant burn must start immediately—preferably at the moment of burning. Unfortunately, this early emergency care is too often administered by well-meaning but terrified family members or bystanders; care may be so poor that caregivers end up *hurting* the victim instead of helping. Remember: A First Aider does not *treat* a burn, but merely cares for the burn until the victim can be transported to a hospital or burn center for thorough treatment.

Your first priority is to prevent further injury to the victim or injury to others and *to stop the burning.* Specific guidelines for the care of other types of burns are listed later in this chapter; regardless of the type of burn, follow these general guidelines:

1. Remove the victim from the source of the burn. Move the victim far enough away from a fire so no smoke is inhaled; remove the victim from the source of a chemical spill; if the victim was struck by lightning, move to shelter.

2. Eliminate the cause of the burn—put out the fire, wash away the chemicals, and so on. Immerse scald or grease burns in cold water to stop the burning (see Figure 24-15); if the victim's clothes are on fire, douse the victim with water and remove all clothing, jewelry, and shoes that are not sticking to the skin. Roll the victim on the ground to extinguish flames only as a last resort; the po-

Figure 24-15. Cooling a burn by submerging the burned area in cold running water

tential for wound contamination is great, and infection is a major killer of burn victims.

3. Assess ABCDs, and manage respiratory and cardiac complications. Immediately assist with breathing if the victim
   - Wheezes or coughs while breathing
   - Has a sooty or smoky smell on the breath
   - Has particles of soot in the saliva
   - Has burned mucous membranes in the mouth or nose

4. Activate the EMS system as soon as possible.

5. Continue to assess the victim's vital signs until medical help arrives; swelling of the respiratory tissues following a burn can cause the vital signs to change suddenly.

6. For a first-degree or mild second-degree burn, cover the burn with a cold, wet cloth or immerse the burned area in cold water until it no longer burns, in or out of the water. Never cool more than 10 percent of a child's body area or 20 percent of an adult's body area. Never break blisters. Apply aloe vera gel or a nonscented moisturizer to keep skin moist. Cover more severe burns with a sterile, nonstick burn dressing or sheet; if less than 10 percent of the body surface is burned, the skin is not broken, and the victim is not in a cold environment, cover the burned area with cool, wet towels or compresses. A standard burn-care kit will contain compresses (see Figure 24-16 on page 398). Never use plastic as a dressing; it traps moisture and encourages the growth of bacteria. *Never use grease or fat on a burn.* Never use ice packs on a burn. (*Note:* There is some disagreement among authorities as to whether a burn dressing should be wet or dry; *follow local protocol.*) Figures 24-17 through 24-24 illustrate care of burns.

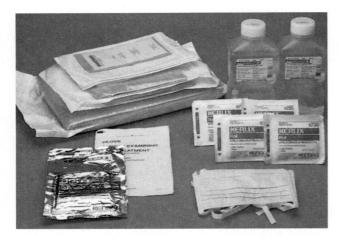

Figure 24-16. *Burn-care kit*

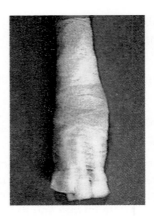

Figure 24-17. *Cover burn with dry dressing.*

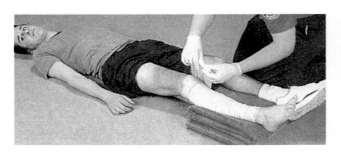

Figure 24-18. *Cover burn and treat victim for shock.*

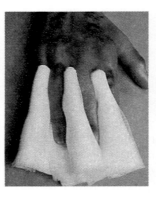

Figure 24-19. *Separate burned fingers with gauze.*

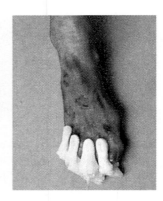

Figure 24-20. *Separate burned toes with gauze.*

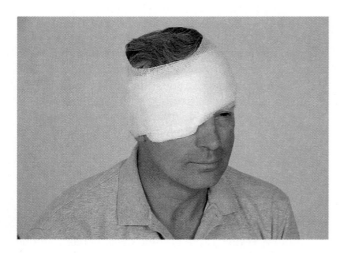

Figure 24-21. *Apply moist, sterile pads to burned eyes.*

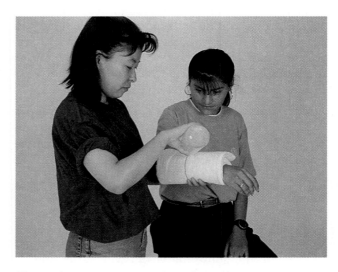

Figure 24-22. *Remoistening a burn dressing*

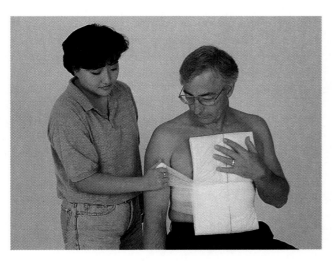

Figure 24-23. Application of bulky burn dressing for moderate and critical burns

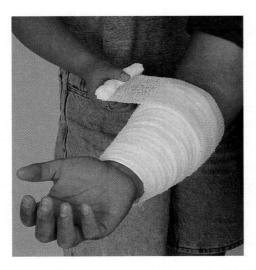

Figure 24-24. Cover moderate and critical burns with thick, clean, dry dressing and loosely bandage in place.

Progress Check

1. One of the most common types of burn is _____ .
   (chemical/thermal/electrical)

2. The first priority in burn care is _____ .
   (preventing further injury/removing the source of the burn/moving the victim away from the source of the burn)

3. You should always check for _____ complications immediately.
   (burn/shock/respiratory)

4. If less than 10 percent of the body surface is burned, cover the burned area with _____ .
   (ice packs/adherent gauze/nonstick dressings)

• Section 3 •
INHALATION INJURIES

More than half of all fire-related deaths are caused by smoke inhalation. Eighty percent of those who die in residential fires do so because they have inhaled heated air, smoke, or other toxic gases—not because they have been burned to death. Suspect **inhalation injury** in any victim of thermal burn, especially if the victim was confined in an enclosed space at any time during the fire.

There are three causes of inhalation injuries that accompany burns:

* Heat inhalation
* Inhalation of toxic chemicals or smoke
* Inhalation of carbon monoxide (the most common burn-associated inhalation injury)

When heat is inhaled, mucous membranes and linings get scorched, and swelling partially blocks the airway. Because edema (swelling) and other damage can be progressive, the inhalation injury may appear to be mild at first, but may become more severe. Depending on what was burned, how completely the materials were burned, how long the victim was exposed to the smoke, and whether the victim was in a confined space, the symptoms may occur within a few minutes, but may not appear for many hours.

Signs and Symptoms

Learning Objective 6 Identify the signs and symptoms of inhalation injuries.

Specific signs and symptoms of inhalation injury (see Figures 24-25 and 24–26 on page 400) are

* Facial burns
* Singed nasal hairs
* Burned specks of carbon in the saliva
* A sooty or smoky smell on the breath
* Respiratory distress, accompanied by
  * Restriction of chest-wall movement
  * Restlessness
  * Chest tightness
  * Difficulty in swallowing
  * Hoarseness
  * Coughing

inhalation injury An injury caused by breathing in heat, toxic chemicals, smoke, or carbon monoxide

- Cyanosis
- Noisy breathing
- Actual burns of the mucous membranes in the mouth or nose

Assume respiratory injury if in doubt, especially if facial burns are present.

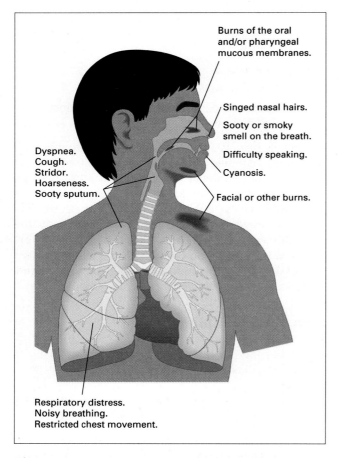

Burns of the oral and/or pharyngeal mucous membranes.

Singed nasal hairs.

Sooty or smoky smell on the breath.

Difficulty speaking.

Cyanosis.

Facial or other burns.

Dyspnea.
Cough.
Stridor.
Hoarseness.
Sooty sputum.

Respiratory distress.
Noisy breathing.
Restricted chest movement.

Figure 24-25. Signs and symptoms of inhalation burns

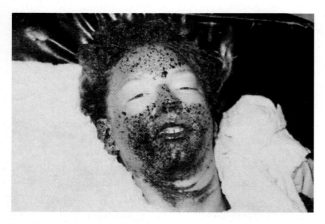

Figure 24-26. Facial inhalation burns

Inhalation of Noxious Fumes

The most critical respiratory injury results from the inhalation of noxious chemicals, **carbon monoxide** fumes, or smoke. **Noxious** fumes can result from the burning of a number of ordinary household objects, such as carpets, draperies, wall coverings, floor coverings, upholstery, and lacquered wood veneer on furniture. There are almost three hundred toxic substances that result from the burning of wood alone.

When noxious fumes are inhaled, mucosa in the lungs swell and break, leaking fluid into the nearby alveolar spaces and damaging the cilia. Mucus builds up and plugs the air passages. The final result is reduced oxygen exchange, which can eventually cause death if left untreated.

Carbon Monoxide

Carbon monoxide is released during the combustion of most things, especially cellulose materials, such as wood, paper, and cotton. Carbon monoxide poisoning is the major cause of death at the scene of a fire. Because carbon monoxide is colorless, odorless, and tasteless, it is extremely difficult to detect.

Because burns usually do not alter levels of consciousness, assume that any burn victim who is unconscious is suffering from carbon monoxide poisoning. Other signs and symptoms include

- Headache
- Weakness
- Nausea and/or vomiting
- Loss of manual dexterity
- Confusion, lethargy, irrational or reckless behavior

Do not wait for the traditional sign of cherry-red skin—it is a very late sign, and may not even occur until after death.

Emergency Care

Learning Objective 7 Describe appropriate emergency care for inhalation injuries.

To prevent further respiratory complications

1. Place the victim in an upright position to allow for easier breathing unless injuries contraindicate it.
2. If respiratory distress occurs, maintain an adequate airway.
3. Remove the victim as far as possible from the source of the toxic fumes, especially if it is a fire; try to situate the victim in fresh air.
4. Give mouth-to-mouth ventilation if the victim has stopped breathing; clear all foreign particles from the airway first.

5. Remove any clothing that may restrict chest movement, including neckties and necklaces, if they are not sticking to the skin.

6. Activate the EMS system immediately.

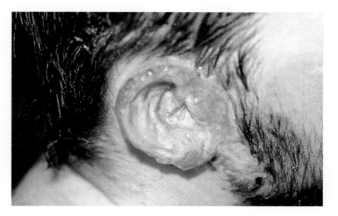

Figure 24-27. Chemical burn

Progress Check

1. Suspect inhalation injury in any victim of thermal burn, especially if the victim was _____ .
   (in contact with chemicals/in an enclosed space/exposed to carbon monoxide)

2. The most common burn-associated inhalation injury is caused by _____ .
   (smoke/heat/carbon monoxide)

3. The signs and symptoms of inhalation injury may be delayed because the _____ associated with it is progressive.
   (mucus buildup/swelling/cilia damage)

4. Always assume respiratory injury if the _____ is burned.
   (face/throat/head)

5. Always assume that any burn victim who is _____ is suffering from carbon monoxide poisoning.
   (in a confined space/burned on the face/unconscious)

• Section 4 •
CHEMICAL BURNS

It is extremely difficult to assess the depth and severity of chemical burns (see Figure 24-27) in a first aid setting; therefore, the general guideline is to *treat all chemical burns aggressively*. Chemicals continue to burn as long as they are in contact with the skin, and chemical burns are considered to be critical burns.

Every victim of chemical burns needs to be transported to a hospital. Speed is essential: The more quickly you are able to remove the source of the burn and initiate care, the less severe the burn will be.

Emergency Care

Learning Objective 8 Describe appropriate emergency care for chemical burns.

Before beginning emergency care, make sure it is safe to approach the victim; if not, wait for trained rescue personnel to arrive. During each step of rescue, make sure to protect yourself from contamina-

tion. If possible, put on latex or rubber gloves to protect yourself from injury before you start caring for the victim.

1. Brush any dry powder off the skin, then flush the burned area vigorously in a steady stream of water; a shower or garden hose is ideal. (The pressure should not be too great; high pressure will drive chemicals into the pores of the skin.) Irrigate the area continuously for at least 20 minutes under a steady stream of water. *There are three important exceptions to this rule:*

   • Lime powder creates a corrosive when mixed with water; make sure that all traces have been removed from not only the skin, but the clothing before flushing with water (see Figures 24-28 through 24-30 on page 402).

   • Phenol (carbolic acid) should be washed off with alcohol; the burn area should then be irrigated with water.

   • Concentrated sulfuric acid produces heat when mixed with water and may cause greater burn injuries unless flushed vigorously with a hose or in a shower. *Follow local protocol.*

2. While flushing the burn area, remove the victim's clothing, shoes, stockings, and jewelry.

3. If the victim is able, have him or her wash with soap and water, then rinse thoroughly, after you have finished irrigating the burn.

carbon monoxide An odorless, colorless, tasteless, poisonous gas resulting from incomplete combustion of anything containing carbon
noxious Poisonous

Figure 24-28. Lime powder should be brushed off the skin before flushing with water.

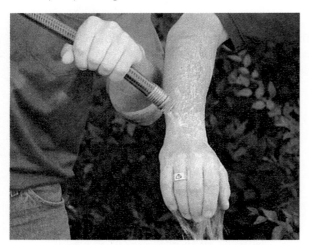

Figure 24-29. After brushing off lime powder, flush the skin with water—if possible, with copious amounts of water, as with a garden hose.

Figure 24-30. A chemical burn victim flushing himself off under an emergency wash/shower system at the worksite. (Courtesy of Lab Safety Supply.)

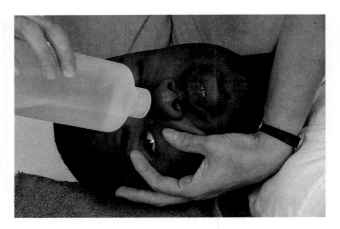

Figure 24-31. Flushing a chemical burn of the eye

4. If any chemicals splash into the victim's eyes, use a faucet or hose on low pressure to irrigate the eyes for at least 20 minutes (see Figure 24-31); make sure contact lenses are removed. You can also use a pan, bucket, cup, or bottle; make sure to irrigate well underneath the lids.

5. When you have finished flushing, cover the burned area with a dry sterile dressing.

6. Activate the EMS system as soon as possible. If you can, get the name of the chemical, or send the container to the hospital with the victim.

Note: Never try to use an antidote, and do not try to neutralize a burned area with alkali or acid solutions; you may intensify the injury.

Progress Check

1. Because it is so difficult to determine the depth and severity of a chemical burn in a first aid setting, the general guideline is to treat all chemical burns

   _____ .
   (by flushing with water/aggressively/immediately)

2. Before beginning emergency care for a chemical burn, you must _____ .
   (activate the EMS system/find the chemical container/ make sure it is safe to approach the victim)

3. Immediately treat a chemical burn by irrigating the area for at least _____ minutes.
   (20/30/40)

4. After you remove the victim's clothing, continue irrigating the area for at least _____ minutes.
   (20/30/40)

5. The most essential part of caring for chemical burns is _____ .
   (speed/accuracy/timing)

• Section 5 •
ELECTRICAL BURNS

Approximately 3,000 electrical injuries each year in the United States cause burns, and approximately 40 percent of all victims die as a result of their injuries. Understanding electrical burns is critical; it will not only enable you to help a victim, but may also save your own life.

Protecting Yourself and the Victim

If you feel a tingling sensation in your legs as you approach the victim, *stop*—that sensation indicates that the ground is energized and that you are at risk of electrocution. When approaching any accident that involves downed power lines or other electrical hazards

- Look for downed wires whenever a vehicle has struck a power pole. If it is dark, use a flashlight to inspect the poles and the surrounding area.

- *Never attempt to move downed wires!* Notify the power company and request an emergency crew.

- If a downed power line is lying across a wrecked vehicle, *do not touch the vehicle,* even if the victims inside are seriously injured. If you touch the vehicle, you will probably die. If the victims in the car are conscious, warn them not to leave the vehicle.

    If the car begins to burn, instruct victims in the car to open the door and jump as far away as they can from the car. If they touch the car and the ground at the same time, the current will kill them.

- If a victim is holding a power tool, look for cords; the tool does not have to be on to present an electrical hazard.

- If a victim is in a pool, turn off all power at the main switch before entering the water.

- If a victim is found in a bathtub with an electrical appliance that has energized the water, *pull the plug of the appliance before you touch the victim.*

Types of Electrical Burns

There are three general kinds of electrical burns:

- **Thermal burns,** caused when electricity causes flames that then burn the skin; with thermal burns, electricity does not actually pass through the body.

- **Contact burns,** which occur where the current is most intense, at the points where electrical current enters and exits the body (see Figure 24-32).

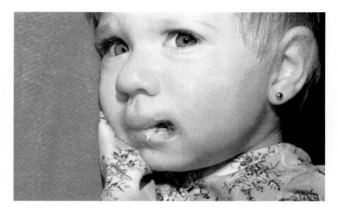

Figure 24-32. Electrical contact burn caused by chewing on an electrical cord

- **Arcing injuries** (or **flash burns**), caused when a current jumps from one surface to another, burning nearby skin, electricity does not actually pass through the body.

Severity of Electrical Shock

The severity of electrical shock is determined by the following factors:

- Voltage and amperage of the current
- Amount of time the victim was exposed to the shock
- Amount of moisture on the victim
- Amount of the victim's body surface that is in contact with water
- Amount of insulation worn by the victim
- Area of the body through which the current passes
- Type of current (AC or DC)

Signs and Symptoms of Electrocution

Learning Objective 9 Understand how electrical energy and lightning can injure the body.

thermal burn A burn caused by flames

contact burns Burns caused by touching either a hot surface or a live electrical circuit

arcing injury (flash burn) An injury caused when an electrical current jumps from one surface to another; nearby skin is burned, but electricity does not actually pass through the skin

If you are unsure whether a person has been shocked, examine the victim for the following signs and symptoms (see Figures 24–33 and 24–34):

- Dazed and confused condition
- Obvious and severe burns on the skin surface
- Unconsciousness
- Weak, irregular, or absent pulse
- Shallow, irregular, or absent breathing
- Possibility of multiple severe fractures due to intense muscular contractions

Emergency Care for Electrical Shock

Learning Objective 10 Describe appropriate emergency care for electrical shock.

To care for a victim of electrical shock

1. Your first priority is to protect yourself; follow the guidelines outlined on page 403. Do not approach the victim unless you can do so safely.

2. Check the victim's breathing and pulse; start CPR immediately, even if you are unsure about the ex-

tent of injury. (Most electrical injury victims—even those in full arrest—can be successfully resuscitated with vigorous CPR.)

3. If the victim fell or was thrown, treat for spinal injuries.

4. Activate the EMS system immediately. If the victim is conscious and his or her condition is not urgent, provide basic burn care for entrance and exit wounds (see Figure 24-35), and splint fractures.

5. Treat the victim for shock.

Note: A victim of electrical shock may become hysterical and start running around in circles; force the victim to lie down and keep quiet; maintain body temperature.

Lightning Injuries

Lightning injures hundreds of people every year in the United States, but approximately two-thirds of those injured can be revived. *Always* assume that a victim of lightning strike has sustained multiple injuries; most are knocked down or thrown, so also assume spinal injury. A victim who has been struck by light-

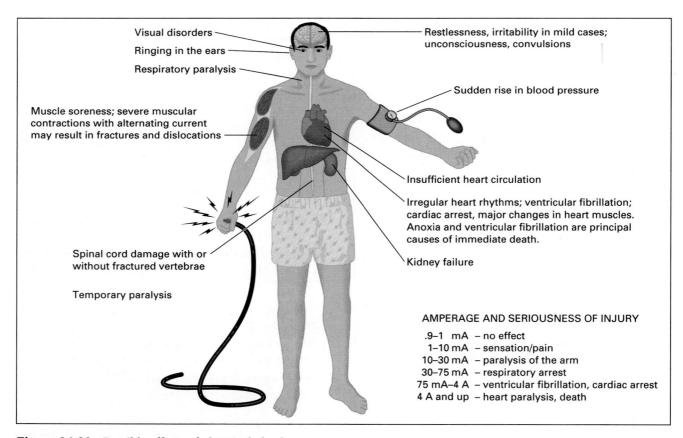

Figure 24-33. Possible effects of electrical shock

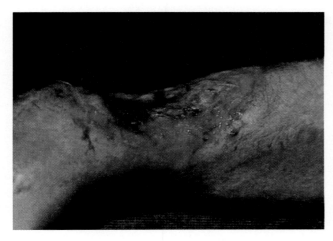

Figure 24-34. Deep third-degree electrical burn

Figure 24-36. Lightning burn

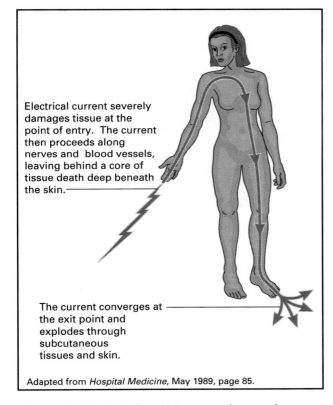

Electrical current severely damages tissue at the point of entry. The current then proceeds along nerves and blood vessels, leaving behind a core of tissue death deep beneath the skin.

The current converges at the exit point and explodes through subcutaneous tissues and skin.

Adapted from *Hospital Medicine*, May 1989, page 85.

Figure 24-35. Look for two separate burns when electricity is the cause of injury.

ning does *not* hold a charge, so it is safe to handle and treat the victim.

In addition to the burn (see Figures 24-36 and 24-37), lightning strike victims usually sustain injury to the following body systems:

- The nervous system
- The sensory system
- The skin
- The heart and the vascular system

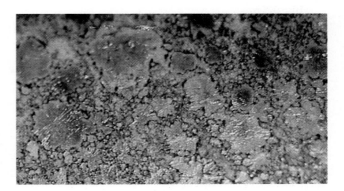

Figure 24-37. Lightning burn

Emergency Care of Lightning Injuries

Learning Objective 11 Describe appropriate emergency care for injuries inflicted by lightning.

The goal of first aid for lightning victims is to oxygenate the heart and the brain until the heart regains its ability to function. You should always continue resuscitation (artificial ventilation and chest compressions) of lightning victims longer than you would victims of other trauma—even if the victim appears lifeless. Victims of lightning strike have a greater chance of resuscitation than victims of cardiac or respiratory arrest due to other causes because when lightning hits the body all metabolism ceases, delaying tissue death. (Victims of lightning strike have been resuscitated as long as 30 minutes after the strike without any residual damage.)

If the strike occurred in an open area, quickly move the victim to a protected area to reduce the chance of a second strike. If a group has been struck, care for the apparently dead first. Those who display vital signs will probably recover spontaneously.

To care for lightning strike victims

1. Activate the EMS system immediately.

2. Survey the scene, assess what happened, and make sure the victim is safe from further injury. Remove

debris that has fallen on the victim, and move the victim away from any source of electricity.

3. Assess breathing and pulse; if appropriate, begin artificial ventilation or CPR. *The key to survival is early, vigorous, prolonged resuscitation efforts.* Hold the head in a neutral position and bring the jaw forward gently in case of spinal injury.

4. Stabilize the victim's neck to prevent aggravating a possible cervical spine injury. If possible, move the victim to dry ground after stabilizing the neck.

5. If the victim is conscious, check movement in all extremities; determine the victim's reaction to pain.

6. While waiting for medical help to arrive, assess the victim for open wounds or fractures, and provide appropriate care.

Progress Check

1. If a downed power line is lying across a vehicle, _____ .
   (have occupants of the car get out/use a wooden pole to move the line/do not touch the vehicle)

2. If a victim is found in the bathtub with an appliance that has energized the water, _____ .
   (unplug the appliance/drain the bathtub)

3. An arcing injury occurs when _____ .
   (an extremity is struck by lightning/a current enters the body/a current jumps from one surface to another)

4. Your first priority in treating an electrical shock victim is to _____ .
   (remove the source of electricity/ protect yourself/get the victim away from the electrical source)

5. Always assume a victim of lightning strike has sustained _____ .
   (multiple injuries/cardiac arrest/internal burns)

6. Victims of lightning strike have a greater chance of resuscitation than victims of arrest from other causes because _____ .
   (tissue death is delayed/body temperature is slightly elevated)

7. The goal of first aid for lightning victims is to _____ .
   (prevent further injury/oxygenate the heart and brain/ restore circulation)

• SUMMARY •

- Burns are classified by the degree of damage to the skin and underlying tissues. First- and second-degree burns are partial-thickness burns (they burn through only part of the skin's layers), while a third-degree burn is a full-thickness burn (involving all layers of the skin).

- You can quickly assess how much of a victim's body surface is burned by using either the Rule of Nines or the palmar surface method.

- Burns of the face, hands, feet, or genitals are always considered critical.

- The first priority in emergency care for burns is to prevent further injury. To treat, begin by removing the victim from the source of the burn and by eliminating the cause of the burn.

- Inhalation injuries cause the majority of deaths from fire; the most common burn-associated inhalation injury is carbon monoxide poisoning. Always assume that an unconscious burn victim has inhaled carbon monoxide fumes.

- Always assume inhalation injury has occurred with any thermal burn, whenever the face is burned, or whenever a victim was confined in an enclosed space.

- The key to treating chemical burns is aggressive, vigorous, prolonged irrigation; the more quickly you initiate care, the less severe the burn will be. Begin by irrigating for at least 20 minutes.

- Before you approach any victim of electrical injury, make sure it is safe to do so.

- The goal of first aid treatment for a victim of lightning strike is to oxygenate the heart and brain until the body resumes circulation on its own.

• KEY TERMS •

Make sure you understand the following key terms:

- first-degree burn
- second-degree burn
- third-degree burn
- Rule of Nines
- palmar surface method
- inhalation injury
- carbon monoxide
- noxious
- thermal burn
- contact burns
- arcing injury (flash burn)

Student: _____   Date: _____

Course: _____   Section #: _____

PART 1 • True/False

If you believe the statement is true, circle the T. If you believe the statement is false, circle the F.

T F **1.** More than half of all fire-related deaths are caused by smoke inhalation.

T F **2.** With an inhalation injury, most of the damage done to the upper airway is a result of inhalation of carbon monoxide.

T F **3.** Common signs and symptoms of upper-airway injury from inhalation include burned specks of carbon in the sputum, hoarseness, coughing, and cyanosis.

T F **4.** Carbon monoxide poisoning is the major cause of death at the scenes of most fires.

T F **5.** First-degree thermal burns should be immersed in cool water.

T F **6.** Second-degree burns should not be immersed in cool water.

T F **7.** Chemical burns should be continuously irrigated for at least 20 minutes.

T F **8.** A lime powder burn should be treated like other chemical burns.

T F **9.** Lightning causes more deaths than any other type of electrical burn.

T F **10.** As many as 70 percent of smoke-inhalation victims have facial burns.

T F **11.** Victims of lightning have been resuscitated as long as 30 minutes after a strike without residual damage.

T F **12.** If a group has been struck by lightning, care for the apparently dead first.

T F **13.** While approximately two-thirds of all those struck by lightning die as a result, approximately one-third can be revived.

T F **14.** Always assume that a victim of a lightning strike has sustained multiple injuries.

PART 2 • Multiple Choice

For each item, circle the correct answer or the phrase that best completes the statement.

1. The First Aider's first action at a burn accident should be to

a. remove the victim from the source of the burn
b. examine the victim for respiratory or cardiac complications
c. determine the severity of the burn
d. open and maintain the victim's airway

2. The first step in caring for a first-degree burn is usually to

a. transport the victim to a medical facility as soon as possible
b. cover the area with a moist, bulky dressing
c. apply grease or petroleum jelly to the area
d. submerge the burned area in cold water

3. Immersion of second-degree thermal burns in cold water can

a. reduce swelling
b. relieve pain
c. prevent infection
d. a and b are correct

4. Emergency care for a chemical burn caused by dry lime is to

a. flush the lime with running water
b. apply a neutralizer to the lime
c. first brush the dry lime from the victim's skin, hair, and clothing
d. apply an occlusive bandage

5. What should be done to care for most chemical burns?

a. neutralize the area with alkali or acid solutions
b. remove clothing while flushing the area with water
c. locate an antidote before treating; water may intensify the reaction
d. cover the area with a dry, sterile gauze

6. Immediate care in the case of a lightning victim should consist of

a. determining the victim's reaction to pain
b. treating for shock
c. getting the victim under cover
d. restoring and maintaining breathing and heartbeat

7. According to the Rule of Nines, which of the following areas is estimated to comprise 9 percent of the body area?

a. one leg
b. back of trunk
c. front of trunk
d. one arm

8. In a serious burn case, pain is best relieved by protecting the burn from air through the application of a

a. burn spray
b. thick, clean, dry dressing
c. thick, petroleum-based burn ointment
d. soybean-oil-based burn ointment

9. Which of the following causes the most damage in upper-airway inhalation injury accompanying burns?

    a. heat
    b. noxious chemicals
    c. carbon monoxide
    d. smoke

10. What care should be given if clothing or debris is sticking to a burn that is not severe?

    a. remove it carefully
    b. soak the involved area in cool salt water
    c. leave it alone
    d. scrub the involved area with a soft brush and water

11. Which of the following comes first in emergency care of an electrical burn victim?

    a. separating the victim carefully from the electrical source
    b. initiating CPR
    c. opening the airway
    d. locating entrance and exit wounds

12. According to the Rule of Nines, the infant's head area represents what percent of the total body area?

    a. 4½ percent
    b. 9 percent
    c. 15 percent
    d. 18 percent

13. What should a First Aider do if he or she comes across a downed power line lying across a wrecked vehicle?

    a. instruct conscious victims to attempt to jump from the vehicle
    b. tell conscious victims to stay inside the vehicle and wait for a power company crew
    c. tell victims to turn on the ignition and move the vehicle
    d. throw a blanket or jacket over the line, and instruct conscious victims to leave the vehicle

14. Possible effects of electric shock include

    a. ringing in the ears
    b. visual disorders
    c. kidney failure
    d. all of the above

PART 3 • Matching

Match each description with a severity level.

A. Critical

B. Moderate

C. Minor

1. _____ Third-degree burns between 2 and 10 percent of the body of an adult (excluding face, hands, and feet)

2. _____ Burns complicated by respiratory tract injury and/or fractures

3. _____ First-degree burns that cover more than 75 percent of the body surface

4. _____ Second-degree burns covering between 15 and 25 percent of an adult's body surface

5. _____ Second-degree burns over less than 15 percent of an adult's body surface

6. _____ Third-degree burns involving more than 10 percent of an adult's body surface

7. _____ Second-degree burns covering more than 30 percent of an adult's body surface

8. _____ Third-degree burns that cover more than 2 to 3 percent of a child's body surface

9. _____ Third-degree burns that involve face, hands, feet, or genital area

10. _____ First-degree burns covering 50 to 75 percent of an adult's body surface

11. _____ Second-degree burns covering less than 10 percent of a child's body surface

PART 4 • What Would You Do If?

- A 10-year-old boy was playing with gasoline and received burns on his abdomen and lower extremities.
- An industrial worker has dry lime powder spilled over his whole body.
- A teenage boy is hit by lightning on a golf course. He is not breathing and has no detectable carotid pulse.

PART 5 • Practical Skills Check-Off

_____ has satisfactorily passed the following practical skills:

Student's Name

Read the following list of first-aid emergency-care skills; indicate with a checkmark which ones you feel prepared to perform. At the end of this course, go back over the list to determine your preparedness.

First Aid Skills	Now	End of Course
1. Describe and demonstrate how to care for first- and second-degree burns of the extremities.	❑	❑
2. Describe and demonstrate how to care for a lime powder burn.	❑	❑

25

Heat and Cold Emergencies

Learning Objectives

When you have mastered the material in this chapter, you will be able to

1 Explain how the body attempts to maintain normal body temperature

2 Explain how the body loses heat

3 Describe and demonstrate appropriate emergency care for heatstroke

4 Describe and demonstrate appropriate emergency care for heat exhaustion

5 Describe and demonstrate appropriate emergency care for heat cramps

6 Identify the signs and symptoms of hypothermia

7 Describe and demonstrate appropriate emergency care for hypothermia

8 Identify the signs and symptoms of frostbite

9 Describe and demonstrate appropriate emergency care for frostbite

SQ3R Plus

- **Survey** to set goals for studying.
- Ask **questions** as you **read.**
- Stop frequently to **recite** and **review.**
- **Write** a summary of key points.
- **Reflect** on the importance of this material and its relevance in your life.

On July 23, 1998, 16-year-old Daniel Stringham and four of his friends were running along a stretch of highway in a rural area of the county, training for an upcoming marathon race. Daniel, a stocky teenager who had not kept up the training schedule of the others for the past few months, was struggling to keep up.

As the rest of the boys rounded a curve in the road, Daniel collapsed. Daniel's skin was dry and red; though he felt extremely hot, he was not sweating. He was breathing rapidly and sounded as if he was snoring. As the boys gathered around him, it was obvious that he was confused—he did not know where he was and seemed very anxious.

Nineteen-year-old Parker Merritt sent one of the runners to a nearby home to call 9-1-1; with the help of the others, Parker moved Daniel into the shade of a tree. The boys removed Daniel's shirt, shorts, socks, and shoes; two of them brought water in their cupped hands from a nearby irrigation ditch and splashed it over Daniel's chest, arms, and legs while Parker fanned him briskly with his running shorts. By the time EMTs arrived on the scene, Daniel's temperature was starting to decrease. Parker's quick action had prevented serious complications.

HEAT AND COLD CAN LEAD TO A NUMBER OF DIFFERENT injuries—some minor, some life threatening. Critical to your ability to care for those injuries is a basic understanding of the way the body maintains its temperature and how it adjusts physiologically to extremes in heat and cold.

MECHANISMS OF HEAT LOSS

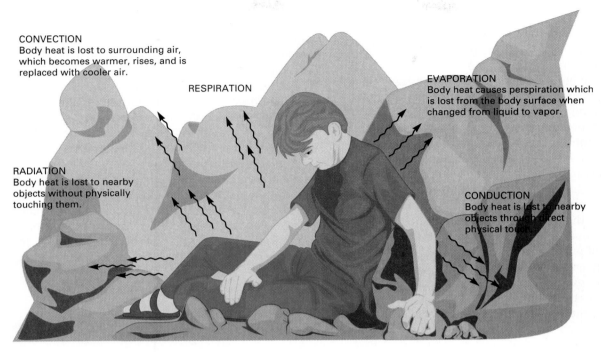

CONVECTION
Body heat is lost to surrounding air, which becomes warmer, rises, and is replaced with cooler air.

RESPIRATION

EVAPORATION
Body heat causes perspiration which is lost from the body surface when changed from liquid to vapor.

RADIATION
Body heat is lost to nearby objects without physically touching them.

CONDUCTION
Body heat is lost to nearby objects through direct physical touch.

Figure 25-1. A wet, poorly dressed climber has taken shelter among cold, wet rocks.

• Section 1 •
TEMPERATURE REGULATION

Learning Objective 1 Explain how the body attempts to maintain normal body temperature.

The human body stubbornly defends its constant core temperature of 98.6 degrees F. If that temperature is to be maintained, heat loss must equal heat production. The body maintains equilibrium by varying blood flow to the outer part of the body. When the core temperature rises, vessels near the skin dilate, and the blood brings increased heat to the skin. If the outside environment is cooler than the skin, the heat is dissipated by radiation and convection; if the environment is hot, heat is dissipated by evaporation of sweat.

How the Body Loses Heat

Learning Objective 2 Explain how the body loses heat.

The body loses heat in the following four ways (see Figure 25-1):

1. **Radiation,** whereby heat is transferred from the surface of one object to the surface of another without actual contact; radiation is the primary way the body loses heat.

2. **Conduction,** whereby heat is transferred from the surface of one object to the surface of another through direct contact; heat loss through conduction can be 25 times greater in cold air than in cold water.

3. **Convection,** whereby cold air in immediate contact with the skin is warmed by the skin; heated molecules move away, cooler ones take their place, and the cycle repeats itself.

radiation The loss of body heat to the surface of another object without physical contact

conduction The loss of body heat to nearby objects through direct physical touch

convection The loss of body heat to surrounding air, which becomes warmer, rises, and is replaced with cooler air

4. **Evaporation,** whereby body heat causes perspiration, which is lost from the body surface when it is changed to vapor; two-thirds of evaporative loss is through perspiration, one-third through respiration.

If the body gets overheated, blood flow is increased to the skin. Vessels at the skin surface dilate, the heat in the blood is taken to the skin surface, and the heat is then lost through radiation, convection, and evaporation (perspiration).

The phenomenon of convection has been incorporated into the concept of windchill (Figure 25-2). A unit of windchill is defined as the amount of heat that would be lost in an hour from a square meter of exposed skin surface with a normal temperature of 91.4 degrees F. In essence, the windchill factor combines the effects of the speed of the wind and the temperature of the environment into a number that indicates the danger of exposure. When the windchill factor is –10, the temperature is bitterly cold; at –20, exposed flesh may freeze; at –70, exposed flesh will freeze in less than 1 minute; and at –95, exposed flesh will freeze in less than 30 seconds. For instance, flesh will freeze in less than 1 minute in only 10-mile-per-hour winds if the temperature is –40° F.

How the Body Conserves Heat

The skin is heated in three ways:

1. Blood rushes to the surface of the skin
2. Hairs stand erect, trapping warm air immediately next to the skin
3. Little or no perspiration is released to the skin surface for evaporation

How Clothing Affects Thermal Equilibrium

Clothing provides thermal resistance to heat loss, insulating the skin by trapping air between its fibers. Unfortunately, most people do not understand how to use clothes to their best advantage in regulating body temperature.

Heat loss needs to be increased when the body is active and decreased when it is inactive. But the way most people wear clothes in cold weather defeats both purposes—they wear too many layers while they are working, and too few layers while they are resting.

Consider what happens when you perspire. In hot weather, clothes act as a barrier to evaporation of perspiration, frustrating the cooling system of the body. In cold weather, a person who wears too many layers of clothing perspires heavily, and the layer of clothing next to the skin stays wet. As a result, the person loses heat 240 times faster than if the clothing remains dry.

Progress Check

1. Heat loss through radiation involves the transfer of heat from the body to another surface without

   _____ .

   (interference/direct contact/evaporation)

2. Convection, central to the concept of windchill, occurs when air molecules surrounding the skin get

   _____ , rise, and are replaced by cooler air.
   (moved by the wind/caught in a draft/warmed by the skin)

WIND SPEED (MPH)	WHAT THE THERMOMETER READS (degrees F.)											
	50	40	30	20	10	0	–10	–20	–30	–40	–50	–60
	WHAT IT EQUALS IN ITS EFFECT ON EXPOSED FLESH											
CALM	50	40	30	20	10	0	–10	–20	–30	–40	–50	–60
5	48	37	27	16	6	–5	–15	–26	–36	–47	–57	–68
10	40	28	16	4	–9	–21	–33	–46	–58	–70	–83	–95
15	36	22	9	–5	–18	–36	–45	–58	–72	–85	–99	–112
20	32	18	4	–10	–25	–39	–53	–67	–82	–96	–110	–121
25	30	16	0	–15	–29	–44	–59	–74	–88	–104	–118	–133
30	28	13	–2	–18	–33	–48	–63	–79	–94	–109	–125	–140
35	27	11	–4	–20	–35	–49	–67	–82	–98	–113	–129	–145
40	26	10	–6	–21	–37	–53	–69	–85	–100	–116	–132	–148

Source: U.S. Army

Little danger if properly clothed	Danger of freezing exposed flesh	Great danger of freezing exposed flesh

Figure 25-2. The windchill index

3. Heat loss through conduction involves the transfer of heat from one surface to another through _____ .
(direct contact/indirect contact/clothing fibers)

4. Through evaporation, perspiration is changed from liquid to _____ and carries heat away with it.
(gas/solid/vapor)

• **Section 2** •

HEAT-RELATED INJURIES (HYPERTHERMIA)

Heat-related injuries (**hyperthermia**) fall into three major categories: heatstroke, heat exhaustion, and heat cramps. They are most common when the temperature and humidity are high and there is little or no breeze. Most susceptible are

- Athletes
- Workers near furnaces or ovens
- Those in poor physical condition
- Alcoholics
- The obese
- The chronically ill
- Those who have not adjusted to the environment
- Those with heart disease
- People using certain drugs (such as diuretics)
- Burn victims

- The elderly
- Children

Heatstroke

Heatstroke—sometimes called "sunstroke"—is a true life-threatening emergency that occurs when the body's heat-regulating mechanisms break down and fail to cool the body. The body becomes overheated, body temperature rises, and about half of all victims do not sweat.

Because no cooling takes place, the body stores increasing amounts of heat, the heat-producing mechanisms speed up, and eventually brain cells are damaged, causing permanent disability or death. Untreated victims die.

There are two kinds of heatstroke: *classic,* in which people lose the ability to sweat (generally affecting the elderly or chronically ill during a heat wave); and *exertional,* in which victims involved in physical exertion and muscle stress retain the ability to sweat. The heat and humidity risk scale (see Figure 25-3) indicates when problems are likely to occur.

evaporation The loss of body heat when perspiration is changed from liquid to vapor

hyperthermia Greatly increased body temperature

heatstroke A life-threatening emergency caused by a disturbance in the body's temperature regulation mechanism, characterized by extreme fever, hot and dry skin, delirium, or coma

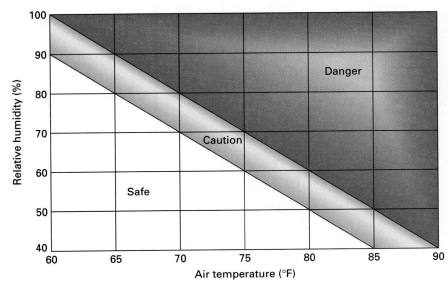

HEAT AND HUMIDITY RISK SCALE

Figure 25-3. The risk of illness is increased when heat and humidity produce dangerous conditions.

(Adapted with permission from William C. Brown Publishers, Dubuque, Iowa. Fox EL, Bowers RW, Foss ML: *The physiological basis of physical education and athletics,* ed. 4. Philadelphia, WB Saunders Co., 1988, p. 503. Reproduced with permission from *Patient Care,* June 15, 1989. Copyright © 1989 Patient Care, Oradell, NJ. All rights reserved.)

Signs and Symptoms

Heatstroke (see Figures 25-4 and 25-5) is indicated by

- Body temperature of 105 degrees F or more
- Hot, red skin
- Initially rapid, strong pulse
- Later rapid, weak pulse
- Initially constricted pupils
- Later dilated pupils
- Tremors
- Mental confusion or anxiety
- Irritability or aggression
- Initially deep, rapid breathing
- Later shallow, weak breathing
- Headache
- Dry mouth
- Shortness of breath

- Loss of appetite
- Nausea and vomiting
- Dizziness and weakness
- Seizures or sudden collapse

All heatstroke victims have compromised levels of consciousness, ranging from disorientation to coma.

Emergency Care

Learning Objective 3 Describe and demonstrate appropriate emergency care for heatstroke.

Heatstroke is a true medical emergency; every minute counts. Emergency care of heatstroke is aimed at *immediate* cooling of the body. Activate the EMS system; then:

1. Establish an airway and, when possible, remove the victim from the source of heat.

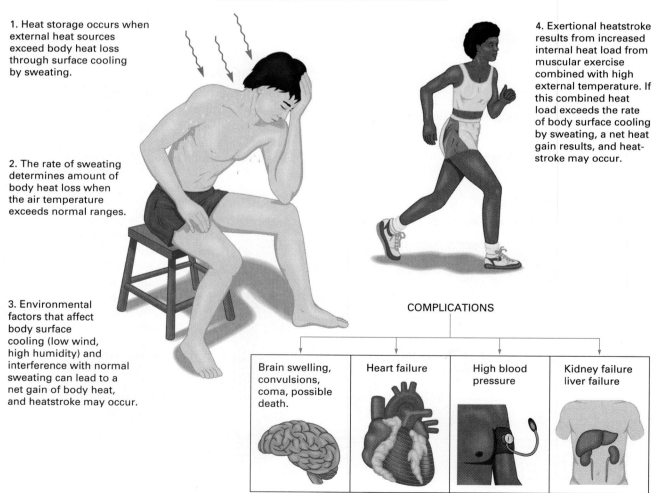

SWEATING: DEFENSE AGAINST HEATSTROKE

1. Heat storage occurs when external heat sources exceed body heat loss through surface cooling by sweating.

2. The rate of sweating determines amount of body heat loss when the air temperature exceeds normal ranges.

3. Environmental factors that affect body surface cooling (low wind, high humidity) and interference with normal sweating can lead to a net gain of body heat, and heatstroke may occur.

4. Exertional heatstroke results from increased internal heat load from muscular exercise combined with high external temperature. If this combined heat load exceeds the rate of body surface cooling by sweating, a net heat gain results, and heatstroke may occur.

COMPLICATIONS

| Brain swelling, convulsions, coma, possible death. | Heart failure | High blood pressure | Kidney failure liver failure |

Figure 25-4. Heatstroke is a true life-threatening emergency.

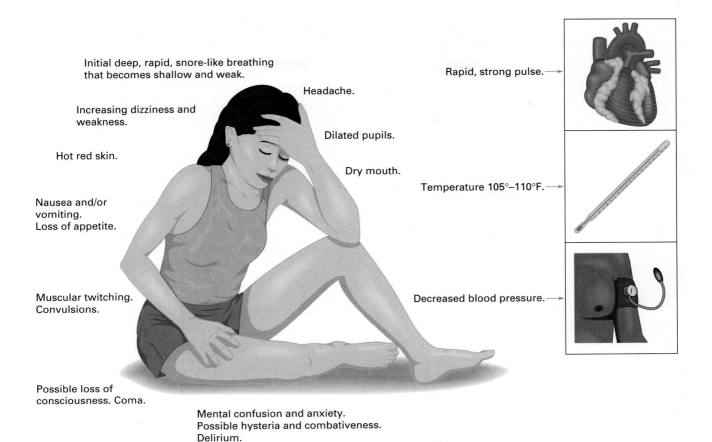

Initial deep, rapid, snore-like breathing that becomes shallow and weak.

Increasing dizziness and weakness.

Hot red skin.

Nausea and/or vomiting.
Loss of appetite.

Muscular twitching.
Convulsions.

Possible loss of consciousness. Coma.

Headache.

Dilated pupils.

Dry mouth.

Rapid, strong pulse.

Temperature 105°–110°F.

Decreased blood pressure.

Mental confusion and anxiety.
Possible hysteria and combativeness.
Delirium.

Figure 25-5. Signs and symptoms of heatstroke

2. Remove as much of the victim's clothing as possible, down to his or her underwear; elevate the victim's head and shoulders slightly, then use a combination of these methods to cool the victim until his or her mental status returns to normal:

   • If humidity is high, put the victim in a tub of cool water (less than 60 degrees F), and stir the water gently so the body doesn't heat a layer of water right around the victim.

   • Pour cool water over the victim's body, or spray the victim with cool water. (These methods are not effective if humidity is high.)

   • Place cold packs or wrapped ice bags under the victim's arms, in the groin, around the neck, behind each knee, and around the ankles to cool the large surface blood vessels (see Figure 25-6).

   • Wrap a wet sheet around the victim, then direct an electric fan at the victim (see Figures 25-7 and 25-8 on page 416).

   • If the victim begins to shiver, slow the cooling method (shivering produces heat).

   • *Never* use isopropyl alcohol to cool the skin; the skin absorbs the alcohol, which can be toxic.

3. Never give the victim stimulants or hot drinks.

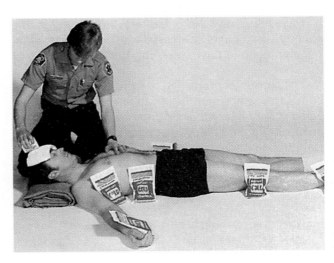

Figure 25-6. Use cold packs on the head and body to cool a victim of heatstroke.

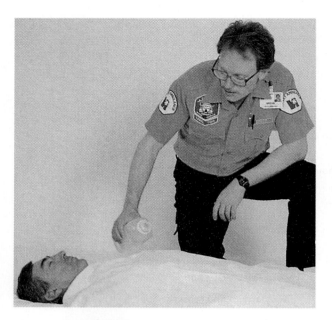

Figure 25-7. *Wrapping a heatstroke victim in a wet sheet can help reduce temperature.*

4. As the body cools, seizures or vomiting may occur. Position the victim to allow for easy drainage.

5. Monitor the victim's temperature while you wait for emergency personnel to arrive. If the temperature starts to climb, start cooling procedures again. (The temperature must drop below 100 degrees F and must stay that low before the danger has passed.)

Heat Exhaustion

The most common heat injury, **heat exhaustion** occurs in an otherwise fit person who engages in extreme physical exertion in a hot, humid environment. It is actually a mild form of shock brought on by the pooling of blood in the vessels just below the skin, causing blood to flow away from the major organs of the body.

As a result of prolonged and profuse sweating, the body loses large amounts of salt and water. When the water is not replaced, blood circulation diminishes, affecting brain, heart, and lung functions. The most critical problem in heat exhaustion is dehydration.

Signs and Symptoms

The primary signs and symptoms of heat exhaustion mimic those of the flu:

*   Headache
*   Weakness
*   Fatigue
*   Nausea and/or vomiting

Figure 25-8. *A wet sheet and a fan can cool the heatstroke victim.*

*   Diarrhea
*   Loss of appetite
*   Dizziness and faintness
*   Profuse sweating
*   Pale, cool, ashen skin
*   Below-normal temperature
*   Dilated pupils
*   Weak, rapid pulse
*   Inelastic skin
*   Thirst
*   Difficulty walking
*   Collapse or brief unconsciousness
*   Possible muscle cramps

See Figure 25-9 for a comparison of the signs and symptoms of heat exhaustion and heatstroke. The two most distinct differences between heatstroke and heat exhaustion are the condition of the skin and the body temperature (see Table 25-1).

Emergency Care

Learning Objective 4 Describe and demonstrate appropriate emergency care for heat exhaustion.

To treat heat exhaustion

1. Move the victim to a cool place, remove as much of the victim's clothing as possible, apply cool wet compresses to the skin, and fan the victim lightly. Make sure the victim does not get chilled.

heat exhaustion A heat-related emergency caused by excessive loss of water and salt through sweating, characterized by cold, clammy skin and a weak, rapid pulse

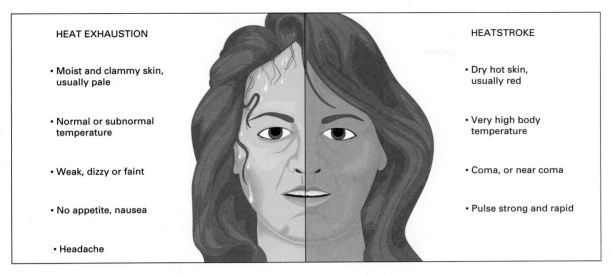

HEAT EXHAUSTION

- Moist and clammy skin, usually pale

- Normal or subnormal temperature

- Weak, dizzy or faint

- No appetite, nausea

- Headache

HEATSTROKE

- Dry hot skin, usually red

- Very high body temperature

- Coma, or near coma

- Pulse strong and rapid

Figure 25-9. *Signs and symptoms of heat exhaustion and heatstroke*

Table 25-1		
Heatstroke and Heat Exhaustion		
Condition	**Skin Condition**	**Body Temperature**
Heatstroke	Flushed, hot to the touch, wet or dry	High—usually 105 to 110 degrees F
Heat exhaustion	Cool, pale, clammy, often ashen	Normal or even below normal

2. Have the victim lie down, raise the feet 8 to 12 inches (see Figure 25-10), and lower the head slightly to help increase blood circulation to the brain.

3. If the victim is fully conscious, give him or her cool water to drink at the rate of half a glass every 10 minutes for 1 hour (see Figure 25-11). If the victim doesn't improve in 20 minutes, add electro-

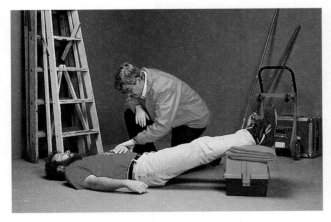

Figure 25-10. *The victim with heat exhaustion should be on the back with feet elevated.*

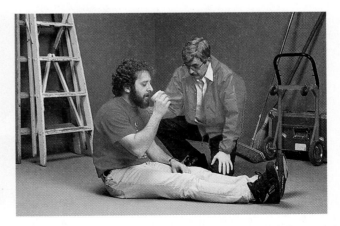

Figure 25-11. *If the victim with heat exhaustion is fully conscious, give him or her cool water.*

lytes (such as a commercial sports drink). *Never give the victim salt tablets.* If the victim vomits, stop giving fluids and activate the EMS system immediately.

4. If the victim is unconscious, sponge the victim off with cool water.

5. Take the victim's temperature every 10 to 15 minutes. If the temperature is above 101 degrees F or is rising, or if the victim does not improve within 30 minutes, activate the EMS system.

Heat Cramps

Learning Objective 5 Describe and demonstrate appropriate emergency care for heat cramps.

The least common and least serious heat injury, **heat cramps** are muscle spasms that occur when

- The body loses too much salt during profuse sweating and not enough salt is replaced
- Calcium levels are low
- Too much water is consumed

Muscles rely on a strict balance of water, calcium, and sodium; whenever that balance is disrupted, heat cramps can result. In essence, the cramp occurs because the muscle contracts but does not relax.

Hot weather is not a prerequisite—a person who exercises strenuously in cold weather and perspires can develop heat cramps if he or she drinks water but does not replace salt.

Signs and Symptoms

Heat cramps can range from mild to extremely painful muscular cramps and pain, and are most common in the legs, calves, and abdomen. Other signs and symptoms include (see Figure 25-12)

- Rapid heartbeat
- Hot, sweaty skin
- Normal body temperature
- Faintness and dizziness
- Exhaustion or fatigue
- Stiff, boardlike abdomen
- Possible nausea and vomiting
- Normal consciousness level

Emergency Care

1. If the victim is in a hot environment, remove him or her from the heat immediately; have the victim rest in a cool place.

2. Administer sips of salt water at the rate of half a glass every 15 minutes; dilute 1 teaspoon salt or

SIGNS AND SYMPTOMS OF HEAT CRAMPS

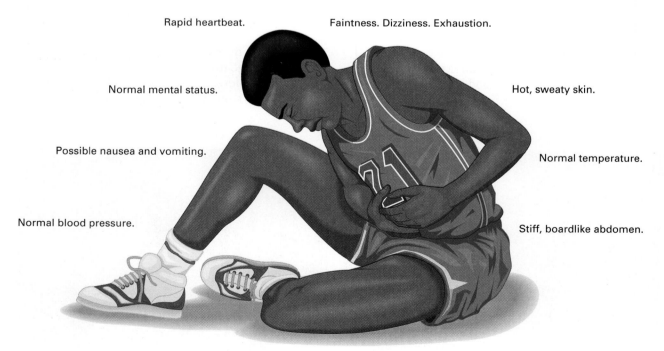

Rapid heartbeat.

Faintness. Dizziness. Exhaustion.

Normal mental status.

Hot, sweaty skin.

Possible nausea and vomiting.

Normal temperature.

Normal blood pressure.

Stiff, boardlike abdomen.

Severe muscular cramps and pain, especially of the arms fingers, legs, calves, and abdomen.

Figure 25-12. Heat cramps are the most common but least serious heat injury.

1 bouillon cube in 1 quart of water. *Do not use salt tablets.*

3. Apply moist towels to the victim's forehead and over the cramping muscles. To relieve pain, try gently stretching the involved muscle groups, or pinch the upper lip just below the nose (an acupuncture technique that helps cramping calf muscles).

4. Explain to the victim what happened and why so the victim can avoid a recurrence; the victim should avoid exertion of any kind for at least 12 hours, or heat cramps will recur. Activate the EMS system if the victim has other illnesses or injuries, if other symptoms develop, or if the victim's condition worsens or does not respond to care.

Follow local protocol regarding massage of cramping muscles. In many cases, massage actually increases the pain of heat cramps.

Progress Check

1. _____ is a life-threatening condition; untreated, all victims die.
   (Heatstroke/Heat exhaustion/Heat cramps)

2. The two most reliable and distinct differences between heatstroke and heat exhaustion are body temperature and _____ .
   (level of consciousness/condition of the skin/pattern of breathing)

3. In heatstroke, the skin is hot, red, and _____ .
   (wet/dry/either wet or dry)

4. The top priority in treatment of heatstroke is _____ .
   (monitoring pulse/immediate cooling of the body/monitoring body temperature)

5. If the victim's temperature starts rising again after you have started treatment for heatstroke, you should _____ .
   (activate the EMS system immediately/submerge the victim in cool water/begin cooling procedures again)

6. Heat exhaustion is actually a mild form of _____ .
   (fatigue/shock/heatstroke)

7. The most critical problem in heat exhaustion is _____ .
   (dehydration/overheating/circulatory disturbance)

8. Heat cramps occur because of disruption in the muscle's balance of calcium, water, and _____ .
   (sodium/potassium/phosphorus)

9. To treat heat cramps, give the victim sips of _____ .
   (hot water/cold water/salt water)

• Section 3 •
COLD-RELATED INJURIES (HYPOTHERMIA)

Major injuries related to extreme cold temperature are general hypothermia, immersion hypothermia, and frostbite. Cold-related injury can occur at any time of year if a person is exposed to the elements for an extended period, is sweating heavily and exposed to wind, or is a victim of near-drowning. Remember: A number of conditions other than cold weather can affect the body's ability to regulate its own temperature.

General Hypothermia

The most life-threatening cold injury, general **hypothermia** affects the entire body with severe generalized cooling; as many as 87 percent of all victims of general hypothermia die (see Figure 25-13 on page 420). In general, thermal control is lost once the body temperature is lowered to 95 degrees F; coma occurs when the body's core temperature reaches approximately 79 degrees F.

Factors contributing to hypothermia, even in the absence of cold environment, include

- Use of drugs
- Surgery
- Water activities
- Existing disease
- Trauma
- Massive blood loss
- Extremes of age
- Immobility

heat cramps Muscle spasms caused by a disturbance in the electrolyte balance of the muscles; generally seen when the body loses too much salt during profuse sweating

hypothermia Greatly decreased body temperature

Predisposing Factors	Signs Others See	Symptoms Victims Feel	Prevention	Emergency Care
Poor physical condition	Loss of coordination slow, stumbling pace	Violent shivering, with muscle tension	Rest and eat before exertion	MINIMIZE HEAT LOSS: Protect victim from cold
Failure to eat and drink enough	Speech distortion	Fatigue	Nibble on high-energy food continuously while outdoors	Place insulating pad between victim and the ground
Little body fat	Forgetfulness	Feeling of extreme cold or numbness		Wrap victim in dry clothing and/or blankets
Inadequate clothing (wool is best)	Lack of judgment; irrational ambition	Loss of coordination; stumbling, thick speech, disorientation	Wear windproof outer clothing, wool underneath	Keep victim dry
Lack of shelter from snow, rain, wind	Overactive imagination; possible hallucinations	Rigidity of muscles after shivering stops	Carry emergency camping equipment	ADD HEAT: Have victim get into sleeping bag with another person
Wetness (from perspiration or precipitation)	Blue, puffy skin	Blue, puffy skin	Make camp immediately if storm arises, injury occurs or you get lost	Give warm liquids
Exhaustion	Dilated pupils	Pulse slow, irregular, or weak		Apply heat, using warmed stones wrapped in cloth, heat packs, or hot water in a canteen
	Slow, shallow breathing		Keep moving; this keeps the body producing heat; if camped, use isometric exercises	Keep victim in physical contact with others for body heat
	Confusion, stupor, possible unconsciousness			Have victim breathe warm, moist air

Figure 25-13 Summary of general hypothermia. Adapted from: Brent Q. Hafen and Brenda Peterson, *First Aid for Health Emergencies,* West Publishing Co., 1980, p. 248.

Basically, hypothermia occurs when the body loses more heat than it produces; death can occur within 2 hours of the first signs and symptoms (see Figure 25-14). However, treatment should always be attempted—cases have been documented in which victims have survived a core temperature as low as 64.4 degrees F.

Signs and Symptoms

Learning Objective 6 Identify the signs and symptoms of hypothermia.

Because it is extremely difficult to measure core body temperature in the field, when you suspect hypothermia you should rely instead on signs and symptoms (see Figures 25-15 and 25-16 on page 422).

- Skin that is cold to the touch; to test, place the back of your hand against the skin of the victim's abdomen
- Trembling on one side of the body without shivering
- Uncontrollable shivering
- Vague, slurred, thick speech
- Amnesia and incoherence
- Disorientation, confusion
- Poor judgment
- Staggering gait
- Dizziness
- Bluish or gray waxen skin
- Semirigid skin
- Disorientation and confusion
- Sluggish pupils
- Bloated face
- Initially increased heart and respiratory rates
- Later decreased heart and respiratory rates
- Dehydration
- Drowsiness and/or stupor
- Apparent exhaustion
- Unconsciousness

STAGES OF HYPOTHERMIA (Cold-Related Injury)

Stage 1: **Shivering** is a response by the body to generate heat. It does not occur below a body temperature of 90°F.

Stage 2: **Apathy and decreased muscle function.** First fine motor function is affected, then gross motor functions.

Stage 3: **Decreased level of consciousness** is accompanied by a glassy stare and possible freezing of the extremities.

Stage 4: **Decreased vital signs**, including slow pulse and slow respiration rate.

Stage 5: **Death**.

Figure 25-14. Hypothermia is an acute medical emergency requiring immediate attention.

Emergency Care

Learning Objective 7 Describe and demonstrate appropriate emergency are for hypothermia.

The basic principles of emergency care for hypothermia include preventing heat loss, rewarming the victim as quickly and safely as possible, and remaining alert for complications (see Figure 25-16 on page 422). Immediately get the victim out of the cold; after activating the EMS system:

1. Check the victim's vital signs. Measure for 1 full minute, because vital signs are slowed in hypothermia. (A hypothermic victim may breathe only three or four times per minute and have a pulse of only 5 to 10 beats per minute.) If there is no pulse, open the airway and begin CPR.

   Note: According to American Heart Association guidelines, you should attempt CPR on a hypothermia victim in cases when you ordinarily would not attempt CPR—even in the presence of fixed and dilated pupils. Do not attempt CPR if there are other obviously lethal injuries, if cold has made the chest wall too rigid to perform CPR, if the victim was submerged in water for more than 60 minutes, or if transport for gradual rewarming will be delayed.

2. Handle the victim *very* gently; jostling can cause ventricular fibrillations. Don't let the victim walk around or move much on his or her own.

3. Keep the victim in a horizontal position to prevent shock and increase blood flow to the brain. *Do not elevate the legs;* doing so causes cold blood to flow to the heart. Elevate the head if the victim has head or chest injuries, shortness of breath, or symptoms of myocardial infarction or if the terrain is extremely steep.

4. Prevent further heat loss:
   • Move the victim to a warm, sheltered place.
   • Insulate the head.

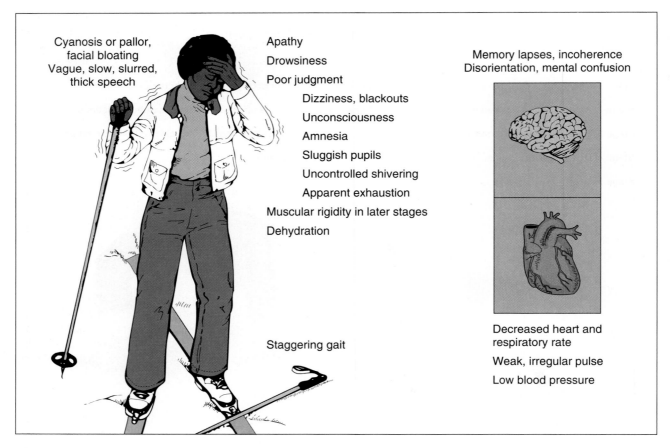

Cyanosis or pallor,
facial bloating
Vague, slow, slurred,
thick speech

Apathy

Drowsiness

Poor judgment

Dizziness, blackouts

Unconsciousness

Amnesia

Sluggish pupils

Uncontrolled shivering

Apparent exhaustion

Muscular rigidity in later stages

Dehydration

Staggering gait

Memory lapses, incoherence
Disorientation, mental confusion

Decreased heart and
respiratory rate

Weak, irregular pulse

Low blood pressure

Figure 25-15. Signs and symptoms of hypothermia

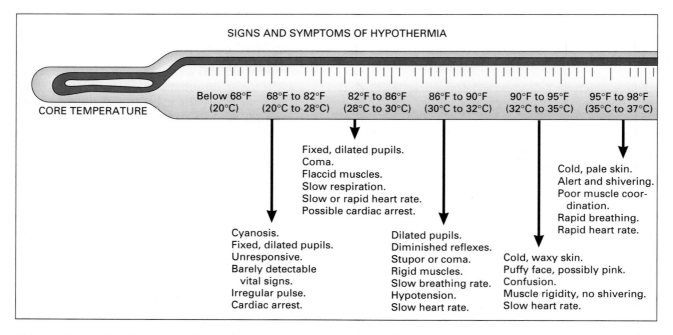

SIGNS AND SYMPTOMS OF HYPOTHERMIA

CORE TEMPERATURE

Below 68°F
(20°C)

68°F to 82°F
(20°C to 28°C)

82°F to 86°F
(28°C to 30°C)

86°F to 90°F
(30°C to 32°C)

90°F to 95°F
(32°C to 35°C)

95°F to 98°F
(35°C to 37°C)

Fixed, dilated pupils.
Coma.
Flaccid muscles.
Slow respiration.
Slow or rapid heart rate.
Possible cardiac arrest.

Cold, pale skin.
Alert and shivering.
Poor muscle coor-
dination.
Rapid breathing.
Rapid heart rate.

Cyanosis.
Fixed, dilated pupils.
Unresponsive.
Barely detectable
vital signs.
Irregular pulse.
Cardiac arrest.

Dilated pupils.
Diminished reflexes.
Stupor or coma.
Rigid muscles.
Slow breathing rate.
Hypotension.
Slow heart rate.

Cold, waxy skin.
Puffy face, possibly pink.
Confusion.
Muscle rigidity, no shivering.
Slow heart rate.

Figure 25-16. Hypothermia victims with a core temperature lower than 90 degrees F require extreme care in handling and rapid transport to the hospital.

- Do not allow the victim's skin to be exposed to wind, cold air, or water spray.

- Squeeze as much water as possible from wet clothing, then layer dry clothing and coverings on top of wet clothing. (The movement involved in removing wet clothing can cause ventricular fibrillation.)

- If the victim is wearing a coat, place the victim's arms next to his or her body instead of in the sleeves of the coat.

- Insulate the victim from the ground with blankets, plastic sheets, newspapers, plastic air-bubble packing material, or a sleeping bag.

5. Never rub or manipulate the arms or legs; you could force cold blood from the veins into the heart, causing cardiac arrest.

6. Never give the victim tobacco, coffee, or alcohol. Give fluids only after uncontrollable shivering stops and the victim is completely conscious (the victim must be able to swallow and cough).

Emergency Care for Severe Hypothermia

Severe hypothermia makes the victim appear dead—the victim may be in a coma, be cold to the touch, have fixed and dilated pupils, be in shock, have slow or no reflexes, breathe only once or twice per minute, be stiff, or assume a fetal position. The key in hypothermia is that *a person is not dead until he or she is warm and dead. Always assume the victim is still alive,* and provide the following care:

1. *Never* try to rewarm a severely hypothermic victim. Insulate the victim against further heat loss, but do not apply any source of heat. Handle the victim *extremely* gently.

2. Assess vital signs over a 2-minute period; if there is no heartbeat during the 2 minutes, start CPR.

3. Use gentle mouth-to-mouth or mouth-to-nose ventilation if the victim is not breathing; rapid mouth-to-mouth breathing can trigger cardiac arrest.

4. Maintain airway, breathing, and circulation until EMTs arrive.

Immersion Hypothermia

Immersion hypothermia—lowering of the body temperature that occurs as a result of immersion in cold water—should be considered in all cases of accidental immersion.

Body temperature drops to equal water temperature within 10 minutes; when the water is 50 degrees F or lower, death can occur within a few minutes.

A number of factors cause more rapid cooling when the body is immersed in the water. They include

- Water temperature (colder water speeds body cooling)

- Body size (small, thin people cool more quickly)

- Clothing (clothing helps insulate the body and slows cooling)

- Physical activity (trying to swim or tread water makes the victim cool off faster)

- Alcohol (alcohol dilates surface blood vessels and promotes rapid cooling)

Emergency Care

The immediate priority in immersion hypothermia is to remove the victim from the water. Do not allow the victim to move rapidly in the water; turbulence and activity decrease survival time by 75 percent. Lift the victim from the water in a horizontal position. Once the victim is out of the water

1. Activate the EMS system immediately.

2. Maintain the victim's airway, breathing, and circulation.

3. Keep the victim still and quiet; the coldest blood is in the extremities, and it will circulate rapidly to the heart with movement.

4. Follow insulating and rewarming guidelines as for general hypothermia, remembering to handle the victim *very* gently.

If a victim in the water cannot be rescued immediately, instruct the victim to exert as little effort as possible, keep head and face out of the water, cross legs under the water, and do as little as possible to stay afloat. If there is more than one victim in the water, have them form a tight circle with their chests together to maintain heat (see Figure 25-17 on page 424).

Frostbite

Frostbite, the freezing of body tissue, and **frostnip,** freezing of the skin surface, often accompany hypo-

frostbite Damage to the tissues resulting from prolonged exposure to extreme cold

frostnip Freezing of the skin surface

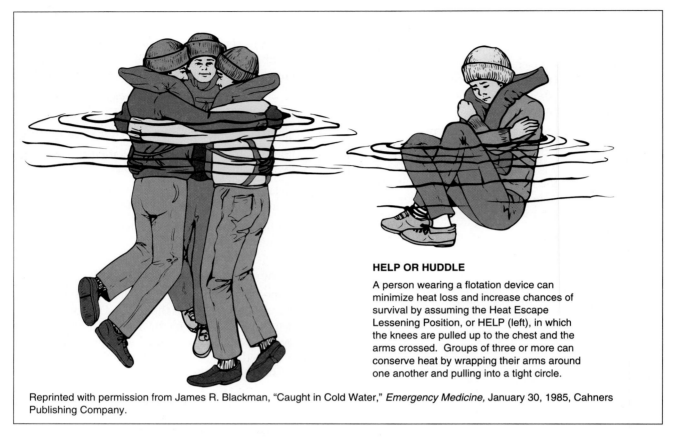

HELP OR HUDDLE

A person wearing a flotation device can minimize heat loss and increase chances of survival by assuming the Heat Escape Lessening Position, or HELP (left), in which the knees are pulled up to the chest and the arms crossed. Groups of three or more can conserve heat by wrapping their arms around one another and pulling into a tight circle.

Reprinted with permission from James R. Blackman, "Caught in Cold Water," *Emergency Medicine,* January 30, 1985, Cahners Publishing Company.

Figure 25-17. Conserving body heat to help prevent immersion hypothermia

thermia. In those cases, care of the hypothermia always takes precedence.

Frostbite, which most commonly affects the hands, feet, ears, nose, and cheeks, occurs when ice crystals form between the cells of the skin and then grow by extracting fluid from the cells (see Figure 25-18). The temperature of the skin must be below freezing—usually at about 28 degrees F or lower—before tissues of the body will freeze. Circulation is obstructed, causing additional damage to the tissue. The likelihood of frostbite is increased by

- Any kind of trauma
- Loss of blood
- Extremes of age
- Tight or tightly laced footwear
- Use of alcohol during exposure to cold
- Wet clothing
- High altitudes

- Race (Blacks are three times more likely than Whites to experience frostbite)

Signs and Symptoms

Learning Objective 8 Identify the signs and symptoms of frostbite.

It is very difficult to assess frostbite; while frozen, even severely frostbitten tissue can appear almost normal. In general, the appearance of the skin varies depending on the extent of injury (see Table 25-2 on page 426).

Figures 25-19 and 25-20 on page 426 illustrate third- and second-degree frostbite.

The signs and symptoms of frostnip include skin that is reddened, swollen, and painful.

Emergency Care

Learning Objective 9 Describe and demonstrate appropriate emergency care for frostbite.

1. FIRST DEGREE (Frost Nip)
   Affects tips of ears, nose, cheeks, fingers, toes, chin - skin blanched white, painless

FROSTBITE is localized cooling of the body

- 70% of the body is composed of water.

- When the body is subjected to excessive cold, the water in the cells can freeze; resulting ice crystals may even destroy the cell.

- Never rub the skin of a victim with frostbite; rubbing can result in permanent tissue damage.

2. SECOND DEGREE
   Affects skin and tissue just beneath skin; skin is firm and waxy, tissue beneath is soft, numb, then turns purple during thawing.

3. THIRD DEGREE
   Affects entire tissue depth; tissue beneath skin is solid, waxy white with purplish tinge.

1. **Emergency Care for First-Degree Frostbite:**
   The skin can be warmed by applying firm pressure with a hand (no rubbing) or other warm body part, by blowing warm breath on the spot, or by submerging in warm water.

2. **Emergency Care for Second-Degree Frostbite:**
   Treatment includes providing dry coverage and steady warmth. Submerging in warm water is also helpful.

3. **Emergency Care for Third-Degree Frostbite:**
   This victim needs immediate hospital care. Dry clothing over the frostbite will help prevent further injury. Submerging in warm water can help thaw. Rewarm by immersion in water heated to 100°–110° F, and maintain body core temperature. The frostbitten part should not be rubbed or chafed in any way. The part should not be thawed if the victim must walk on it to get to the medical facility. Do not delay activating the EMS system for rewarming.
   Follow local protocol.

Figure 25-18. *The three stages of frostbite*

Table 25-2
Stages of Frostbite

Extent of Injury	Appearance of Frozen Skin	Appearance of Skin after Rewarming
First degree (layers of skin only)	White, plaquelike	Red, hot, and dry, with itching, burning, and swelling
Second degree (skin and the layer just beneath the skin)	White with blisters filled with clear fluid	Blisters filled with straw-colored fluid; swelling and intense burning
Third degree (skin and the layers beneath the skin)	Discolored, fails to blanch with pressure, deep small blisters filled with dark fluid	Blisters filled with bloody fluid; severe swelling, with some tissue death
Fourth degree (skin, muscle, and bone)	White to deep purple skin; no pain, swelling, or blisters; full-thickness freeze	Numbness; significant death of the skin, muscle, and bone

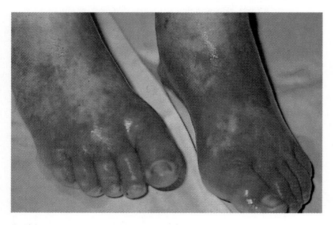

Figure 25-19. Third-degree frostbite

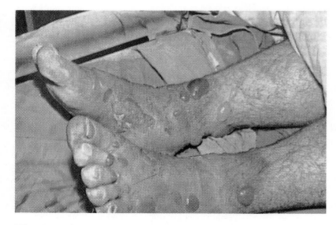

Figure 25-20. Second-degree frostbite

To care for frostnip, gently rewarm the affected skin by placing it against warm skin (the skin of the abdomen, or in the armpit or groin). Never rub the skin. It will tingle when it is warm.

To care for frostbite, activate the EMS system immediately; then:

1. Immediately remove the victim from the cold environment.

2. Keep the tissue frozen until you can initiate care; *never thaw tissue if there is any chance of its refreezing.* If the tissue refreezes, the ice crystals will be larger and will do greater damage to the tissues.

3. Protect the injured tissue from friction or pressure; never poke or squeeze the tissue. Remove constricting clothing or jewelry that is not sticking to the skin.

4. Thaw frostbitten tissue *rapidly* in water just above normal body temperature (see Figure 25-21). Fully immerse the frozen extremity without allowing it to touch the sides or bottom of the container; check the water temperature with a thermometer, and keep it between 100 and 110 degrees F by adding warm water. Never use any kind of flame or electric heat, and never use dry heat. *Never* rub or massage frostbitten skin or rub it with snow or alcohol. Never break any blisters caused by frostbite.

5. Keep rewarming until the skin color no longer improves (rewarming to this point may take as long as 40 minutes).

6. Once the skin is thawed, any solution that comes in contact with it must be sterile. Cover the thawed parts with loose, dry, sterile dressings and elevate the extremities. Place sterile gauze between the fingers and toes to reduce the risk of increased injury.

7. While waiting for emergency personnel to arrive, monitor vital signs and keep the victim warm. Do not let the victim walk if the feet are involved, and do not let the victim smoke.

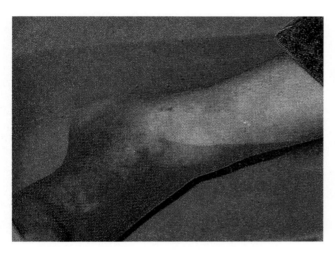

Figure 25-21. *Thaw the frostbitten part rapidly in water just above normal body temperature (100–110 degrees F).*

Progress Check

1. Because taking core temperature is difficult in the field, you should rely on _____ to identify hypothermia.
   (skin temperature/signs and symptoms/what the victim tells you)

2. The key to treating hypothermia is never to _____ .
   (start rewarming right away/allow the victim to stay in a cold environment/rewarm too rapidly)

3. Rewarm a hypothermia victim only if the victim _____ .
   (does not respond to other treatment/has a further temperature drop/cannot be transported immediately)

4. The key in treating immersion hypothermia is _____ .
   (getting the victim out of the water/preventing drowning/drying the victim)

5. You should never thaw frostbitten tissue if there is any danger of _____ .
   (refreezing/delayed transport/increased injury)

6. Frostbitten tissue should be thawed _____ .
   (gradually/rapidly/with high heat)

• SUMMARY •

- The body maintains its temperature by variations in the blood flow.

- Body heat can be lost through radiation, conduction, convection, and evaporation.

- There are three kinds of heat-related injury, or hyperthermia—heatstroke, heat exhaustion, and heat cramps.

- Heatstroke is a life-threatening emergency; untreated victims die.

- Heatstroke occurs when the temperature-regulating mechanisms of the body fail and the body can no longer cool itself.

- Heat exhaustion is a mild state of shock that occurs when profuse sweating results in severe loss of salt and water.

- Heat cramps occur when the balance of water, salt, and calcium in the muscles is disrupted.

- A victim of general hypothermia can appear to be dead, but you should give emergency care unless there are other obviously lethal injuries. A victim should never be considered dead until he or she is *warm* and dead.

- The key in treating immersion hypothermia is to get the victim out of the water.

- Frostbite is freezing of body tissues; never warm or thaw frostbitten tissue if there is any danger of its refreezing.

• KEY TERMS •

Make sure you understand the following key terms:

- radiation
- conduction
- convection
- evaporation
- hyperthermia
- heatstroke
- heat exhaustion
- heat cramps
- hypothermia
- frostbite
- frostnip

Student: _____   Date: _____

Course: _____   Section #: _____

PART 1 • True/False

If you believe the statement is true, circle the T. If you believe the statement is false, circle the F.

T F **1.** Heatstroke commonly occurs under conditions of high temperature, high humidity, and low wind velocity.

T F **2.** Emergency care of heatstroke is aimed at immediate cooling of the body.

T F **3.** To treat heatstroke, remove the victim's clothing, moisten the skin with cool water, and direct a fan at the skin.

T F **4.** Heat exhaustion is the most common heat injury.

T F **5.** The most critical problem in heat exhaustion is dehydration.

T F **6.** In heat exhaustion, the skin is flushed and hot; in heatstroke, the skin is cool and pale.

T F **7.** Do not give a heat exhaustion victim fluids by mouth.

T F **8.** Heat cramps are the least common and least serious heat injury.

T F **9.** Heat cramps occur only in hot weather.

T F **10.** Death can occur within 2 hours of the first signs and symptoms of hypothermia.

T F **11.** Hypothermia can occur even in warm weather.

T F **12.** Whenever possible, keep a hypothermia victim in a sitting position.

T F **13.** If a hypothermia victim is not shivering, do not try to rewarm the victim.

T F **14.** Active rewarming of a hypothermia victim should always be attempted before transporting the person to a hospital.

T F **15.** Never try to rewarm a severely hypothermic victim.

T F **16.** A victim of immersion hypothermia should be encouraged to increase physical activity.

T F **17.** Always thaw a frostbitten part.

T F **18.** Frostbite should be thawed gradually.

T F **19.** If possible, use dry heat to thaw frostbitten parts.

PART 2 • Multiple Choice

For each item, circle the correct answer or the phrase that best completes the statement.

1. Which of the following is *not* a means for the body to lose heat?

 a. evaporation
 b. osmosis
 c. convection
 d. radiation

2. The phenomenon of convection has been incorporated into the concept of

 a. windchill
 b. evaporation
 c. perspiration
 d. hyperthermia

3. The most important characteristic of heatstroke is

 a. profuse perspiration
 b. dizziness
 c. very hot skin
 d. painful muscle cramps or spasms

4. The most important emergency care procedure for victims of heatstroke is to

 a. treat for shock
 b. replace lost body fluids
 c. cool the body in any way possible
 d. give the victim salt-and-sugar water

5. The two most distinct differences between heatstroke and heat exhaustion are

 a. pulse rate and presence of perspiration
 b. skin condition and pupil reaction
 c. body temperature and presence of perspiration
 d. body temperature and skin condition

6. The victim suffering from heat exhaustion can be identified by

 a. hot, dry, flushed skin
 b. cool, moist skin and shallow breathing
 c. cool, dry skin; dizziness; and headache
 d. hot, moist skin; labored breathing; and slow pulse

7. The most serious heat-related emergency is
   a. heat exhaustion
   b. heatstroke
   c. heat cramps
   d. all are equally serious

8. Which of the following is *not* a procedure for care of a victim of immersion hypothermia?
   a. handle the victim very gently
   b. encourage the victim to walk around to increase circulation
   c. layer dry clothing over the victim's wet clothing
   d. protect the victim from the wind

9. For which of the following reasons should a frostbitten part be left frozen?
   a. assessment has not been confirmed
   b. pain becomes severe as thawing takes place
   c. there is a possibility of refreezing
   d. acclimatization needs to be increased

10. A frostbitten part should be rewarmed
   a. by rubbing
   b. with water between 100 and 110 degrees F
   c. with heat from a fire or stove
   d. with water between 75 and 85 degrees F

PART 3 • Matching

Match the type of emergency with the appropriate signs/symptoms and emergency care.

Type of Emergency

A. Heatstroke
B. Heat exhaustion
C. Heat cramps
D. Frostbite
E. Hypothermia

Signs/Symptoms and Care

_____ 1. Pale, clammy skin

_____ 2. Firm, waxy, white skin

_____ 3. A dangerous medical emergency

_____ 4. Hot, flushed, dry skin

_____ 5. Painful abdomen

_____ 6. Body temperature of 106 degrees F

_____ 7. Do not rub or chafe

_____ 8. Give sips of cool salt water

_____ 9. Slow, slurred speech

_____ 10. Wrap in wet sheet

_____ 11. Sweating mechanisms fail

_____ 12. General cooling of entire body

_____ 13. May require CPR

PART 4 • What Would You Do If?

• A middle-aged man who is playing baseball on a hot and humid day becomes dizzy and weak. He has moist, pale, clammy skin; complains of a headache; and is nauseous.

• You arrive at a winter campout area and find a victim who is confused and disoriented. She has a stumbling gait, and her face appears bloated and cyanotic. She also seems irrational, and her speech is thick and slurred.

Water Emergencies

Learning Objectives

When you have mastered the material in this chapter, you will be able to

1 Explain the difference between drowning and near-drowning

2 Explain the difference between "wet" and "dry" drowning

3 Explain why you should always try to resuscitate someone who has had an accident in cold water

4 Explain how to safely reach someone in trouble in the water

5 Describe and demonstrate how to protect a victim in the water if you suspect spinal injury

6 Describe and demonstrate the emergency care for a near-drowning victim

7 Describe the various kinds of diving emergencies

8 List the signs and symptoms of air embolism and decompression sickness

9 Describe and demonstrate the emergency care for a victim of air embolism or decompression sickness

10 Describe and demonstrate the emergency care for a victim of barotrauma

SQ3R Plus

- **Survey** to set goals for studying.
- Ask **questions** as you **read.**
- Stop frequently to **recite** and **review.**
- **Write** a summary of key points.
- **Reflect** on the importance of this material and its relevance in your life.

On July 24, 1998, Daniel Martin and his two young children were enjoying relief from the searing summer heat at a mountain lake 30 miles outside of town. As his youngest child grasped a rope swing for a turn over the water, Daniel saw a teenage girl struggling to stay afloat about 15 feet from shore.

Daniel knew the water was too deep for him to touch bottom, and he had limited confidence in his own swimming skills. Acting quickly, he tied a large thermos jug to the long tow rope from his car trunk. Positioning himself solidly against a tree at the lake's edge, he threw the object out to 13-year-old Karen Francis. When she grasped it and clung to it for buoyancy, Daniel pulled Karen to shore.

She was weak and shaken. Daniel had her lie down on a grassy area at the lake's edge. She seemed to be breathing well and had a pulse; a quick primary survey revealed no bleeding or suspected fractures. Using his two sons' beach towels, Daniel covered Karen to help preserve her body heat. Following Karen's directions, Daniel sent a nearby woman to find Karen's parents, who gently helped her into their motor home and took her into town for evaluation at an emergency room.

NEARLY 9,000 PEOPLE DIE EACH YEAR IN THE UNITED States from water accidents. While drownings are most commonly associated with water emergencies, drownings actually cause only about one in twenty water-related deaths. The rest are mostly caused by accidents suffered while diving or during deep-water exploration, boating, and water skiing. Water-related deaths may also result from motor vehicle accidents. In addition to drowning and near-drowning, water-related accidents can cause bleeding, soft-tissue injuries, and fractures.

This chapter details water-safety techniques to protect you as a First Aider, outlines first aid procedures to use with drowning and near-drowning victims, and explains appropriate care for victims of diving accidents.

Note: Unless a water emergency occurs in open, shallow water that has a stable, uniform bottom, never go out into the water unless you are

- a good swimmer;
- specially trained;
- wearing a personal flotation device; and
- accompanied by other rescuers.

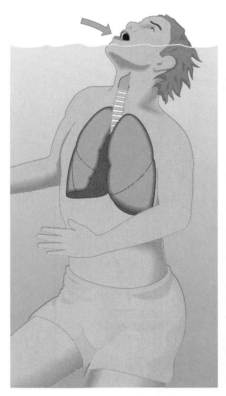

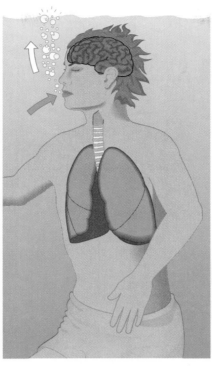

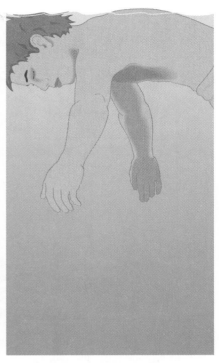

Drowning can be the result of cold, fatigue, injury, disorientation, intoxication, or limited swimming abilities.

The drowning victim struggles to inhale air as long as possible. Eventually the victim inhales water or a muscle spasm of the larynx closes the airway.

Loss of consciousness, convulsions, cardiac arrest, and death may follow.

Figure 26-1. Drowning

• Section 1 •
DROWNING AND NEAR-DROWNING

Learning Objective 1 Explain the difference between drowning and near-drowning.

Drownings and near-drownings do not always occur in large bodies of water: an adult can drown in just a few inches of water, and an infant in even less. Recent studies indicate that one-fourth of all infants who drown do so in 5-gallon buckets; others drown in bathtubs and toilets.

Near-drowning is defined as at least temporarily surviving near suffocation due to submersion. **Drowning** is death from suffocation due to submersion.

Learning Objective 2 Explain the difference between "wet" and "dry" drowning.

"Wet" drowning occurs when a victim aspirates fluid into the lungs. **"Dry" drowning** occurs when a severe muscle spasm of the larynx cuts off respiration

but does not allow aspiration of a significant amount of fluid into the lungs (see Figure 26-1). It is estimated that approximately 10 to 40 percent of all drownings are "dry"—and autopsies reveal that only about 15 percent of all drowning victims aspirate enough water to cause death directly. Panic can often contribute to the death of the person who loses self-control in a water accident (see Figure 26-2 on page 434). In **secondary drowning,** the victim is resuscitated but later

near-drowning Survival, at least temporarily, of near suffocation due to submersion

drowning Death from suffocation due to submersion

"wet" drowning Drowning in which water enters the lungs

"dry" drowning Drowning in which little or no water enters the lungs

secondary drowning Death from aspiration pneumonia following resuscitation after a water accident

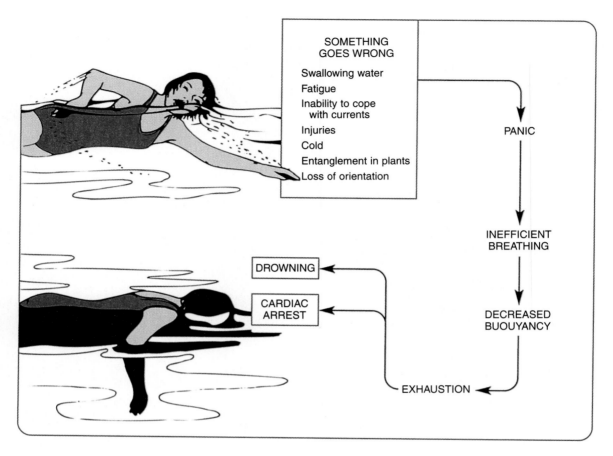

Figure 26-2. *In water accidents, panic can often contribute to the death of the person who loses self-control.*

dies from the incident, usually as a result of breathing water into the lungs and developing aspiration pneumonia.

Among victims of water-related accidents, those with the poorest prognosis are older victims, those who struggle in the water, those who suffer associated injuries, those who are submerged for a long time, and those who are in warm, dirty, or brackish water. Standard water-safety precautions can be taken to prevent near-drowning accidents (see Figure 26-3).

Resuscitating Cold-Water Submersion Victims

Learning Objective 3 Explain why you should always try to resuscitate someone who has had an accident in cold water.

There is a significant difference between warm-water and cold-water drownings: When a person dives into cold water (below 68 degrees F), the **mammalian**

diving reflex can prevent death, even after prolonged submersion.

Here is how it works: When the face is submerged in cold water, breathing is inhibited, the heart rate slows, and the blood vessels throughout most of the body constrict. However, blood flow to the heart and brain is maintained. In this way, oxygen is sent and used only where it is needed immediately to sustain life.

The colder the water, the more oxygen is diverted to the heart and brain. The diving reflex is more pronounced, and cooling is more rapid, in the young. In water at or below 68 degrees F, the body's metabolic requirements are only about half of normal.

Note that the notion of the mammalian diving reflex is somewhat controversial. Recent research suggests that the mammalian reflex works in a number of mammals, such as whales, but does not apply to humans. Some researchers suggest that cold-water survival is due to hypothermia, which slows the metabolism and reduces the body's need for oxygen.

Generally, you can resuscitate victims who have been submerged in cold water even after 30 minutes

The vast majority of drowning and near-drowning incidents (see table) could be prevented if people would remember three basic rules:

- *Children should be under constant supervision if a lake, pool, or pail of water of any size is nearby.*
- *Water sports and alcoholic beverages never mix.*
- *Life preservers or life jackets should always be worn when boating.*

These and other standard water safety precautions for swimming, diving, and boating should be made clear and repeated frequently.

Where People Drown

Type of water or site	Drownings (%)
Salt water	1–2
Fresh water	98–99
Swimming pools	
Public	50
Private	3
Lakes, rivers, streams, storm drains	20
Bathtubs	15
Buckets of water	4
Fish ponds or tanks	4
Toilets	4
Washing machine	1

Adapted with permission from Orlowski, JP: Drowning, near-drowning, and ice-water submersions. *Pediatr Clin North Am* 34(1):77.

Effective prevention in children requires constant supervision and common sense. A young child can find and fall into water in just a minute or two—less time than anyone would realize he or she is gone unless attention is continuous—and fences are not always effective in keeping children out of places where they should not go. A fence may appear to enclose a pool completely, but the gate may not be self-closing or the lock may be broken. The vast majority of children who drown in swimming pools do so in the backyards of their own homes, usually in the later afternoon on summer weekends. And isn't it sensible to require that babysitters know CPR?

Programs that claim to "drown-proof" or teach young children to swim are controversial, and many experts feel they provide a false sense of security. The American Academy of Pediatrics does not recommend teaching children younger than 3 years of age to swim, although some regional programs take children as young as 6 months. Drown-proofing programs fail—studies indicate that a significant number of children have submersion accidents despite their training—because the sequential patterning approach used to teach the very young in a structured environment engenders, in effect, learned helplessness. The cues a child learns in the class or pool setting are missing in the real-life crisis.

A large number of adult drowning victims have detectable levels of blood alcohol. Swimmers should be warned about diving in shallow or unexplored water. Boating precautions should be heeded by all boaters. Seizure disorders are an important but easily overlooked risk factor in persons of all ages.

Figure 26-3. Preventing near-drowning accidents (Adapted with permission from *Patient Care,* January 15, 1989. Copyright © 1989, Patient Care, Oradell, NJ. All rights reserved.)

or longer in cardiac arrest. As a guideline, any pulseless, nonbreathing victim who has been submerged in cold water should be resuscitated.

Some experts advise providing resuscitation to every drowning victim, regardless of water temperature—even those who have been in the water for a prolonged period. *Follow local protocol.*

Ensuring Your Own Safety

Learning Objective 4 Explain how to safely reach someone in trouble in the water.

In any water emergency, you need to reach the victim, but *you must do so with utmost concern for your own safety.*

Never enter anything but very shallow water with a stable, uniform bottom unless

- You know how to swim
- You have been trained in water-rescue techniques
- You are wearing a personal flotation device
- You are accompanied by other rescuers.

If the victim is conscious and close to shore

- Make sure you have firm, solid footing and cannot slip into the water.
- Hold out an object for the victim to grab; the best thing to use is a rope. You can also use an oar, branch, fishing pole, towel, shirt, or other strong object that will not break.

mammalian diving reflex A reflex that prevents death after submersion in cold water

- Once the victim has grabbed the object, pull the victim to shore.

   If the victim is conscious but too far away to reach

- Make sure you have firm, solid footing and cannot slip into the water.
- Tie a long rope or line to an object that floats and is heavy enough to throw, such as an inflatable ball, log, thermos jug, picnic cooler, or capped empty milk jug.
- Throw the object near the victim.
- Once the victim has grabbed the floating object, tow the victim to shore.

   If the victim is unconscious or too far to reach with a line, you will need to go to the victim. If at all possible, use a boat. Otherwise, never try to go to the victim unless you meet the safety criteria listed above.

Caring for Spinal Injury

Learning Objective 5 Describe and demonstrate how to protect a victim in the water if you suspect spinal injury.

If the victim may have been involved in a diving accident, you should suspect spinal injury. You should also suspect spinal injury in any swimmer who is unconscious (especially one in shallow, warm water).

   In the case of possible spinal injury, the goal is to support the back and stabilize the head and neck as other care is given. It is important to stabilize the victim in the water properly, then to remove the person carefully from the water. The American National Red Cross suggests that the victim not be removed from the water until a backboard or other rigid support can be used as a splint.

   If you are not specially trained in water rescue

- Do not remove the victim from the water.
- Keep the victim afloat on his or her back.
- Always support the head and neck level with the back.
- Maintain the airway and support ventilation in the water.
- Wait for help.

Progress Check

1. _____ is death from suffocation due to submersion.
   (Near-drowning/Drowning/Asphyxia)

2. Victims submerged in _____ water have the poorest prognosis.
   (cold/warm/deep)

3. "Dry" drowning occurs when a severe spasm of the _____ cuts off respiration, but water does not enter the lungs.
   (trachea/bronchioles/larynx)

4. The _____ reflex helps victims submerged in cold water survive longer.
   (mammalian/Freudian/subdiaphragmatic)

5. Never go in the water unless you can swim and have been trained, and are _____ .
   (in good health/prepared to perform rescue breathing/wearing a flotation device)

• Section 2 •

EMERGENCY CARE FOR NEAR-DROWNING

Learning Objective 6 Describe and demonstrate the emergency care for a near-drowning victim.

To care for near-drowning victims, activate the EMS system; then:

1. Remove the victim from the water as quickly and safely as you can.
   - If you suspect that the victim has spinal injury, maintain in-line immobilization and secure the victim to a backboard before removing the person from the water.
   - If you find the victim face down, splint the victim's head and neck with your arms or the victim's arms (see Figure 26-4), then roll the victim over, supporting the back and stabilizing the head and neck. Keeping the head and neck in line with the back, slide a backboard under the victim; secure the victim to the backboard (see Figure 26-5 on page 438).
   - If possible, apply a rigid cervical collar or place padding at the sides of the victim's head to keep it from moving.
   - Float the board to shore or poolside and lift the victim from the water.

2. If you do not suspect spinal injury, place the victim on the left side so that water, vomitus, and secretions can drain from the upper airway.

HEAD SPLINT TECHNIQUE

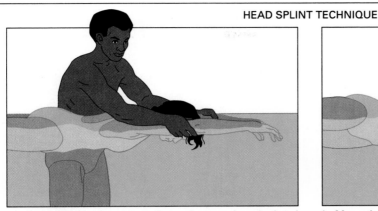

a. Extend the patient's arms. Press them against the head to create a splint.

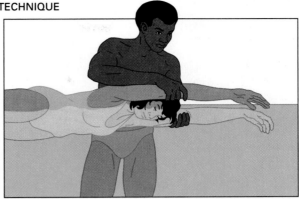

b. Move the patient forward to a horizontal position. Begin to rotate the patient.

c. Lower yourself until the water is at shoulder level and the patient is face up.

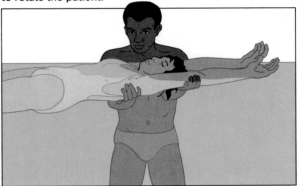

d. Bring the patient's head to rest in the crook of your arm until help arrives.

Adapted from Pat Samples, Spinal Cord Injuries: "The High Cost of Careless Diving," *The Physician and Sportsmedicine*, July 1989.

Figure 26-4. The head-splint technique immobilizes the head and neck while the victim is being turned in the water.

3. Assess for breathing and pulse.

4. If there is no breathing, establish an airway as rapidly as you can and begin ventilations.
   Note: Water in the airway can cause resistance to ventilations. Once you have determined that there are no foreign objects in the airway, apply ventilations with more force until you see the victim's chest rise and fall.

5. If there is no pulse, begin chest compressions and perform CPR, as described in Chapter 5. Continue resuscitation until emergency personnel arrive.

A near-drowning victim needs to be taken to a hospital or medical facility, even if you think the danger has passed. A near-drowning victim can develop complications and die as long as three or four days after the incident. (Approximately 15 percent of all drowning deaths are due to secondary complications.)

Progress Check

1. If you suspect spinal injury, stabilize the neck and spine _____ you remove the victim from the water.
   (before/after/while)

2. If you suspect spinal injury, apply a cervical collar and secure the victim to a _____ .
   (buoyant device/stable object/spine board)

3. _____ can cause resistance to ventilations.
   (Spasms/Swelling of the airway/Water in the airway)

4. Near-drowning victims should always be taken to the hospital; 15 percent of all drowning deaths are due to _____ .
   (aspiration/laryngeal spasm/secondary complications)

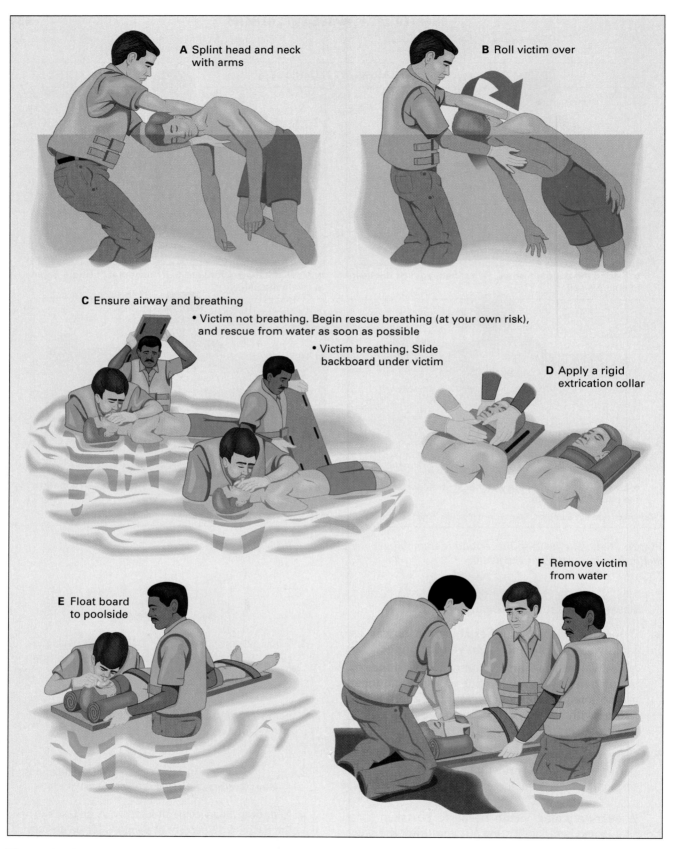

A Splint head and neck with arms

B Roll victim over

C Ensure airway and breathing
- Victim not breathing. Begin rescue breathing (at your own risk), and rescue from water as soon as possible
- Victim breathing. Slide backboard under victim

D Apply a rigid extrication collar

E Float board to poolside

F Remove victim from water

Figure 26-5. Immobilizing suspected diving accident victim, using a backboard or firm flat object, such as a door. Follow local protocols.

• Section 3 •
DIVING EMERGENCIES

Learning Objective 7 Describe the various kinds of diving emergencies.

Diving emergencies can result either from diving into a pool or other relatively shallow body of water or from diving in deep water with scuba gear.

Diving in Shallow Water

Injuries to the head and neck and fractures of the arms, legs, and ribs can be sustained when diving into water from a diving board, shore, poolside, boat, or dock.

You should always assume that the diver has sustained neck and spinal injuries, even if the diver is still conscious. If the victim is still in the water, provide care as you would for a near-drowning, stabilizing the neck and spine as described on page 436. If the victim has left the water, provide care as you would for any other victim with suspected neck and spinal injuries.

Deep-Water Diving

A major complication of deep-water diving emergencies is coma, which may result from asphyxiation, head injury, heart attack, air tank contamination, intoxication, or aspiration. It can also result from air embolism or decompression sickness, two emergencies that require recompression.

Air Embolism

Air embolism generally occurs when a diver holds a breath during a dive. Pressure exerted on the body is rapidly reduced the farther the diver descends, and the air in the lungs expands rapidly, rupturing the alveoli and damaging adjacent blood vessels. As a result, air bubbles enter the bloodstream, making it difficult for the blood to perfuse body tissues with oxygen and nutrients. The onset of air embolism is rapid.

Decompression Sickness

Decompression sickness ("the bends") usually occurs when a diver comes up too quickly from a deep, prolonged dive. Gases (usually nitrogen) breathed by the diver are absorbed into the bloodstream; as the diver comes up, the nitrogen is transformed into tiny bubbles, which lodge in body tissues and enter the bloodstream. Decompression sickness is gradual in onset, and symptoms usually occur 12 to 24 hours after the dive.

Signs and Symptoms

Learning Objective 8 List the signs and symptoms of air embolism and decompression sickness.

Following are signs and symptoms common to both air embolism and decompression sickness:

- Itchy, blotchy, or mottled skin
- Difficulty breathing
- Dizziness
- Chest pain
- Severe, deep aching pain in the muscles, joints, and tendons
- Blurred or distorted vision
- Partial deafness, distortion of senses
- Nausea and vomiting
- Numbness or paralysis
- Staggering gait or lack of coordination

In addition, air embolism can cause

- Frothy blood in the nose and mouth
- Swelling and crepitus in the neck
- Loss or distortion of memory
- Cardiac or respiratory arrest
- Behavioral changes (sometimes the only sign)

In addition, decompression sickness can cause

- Swelling of the extremities
- A migrainelike headache
- Choking or coughing
- Inability to void the bladder
- Hallucinations

Emergency Care

Learning Objective 9 Describe and demonstrate the emergency care for a victim of air embolism or decompression sickness.

To care for a victim of air embolism or decompression sickness, activate the EMS system; then:

1. If there is no sign of neck or spine injury, position the victim on the left side; slant the entire body

air embolism A diving injury in which air bubbles enter the bloodstream

decompression sickness A diving injury in which gases (usually nitrogen) enter the bloodstream

15 degrees with the head down to force air or gas bubbles to stay in the abdomen.

2. Provide basic life support; administer ventilations and initiate CPR if needed. Life support is critical in these cases because oxygen reduces the size of nitrogen bubbles and improves circulation.

3. Monitor the victim continuously until emergency personnel arrive. The victim needs to be taken to a recompression chamber for treatment.

Barotrauma

> **Learning Objective 10** Describe and demonstrate the emergency care for a victim of barotrauma.

Sometimes called "the squeeze," **barotrauma** occurs during ascent or descent when air pressure in the body's air cavities (such as the sinuses or middle ear) becomes too great. As a result, tissue in the air cavities is injured; for example, the eardrum or sinus may rupture.

Barotrauma is marked by mild to severe pain in the affected area, possible discharge from the nose or ears, extreme dizziness, nausea, and disorientation.

Victims of barotrauma must be cared for at a medical facility immediately to prevent permanent blindness, deafness, residual dizziness, or the inability to dive in the future. Provide the same care as you would for air embolism or decompression sickness.

Progress Check

1. Always assume that someone who dived in shallow water has sustained _____ .
   (*respiratory injury/abdominal injury/spinal injury*)

2. A major complication of deep-water diving emergencies is _____ .
   (*coma/head injury/spine injury*)

3. Decompression sickness is sometimes called _____ .
   (*"the squeeze"/"the bends"*)

4. Victims of air embolism or decompression sickness need treatment in a _____ .
   (*recompression chamber/iron lung/resonance imager*)

> **barotrauma** A diving emergency in which body cavities are subjected to extreme pressure

• SUMMARY •

- Drowning is death from suffocation due to asphyxiation; near-drowning is survival, at least temporarily, from near suffocation due to submersion.

- In 10 to 40 percent of all drownings, water did not enter the lungs; instead, the victim died because a spasm of the larynx cut off respiration.

- Among victims of water accidents, those with the poorest prognosis include older victims, those who struggle in the water, those who suffer associated injuries, those who have prolonged submersion time, and those who are in warm, dirty, or brackish water.

- The mammalian diving reflex may enable victims in cold water to survive far longer than those in warm water.

- Never go into water to rescue a swimmer unless you can swim, have been trained in water-rescue techniques, are wearing a personal flotation device, and are accompanied by other rescuers.

- If you suspect that a near-drowning victim has sustained spinal injuries, immobilize the spine before you remove the victim from the water.

- If you can, immobilize the spine before you perform other rescue operations, such as giving rescue breathing in the water.

- A near-drowning victim should always be taken to a hospital; complications can occur as much as 3 or 4 days later and are the cause of 15 percent of all drowning deaths.

- Always assume that a victim of a diving accident has sustained neck and spinal injuries, even if the diver is still conscious.

- A major complication of deep-water diving emergencies is coma.

- Victims of deep-water diving emergencies need rapid transportation to a medical center; many need treatment in a recompression chamber.

• KEY TERMS •

Make sure you understand the following key terms:

- near-drowning
- drowning
- "wet" drowning
- "dry" drowning
- secondary drowning
- mammalian diving reflex
- air embolism
- decompression sickness
- barotrauma

Student: _____ Date: _____

Course: _____ Section #: _____

If you believe the statement is true, circle the T. If you believe the statement is false, circle the F.

T F **1.** Drowning always results from inhaling water, and a drowning victim's lungs always contain water.

T F **2.** Warm-water drowning and cold-water drowning are virtually the same.

T F **3.** If you suspect that a victim of a water accident has sustained a back or neck injury, you should *not* move him or her from the water before strapping to a backboard.

T F **4.** A near-drowning victim may still die up to 2 days following successful resuscitation.

T F **5.** If a victim is in trouble near a deck or the pool's edge, it is always best to rescue the person by getting into the water yourself.

T F **6.** A spinal injury victim who is in the water should be removed from the water immediately, then splinted on shore.

T F **7.** The diving reflex causes blood to be shunted from the body core into the extremities.

T F **8.** An estimated 10 to 40 percent of all drownings are "dry."

T F **9.** A near-drowning victim should always be transported to a hospital, even if the victim appears to have recovered.

T F **10.** Fifteen percent of all drowning deaths are the result of secondary complications.

• You are at a mountain lake and see a child floating face down, 20 to 30 feet offshore.

27

Wilderness Emergencies

Learning Objectives

When you have mastered the material in this chapter, you will be able to

1   List the specific information you should have about the wilderness area you will visit before you leave home

2   Explain what kinds of information the first aid leader should have about each member of the group

3   Outline basic survival techniques for cold weather

4   Discuss special ways of handling food and water while in the wilderness

5   List the signs and symptoms of the major altitude-related emergencies

6   Discuss special assessment techniques to use in a wilderness setting

7   Discuss special considerations for managing shock in a wilderness setting

8   Discuss special considerations for performing CPR in a wilderness setting

9   Discuss special considerations for management of soft tissue and musculoskeletal injuries in a wilderness setting

10   Discuss special considerations in immobilizing a victim in a wilderness setting

SQ3R Plus

- **Survey** to set goals for studying.
- Ask **questions** as you **read.**
- Stop frequently to **recite** and **review.**
- **Write** a summary of key points.
- **Reflect** on the importance of this material and its relevance in your life.

This chapter was written by Chad N. Smith.

*O*n June 6, 1998, four college students set out before dawn to climb to the summit of Mount Timpanogos, the highest peak of the Wasatch Range of the Rocky Mountains. The hike to the 12,000-foot summit, though rigorous, was frequently completed by climbers in a single day.

The group made good time throughout the morning, stopping only occasionally to eat a piece of fruit or adjust their gear. When the four stopped about noon to eat lunch, 21-year-old Brock Miller, who had been lagging behind, complained of a severe headache. When the other three suggested that he might have low blood sugar from not eating much all morning, he said he felt nauseated and did not want to eat. Brock leaned against an outcropping of granite while the others ate a hearty lunch.

When it was time to go, Brock resisted. He felt too fatigued, he said. On closer observation, Brock's friend Curtis Carson noticed that, even though Brock had been resting for almost an hour, he was having difficulty breathing. His headache and nausea had both intensified.

Curtis recognized Brock's signs and symptoms as those of acute mountain sickness that had progressed into high altitude pulmonary edema, and he knew that Brock's condition could deteriorate rapidly unless he was taken to a lower altitude immediately. Curtis took Brock's gear, and all three hikers assisted him several miles to the nearest ranger station, where a Forest Service employee drove him to an area hospital for treatment that reversed the potentially fatal condition.

CONFRONTING ANY MEDICAL EMERGENCY CAN BE challenging, but it can be especially difficult in a wilderness setting—in the mountains, in the desert, on the water, or in any other isolated area.

In a wilderness setting you are generally at increased risk for injury, are far from the comfort and safety of the 9-1-1 system, and are in potentially hostile environments. You may have very limited resources for dealing with any medical emergencies.

Besides coping with limited equipment or supplies, you may be 8 to 12 hours away from the nearest phone or radio. Even if you can quickly call for emergency help, it may take hours for the help to reach you, and it may be extremely difficult to describe exactly where the emergency scene is in terms that will help personnel find you without delay. In many cases, you will be the only help the victim has for hours—or, possibly, days.

This chapter explains the importance of working to prevent problems in the wilderness, reviews basic survival techniques, discusses common outdoor first aid problems, and outlines special considerations for first aid treatment in the wilderness.

• Section 1 •
PREVENTION OF WILDERNESS EMERGENCIES

> **Learning Objective 1** List the specific information you should have about the wilderness area you will visit before you leave home.

Most wilderness emergencies are preventable, and the impact of most medical emergencies in the wilderness can be reduced through proper planning and preparation.

Proper preparation includes being properly equipped—not only with first aid supplies, but with food, water, extra clothing, and materials for constructing shelter. Always be prepared for a change in the weather. And always travel with at least one other person, let people at home know exactly where you are going, and give an estimated time of return.

Never enter a wilderness area without at least one leader who has been to the area before, who knows the way, and who has information on

- What terrain can be expected
- What weather conditions are likely
- How long the trip will take
- What hazards may be encountered
- What resources will be available in case of emergency

This leader should have final say about the equipment, route, camp, daily goals, and so on.

> **Learning Objective 2** Explain what kinds of information the first aid leader should have about each member of the group.

A *first aid leader* (who may be the same person as the group leader)

- Determines what first aid supplies are needed
- Ensures that adequate and appropriate first aid supplies are available
- Knows the previous experience and pertinent medical history of each member of the party, including preexisting medical conditions, prescribed medications, and allergies
- Ensures that any required medications or appropriate supplies are taken into the wilderness (though he or she does not necessarily need to carry those supplies)
- Understands appropriate wilderness first aid procedures and has training and experience in using them

Part of the planning for any trip into a wilderness area should include deciding how the group will handle a serious medical emergency. Wilderness first aid kits should be carefully stocked to handle the *long-term care* of potential victims, because you may be hours from medical help when emergencies occur. Ideally, First Aiders in the wilderness setting should have a thorough understanding of human anatomy and physiology as well as knowledge of some basic nursing principles.

> ### Progress Check
>
> 1. Before entering a wilderness area, you should specifically plan how you will handle _____ .
> *(animal attacks/food shortages/serious medical emergencies)*
>
> 2. The first aid leader should know the _____ of each member of the party.
> *(medical history/name/next of kin)*
>
> 3. First aid in wilderness settings often involves _____ care.
> *(advanced/long-term/specialized)*
>
> 4. A wilderness first aid kit should be packed to allow the group to handle a _____ .
> *(trauma/serious medical emergency/disaster)*

• Section 2 •
BASIC SURVIVAL

> **Learning Objective 3** Outline basic survival techniques for cold weather.

Physiologically, the human body requires shelter, water, and food, in that order. Severe weather conditions can incapacitate—and possibly kill—a person in about 3 hours. Without water, a person will die in 3 days. A normally healthy individual can survive for about 3 weeks without food.

In the wilderness, you need to remember the **Rule of Threes**—when a person faces a combination of all three conditions—severe weather, no water, and no food—survival time is considerably reduced.

> **Rule of Threes** A rule stating that survival time is considerably reduced if a victim is without all three factors required for survival: shelter, water, and food

Shelter

Ideally, shelter should do just that: *shelter* you from heat, wind, cold, and/or moisture. As you seek shelter in the wilderness, remember the principles of how the body loses heat that were discussed in Chapter 25. To begin with, dress appropriately; use layers of clothing to maximize your ability to stay warm, and to increase your flexibility in changing weather. Wear synthetic long underwear; cotton, although absorbent, loses the ability to insulate as soon as it gets damp. Use natural-fiber pants, sweaters, and jackets to insulate. As an outer layer, wear fabric that is breathable, windproof, and waterproof. Wear a synthetic liner under fleece socks, and use water-repellent footwear with good traction. Use windproof and waterproof mittens and a wool hat that covers your entire head, including your ears.

Various kinds of shelter will work to keep you warm as long as you

- Stay out of the bottom of valleys or canyons; heat rises, and the lowest area will also be the coldest.

- Avoid setting up a shelter on a ridge or the top of a mountain where you would be exposed to wind.

- Place your shelter downwind of some sort of windbreak, such as a large rock, mound of dirt, or bank of trees or bushes.

You can seek shelter in a natural cave, or you can construct your own shelter. A snow cave or snow trench can keep you warm, as can plastic garbage bags. A tent is ideal *if* it is located out of the wind. If a tent is placed in a windy area, it will actually increase heat loss by convection through a process called **"billowing."** Body heat warms the inside of the tent; as the wind flaps the sides of the tent, the warm air gets blown away and is replaced by cold air.

> **Learning Objective 4** Discuss special ways of handling food and water while in the wilderness.

Water

Plan for water purification before you enter a wilderness area. The best method is to strain the water for large particles, then bring it to a full boil for 2 to 8 minutes, depending on the altitude. The higher the altitude, the longer you need to boil the water to destroy all microorganisms effectively.

The second best method of purifying water is with a commercially manufactured filter. Ideally, choose one that filters out organisms as small as 2 microns in size, which will eliminate *Giardia lamblia*, a cause of profuse diarrhea. Carefully follow manufacturer's instructions for use.

If you are forced to use snow as a water source, melt it before purifying and drinking it. While it seems a simple way to add water to the body, eating snow carries a high price in terms of heat loss. You can melt snow with a stove, over a campfire, or with a candle.

Food

Before entering the wilderness, plan for plenty of nutritious food for each member of your party. Pack the correct kinds of food in adequate amounts, then protect it as if your life depends on it. It does.

Eating is one way the body produces energy, which also produces heat. Make sure there is enough food for each member of your party to eat three nutritious meals each day, as well as for each person to have several high-energy snacks. If you are likely to face uncertain weather or terrain conditions that could delay your party by even 1 day, allow for extra food.

Improper handling and storage of food in a wilderness setting can have both simple consequences (you could lose your food) and dangerous results (you could be attacked and severely injured by animals foraging for your food). Wilderness animals that commonly steal food range from the nonthreatening (pack rats, squirrels, birds, and weasels) to the dangerous (bears, wolves, and coyotes).

To keep your food safe and protect yourself from injury

- Store food supplies some distance from your campsite.

- Store food supplies off the ground; hanging food in stuff sacks is advised.

- Avoid cooking foods with especially strong odors, such as bacon.

- Remember that food refuse also will attract wildlife; burn as much as you can, then keep remaining garbage a safe distance from your campsite and off the ground.

> ## Progress Check
>
> 1. A person can survive for approximately _____ days without water.
>   (2/3/4)
>
> 2. The most important factor for survival in cold weather is _____ .
>   (food/water/shelter)

3. When a victim faces a combined lack of shelter, water, and food, the "rule of _____" goes into effect.
   (survival/threes/convection)

4. Always try to construct a shelter _____ .
   (in the bottom of a canyon/downwind of a windbreak/on top of a ridge)

5. Tents do not provide any _____ .
   (moisture resistance/security/insulation)

6. The best method of purifying water in the wilderness is _____ .
   (purification tablets/filtration/boiling)

7. The higher the altitude, the _____ you should boil water to kill organisms.
   (longer/less time)

8. To protect yourself from predators, _____ your food away from your campsite.
   (bury/hang/cover)

• Section 3 •
ALTITUDE PROBLEMS IN THE WILDERNESS

Learning Objective 5 List the signs and symptoms of the major altitude-related emergencies.

Almost all serious wilderness emergencies can be prevented with proper planning. Hypothermia and heat stroke—both potentially fatal—are generally preceded by milder conditions. The key in the wilderness setting is to act rapidly at the first sign or symptom of a problem (such as shivering) so that a victim does not begin to deteriorate. For information on heat and cold emergencies, see Chapter 25.

Victims of heat or cold injury ideally should remain stabilized and at rest for at least 12 hours after appropriate first aid treatment. Because that may not always be possible in a wilderness setting, monitor the victim closely; relapse is common.

Altitude-related illness generally occurs at altitudes of more than 8,000 feet, though it has been recorded at altitudes of 6,000 feet. It is caused by a lack of oxygen: There is plenty of oxygen in the air, but the lower atmospheric pressure at higher elevations does not provide as much pressure to drive oxygen into the body.

It *is* possible to acclimate to higher elevations. Over time, the body produces more red blood cells and increases the chemicals that allow oxygen to transfer to the body cells. The body also develops more blood

vessels, especially in muscle tissue. In the meantime, respiratory and heart rates and volumes increase. It takes approximately 6 weeks for the acclimatization process to occur. Most victims of altitude-related illness ascended too high, too quickly. Dehydration aggravates altitude-related illness.

Acute Mountain Sickness

The mildest form of altitude sickness is **acute mountain sickness,** which mimics a severe hangover. Signs and symptoms include

- Headache that develops during the night and is present when the victim wakes up in the morning
- Swollen face and puffiness under the eyes
- Nausea and loss of appetite
- Fatigue that is out of proportion with the amount of exertion
- Shortness of breath with even mild exertion

Mild acute mountain sickness generally occurs at altitudes above 8,000 feet among those who have climbed too quickly. Acute mountain sickness occurs more often when the weather is cold and windy, when hikers are fatigued or anxious, or when hikers are dehydrated or have upper respiratory infections.

To treat acute mountain sickness:

1. *Stop climbing immediately;* rest and see whether symptoms improve.

2. If symptoms do not improve, descend 2,000 to 3,000 feet as quickly as possible.

3. Prevent or correct dehydration by drinking at least 4 quarts of fluid every day; eat a high-carbohydrate, high-calorie diet while climbing.

High Altitude Pulmonary Edema

In **high altitude pulmonary edema** (HAPE), fluid from the body is slowly transferred to the lungs; the body's ability to take on oxygen is diminished. HAPE is caused by reaching a new altitude too quickly, and

billowing Loss of heat inside a tent when the wind flaps the sides of the tent and warm air is replaced with cold air

acute mountain sickness An altitude-related illness that resembles a severe hangover

high altitude pulmonary edema An altitude-related illness that causes fluid to go into the lungs from body cells although it can occur at lower altitudes, it generally starts at about 10,000 feet. Unlike acute mountain sickness, which usually causes symptoms within a few hours, the signs and symptoms of HAPE do not develop until as long as 72 hours after reaching the new altitude. Untreated, HAPE can cause death in fewer than 12 hours after symptoms begin.

The signs and symptoms of HAPE include

- Severe shortness of breath, even when resting
- Cyanosis (bluish discoloration of the lips, fingernails, and mucous membranes lining the mouth)
- "Moist" breathing that produces rattling and crackling
- Cough that produces pink, frothy sputum

A victim of HAPE needs *immediate* medical treatment in a compression chamber. *The most important thing you can do is descend immediately* and seek medical help for the victim.

High Altitude Cerebral Edema

High altitude cerebral edema (HACE) causes a dangerous buildup of fluid levels in the brain, resulting in swelling of the brain tissue and increased pressure inside the skull. The brain has nowhere to expand other than downward, through the **foramen magnum**—the hole at the base of the skull that houses the brain stem. Pressure on the brain stem affects cardiac function, respiratory function, and blood pressure; associated pressure on the cerebellum affects balance and motor dexterity.

Signs and symptoms include the following:

- Severe headache
- Severe nausea and vomiting
- **Ataxia** (inability to maintain balance)
- Dizziness
- Extreme fatigue, progressing to coma

Untreated, HACE can cause death within a few hours after the onset of symptoms.

Emergency Care

To care for victims of altitude-related illness, *get the victim to a lower elevation as quickly as possible.* If the victim cannot walk, the victim must be carried or transported on an improvised stretcher. Encourage the victim to drink as much water as possible.

Once the victim is at a lower altitude and symptoms have eased, keep the victim at rest for 12 to 24 hours.

Progress Check

1. Altitude-related illness is caused by a lack of
_____ .
(oxygen/fluids/nutrients)

2. Acute mountain sickness causes symptoms much like those of a severe _____ .
(cold/hangover/migraine headache)

3. High altitude pulmonary edema is characterized by _____ , even after rest.
(fatigue/muscle soreness/difficulty breathing)

4. High altitude cerebral edema is characterized by
_____ .
(ataxia/muscle cramping/double vision)

5. Regardless of the illness, treat altitude problems by getting the victim to _____ .
(rest/lie down/a lower altitude)

• Section 4 •
SPECIAL WILDERNESS CONSIDERATIONS

Almost any accident or illness that can occur under regular conditions can occur in the wilderness. Although the same general principles of assessment and care should be used in the wilderness, some special considerations apply.

Assessment

Learning Objective 6 Discuss special assessment techniques to use in a wilderness setting.

The primary difference between assessment in the wilderness and elsewhere is time; the primary survey should be the same, but you should spend more time doing a detailed secondary survey in a wilderness setting.

Under normal circumstances, the role of a First Aider is to identify and stabilize the most serious injuries while activating the EMS system (see Figure 27-1). In such situations you generally do not have to worry about cleaning wounds, changing dressings, or adjusting splints, for example. In the wilderness, on the other hand, you will probably have to assume responsibility for the victim for a longer period of time, and the treatment you give based on the secondary survey may be the only treatment the victim receives for 12 hours or longer (see Figure 27-2).

Figure 27-1. *First Aider approaching a victim in a wilderness setting*

Figure 27-2. *Assessing a victim in a wilderness setting*

Your assessment is especially vital in getting the right kind of help for the victim: first responders may have to carry the appropriate equipment over miles of rough terrain to treat the victim; you want to make sure it is done right the first time. Your assessment should include detailed and accurate information about the mechanism of injury, the victim's wounds, what is being done for the victim, and—most important— where you are. Always send at least two people for help; if possible, identify your location on a spare map that you send along.

One of the most essential parts of assessment in the wilderness is "charting"—accurate documentation of

• The mechanism of injury or illness

• The victim's vital signs, taken periodically the entire time the victim is under your care

• Your observation of the victim's condition, given periodically

• Your treatment plan and how it was carried out

This kind of information is vital to medical personnel, who will use it to establish *their* treatment plan. If you cannot provide a record of the victim's condition from the time of injury or illness until the victim arrives at the hospital, then the victim's "baseline" vital signs may be hours—or possibly days—old.

To determine the type of records you should keep, remember the mnemonic, C-H-A-R-T:

C	Chief complaint (What did the victim tell you?)
H	History (What happened?)
A	Assessment (What signs and symptoms did you find?)
R$_x$	Treatment (What did you do for the victim?)
T	Transport and disposition (After you cared for the victim, where did the victim go? Did the victim leave? Was it on foot, in a car, in an ambulance, in a helicopter?)

Finally, assessment in the wilderness setting is important because it allows you to determine whether the injury or illness is serious enough to abandon the trip. Some injuries or illnesses may cause discomfort but can safely be treated at the site; others call for aggressive action aimed at evacuating the victim and transporting the person to a hospital. Adequate assessment lets you know the difference.

Management of Shock

Learning Objective 7 Discuss special considerations for managing shock in a wilderness setting.

There are two goals of shock management:

1. Increase and maintain the effective circulating volume of blood

2. Reduce the oxygen debt being incurred by the body.

high altitude cerebral edema An altitude-related illness that causes swelling of the brain and increased pressure inside the skull

foramen magnum The opening at the base of the skull that houses the brain stem

ataxia Inability to keep balance

Figure 27-3. First Aider in wilderness area, treating a victim for shock and maintaining temperature

You need to place the victim in the correct position, maintain a normal body temperature, and replace lost fluids.

Management of shock is detailed in Chapter 6. Special considerations in the wilderness setting include the following:

• *Maintaining temperature.* If you have placed the victim on the cold ground, you must provide insulation; place a blanket, coat, layers of pine needles, or other material between the victim and the ground (see Figure 27-3). If you are in a hot climate, shade the victim from the sun.

• *Replacing fluids.* If you have access to the EMS system, you should never try to replace fluids; if you are in a wilderness setting hours from medical help and shock is progressing, give the victim small sips of water *if the victim is fully conscious.* Monitor closely for nausea, and be prepared to turn the victim on his or her side if vomiting occurs.

Cardiopulmonary Resuscitation

Learning Objective 8 Discuss special considerations for performing CPR in a wilderness setting.

The most daunting aspect of performing CPR in a wilderness setting is the fact that advanced cardiac life support is *not* simply a phone call away. Because victim survival depends on immediate defibrillation, advanced life support, and rapid transport, the prognosis for a victim of cardiac arrest in the wilderness is grim.

Regardless of that fact, begin CPR as soon as assessment indicates it, and continue aggressive and *prolonged* CPR, especially in cases of cold-water drowning or lightning strikes; spontaneous resuscitation can often occur in these cases.

Learning Objective 9 Discuss special considerations for management of soft-tissue and musculoskeletal injuries in a wilderness setting.

Management of Soft-Tissue Injuries

If a laceration, incision, avulsion, puncture, or abrasion is large enough or dirty enough to overwhelm the body's immune system, you will have to deal with the threat of infection—and what you do during the first few hours is critical. To prevent infection:

1. Irrigate the wound immediately to flush out as much bacteria, dirt, and debris as possible. Use boiled water or saline; ideally, squirt the water or solution from a squeeze bottle to provide some pressure, which will help remove dirt and debris from the wound. *Do not use hydrogen peroxide, alcohol, or povidone-iodine directly on the wound.*

2. If tissue has been completely avulsed, wipe or scrub it away with a gauze pad and sterile water or saline; if an avulsion is only partial, clean the tissue thoroughly and place it in its normal anatomical position.

3. Bring the edges of the wound together as closely as you can to the position they were in before the skin was separated. Use commercially prepared tapes, strips, or pieces of adhesive tape to hold the edges of the wound together.

4. Dress and bandage the wound.

If you are a day or more away from medical care, you will need to inspect the wound periodically for signs and symptoms of infection and change the dressing. Follow these guidelines:

• Always wash your hands thoroughly before removing the dressing.

• Keep all dressing materials sterile.

• If necessary, reclean the wound.

• If signs of infection are present (an expanded area of redness, red streaks, heat, pulsating localized pain, pus, or a foul odor), apply a warm, moist compress to the wound for 20 minutes. Remove the compress for 20 minutes; repeat. If there are signs of infection, you should inspect the wound every 4 hours.

• Apply a sterile dressing, then bandage.

Management of Musculoskeletal Injuries

Splinting a fracture in a wilderness setting (see Figure 27-4) requires more than the usual amount of care and consideration: the victim may be in the splint for several days. Follow these guidelines:

• If you do not have access to a splint, improvise with tree limbs, smaller branches lashed together, camp shovels, paddles, oars, skis, ski poles, walking sticks, tent poles, or similar objects.

• Victim comfort is essential, because medical help may be delayed. Make sure you pad the splint well.

• It is vital that you check often for signs of impaired circulation or nerve function.

• While you should *not* normally try to realign an angulated fracture, you may have to do so in a wilderness setting—splinting a severely angulated fracture in the position found and leaving it that way for many hours or even days will almost certainly result in permanent loss of function. Realign as soon after the injury as you can; do not try to "set" the bone, but make sure the normal circulation and nerve function are intact.

• If you are fewer than 3 hours from a hospital, cover the wound from an open fracture with a dry, sterile dressing and splint the fracture. If you are more than 3 hours from a hospital, gently clean the wound and exposed bone ends with a sterile dressing soaked with sterile water. *Do not irrigate the wound.* Cover with a dry, sterile dressing, then splint. All open fractures require immediate medical attention, so arrange to evacuate the victim.

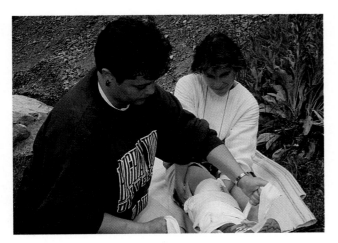

Figure 27-4. Splinting a leg fracture in the wilderness

Immobilizing a Victim

> **Learning Objective 10** Discuss special considerations in immobilizing a victim in a wilderness setting.

To immobilize a victim in a wilderness setting without a commercial backboard:

• Remember that the victim may have to be secured to your improvised backboard for many hours, or even days. You will have to make allowances for eliminating waste (leave a strategically placed hole or space), sliding the victim into a sleeping bag, and feeding the victim.

• Improvise a backboard by lashing together tree branches, walking sticks, the external frames of backpacks, or other similar objects.

• Use a rolled-up blanket to immobilize the neck. Place the blanket behind the victim's head, allowing both long ends to fall across the victim's chest; cross the ends on the chest; applying gentle tension on both long ends, pass them under the victim's opposite arms; attach the ends securely to the blackboard.

• Make sure you pad thoroughly to keep the victim comfortable. Provide plenty of padding over bony prominences and under the buttocks. Do not tie the legs absolutely flat; place a small amount of padding under the knees. Unless absolutely necessary, do not tie down the hands.

Death of a Victim

If a victim dies in the wilderness, you will have to manage a situation that First Aiders in urban areas are unlikely to face. Follow these guidelines:

• Immediately following the death, provide emotional and psychological care to survivors, who will undoubtedly be disturbed by the death. See Chapter 28 for information on psychological emergencies.

• Depending on the religious beliefs of others in the group, some sort of ceremony may be appropriate and comforting. Improvise; if possible, do not remove religious jewelry from the body.

• Note the time, cause, and location of the death. If you can, note the place on a map; if you have to transport the body across county or state lines, you may need to notify authorities in each jurisdiction later.

- Protect the body from predators and from the elements until you can transport it or until authorities arrive. *Do not encase a body in a sleeping bag;* the goal is to cool the body as rapidly as possible. Wrap the body in a tarp, groundcloth, or tent; if someone cannot stay with the body to protect it, hang it from a sturdy tree or over a ledge, or cover it with large stones.

- Notify authorities as quickly as possible. If they can, they should come to you. Packing a body out can be extremely difficult: search and rescue handbooks advise that, depending on terrain, it requires *at least* eight healthy people to carry a body 1 mile. Those eight must then rest while eight *additional* rescuers carry the body the next mile.

Progress Check

1. When assessing a victim in the wilderness, spend more time on the _____ survey than you otherwise would.
   (initial/primary/secondary)

2. To manage a shock victim, insulate the victim from _____ .
   (the air/the ground/moisture)

3. Replace fluids in a shock victim by giving the victim _____ of water.
   (small sips/one glass/large amounts)

4. Wound management in the wilderness involves cleaning the wound and _____ .
   (removing dead tissue/suturing the wound/changing the dressings)

5. Whenever you splint a fracture or immobilize a victim to a backboard, pay special attention to _____ .
   (strapping/padding/lashing)

6. If a victim dies in the wilderness, it's easiest to _____ .
   (have authorities come to the scene/carry the victim out)

• SUMMARY •

- Never enter the wilderness without a leader who has been to the area before and who can predict probable terrain, weather conditions, and hazards.

- Before entering a wilderness area, make a specific plan about how you will handle serious medical emergencies.

- Most wilderness emergencies are preventable. Protect yourself and others from the elements by setting up camp downwind from a windbreak. Avoid setting up camp in the bottom of a canyon or on a ledge.

- Plan for plenty of food and water for every member of your party; purify water by boiling it or filtering it, and keep food well secured and at a distance from your campsite.

- Altitude-related illness can occur at altitudes as low as 6,000 feet; the key to treatment is to get the victim to a lower altitude quickly.

- Because you are likely to be many hours—or even days—from medical help, you need to take special considerations in the assessment and treatment of victims in a wilderness setting. Examples include conducting a more detailed assessment; replacing fluids for shock victims; cleaning wounds; reducing fractures; and taking responsibility for the body of someone who has died.

• KEY TERMS •

Make sure you understand the following key terms:

- Rule of Threes
- billowing
- acute mountain sickness
- high altitude pulmonary edema
- high altitude cerebral edema
- foramen magnum
- ataxia

Student: _____   Date: _____

Course: _____   Section #: _____

PART 1 • True/False

If you believe the statement is true, circle the T. If you believe the statement is false, circle the F.

T F   **1.** When entering the wilderness, you should always go with someone who has been to the area before.

T F   **2.** You will get the most effective shelter if you set up camp in the bottom of a canyon.

T F   **3.** Tents provide adequate shelter from moisture and insulation from wind.

T F   **4.** People can get altitude-related illness at altitudes as low as 6,000 feet, though it is more common at altitudes of 8,000 feet and higher.

T F   **5.** The best treatment for a victim of altitude-related illness is to stop for a day; the victim will "acclimate" and recover in that period.

T F   **6.** When conducting victim assessment in the wilderness, spend more time on the secondary survey than you normally would.

T F   **7.** Do not even attempt CPR in a wilderness setting; because paramedics are so far away, the victim probably will not survive anyway.

T F   **8.** Even if you are several days from help, do not give fluids to a shock victim.

T F   **9.** Help prevent wound infection by irrigating the wound with sterile water.

T F   **10.** Make a victim on a backboard more comfortable by strapping the legs down flat.

PART 2 • Multiple Choice

For each item, circle the correct answer or the phrase that best completes the statement.

1. If you are more than 3 hours away from medical help, treat an open fracture by
   a. irrigating the wound
   b. gently cleaning the wound and bone ends
   c. setting the bone
   d. placing the limb in traction

2. All but which of the following indicate wound infection?
   a. pus
   b. red streaks
   c. confined area of redness
   d. pulsating localized pain

3. If a wound develops signs of infection
   a. irrigate the wound with a disinfectant, such as hydrogen peroxide
   b. apply a topical antibiotic salve to the wound
   c. apply a warm, moist compress to the wound
   d. cut away any decaying tissue

4. CPR in a wilderness setting should be aggressive and prolonged, especially in cases of
   a. warm-water drownings
   b. falls
   c. lightning strikes
   d. animal attacks

5. An essential part of assessment in the wilderness setting is
   a. charting
   b. billowing
   c. testing reflexes
   d. determining the level of consciousness

6. Before entering a wilderness area, a first aid leader should
   a. purchase a commercial wilderness first aid kit
   b. review a good first aid text
   c. make specific plans about how he or she will handle a serious medical emergency
   d. map out the terrain

7. Because tents do not provide adequate insulation against the wind, you should pitch your tent
   a. in the bottom of a canyon
   b. at the top of a ridge
   c. downwind from a windbreak
   d. with extra-long stakes

8. The preferred method of purifying water in a wilderness setting is
   a. boiling it
   b. using water purification tablets
   c. filtering it
   d. using household bleach

9. High altitude cerebral edema causes
   a. stroke
   b. increased pressure inside the skull
   c. impaired circulation
   d. double vision

10. High altitude pulmonary edema results when fluid is forced from body cells into the
   a. bloodstream
   b. brain
   c. heart
   d. lungs

11. A characteristic sign of high altitude pulmonary edema is

    a. coughing
    b. frothy sputum
    c. difficulty breathing, even at rest
    d. chest pain

12. High altitude cerebral edema, which can cause death within a few hours, forces the brain through the foramen magnum, affecting functions regulated by the

    a. cerebrum
    b. cerebellum
    c. brain stem
    d. meninges

13. The most crucial treatment for any altitude-related illness is

    a. rapidly getting the victim to a lower altitude
    b. encouraging the victim to drink plenty of fluids
    c. keeping the victim at rest
    d. keeping the victim at the current altitude so he or she can become acclimated

14. When immobilizing a victim to a backboard in a wilderness setting, you must plan and allow for

    a. elimination of wastes
    b. rapid evacuation
    c. improvised strapping
    d. intravenous lines

15. If a victim dies in a wilderness setting, you should

    a. allow the body to cool as quickly as possible
    b. encase the body in a sleeping bag
    c. bury the body
    d. tag the body, then go for help

PART 3 • What Would You Do If?

- While hiking in a wilderness area, a member of your party falls and lacerates her arm on the jagged edge of a rock. The 2-inch wound is contaminated with dirt and small pieces of bark; it is bleeding moderately.

- On the third day of a week-long trip into a remote mountainous area, one of your hiking companions sustains an open fracture of the lower leg. You are at least a day and a half from medical help.

Psychological Emergencies and Disasters

Learning Objectives

When you have mastered the material in this chapter, you will be able to

1   Discuss the goals of psychological emergency care

2   Outline the basic principles of psychological emergency care

3   List the factors that cause psychological changes

4   Distinguish between psychological and physical emergencies

5   Discuss common psychological emergencies, including panic, agitation, and bizarre thinking and behavior

6   Discuss the risk factors for suicide

7   Describe how to manage a suicidal person

8   Discuss the principles of assessment for psychological emergency

9   Discuss the legal considerations involved in managing psychological emergencies

10 Describe how to manage a violent victim

11 Describe and demonstrate methods of calming a person undergoing a psychological emergency

12 Describe and demonstrate how to restrain a violent victim

13 Discuss how to manage mass casualties and disasters

14 Describe how to perform triage

*O*n December 14, 1998, 21-year-old Jeffrey Huntington was called to a neighbor's apartment; a middle-aged man sat quietly at the far end of the living room. Fearing that her husband was extremely ill, his wife asked Jeffrey for help in determining what was wrong.

Jeffrey did a quick primary survey that turned up no evidence of life-threatening problems. He then did a secondary survey while he obtained a history from 52-year-old Helen Canterbury. Her husband's symptoms had developed fairly slowly, she said. He was "hearing voices," though he was oriented to time and place, and his pupils were even and responded to light.

With a calm and direct manner, Jeffrey started talking to Clifton Canterbury. Jeffrey expressed confidence in Clifton's ability to maintain control of his situation, and together they discussed the symptoms that were bothering Clifton. Through keen observation and knowledge of behavioral emergencies, Jeffrey was able to accurately assess Clifton as a victim of a psychological—not a physical—emergency.

Working with Helen, Jeffrey was able to convince Clifton that he needed to see a physician about the symptoms that were bothering him. While Helen called for an ambulance, Jeffrey waited with Clifton, listened to his story, and empathized with his situation. When paramedics arrived, Clifton was calm enough to be transported without resistance or restraint.

Physical first aid is tangible—it involves bandaging wounds, splinting bones, or restoring breathing. You perform physical care, and you can immediately see the results of your efforts.

Caring for psychological emergencies is different. You cannot readily see the comfort that you provide to someone who is panicked or agitated. It is hard to gauge immediately the results of caring for someone who is depressed and suicidal. But in terms of victim care, psychological support is often as important and life saving as is first aid for physical trauma.

This chapter outlines the goals and basic principles of psychological care, teaches how to distinguish between physical and psychological emergencies, discusses important assessment considerations, details legal considerations, and details methods of care. It also gives important information about mass-casualty situations and teaches how to perform triage.

• Section 1 •
GOALS AND BASIC PRINCIPLES

A psychological emergency is a situation in which a person exhibits "abnormal" behavior—behavior that is unacceptable or intolerable to the victim, the family, or the community. The abnormal behavior may be due to a psychological condition (such as a mental illness), to extremes of emotion, or even to a physical condition (such as a lack of oxygen or low blood sugar).

Goals of Psychological Care

Learning Objective 1 Discuss the goals of psychological emergency care.

Psychological emergency care should be planned and developed with four goals in mind:

1. To help the person begin functioning normally again as soon as possible

2. When the victim cannot be returned to normal quickly, to minimize as much as possible the victim's psychological disability

3. To decrease the intensity of the victim's emotional reaction until professional help is available

4. To keep the victim from hurting self or others

Figure 28-1 lists signs and symptoms that may indicate a psychological emergency.

Basic Principles of Care

Learning Objective 2 Outline the basic principles of psychological emergency care.

Providing care in psychological emergencies requires that you understand the following basic principles:

• Every person has limitations. In a psychological emergency, every person there—including you—is susceptible to emotional injury.

• Each person has a right to his or her feelings. A person who is emotionally or mentally disturbed does not want to feel that way, but at that particular time, those feelings are valid and real.

• Each person has more ability to cope with crisis than he or she might think. For every manifestation of crazed emotion, the victim no doubt has some strength left within.

SIGNS AND SYMPTOMS OF
PSYCHOLOGICAL EMERGENCIES

FEAR

ANXIETY

CONFUSION

BEHAVIORAL DEVIANCE

ANGER

MANIA

DEPRESSION

WITHDRAWAL

LOSS OF CONTACT
WITH REALITY

Figure 28-1. One or more of the signs and symptoms listed above may indicate a psychological emergency.

- Everyone feels some emotional disturbance when involved in a disaster or when injured. A particular physical injury might be especially devastating to a certain person—for example, a relatively minor hand injury may seem of little consequence, but it could ruin the career of a concert violinist.

- Emotional injury is just as real as physical injury. Unfortunately, physical injury is more visible, so it is more often accepted as being "real."

- People who have been through a crisis do not just "get better." Do not expect automatic results; you are first on the scene, and your role is to provide a positive beginning to a long, difficult healing process.

- You will encounter people of all races and cultural backgrounds (see Figure 28-2). Come to terms with your own feelings as you approach a situation, and take the time to understand the victim's perspective.

The main consideration in giving psychological emergency care is to develop confidence and rapport with the victim by:

- Identifying yourself
- Expressing your desire to help
- Using understandable language
- Maintaining eye contact
- Listening intently and being empathetic
- Acting interested and concerned
- Giving calm and warm reassurance
- Not invading the victim's "space" until the person feels comfortable
- Never using any physical force unless the victim is a threat to self or others
- Never lying to or misleading the victim
- Not engendering false hope
- Not judging, criticizing, arguing, or being overly sympathetic
- Explaining the situation to the victim and your plan of action; letting the person know that you are in control
- Avoiding stock phrases like "everything will be o.k."

Victims with Special Communication Needs

Geriatric	Pediatric	Deaf	Blind

• Do not assume senility or lack of understanding.
 • Use victim's name.
 • Check for hearing deficiency.
 • Allow extra time for response.
 • Ask victim what makes him or her most comfortable.
	• Victim may be frightened.
	 • Victim may be modest.
	 • Move slowly.
	 • Explain procedures.
	 • Use simple terms.
	 • Allow child to keep toy, blanket, etc.
	 • Be honest about pain caused by procedure.
	 • Dolls may be useful to demonstrate procedure.
	 • Parents and siblings may be useful to help calm and explain.
		• Determine if victim can read lips.
		 • Position yourself properly.
		 • Use interpreter if necessary and possible.
		 • Use universally understood signs:
		   sick
		   hurt
		   help
		   etc.
		 • Use written messages.
			• Determine if victim has hearing impairment.
			 • Do not shout.
			 • Explain incident and procedures in detail.
			 • Lead victim if ambulatory, alerting the person to obstacles.

Non–English Speaking	Confused and/or Developmentally Disabled
• Use interpreter if possible. • Use gestures. • Refer to illustrated charts.	• Determine level of understanding. • Speak at appropriate level. • Wait for delayed response. • Evaluate understanding and explain again if necessary. • Listen carefully.

Figure 28-2. Victims of psychological emergencies may have special communication needs.

• **Section 2** •

PSYCHOLOGICAL CRISES

Learning Objective 3 List the factors that cause psychological changes.

A number of factors can cause a change in a person's behavior, among them situational stresses, medical illnesses, psychiatric problems, alcohol, or drugs. Some of the most common reasons behavior may change are

- Low blood sugar in a diabetic, which can cause delirium, confusion, and even hallucinations
- Lack of oxygen

- Inadequate blood flow to the brain
- Head trauma
- Mind-altering substances, such as alcohol, depressants, stimulants, psychedelics, and narcotics
- Psychogenic substances, which can cause psychotic thinking, depression, or panic
- Excessive cold
- Excessive heat

Distinguishing between Physical and Psychological Causes

Learning Objective 4 Distinguish between psychological and physical emergencies.

As obvious as it sounds, you need to be sure you are dealing with a psychological, and not a physical, emergency. For example, you may detect what smells like alcohol on a victim's breath, but do not assume the victim is simply intoxicated. Diabetic coma can cause an odor on the breath that smells like alcohol. Antabuse, a drug used by alcoholics to decrease alcohol dependency, can also cause a breath odor similar to that of alcohol.

Table 28-1 can help you distinguish between physical and psychological problems.

Remember that psychological changes and crises often follow (or are a result of) physical trauma or illness. Even if all the clues point to strictly a psychological problem, assess adequately to rule out a physical cause.

Table 28-1

Psychological and Physical Emergencies

Psychological	Physical
The onset of symptoms is usually gradual, developing over a number of months	The onset of symptoms can be sudden
Hallucinations are usually auditory	Hallucinations are usually visual
Memory remains intact, and the victim is usually oriented to time, location, and events	There is memory loss or impairment, and the victim may be disoriented
Pupils are normal	Pupils may be dilated, constricted, or uneven, or they may respond differently to light
Salivation is not excessive	Salivation may be excessive
Incontinence is unusual	Incontinence is more common
Breath odor is normal for the victim	The breath may smell like fruit, acetone, or alcohol

Table 28-2
Common Psychological Emergencies

Disorder	Description	Manifestations
Panic	A response to stress that results in overwhelming feelings of helplessness; victims fear losing control	Intense fear, tension, restlessness, dizziness, hyperventilation, tingling around the mouth and fingers, spasms of the hands and feet, feelings of choking or smothering, irregular heartbeat
Agitation	Response to a situation that causes uneasiness or upset	Resentment, suspicion, impatience, irritability, anxiety, anger directed at an inappropriate source
Bizarre thinking and behavior	Thought or behavior patterns that are inappropriate	Highly exaggerated mistrust, hostility, elaborate delusions, coldness, antagonism, debilitating distortions of speech and thought, bizarre delusions, social withdrawal, lack of emotional expression
Danger to self	Depression causes the desire to harm self	Sad appearance, crying spells, listlessness, withdrawal, despondence, severe restlessness, feelings of worthlessness, helplessness, and hopelessness
Danger to others	Violence precipitated in an attempt to gain security or control	Nervous pacing, shouting, threatening, cursing, throwing objects, clenched teeth or fists

Specific Crises

Learning Objective 5 Discuss common psychological emergencies, including panic, agitation, and bizarre thinking and behavior.

Specific crises you may be confronted with as a First Aider include panic, agitation, bizarre thinking and behavior, victims who pose a danger to themselves (such as those who are suicidal), and victims who pose a danger to others (such as those who are violent). See Table 28-2 for a comparison of these emergencies.

Progress Check

1. Hallucinations caused by a psychological problem are almost always _____ .
   (*visual/auditory/olfactory*)

2. Symptoms of physical disorders are more _____ in onset than those due to psychological disorders.
   (*gradual/rapid*)

3. Memory loss is _____ among those with psychological disorders.
   (*common/sudden/uncommon*)

4. A person with unusual breath odors and dilated pupils probably has a _____ problem.
   (*physical/psychological/memory*)

● Section 3 ●
SUICIDE

Suicide is any willful act designed to end one's own life. Suicide is now the tenth leading cause of death in the United States among all ages and the second leading cause of death among college-age students. Three times more women than men *attempt* suicide, but three times more men are successful. Suicide peaks in the spring and again in the fall, and is lowest during the month of December. Many believe that suicide is vastly underreported because of the stigma that still surrounds it.

Many suicide victims make last-minute attempts to communicate their intentions; most do not really want to die, but use the suicide attempt as a way to get attention, receive help, or punish someone. Every suicidal act or gesture should be taken seriously, and the victim should be transported for evaluation (see Figure 28-3).

suicide Any willful act designed to end one's own life

Suicide Emergencies

Misconception	Fact
People who talk about suicide don't commit suicide.	Eight out of ten people who commit suicide have given definite warnings of their intentions. Almost no one commits suicide without first letting others know how he or she feels.
You can't stop a person who's suicidal—he or she is fully intent on dying.	Most people who are suicidal can't decide whether to live or die. Neither wish is necessarily stronger.
Once a person is suicidal, he or she is suicidal forever.	People who want to kill themselves are only suicidal for a limited time. If they're saved from feelings of self-destruction, they can often go on to lead normal lives.
Improvement after severe depression means that the suicidal risk is over.	Most persons commit suicide within about 3 months of the beginning of "improvement," when they have the energy to carry out suicidal intentions. They can also show signs of apparent improvement because their ambivalence is gone—they've made the decision to kill themselves.
If a person has attempted suicide, he or she won't do it again.	More than 50 percent of those who commit suicide have previously attempted to do so.

ASSESSING LETHALITY

Age and Sex
- Incidence of suicide is highest in adolescents (ages 15 to 24) and in persons age 50 and over.
- Men succeed at suicide more often than women.

Plan: Remember these points:
- Does the victim have a plan? Is it well thought out?
- Is it easy to carry out (successfully)?
- Are the means available? (For example, does the victim have pills collected, or a gun?)
- A detailed plan and available means carries maximum potential for lethality.

Symptoms
- What is the victim thinking and feeling?
- Is the person in control of his or her behavior? (Being out of control carries higher risk.)
- Alcoholics and psychotics are at higher risk.
- Depressed people are most at risk at the onset and at decline of depression.

Relationships with Significant Others
- Does the person have any support? Family, friends, therapist?
- Has the person suffered any recent losses?
- Is the person still in contact with people?
- Is the person telling family he or she has made a will?
- Is the person giving away prized possessions?

Medical History
People with chronic illnesses are more likely to commit suicide than those with terminal illnesses. Incidence of suicide rises whenever a victim's body image is severely threatened—for example, after surgery or childbirth.

The goal is to shift the intensity of a suicidal act from a desire to commit suicide to conflict over the need to commit suicide. The following guidelines can help:

- Specifically talk to the person about his or her intent.
- Ask the person how serious he or she is about killing himself or herself.
- Ask what concerns the person has about taking his or her life. The person will probably have some conflict.
- Ask the person why suicide is the answer to his or her problems.
- Ask what other alternatives the person has considered and what problems block the choice of other alternatives.
- Ask what hope the person has—even if it seems remote or blocked.
- By this time you may have helped decrease the intensity of the person's need to commit suicide, even though this change may be temporary.
- Always get professional help.
- A suicidal person should be transported to the hospital for evaluation even if he or she says everything is okay. Police assistance may be necessary.

Figure 28-3. Suicide emergencies

Risk Factors

Learning Objective 6 Discuss the risk factors for suicide.

The risk factors for suicide include the following:

- Being a male over 40 and being single, widowed, or divorced; men account for 70 percent of all suicides, and suicide is five times higher among people who are widowed or divorced.
- Alcoholism or drug abuse
- Depression; suicide is 500 times more common among people who are severely depressed.
- Suicidal gestures; approximately 80 percent of people who succeed in committing suicide made previous attempts.
- A plan; at highest risk are victims who have formulated a highly lethal plan and told others about it.
- An unusual gathering of articles that could be used to commit suicide (such as a gun or a large quantity of pills) or immediate access to a device that could be used to commit suicide
- A previous history of self-destructive behavior, even if that behavior was not overtly suicidal
- A recent diagnosis of serious illness, especially an illness that signals a loss of independence (suicide is especially high among homosexuals who are HIV-positive and among the elderly who have been diagnosed with chronic disease).
- The recent loss of a loved one; suicides also occur when a person's close emotional attachments are perceived to be in danger.
- An arrest, imprisonment, or the loss of a job (general signs that the victim has lost control or is unable to manage life).

During assessment, you may notice that

- The victim is in an unsafe environment or is holding a dangerous object (such as a gun, knife, or rope).
- The victim displays self-destructive behavior, either before you arrived or during your assessment.

Emergency Care

Learning Objective 7 Describe how to manage a suicidal person.

To manage a suicide emergency, activate the EMS system; then:

1. Make sure you are safe—your safety is of utmost importance. If you cannot guarantee your own safety, call the police and wait for them to arrive. Once the scene is safe for you, quickly survey for instruments the person might use to cause self-injury; discreetly remove any dangerous articles.

2. Assess the person for physical injury; first aid treatment for physical injury has priority.

3. Assess the seriousness of the person's thoughts and feelings. Do not be afraid to ask the person directly about suicidal thoughts. Always take a suicide threat seriously; if the person has a plan, the problem is more serious than it would be with someone who has considered suicide but has not figured out how.

4. Calm the person and stay with him or her. Never leave a suicidal person alone.

5. If it is necessary to protect the person from self-harm, use restraints. Never use restraints as a substitute for observation, and never use metal handcuffs.

As you deal with a suicidal person (see Figure 28-4), follow these guidelines:

- Listen carefully.
- Accept all the person's complaints and feelings; do not underestimate what the person may be feeling.
- Do not trust "rapid recoveries." The person needs to be taken to the hospital even if he or she seems to be "better."
- Be specific in your actions; do something tangible for the person, such as arranging for a clergyman to meet the person at the hospital.
- Never show disgust or horror when you care for the person.
- Never try to shock a person out of a suicidal act. Never argue or challenge the person to go ahead.

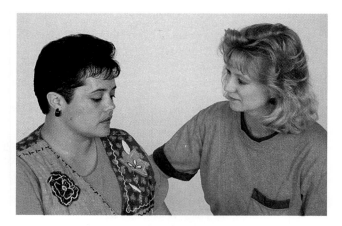

Figure 28-4. Approach the potential suicide victim with empathy and concern.

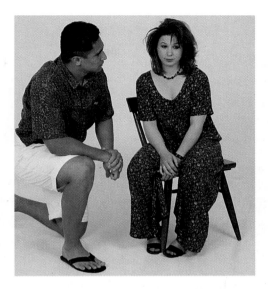

Figure 28-5. When dealing with a psychological emergency, be calm and show through your actions that you have confidence in the victim's ability to maintain self-control.

• Section 4 •
ASSESSMENT

Learning Objective 8 Discuss the principles of assessment for psychological emergency.

When assessing victims of a psychological emergency, follow these guidelines:

1. Identify yourself and let the victim know you are there to help. Show through your actions that you have confidence in the victim's ability to maintain self-control and control of the situation (see Figure 28-5).

2. Tell the victim what you are doing; be honest, but do not frighten the victim.

3. Ask questions in a calm, reassuring voice. Be polite, use good manners, show respect, and make no assumptions or judgments.

4. Allow the victim to tell you what happened. If you can, interview the victim in a quiet room where the victim has privacy. Show you are listening by rephrasing or repeating part of what the victim says.

5. Acknowledge the victim's feelings. Use phrases such as, "I can see that you are very depressed," or "I understand that you must feel frightened."

6. Assess the victim's mental status by asking specific questions that will help you measure the victim's level of consciousness, orientation, and contact with reality.

Assessing the Potential for Violence

Violence is generally an attempt to gain security or control; 60 to 75 percent of all psychological emergency victims become assaultive or violent. Anger or violence may be a response to illness or the victim's way of coping with feelings of helplessness. It can also be precipitated by victim mismanagement (real or perceived), psychosis, alcohol or drug intoxication, fear, panic, or head injury.

To determine the potential for violence (see Figure 28-6 on page 464):

- Size up the scene. Locate the victim visually before you approach. Determine whether the victim is disoriented, whether drugs or alcohol are involved, whether the victim has a gun or other weapon, whether the situation involves a hostage, and whether others are involved.

- Early in that assessment—before you physically approach the victim—determine whether you can handle the situation alone. Even a small person who is sufficiently agitated can be very difficult to handle. If you doubt that you can handle the victim alone, call the police and wait for them to arrive.

- Take a history. Ask bystanders what has been going on. Has the victim been violent or threatened violence? Does the victim have a history of violence, aggression, or combativeness?

- Anticipate violence if the victim is standing or sitting in a way that threatens self or others, if

---

Disruptive and Aggressive Victims: Assessment Guidelines

Any behavior that presents a danger to the victim or others or that delays or prevents appropriate care is disruptive and may precipitate a psychological emergency. Common causes of disruptive behavior include stress-induced hysteria; aggression, alcohol or drug problems; neurological trauma; metabolic imbalances; organic brain syndromes; psychological disorders.

Assessing the Situation

- What information do you have from the situation—what happened?
- Is the environment (emotional, social, and/or physical) dangerous to you and/or others?
- Does the victim seem agitated, elated, depressed, or restless?
- Has the person already demonstrated aggressive or violent behavior?
- Does the person talk loudly and in sarcastic terms?
- Does the person use vulgar language?
- Is the person easily provoked to anger?
- Does the person have a limited attention span?
- Does the person seem to be out of control or disoriented?
- Does the person seem to be afraid or panicky?
- Does the person have a weapon?
- Is there evidence of alcohol or drug abuse?
- Is a domestic disturbance involved?
- Has criminal activity occurred?

If you answer **yes** to several or most of the above questions, use extreme caution. If possible, try not to control or suppress the victim's behavior. Rather, allow the person to express feelings. Remember—the most effective way to deal with a victim who exhibits aggressive and/or violent behavior is to reduce the crisis and prevent further disruptive behavior. The safest thing to do in these situations is to call the police.

Figure 28-6. Assessing disruptive and aggressive victims

the victim's fists are clenched, or if the victim is holding anything that could be used as a lethal weapon.

- Anticipate violence if the victim is yelling, cursing, arguing, or verbally threatening to hurt self or others.
- Monitor the victim's physical activity. Signs of potential violence include moving toward the caregiver, carrying a heavy or threatening object, using quick or irregular movements, and having muscle tension.

Progress Check

1. When you approach the victim, you should _____ .
(tell the victim what you are doing/try to take the victim by surprise/divert the victim's attention)

2. A good assessment strategy is to _____ the victim's feelings.
(deny/try to change/acknowledge)

3. A risk factor for violence is a history of
_____ .
(head injury/arrest/aggression)

4. Anticipate violence if the victim has
_____ .
(head injury/clenched fists/run away)

5. Anticipate violence if the victim is _____ .
(cursing/disoriented/hallucinating)

6. A person with quick, _____ moves is at risk for becoming violent.
(dramatic/sweeping/irregular)

• Section 5 •
LEGAL CONSIDERATIONS

Learning Objective 9 Discuss the legal considerations involved in managing psychological emergencies.

Every time you respond as a First Aider, you have a chance of encountering the legal system. That chance becomes greater when you are responding to victims with psychological problems. To reduce your legal liability, follow these guidelines:

- *When possible, get consent.* Simply stated, consent is permission to treat. In most states, you could be charged with assault and battery if you force a person to have treatment against his or her will. Review the consent information in Chapter 1.

- *If a victim refuses care,* carefully document what has happened. If the victim threatens to hurt self or others and you can demonstrate reason to believe that the victim's threats are real, the victim can be transported by EMTs or law enforcement without consent. Remember—you must be able to document your belief that the victim is a threat.

- *Avoid unreasonable force.* If it's necessary to restrain a victim, use **reasonable force**—only the amount of force required to keep the victim from injuring self or others. The amount of force considered reasonable depends on the victim's size and strength, behavior, gender, and mental state and the method of restraint (soft restraints or straps are usually considered reasonable; metal cuffs are not).

  In most areas, you need police authorization to use reasonable force in restraining a victim without consent. In most areas, First Aiders can use reasonable force to defend against an attack by an emotionally disturbed victim without fearing legal consequences. The basic guideline is to avoid any act or physical force that may injure the victim during restraint.

- *Seek police direction.* It is always a good idea to involve law enforcement if there is any threat of violence. Police officers serve a twofold purpose in cases such as this: They provide protection from injury, and they serve as credible witnesses if a victim later tries to sue you.

- *Protect yourself against false accusations.* Carefully and completely document everything that happens during the situation; include details of the victim's abnormal behavior. In most jurisdictions, anything documented at the scene is considered legally admissible evidence, and anything not documented is hearsay.

- *Manage a crime scene.* You may find, when called to the scene of a psychological emergency, that the person has either committed or been the victim of a crime or harmed himself or herself. If you help at the scene of a criminal act, your first concern is to care for the injured victims.

  - Always cooperate with local law enforcement.
  - Disrupt or touch evidence as little as possible.
  - If the victim is moved, mark the original body position.
  - Provide reassurance and emotional support. Common victim responses include outrage, disbelief, withdrawal, hysteria, and depression.

To avoid disturbing crucial evidence that is needed by law enforcement in investigating the crime, follow these guidelines:

- Do not allow bystanders into the area.
- Where appropriate, assist police in collecting and recording anything on the victim, such as blood, hair, seminal fluid, gunpowder residue, or clothing fibers.
- Take extreme care not to disturb any evidence that is not on the victim's body (footprints, soil, broken glass, tire tracks, and so on).
- Never touch or move suspected weapons unless it is absolutely necessary in treating the victim's injuries.
- If you need to tear or cut away clothing to expose a wound, do not cut through a bullet hole or knife slash in the clothing.
- If the victim was strangled and still has the rope or cord around the neck, cut it instead of untying it—the knot can be used as evidence and may identify the perpetrator.
- Document in writing who is at the crime scene when you arrive.
- If the victim is obviously dead when you arrive, do nothing and disturb nothing. Call the police and wait for them to arrive.

---

reasonable force The amount of force required to keep a person from injuring self or others

---

Progress Check

1. Whenever possible, get _____ before you care for a victim.
   (help/protection/consent)

2. Use _____ only to restrain a victim.
   (metal cuffs/ropes/reasonable force)

continued

3. The amount of force that is reasonable to restrain a victim depends in part on the victim's

_____ .
(history/size/illness)

4. If you have to restrain a victim, try to involve the

_____ .
(police/victim's family/bystanders)

5. To protect yourself against false accusations, _____ everything that happens while you are at the scene.
(photograph/document/think about)

6. If a victim was involved in a crime, take extra care not to disturb _____ .
(the police investigation/the evidence/the next of kin)

• Section 6 •
EMERGENCY CARE FOR PSYCHOLOGICAL EMERGENCIES

Managing a Violent Victim

Learning Objective 10 Describe how to manage a violent victim.

Your first priority is to protect yourself. Never go into a potentially violent situation by yourself. To keep yourself safe and protect the victim (see Figure 28-7), do the following:

• If you are outdoors and can do so, walk on the grass, not the sidewalk.

• If you are using a flashlight, hold it beside—not in front of—your body.

• If you are walking with someone else, walk single file; only the first person in line should carry a flashlight.

• As you approach the scene, make a mental map of all possible places for **concealment** (objects that will hide you, such as shrubbery) and **cover** (objects that will both hide you and stop bullets, such as trees). Keep scanning the area for movement.

• Stand to the side of a door when you knock on it; never stand in front of it.

• As soon as the door is open, assess the situation before you decide whether to retreat and call for help.

• Negotiate with the victim from a safe distance (at least 6 feet away) and position (facing the victim). Never turn your back on the victim.

• Keep the door to the room open, and identify as many exits as possible. Regardless of the situation, make absolutely sure you have at least one certain route of escape.

• Always follow a victim down a hallway or stairway. Never lead the way.

• Never ignore or disregard a weapon. In a calm and nonconfrontational way, tell the victim that you want to help, but you cannot do so until the weapon is released. Ask the victim to put the weapon in a neutral place.

How to Calm Psychological Emergency Victims

Learning Objective 11 Describe and demonstrate methods of calming a person undergoing a psychological emergency.

Because psychological emergencies are difficult, you may need to use techniques you would not consider with victims of other kinds of emergencies. Following are some techniques to use in addition to the typical techniques used during assessment:

1. Maintain a comfortable distance from the victim; many victims are threatened by physical contact.

2. Do not make any quick movements. Act quietly and slowly; let the victim see that you are not going to make any sudden moves (a fear that can precipitate violence).

3. Respond honestly to the victim's questions, but do not foster unrealistic expectations. Instead of saying, "You have nothing to worry about," say something like, "Despite all the problems you've had, you seem to have lots of people around you who really care about you." Reassure the victim that visual or auditory disturbances are temporary and will clear up with treatment. Always tell the truth.

4. Never threaten, challenge, or argue with disturbed victims. Many psychologically disturbed victims will be adept at picking out your weaknesses; remain kind and calm.

concealment A place or an object that will hide you, such as shrubbery

cover An object that will both hide you and stop bullets, such as a tree

Disruptive and Aggressive Victims: Management Guidelines

Don'ts

- Don't put yourself in a position of danger.
- Don't attempt to diagnose, judge, label, or criticize the victim.
- Don't isolate yourself from other helpers.
- Don't isolate yourself with a victim who has a record of potential violence.
- Don't disturb a victim with emergency care or taking vital signs any more than is necessary.
- Don't turn your back on the victim.
- Don't position yourself between the victim and the only doorway.
- Don't forget that a disturbed victim's moods can fluctuate rapidly.
- Don't reject any of the victim's complaints— acknowledge them.
- Don't threaten, lie, bluff, or deceive the victim.
- Don't take insults personally.
- Don't rush into action.
- Don't show hostility toward the victim's words or actions.
- Don't appear aggressive or defensive.
- Don't be overly friendly.
- Don't sound authoritarian or demanding when you speak to the victim.
- Don't attempt to restrain a victim unless you have adequate assistance to do so safely. It is best to call the police.

Do's

- If danger exists, create a safe zone and wait for assistance (police and/or emergency units).
- Keep bystanders outside of safe zone.
- Remove any person or object from the environment that seems to be triggering the victim's aggression.
- Convey a sense of helpfulness rather than hostility or frustration.
- Establish voice control by asking bystanders what the problem is loud enough so that the victim can hear you.
- Identify yourself.
- Let the victim know what you expect.
- Present a comfortable, confident, and professional manner.
- Ask the victim his or her name and what the problem is.
- Listen to, but do not respond to insults and abusive language or take them personally.
- Be honest.
- Speak in short sentences with simple ideas and explanations.
- Remain relaxed and confident.
- Adjust your physical distance from the victim to a safe range—at first no closer than approximately 10 or 15 feet. Move closer only after adequate assessment reveals that it's safe to do so.
- Respect the victim's difficulty in maintaining self-control. Tell the person that you are aware of the problem, and acknowledge her or his attempt to deal with it.
- Acknowledge the victim's complaints—you do not have to agree, but acknowledge that the person has a reason to be upset.
- Use gestures and other nonverbal messages carefully. They may communicate the opposite of what you intend. A disturbed victim may interpret friendliness and smiling as an attempt at trickery.
- If your preventive actions fail to reduce hostile, violent, and combative behavior, the victim is in control and it may be necessary to restrain the victim to protect self and others.
- Assess the victim's strengths.
- Make certain that you have a plan and sufficient help to prevent injury to the victim and yourself.

Figure 28-7. Managing disruptive and aggressive victims

5. When you can, involve trusted family members or friends.
6. Never leave the victim alone; all psychological emergency victims are escape risks. Once you have responded to the emergency, the victim's safety is legally your responsibility.

7. Maintain good eye contact with the victim, for two reasons: First, direct eye contact communicates your control and confidence. Second, the victim's eyes can reflect emotions and tell you whether the victim is terrified, confused, struggling, in pain, or dying.

8. Do not force the victim to make decisions, because the victim has probably lost the ability to cope effectively.

9. If the victim has attracted a crowd, do what you can to disperse it so you can deal with the victim on a one-to-one basis.

Restraining a Victim

Learning Objective 12 Describe and demonstrate how to restrain a violent victim.

A difficult situation arises when a victim is out of control. If you believe the victim may be dangerous to self or others, you must notify the police. Never leave a violent victim alone; watch the victim constantly, and stay alert.

Restraint should be avoided unless the victim is a danger to self and others. Use of restraints may require police authorization; if you are not authorized by state law to use restraints, wait for someone with authority.

A violent physical struggle is usually brief, because most people cannot sustain the intensity needed; however, if you still feel the need for restraints

1. Gather enough people to overpower the victim clearly before you attempt restraint.

2. Plan what you are going to do before you attempt restraint. Everyone involved should know what is going to happen.

3. Use only as much force as needed for restraint; never inflict pain or use unwarranted force in restraining a victim.

4. Estimate the range of motion of the victim's arms and legs, and stay beyond that range until you actually are ready to begin restraint.

5. Once you have made the decision to restrain, act quickly. Part of restraint involves taking the victim by surprise; your delay or indecision could allow the victim to get the upper hand.

6. Approach the victim with at least four people, one assigned to each limb, at the same time. Secure the victim's limbs together with restraints of soft leather or cloth.

7. If the victim's physical injuries do not contraindicate it, turn the victim face down.

Once you have applied restraints, do not remove them. Reassess the victim's circulation frequently to make sure the restraints are not binding. Document the reason you felt it necessary to restrain the victim, and thoroughly document the technique you used for the restraint.

Progress Check

1. After you have knocked on the door at a site where there is a potential for violence, stand _____.
   (in front of the door/away from the door/to the side of the door)

2. When dealing with a violent person, _____.
   (use a gentle touch on the arm/hold the arm firmly/avoid physical contact)

3. Use soft leather or _____ to restrain a victim. *(cloth/wire/metal cuffs)*

4. At least _____ people should be involved in restraining a victim. *(two/three/four)*

• Section 7 •
MASS CASUALTIES AND DISASTERS

When the situation involves more than one casualty, people may become dazed, disorganized, or overwhelmed. The American Psychiatric Association has identified five possible types of reactions (see Figure 28-8) in such situations:

1. *Normal*
2. *Blind panic*
3. *Depression*
4. *Overreacting*
5. *Conversion hysteria*

With **conversion hysteria,** the victim's mood may shift rapidly from extreme anxiety to relative calmness; the victim may then convert anxiety to a physical dysfunction, such as hysterical blindness, deafness, or paralysis.

Managing Mass Casualty or Disaster Situations

Learning Objective 13 Discuss how to manage mass casualties and disasters.

conversion hysteria Converting anxiety to a physical dysfunction, such as blindness or deafness

Emotional Reactions in Mass Casualties and Disasters

Reactions	Signs and Symptoms	Do's	Don'ts
Normal	Fear and anxiety Muscular tension followed by trembling and weakness Confusion Profuse perspiration Nausea, vomiting Mild diarrhea Frequent urination Shortness of breath Pounding heart These reactions usually dissipate with activity as the person gains self-control	Normal reactions usually require little emergency care Calm reassurance may be all that is necessary to help a person pull himself together Watch to see that the individual is gaining composure, not losing it Provide meaningful activity Talk with the person	Don't show extreme sympathy
Panic (blind flight of hysteria)	Unreasoning attempt to flee Loss of judgment—blindness to reality Uncontrolled weeping or hysteria often to the point of exhaustion Aimless running about with little regard for safety Panic is contagious when not controlled. Normally calm persons may become panicked by others during moments when they are temporarily disorganized	Begin with firmness Give something warm to eat or drink Firmly, but gently, isolate the person from the group. Get help if necessary Show empathy and encourage the person to talk Monitor your own feelings Keep calm and know your limitations	Don't brutally restrain the person Don't strike the person Don't douse the person with water Don't give sedatives
Overactive	Explodes into flurry of senseless activity Argumentative Overconfident of abilities Talks rapidly—will not listen Tells silly jokes Makes endless suggestions Demanding of others Does more harm than good by interfering with organized leadership Like panic, overactivity is contagious if not controlled	Let the person talk and ventilate feelings Assign and supervise a job that requires physical activity Give something warm to eat or drink	Don't tell the person he is acting abnormally Don't give sedatives Don't argue with the person Don't tell the person he or she shouldn't act or feel this way
Underactive (daze, shock, depression)	Cannot recover from original shock and numbness Stands or sits without talking or moving Vacant expression Emotionless "Don't care" attitude Helpless, unaware of surroundings Moves aimlessly, slowly Little or no response to questioning Pulls within self to protect from further stress Puzzled, confused Cannot take responsibility without supervision	Gently establish contact and rapport Get the person to ventilate feelings and let you know what happened Show empathy Be aware of feelings of resentment in yourself and others Give the person warm food or drink Give and supervise a simple, routine job	Don't tell the person to "snap out of it" Don't show extreme pity Don't give sedatives Don't show resentment
Severe physical reaction (conversion hysteria)	Severe nausea Conversion hysteria—the victim converts anxiety into a strong belief that a part of his body is not functioning (paralysis, loss of sight, etc.). The disability is just as real as if the person had been physically injured	Show interest Find a small job for the person to do to take his or her mind off the injury Make the person comfortable and summon medical aid Monitor your own feelings	Don't say, "There's nothing wrong with you" or, "It's all in your head" Don't blame or ridicule Don't call undue attention to the injury Don't openly ignore the injury

Source: American Psychiatric Association

Figure 28-8. *Emotional reactions in mass casualties and disasters*

Although each disaster presents individual problems, these general guidelines will usually apply to any disaster you may be called to respond to:

1. Don't let yourself become overwhelmed by the immensity of the disaster. Administer aid to those who need it. Carefully evaluate the injuries, and determine which victims should be treated first. Then set about administering the aid, treating victims one by one. This will help you maintain some calm and feel that you are making progress, despite the immensity of the disaster.

2. Obtain and distribute information about the disaster and the victims. The families of victims deserve accurate information about both the disaster and the victims themselves.

3. Reunite the victims with family members as soon as possible. There are two benefits of this: first, emotional stress will be lessened once victims are with family members. Second, family members may be able to provide you with critical medical history that may affect your ability to treat the victims.

4. Encourage victims or bystanders who are able to do necessary chores at the scene. Work can be therapeutic.

5. Identify yourself; stay self-assured, sympathetic, and businesslike, and reassure anxious victims or bystanders.

6. Assess and care for physical injuries immediately.

7. Keep spectators away from the victims, but do not leave the victims alone. If all rescue personnel are busy dealing with physical injuries, assign a responsible bystander to stay with anyone showing unusual behavior.

8. Respect the right of victims to have their own feelings, and accept the physical and emotional limitations of victims.

9. Accept your own limitations; there are limits to what can be done. You will provide more effective care if you establish priorities and refuse to overextend yourself.

Triage

All the medical knowledge in the world and the finest care by a First Aider will not help if priorities are not properly ordered. It is critical that you know which victims of a multiple-victim accident or disaster require emergency care first and that you classify those who need attention and care the most desperately.

Triage, a French term meaning picking or sorting, is a process of sorting and classifying sick and injured victims. Triage is a procedure by which the sick and wounded are classified as to type and urgency of condition and, based on the assigned priorities, are sent to facilities where they can receive care.

Conducting Triage

Learning Objective 14 Describe how to perform triage.

Triage should be conducted by the most experienced First Aider as soon as the scene is secured (traffic is controlled, the fire is out, and so on). Move from victim to victim, performing a limited amount of lifesaving care and tagging the victims for later care. This sets the stage for the next arriving rescuers, who can focus on caring for salvageable victims.

The three-level method of triage uses different tags for life-threatened (highest priority), urgent (second priority), and delayed (lowest priority) (see Table 28-3). Those who are dead are taken to a morgue in a different area of the disaster scene. The two-level method (see Table 28-4) uses separate tags for immediate (first priority) and delayed (second priority).

To conduct triage:

1. Move quickly from one victim to the next; complete a primary survey on each.

2. Correct immediate life-threatening problems. Apply the ABCs (caring for airway/breathing/circulation) on a limited basis, depending on the availability of rescuers who can help with triage and treatment. *You should not spend more than 30 to 60 seconds per victim during the actual triage.*

3. Tag each victim as to priority.

4. Ask for additional assistance if needed.

5. Assign available manpower and equipment to highest priority victims.

6. When additional help arrives, arrange for treatment and transport of highest priority victims first.

7. If possible, notify emergency personnel and/or hospital(s) of number and severity of injuries.

8. Triage rescuer remains at scene to assign and coordinate manpower, supplies, and vehicles.

9. Reassess victims regularly for changes in status.

triage A system of sorting victims into categories by treatment priority

Table 28-3
Three-Level Triage

	Highest Priority	Second Priority	Lowest Priority
Level of emergency	Critically injured but can recover if treated immediately	Seriously injured; may die without further treatment	Noncritical injuries or minor wounds
Examples	Airway and breathing difficulties, cardiac arrest (treat if enough personnel available), uncontrolled or severe bleeding, severe head injuries, severe medical problems (poisoning and diabetes), open chest or abdominal wounds, shock	Burns, major or multiple fractures, back injuries with or without spinal cord damage	Fractures, minor injuries, obviously mortal wounds making death reasonably certain, cardiac arrest if there are not enough personnel

Note: Dead victims will be taken to a morgue in different location. Victims requiring vigorous care for cardiac arrest should be treated as dead.

Table 28-4
Two-Level Triage

Immediate (First Priority)	Delayed (Second Priority)
Includes those who have critical injuries that threaten life but are salvageable; those requiring immediate medical care (within five to fifteen minutes) to survive	Includes those who are seriously injured but whose lives are not threatened; those whose injuries are minor and whose treatment can be delayed; and those who are very critically injured—non-salvageable or dead; also includes those with no injuries or only minor injuries requiring emergency care

Progress Check

1. In a mass casualty or disaster, extreme anxiety, sweating, and vomiting are _____ reactions.
   (normal/abnormal/delayed)

2. Becoming blind or deaf after a mass casualty or disaster is a sign of _____ .
   (physical injury/conversion hysteria/sensory trauma)

3. During a mass casualty, you should keep spectators away and _____ .
   (give victims privacy/isolate victims/stay with the victims)

4. A victim with obviously mortal wounds should be classified in the _____ triage priority.
   (highest/second/lowest)

5. A victim with a life-threatening condition that could be saved if treated immediately should be classified in the _____ priority.
   (highest/second/lowest)

6. A victim who is seriously injured and who may die without treatment should be classified in the _____ priority.
   (highest/second/lowest)

• SUMMARY •

- The goals of psychological emergency care are to help the person begin functioning normally as soon as possible, to minimize psychological disability, to decrease the intensity of emotional reaction until professional help is available, and to keep the victim from hurting self or others.

- A number of physical disorders can create symptoms that mimic psychological disorders; assess the victim carefully to make sure there is not a physical problem that needs to be cared for.

- The most common psychological crises include panic, agitation, bizarre thinking and behavior, danger to self, and danger to others.

- Take every suicide threat seriously; the threat is particularly serious if the victim has a plan.

- Never try to argue someone out of committing suicide, and never challenge someone to go ahead.

- People who are about to become violent manifest certain behaviors, such as clenching the fists, moving in quick and irregular ways, shouting, cursing, and so on. Become familiar with these signs and act quickly to protect yourself.

- Always try to get consent before you care for or transport a victim.

- If you have to restrain a victim who is threatening to hurt someone (including self), use reasonable force based on the victim's size, strength, gender, mental status, and behavior.

- If you arrive at a crime scene, make sure the scene is safe before you enter; take care to preserve the chain of evidence for the police.

- Use professionalism, empathy, and courtesy to help calm the victim of a psychological emergency. Use restraints only when absolutely necessary, and always use soft restraints.

- Victims of a mass casualty or disaster are normally extremely anxious, weak, shaky, and nauseated; they can be helpful if given specific tasks.

- Triage is a system of identifying and prioritizing victims so that the most effective care can be given to the largest number of victims. Those who have life-threatening injuries but who can recover with treatment should be treated and transported first; those with minor or obviously mortal injuries should be treated and transported last.

• KEY TERMS •

Make sure you understand the following key terms:

- suicide
- reasonable force
- concealment
- cover
- conversion hysteria
- triage

Student: _____   Date: _____

Course: _____   Section #: _____

PART 1 • True/False

If you believe the statement is true, circle the T. If you believe the statement is false, circle the F.

T   F   **1.** While talking to a victim, ask questions that are direct and specific to measure the victim's contact with reality.

T   F   **2.** Do *not* leave a victim of a psychological emergency alone.

T   F   **3.** It is appropriate to lie to a victim to protect the victim from unpleasant facts.

T   F   **4.** Suicide threats do not need to be taken seriously.

T   F   **5.** Few people have as much ability to cope with crisis as they think they do.

T   F   **6.** People under severe emotional stress usually feel that they are in complete control.

T   F   **7.** Violent behavior is often an attempt to gain control.

T   F   **8.** Burns are in the highest priority of care in triage.

T   F   **9.** If a person is having a psychological emergency, you do not have to obtain consent to treat because the person is not lucid anyway.

T   F   **10.** It is impossible to tell by a person's behavior whether the person is about to become violent.

PART 2 • Multiple Choice

For each item, circle the correct answer or the phrase that best completes the statement.

1. In dealing with a mass casualty, you should *not*
   a. remain self-assured and businesslike
   b. feel responsible for treating every victim
   c. assign tasks to bystanders
   d. make clear that you understand the victim's feelings

2. How should you handle the emotional reactions of victims of mass casualties and disasters?
   a. show extreme sympathy
   b. douse the person with water
   c. firmly but gently isolate the person
   d. administer mild sedatives

3. A victim who is talking compulsively and joking inappropriately is having what kind of reaction?
   a. normal
   b. panic
   c. overreacting
   d. conversion hysteria

4. Which guideline for psychological care is *not* correct?
   a. establish rapport with the victim
   b. encourage the victim to talk out feelings and fears
   c. slap the victim to bring him or her around
   d. encourage an exhausted victim to sleep

5. Which is *not* a principle of psychological emergency care?
   a. every person has limits
   b. emotional trauma is less serious than physical trauma
   c. every person has the right to his or her feelings
   d. everyone feels emotionally distraught as a result of physical injury

6. What is a sound way to deal with a suicidal person?
   a. trust rapid recoveries
   b. try to shock the person out of a suicidal act
   c. show the person you are disgusted with his or her actions
   d. ask the victim directly about suicidal thoughts

7. What physical illness would most likely appear to be psychological?
   a. cardiac arrest
   b. epilepsy
   c. diabetic coma
   d. shock

8. Which of the following should you *not* do when dealing with a potentially violent victim?
   a. position yourself between the victim and the door
   b. present a comfortable, confident, professional manner
   c. keep a safe distance from the victim
   d. let the victim know what you expect

9. Triage means
   a. giving emotional support to victims
   b. mobilizing available rescue personnel
   c. establishing a community plan
   d. assessing and categorizing the injured so treatment can begin

10. Which of the following is *not* in the highest-priority category of triage?
   a. airway and breathing difficulties
   b. severe bleeding
   c. fracture
   d. open chest wound

Match the type of reaction at the left with the correct definition at the right.

Reaction

Normal reaction
Blind panic
Depression
Overreaction
Conversion hysteria

Definition

_____ Mood may shift rapidly from extreme anxiety to relative calmness.

_____ The individual remains motionless and looks numbed and dazed.

_____ Extreme anxiety, including sweating, shaking, weakness, nausea, and sometimes vomiting

_____ Judgment seems to disappear completely.

_____ Person talks compulsively, jokes inappropriately, and races from one task to another, usually accomplishing little.

• You are a pedestrian at a busy downtown intersection where a person is wandering dangerously among the traffic and seems to be oblivious to what is going on around him. He is anxious and withdrawn and is talking to himself. He also seems to be very fearful of something.

29

Lifting and Moving Victims

Learning Objectives

When you have mastered the material in this chapter, you will be able to

1 Discuss the general guidelines for moving victims

2 Identify the situations in which an emergency move must be made

3 Describe and demonstrate the walking assist

4 Describe and demonstrate the blanket drag

5 Describe and demonstrate the shirt drag

6 Describe and demonstrate the sheet drag

7 Describe and demonstrate the fireman's carry

8 Describe and demonstrate seat carries

9 Describe and demonstrate the extremity lift

10 Describe and demonstrate the chair litter carry

11 Describe and demonstrate the flat lift and carry

12 Describe and demonstrate how to use backboards to move a victim

13 Describe and demonstrate how to use a blanket stretcher

14 List objects that can be used for improvised stretchers

15 Discuss the guidelines for moving a victim on a stretcher

SQ3R Plus

- **Survey** to set goals for studying.
- Ask **questions** as you **read.**
- Stop frequently to **recite** and **review.**
- **Write** a summary of key points.
- **Reflect** on the importance of this material and its relevance in your life.

On his way to university classes one morning, 23-year-old Kent Ashby came upon a two-car accident in which one vehicle had broadsided another. Two victims had been ejected from the vehicles. A third, a woman about 30 years old, had unfastened her seat belt and managed to get out of one of the cars; she was leaning against it and cradling her right arm against her chest.

Running to the scene, Kent could see that one of the victims was lying in a pool of gasoline that had streamed from the ruptured tank of one of the cars. The other victim was quite a distance away. Kent knew that the first victim had to be moved—there was danger of the gasoline igniting.

By this time, two other vehicles had stopped. Kent sent the driver of one to call for emergency personnel. He asked the driver of the other, 46-year-old Judith Sterling, to help in the move. She refused, stating that she had just recovered from back surgery. Kent was on his own.

Because spinal damage was likely, Kent knew he had to pull the victim in the direction of the long axis of the body, to provide the greatest possible protection for the spine. Kent quickly removed his own belt and used it to fasten the victim's hands loosely together, then to the victim's belt—a move that would prevent the victim's arms from flopping around or slipping out of his shirt. Then, using his forearms as a support on each side of the victim's head, Kent grasped the shoulders of the victim's shirt firmly. Using the shirt as a handle, he pulled the victim toward him and out of the pool of gasoline.

When emergency crews arrived a minute or two later, Kent was already starting a primary survey and had identified life-threatening problems that emergency medical personnel needed to address immediately.

AN INJURED PERSON OFTEN NEEDS TO BE MOVED. IT IS your responsibility to see that the victim is moved in a way that will prevent further injury and will not cause unnecessary pain and discomfort. Improper moving can add to the original injuries, increase shock, and endanger life.

Under normal circumstances, a victim should not be moved until a thorough assessment has been made and emergency care has been given; ideally, you should leave moving a victim to professional emergency teams. Under some situations, however, you will need to move the victim *before* assessment and care in order to remove the victim from a potential hazard or to reach other, more seriously injured people. This chapter discusses the general guidelines for moving victims and details various rescue moves.

• Section 1 •
GENERAL PRINCIPLES OF MOVING

Learning Objective 1 Discuss the general guidelines for moving victims.

Although speed is important in cases where a victim is exposed to environmental hazards, it is always more important to accomplish the handling and moving of a victim in a way that will not further injure the victim. As a basic rule of thumb, you should not move a victim until you absolutely have to or until you are completely ready to—and, if you can avoid it, you should not try to move a victim by yourself if you can wait and get help.

When moving a victim, follow these guidelines:

- If you find a victim in a face-down position, move the person to an assessment position *after* doing the ABCD assessment and checking for possible neck and spinal injury (see Figures 29-1 through 29-5).

- Generally, you should not move a victim if moving the person will make injuries worse.

- Provide all necessary emergency care; splint all fractures, especially those of the neck and back.

- Move a victim only if there is immediate danger (see the section that follows). Only when there is a threat to life should a victim be moved before the ABCDs are completed.

- If it is necessary to move a victim, your speed will depend on the reason for the move. For example, a victim who needs to be moved away from a fire should be moved as quickly as possible; a victim who needs to be moved so you have access to another victim should be moved with due consideration to his or her injuries before and during the move.

When to Make an Emergency Move

Learning Objective 2 Identify the situations in which an emergency move must be made.

Normally, top priorities in emergency care are maintaining the victim's airway, breathing, circulation, and spinal status and controlling hemorrhage. But when the scene of an accident is unstable, threatening your life as well as that of your victim, your priority changes—you must first move the victim.

Under life-threatening conditions, you may have to risk injury to the victim in order to save his or her life. *You should make an emergency move only when no other options are available,* such as in situations involving

- Uncontrolled traffic
- Physically unstable surroundings (such as a vehicle that you cannot stabilize and that is in danger of toppling off an embankment)
- Exposure to hazardous materials

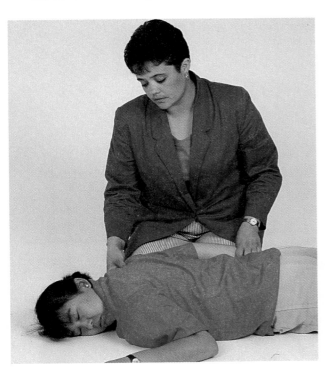

Figure 29-1

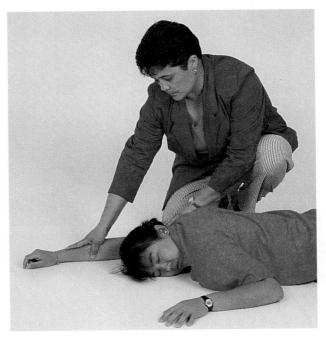

Figure 29-2

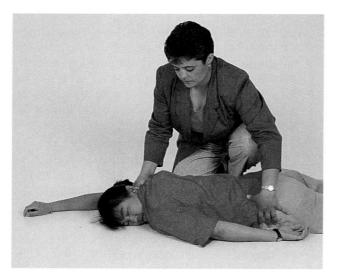

Figure 29-3

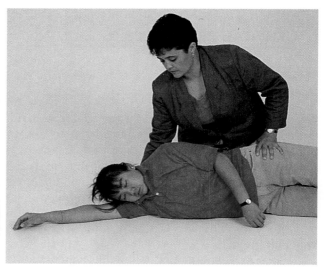

Figure 29-4

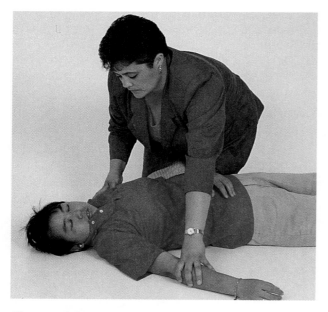

Figure 29-5

Figures 29-1 through 29-5. *Moving victim from a face-down position to an assessment position after doing the ABC assessment and checking for possible neck injury. First, move the victim's nearer arm above the head; then place one hand behind the victim's head and neck and the other hand on the distant hip; roll the victim toward you by pulling the hip. Once the victim is flat, the extended arm is brought back to the side. Seek additional help, and move the victim only in case of life-threatening emergency. When possible, a victim should be moved only by trained professionals.*

- Fire or threat of fire (fire should always be considered a grave threat)
- Hostile crowds
- The need to reposition the victim in order to provide life-saving treatment (such as moving to a firm, flat surface to perform CPR)
- The need for access (you may need to move one victim to gain access to another)
- The victim's demanding to be moved
- Weather conditions (you need to control exposure if the weather is very cold, wet, or hot, or windy enough to turn objects into projectiles)

Progress Check

1. In general, you should move a victim to an assessment position only after checking for possible _____ injury.
   (head/spinal/chest)

2. Unless there is a pressing reason, you should move a victim only after _____ .
   (necessary emergency care/thorough assessment/help arrives on the scene)

3. The speed with which you move a victim depends on _____ .
(the victim's injuries/the victim's desires/your reason for moving)

4. You should move a victim before assessment or care if the scene _____ .
(is especially unpleasant/threatens life/is crowded)

• Section 2 •
ONE-RESCUER TECHNIQUES

Although two or more people should be available to move injured victims, you may be faced with moving a victim by yourself—usually because of a flood, fire, building collapse, or some other life-threatening situation. Use the following techniques.

Walking Assist

Learning Objective 3 Describe and demonstrate the walking assist.

The **walking assist** (see Figure 29-6) is a method of moving a victim in which a single rescuer functions as a "crutch" in assisting the injured victim to walk.

1. Stand at the victim's side and drape the victim's arm across your shoulders.

2. Support the victim by placing your arm around his or her waist.

3. Using your body as a "crutch," support the victim's weight as you both walk.

Blanket Drag

Learning Objective 4 Describe and demonstrate the blanket drag.

The **blanket drag** (see Figure 29-7) is a method of moving an injured victim in which a rescuer places the victim on a blanket and drags the victim to safety.

1. Spread a blanket alongside the victim; gather half the blanket into lengthwise pleats.

2. Roll the victim away from you, then tuck the pleated part of the blanket as far beneath the victim as you can.

3. Roll the victim back onto the center of the blanket on his or her back; wrap the blanket securely around the victim.

4. Grab the part of the blanket that is beneath the victim's head and drag the victim toward you; if

Figure 29-6. One-rescuer walking assist

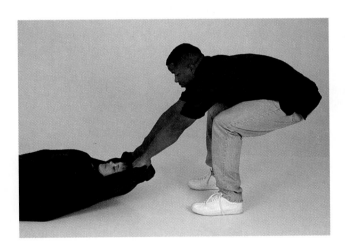

Figure 29-7. Blanket drag

walking assist A method of moving a victim in which a rescuer functions as a crutch in assisting the injured victim to walk

blanket drag A method of moving an injured victim in which a rescuer places the victim on a blanket and drags the victim to safety

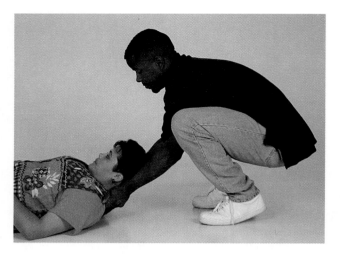

Figure 29-8. Shirt drag

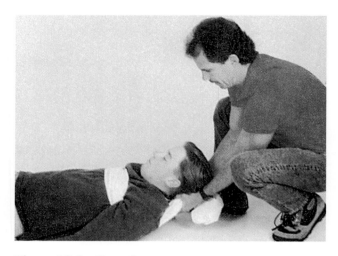

Figure 29-9. Sheet drag

you have to move on a stairway, keep the length of the victim's body in contact with several stairs at once to prevent the victim from bouncing on the steps.

Shirt Drag

Learning Objective 5 Describe and demonstrate the shirt drag.

The **shirt drag** (see Figure 29-8) is a method of moving a victim in which a single rescuer uses the victim's shirt as a handle to pull the victim.

A t-shirt won't work for a shirt drag because it stretches too much to work well. If the victim is wearing a shirt other than a t-shirt

1. Fasten the victim's hands or wrists loosely together, then link them to the victim's belt or pants to keep the arms from flopping or coming out of the shirt.
2. Grasp the shoulders of the victim's shirt under the head; use your forearms to support both sides of the head.
3. Using the shirt as a handle, pull the victim toward you; the pulling power should engage the victim's armpits, not the neck.

Sheet Drag

Learning Objective 6 Describe and demonstrate the sheet drag.

The **sheet drag** (see Figure 29-9) is a method of moving a victim in which a single rescuer forms a drag harness out of a sheet, passes it under the victim's arms at the armpits, and uses it to pull the victim.

1. Fold a sheet several times lengthwise to form a narrow, long "harness"; lay the folded sheet centered across the victim's chest at the nipple line.
2. Pull the ends of the sheet under the victim's arms at the armpits and behind the victim's head; twist the ends of the sheet together to form a triangular support for the head. Be careful not to pull the victim's hair.
3. Grasping the loose ends of the sheet, pull the victim toward you.

Fireman's Carry

Learning Objective 7 Describe and demonstrate the fireman's carry.

The **fireman's carry,** a method of lifting and carrying a victim in which one rescuer carries the victim over his or her shoulder, is not as safe as most ground-level moves because it places the victim's center of mass high—usually at the rescuer's shoulder level—and because it requires a fair amount of strength. However,

shirt drag A method of moving a victim in which a single rescuer uses the victim's shirt as a handle to pull the victim

sheet drag A method of moving a victim in which a single rescuer forms a drag harness out of a sheet by passing it under the victim's arms at the armpits, and uses it to pull the victim

fireman's carry A method of lifting and carrying a victim in which one rescuer carries the victim over his or her shoulder

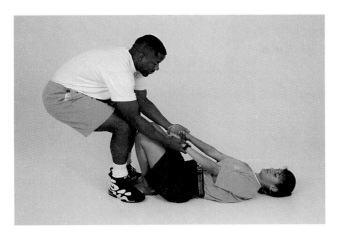

Figure 29-10

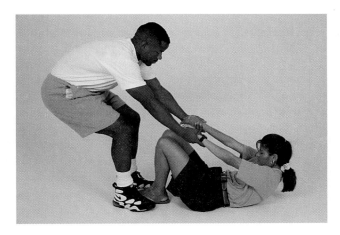

Figure 29-11

Figure 29-12

Figure 29-13

Figures 29-10 through 29-13. *Fireman's carry*

it is preferred if a single rescuer has to move a victim over irregular terrain.

Unless there is a life-or-death situation, do not attempt a fireman's carry if the victim has suspected spinal injury or fractures of the extremities. To perform the fireman's carry (see Figures 29-10 through 29-13):

1. Position the victim on his or her back with both knees bent and raised; grasp the back sides of the victim's wrists.

2. Stand on the toes of both the victim's feet; lean backward and pull the victim up toward you. As the victim nears a standing position, crouch slightly and pull the victim over your shoulder, then stand upright.

3. Pass your arm between the victim's legs and grasp the victim's arm that is nearest your body.

Progress Check

1. Use the walking assist to help a _____ victim walk.
   (slightly injured/conscious/spinal-injured)

2. You can roll a victim onto a _____ , then drag him or her to safety.
   (chair/stretcher/blanket)

3. In the shirt drag, make sure the pulling power engages the victim's _____ .
   (neck/shoulders/armpits)

(continued)

4. The sheet drag involves creating a "harness" that is twisted under the victim's arms and behind the

_____ .

(head/neck/shoulders)

5. Unless you are in a life-and-death situation, you should not use the fireman's carry to move a victim with suspected _____ .

(spinal injury/head injury/chest injury)

• Section 3 •

TWO- AND THREE-RESCUER TECHNIQUES

Seat Carries (Two Rescuers)

Learning Objective 8 Describe and demonstrate seat carries.

A seat carry (see Figures 29-14 through 29-16) is a method of lifting and moving a victim in which two rescuers form a "seat" with their arms.

Figure 29-14

Figure 29-15

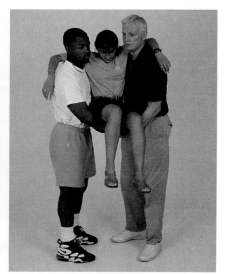

Figure 29-16

Figure 29-17

Figure 29-18

Figure 29-19

Figures 29-14 through 29-19. _Seat carries_

1. Raise the victim to a sitting position; each First Aider steadies the victim by positioning an arm around the victim's back.

2. Each First Aider slips his or her other arm under the victim's thighs, then clasps the wrist of the other First Aider. One pair of arms should make a seat, the other pair a backrest.

3. Slowly raise the victim from the ground, moving in unison. In one variation of the technique (Figures 29-17 through 29-19), the First Aiders make a seat with all four hands; the victim then supports him or herself by placing his or her arms around the First Aiders' shoulders.

Extremity Lift (Two Rescuers)

Learning Objective 9 Describe and demonstrate the extremity lift.

The **extremity lift** is a method of lifting and carrying a victim in which two rescuers carry the victim by the extremities. Do not use this method if the victim has back injuries.

1. One First Aider kneels at the victim's head; the other kneels at the victim's knees.

2. The First Aider at the victim's head places one hand under each of the victim's shoulders; the second First Aider grasps the victim's wrists.

3. The First Aider at the victim's knees pulls the victim to a sitting position by pulling on the victim's wrists; the First Aider at the victim's head assists by pushing the victim's shoulders and supporting the victim's back.

4. The First Aider at the victim's head slips his or her hands under the arms, and grasps the victim's wrists (see Figure 29-20).

5. The First Aider at the victim's knees slips his or her hands beneath the victim's knees.

6. Both First Aiders crouch on their feet and then simultaneously stand in one fluid motion (see Figure 29-21).

Chair Litter Carry (Two Rescuers)

Learning Objective 10 Describe and demonstrate the chair litter carry.

If the victim does not have contraindicating injuries and if a chair is available, you can use the **chair litter carry**. Sit the victim in the chair. One First Aider then carries the back of the chair while the other carries the legs; the chair itself is used as a litter (see Figures 29-22 and 29-23 on page 484). Be sure the chair is sturdy enough to support the weight of the victim.

> **seat carry** A method of lifting and moving a victim in which two rescuers form a "seat" with their arms
>
> **extremity lift** A method of lifting and carrying a victim in which two rescuers carry the victim by the extremities
>
> **chair litter carry** A method of lifting and moving a victim in which the victim is seated in a chair and two rescuers carry the victim in the chair

Figure 29-20

Figures 29-20 and 29-21. Extremity lift

Figure 29-21

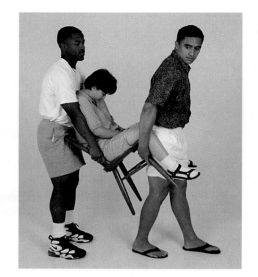

Figure 29-22   *Figure 29-23*

Figures 29-22 and 29-23. *Chair litter carry*

Flat Lift and Carry (Three Rescuers)

Learning Objective 11 Describe and demonstrate the flat lift and carry.

The three-rescuer **flat lift and carry,** when three rescuers lift and carry the victim to a stretcher, is an effective way to move a severely injured victim who cannot sit in a chair or when a cot cannot be moved close to the victim (see Figures 29-24 through 29-27). It has the advantage of permitting you to move the victim through narrow passages and down stairs. Use this method only if the victim does not have spinal injury.

1. Three First Aiders line up on the least injured side of the victim; if one First Aider is noticeably taller, that person stands at the victim's shoulders; another stands at the victim's hips, and the third at the victim's knees.

2. Each First Aider kneels on the knee closest to the victim's feet.

3. The First Aider at the victim's shoulders works his or her hands underneath the victim's neck and shoulders; the next First Aider's hands go underneath the victim's hips and pelvis; and the final First Aider's hands go underneath the victim's knees.

4. Moving in unison, the First Aiders raise the victim to knee level and slowly turn the victim toward themselves until the victim rests on the bends of their elbows.

5. Moving in unison, all three rise to a standing position and walk with the victim to a place of safety

or to the stretcher. To place the victim on the stretcher, simply reverse the procedure.

This move can also be done with four First Aiders: position them at the victim's head, chest, hips, and knees. Support is then given to the head, chest, hips, pelvis, knees, and ankles.

Progress Check

1. In seat carries, a "chair" can be formed by a pair of arms or by _____ .
    (two hands/four hands/a pair of shoulders)

2. Never use the extremity lift if the victim has

    _____ .

    (head injuries/back injuries/fractures)

3. If you have access to a sturdy chair and the victim does not have contraindicating injuries, use the

    _____ .

    (chair lift/chair carry/chair litter carry)

4. If you have at least three rescuers, use the _____ to move a severely injured victim.
    (flat lift and carry/extremity lift/chair carry)

flat lift and carry A method of lifting and moving a victim in which three rescuers or more lift and carry the victim to a stretcher

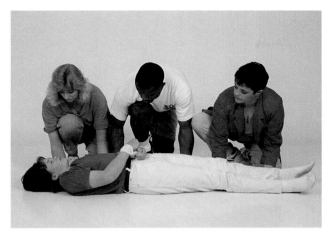

Figure 29-24

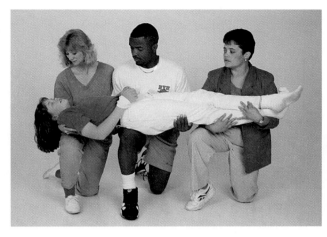

Figure 29-25

Figure 29-26

Figure 29-27

Figures 29-24 through 29-27. *Flat lift and carry*

• Section 4 •
EQUIPMENT

Canvas Litter/Pole Stretcher

Canvas litters (see Figure 29-28) have been used by armies worldwide for at least two centuries. The modern tubular-framed, vinyl-coated nylon version accommodates victims weighing as much as 350 pounds.

Use a canvas litter when a victim can be rolled in a single unit, without moving one end of the body ahead of the other (a method called a "logroll"). Do *not* use one when the victim has to be moved lengthwise or when spinal immobilization is needed.

Figure 29-28. *Canvas litter or stretcher*

Figure 29-29. Short backboard

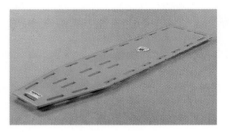

Figure 29-30. Long backboard

Backboards

Learning Objective 13 Describe and demonstrate how to use backboards to move a victim.

If you need to immobilize the spine, manually support the victim's head and neck in normal anatomic position until the victim is supine on the backboard; if possible, apply a rigid cervical collar to the victim's neck. Figures 29-29 and 29-30 illustrate short and long backboards, respectively.

There are several ways to get a victim onto a backboard; both require two First Aiders. If the victim is sitting:

1. Approach the victim from behind; slide a short board carefully behind the victim's back.
2. Tell the victim to lean against the board; anchor the bottom of the board with your knee to keep it from shifting position.
3. Slowly lower the board, maintaining manual support of the victim's head and neck. As the victim becomes supine, slide his or her lower body onto the board. Move in several short steps instead of one long one.

If the victim is supine:

1. Bring a long board to within arm's reach.
2. Kneeling at the victim's side, grasp the victim's forearm closest to you and lay it across the victim's chest; grasp the elbow of the same arm. With your other hand, grasp the victim's knee on the same side, bringing the knee into a raised position. Grasp the knee.

3. Holding onto the victim's elbow and knee, push away from you while a second First Aider gently rotates the head in the same direction.
4. With the victim on his or her side, examine the victim's back; then pull the backboard toward you and place it on edge against the victim's back. Roll the victim toward you and onto the board.
5. Strap the victim securely to the board, using at least three straps and preferably four.

If the victim is in a prone position, logroll the victim onto a spine board.

Blanket Stretcher

Learning Objective 14 Describe and demonstrate how to use a blanket stretcher.

When space is limited or you need to traverse stairs or cramped corners, you can use a blanket as a stretcher *if* the victim has no neck, back, or pelvic injuries or a fractured skull.

Use a blanket that is strong, free of holes and in good condition, and large enough to support the victim's entire body.

To use a blanket as a stretcher (see Figures 29-31 through 29-36), logroll or slide the victim onto the center of the blanket; tightly roll the side edges of the blanket toward the victim to form handholds. Position as many First Aiders around the victim as needed to distribute the hands evenly. If the weather is cold, use two blankets instead of one, folding one around the victim for warmth.

You can also fold and roll blankets to immobilize the head or other body parts.

Improvised Stretchers

Learning Objective 15 List objects that can be used for improvised stretchers.

You can improvise a stretcher with any of the following:

• A blanket, canvas, or sheet and two poles (fold the sides of the blanket or other material over the two poles; see Figures 29-37 through 29-40 on page 488).
• Cloth bags or sacks and two poles (cut holes in the bags to accommodate the poles)
• Three or four coats or jackets and two poles (fasten the jackets, turn the sleeves inside out, and pass the poles through the sleeves)

You can move an infant or toddler in an infant car seat; it also acts to immobilize the child.

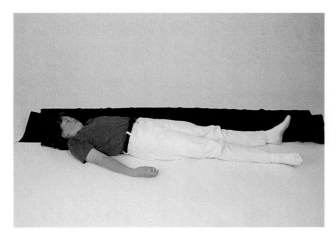

Figure 29-31

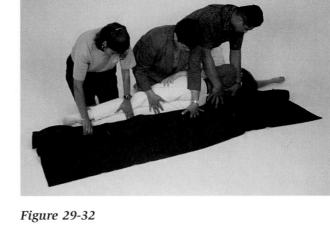

Figure 29-32

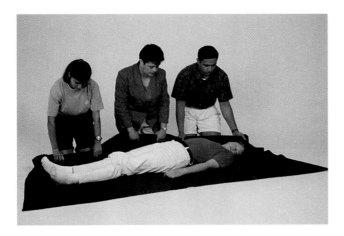

Figure 29-33

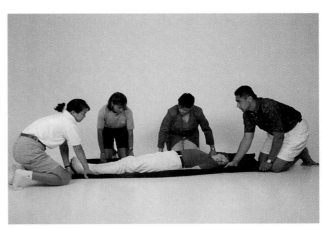

Figure 29-34

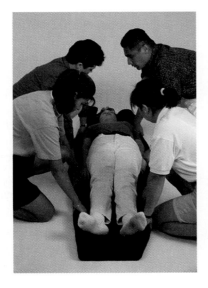

Figure 29-35

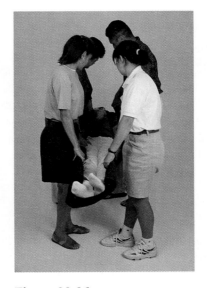

Figure 29-36

Figures 29-31 through 29-36. *Proper use of a blanket stretcher*

Figure 29-37

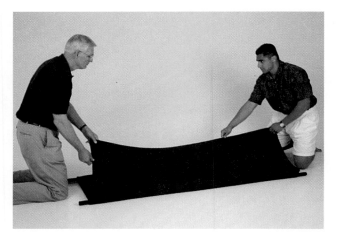

Figure 29-38

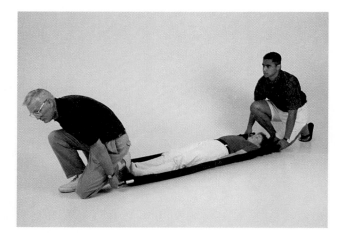

Figure 29-39

Figures 29-37 through 29-40. Improvised stretcher

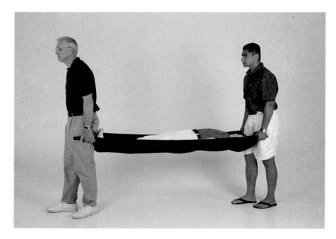

Figure 29-40

Stretcher Transportation

Learning Objective 16 Discuss the guidelines for moving a victim on a stretcher.

Before you use a stretcher, lock the crosspieces in place, test it by placing an uninjured person of the same weight as the victim on it, and pad it with a blanket or similar material. To move a victim on a stretcher

1. Three First Aiders position themselves on the victim's least injured side at the victim's knees, hips, and shoulders; the fourth is positioned at the victim's hips on the opposite side. Each First Aider rests on the knee nearest the victim's feet.

2. The hands of the First Aider at the shoulders are placed under the victim's neck and shoulders; the First Aider at the victim's knees places his or her hands under the victim's knees and ankles; and the First Aider at the victim's hips places his or her hands under the victim's pelvis and small of the back.

3. Moving in unison and keeping the victim's body level, the four slowly lift the victim and rest him or her on the knees of the three First Aiders. The fourth First Aider places the stretcher under the victim, then returns to his or her original position.

4. Moving in unison, the four gently lower the victim to the stretcher and cover the victim with a blanket.

5. The four position themselves, one at each end and one at each side of the stretcher, facing the victim.

6. All four First Aiders grasp and lift the stretcher. The two First Aiders on either side each shift one hand and support the end of the stretcher nearest

Figure 29-41. Stretcher transportation

the victim's feet, allowing the First Aider at that end to turn around with his or her back to the stretcher. Then, the First Aiders at the sides of the stretcher move in unison, one to the end near the victim's head, and one to the end near the victim's feet; all four First Aiders then grasp an end of a stretcher pole. The First Aiders are now ready to transport the stretcher. The victim is transported feet first (see Figure 29-41); the First Aider at the victim's head constantly monitors the victim's condition.

Progress Check

1. You should maintain manual support of the _____ until the victim is supine on a backboard.
   (backboard/head/head and neck)

2. Use a blanket as a stretcher only if you do not suspect a _____ .
   (pneumothorax/hemothorax/fractured skull)

3. Before you place a victim on a stretcher, you should test it with an uninjured person of the same _____ .

   (height/weight/gender)

• SUMMARY •

- Unless you are facing life-threatening conditions, you should not move a victim until assessment and care are completed. Ideally, leave moving to professional emergency teams.

- You should move a victim before assessment and care if there is a threat to life, such as uncontrolled traffic, physically unstable surroundings, exposure to hazardous materials, fire, or bad weather conditions. You may also have to move one victim to get access to another.

- The speed with which you move a victim depends on your reason for moving the victim.

- Ideally, two or more First Aiders should help move a victim; if you are on your own, you can use any of several one-rescuer techniques, such as the walking assist, blanket drag, shirt drag, sheet drag, or fireman's carry.

- If you suspect neck or spinal injuries, do *not* use the fireman's carry, extremity lift, chair litter carry, or flat lift and carry.

- If you do not have a commercial stretcher, you can improvise a stretcher from a blanket, canvas, or strong sheet and two poles. You can also make a stretcher from cloth bags or sacks or several jackets and a pair of poles.

- One of the most versatile pieces of equipment in caring for and moving the victim is the backboard.

• KEY TERMS •

Be sure you understand the following key terms:

- walking assist
- blanket drag
- shirt drag
- sheet drag
- fireman's carry
- seat carry
- extremity lift
- chair litter carry
- flat lift and carry

Student: _____   Date: _____

Course: _____   Section #: _____

If you believe the statement is true, circle the T. If you believe the statement is false, circle the F.

T   F   **1.** Usually, all necessary care should be provided before moving a victim.

T   F   **2.** Only when you are facing a threat to life should a victim be moved before the ABCDs are completed.

T   F   **3.** The extremity lift is a good lift to use if the victim has back injuries.

T   F   **4.** The three-rescuer flat lift is not a good move to use for a severely injured victim.

T   F   **5.** A victim should be transported head first on a stretcher.

T   F   **6.** The blanket drag is an effective way for a single rescuer to move a victim to safety.

T   F   **7.** The shirt drag cannot be used if the victim is wearing only a t-shirt.

T   F   **8.** The fireman's carry is considerably safer to use than most other ground-level moves.

T   F   **9.** If you find a victim face down, immediately move the victim into the assessment position before doing any kind of assessment.

For each item, circle the correct answer or the phrase that best completes the statement.

1. Two or more rescuers can use a blanket to transport an injured victim safely as long as the victim does not have

   a. a fractured pelvis
   b. a spinal injury
   c. a skull fracture
   d. any of the above

2. When carrying a victim on a litter, how many rescuers should ideally lift and carry?

   a. two
   b. three
   c. four to six
   d. eight

3. An injured victim may be moved by a First Aider only if the victim's position

   a. creates the risk of shock
   b. endangers the victim's life
   c. is inconvenient for giving first aid
   d. prevents the victim from receiving first aid

4. If you use a shirt drag to move an injured victim, pull the victim on his or her

   a. back, feet first
   b. back, head first
   c. stomach, feet first
   d. stomach, head first

5. When is it appropriate to move a victim away from the emergency site before giving emergency care?

   a. when there is danger of fire or explosion
   b. when the victim is blocking another victim who needs life-saving care
   c. when it is impossible to protect the scene
   d. all of the above

6. A victim who is slightly injured may be moved by one rescuer using the

   a. walking assist
   b. logroll
   c. shoulder drag
   d. extremity lift

7. If the move is a nonemergency move, you should

   a. treat for shock before moving the victim
   b. complete emergency care before moving the victim
   c. only move the victim if it is impossible to give first aid
   d. all of the above

8. The primary consideration in an emergency move is protecting the

   a. head
   b. extremities
   c. heart
   d. spine

- You must move a severely injured trauma victim who is unconscious; other First Aiders are available.
- You must move an unconscious victim away from a burning automobile.

Vehicle Stabilization and Victim Extrication

Learning Objectives

When you have mastered the material in this chapter, you will be able to

1 Discuss how to locate all victims of a vehicle accident

2 Discuss how to deal with dangers at the scene of a vehicle accident

3 Describe how to stabilize a vehicle

4 List the basic tools and equipment needed to rescue a victim from a vehicle

5 Describe how to gain access to a victim who is trapped in a vehicle

6 Describe and demonstrate how to stabilize a victim trapped in a vehicle

7 Describe and demonstrate how to remove a victim who is lying on the seat of a vehicle

8 Describe and demonstrate how to remove a victim who is lying on the floor of a vehicle

SQ3R Plus

- **Survey** to set goals for studying.
- Ask **questions** as you **read.**
- Stop frequently to **recite** and **review.**
- **Write** a summary of key points.
- **Reflect** on the importance of this material and its relevance in your life.

On March 10, 1998, 33-year-old Karen Norton was pulling around the corner into the grocery store parking lot when a car struck her from behind with tremendous force. Though Karen was secure in a seat belt, her 6-year-old daughter Amy had unbuckled her restraint in the back seat and was trying to find some crayons at the time of the accident. The impact slammed her into the front seat, then hurled her onto the floor in the back seat.

Twenty-two-year-old Brian Millgate was just loading his own groceries into his car when he heard the impact. He ran to the scene; the driver of the second car was still in his seat belt and appeared to have only minor injuries. Karen, concerned for Amy, had left the car and was running around the smashed vehicle, screaming. Brian could smell gasoline.

Brian immediately enlisted the help of another shopper to calm Karen down. A store employee came running toward them, announcing she had already called 9-1-1. Brian asked her and a middle-aged man to help him reach Amy.

Both rear doors opened, despite damage to the vehicle. Amy was lying across the floor. Brian positioned himself at Amy's head and held her head and neck in alignment; he instructed the store employee to hold Amy's feet and legs in alignment. Finally, he instructed the middle-aged man to lean over the front seat and grasp Amy's clothing at her waist, hips, and thighs. At Brian's instruction and on the count of three, all three lifted Amy to the back seat, maintaining body alignment. Brian had just started a primary survey when paramedics arrived on the scene; his quick action enabled them to begin assessment and care immediately.

EXTRICATION IS THE PROCESS OF REMOVING A VICTIM OR victims from a dangerous, life-threatening situation, typically, from inside a wrecked car. Ideally, **extrication** should be performed by trained or professional emergency crews. However, if a victim faces danger and emergency crews have not arrived, you may need to extricate the victim from the vehicle yourself.

This chapter explains how to locate victims and deal with dangers at the scene of a vehicle accident, and gives basic guidelines on victim extrication.

• Section 1 •
BASIC GUIDELINES

In most cases, a victim will not have to be moved immediately, and you will be able to wait for an emergency team to arrive. In those cases

- Control the hazards and stabilize the accident scene (see Figure 30-1)—shut off engines, set flares, douse fires, and so on. Allow no one to smoke because of the possibility of spilled gasoline.
- Gain access to the victim if it is possible and safe to do so.
- Perform life-saving care to stabilize the victim.
- Stay with the victim until the emergency team arrives.

Locating the Victims

> **Learning Objective 1** Discuss how to locate all victims of a vehicle accident.

Care first for all victims you can locate immediately—then scour the area for any victim who might be hidden. Use a systematic approach to increase your odds of finding all the victims:

- Ask coherent, conscious passengers how many were in the car (see Figure 30-2).
- Ask witnesses if someone left the site or took a victim away.
- In high-impact accidents, search the vehicle and area carefully, especially in ditches and tall weeds. A victim may even be wedged under the dashboard.
- Look for tracks in the earth or snow.

Figure 30-1. Placing a flare at the accident scene

Figure 30-2. Gathering information at the accident scene

Dealing with Dangers

> **Learning Objective 2** Discuss how to deal with dangers at the scene of a vehicle accident.

If a car is on fire and fire-fighting personnel have not arrived

- If passengers are not trapped, move them first.
- If passengers are trapped, deal with the fire.

If you approach an accident with downed power lines

- Assume all downed lines are live; call for expert assistance.
- Park your vehicle at a safe distance from the power line.
- Warn bystanders to stay clear.
- Tell victims to stay inside their vehicles.
- *Never try to handle a live wire yourself* (see Chapter 24).

Progress Check

1. To help locate all victims, look for _____.
   (blood/torn clothing/tracks in the earth or snow)

2. If a vehicle is on fire and the victims are not trapped, first _____.
   (call the fire department/move the victims/fight the fire)

3. If there are downed power lines, have the victims

   _____.
   (jump clear of the car/step out of the car/stay in the car)

---

extrication The process of removing a victim from a dangerous situation or wrecked car

• Section 2 •
STABILIZING THE VEHICLE

> **Learning Objective 3** Describe how to stabilize a vehicle.

After all possible hazards have been controlled, make the rescue setting as safe as possible. Consider any vehicle unstable until you have made it stable, regardless of how it came to rest after the collision.

If the vehicle is overturned, place a solid object—such as a wheel chock, spare tire, cribbing, or timber—between the roof and the roadway (see Figures 30-3 and 30-4). Hook a chain to the vehicle's axle, then loop the chain around a tree or post.

If the vehicle is resting on all four wheels, place the gear selector in park; on a standard shift, place the vehicle in reverse. Use blocks or wedges at the wheels to prevent unexpected rolling.

Figure 30-3. *Stabilizing an overturned vehicle with cribbing*

Figure 30-4. *Spare wheels can be used when cribbing is not available.*

If the air bag has not deployed, disconnect the negative side of the battery and the yellow air-bag connector, which in most cars can be found where the steering column meets the dashboard. If the air bag did deploy, expect harmless cornstarch residue in the passenger area.

Tools and Equipment

> **Learning Objective 4** List the basic tools and equipment needed to rescue a victim from a vehicle.

Have the following basic tools on hand for possible vehicle stabilization and victim extrication:

- Hammer
- Screwdriver
- Chisel
- Crowbar
- Pliers
- Linoleum knife
- Work gloves and goggles
- Shovel
- Tire iron
- Wrench
- Knife
- Car jack
- Rope or chain

If you include some or all of these in your first-aid kit, you can use them to help extricate victims safely and effectively.

Progress Check

1. You should consider _____ vehicle unstable.
   (an overturned/a stacked/any)

2. To stabilize an overturned vehicle, chain the _____ to a post or tree.
   (frame/axle/door)

3. If a vehicle rests on all four tires, place an automatic gear selector in _____ .
   (reverse/overdrive/park)

4. To stabilize an upright vehicle that is resting on all four tires, use blocks or wedges at the _____ .
   (frame/bumpers/wheels)

• Section 3 •
GAINING ACCESS TO THE VICTIM

Learning Objective 5 Describe how to gain access to a victim who is trapped in a vehicle.

To gain access to a victim

- Attempt to open the door nearest the victim by using the door handle.

- If doors are locked, ask a person inside the car to unlock them; if necessary, slide a coat hanger between the door frame and window to force the lock.

- If the doors cannot be opened, determine the next best point of entry.

- If you have to break a window (see Figure 30-5), wear gloves to protect yourself.

- Always break the window farthest from the victim.

- If possible, put strips of broad tape over the glass before you break the window to keep broken pieces of glass from spraying the victim.

- To break a window, give a quick, hard thrust in the lower corner with a spring-loaded punch, screwdriver, or other sharp object.

- Once the window is broken, use your gloved hand to pull glass outside the vehicle.

- Clear all glass away from the window opening.

Figure 30-5. Gaining access to the victim through a window

- Before you crawl through a broken window, drape a heavy tarp, blanket, or coat over the edge of the window and on the interior of the car just below the window. Cover the victim with a blanket to protect against broken glasss.

Progress Check

1. The first step in trying to gain access to a victim is to try the _____ .
   (door nearest the victim/window nearest the victim/window farthest from the victim)

2. Try to open the door with _____ .
   (a crowbar/a tire iron/the door handle)

3. If you need to break a window, choose the one _____ the victim.
   (closest to/farthest from/across from)

4. If you can, put strips of _____ over the window before you break it.
   (tape/aluminum foil/webbing)

• Section 4 •
STABILIZING THE VICTIM

Learning Objective 6 Describe and demonstrate how to stabilize a victim trapped in a vehicle.

Note: You should use backboards only if you have been specifically trained in their use; use of backboards and spineboards is not considered a usual first aid skill.

Once you are inside the vehicle with the victim

1. Conduct a quick but thorough primary survey; if more than one victim is involved, perform triage.

2. Stabilize airway, breathing, circulation, and hemorrhage; correct any life-threatening problems, then provide other care as needed. Bandage all wounds, splint all fractures, and give psychological support.

3. If you need to move the victim before you have immobilized him or her because of threat to life

   - Cut away any jammed seat belts.

   - Immobilize the neck with a rolled blanket (see Figure 30-6 on page 498): Place the blanket behind the victim's head, allowing both long ends to fall across the chest; cross the ends on the chest; applying gentle tension on both long

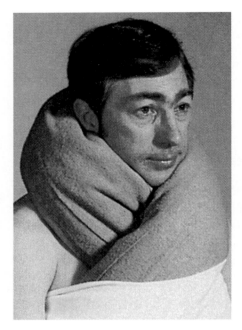

Figure 30-6. Rolled blanket used as improvised cervical collar

Figure 30-7. Moving the victim onto a long backboard

ends, pass them under opposite arms; gather the blanket behind the victim and rotate him or her from the seat into your arms.

4. Once the victim has been stabilized and moved, continue to monitor airway, breathing, circulation, bleeding, and temperature.

Be aware that during a long extrication procedure, shock combined with temperature extremes can be fatal. Maintain body temperature with blankets if necessary, and provide shade during the summer.

Removing a Victim on the Seat of a Vehicle

Learning Objective 7 Describe and demonstrate how to remove a victim who is lying on the seat of a vehicle.

1. One First Aider maintains stabilization of the head and neck to keep the victim's head in normal alignment with the body.

2. Apply an improvised or rigid cervical collar.

3. A second First Aider carefully moves the victim's legs and body into alignment while the first rescuer maintains head stabilization. At least one other First Aider then moves the victim slightly away from the seat to allow a long backboard to be slipped beneath the victim's back (see Figure 30-7).

4. Ease the victim against the backboard. On signal from the First Aider at the victim's head, hold the victim snugly against the backboard and push the backboard down until the backboard and victim are flat on the seat. Secure the victim to the backboard and remove from the car.

If the victim is found face down, give urgent first aid without moving the victim more than necessary.

Removing a Victim Lying on the Floor

Learning Objective 8 Describe and demonstrate how to remove a victim who is lying on the floor of a vehicle.

If the victim is on the floor of the vehicle:

1. Place the backboard flat on the seat.

2. One First Aider should keep the victim's head and neck in alignment with the body while another First Aider maintains alignment of the feet and legs (see Figure 30-8); if possible, secure the victim's legs together with a bandage.

3. While the body is kept in alignment, at least one other First Aider reaches over the seat and grasps the victim's clothing at the waist, hips, and thighs.

4. On signal from the First Aider at the victim's head, lift the victim onto the backboard, maintaining body alignment. Secure the victim to the backboard and remove the person from the car.

Progress Check

1. Your first priority once you are in the vehicle with the victim is to _____ .
(secure the person to a backboard/give psychological support/perform a primary survey)

2. If more than one victim is involved, _____ .
(send for help/perform triage/stay out of the vehicle)

3. If necessary, you can immobilize the victim's neck with a _____ .
(blanket/seat belt/bandage)

4. _____ combined with weather extremes can be fatal during long extrication.
(Bleeding/Shock/Head injury)

Figure 30-8. Keeping head, neck, and legs in alignment in preparation for application of long spine backboard

• SUMMARY •

- Whenever possible, leave vehicle stabilization and victim extrication to trained or professional emergency crews.

- If you can wait for emergency crews to arrive, control the hazards, stabilize the accident scene, gain access to the victim, and perform life-saving care—but do not try to extricate the person from the vehicle.

- Make sure you look for all the victims who could have been involved; look in ditches, tall weeds, and under the dashboard.

- If the vehicle is on fire and the passengers are not trapped, move them first; if they are trapped, deal first with the fire.

- If there are downed power lines at the scene, tell the victims to stay in the vehicle; never try to manage downed power lines by yourself.

- Consider any vehicle unstable until you have stabilized it, regardless of how it came to rest after a collision.

- The first thing you should try in gaining access to a victim is to open a door with the door handle.

- Once you are inside the car with the victim, complete a rapid primary survey, perform the ABCs, correct life-threatening conditions, provide other emergency care as needed, and continue to monitor the victims.

• KEY TERM •

Make sure you understand the following key term:

- extrication

Student: _____ Date: _____

Course: _____ Section #: _____

If you believe the statement is true, circle the T. If you believe the statement is false, circle the F.

T   F   **1.** Suspect any vehicle of being unstable until you have made it stable.

T   F   **2.** Part of stabilizing a victim is to splint all fractures.

T   F   **3.** A victim's head and neck should be stabilized before a cervical collar is applied.

T   F   **4.** When you gain access to an accident victim, you should first establish an open airway.

T   F   **5.** *Extricate* means to pull a person quickly out of a wrecked vehicle.

T   F   **6.** Do not worry about a downed power line unless it is sparking.

T   F   **7.** Stabilize a standard-transmission vehicle by putting the transmission in first gear.

T   F   **8.** Break the window nearest the victim so you will have immediate access to the victim.

For each item, circle the correct answer or the phrase that best completes the statement.

1. Cars that are upside down or lying on their side should be
   a. turned upright
   b. taken apart
   c. stabilized as is
   d. left untouched

2. Once you have gained access to the victim, you should
   a. check for breathing and heartbeat
   b. control severe bleeding
   c. splint fractures
   d. treat for shock

3. When a victim is lying on the seat of a car, what is the first step involved in removing the victim from the car?
   a. move the legs and body into alignment
   b. maintain slight and gentle traction on the head
   c. apply a cervical collar
   d. move the victim slightly away from the seat

4. *Extrication* means
   a. picking and sorting the injured
   b. gaining access to the accident scene
   c. moving and transporting the injured
   d. disentangling or freeing a trapped victim

5. What should you do if the victim does not need to be rescued immediately and a rescue team will be arriving soon?
   a. control the hazards and stabilize the accident scene
   b. gain access to the victim if possible
   c. give emergency care to stabilize the victim
   d. all of the above

6. What part of the vehicle should you check first to gain access to a trapped victim?
   a. windows
   b. floor
   c. roof
   d. doors

- A 65-year-old driver has run his vehicle into a parked car, then skidded sideways into traffic where his car was broadsided on the passenger side. When you arrive, he is unconscious and pale and slumped into the steering wheel. He is not wearing a seat belt. Both doors are jammed, but the window on the passenger side is knocked out.

  What two factors concerning extrication would you consider first? How would you gain access to the victim?

Glossary..

A

abdomen The area of the body between the nipples and the groin

abdominal aortic aneurysm A section of the wall of the aorta in the abdomen that weakens, dilates, and eventually ruptures

abrasion A superficial wound caused by rubbing, scraping, or shearing

abruptio placenta A condition in which a normally positioned placenta separates from the uterine wall during the last 3 months of pregnancy

absorption Taking a substance into the body through the skin

acromioclavicular joint The joint in the shoulder where the clavicle, scapula, and humerus join

activated charcoal A special steam-distilled charcoal that can absorb many times its weight in contaminants because of its porous surface

actual consent Informed consent

acute mountain sickness An altitude-related illness that resembles a severe hangover

air embolism A diving injury in which air bubbles enter the bloodstream

amniotic sac A plasticlike sac of fluid in which the baby floats

anatomical position Standing erect with the arms down at the sides, the palms facing forward

anatomical snuffbox The area of the wrist through which the radial artery passes

angina pectoris Chest pain caused when the heart's need for oxygen is not met

anterior Toward the front

arcing injury (flash burn) An injury caused when an electrical current jumps from one surface to another; nearby skin is burned, but electricity does not actually pass through the skin

arteriosclerosis A disease condition in which the arteries lose their elasticity

articulate To fit into each other

aseptic Free of bacteria

aspiration Breathing foreign matter into the lungs

ataxia Inability to keep balance

atherosclerosis A condition in which fatty substances and other debris are deposited on the arterial walls

atonic seizure Also called a "drop attack," a seizure in which the legs of a child suddenly and temporarily collapse

aura The first phase of a seizure that lasts only a few seconds and involves a peculiar sensation that may be psychic or sensory in nature

autonomic discharge A stage in a grand mal seizure that lasts for a few seconds and includes hyperventilation, salivation, and rapid heartbeat

autonomic nervous system The part of the nervous system that influences the activities of involuntary muscles and glands

avulsion The tearing loose of a flap of skin, which may either remain hanging or be torn off altogether

B

ball-and-socket joint The type of joint that permits the widest range of motion

bandage Material used to hold a dressing in place

barotrauma A diving emergency in which body cavities are subjected to extreme pressure

basic life support A term that describes the first aid procedures necessary to sustain life in an emergency situation

Battle's sign Bruising behind the ears (mastoid process); a sign of skull fracture

billowing Loss of heat inside a tent when the wind flaps the sides of the tent and warm air is replaced with cold air

birth canal The vagina and lower part of the uterus

black widow spider A poisonous spider identified by a red mark shaped like an hourglass on its underside

blanket drag A method of moving an injured victim in which a rescuer places the victim on a blanket and drags the victim to safety

bloody show Pink-tinged mucus in the vaginal discharge that is evident as labor begins

"blue bloater" A victim of chronic bronchitis

breech birth A situation in which the buttocks of the baby present first through the birth canal

bronchiolitis A viral infection that inflames the bronchioles

bronchospasm Generalized spasm of the bronchi

brown recluse spider A brown poisonous spider identified by a violin-shaped mark on its back; brown recluse spider bites do not heal and require surgical grafting

C

carbon monoxide An odorless, colorless, tasteless, toxic gas resulting from incomplete combustion of anything containing carbon

cardiac arrest The heart stops beating

cardiac muscle The muscle that makes up the walls of the heart

carpopedal spasm Drawing up of the hands at the wrists and knuckles with flexed fingers

carotid pulse The pulse at the groove on either side of the neck

central nervous system The part of the nervous system that consists of the brain and the spinal cord

central vertigo The least common type of vertigo (dizziness), which mimics a transient ischemic attack or stroke; victims do not experience nausea, vomiting, hearing loss, or a whirling sensation

cerebral embolism A clot that forms elsewhere in the body, travels through the bloodstream, and lodges in a cerebral artery

cervix The neck of the uterus

chair litter carry A method of lifting and moving a victim in which the victim is seated in a chair and two rescuers carry the victim in the chair

chronic obstructive pulmonary disease A range of diseases including emphysema, chronic bronchitis, and asthma

clonic phase The phase of a seizure characterized by muscular rigidity and relaxation that alternate rhythmically in rapid succession

colicky pain Cramplike pain that occurs in waves

Colles's fracture A displaced fracture of the forearm caused when the victim falls on the palm of the hand with the wrist extended

compensatory shock The first stage of shock, in which the body attempts to overcome problems with normal defenses

concealment A place or an object that will hide you, such as shrubbery

conduction The loss of body heat to nearby objects through direct physical touch

condyloid joint A modified ball-and-socket joint

conjunctiva The transparent mucous membrane lining the eyelids and covering the outer surface of the eyeball

contact burns Burns caused by touching either a hot surface or a live electrical circuit

contusion A bruise

convection The loss of body heat to surrounding air, which becomes warmer, rises, and is replaced with cooler air

conversion hysteria Converting anxiety to a physical dysfunction, such as blindness or deafness

coral snake A type of poisonous snake that does not have a pit or fangs

coronary artery disease A condition in which a coronary artery has been damaged

coup-contrecoup A mechanism of brain injury in which the head comes to a sudden stop but the brain continues to move back and forth inside the skull

cover An object that will both hide you and stop bullets, such as a tree

cramp Uncontrolled spasm of a muscle

cravat A folded triangular bandage

crepitus A sandpaperlike grating sound made by the ends of a broken bone as they rub together

croup A viral infection that causes swelling beneath the glottis and progressive narrowing of the airway

crowning The emergence of the baby's head at the vaginal opening

cyanosis Bluish discoloration from lack of oxygen

D

decompression sickness A diving injury in which gases (usually nitrogen) enter the bloodstream

deep Remote from the surface

delirium tremens A life-threatening condition causing delirium that usually occurs within 5 days of an alcoholic's last drink

dermis The second layer of skin, which contains the hair follicles, sweat glands, oil glands, and nerves

diabetic coma A condition that results from too little insulin and too much sugar

dilation The stage of labor during which the cervix dilates and contractions occur

dislocation The displacement of a bone end from a joint

distal Farther from the point of reference

distraction The sudden pulling apart of the spine that stretches and tears the cord, as in hanging

dressing A sterile covering for a wound

drowning Death from suffocation due to submersion

"dry" drowning Drowning in which little or no water enters the lungs

duty to act The legal obligation to give aid or perform emergency care

dyspnea Shortness of breath or difficulty in breathing

E

eclampsia The second stage of toxemia

ectopic pregnancy A pregnancy in which the fertilized egg is implanted outside the uterus

elliptical pupils Pupils that are vertical slits, like those of a cat

emphysema A respiratory disease characterized by overinflated alveoli

endocrine glands The ductless glands that regulate the body by secreting hormones

epidermis The outermost layer of the skin

epiglottitis A bacterial infection that causes swelling of the epiglottis and blocking of the airway

epilepsy A chronic brain disorder characterized by recurrent seizures not caused by acute problems, with or without loss of consciousness

esophageal varices Bulging, engorged, weakened blood vessels in the lining of the wall of the lower one-third of the esophagus

evaporation The loss of body heat when perspiration is changed from liquid to vapor

evisceration The protrusion of abdominal contents through a laceration or other wound

exhalation The act of breathing out (expiration)

expiration The act of breathing out (exhalation)

external Outside

extremity lift A method of lifting and carrying a victim in which two rescuers carry the victim by the extremities

extrication The process of removing a victim from a dangerous situation or wrecked car

extruded Forced out of position; an extruded eyeball has been forced out of the socket

F

face mask A barrier device that covers a victim's mouth and nose

face shield A barrier device that covers a victim's mouth

fetus The developing unborn baby

fireman's carry A method of lifting and carrying a victim in which one rescuer carries the victim over his or her shoulder

first aid The temporary and immediate care given to a person who is injured or who suddenly becomes ill

first-degree burn A burn that involves only the epidermis, or outer layer of skin, characterized by pain and redness

flail chest Instability of a section of chest wall

flat lift and carry A method of lifting and moving a victim in which three or more rescuers lift and carry the victim to a stretcher

foramen magnum The opening at the base of the skull that houses the brain stem

fracture A crack or break in a bone

frostbite Damage to the tissues resulting from prolonged exposure to extreme cold

frostnip Freezing of the skin surface

G

gastric distention Inflation of the stomach with air

gauze pads Commercially manufactured and individually wrapped sterile pads made of gauze

gestational diabetes Temporary diabetes that develops in a pregnant woman

gliding joint A joint that permits a gliding motion

globe The eyeball

glucose Sugar

Good Samaritan laws Laws that protect health care personnel and provide guidelines for care

grand mal seizure A convulsive seizure characterized by alternating muscle rigidity and jerking, temporarily suspended breathing, and unconsciousness

H

heat cramps Muscle spasms caused by a disturbance in the electrolyte balance of the muscles; generally seen when the body loses too much salt during profuse sweating

heat exhaustion A heat-related emergency caused by excessive loss of water and salt through sweating, characterized by cold, clammy skin and a weak, rapid pulse

heatstroke A life-threatening emergency caused by a disturbance in the body's temperature regulation mechanism, characterized by extreme fever, hot and dry skin, delirium, or coma

Heimlich maneuver A system using abdominal thrusts to remove foreign objects from the airway

hematoma A collection of blood beneath the skin

hemophiliac A person whose blood will not clot because of congenital abnormalities in the clotting mechanism

hemoptysis Coughing up of blood

hemothorax An accumulation of blood in the chest cavity

hemorrhage Uncontrolled bleeding

hernia Protrusion of an internal organ through the abdominal wall or into another body cavity

high altitude cerebral edema An altitude-related illness that causes swelling of the brain and increased pressure inside the skull

high altitude pulmonary edema An altitude-related illness that causes fluid to go into the lungs from body cells

hinge joint A joint that permits a one-way hinge motion

hyperthermia Greatly increased body temperature

hypothermia Greatly decreased body temperature

hypertonic phase The phase in a seizure that signals the end of continuous muscle contractions, characterized by extreme muscle rigidity and hypertension

hyperventilation A condition characterized by overbreathing or breathing too rapidly

hyperventilation syndrome An abnormal state in which rapid breathing persists

I

implied consent Assumption that a victim of life-threatening injury or illness would give consent

infantile seizure A seizure in an infant characterized by falling forward of the head and flexing forward of the arms

infectious disease A disease that can be transmitted from one person to another or from an insect or animal to a person

inferior Toward the feet

ingestion Taking a substance into the body through the mouth

inhalation The act of breathing in (inspiration), or the drawing of air or other gases into the lungs

inhalation injury An injury caused by breathing in heat, toxic chemicals, smoke, or carbon monoxide

inspiration The act of breathing in (inhalation)

insulin A hormone needed to facilitate movement of glucose out of the bloodstream, across the cell membranes, and into the cells

insulin shock A condition that results from too much insulin and too little food

internal Inside

involuntary muscle Smooth muscle over which a person has no voluntary or conscious control

irreversible shock The final stage of shock, in which body organs start to die

ischemic stroke A stroke caused by a clot inside the brain

ischial tuberosity The spot where the top of the hamstring attaches

J

Jacksonian seizure A simple, partial seizure characterized by jerking in the fingers and toes; the jerking may spread to involve the entire arm or leg, or even the entire body, but the victim stays awake and aware

L

labor The process that begins with the first uterine contraction and ends with delivery of the baby and placenta

labyrinthine vertigo The most common kind of dizziness, caused by a disturbance in the inner ear and characterized by nausea, vomiting, and a whirling sensation

laceration A break in the skin; lacerations can have either smooth or rough edges and can be of varying depth

larynx The voice box

lateral To the right or left of the midline (center) of the body

lateral recumbent position Lying on the right or left side

M

mammalian diving reflex A reflex that prevents death after submersion in cold water

mandible The lower jaw

maxilla The upper jaw

meconium The feces of a fetus; greenish or brownish-yellow amniotic fluid indicates that the baby had a bowel movement in the uterus before delivery

medial Toward the midline (center) of the body

minor's consent The right of consent given to a parent or guardian

miscarriage Loss of pregnancy before the baby is able to survive, usually before 20 weeks of gestation; also called "spontaneous abortion"

"mules" Individuals who swallow latex containers filled with cocaine in an attempt to smuggle the drug

myocardial infarction Heart attack, caused when the blood supply to the heart is restricted or cut off

myocardium The heart muscle

myoclonic seizure A seizure characterized by sudden, brief, massive muscle jerks that involve part or all of the body

N

near-drowning Survival, at least temporarily, of near suffocation due to submersion

negligence Acting with carelessness, inattention, disregard, inadvertence, or avoidable oversight

nitroglycerin Medication prescribed to ease the pain of angina pectoris

noxious Poisonous

O

occlusive Waterproof and airtight

ocular Having to do with the eye

orbit The bony socket that holds the eyeball

P

pallor Paleness

palmar surface method A method of using the size of the victim's palm to estimate the percentage of body surface that has been burned

palpable Able to be felt by the First Aider

paradoxical breathing A condition in which the injured area of the chest moves opposite the rest of the chest during breathing

paresthesia Pricking or tingling sensation that indicates loss of circulation

parasympathetic nervous system The part of the autonomic nervous system seated in the midportion of the brain, brain stem, and lower spinal cord

patella The kneecap

PCP Phencyclidine, a hallucinogenic drug that acts as an anesthetic

perfusion Circulation of oxygen-rich blood through organs and tissues

perineum The area of skin between the vagina and the anus

peripheral nervous system Structures of the nervous system (especially nerve endings) that lie outside the brain and spinal cord

peristalsis The rhythmic movement of matter through the digestive tract

peritonitis Inflammation of the lining of the abdomen

petit mal seizure A seizure characterized by a blank stare that lasts only a few seconds, most common in children; a petit mal seizure does not involve convulsions

"pink puffer" A victim of emphysema

pit viper snake A type of poisonous snake such as a rattlesnake, characterized by a pit between the eyes and mouth

pivot joint A joint that allows a pivotal motion

placenta Structure on the inner lining of the uterus that provides the fetus with nourishment

placenta previa A condition in which the placenta is positioned abnormally

plaque Fatty deposits on the arterial walls

pneumothorax A condition in which air from a lung or from the outside fills the chest cavity, but does not fill the lung

posterior Toward the back

postictal stupor The phase following a seizure, during which all muscles relax and the victim falls into a deep sleep

postseizure phase One of the final phases of a seizure, during which the victim progresses into a coma

preeclampsia The first stage of toxemia

premature baby A baby that weighs less than 5½ pounds and/or is born after less than 36 weeks' gestation

presenting part The part of the baby that emerges first through the birth canal; in a normal birth it is the head

pressure point A place where an artery is close to the skin surface and lies over a bone

progressive shock The second stage of shock, in which the body shunts blood away from the extremities and abdomen

prolapsed cord The presentation of the umbilical cord at the vaginal opening before the baby

prone position Lying on the stomach (face down)

proximal Near the point you are referring to

psychomotor seizure A seizure that starts with a blank stare, then progresses into chewing and random activity; the victim seems dazed

pulmonary edema A condition in which plasma seeps out of the capillaries into the lungs as a result of pressure from a failing heart

Q

quadrants Sections; the abdomen is divided into four quadrants

R

raccoon eyes Bruising around the eyes in the absence of trauma to the eyes; a sign of skull fracture

radial pulse The pulse at the wrist

radiation The loss of body heat to the surface of another object without physical contact

reasonable force The amount of force required to keep a person from injuring self or others

"reasonable-man" test Did the First Aider act the same way a normal, prudent person with similar training would have acted under the same circumstances?

reduce To straighten

respiration The act of breathing

roller bandage A form-fitting bandage designed to be wrapped around a wound site

Rule of Nines A method of estimating how much body surface was burned by mentally dividing the body into regions, each representing 9 percent (or a multiple of 9 percent) of the body surface

Rule of Threes A rule stating that survival time is considerably reduced if a victim is without all three factors required for survival: shelter, water, and food

S

saddle joint A type of joint that permits up-and-down and side-to-side movement

sclera The white of the eye

seat carry A method of lifting and moving a victim in which two rescuers form a "seat" with their arms

secondary drowning Death from aspiration pneumonia following resuscitation after a water accident

second-degree burn A burn that involves both the epidermal and dermal layers of the skin, characterized by blistering, swelling, and pain

seizure An involuntary, sudden change in sensation, behavior, muscle activity, or level of consciousness that results from irritation or overactivity of brain cells

sheet drag A method of moving a victim in which a single rescuer forms a drag harness out of a sheet by passing it under the victim's arms at the armpits, and uses it to pull the victim

shirt drag A method of moving a victim in which a single rescuer uses the victim's shirt as a handle to pull the victim

shock The collapse and progressive failure of the cardiovascular system

signs Things you can observe about the victim, such as bleeding

silent myocardial infarction A heart attack that does not cause chest pain

skeletal muscle Voluntary muscle

Smith's fracture A displaced fracture of the forearm caused when the victim falls on the back of the hand with the wrist flexed

smooth muscle The muscles found in the walls of the internal organs and blood vessels, generally not under voluntary control

special pads Large, thickly layered, bulky pads used to control bleeding and stabilize impaled objects

sprain An injury in which ligaments are stretched and partially or completely torn

status asthmaticus A severe, prolonged asthma attack that represents a dire medical emergency

status epilepticus A severe, prolonged seizure or a series of seizures that occur without the victim's regaining consciousness between them

sterile Free of all microorganisms and spores

stoma A surgical opening in the neck

strain A soft-tissue injury or muscle spasm around a joint

stroke Any disease process that impairs circulation to the brain

substernal notch The notch at the spot where the ribs join the sternum

sudden infant death syndrome Sudden death of an apparently healthy infant, usually while asleep

suicide Any willful act designed to end one's own life

superficial Near the surface

superior Toward the head

supine position Lying on the back

sympathetic nervous system The part of the autonomic nervous system that causes blood vessels to constrict, stimulates sweating, increases the heart rate, causes the sphincter muscles to contract, and prepares the body to respond to stress

symptoms Things the victim describes to you, such as abdominal pain

syncope Fainting

T

tennis elbow Inflammation of the bony protrusion of the elbow

tension pneumothorax A situation in which air enters the pleural space through a one-way defect in the lung, resulting in a progressive increase in pressure in the pleural cavity that causes the lung to collapse and that impairs circulation

thermal burn A burn caused by flames

third-degree burn A full-thickness burn, involving all layers of the skin as well as fat, muscle, and bone; a third-degree burn is characterized by dry, leathery, charred skin

thrombus A clot that forms in a cerebral artery

tonic phase The early stage of a seizure during which the victim loses consciousness, the eyes roll upward, and the body is completely rigid with continuous muscular contraction

toxemia Poisoning of the blood during pregnancy

tracheal deviation Displacement of the trachea to one side or the other

transient ischemic attack Brief attacks similar to strokes that occur when arterial blockage is partial or brief

traumatic asphyxia Sudden compression of the chest wall that forces blood the wrong way out of the heart

triage A system of sorting victims into categories by treatment priority

triangular bandage Triangle-shaped piece of cloth used to apply splints and form slings

Type I diabetes Diabetes that results when the body produces little or no insulin

Type II diabetes Diabetes that results when the body cannot utilize the insulin it produces

U

umbilical cord An extension of the placenta that resembles a sturdy rope, through which the fetus is nourished

urushiol The toxic element of poison ivy, which can be carried on animal fur, tools, clothing, and, when the plant is burned, in the air

uterus The organ in which the baby grows

V

vagina The passage for childbirth

vernix caseosa The white, cheeselike covering on a newborn's skin

vertigo Dizziness

voluntary muscle "Skeletal muscle"; muscle that is under direct voluntary control of the brain

voluntary nervous system The part of the nervous system that influences activity of the voluntary muscles and movements throughout the body

W

walking assist A method of moving a victim in which a rescuer functions as a crutch in assisting the injured victim to walk

"wet" drowning Drowning in which water enters the lungs

withdrawal syndrome A four-stage syndrome that occurs after a cutback in the amount of alcohol a person is used to or when blood alcohol levels start to fall after severe intoxication

wound An injury to the skin and underlying musculature that disrupts the normal continuity of the affected tissue, organ, or bone

X

xiphoid process The lower tip of the sternum

Index ....